Karen Blom

YMCA Aquatic Management:
A Guide to Effective Leadership

YMCA of the USA

Library of Congress Cataloging-in-Publication Data

YMCA of the USA.
   YMCA aquatic management : a guide to effective leadership /
YMCA of the USA.
     p. cm.
  Includes index.
  ISBN 0-7360-4475-2
   1. Aquatic sports--Management--Handbooks, manuals, etc. 2.
Swimming--Management--Handbooks, manuals, etc. 3. YMCA of the USA--Handbooks,
manuals, etc. I. Title.
GV770.5 .Y62 2002
797'.068--dc21

2002017321

ISBN: 0-7360-4475-2

Published for the YMCA of the USA by Human Kinetics Publishers, Inc.

YMCA staff credits: Laura Slane; **Acquisitions Editor:** Patricia Sammann; **Managing Editor:** Wendy McLaughlin; **Assistant Editors:** Dan Brachtesende and Kim Thoren; **Copyeditor:** Barb Field; **Proofreader:** Sara Wiseman; **Permission Manager:** Toni Harte; **Graphic Designer:** Fred Starbird; **Graphic Artist:** Tara Welsch; **Photo Manager:** Carl Johnson; **Cover Designer:** Jack W. Davis; **Photographer (cover):** Tracy Frankel; **Photographer (interior):** Tracy Frankel, Laura Slane, Rhonda Rule, and David Barnes; **Art Manager:** Carl Johnson; **Illustrator:** Mic Greenberg; Figures 3.5-3.13 by Cindy Wrobel and Larry Nolte. Figures 9.3, 9.5, 10.1, 10.5, 10.16, 10.17, 10.19-10.21, 11.1, and 11.2 by Roberto Sabas based on illustrations by Keith Neely. **Printer:** Sheridan Books

Human Kinetics books are available at special discounts for bulk purchase. Special editions or book excerpts can also be created to specification. For details, contact the Special Sales Manager at Human Kinetics.

Printed in the United States of America

10 9 8 7 6 5 4 3 2 1

Copies of this book may be purchased from the YMCA Program Store, P.O. Box 5076, Champaign, IL 61825-5076, 800-747-0089.

The YMCA of the USA is a not-for-profit corporation that provides advice and guidance, but not rules of compliance, for member associations of the National Council of YMCAs.

Contents

Chapter 20   Scuba Programs   605

Chapter 21   YMCA Synchronized Swimming   625

Chapter 22   YMCA Wetball/Water Polo   637

Preface

Being an aquatics director is not easy. You have the responsibility for developing and running programs, hiring and guiding staff, balancing your budget, promoting your programs and department, and making sure the pool and pool areas are always safe, clean, and comfortable. You are constantly in contact with children, parents, members, and community agencies, as well as the staff members within your own YMCA. You have to wear many different hats.

To wear those hats well, you have to have the necessary knowledge and skills. That's what this book is meant to help provide. *YMCA Aquatic Management* is the manual for the YMCA Aquatic Management course, but it can also be an essential handbook for every YMCA aquatics director. It brings together information about many areas of management expertise and YMCA aquatics programs in one volume for the first time.

YMCA Aquatic Management is divided into two parts. Part I covers what you need to know to run a YMCA aquatics department. It includes information on program development and management; staff development and membership service and involvement; and personal skills for working with YMCA staff and volunteers, handling problems, scheduling time efficiently, fundraising, and more. It also includes the basics of budgeting and budget management, program promotion, and emergency and risk management. Rule setting and lifeguarding procedures follow, along with facility management and development.

In part II we discuss in depth 11 different types of YMCA aquatic programs, both instructional and recreational. For each, we describe the program's structure, content, benefits, instructor training, and promotional ideas. Start-up or transitional tips are often included, as well as references to additional program resources.

Several appendixes are included to give you additional resource materials. They include the Developmental Assets, YMCA Child Abuse Identification and Prevention Guidelines, YMCA Aquatics Guidelines, and the Aquatic Emergency Preparedness Self-Assessment.

Being a YMCA aquatics director is difficult but also wonderful. Every day you get to help others reach their potential in any number of ways, and every day is a new challenge. We hope that this book will give you the tools you need to succeed and to continue the lifelong learning required to be an excellent YMCA aquatics director.

Acknowledgments

The YMCA of the USA would like to acknowledge the contributions of the following individuals to *YMCA Aquatic Management*. Staff leadership for this project was coordinated by Laura J. Slane.

Kevin Bottomley
Greensboro Central YMCA
Greensboro, NC

Sean Cogan
Shady Grove YMCA
Richmond, VA

Chris Coker
YMCA of the Ozarks
Potosi, MO

Holly Colon
Countryside YMCA
Lebanon, OH

Kayla Conger
Maryland Farms YMCA
Brentwood, TN

Bridget Cullen
Oshkosh Community YMCA
Oshkosh, WI

Jerry DeMers
Professional Aquatic Consultants International
and
California Polytechnic State University
San Luis Obispo, CA

Vernon Delpesce
YMCA of Greater Des Moines
Des Moines, IA

Deb Duffy
Northwest YMCA
Rochester, NY

Margo Erickson
US Synchronized Swimming (Synchro USA)
Indianapolis, IN

Beth Fugate
Clermont YMCA
Cincinnati, OH

Mauricio Gonzalez
Border View YMCA
San Diego, CA

Georgia Harrison
Cresenta Canada YMCA
Flintridge, CA

Elaine Helm
Gloucester County YMCA
Woodbury, NJ

Henry Helton
Claremont, NC

Theresa Hendrix
Putnam County YMCA
Crescent City, FL

Donna Hirt
Billings YMCA
Billings, MT

Ralph Johnson
Professional Aquatic Consultants International
and
North Greenville College
Tigersville, SC

Terri Johnson
YMCA of Greater Oklahoma City
Oklahoma City, OK

Suzanne King
St. Joseph YMCA
St. Joseph, MO

Tatiana Kolovou
Indiana University
Bloomington, IN

Kathy Kuras
YMCA of Metropolitan Dallas
Dallas, TX

Tomas LeClerc
Professional Aquatic Consultants International
and
Texas Technical University
Lubbock, TX

Beth LeConte
South County Branch YMCA
Peace Dale, RI

Monica Lepore
West Chester University
West Chester, PA

Anthony Lisinicchia
Lake View YMCA
Chicago, IL

Craig Maachi
USA Water Ski
Polk City, FL

Suzanne Mabee
YMCA of the Greater Houston Area
Houston, TX

Gayle Magee
Glenwood Park YMCA
Erie, PA

Karen Martorano
YMCA of Metropolitan Detroit
Detroit, MI

Kim Nutter
Arthur Jordan YMCA
Indianapolis, IN

John Nystrom
YMCA of Greater New York
New York, NY

Terri Pagano
Professional Aquatic Consultants International
and
University of North Carolina
Chapel Hill, NC

Bruce Pearl
YMCA of Montclair
Montclair, NJ

Jay Pecovish
YMCA of the Greater Houston Area
Houston, TX

Kathy Pszolkowski
Allegheny Valley YMCA
Natrona Heights, PA

Nancy Reece
YMCA of Middle Tennessee
Nashville, TN

Kathy Ritter
Central Douglas YMCA
Roseburg, OH

Mark Rutkowski
Silver Bay YMCA and Conference Center
Silver Bay, NY

Mary Sanders (author, chapter 16)
WaterFit and University of Nevada
Reno, NV

Cathy Scheder
American Camping Association
Martinsville, IN

Mikos Sepko
Professional Aquatic Consultants International
and
North Greenville College
Tigersville, SC

Kay Smiley
Edward Jones YMCA
Maryland Heights, MO

Steven Smith
Southwest YMCA
Milwaukee, WI

Bruce Wigo
U.S. Water Polo
Ft. Lauderdale, FL

John Wingfield
U.S. Diving
Indianapolis, IN

YMCA of the USA

Krystal Canady

Tec Clark

Richard Clegg

Arnie Collins

Leslie Coneely

Melissa Davis

Janet Dunn

Curt Fatyol

Gary Forster

Laura Fortson

Carmelita Gallo

Tony Ganger

Janet Koran

Don Kyzer

Augie Mendoza

Julie Mulzoff

Tim O'Brien

Andy Sullivan

Celeste Wroblewski

Credits

Chapter 5

The section on "Hiring Under the Americans With Disabilities Act (ADA)" (pages 134-135) and the second paragraph under "Reference and Background Checks" (page 135) are adapted with permission from Chrys A. Martin, shareholder, Bullivant Houser Bailey, Portland, Oregon.

Chapter 6

The "Grants" section (pages 203-204) is reprinted, by permission, from Center for Nonprofit Management, "Elments of a Proposal," Document FR-PW-009, Los Angeles, CA ©1995. **www.nonprofit.org**

Chapter 7

The section "Operating Plan" (pages 215-216) is adapted from Copyright © 1994-95 Support Center, 706 Mission Street, 5th Floor, San Francisco, CA, USA 94103-3113. 415-974-5100. Distribution and reprinting permitted as long as this copyright notice is included. All Rights Reserved. **http://www.supportcenter.org/sf/genie.html**

Chapter 8

The part of the section "Focus Groups/Individual Depth Interviews" from the line "Use focus groups when ..." (page 257) to "If you choose to conduct a focus group ..." (page 258) and the list of sample types of questions that might be asked of YMCA or community members in a focus group (page 260) is adapted, by permission, from Mary Debus, 1988, *Methodological review: A handbook for excellence in focus group research.* Washington, DC: Academy for Educational Development. Publication done for a U.S. Government-funded project.

Chapter 9

The "What Is Risk Management?" section up through the four basic risk management techniques (pages 261-263) is adapted, by permission, from the website of the Nonprofit Risk Management Center, **www.nonprofitrisk.org.** For more information call (202) 785-3891.

The director's role in creating a risk management plan within the "Hazard Identification and Analysis" section (pages 269-270) is adapted, by permission, from Clayton and Thomas, 1989. *Professional aquatic management* (2nd ed.). (Champaign, IL: Human Kinetics). Pages 60, 61, 62, and 65.

The sections "Informing Relatives," "Transporting Victims to a Hospital," and "Staff Posttraumatic Stress" (pages 284, 286-288) are adapted with permission from Gruber, F.W., and DeMers, G.E. 1999. Emergency plans. In Gabriel, J.L., Leas, D.E., and George, G.S. (Eds.) *U.S. Diving Safety Training Manual* (2nd ed.). Indianapolis: U.S. Diving Publication, pp. 42-43.

The section "Accident Investigation" (pages 288-290) is adapted with permission from Ralph Johnson. (From Johnson, Ralph. 1997. R.E.A.D.Y.: Reacting Expectantly and Defensively Yourself. Presentation at the National AAHPERD Convention in St. Louis, April.)

Chapter 10

Information on permanent slides in the section "Serpentine Slides and Rapids" (pages 308-311) is taken from *Swimming Pool Slides Safety Standard,* Consumer Product Safety Commission.

The "Inflatable Safety" section (pages 318-325) is adapted, by permission, from *The use of play equipment and water features in swimming pools: A recommended code of practice.* (Melton Mowbray, UK: The Institute of Sport and Recreational Management).

Chapter 12

The section "Fecal Contamination of Pool Water" from the third paragraph on (pages 354-355) is adapted from the Division of Parasitic Diseases, Centers for Disease Control. 2001. What every pool operator should know! (On-line newsletter) *Healthy swimming 2001*, Vol. 1, No. 1. Retrieved from **www.cdc.gov/healthyswimming/newsletters/vol1no1.htm.**

The "Springboard Diving Safety" section (pages 355-359) is adapted with permission from Gerald DeMers.

Chapter 16

The section "Becoming Responsive Instructors" (pages 445-447) is adapted, by permission, from Mary Sanders, 2000. "See and hear every participant" *ACSM Health and Fitness Journal*, 4(4): 27-28.

Chapter 16 is adapted with permission from Mary Sanders and Tatiana Kolovou.

Chapter 17

Chapter 17 is adapted from chapters 2 and 4 of *Principles of YMCA competitive swimming and diving* (2nd ed.), with permission from Bruce Griffin.

Figure 17.6 is reprinted, with permission, by the National Collegiate Athletic Association and the NCAA Men's and Women's Swimming Committee.

Chapter 18

The sidebar within the "Working With People With Disabilities" section (pages 534-535) is adapted, by permission, from Disability etiquette tips, 2002. National Organization on Disability (NOD). Washington, DC. **www.nod.org.**

Guidelines for addressing people with disabilities respectfully (page 533) is adapted with permission, © 1996, Goodwill Industries International, Inc.

The section "Facilities, Equipment, and Supplies" (pages 516-533) and figures 18.2-18.19 are adapted, by permission, from Lepore, Gayle, and Stevens. 1998. *Adapted aquatics programming: A professional guide.* Champaign, IL: Human Kinetics. Pages 82, 89, 90, 91, and 97-111.

Figure 18.4 is adapted from functions of physical educators as presented in Randall, L.E. 1992. *Systematic supervision for physical education* (Champaign, IL: Human Kinetics).

Figure 18.12 is by Aquatic Access, Louisville, KY.

Figure 18.16 is by Triad Technology, Syracuse, NY.

Figure 18.18 is courtesy of Aquatic Therapy, Kalamazoo, MI.

Figure 18.19 is courtesy of Excel Sports Sciences, Inc., Eugene, OR.

Table 18.1 is adapted from the Department of Justice, Office of the Attorney General. 1991. Nondiscrimination on the basis of disability by public accommodations and in commercial facilities: Final rule, Part III of the Americans With Disabilities Act. *Federal Register* 56(144): 35544-35691.

Chapter 19

The portion of this chapter from the heading "Boating Programs" (page 564) on (including figures 19.4-19.8) is from *Camp boating*, 1993, Martinsville, IN: American Camping Association. Adapted by permission from the publisher. For permission to reprint beyond limited personal use, please contact the publisher at 765-342-8456. The original material taken from *Camp boating*, copyright 1993 American Camping Association, has been updated to meet current practice.

The checklist on pages 543-544 and figure 19.2 are from Pohndorf, Richard H. 1960. *Camp waterfront programs and management.* (New York: Association Press)

Table 19.1 is from the U.S. Coast Guard (n.d.) *Federal requirements – Quick reference.* Retrieved from **http://www.uscgboating.org/reg/reg_fr_equipReq_quickref.asp**

Table 19.2 is from the American White Water. 1998. *Safety code of American whitewater*, VI. International Scale of River Difficulty. Information courtesy of American Whitewater, 1424 Fenwick Lane, Silver Spring, MD, **Nick@amwhitewater.org.**

The section "Characteristics of a Good Waterfront Site," (pages 541-543) paragraphs six through eight under "Activity Areas," (page 547) and figures 19.1 and 19.5 are from U.S. Army Corps. 1987. *Engineering and design – Recreation planning and design criteria* (Publication number EM 1110-1-400). Retrieved from **www.usace.army.mil/inet/usace-docs/eng-manuals/em1110-1-400/toc.htm.**

The section "Basic Sailing – Level One" (pages 589-591) is adapted, by permission, from Derrick Fries, 1988, *Start Sailing Right: The national strandard for quality sailing instruction.* © **United States Sailing Association.**

Chapter 21

Chapter 21 is adapted, by permission, from US Synchronized Swimming, Indianapolis, IN. **www.usasynchro.org.**

Chapter 22

Figure 22.1, "Introduction to Water Polo", is adapted from USA Water Polo. 1993. *United States water polo level one coaching manual.* Ft. Lauderdale, FL: USA Water Polo.

The two-column list of reasons why water polo can be advantageous (pages 640-641) is adapted from the July 1993 issue of *Swimming World and Junior Swimmers* with permission from Sports Publications.

The section "Water Polo Safety Rules" (page 651) is adapted from USA Water Polo. 1993. *United States water polo level one coaching manual.* Ft. Lauderdale, FL: USA Water Polo.

Appendixes

Appendix 1, "Developmental Assets", is reprinted, by permission, from *The troubled journey: A portrait of 6th-12th grade youth.* (Minneapolis, MN: Search Institute). © Search Institute, 1990, **www.search-institute.org.**

Appendix 2, "Child Abuse Identification and Prevention: Recommended Guidelines for YMCAs." The list entitled "Possible Indicators of Abuse" is reprinted, by permission, from Becca Cowan Johnson, 1992, *For their sake: Recognizing, responding to and reporting child abuse.* (Martinsville, IN: American Camping Association).

The "Family Characteristics" portion of the list "Possible Indicators of Abuse" is excerpted from "What do I do now? Indicators of child sexual abuse and guidelines for mandated reporters" by Tracy Flynn, M.Ed. © 2002 Committee for Children. Reprinted by permission from Committee for Chidren.

YMCA Credits

The following YMCA resources were used in developing this book. (The chapters in *YMCA Aquatic Management* in which the materials were used follow each reference.):

Cason, Dave, and Larry Rosen. n.d. *Image development guide.* Los Angeles: YMCA of Metropolitan Los Angeles. (Chapter 8)

Goodrich, Michelle. n.d. *Developing and implementing a quality program.* Handout from YMCA presentation. (Chapter 2)

Kuenzli, Gary. n.d. *Successful board leadership.* San Mateo, CA: Southern California MRC. (Chapter 2)

National Board of YMCA. 1962. *Basic physical education in the YMCA.* New York: Association Press. (Chapters 1 and 2)

Pohndorf, Richard H. 1960. *Camp waterfront programs and management.* New York: Association Press. (Chapter 19)

YMCA of the USA. n.d. YMCA financial management guidelines for accounting and financial activity (YMCA Intranet website). Located at **http://www.ymcausa.org/Fiscalops/Accounting/guidelines.htm.** (Chapter 7)

— 1987. *Aquatics for special populations.* Champaign, IL: Human Kinetics. (Chapter 18)

— 1990. *YMCA communications: A handbook.* Chicago: YMCA of the USA. (Chapter 8)

— 1994. *The seven R's of volunteer development: A YMCA resource kit.* Chicago: YMCA of the USA. (Chapter 5)

— 1995. *YMCA Youth Sports Director's Manual* (2nd ed.). Champaign, IL: Human Kinetics.

— 1996. *Fun, function, and safety: Improving and expanding your YMCA aquatic center.* Chicago: YMCA of the USA. (Chapters 7, 10, and 12)

— 1997. *Principles of YMCA aquatics.* Champaign, IL: Human Kinetics (Part II opening, Chapter 2)

— November 1997. Resource information regarding focus groups and in-depth interviews. (YMCA Intranet website). (Chapter 8)

— 1999. *Teaching swimming fundamentals.* Champaign, IL: Human Kinetics. (Chapters 2, 3, and 18)

— 1999. *YMCA day camp manual* (2nd ed.). Champaign, IL: Human Kinetics. (Chapters 8 and 9)

— 1999. *YMCA Swim Lessons administrator's manual.* Champaign, IL: Human Kinetics. (Chapters 2, 3, 4, 5, 7, and 8)

— 1999. *The Youth and Adult Aquatic Program manual.* Champaign, IL: Human Kinetics. (Part II opening)

— October 2000. *One for the movement.* Paper issued by the YMCA of the USA. (Chapter 1)

— November 2000. *People management resource tool.* CD-Rom prepared by Arthur Andersen for the YMCA. (Chapter 5)

— 2000. *Principles of YMCA competitive swimming and diving* (2nd ed.). Champaign, IL: Human Kinetics. (Chapter 17)

— 2000. *Ready to respond: YMCA aquatics in the 21st century.* (Critical Issues paper). Chicago: YMCA of the USA, Association Resources. (Chapters 5 and 9)

— 2000. *The YMCA guide to managing multisite child care programs.* Chicago: YMCA of the USA. (Chapter 5)

— 2000. *The YMCA service-learning guide: A tool for enriching the member, the participant, the YMCA, and the community.* Chicago: YMCA of the USA. (Chapter 2)

— 2001. *On the guard II: The YMCA lifeguard manual* (4th ed.). Champaign, IL: Human Kinetics. (Part II opening, chapters 6, 9, 10, and 12)

— 2001. *YMCA membership by design manual.* Chicago: YMCA of the USA, Association Resources, Membership and Program Development Group. (Chapters 2, 4, 5, and 8)

YMCA of the USA Program Development. 1995. Compensation of child care staff and the relation to quality (Child Care technical assistance paper). Chicago: YMCA of the USA. (Chapter 5)

Y Services. n.d. Program risk management handout. (Chapter 9)

Y Services. n.d. Suggested program for YMCA emergency procedures. (Chapter 9)

Zoller, Mary. 1989. *Guide for program assessment based on the development and implementation of quality standards.* Chicago: YMCA of the USA. (Chapter 2)

Other unpublished YMCA resources used in this manual include the following:

- Aquatic Facility Management Training Design and handouts (Chapters 2, 5, 7, 8, and 9)
- LTP PMP Training Design (Chapter 2)
- LTP PPM Module (Chapters 2 and 5)
- LTP Group Work Module (Chapter 5)
- Recovery Strategies Y Training Design (Chapter 4)
- Power of Positive Workplace Training Design (Chapter 5)
- Ready to Respond Training Design (Chapter 5)
- Youth Governors' handout (Don Kyzer) (Chapter 5)
- Working With Program Volunteers Training Design (Chapter 5)
- Working With Program Volunteers Handout Book (Chapter 5)
- Supervision LTP Module (Chapter 6)
- Storytelling Training Design (Chapter 6)
- Y Core Competency Training (Chapter 6)

These figures and tables in *YMCA Aquatic Management* are from the following YMCA books:

On the guard II (4th ed.): Figures 9.1-9.5; figure 10.1; figures 11.1-11.3; figures 12.1-12.19; table 10.1; tables 12.1-12.3; tables 14.1 and 14.2

Principles of YMCA competitive swimming and diving: Figure 17.1 and 17.2

YMCA scuba standards and procedures (2000 Edition): Appendixes 6, 7, and 9

YMCA Swim Lessons administrator's manual: Figures 2.4 and 2.5; figures 3.1-3.5 and 3.14-3.21; figures 5.1-5.5 and 5.9; figure 7.3

YMCA Swim Lessons teaching swimming fundamentals: Figures 3.6-3.13

YMCA Swim Lessons: The Parent/Child and Preschool Aquatic Program Manual: Table 13.1

YMCA water fitness for health: Figure 16.1

YMCA Aquatics Department Management

In this part of the book, which includes chapters 1 through 12, we cover the skills and knowledge you need to be a good aquatics director. We begin with an overview of the YMCA, what it is, and what programs it offers. In the next two chapters, we describe programming. Chapter 2 is on program development, from how to select or create programs to setting up the structure for monitoring and managing them. It also includes sections on working developmental assets and impact research into programs and how to work with aquatics or program committees. In chapter 3, we discuss the nuts and bolts of running programs. The first part of the chapter relates to program preparation: timetables for performing tasks, necessary policies, registration, class levels and organization, and first-day orientation. The second half has to do with class supervision, student evaluation, and gathering program statistics. A final section describes special events.

Next we turn to people skills. In chapter 4, we focus on member service and involvement. After discussing how to provide excellent service to members and how to deal with member complaints, we describe how to work with members to get them more deeply involved with the YMCA. Chapter 5 is devoted to staff development. It starts with structuring positions, recruiting, and hiring. Then it moves on to the continuous tasks of supervising and training staff and scheduling staff for duty, as well as methods of staff retention. If staff members aren't performing well, we offer advice in sections on coaching and disciplining staff. Chapter 6 is oriented toward your own personal skills. This includes staff management skills such as supervising, intervening, and monitoring your department and providing leadership. It also includes professional skills such as avoiding burnout, problem solving and negotiating, time management, and others. Crucial skills for working within the organization are fundraising, interacting with your boss and others in the YMCA, facilitating meetings, and storytelling for the YMCA. Finally, we talk about how you can develop your own career by developing a training plan, gathering new experience, finding a mentor (or mentoring), and planning.

Two important skills for running your department are budget management and program promotion. We address these in chapters 7 and 8. In chapter 7, we introduce you to the concepts of an operating plan, budgeting, and the budget process. We then discuss how to create a budget, looking at direct and indirect income and expenses, break-even analysis, and probable income sources and expenses. Budget spreads and tips for good budgeting are included, as well as ideas on how to defend your budget requests. Finally, we turn to how you monitor and adjust your budget, ending with a short section on financial aid.

In the chapter on program promotion, chapter 8, we give you some basic concepts for clear communication of program benefits and a promotional plan framework. We also talk about some methods of improving promotion, such as focus groups, direct communication, and image. The last part of the chapter contains ideas for promoting various aquatics programs and some sample promotional materials.

The next four chapters are concerned with various facets of risk management. Emergency management is the key concept in chapter 9. We review risk management, list potential types of emergencies you should prepare to handle, and describe hazard identification and analysis, including insurance. Next we get into emergency procedures, policy guidelines, and plans, as well as the need for good record keeping. This chapter ends with information on crisis management and the legal issues you are responsible for as an aquatics director.

The topic for chapter 10 is rules and regulations. We describe how to establish and communicate rules, then list common rules you might want to set for high-risk locations and starting blocks and platforms. We also include a large section on how lifeguards should guard each of several water recreation attractions, as well as information on inflatables safety. Chapter 11 continues with more on how to set up lifeguarding procedures. We tell you how to teach your lifeguards to enforce rules, and how to set up scanning areas and rotation for the guards. Finally, we end this chapter with ideas for how you might plan ahead to help your lifeguards know how to handle special situations that may come up, such as violent confrontations and what to prepare your guards for in some special guarding situations.

We end this part of the book with a chapter on facility management. Chapter 12 includes information on how to maintain the pool and pool water and how to improve the facility with additions or renovations. Topics covered in the first part of the chapter are safety inspections, safety and sanitation precautions, signage, water filtration and chemistry, care of spas, and maintenance record keeping. In the second part of the chapter, we discuss how to analyze your facility to determine what is needed, then either create a new facility or improve the existing one.

An Overview of the YMCA

Together, YMCAs make up the largest not-for-profit community service organization in America. They are at the heart of community life in neighborhoods and towns across the nation, working to meet the health and social service needs of over 18 million men, women, and children. The YMCA mission is to put Christian principles into practice through programs that build healthy spirit, mind, and body for all.

Local YMCAs help people develop values and behavior that are consistent with Christian principles. They focus on fostering four core values:

- *Caring:* to love others; to be sensitive to the well-being of others; to help others
- *Honesty:* to tell the truth; to act in such a way that you are worthy of trust; to have integrity, making sure your choices match your values
- *Respect:* to treat others as you would have them treat you; to value the worth of every person, including yourself
- *Responsibility:* to do what is right, what you ought to do; to be accountable for your behavior

YMCAs believe we all need a place to belong—a place where we genuinely care about one another; where we pull together for a common cause; where we treat each other with loving kindness, open communication, and support; where we share in decisions—a community. YMCAs nurture children, support families, and strengthen society. They are a force for hope.

YMCAs are for people of both genders and all faiths, races, abilities, ages, and incomes. By law, the fees that YMCAs charge for some services must be affordable to a significant segment of the people in the communities in which they are located. For those who demonstrate financial hardship, assistance programs are available. The YMCAs' strength is in the people they bring together.

Volunteering is at the heart of local YMCAs. They offer people a chance to get involved in community life and to show how much they care for others by running programs, setting policies, raising money, and solving neighborhood problems. By giving their time to others, volunteers also give themselves a chance to learn, grow, and have fun.

Local YMCAs meet community needs through organized activities called programs. Best known, perhaps, for community-based health and fitness programs, local YMCAs

teach kids to swim, organize youth basketball games, offer exercise classes for people with disabilities, and lead adult aerobics. They also offer hundreds of other programs, including day and resident camp for kids, child care (YMCAs make up the largest not-for-profit provider in the United States), teen clubs, environmental programs, substance abuse prevention, family nights, job training, international exchange, and many more.

THEN AND NOW

The first YMCA was founded in London, England, in 1844 by George Williams and a dozen or so friends who lived and worked as clerks in a drapery, a forerunner of dry-goods and department stores. Their goal was to save fellow live-in clerks from the wicked life on the London streets. The first members were evangelical Protestants who prayed and studied the Bible as an alternative to vice. YMCAs have always been nonsectarian and today accept those of all faiths at all levels of the organization, despite their unchanging name: the Young Men's Christian Association.

The first U.S. YMCA started in Boston in 1851, the work of Thomas Sullivan, a retired sea captain who was a lay missionary. Local YMCAs spread fast and soon were serving boys and older men in addition to young men. Although 5,145 women worked in YMCA military canteens in World War I, it wasn't until after World War II that women and girls were admitted to full membership and participation in U.S. YMCAs. Today, half of all YMCA constituents and staff members are women. Also, half of the YMCAs' constituents are 18 or younger.

In 2001, a total of 973 member YMCAs (also called corporate YMCAs) operated 1,520 branches, operating units, and camps. These 2,493 YMCAs were run by 55,961 volunteer policymakers serving on YMCA boards and committees and 540,672 volunteer program leaders and countless other volunteers, all of whom worked with 16,910 paid professional staff members. These volunteers and staff members worked not only out of YMCA buildings and resident camps, but also out of rented quarters, parks, and playgrounds. Some YMCAs have no building at all.

Combined, YMCAs had a total operating budget of $3.7 billion from the following sources: 33 percent from fees paid to take part in YMCA programs, 34.4 percent from membership dues, 11 percent from charitable contributions, 6 percent from fees paid for resident camping and for staying in YMCA rooms and other living quarters, 11.6 percent from government contracts, and 4 percent from miscellaneous sources.

During the year, local YMCAs also received contributions, not included in operating income, for capital improvements and debt reduction. Of 944 member YMCAs reporting, 527 had capital gifts totaling $325 million. If this sum is included in total contributed income for 2001, the portion of YMCAs' income that is contributed rises from 11 percent to 18 percent.

ORGANIZATION

By law, YMCAs are led by volunteers. A volunteer policy-making board of directors holds title to YMCA assets and sets policy for its executive, who manages the operation with full- and part-time staff and volunteer leaders. The board is elected by, and in turn responsible to, the membership. It is guided by a written constitution and is able to do the following:

- Appoint major committees
- Select and employ the chief executive officer
- With the advice of its personnel committee and upon the recommendation of the chief executive officer, employ other staff members

Volunteers are involved in all aspects of a YMCA's operations, from leading programs to raising money. All YMCA activities should contribute to the mission of the YMCA. Board, committee, and staff members, volunteer leaders, and the members themselves need to keep this in mind. Volunteer YMCA leaders should not only accomplish the specific tasks for which they were recruited and trained but also help achieve the YMCAs' purpose. They also should experience personal growth as they prepare for and perform their assigned tasks.

Volunteers and employed staff mentors work as partners, but distinctions are made between them. Employed officers carry out the policies developed by the authorized volunteer committees and boards. The committees are guided by written policies or commissions (or both, in most cases) that outline their duties and responsibilities, indicate lines of authority, and specify the length of appointments. Similarly, employed officers are guided by written job descriptions. In both cases, clearly defined statements are the basis for evaluating people or appraising their accomplishments.

Each local YMCA is an independent charitable not-for-profit organization, qualifying under Section 501(c)(3) of the U.S. Tax Code. (This means that donations to YMCAs are tax-deductible.) YMCAs are required by the national constitution to pay annual dues, to refrain from discrimination, and to support the YMCA mission. All other decisions are local choices, including programs offered, staffing, and style of operation.

Geographical groupings of associations account for the organizational structure of YMCAs. These units in turn are combined to form the National Council of the YMCAs of the USA, headquartered in Chicago. The national office, called the YMCA of the USA, serves member associations in three ways:

- Connecting YMCAs to one another, to the greater movement, and to society at large

- Serving member associations and responding to their changing needs
- Leading and focusing the collective efforts and strengths of member associations on important issues and opportunities

A WORLDWIDE MOVEMENT

Local YMCAs are at work in 130 countries around the world. YMCAs have reopened in China, Russia, Poland, the Czech Republic, Slovakia, Hungary, Bulgaria, Ethiopia, Zaire, and Liberia and are emerging in Armenia, Estonia, and Latvia. More than 316 local U.S. YMCAs maintain relationships with YMCAs in other countries. Like other national YMCA movements, the YMCA of the USA is a member of the World Alliance of YMCAs, headquartered in Geneva, Switzerland.

YMCA PROGRAMS

Local YMCAs meet community needs through organized activities called programs. Each YMCA program is intended to do three things: (1) build spirit, mind, and body; (2) offer a place to belong, people who care, activities that build skills and assets, and fun; and (3) provide effective solutions to social problems.

First, all programs build spirit, mind, and body. There's a great sense of self-esteem that kids and adults get when they learn to swim. And like all exercise programs, aquatics and scuba contribute to good health. Some say that connection with the water, which covers 70 percent of the world's surface and makes up 60 percent of our bodies, offers an unparalleled sense of well-being. Surely it offers a relaxing environment for safe exercise, physical therapy, and play.

Second, YMCA programs offer a place to belong, people who care, activities that build skills and assets, and fun. Everyone in the pool: that's not just a saying at YMCAs—it's a philosophy. YMCAs open their doors to kids and adults with all levels of abilities, and to people of all ages, incomes, races, and religions. Caring staff don't just teach important swimming and scuba skills; they teach YMCA core values, too, encouraging everyone to achieve his or her personal best. And it's all done in a fun way that keeps people coming back, resulting in lifelong enjoyment and health benefits.

Finally, all YMCA programs provide effective solutions to social problems. When you have caring adults creating a safe and inclusive environment, aquatics and scuba—like any other wholesome activity—are tools for youth and community development. YMCA aquatics programs help prevent drownings and water-related deaths. Many aquatics programs are therapeutic. Like other YMCA health and fitness programs, aquatics and scuba contribute to good physical, mental, and spiritual health, which lowers health care costs and contributes to a better quality of life for everyone.

Now let's take a look at YMCA goals for members and the many categories of YMCA programming.

YMCA Goals for Members

Because many organizations offer their own programs, the question is often asked, "What is different about YMCA programs?" In aquatics, as well as in other program areas, YMCAs have a longer history than many other organizations and often have higher-quality guidelines for programming and more extensive training and re-

sources. However, these are not the primary differences between YMCA programs and those offered by other organizations.

Many organizations offer their programs as an end in themselves, but YMCAs use programs as a vehicle to deliver their unique mission. It is not the programs themselves that develop people to their fullest potential; it is the activities within the programs that make the difference for YMCA members and program members (participants).

To help people grow spiritually, mentally, and physically, all YMCA programs address eight specific goals as outlined in the constitution of the National Council of YMCAs, to which all YMCAs belong. Through planned activities, YMCA programs seek to help people improve in the following areas:

- **Self-worth:** To develop self-confidence and self-respect and an appreciation of their own worth as individuals.

- **Christian Principles:** To develop a faith for daily living based upon the teachings of Jesus Christ, that they may thereby be helped in achieving their highest potential as children of God.

- **Positive Relationships:** To grow as responsible members of their families and citizens of their communities.

- **Holistic Health:** To appreciate that health of mind and body is a sacred gift and that physical fitness and mental well-being are conditions to be achieved and maintained.

- **Appreciation of Diversity:** To recognize the worth of all persons and to work for interracial and intergroup understanding.

- **International Awareness:** To develop a sense of world-mindedness and to work for worldwide understanding.

- **Leadership and Service:** To develop their capacities for leadership and use them responsibly in their own groups in community life.
- **Environmental Stewardship:** To appreciate the beauty, diversity, and interdependence of all forms of life and all resources that God has provided in this world, and to develop an ethical basis for guiding their relationships of mankind with the rest of God's natural community.

YMCA Program Categories

YMCAs in the United States do hundreds of things, and there are many ways to classify the programs they offer. Here is one way of outlining the wide array of activities and services. The major program categories are in bold type, accompanied by examples of specific kinds of programs in that category.

Character development, member involvement, international education, volunteer development, and service-learning are not listed here because they are not stand-alone programs—they are integrated into programs.

Adult Development
Leadership, enrichment, or development programs for people 18 and older

- Active Older Adults, a multifaceted program of activities such as travel, social clubs, exercise, volunteering, and camping for adults 55 and older
- Continuing education, e.g., computer skills, language classes
- Financial development and support canpaigns
- International education, e.g., partnerships and exchanges with YMCAs in other countries
- International Management Council (leadership and career program)
- Participation in financial development campaigns: annual support, capital, endowment, etc.
- Student YMCAs (for college students)
- Social and support groups based on age or interests
- Travel clubs
- Volunteer and service-learning projects; service clubs for adults, e.g., Y's Men's Clubs
- Young adult programs for 18- to 29-year-olds, e.g., Young Adult Civic Connector Initiative

Aquatics and Scuba
Water-based safety, skill, sport, or exercise programs for all ages

- Arthritis classes; other specialty water fitness classes
- Classes for people with disabilities: kids, adults
- Competitive swimming and diving: youth (under 18), masters (18 and over), triathlons
- Lifeguarding; aquatic safety assistant classes
- Scuba; snorkeling; skin diving; technical diving
- Sports: kayaking, synchronized swimming, water polo, wetball, etc.
- Swim lessons: parent/child, preschool, youth, family, teen, adult, older adult, adaptive

- Swims: family, lap, open
- Water and boating safety
- Water fitness, including classes for people with disabilities, arthritis, etc.

Arts and Humanities

Art and humanities lessons, performances, shows, clubs, and groups for all ages

- Literary arts: YMCA Writer's Voice, reading and discussion groups, storytelling, public readings
- Humanities workshops and readings, e.g., in history, philosophy, ethics
- Performing arts: music, dance, poetry, performance, theatre
- Popular crafts: scrapbooking, knitting, doll-making
- Visual arts: ceramics, drawing, painting, photography, sculpture, murals, textiles, multimedia

Camping and Outdoor Enrichment

Programs for all ages that use the outdoors as a primary venue or main theme

- Camping for special populations: burn victims, those with spina bifida or cancer, etc.
- Conferences: youth, teen, adult, older adult
- Counselor-in-training programs for youths and teens
- Day camping: youth, teen
- Family camping
- High adventure programming
- International Camp Counselor Exchange
- Outdoor and environmental education
- Reunions: families, clubs, colleges
- Resident camping: youth, teen, older adult
- Retreats: youth, teen, adult, older adult
- Specialty camping: computers, sailing
- Travel and caravan camping
- World Camp

Child Care

Programs that provide out-of-home care and support the development of children from birth to age 11

- Alternative hours child care for nontraditional schedules, e.g., nightshift
- Full-day infant care
- Full-day toddler care (ages 1–2)
- Full-day preschool (ages 3–5)
- Part-day preschool programs
- School-age child care (before or after school, on breaks)
- KidzLit literacy program (component of after-school programs)

Community Development and Resources
Programs that address special issues faced by communities, families, or individuals of all ages

- Asset-based community development
- Charter schools; school partnerships
- Collaborations and alliances with private, not-for-profit, and public sector partners
- Economic development; job creation programs , transportation
- Elder care for sick or fragile older adults
- Employment and job readiness and training
- Foster care programs
- G.E.D. preparation; tutoring
- Housing: runaway/homeless, low-income, short-term, long-term
- Pregnancy prevention and support
- Prevention, intervention, and care: HIV/AIDS, alcohol, tobacco, drugs
- Technology skills programs
- Violence and gang prevention and intervention

Family Strengthening
Programs that strengthen bonds between two or more family members, or that support family members in fulfilling their responsibilities

- Family activity programs: family nights, family volunteering
- Family counseling and referrals

- Family support groups
- Intergenerational programs with children, parents, grandparents
- Parent/child programs: Y-Guides, Dads and Daughters, nature programs, Y-Trails
- Parenting skills programs
- Social and support groups, e.g., for single parents and multiracial families

Health and Fitness
Land-based exercise, skill, safety, and behavioral modification programs for all ages

- CPR and first aid
- Group exercise: step, hi/lo aerobics, indoor cycling, kickboxing
- Health risk/lifestyle assessment; fitness testing
- Low-impact exercise; older adult exercise
- Personal fitness programs for those starting out
- Personal training
- Smoking cessation programs
- Specialty exercise classes: healthy back, prenatal, people with disabilities
- Sports medicine programs: cardiac rehabilitation, physical therapy
- Strength training
- Stress management
- Walking classes and clubs
- Weight management and nutrition, including Get Real
- Yoga
- Youth health and fitness, including preschool movement, parent-child, teen exercise

Sports and Recreation
Sport and recreation leagues, lessons, clubs, and competitions for all ages

- Adult leagues: basketball, softball, volleyball
- Corporate challenges
- Cycling
- Extreme sports
- Family sports
- Gymnastics: progressive, competitive
- Martial arts
- Special Olympics
- Teen sports of all kinds, teen adventure programs, skateboarding
- Tennis, racquetball
- Youth baseball, softball, T-ball
- Youth basketball, volleyball, soccer
- Youth hockey, flag football, wrestling
- Youth Super Sports: Rookies, Winners, Champions

Youth Development
Leadership, enrichment, and development programs for young people under 18

- Black Achievers, Minority Achievers, Hispanic Achievers, Youth Achievers
- Earth Service Corps
- Hi-Y, Tri-Hi-Y, Gra-Y clubs
- Leaders Clubs
- Mentoring programs for teens
- Model United Nations
- Service-learning clubs, corps, etc. for teens
- Social and support groups
- Special interest clubs, e.g., international or multicultural clubs
- Teen Club (middle-school afterschool program)
- Teen leadership programs
- Youth and Government

Program Development

Successful programming is one of your biggest concerns as aquatics director. Choosing appropriate programs, developing them properly, and seeing that they run well will take a lot of time and effort. This chapter gives you guidance on selecting programs and creating new ones, as well as adjusting them to meet changing times and needs. It also covers methods for monitoring and evaluating programs to maintain high quality and determine future programming. Finally, the chapter ends with a description of how program and aquatics committees work and advice on how they can best assist you and your department.

Let's begin by talking about why your programs should be YMCA aquatic programs.

WHY YMCA AQUATICS?

Since 1885, the YMCA has been an innovator and leader in aquatic program development for the world. Figure 2.1 shows some of the key dates and developments.

Although the YMCA has been a leader in aquatics and water safety for a long time, it is more than just tradition that keeps aquatics programs an important part of the YMCA; it is the benefits that people can obtain from participating in those programs. Here are some examples.

- *Meeting community needs.* Today people need a readily accessible resource for learning about water safety. Because public schools have cut back on physical education and aquatics courses, many Americans do not know how to swim or to be safe around water. This is happening even as water recreation activities are becoming more popular.

- *Teaching personal safety and rescue skills.* Thousands of people drown annually, but the YMCA can help prevent such drownings by offering water safety, swimming, and safe boating classes. Knowing how to protect themselves from dangers in the water and how to save others also gives participants more self-confidence.

- *Developing social skills.* Aquatics classes give participants of all ages an opportunity to make friends and meet people of diverse backgrounds. They also provide participants opportunities to work together cooperatively.

1885	The first YMCA swimming pool was built in the Brooklyn YMCA in New York.
1904	The first YMCA lifesaving corps was organized in 1904 at Camp Dudley in upstate New York.
1910	George Corsan used group teaching methods instead of teaching individuals. He taught crawl stroke first, contrary to the practice of the day. The YMCA and the Red Cross (U.S.A.) commenced co-operatively to promote first aid. Shortly afterwards, the Red Cross hired Commodore Longfellow to study the drowning situation, and Longfellow developed a lifesaving corps in the YMCA (Baltimore, Maryland). From this point, both organizations proceeded to develop their own lifesaving programs.
1912	The National YMCA Lifesaving Service was organized.
1923	The first YMCA swimming championships were held at the Brooklyn YMCA.
1938	The new YMCA aquatics program was published. Swimmers at varying degrees of ability were known as Minnows, Fish, and Sharks.
1956	The YMCA introduced the idea of "Learn to Swim Month."
1959	The YMCA Scuba program was developed.
1964	The National YMCA Aquatic Conference adopted the Porpoise and Springboard Diving programs.
1972	The Progressive Swimming and Springboard Diving Program manual was published. The new program used the "whole-part" rather than the "part-whole" method of instruction. Activities were pupil-centered rather than teacher-centered, and problem solving was emphasized rather than skill instruction and drills. Tadpoles, a preschool program, was introduced. Polliwog and Flying Fish were added to the Progressive Swimming program. A synchronized swimming program was also introduced.
1973	The YMCA began its first national emphasis on aquatic activities for the disabled.
1975	The National YMCA Swimming and Diving Championship became the largest swimming championship in the world, with over 1,500 participants.
1981	A new level of the progressive swim system, Guppy, was introduced.
1982	The National Physical Fitness Through Water Exercise and the Arthritis Foundation YMCA Aquatic programs were launched. The Aquatic Facility Manager course was adopted as a certification course.
1987	The YMCA of the USA adopts the Pool Operator on Location course. The manual was published in 1989.
1988	Y's Way to Water Exercise was released as a new manual and specialty instructor course certification.
1992	The YMCA operated over 1,700 pools. The YMCA of the USA maintained records of over 25,000 lifeguards and instructors.
1994	On the Guard II: The YMCA Lifeguard Program was introduced. This edition emphasizes the decision-making skills needed to prevent accidents and how to safely and most effectively perform rescues. Aquatic Safety and Aquatic Personal Safety and Survival are two programs included in the lifeguard program to be used when teaching a variety of groups about water safety and accident prevention. YMCA Synchronized Swimming Instructor and YMCA Wetball (Water Polo) Instructor/Coach were introduced through the cooperation of the U.S. Olympic Committee and the national governing bodies of the sports.
1995	The 12th National Aquatic Conference was held in Ft. Lauderdale to celebrate the 110th anniversary of YMCA swimming.
1996	YMCA Splash, a community-based learn-to-swim program was released. This program's purpose was to help people of all ages, especially children and families, learn some basic swimming skills and water-safety practices.
1999	Four new books were released as the foundation for the new Y Swim Lessons Program: *Teaching Swimming Fundamentals, The Youth and Adult Aquatic Program Manual, The Parent/Child and Preschool Aquatic Program Manual,* and *YMCA Swim Lessons Administrator's Manual.* A new instructor training program was also released.
2000	The *YMCA Water Fitness for Health* program and manual were released in conjunction with an instructor training program for water fitness and active older adult water fitness.
2001	*On the Guard II* (4th ed.) was released. The new participant manual included a CD-Rom with video clips of skills. The instructor manual was also updated and released.
2002	*YMCA Aquatic Management: A Guide to Effective Leadership* was released, along with a new training program for aquatic professionals. The Arthritis Foundation YMCA Aquatic program was updated and new manuals were released.

Figure 2.1 YMCA aquatics programs.

- *Promoting character development.* Classes include many situations in which instructors can recognize, teach, and celebrate the values of caring, honesty, respect, and responsibility and encourage participants to follow those values.
- *Maintaining health.* Teaching people the skills they need for water activities provides them with a form of physical activity they can enjoy throughout their lives. And YMCA pools give people a place to enjoy them!
- *Promoting leadership.* Teen and adult volunteers can fill many leadership roles in aquatic programs as aquatic assistants, lifeguards, and instructors. Swim team parent supporters may help with fundraising and program promotion. In classes and programs, students are given the opportunity to learn about being a leader and a follower.
- *Developing life skills.* For many teens, becoming a lifeguard is their first job experience. It gives them a chance to become responsible employees and to learn important rescue and first aid skills. Others may become assistants or instructors in swimming or diving programs. In classes/programs, students also learn about life skills through getting along with others, developing new skills, challenges, etc.
- *Building confidence and self-esteem.* From preschoolers to adults, overcoming fears of the water and developing water and swimming skills is rewarding.
- *Having fun!* People of any age can use aquatic activities for recreation and relaxation. These are also fun pastimes that families can enjoy together.

The main purpose of YMCA aquatics programs is to help meet the YMCA's mission. We can accomplish this by

- focusing on members' needs;
- developing swimming skills;
- teaching water safety;
- maximizing the use of facilities;
- valuing our aquatic staff and volunteers;
- developing training that is accessible to the whole community; and
- collaborating with others to strengthen the programs and involve more people.

CHOOSING PROGRAMS FOR YOUR YMCA

Aquatics directors usually come to a facility that is already scheduled. Often that schedule has not changed much over the years. This is a very different experience from being part of opening a new pool that does not have tradition driving when and what programs are offered.

In either case, you first need to know about the function of the facility. The best way to get this information is to look at the association's strategic plan, operating principles, and annual goals and objectives. These documents will tell you the direction in which the association is going and can help you put together a program plan to meet those goals and objectives.

The next step is to talk to your program committee and your board about what they believe the function of the pool should be in their community. Ask them:

- What is the pool's role in the community?
- Is it for recreation, swimming instruction, fitness swimming, or competition?
- If the answer is "all of the above," then which goals get top priority? What percentage of time should be allocated to each?

These questions will create good discussion and reflection on what the YMCA aquatics program should be doing in the community. This also ties into the key issues worked on by our volunteers. By allowing them to review the strategic plan, operating principles, and annual goals and objectives, then asking these questions, you can help them see the impact of those decisions on the facility. Most volunteers normally don't realize this connection. Have this discussion with your volunteers annually when goals and objectives are being developed and before the budgeting for the next fiscal year.

Once these questions are answered, you can figure out the program mix for your pool. Then you can begin putting together the balanced program schedule your YMCA needs. Besides following your YMCA's and department's priorities, you will also have to divide pool time among many different groups of members. Traditionally, adult members want increased time for lap swimming, families want more time to spend in the pool with their small children, swim teams (both YMCA and other organizations) want more practice time, and programs are always expanding. To best serve *all* members, make sure that each segment is duly represented in your programming. This can be a very complex task, especially if the goals of your YMCA or department are not clearly defined.

The bottom line is that your facility schedule should reflect the goals and priorities of the organization while meeting members' needs. Table 2.1 lists numerous YMCA aquatics programs from which you can choose.

Table 2.1   Sample Program Offerings

INSTRUCTION

YMCA Swim Lessons: Parent/Child

- Shrimps
- Kippers
- Inias
- Perch

YMCA Swim Lessons: Preschool

- Pike
- Eel
- Ray
- Starfish

YMCA Swim Lessons: Youth

- Polliwog
- Guppy
- Minnow
- Fish
- Flying Fish
- Shark
- Porpoise

YMCA Swim Lessons: Adult

- Terrified of water
- Beginning

- Intermediate
- Advanced
- Teen beginner

YMCA Swim Lessons: Individuals with Disabilities

- Youth
- Adult
- Specialty classes for people with physical or mental disabilities

YMCA Synchronized Swimming

- Level One—Oyster
- Level Two—Lobster
- Level Three—Dolphin

YMCA Water Polo

- Level One
- Level Two
- Level Three

Competitive Readiness

YMCA Springboard Diving

- Level One
- Level Two
- Level Three

YMCA Skin Diving

YMCA Scuba

Kayaking

Underwater Photography

YMCA Lifeguard and Aquatic Safety Programs

- Aquatic Personal Safety
- Aquatic Personal Safety and Survival
- YMCA Aquatic Safety Assistant
- YMCA Splash

FITNESS

Lap Swimming

YMCA Water Fitness (Vertical)

- Shallow
- Deep
- Sport conditioning
- Post rehab
- Arthritis
- Multiple sclerosis
- Prenatal
- Personal training
- Water walking
- Water running
- Deep water running

COMPETITIVE

- Swim team
- Synchronized swimming team
- Water polo team
- Springboard diving team
- Masters swim team
- Masters synchronized swimming team
- Masters water polo team
- Masters springboard diving team
- Innertube water polo
- Water volleyball
- Water basketball
- Triathlete training
- Lifeguard competitions
- Family obstacle courses
- Swim meets

RECREATION

- Family swims
- Youth swims
- Adult swims
- Teen swims
- Day care swims
- Day camp swims
- Rental groups
- Birthday parties
- Inflatables
- Dive-in movies
- Innertube water polo
- Water volleyball
- Water basketball
- Underwater hockey
- Games night

LEADERSHIP DEVELOPMENT

- Aquatic Leadership Program
- Leaders Club
- Scuba Club

INSTRUCTOR DEVELOPMENT PROGRAMS

- YMCA Swim Lessons
- YMCA Water Fitness
- YMCA Lifeguard Instructor

SPECIAL EVENTS

- YMCA Splash
- Healthy Kids Day
- Open house
- Water shows
- Birthday parties
- Church groups
- Rentals
- Swim meets
- Family Nights
- Teen Nights

If you have a new pool, look at the priorities that have been set and begin to select programs and put together a balanced schedule. If it is an existing pool, evaluate the program schedule and see what needs to be modified. You can begin to make changes with the next program session or season.

Once you realize what changes need to be made, you can begin to achieve your objectives. For a successful transition, do the following:

• Develop a proposal to submit first to your supervisor and then to your program or aquatics committee for discussion and to gain their support. This proposal should include the programs affected, the number of staff and volunteers involved, and how the change will help achieve goals. In addition, include what the new program schedule would look like, the number of new participants, and the financial impact. Gain your supervisor's and committee's support before you communicate with the groups affected by your changes.

• Talk to the members and participants in the affected groups and let them know when and why these changes are going to be made. Also tell them how the YMCA will be able to continue to serve them. No matter how well you do this, some people will be upset and will decide to leave the YMCA.

YMCA Pinnacle Programs

As you prepare to develop new programs, think about whether those programs should be Pinnacle Programs. Pinnacle Programs are those YMCA programs that broadly and deeply integrate the Y's mission and goals into every aspect of their program through endeavors such as:

• *Community development.* Identifying issues and challenges in water safety for the entire community and acting as a catalyst for change. Organizing and offering programs outside of their YMCA site in areas where people need water safety education.

- *Environmental awareness.* Evaluating and educating the community about water quality and safe swimming areas. Providing information on environmental protection in boating and backyard pool safety classes.

- *Group leadership.* Organizing communitywide efforts to address water safety concerns.

- *Programming for special populations.* Mainstreaming individuals with disabilities into regular aquatics classes and offering special programs for those with specific needs.

- *Collaboration.* Collaborating with other departments within the local YMCA and with other community agencies and organizations to expand services and meet community needs.

- *Substance abuse prevention.* Incorporating awareness education into existing aquatics programs, such as talking about safety issues in connection with drug and alcohol use during aquatic activities and discussing and providing activities on healthy lifestyles.

- *Volunteer development.* Providing opportunities for youth, adults, and families to volunteer to help with classes and swim teams, as well as to serve on committees and assist with special events.

- *Youth development.* Expanding youth and teen programs to include self-awareness activities, empowerment, leadership, and service.

These programs are called Pinnacle Programs because they are taken to the highest level of program development. When a local YMCA chooses to go beyond teaching swimming and becomes a leader through its activities, collaborating with and showing concern for the entire community, that YMCA is offering a Pinnacle aquatics program. The YMCA Program Store offers resources to assist staff and volunteers in implementing initiatives that address Pinnacle Program issues.

The following paragraphs explain the differences among programs, YMCA programs, and YMCA Pinnacle Programs:

Programs	Any agency or organization can offer programs. Given a pool, a gym, a strength training center, or a classroom, just about anyone can teach a stroke, an exercise, a technique for lifting weights, or a safety concept.
YMCA programs	Local YMCAs take the same programs and integrate the YMCA mission and YMCA goals into program activities, which makes the programs a conduit for the unique YMCA mission of developing the spirit, mind, and body.
YMCA Pinnacle Programs	These are YMCA programs that broadly and deeply integrate and demonstrate the Y's mission and goals for members into every aspect of their program.

Throughout this manual you will find ways that you can "plus" your program to enhance its quality and meaningfulness to participants and their families. Doing this will allow you to offer the members of your local YMCA and your community a fully integrated program that truly meets the YMCA's mission and benefits your community. Figure 2.2 illustrates these differences.

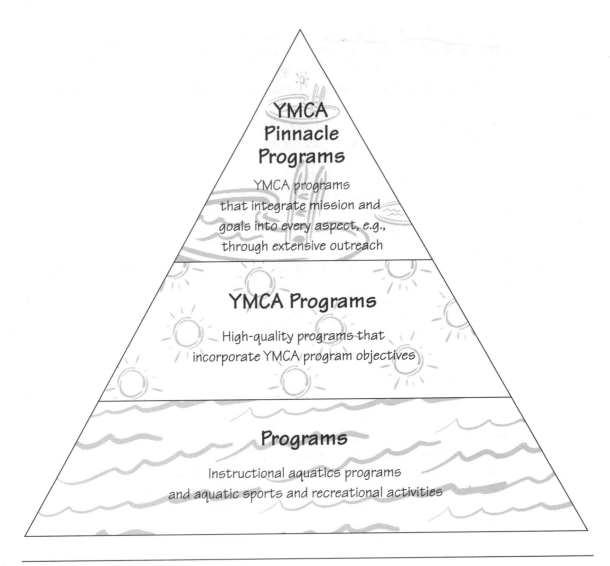

Figure 2.2   The three levels of programs.

CREATING NEW PROGRAMS

Program development is a regular function of YMCA aquatics directors, so you need to know how to do this effectively. The program development process described in this section can be used for any program category.

Program development is everything that is done to conceive, operate, and continuously upgrade programs that most effectively achieve YMCA purposes. This process applies equally to new programming and the revitalization of old programs. It is a formal and deliberate process requiring thorough documentation. The YMCA staff follow this process, with considerable involvement of policy-making volunteers and community resource experts.

In this process, the association's strategic plan—including the mission statement, long-range strategic plan, and operating principles that have been developed by the staff and approved by the board—must be used as the basis for program development:

• The mission statement provides overall guidance and direction for the organization. It is the inspirational purpose of the organization, and it is continuously being achieved. It is what we try to do every day.

• Goals are a further definition of the mission, more specific yet still general enough to be difficult to measure. Association goals are generally found in the strategic plan of a YMCA; they are the steps taken to meet the strategic plan. Goals should be set for each program.

• Operating principles are a step between goals and objectives that serves as a screen against which to test the operating procedures and systems of programs. They are guidelines to help key leadership make choices about what their YMCA should and should not be doing. They help give direction to staff and volunteers involved in the delivery program.

• Objectives are the steps taken to meet each goal of each program.

To view sample strategic plan goals, operating principles, and objectives, go to the YMCA of the USA Web site **(www.ymcausa.org).**

Each program operated by YMCAs should reflect the mission and values of the organization, as well as be congruent with the strategic plan and operating principles.

Program development is a six-step process:

• Identify need or opportunity.
• Collect data.
• Test possible ideas.
• Pilot the design.
• Implement the program.
• Monitor and evaluate the program.

Identify Need or Opportunity

The first step in the program development process is to identify an important prevailing need in your community. Program development occurs to meet organizational or societal needs. But some of the needs in your community are not within the mission of the YMCA—they are somebody else's business. The need you select must be one that is consistent with your YMCA's mission and for which you are able to do something significant.

How do you determine what is needed in your community? Following are some ways that others have found useful:

• Study community demographics.
• Study social trends.
• Interview current members.
• Meet with other organizations and agencies.
• Meet with religious leaders, community leaders, and business people.
• Talk to school administrators and educators.

To gather information, you might do a community analysis, which should include the following:

• Service area demographics
• Accident statistics, including those that are water-related

- Needs-based surveys
- An analysis of relevant local and national social trends
- Surveys or interviews with community leaders
- Details of your current aquatics program and facilities
- Details of other aquatics programs and facilities available to the community
- Member input through focus groups involving people of all ages who use the pool and some of those who don't (See how to run a focus group in chapter 8.)

Contact the YMCA of the USA Research and Planning department for assistance in gathering some of the information mentioned in this list

Once you've compiled all your information, analyze it, keeping these questions in mind:

- Are the pool and programs meeting the needs of the community?
- How do your pool schedule and programs reflect the priorities and goals of your YMCA?
- Are the needs of special groups (such as swim teams, lap swimmers, or active older adults) your top priority or the needs of your membership as a whole?
- Are programs available for all age groups?

Once you've considered these questions, you may need to invest in new program development at your facility at this time. Determine when you will go through the identification step again.

If you identify a new area of need in your community or a current major program that needs revitalization, describe this need. It will provide the target or objective on which you will focus the rest of the development process.

As program development is expensive, ask yourself some initial questions before you go too far:

1. Could an existing program be revised to include this need?
2. Who else in the community is addressing this need?
3. How would a YMCA program dealing with this need be different from what is already available?
4. Could the YMCA collaborate with others who are attempting to meet this need?

Collect Data

In this step in the process, you are focused on gathering information and ideas about possible solutions from as wide a variety of perspectives as possible. In the beginning of this process, your efforts should be spent on data collection and the generation of new information and ideas. After this exercise has been completed, you should switch to the identification of possible solutions.

If the need you have chosen involves a particular group or clientele, make sure that data collection includes that group. Remember that it is easy to get caught up in the data collection phase and collect more than you need.

Data collection may include the following:

- Determining the YMCA's strengths, weaknesses, and uniqueness.
- Assessing current program offerings for compatibility with mission, operating principles, and thrusts and effectiveness of delivery.

- Surveying YMCA members' attitudes and interests to learn what they like and dislike about their involvement, why they joined, why they stay (or leave), what other interests they have, and who they are.
- Identifying the characteristics of the community to be served—including demographic, economic, and social trends, understanding what non-YMCA participants do, and an assessment of the competition. Refer back to the demographic, economic, and social data you collected in the first step to identify key unmet needs that are compatible with the YMCA's mission and within its capabilities.
- Surveying target groups identified for service by YMCA programming to develop a profile that includes interests, attitudes, abilities, limitations, current activities, growth-decline trends, and so on.

You can use some of the material previously collected, as well as county records, United Way reports, and other existing data.

Test Possible Ideas

In this step, you use your research to identify a possible program idea to develop. You need to generate one or more general program formats in enough detail that they can be tested with potential participants. This provides you with a reality check, helps you refine and reshape the original idea, and allows you to begin developing a consumer support base for the program.

First, create a proposal for the best response to the problem or need identified. The proposal should cover the following points:

- What will happen
- When it will happen
- Where it will happen
- How it will happen
- Who will be involved
- How much it will cost
- How long it will last
- What is unique and different about it
- How it will benefit those who participate
- How it will address the problem or need
- How it will meet the association's mission, goals, and operating principles

Then evaluate your proposal by asking yourself the following questions:

- What strengths does this program have that indicate it could be delivered successfully?
- What organizational issues need to be addressed for the program to work?
- What problems within the program must be solved before proceeding?
- If this program succeeds, how will it affect other YMCA programs, the YMCA members, or the community?
- If this program succeeds, what new opportunities will become available?

When you're confident of the proposal, outline a program development chart of work that includes the following:

- Program format
- Leadership
- Participant materials, if any
- A leadership training and development plan
- Enrollment projections for the first year
- Operating budgets
- A description of the test model
- Identification of the test model target group
- A promotion plan
- An evaluation plan and tools
- A list of needed facilities and equipment
- Staff assignments and a supervision plan

Pilot the Design

Pilot testing allows you to try a small, controlled version of the new or revised program with potential participants. This will help you learn the strong and weak points of the new design and allow you to make necessary refinements as it operates. Key questions to ask yourself during the pilot test are these:

- Will it work? If so, how, where, with whom, and under what conditions?
- In what ways could the design be modified to get better results at less cost?
- How could it work better?

You should come up with a refined, clearer, cleaner program after this step.

Implement the Program

At this step, give final consideration to how the program will be presented and operated. Review the how and why of each of the preceding steps, and make sure the program committee members and others crucial to the success of the program are fully on board.

Make any necessary modifications in the program development chart of work that was completed for the pilot program. During this step, you will select marketing strategies, complete the budget, set quantity and quality goals, and finalize plans for obtaining the necessary facilities, equipment, and leaders.

Monitor and Evaluate the Program

Once a program has been implemented, you will need to monitor it. As you learn more, you will want to introduce changes and improvements. Key program leadership and responsible committees should review the performance of major programs regularly. Quality control happens at this point of delivery. Make sure that systems and supports are in place to ensure that programs do what they were created to do and have enough participants to justify their existence. Be willing to eliminate programs that no longer meet a community need or have become too costly to attract participation (see the "Program Life Cycle" section).

DEVELOPING A VISION FOR YOUR AQUATICS DEPARTMENT

Working within the boundaries of your association's strategic plan, branch goals, and performance standards, you can still have your own personal vision for your department that complements the association's larger vision. Using much of the same information and research that is used in the program development process, you should develop a vision for your department. This vision is a realization of your department's potential and helps illustrate your leadership skills.

Here are some questions to use in considering your aquatics department:

- What would your department and programs look like in your ideal world?
- What are the goals?
- What are the core values? How will they be demonstrated?
- What other programs could you be offering based on the needs of the community and the members?
- Are there segments of the community that you could be serving better?
- How will your programs serve the members?

After you start seeing what your department could be, you can start developing your action plan and communicating your vision to the staff and volunteers. Under your leadership, you can make this vision become a reality. This is one of the characteristics that illustrates the difference between a manager and a leader.

Figure 2.3 is an example of a vision statement.

ADJUSTING PROGRAMS

Once a program has started, your work has just begun. You need to oversee all your programs to ensure their quality and their ongoing value in terms of your YMCA's

Aquatics Vision Statement

The main purpose of YUSA aquatics is to help meet the mission of the organization. We will do this by

✔ Focusing on members' needs

✔ Developing swimming skills

✔ Teaching water safety

✔ Maximizing the use of facilities

✔ Valuing our aquatic staff and volunteers

✔ Developing training that is accessible to the whole community

✔ Collaborating with others to strengthen the program and involve more people

As a result of this, YUSA aquatics will be recognized as a leader by the profession and the general public.

Figure 2.3   Sample aquatics vision statement.

mission and goals. One way to do this is to be aware of each program's place in the program life cycle. If you want to extend the life of existing programs that still have merit, you can "plus" them, and one good way to do so is to add service-learning components.

Program Life Cycle

The program life cycle is an effective tool for evaluating your programs. It is based on the idea that programs and services go through discernible stages in response to consumer demand. The interest level and involvement of members in a program vary over time, and we need to be sensitive to that. The five stages in the lifetime of a program are the following (see figure 2.4):

- Birth
- Rapid growth
- Maturity
- Decline
- Death

New programs require a lot of nurturing and probably will not pay off financially right away. Decline in programs over time is inevitable unless something is done to plus or bring innovation to those programs. However, the longer a program can be kept in the maturity phase, the greater the return on investment will be. Programs on the decline can be harvested for immediate gain, can be given more resources to sustain their health, or can simply be allowed to die. The time frame for this process varies.

Here are brief descriptions of each of the stages:

- *Birth stage.* When a program is new, it requires a lot of attention from staff. Considerable testing is done, and modifications are made to the program based on evaluations. The program also usually requires subsidy during this stage.

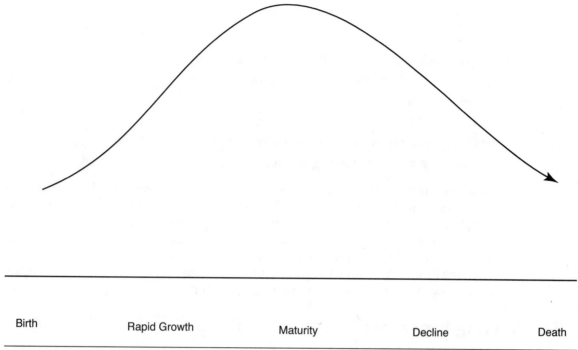

| Birth | Rapid Growth | Maturity | Decline | Death |

Figure 2.4   Program life cycle.

- *Rapid growth stage.* At this stage, a program is part of a trend, has its own life, attracts many people, and requires a lot of problem solving (e.g., need for additional staff, equipment, and space). The program begins to break even or generate surpluses. The length of this stage varies.

- *Maturity stage.* A program at this stage has significant support from volunteers and has stable growth in participation and leadership. The program can produce surpluses and has a positive reputation in the community. It is evaluated regularly.

- *Decline stage.* The program has become routine. Participation has declined continuously over a number of sessions, and staff and volunteers are frustrated and bored with the program. The budget declines, and the program needs revision. This may result from a trend passing or a decline in the quality of the program being offered.

- *Death stage.* Ending a program is difficult to do. Typically, a small number of participants want the program to continue, but usually another program that could use the resources (pool time, equipment, and staff) is ready to replace it.

Staffing, programming, and financial decisions hinge on where a program is in the life cycle.

You need to consider when you should intervene to enhance a program during its life cycle. You can enhance a program using the following methods:

- Adjusting the fee
- Adjusting the participant-to-instructor ratio
- Adding educational components (seminars or handouts)
- Adjusting the schedule
- Plussing the program (see next section)
- Target marketing the program to another audience
- Evaluating your marketing strategy

You also need to cancel when the program

- has a lack of interest,
- has a lack of program and staff quality and service,
- has low participation over a period of time,
- does not meet its financial objectives,
- does not fulfill the mission of the organization,
- does not fulfill the goals and objectives of the YMCA, or
- fails even after repackaging and repricing.

Developing programs is an ongoing process. Your awareness of this fact is important for continuing success. Instead of waiting for a program to decline, you can keep the program in the rapid growth and maturity phases as long as possible through your observations and evaluations. In addition, continuously develop new programs or add additional services for your members and community.

See the "Comprehensive Program Audit/Analysis" section later in this chapter for more on how to assess when to cancel a program.

Plussing Programs

If you have a YMCA program that is not meeting expectations or is in the maturity stage and you want it to continue, evaluate it to determine how you can make it unique or enhance the quality of the program. Ask the following questions:

- What do we have to do to enhance the program?
- What needs to be changed?
- What needs to be considered?
- How can we make it special?
- How can we incorporate the "Wow!" and "Gee-whiz!" factors?

When you analyze a program this way and actually make changes to make it more unique, you have engaged in program "plussing." Some call it "romancing," others call it "re-packaging." But regardless of what you call it, you've improved a YMCA program to make it unique for your members.

Ask yourself the following questions:

- What needs to be done to this program? (Should it be continued? Cancelled? Plussed?)
- Who should be consulted for help? (Accounting, Purchasing, Human Resources)
- Who should be involved in making changes? (members, aquatics staff, volunteers, frontline staff, program participants)
- What are the financial, human, and political (internal/external) resource implications?
- When should changes be implemented?
- Who can I get to champion this with me? (volunteer, staff member)

As an example, here are some suggested activities and services that can add fun and interest to aquatics programs:

- Offer synchronized swim lessons that can lead to a synchronized swim team.
- Have a Halloween costume party in the pool.

- Have a night of "wild water mania" for families, with inflatable toys, Water logs, and other surprises and activities.
- Make Y Pal Play available: Staff members swim with kids while their parents participate in a different pool activity.
- Host celebration nights for high school graduates, giving them access to the full facility for the entire night.
- Host an Easter egg float, with small prizes inside the plastic eggs.
- Schedule interactive games in the pool, such as wetball, basketball, volleyball, or even bingo.
- Encourage staff members to actively suggest appropriate activities to families in the pool.

Service-Learning

Service-learning projects, in which people volunteer to provide assistance to others, are a great way to plus existing programs. The YMCA defines *service-learning* as a deliberate process through which people of all ages—and in all parts of the YMCA—can develop membership- and program-specific skills, knowledge, and behaviors while contributing to their communities and developing civic awareness.

Service-learning is a tool for putting the YMCA's mission into action. It is one of the methods that can move a YMCA program to a pinnacle program. It can also strengthen all aspects of a YMCA's operations, including membership, volunteering, and staff and board development.

The three main components of the service-learning process are

- establishing learning objectives,
- performing meaningful service based on the objectives, and
- reflecting on the experience in a structured way.

Establishing Learning Objectives

Setting learning objectives establishes purpose and is the critical first step from which every other element of the service-learning process flows. Learning objectives describe reinforcement of and changes in the skills, knowledge, attitude, or behavior of the participants as a result of the process.

Establishing learning objectives allows us to see if we have achieved our goals, helps us evaluate our process, and lets us know if we have responded effectively to our participants' needs. By establishing learning objectives with the help of the leader, participants walk away with expanded knowledge and the skills necessary to make a positive difference.

Every YMCA program is designed to help participants build specific skills, knowledge, attitudes, and behaviors. By integrating service-learning into any YMCA program, you can help participants develop those program-specific objectives while also engaging them in helping others and developing civic awareness.

For example, a health and fitness director could use a fundraising exercise-a-thon to help fund research to cure breast cancer. Participants would learn exercise principles (as they would in a regular YMCA class), but they would also learn about breast cancer and get an opportunity to help cure it. Another example would be a preschool service-learning project that would help young children develop fine motor skills (an existing goal of many YMCA preschool programs) by drawing pictures for kids in the hospital or the elderly. The possibilities are endless—service-learning can be used to enhance the preexisting goals and objectives of any and every YMCA program. The trick is to ask, "What are this program's goals and objectives? How could a service-learning project reinforce those goals and objectives? What else could service-learning help our participants in this program learn?"

Performing Meaningful Service

Meaningful service is the active part of the service-learning process and should be connected to the learning objectives. Service is generally considered meaningful if it meets a need that the service beneficiaries believe is important or valuable. The service may be either community or YMCA service.

Community service takes place at a site that is not on YMCA property or is somewhere other than where YMCA members and participants normally gather. Examples would include cleaning up a local park, tutoring children in a low-income neighborhood, or buying groceries for seniors. Because it takes participants out of their normal environment, community service is useful at broadening participants' civic awareness. It's also another way that YMCAs can connect with and understand their communities.

YMCA service takes place on YMCA property or on or near the site where YMCA members and participants usually gather. Examples would include older adult YMCA members painting the walls of the YMCA teen center, families restoring trails at a YMCA camp, or youth holding a swimming marathon in the YMCA pool to raise money for childhood leukemia research. Since YMCAs are of, by, and for the community, all YMCA service is essentially community service.

Whether it's YMCA service or community service, the *service* in service-learning is not one-way. Ideally, it should begin with a mutual exchange of thoughts and actions between the participants and the service beneficiaries that results in community solutions. One step in creating this kind of experience is to identify service projects that are meaningful to both the participants and the service beneficiaries.

The list of possible service projects is infinite: community gardens, mural painting at the YMCA, brown-bag healthy lifestyle lunches, tutoring, water testing, chores for the homebound, beautification projects, storm drain labeling, tree planting, performing arts in nursing homes, recycling . . . the sky is the limit! Anything goes, as long as it meets a real need and is significant to the participants involved. Here are some additional ideas for meaningful service projects:

Help for the Hungry/Homeless

- Help cook or serve a meal at a homeless shelter.
- Gather clothing from your neighbors and donate it to a shelter.
- Help with repairs at a local homeless shelter.
- Make a care package with mittens, socks, T-shirts, long underwear.
- Work with local officials to start a community foodbank, if one is needed.
- Organize a neighborhood group to plant, tend, harvest, and donate a vegetable garden.

Senior Citizens

- Rake leaves, shovel snow, clean gutters, or wash windows for senior citizens.
- Write a "grandfriend" a letter, or write letters for an elderly person.
- Go for a walk with a senior citizen in your community.
- Hold an afternoon dance for your local nursing home.
- Deliver meals or groceries to homebound individuals.
- Help senior citizens in your neighborhood obtain and install locks or smoke alarms.
- Teach a senior friend how to use a computer or the Internet.
- Get a group together to sing or present a play at a nursing home.

Neighborhood Enhancement

- Clean up a vacant lot.
- Organize a campaign to raise money to purchase and install new playground equipment.
- Campaign for additional lighting along poorly lighted streets.
- Paint a mural or clean up in a local park.
- Plant flowers in public areas that could use some color.
- Set up a neighborhood curbside recycling pickup.
- Create a campaign to encourage biking and walking.

For Those With Special Needs

- Volunteer to help at a Special Olympics event.
- Raise money for braille or large-print books for those with visual impairment.
- Volunteer at an agency that works with children who have physical disabilities.
- Read books or the newspaper on tape for people with visual impairment.
- Bring toys to children in the cancer ward of a hospital.

Reflecting in a Structured Way

Reflection is the process of engaging participants' critical thinking skills to prepare for and learn from the service activity. Reflection is an essential component of effective service-learning, yet it is often neglected. Many feel that it is the most important step in the process. It provides a time for participants to capture valuable knowledge and integrate it into their thinking.

One reason reflection is important is that service-learning often introduces participants to new relationships, experiences, questions, and feelings. There is no way of knowing how the participants are reacting to these new experiences or what they are learning unless participants get an opportunity to share. What is not addressed may not be understood.

Reflection provides the project coordinator with an opportunity to check on how the group is doing on the established learning objectives and to evaluate the project. Those who are giving gain knowledge and skills as they actively engage in preparing for the project and look back at what they have accomplished. This process extends the experience of giving from being a one-sided venture to true sharing, in which the giver gets as much as the one on the receiving end. By adding reflection, we can create deeper, long-lasting, positive outcomes for participants. Here are a few examples of reflection activities:

- *Journal writing.* This is an opportunity for participants to capture their experiences, to hold on to what they have experienced, and to think about what they want to take home with them. Ask them to respond to each of the following guided questions, then write down or draw other thoughts that occur to them:

  a. Take a few minutes to think about the experiences you have had today. Think about the feelings, ideas, concerns, and dreams that you will take away with you as a result of your experience. Please write down some of the key things you want to remember about the experience.

  b. Think about and describe the most significant idea, concept, or insight you have discovered today. Why is it important to you?

  c. What is one thing you are going to do that is new or different as a result of this experience?

- *Bumper stickers.* Ask participants to find partners and talk together for a few minutes about the experiences they have had. They should share their ideas about the most important things they have learned. Then they should create a bumper sticker that captures the "essence" of their experience.

- *Commercial.* Divide participants into small groups, then ask each group to create a service-learning commercial to act out for the entire group. It should reflect some of the insights they have gained. The purpose of this commercial is up to them. They may want to convince their community to support service-learning . . . they may want to sell their project to the next group of people to participate . . . and so on. The commercial may be serious or humorous. As with real TV, they can have up to one minute of airtime for their commercial.

- *Group banners.* If you do service projects in teams, or have several participants in the same service activity, break the group into teams or groups. Supply each team with a piece of banner paper and markers and ask them to depict their experience using a combination of words and pictures. Give them about 10-15 minutes. When they have finished, ask each group to share their banner with the whole group. Use their banners as a starting point for processing the experience.

- *Ball of string.* Have the group stand in a circle. Give someone the ball of string and ask that person a question ("What was one thing you learned today?"). Once the person has answered the question, ask him or her to hold onto one end of the string and throw the ball to someone else. Have the second person answer the same question, hold onto one end of the string, and pass it on to the next person. Continue the process until everyone has reflected on the question. When done, you should have something that looks like a web. When the group is done talking, make points about the interconnectedness of people, how they were all part of the solutions, how the outcome would be different if everyone had not participated, and so on.

- *Discussion groups.* In small or large groups, ask participants questions that will help them process their service experience. Some sample questions might include the following:

    a. What difference have we really made in our community?

    b. Where might you apply this new knowledge to other parts of your life?

    c. What things do you see differently as a result of your service?

    d. What have you learned about yourself?

    e. What new views do you have of groups and individuals?

- *Time capsule.* As participants are preparing for a project, have them put together memorabilia related to the process in the form of a time capsule. This could include information about the topic they had researched, a training agenda, dirt from a gardening project, and so on. In addition to including objects, have students write down how they are feeling at different points of the project (what they expected before they began, how they felt about the preparation, how they felt the first time they did service as part of the project). Put everything into a "capsule" that will be opened and read aloud and discussed (perhaps anonymously) at the end of the experience.

- *Before-and-after pictures.* This activity is especially effective for cleanup or renovation projects. Ask participants to draw, color, or paint pictures of the cleanup area before they begin. Chances are, the pictures will include trash, broken bottles, rusty playground equipment, and so on. After the project is complete, have the participants create another picture. Lay the pictures side by side and let them discuss the changes and positive impact they made.

Service-Learning in Aquatics

Here are some examples of service-learning projects that could be incorporated into YMCA aquatics programs.

- *YMCA Swim Team.* Swim team members could hold an annual fundraiser for a local or national cause. For example, on one team, a team member has a brother with Down syndrome. The swim team members decide that they want to hold a swimming marathon to raise funds to support the development of educational materials about Down syndrome and to provide scholarships for families of children with Down syndrome to attend a camp program. To learn more about the syndrome, swim team members invite family members of Down syndrome children to teach them about the disorder. The swim team also partners with a local support agency and provides swim days for children with Down syndrome. Later, team members solicit sponsorships from individuals, businesses, and organizations in the community—$1.00 for each lap—and hold the swimming marathon. Team members are asked to reflect on their experiences by keeping an ongoing journal to record their thoughts and feelings about the experience and what they have learned.

- *Arthritis Foundation (AFYAP) Exercise Class.* Class members are asked to assist with the Polliwog swim lesson group. The swim lesson instructor trains the class members to play skill-related games with the Polliwogs, reviewing the objectives of each game and indicators of skill mastery. The YMCA's pool schedule is coordinated so the AFYAP class follows the Polliwog swim lessons. Class members arrive a half hour before the start of the AFYAP class to play games with the Polliwogs. While they complete their own exercises, class members discuss the progress of the Polliwogs and explore the success of their own teaching skills.

• *Scuba.* This is an actual example from the Southwest Branch YMCA of Metropolitan Atlanta. The scuba club studied the history of slavery and the slave trade during the 16th and 17th centuries. The club then traveled to Key West, Florida, to dive to the remains of a 300-year-old sunken vessel used to transport slaves from the West Indies to Britain. Club members held a memorial service below the surface of the water and placed a memorial plaque at the site of the shipwreck to educate future divers. Each club member kept a journal of the experience, and the club held group discussions to reflect on the personal impact of the event.

The information in this section was excerpted from *The YMCA Service Learning Guide,* available through the YMCA Program Store (Item no. 0-7360-3757-8). The guide provides additional details and resources to help you integrate quality service-learning into the life of your YMCA.

You may also contact the YMCA of the USA at 800-872-9622 or become part of the YMCA service-learning listserv. As a subscriber to the listserv, you can send and receive e-mail to and from YMCA colleagues across the United States. To sign up, send an e-mail message with the word *subscribe* in the body of the text to **Service-Learning@ymca.net.**

PROGRAM MONITORING AND EVALUATION

Measuring program performance is an important role of aquatics directors. Not only do we need to determine the value of our programs, we need to determine their value to our members and participants and be able to describe this value and how much it costs.

Regular monitoring of programs can meet two basic needs:

1. It provides a meaningful way for committee members to be part of the ongoing operation of the YMCA. It allows for broad participation in the decision-making process by key volunteer and community leaders, thus increasing the sense of ownership and investment on the part of those with the power to make things happen.

2. It makes quality control and change or revision of programs a regular, planned part of the ongoing operation of the YMCA. It avoids a problem-oriented, crisis approach to management. Program quality monitoring, properly conducted in a consultative, cooperative way, can be as much a celebration of what is being done right as an analysis of what is being done wrong.

Monitoring program quality includes a variety of assessments:

Objective Analysis
- What is the program designed to do?
- How well is it achieving the mission and functioning within the operating principles of the YMCA?
- How well is it meeting the current community needs?
- Is it achieving its objectives with current participants?

Financial Analysis
- What is the enrollment picture for the last three years?
- Is it meeting its revenue goals? Why or why not?
- What is the balance of earned to contributed income?
- What is the cost per participant?

- Is the trend line of cost per participant moving up or down?
- How much financial assistance has been given each year?

Market Share Analysis

- What is the total market for the program?
- What percentage of that market is the program serving?
- Over the past three years, is the percentage increasing or decreasing?
- What is the market share goal for the program?
- Where is the program on the program life cycle?
- What new features have been added recently?
- What are the program's real benefits to participants?

Leadership Analysis

- What is the quality level of the current leadership?
- Does the present leadership have a good understanding of the YMCA's mission and the program objectives, as well as the skills necessary to deliver the program?
- How many volunteers are involved in leadership or operational positions in the program? How could more volunteers be involved in its delivery?
- Are there regular opportunities for training and evaluation of program leaders?

Related Service Analysis

- What other service-related programs are available in the community (government, schools, churches, parks and recreation departments, other agencies)?
- Where are the services located? What times and days are they offered?
- How do those programs market their services? What are their results?
- How does the quality of their program compare with that of the YMCA?
- When was the last time someone "shopped" those services?

Quality Analysis

- How do key program decision makers and participants rate the program in areas such as administration, promotion and marketing, volunteer and professional staff training and supervision, family or support group involvement, participant evaluation and retention?
- Are you proud of the program?
- Are participants so sold on the program that they are willing to help promote it to others?
- Does it really do what we claim it does?
- Does the program comply with each of the operating standards of the association?
- How does the program rate against the YMCA of the USA program guidelines?
- Is the program safe, with minimal injuries and risks?

To have quality programming, a YMCA needs programs that

- have been developed and implemented by people with passion, persistence, and a commitment to quality;
- have had a consistently good level of quality;

- are constantly being improved; and
- help the organization meet its goals for mission, service, image, and finances.

You get there by following the process of development, adhering to your operational standards, and being committed to continuously improving and building program value for members. It helps to approach quality improvement as an attitude, an art, and a process. Intensely focus on members to try to discover what they want from your program and how they perceive it. Consider even small details that may make a big difference to them. Empower your frontline staff to deliver quality, and give your staff feedback to encourage continuous improvement. (See chapter 5 for more on member service.)

Programs can be monitored using a variety of methods:

- Observation of classes
- Evaluation and feedback from parents, participants, and staff, as well as peers
- Validation reviews
- Comprehensive program audit/analysis

Observation of Classes and Programs

One of the best ways to monitor is to drop in on classes and programs informally. While you observe, pay attention to the following:

- The cleanliness of the area
- The sounds of the program
- The expressions on the faces of participants
- How staff are interacting with participants
- Safety of participants

If a quality YMCA experience is happening, one in which all participants are growing toward the best in themselves, you will see the following:

- Warm relationships
- Enthusiasm for the program
- A number of people staying with the program
- One-to-one relationships
- Openness
- Fun and enjoyment
- A high percentage of those involved sharing program responsibility
- Freedom and creativity
- Feelings of self-mastery and accomplishment
- Feelings of safety

Program Evaluation

We recommend that you formally evaluate each aquatics class each session. This allows you to find out whether participants and parents were satisfied with their experiences, whether the quality of the instruction and facilities was maintained, and what you might do to make the program better next time. It also fosters good public relations between your YMCA and your participants.

Tally and review the evaluation forms. Evaluation allows you to see what changes to make in the future or to correct any ongoing problems or make adjustments in administering or presenting programs. Ensure that every constructive criticism or suggestion is addressed by someone on your staff. Develop a system for responding, such as posting the responses on a bulletin board or calling the individual who made the criticism or suggestion.

Give each of the groups involved in the program the opportunity to provide feedback, including parents, participants, and staff. It is also a good idea to have a group of knowledgeable outsiders review your program at least once a year to see if it is meeting your YMCA standards.

Evaluation of the Program by Parents

During each session, give parents the opportunity to complete an evaluation form about the program. This lets parents know that your YMCA cares about their thoughts and feelings. It also gives you feedback for improving your program and evaluating your instructors. Parents often have wonderful insights that instructors and directors cannot see because they look at the program from a different perspective.

A good time to distribute evaluation forms is about halfway through the session. This gives you feedback in time to make changes before the session is over. The following figures show sample evaluation forms for parents. Figure 2.5 is a short form that is best used when time is scarce; figure 2.6 is an open-ended form that allows parents to provide as much information as they like.

You can distribute the evaluation forms in several ways. You can hand them out to students so they can take them home and return them to the front desk after their parents have completed them. Alternatively, you can take the forms directly to the parents in the observation area and have them complete them in 5 or 10 minutes, collecting the completed forms directly from the parents. Last, you can mail them to the parents at home, along with stamped, self-addressed envelopes in which they can return the completed forms.

Still another option for making evaluation forms available is to keep them in a box placed where parents wait for or watch their children during class. In that way, parents can give the YMCA feedback whenever they like.

Short Program Evaluation Form

Program Feedback Sheet

Please help us to serve you better. We need your feedback—good or bad. Thank you.

Program _____

Instructor _____

Please rate your satisfaction on a scale from 1 to 5, where 1 is very dissatisfied and 5 is very satisfied.

Check the appropriate boxes.

	1	2	3	4	5
Staff's responsiveness	☐	☐	☐	☐	☐
Staff's courtesy	☐	☐	☐	☐	☐
Instructor's knowledge of class material	☐	☐	☐	☐	☐
Instructor's helpfulness and consideration	☐	☐	☐	☐	☐
Cleanliness and condition of area where class met	☐	☐	☐	☐	☐
Precautions taken to ensure safety and prevent injury	☐	☐	☐	☐	☐
Value of class for the price	☐	☐	☐	☐	☐
Expectations met	☐	☐	☐	☐	☐
Overall satisfaction	☐	☐	☐	☐	☐

If you marked dissatisfied or very dissatisfied for any of the above items, could you please explain?

Would you like a staff person to contact you? No   Yes

Which staff person?_____
(If you want us to contact you, please give us your name and a daytime phone number at the bottom of the card.)

How did you hear about our program? _____

Would you be interested in becoming a volunteer instructor for any of our programs? No Yes

Please give us your name and daytime phone number.

Name _____

Daytime phone number _____   Date _____

Figure 2.5   Sample short program evaluation form for parents.

YMCA Program Evaluation Form

The board and staff of the _____ YMCA are striving to maintain the highest standards of friendliness and efficiency. We feel that our participants can help us by letting us know how they feel about our program. Please help us by filling in the information below. We appreciate any and all comments. Thanks for your support and interest in the _____ YMCA.

Program or activity _____

Age/grade of participant _____

What part of this program did you or your child enjoy best? _____
_____
_____

What part of this program did you or your child enjoy the least? _____
_____

Was the program what you thought it would be when you signed up? _____
_____

If not, why not? _____
_____

How well did our staff members perform? Rate your satisfaction on a scale from 1 to 5, where 1 is very dissatisfied and 5 is very satisfied. (If enrolled in a class, please rate the instructor; if enrolled in sports, please rate the officials and coaches; if enrolled in child care, please rate the counselors.)

    Instructor   _____

    Coaches   _____

    Officials   _____

    Counselors   _____

Why did you rate the staff the way you did? _____

What suggestions would you make to the staff? _____

Would you enroll in this program again? _____ Would you recommend it to others? _____

Why or why not? _____

Was the program priced fairly? _____

Please rate the following:

    Staff responsiveness   _____

    Desk service   _____

    Staff courtesy   _____

    Telephone service   _____

    Program scheduling   _____

    Condition of facility   _____

Name (Optional) _____

Comments:

Figure 2.6 Sample long program evaluation form for parents.

Evaluation of the Program by Students

From time to time, you can ask students informally what they like about a class. At the end of each session, you can also have students who are old enough to write complete a simple evaluation form. You can ask younger children the same questions and record their answers.

Evaluation of the Program by Staff

At the end of each session, hold a staff meeting to review how well the session went and to suggest improvements in the program. Have instructors discuss questions such as the following:

- How did your lesson plans for the session go? How could you improve them?
- What games or activities worked really well for you?
- What problems arose, and how did you solve them?
- How well did the pool use patterns work? Could they be changed to be more effective or safer?
- Do we have sufficient equipment for the activities you've planned?
- Are there any steps we could take to make classes safer? Can we make them more fun?
- What worked well (or not) in the schedule of classes? Of instructors? Of assistants?

Evaluation of the Program by Peers

We recommend that you seek an outside evaluation of all your aquatics programs at least annually. This is similar to but less formal than a validation review (discussed in the next section); it may not go to supervisors or the board. You may ask a group of three or four staff members from other YMCAs to evaluate your programs, using the YMCA of the USA Aquatics Guidelines and your association's aquatics policy to guide their review. Doing so ensures that your program is following the set guidelines and policies and that the high quality of your aquatics programming is being maintained.

The group should submit their evaluation report to your YMCA's administrative staff with a checklist that indicates your program's strengths and areas where improvement is needed. Share this checklist with your executive director and program committee.

For additional sample evaluation forms, see the YMCA of the USA Web site (**www.ymcausa.org**).

PROGRAM OPERATIONAL STANDARDS

Program success can be measured in several ways: achievement of quality standards, number of people served, or the amount of revenue generated by the program (in relation to expenses) or funds generated to subsidize the program. However, quality programming can be achieved only when "quality" has been defined. The greatest increase in program quantity and improvement in program quality takes place when standards are developed and implemented in conjunction with the long-range planning process, the budget plan, and the performance appraisal system.

Before we continue, we need to differentiate between guidelines and standards. *Guidelines* are recommendations from the YMCA of the USA to be considered by local YMCAs. The YMCA of the USA Aquatics Guidelines (see appendix 4) will help local YMCA staff, key volunteer decision makers, and program participants assess the quality of their aquatics programs. Used as a tool for self-assessment, the guidelines can point out both areas that need improvement and areas of excellence. Intended for use in conjunction with YMCA of the USA aquatics program manuals, the guidelines have been compiled from suggestions and evaluation instruments contributed by many local YMCAs.

Standards are rules or policies governing any particular program that can only be set by the local association. Program standards provide a definition of quality and serve as operating guidelines by which programs can be evaluated. In an organization based on the principle of local autonomy, local YMCAs are expected to establish standards consistent with National YMCA guidelines but tailored to their own methods of operation and the specific needs and legal requirements of their communities.

It is helpful to have guidelines and association standards as an operating principle. The time and effort invested in this process is well worth it because it helps the YMCA provide consistent quality of programs from one location to another or one session to another. Written standards can be used as a tool for orienting new staff, ensuring a safe environment for participants and staff, and communicating about the program and promoting it to members and the community.

Successful implementation of local standards begins with the development process. Because quality should be perceived as everyone's concern, input from all levels of the organization (e.g., part-time staff, professional staff, volunteer committees) should be incorporated into the development of standards.

Once you have standards, they should be operationalized into the entire organization. If they are not, problems can arise. For instance, if they are not taken into account during the budget process, then financial resources will not be allocated to cover the costs of implementing standards. Also, if staff are not held accountable in their performance objectives and appraisal for compliance with the standards, those standards may not be met.

Review and update your association's standards regularly. Failure to comply with them increases your association's liability in cases of lawsuits.

When developing your standards, keep in mind that there may be local or state regulations that must legally be met. All YMCA programs must comply with the current laws, codes, or ordinances of their city, county, and state. Because regulations vary from place to place, each YMCA is responsible for knowing and abiding by the requirements in its locale. However, state and local standards may be only minimum requirements for operation and may not fully address the quality of the program desired by participants and the YMCA. The goal of a YMCA should be to offer programs of the highest possible quality.

The following are the steps in the process of developing association standards and policy:

- *Identify policy and standards needs.* This is the beginning, the first step, where problems, ideas, concern, challenges, and tasks surface and become agenda items for the appropriate committee. This step involves both staff and board jointly.

- *Formulate policy options.* This second step is where volunteers and staff, working together and sharing their skills and convictions, identify options and alternatives that respond to the problem, concern, or task. This step involves the appropriate committees or board and staff together. This step also includes the following:

    a. Assembling a task force to develop and recommend specific standards.

    b. Providing the task force with information on national YMCA guidelines.

    c. Establishing a process to involve all levels of the organization and clarify their roles.

    d. Pilot testing the standards before final presentation to the board.

    e. Having each program unit complete and submit a self-audit identifying which standards are presently being met and what is needed to meet the other standards.

• *Determine policy.* The actual selection of the options and alternatives, the third step in the process, is generally decided by the volunteers through voting at board or committee meetings.

• *Implement policy.* The next to last step is where staff—paid or volunteer—carry out the selected alternative (voted on at board or committee meetings) in response to the identified problem, concern, or task. They should develop a realistic timetable for implementation and identify who will monitor and drive the implementation process.

They also should establish a written format for presentation of the standards. The standards should be written in such a way that they can be easily measured and should be limited to only those things that really make a difference in delivering a quality program experience.

• *Monitoring policy.* The final step, and one often overlooked, is the joint responsibility of board and staff to keep track of and appraise the outcome of policy implementation. This step "closes the loop," beginning a new cycle of identifying specific policy needs based on what was learned from the previous action.

To ensure that program operational standards are followed, you should set up annual validation reviews. These will include a comprehensive program audit/analysis.

Validation Reviews

Once program operational standards have been developed, your YMCA will need to create a process to assess programs annually using the standards. This process uses an outside validation team recruited from the community, which may include program participants, experts in aquatics, directors of other aquatics facilities, YMCA board members, or staff from other YMCAs. Following is a recommended six-step approach:

1. The association CEO or executive director explains the assessment process to staff and volunteers.

2. The aquatics director, with the help of other staff, conducts a review of all programs using the standards and reports areas needing improvement.

3. The aquatics director or executive director recruits a validation team from the community. This team may include program participants, experts in aquatics, directors of other aquatics facilities, YMCA board members, or staff from other YMCAs.

4. The aquatics director or executive director conducts an orientation for the validation team to review the association's aquatics program standards.

5. The validation team conducts a review of each program.

6. The validation team reports its findings to the YMCA Board of Directors through the appropriate committee structure

Using a validation team provides good community publicity for your YMCA. It familiarizes key people with YMCA aquatics programs and impresses on them your concern for quality. During assessment, each standard should be considered important and should be addressed at the appropriate staff level. This assessment process should not only provide an overview of each program, but should also reinforce the specific standards.

After the assessment is completed, staff and volunteers should determine what corrective action, if any, is needed to bring programs in line with the standards. They should establish a realistic timetable for implementation and create a monitoring system that focuses on rewards for achievement rather than punishment for non-compliance. Maintaining high quality in programs is an ongoing job; assess programs regularly to maintain or improve standards.

Comprehensive Program Audit/Analysis

Before staff and key volunteer program leaders can decide whether to maintain, change, or discontinue an existing program or even to replace it with a new one, they need the best possible overall picture of the program. To perform a comprehensive program audit/analysis, program committees and volunteer and staff leadership should gather and review the following information:

- Program title
- Program life-cycle stage
- How program achieves mission of the YMCA and why it is believed to be in this stage
- Developmental YMCA goals achieved by this program
- Measurable program objectives
- Assessment program demographics
- Constituency
- Annual participation for previous three years and increase/decrease over previous year
- Program target analysis (target market, market penetration, program life span)
- Features and benefits of the program
- Time and space requirements (facility needs, length of each session, number of classes/sessions, equipment, and percentage of professional staff time)
- Leadership (number of part- or full-time staff and number of volunteers, percentage of professional staff time)
- Financial considerations (income and expenses)
- Similar activities available in community (where, cost to participants, enrollment)
- How the program fits into the present mix of offerings
- Future issues or concerns that need to be addressed (external influences effect relating to technical, education, societal, consumer, legal, or political)
- What has been done recently to push the program

This process is very similar to the one conducted by staff as part of the regular monitoring and evaluation of programs (see page 34).

DEVELOPMENTAL ASSETS AND IMPACT RESEARCH

A simple, relatively inexpensive, and thoroughly documented way to prove that YMCA youth programs work is impact research. The YMCA of the USA and Search Institute, a private not-for-profit organization based in Minneapolis, have combined research and resource development to come up with material that proves that youth programs make a measurable, provable difference. The research is based on what's called the asset-development approach, one that identifies the 40 assets that youth need for healthy development. Kids who have more assets are more likely to be involved in positive behaviors such as volunteering and are less likely to be involved in negative behaviors.

A list of the assets appears in appendix 1. The categories of assets are support, empowerment, boundaries and expectations, constructive time use, commitment to learning, positive values, social competence, and positive identity. These 40 assets are the developmental building blocks that young people need to grow, develop, and succeed. The program evaluation process can measure how YMCA programs contribute to asset development; the YMCA youth survey is the way to measure.

Since the correlation between the number of assets and these characteristics is proven, all you have to do to prove that your programs work is to show that they provide kids with developmental assets.

Program leaders in aquatics and scuba focus on skill development and safety. Getting them to see that their programs and activities have a deeper impact than they realize is key. If these program leaders can begin to think how to use the asset approach to express what they do to promote healthy lifestyles, then they will be on their way. They may even begin experiencing something more fulfilling themselves while filling in some essential gaps that might be missing in their programming for young people. Aquatics and scuba program leaders can help build assets in the following ways:

- Make connections between typical activities and the assets. For example, standing in a line is about being responsible (asset #30). Not doing horseplay in the water is about creating safety (asset #10) and caring (asset #26).

- Get to know the young people in your program. Learn their names. Find out about their interests, and help them feel welcome. Encourage their progress.

- Encourage participants to try new things and take healthy risks. Help them see the difference between positive and negative risks (asset #32: planning and decision making).

- Look for opportunities to build leadership skills. For example, a young person can lead the group in a warm-up exercise. An accomplished diver can assist the instructor in teaching other participants how to dive.

- Notice the positive, caring ways young people treat each other during your program.

For more information, contact the YMCA of the USA Research and Planning department or review their materials on the YMCA of the USA Web site.

WORKING WITH AQUATICS AND PROGRAM COMMITTEES

A program committee is typically one of the standing committees of any YMCA board, as it is through our programs that we accomplish our mission in local communities. Therefore, the program committee plays an important role, guiding and monitoring programs to ensure that the association is meeting its mission in a quality manner. Basically, everything else we do exists only to support our membership and programs.

In this section, we first look at how committee members are chosen and the relationship between staff and the committee. We then talk about the purpose of the committee and the development of an annual plan. After discussing committee meetings, we finish with some tips on working with a committee.

Committee Members

In consultation with the YMCA executive and the program director who relates to the committee, the board chairperson appoints a member of the board to chair the program committee. An additional five to eight people should serve on the committee. These members are considered policy volunteers. The other members of the committee do not need to be members of the board; however, they should be involved with the programs of the association in order to understand the issues. Appointments are normally for a term of one year; however, they are generally renewable.

Seek committee members who will look at the "big picture," who recognize the role of the program in the association's overall plan and will not focus on just the one or two programs that they are involved in or are knowledgeable about. Try to achieve a balance of representation. Hold an orientation for new committee members so that they understand the role of the committee, and integrate continuing education into the committee's work where pertinent.

Some associations may have a need for subcommittees of the program committee, such as an aquatics committee, a child care committee, or a health and fitness committee, or for ad hoc committees or task forces to address specific tasks on a short-term basis. The chairperson of each subcommittee should be a member of the program committee, and these subcommittees should report to the program committee; the chairperson of the ad hoc committee or task force should be a member of the committee that commissions it.

The aquatics committee may also have a need for subcommittees, such as a swim team parents' advisory committee or a water fitness committee, or for task forces. A task force is a subcommittee that has a specific job to perform. For example, a task force may look at the future development of facilities or programs in a new community. The task force should complete their work within a specific time frame.

Program Committee/Staff Relationship

The staff and the program committee should have a strong working partnership; however, each has its separate role. The program staff (and sometimes the executive) should be present at all meetings, but the committee chairperson should lead the meetings. Working with a program committee is an important part of the education and professional development of a program director.

As an aquatics director, you should have an active role in the committee process, as the work of these committees contributes greatly to the quality and success of your programs. You may be one of the staff working with the program committee or have your own responsibilities on an aquatics committee. Also try to work toward having key aquatics volunteers serve on various committees and on the board.

Purpose of a Program Committee

The bylaws of an association should give a broad commission or purpose for each of the standing committees; however, the ultimate purpose of a program committee is to make recommendations to the board on future directions for programs and policies that affect those programs. These recommendations are based on careful study and input from committee members, board members, YMCA members and participants, YMCA staff, and other community resources.

A typical program committee will do the following:

- Clarify purposes and set goals
- Recommend priorities and policies to the board
- Adopt standards for operation of various parts of the program
- Request appropriations in the budget for special needs
- Consider requests from members for new programs
- Monitor program quality and program evaluation
- Perform a community-needs assessment
- Assist with program cost studies
- Suggest program schedules
- Consider new equipment needs
- Plan strategies for expanding programs
- Discuss whether a program should be dropped
- Propose program marketing
- Assess risk management and safety
- Review the financial assistance policy
- Review programs to see if they foster Christian values

An aquatics committee may have the following purposes:

- Gathering input from people in the program
- Developing volunteers for future committee and board responsibilities
- Getting support for other projects, such as annual campaigns
- Helping the aquatics director learn how to work with volunteers and act as an executive

The following are some examples of aquatics committee tasks:

- Evaluate aquatics program offerings to ensure achievement of association goals
- Provide input on scheduling
- Deal with conflicts between and grievances from members
- Be a "secret shopper" on aquatics programs
- Evaluate program quality (for example, participate in the assessment process or follow up with individuals who have dropped out of programs)
- Participate in fundraisers
- Volunteer for special events

An important role for the YMCA aquatics (or health and fitness) committee and appropriate staff is to develop a written philosophy and goals, which should be shared with staff, program participants and their family members, committees and boards, and appropriate community agencies.

Some recommendations of the committee may not need board approval and may go directly to staff for implementation. Committees do not implement or administer policies or recommendations; this is the role of the staff. However, committee members may assist with programs as volunteers under the direction of the staff.

Annual Plan or Chart of Work

At the beginning of the board planning year, the program committee (and every committee) should develop, in writing, an annual plan or chart of work. This will help guide the activities of the committee throughout the year, and it should be consistent with the association's overall plan.

The annual plan should be prepared before consideration of specific issues and in collaboration with the committee, its chairperson, and YMCA staff. It should identify and schedule the accomplishment of specific objectives during specific time frames (for example, quarterly, semiannually, or seasonally). The annual plan should reflect implementation of the association's long-range or strategic plan.

Generally, the annual plan is developed at the first meeting of the year. Before the meeting, the committee chair should meet with the staff related to the program committee to draft a plan to be finalized at that meeting. During the year, other issues will probably surface and need to be added to the plan. At that time, the committee should reassess the reasonableness of the plan and make any modifications necessitated by additions or changes (e.g., major loss of funding or cancellation of a program site).

Committee Meetings

The program committee should meet during the year as often as needed to accomplish its objectives. Generally, a program committee meets monthly, bimonthly, or quarterly. The meeting schedule may be slightly irregular depending on YMCA program schedules and planning cycles.

A schedule should be developed for the entire year, listing specific dates and times; however, if a meeting date is approaching and no specific purpose exists for the meeting, it should be canceled.

While meetings can be conducted in a relaxed, informal manner, each meeting should have a written agenda and should begin and end on time. Staff should develop the meeting agendas in collaboration with the committee chairperson, and the staff's immediate supervisor should approve the agendas. The agenda for each meeting should be mailed to committee members at least one week before the meeting and should include all supporting documents and supplementary information. This will allow members adequate time for preparation.

Someone should call committee members before the day of the meeting to confirm that they will be attending and should keep records of member attendance throughout the year. If a member misses a meeting, someone should contact that member to follow up. (Each committee should agree on a protocol for contacting absent members.) Phone calls, notes, and mailings from the staff or chairperson containing the minutes and any additional information are all appropriate methods of follow-up.

Committee members should handle most of the agenda. The agenda should state when a decision is to be made regarding a solution to a problem or an answer to a question. The staff, in collaboration with the committee chairperson, should bring recommendations to the committee for consideration. They should provide sufficient information on alternatives.

The following guidelines are designed to assist you in working with various YMCA decision-making groups, including boards of directors (managers), councils, and committees. You should be prepared to work with a Program, Aquatics, or Health and Fitness committee.

- Each committee has a written commission describing its purpose and function.

- The committee chairperson and members are interested and capable.

- Committee members receive an orientation to the purpose of the committee, as well as to their individual roles and duties and to the YMCA's Mission, as well as continuing education throughout their tenure.

- A staff person maintains a current mailing list of committee members. This list may include the members' home, e-mail, and business addresses and telephone numbers, with designated choices for where to receive mail and calls.

- During meetings the committee is usually focused on decisions and problem solving. Items of general interest or information are written exhibits not for discussion.

- The chairperson brings in outside resource people to provide training for the committee.

- Staff remain attentive to the decision-making process during committee deliberations and make the chairperson aware of their interest.

- Agenda items include some "team and trust building time" in order to stimulate greater committee participation.

- The board, staff, and chair regularly acknowledge the contributions by members of the committee. Appropriate recognition and expressions of appreciation are rewarding to members and encourage them to contribute more fully.

- A staff person is responsible for being sure the minutes are completed for each meeting, either by taking the minutes or getting them from an assigned committee member. The staff person should mail the minutes to committee members within ten business days of the meeting.

- A staff person maintains complete records of committee activities (minutes, agendas, attendance, exhibits, evaluations, history and historical decisions, background and research documents, etc.).

- Committee members evaluate (verbally or in writing) each committee meeting. They also periodically evaluate progress toward established objectives and perform a yearly evaluation.

- The committee chair presents a report on the committee's chart of work to the board.

Program Management

As much planning must go into how to run a program as goes into designing it. The best-conceived plan for a program will fail if it is not executed well. In this chapter, we highlight some of the common policies and tasks that must be completed if programs are to run smoothly.

The chapter begins with a planning timetable for an aquatics program to help you see what needs to be done when. We then turn to program policies that must be set and planning for program registration, including determining children's class levels. Class organization is next, followed by student and parent orientation, class supervision, and student evaluation. Plans are needed for keeping good program statistics, and special events can be used to bring in new program participants. The final section covers issues you may encounter while doing outreach programming.

PLANNING TIMETABLE FOR AN AQUATICS PROGRAM

Managing a YMCA aquatics program takes a lot of advance planning. From the early stages of budgeting to the final student evaluation, you'll need to develop and follow procedures to make the program run smoothly. A better prepared program is a better run program. Also, as you develop a new program, don't forget the day-to-day operations of all your programs.

The following list should give you an idea of which tasks need to be performed at what time to have a strong aquatics program. Procedures may already be in place at your YMCA for some of these tasks; if not, you may need to discuss them with the other staff at your facility. Even if you aren't performing some of these tasks yourself, you should still be familiar with them and make sure they are all carried out.

Twelve Months Before the Session Begins

- Perform a needs assessment and demographic analysis (for a first-time program in a new community).
- Develop relationships in the community.
- Research other aquatics programs.
- Analyze past program history, which may include past participant, parent, and staff evaluations, as well as program participation statistics.
- Set program goals and objectives.

- Develop a budget.
- Design program policy and procedures (make-up classes, drops and changes in registration, waiting list, credit/refund policy).
- Develop job descriptions for staff.
- Plan the class schedule.
- Plan the marketing and promotion of the program, including brochure development and printing.
- Design a registration system (if one is not already in place).
- Establish emergency procedures.

Three Months Before the Session Begins

- Design and print promotional pieces.
- Update and prepare printed materials (skill sheets, progress reports, Family Huddles, Parent Handouts).
- Schedule training meetings for staff and volunteers.
- Begin recruiting and scheduling instructors and lifeguards to implement the program.
- Set registration limits for each class based on available instructors and pool space.
- Order needed equipment and supplies.

Four to Six Weeks Before the Session Begins

- Contact newspapers and radio and TV stations according to your promotional plan.
- Distribute your promotional piece internally to YMCA program participants, members, and previous program participants and externally to schools, businesses, community groups, and new residents as identified in the promotional plan.
- Provide staff orientation.
- Set up registration for off-site locations and begin registration.
- Orient front-desk staff on registering participants in the program.
- Provide parents with program information.

Two to Three Weeks Before the Session Begins

- Develop and print additional resource materials for instructors, such as rosters, schedules, and skill sheets.
- Organize handouts for easy distribution during the session.
- Monitor and modify class registration limits for classes based on preregistrations.
- Hold a staff and volunteer orientation meeting.
- Provide parent orientation along with a standard handout.

After Registration

- Make up class rosters.
- Keep the front-desk staff informed of any changes.

First Day of the Session

- Remind the front-desk staff that it is the first day of a session and provide them with a list of answers to commonly asked questions.

- Provide assistance to members/participants to get to the right place (through the facility, to the pool, and to the right class).
- Communicate with parents/members and give them an overview of what is happening in the pool.
- Troubleshoot problems that arise.

Throughout the Session

- Communicate with parents/participants.
- Troubleshoot problems that arise.
- Monitor performance of staff and coordination of classes.
- Conduct program evaluations.
- Monitor expenses.

First Week of the Session

- Post notices in the facility to encourage last-minute registration.
- Check waiting lists to place students after combination and cancellation of classes have been done.
- Distribute handouts for class participants and parents as planned.

Third Week of the Session

- Begin to advertise for the next session's programs and activities at the following events or within the following programs:

    Swim team

    Child care lessons

Swim lessons

Special-needs swim lessons

Birthday parties

Home schools

Backyard pool programs

Healthy Kids Day

Summer Sign-Up

Open House

YMCA Splash Week

Family Night

Also place flyers/posters in the locker rooms, at the front desk, and on bulletin boards. Advertise to youth sports teams, family programs, and other branch programs, and in any YMCA newsletters.

- Run public service announcements (PSAs) for the next session.
- Develop press releases and flyers to advertise the next session.

Fourth Week of the Session

- Have the aquatics director/supervisor double-check instructors' evaluations of students to confirm the students' class levels for the next session.
- Hand out reenrollment special promotion cards to class participants.

Fifth Week of the Session

- Post registration dates and communicate with participants and parents about their or their children's progress (if applicable).
- Follow up on program evaluation comments to address areas of concern.

Near the End of the Session

- Distribute progress reports and recognition items in YMCA Swim Lessons programs.
- Schedule focus groups (see chapter 8).
- Encourage registration for the next session.

After the Session Has Ended

- Communicate with participants/parents.
- Troubleshoot problems that arise.
- Compile program participation statistics.
- Analyze the budget.
- Compile program evaluations and summarize proposed changes for the next program session (see chapter 2).
- Share program evaluations with instructors.
- Inventory supplies and reorder as needed.

Keep in mind that your individual programs will be in different phases of this 12-month calendar.

PROGRAM POLICIES

Before any program begins, you will need to determine program policies such as the length of classes and the number of classes per session, program scheduling, and methods for dealing with canceled classes.

Length and Number of Classes

Most YMCAs schedule 45-minute youth and adult classes and 30-minute parent/ child and preschool classes. You can schedule classes effectively either back-to-back or with a few minutes between each class.

If classes are back-to-back, assign a staff member to organize how participants enter and exit. This minimizes confusion and helps ensure that classes start and end on time. This type of scheduling keeps staffing costs to a minimum and maximizes pool use.

Scheduling time between classes allows instructors to dismiss the first class, get the equipment organized for the next class, talk to parents if necessary, take care of any personal needs, and be ready to greet the next class. This method does, however, increase staff costs and take up more pool time.

Scheduling of Classes

Scheduling is a delicate balance between meeting the needs of class participants and those of members and the community at large. Look at your pool schedule and ask yourself if you are providing members and the community a mix of programs and activities that includes recreation, instruction, fitness, and competition. You can offer many options, but those that best meet the goals of your YMCA should get top priority.

Over time, a YMCA's goals change; so should your facility schedule. A regular review of your schedule can ensure that your YMCA's goals can be achieved. Look at your current schedule and answer the following questions:

- Are your programs meeting the needs of the community?
- How do your programs and schedule reflect the priorities and goals of your YMCA?
- Are the needs of special groups (swim team, fitness classes, lap swimmers, open swimmers) your top priority or the needs of your membership as a whole?
- Are programs available for all age groups?

Once you have determined the amount of time that will be allocated to instructional programs, you can begin putting together the balanced program schedule your YMCA needs by considering the following:

- How much time should be allocated for each program based on the program's goals?
- When is it convenient for the target market for this program to come to the facility? For example, not many school-age children could attend an open swim held at 11:00 A.M. during the regular school year.
- What other activities are scheduled for this market within your YMCA?
- Is there competition for this type of program from programs sponsored by other organizations?

Be flexible and creative in your scheduling to allow as much activity in the pool as is safely possible. Doing so will make the best use of your staff, utilize pool space efficiently, and increase revenue.

After your schedule is complete, take a step back and look at the whole facility:

- What opportunities exist for families to participate together in different programs at the same time or in the same activities?
- Are any time periods open that could provide opportunities to develop new programs?
- Are programs offered for the same age groups at conflicting times?

Parent/child classes offer some unique scheduling possibilities. Several options are available to you on how to offer the program to your members and participants. The four levels offered through parent/child classes cover these age groups:

Shrimps	6-8 months
Kippers	9-12 months
Inias	13-18 months
Perch	19-36 months

You can choose to offer these levels in four different ways:

1. Each level separately
2. Shrimps/Kippers and Inias/Perch
3. Shrimps/Kippers/Inias and Perch
4. All levels together

The basic deciding factors are the size of your program and the amount of pool space available. If your program is small and has only one or two classes scheduled weekly, offering all the parent/child levels together is a good choice. If you have enough participants to fill a class at each level, it is a good idea to offer the levels separately. When you combine levels, your instructors should plan their classes so they can meet the needs of children at different age levels and their parents.

Once you've determined the number and size of your classes, you can set up a chart to help you schedule staff for those classes. The chart should include the time, type of class or program, maximum enrollment for each class, and the names of the staff scheduled for each time period. Figure 3.1 is a sample staff scheduling chart.

Canceled or Missed Classes

You need to have a set procedure for canceling classes. Cancellation may be due either to insufficient enrollment, in which case you will need to cancel the class for the entire session, or to problems with the pool or inclement weather such as rain, fog, snow, cold, or darkness (especially for outdoor pools), in which case you may need to cancel just one class. For classes canceled due to pool problems or weather, you will need to schedule make-up classes. The procedures for canceling a class or making one up should be outlined in your program brochure and in any information materials given to students when they register. Discuss the procedure with parents during their orientation session.

- Classes canceled for insufficient enrollment. As soon as you have decided that a class will be canceled, contact those who have registered for the class. Try to find another class for them, or process a refund or credit. This should be done before the start of the session, giving the participants as much notice as possible.

Day: Saturday

Time	Class	Max.	Amy	Bob	Cami	Don	Fran	Emilio	Sue
9:00	PGM	24	X	X	X			Guard	Guard
9:00	PRE	12				X	X	Guard	Guard
9:30	PRE	12				X	X	Guard	Guard
9:45	FFFS	24	X	X	X			Guard	Guard
10:00	PRE	12				X	X	Guard	Guard
10:30	PRE	12	X	X					
10:30	PGM	24			Guard	Guard	X	X	X
11:00	P/C	12	X	X	Guard	Guard			

PGM = Polliwog, Guppy, Minnow   PRE = Preschool

FFFS = Fish, Flying Fish, Shark   P/C = Parent/Child

Figure 3.1   Sample staff scheduling chart.

• Classes canceled because of pool problems or inclement weather. Try to cancel classes in enough time to catch participants before they leave home for class. Notify them 30 to 60 minutes before the class by having someone call each class member. Make sure the person doing the calling is familiar with the class cancellation policy and can provide information on how and when the class will be rescheduled.

• Your YMCA may want to set up a weather line for participants to call to hear a recorded message about canceled classes. You also may want to contact your local radio and TV stations to get information about their procedures for reporting canceled classes or programs due to bad weather conditions.

• It may also happen that you start a class but have to stop it because of pool or weather conditions. You need to have a procedure in place for instructors to follow under these circumstances. You may be able to bring the students to another area of your facility and engage in out-of-water activities. However, if the class cannot be completed, you may have to schedule a make-up class.

Part of your policy should concern whether make-up classes will be offered to replace canceled or missed classes or whether participants are instead entitled to a credit or refund. Any credit or refund given should follow your association's policy on such payments. Whatever the policy, make sure that it is included in your program brochure and other promotional materials and that participants are made aware of it at the time they register.

Make-up classes are provided in several ways by YMCAs:

• In some YMCAs, make-up classes are offered only for those classes canceled by the YMCA, not for classes that individual participants missed because they were unable to attend.

- Other YMCAs regularly schedule a class time during the week for any students who miss a class. For example, classes could be scheduled Monday through Thursday, with Friday being the day for make-up classes.

- In some areas where cancellation due to weather is common, the YMCA may schedule 10 classes and guarantee 8. If no classes are canceled, participants receive all 10; if cancellations are necessary, two make-ups are already scheduled.

PROGRAM PARTICIPATION AND THE AMERICANS WITH DISABILITIES ACT (ADA)

YMCAs fall within the definition of the Public Accommodation under Title III of the Americans With Disabilities Act (ADA) and are therefore required to comply with its provisions. The purpose of the ADA is to fully integrate people with disabilities into activities the rest of the society enjoys. This goal of inclusiveness is consistent with the YMCA mission and with YMCA core values.

An individual with a disability is one who has a physical or mental impairment (such as contagious diseases, HIV, multiple sclerosis, mental retardation, emotional illness, specific learning disabilities), and the impairment substantially limits one or more major life activities (such as walking, seeing, hearing, speaking, breathing, learning, working, caring for oneself), or has a record of such impairment, or is regarded as having such an impairment. Homosexuality or bisexuality are not physical or mental impairments, nor is the use of illegal drugs.

The ADA requires that the YMCA do the following:

- Provide goods and services in an integrated setting
- Eliminate unnecessary eligibility standards
- Make reasonable modification in policies, practices, and procedures that deny people with disabilities equal access, unless it would cause a fundamental alteration in the nature of the goods and services provided
- Furnish auxiliary aids (interpreters, readers, assistive listening devices) to ensure effective communication, unless an undue burden or fundamental alteration would result
- Remove architectural and structural barriers if readily achievable or, if not readily achievable, provide readily achievable alternative measures
- Provide equivalent transportation services and accessible vehicles in certain circumstances
- Design and construct new facilities and undertake any alterations in conformity with the requirements of the ADA

The YMCA is not required to do the following:

- Provide personal devices such as wheelchairs, prescription eyeglasses, or hearing aids or services of a personal nature, unless these are provided to others in the program
- Permit a person to participate in or benefit from goods or services it offers when that individual poses a direct threat to the health or safety of others
- Make modifications that fundamentally alter the nature of the goods and services provided, that create an undue burden, or that are not readily achievable

YMCAs should establish policies and procedures regarding the ADA and should educate staff, volunteers, and members as to the purpose and requirements of the

ADA. If there is a question about a participant wanting to register for a program and what the YMCA needs to do to comply, you should consult with your executive director before making any statements. ADA training and additional information are available through the YMCA of the USA Office of the General Counsel at 800-872-9622. (*Note:* This section was provided for general information purposes only and is not intended to substitute for legal advice on specific issues.)

PROGRAM REGISTRATION

Your association should have a written enrollment and admission policy for your program and make it available to program participants or their parents. In most cases, this information is communicated through your program brochures, registration forms, and parent orientations. It includes the fee structure and payment policy and other program information such as the following:

- Goals
- Description of program activities and operation
- Hours of operation
- Participant-to-staff ratio
- Staff qualifications
- Benefits to participants and their families
- Parental involvement
- Other YMCA programs and services
- The attendance and illness policy
- Policy regarding refunds, canceled classes, credits, and make-ups
- Policy regarding parental observation of classes or programs

Have an enrollment form that includes the following information on the participant:

- Full name
- Address
- Phone number
- Emergency phone number
- Participant's or parent's signature
- Health screening form
- A nondiscrimination clause/policy
- A transportation release (if applicable)
- An authorization for release of a child to an adult other than a parent
- Parent options for involvement and volunteer opportunities
- A plan for communicating progress to participants
- A policy statement on enrollment of participants with special needs, disabilities, chronic illnesses, medically fragile conditions, and so on
- A policy statement on behavior management, including your YMCA's approach to discipline, grounds for enrollment termination, and steps that need to be taken for termination
- A financial aid statement

Much of this may already be a part of your YMCA's overall program registration process. Discuss your enrollment and admission policies with your executive and other directors, as your YMCA will want to make policies among departments as consistent as possible. Also discuss how to ensure that the policies are implemented consistently and how staff can obtain necessary information when needed. For instance, if a parent or participant indicates a medical condition on the registration form, the appropriate staff members must be made aware of it so they can be prepared to respond appropriately to any emergency.

Registration procedures vary a great deal from one YMCA to another. Some YMCAs allow members and nonmembers to register at the same time for any published schedule of classes, one or more classes at a time. This makes registration first-come, first-served, with members having no advantage over nonmembers in getting the class and session of their choice. Other YMCAs prefer to give members a chance to register one or two weeks before open registration. Although this gives members an advantage, it can create long lines and increase the frustration and inconvenience for all because of the need to register only on certain dates. Discuss this issue with your management and your board or program committees to determine what will work best for your YMCA.

Another option you may want to consider is allowing currently registered participants to reenroll for the next session. Reenrollment ensures that they can register for the classes they want without being put on a waiting list. YMCAs that do this sometimes give current participants a coupon that allows them to register before other members or nonmembers and sometimes includes a discount on registration fees.

Regardless of the procedures you use, you should prepare for registration, know your procedures for awarding financial aid, and watch how registrations proceed. Make sure the number of participants accepted does not exceed your YMCA's space and staffing capacity to handle them. If you are looking for additional participants, however, you may want to consider some methods for increasing enrollments.

Preparing for Registration

Even if your YMCA has a standard program registration procedure, it is worthwhile to take time to prepare for registration for your program. For example, you may want to add a space or attach an additional sheet to the registration form where parents can indicate the child's current level or swimming experience for your YMCA Swim Lessons program. You should meet with front-desk staff before registration begins to discuss the benefits of the program and ways they can help parents determine the level at which their child belongs. Staff also should be aware of the maximum number of participants allowed per class so they can indicate when a class has been filled. Those who wished to register for that class can then either sign up on a waiting list or contact you. You must be the one to make the decisions on changing class size limits so the right instructor-to-participant ratio can be maintained.

A sample registration form for a YMCA Swim Lessons program is shown in figure 3.2.

After parents have registered their children for the program, make sure someone on staff tells them the date and time for the parent orientation session. Have a handout available with essential information such as the following:

- The YMCA's mission, philosophy, and program goals
- What the program should be expected to offer
- What the child should bring to class (towel, bathing cap)
- How to get to the pool

Program Registration

Program/Class no.:_____   Program name:_____   Program cycle:_____

Regular member program fee:_____   Begin:_____   Max enrollment:_____

Basic membership fee:_____   End:_____   Slots open:_____

Participant fee:_____   Instructor:_____   Location:_____

Day(s):_____   Time:_____

Master ID: ☐ ☐ – ☐ ☐ ☐ ☐ ☐ – ☐ ☐
Full and program members need indicate only ID name

Name _____   Birthdate _____

Address _____   Sex (Male/Female) _____

_____   Home phone _____

City, State _____ ZIP _____   Work phone _____

Join/Exp. date _____ Participant status: ☐ Member   ☐ Nonmember

Emergency contact person _____   Emergency phone _____

For office use only   Mail list: ☐
Membership code: _____

C _____

V _____ MC _____ AE _____ D _____

Card #: _____

Exp. Date: _____ Amount: _____

Date: _____

_____
                    Initial

Figure 3.2   Sample registration form for YMCA Swim Lessons program.

- If the program is at a non-YMCA facility, where they should enter the building
- What time lessons start and finish and when they should arrive
- Procedures for application of sunscreen, showering, dropping off and picking up children, and other class-related information
- Pool rules and regulations
- Program registration policy (make-ups, canceled classes, refunds)

You may want to schedule yourself or some of your aquatics staff to be available around the front-desk area during peak registration times to help answer specific questions regarding the program.

Some YMCAs schedule registration events for their summer swim season in conjunction with YMCA events such as Healthy Kids Day or a Summer Splash Day that includes fun activities, refreshments, and registration for both summer day camp and swim programs.

Granting Financial Aid

Most YMCAs offer financial aid for those who can't afford to attend YMCA programs. This aid is usually a partial- or full-fee waiver for a program. This policy supports the YMCA's commitment to welcoming everyone from all socioeconomic backgrounds and helping children develop their spiritual, mental, and physical potential. The amount of financial aid available is based on your association's ability to secure funds.

Families who apply for financial aid must demonstrate economic and social need. Those children who have the greatest need and who can most benefit from the program are the ones granted aid. Usually, families end up paying a percentage of the fee based on the family's income and the number of family members. Parents may be required to fill out an application listing income sources and the number of family members, and they may also be asked to provide federal income tax returns or proof of government assistance as documentation. A sample financial aid form appears in figure 3.3.

Your association should have a written financial aid policy and should publicize the availability of financial aid.

Watching Registration Levels

During the weeks before a session, check registration levels for each time period. Monitoring registration levels helps you avoid overcrowding of classes and

Financial Aid

Although the YMCA is a not-for-profit agency, we depend on participant fees to help maintain our service. We are committed to serve people regardless of their income level, but we expect participants to pay based on their financial ability. Contingent upon financial resources of the association and verification of personal information, YMCA scholarships will be awarded to applicants.

Child's name: Last _____ First _____

School _____ Age _____ M/F _____

Address _____

City, State _____ ZIP _____ Home phone _____

Mother's name: Last _____ First _____

Employer _____ Work phone _____ Mo. gross income _____

Father's name: Last _____ First _____

Employer _____ Work phone _____ Mo. gross income _____

Other income (child support, etc.) _____

Emergency contact name _____ **Phone** _____

Relationship to child _____

Names and ages of other members of the household:

Name	Age	School
_____	_____	_____
_____	_____	_____
_____	_____	_____
_____	_____	_____
_____	_____	_____

Income:

1. Are you receiving government financial assistance? Yes No $_____/month
2. Are you receiving food stamps? Yes No $_____/month
3. Are you receiving Social Security benefits? Yes No $_____/month
4. Are you receiving veteran's benefits? Yes No $_____/month
5. Are you receiving child support? Yes No $_____/month

(continued)

Figure 3.3 Sample financial aid form.

6. Are you receiving spousal support?	Yes	No	$_____/month
7. Are you employed?	Yes	No	$_____/month
8. Is your spouse employed?	Yes	No	$_____/month
9. Are any of your children employed?	Yes	No	$_____/month
10. Are you or your spouse receiving unemployment benefits?	Yes	No	$_____/month

Indicate the attached documentation:

___ Copy of payroll check stub (one for the last 3 months)—mother

___ Copy of payroll check stub (one for the last 3 months)—father

___ Copy of most recent federal income tax return

___ Unemployment card and check stubs and statements

___ AFDC check stubs and statements

___ List of extraordinary expenses including court decisions and medical bills

___ Anything to help with determination of assistance amount (describe)

_____

_____

Type of membership requested (circle one):   Adult   Youth   Family

☐ New   ☐ Renewal

Amount requested _____ Amount you are able to pay _____

Program _____

☐ New   ☐ Renewal

Amount requested _____ Amount you are able to pay _____

Attach a brief description of why you want YMCA financial assistance. Include financial, family, and medical information or other facts relevant to your situation.

Would you be willing to volunteer time?   Yes   No

If yes, what type of activities would you be interested in doing? _____

In accordance with YMCA policy, NO application will be considered without accompanying verification of income. We require IRS Form 1040 and current Employer Status Report or Public Aid Disclosure.

Please read the following:

I, hereby, certify that the information supplied herein is true, accurate, and complete to the best of my knowledge. I am also aware that it is my responsibility to notify the YMCA, in writing, of any change in information supplied in this application, such as income, address, living arrangements, or other matters which might affect my eligibility for financial assistance. I understand that failure to comply with YMCA policies can result in immediate revocation of scholarship privileges.

Figure 3.3   *(continued)*

Signature of parent/legal guardian if applicant is a minor:

_____ Date _____

Interview conducted by:

_____ Date _____

☐ Approved   Amount _____

☐ Not approved   Comments _____

_____ Date _____
Executive signature

Figure 3.3   _(continued)_

maintain proper instructor-to-student ratios. When you see that some class times are beginning to fill, you may be able to find additional instructors or tell front-desk staff to mention to registrants that other time slots are available. If possible, make adjustments in the limits of that class time. If some class times are not filling, you may be able to cancel them and move those participants to other classes. Contact participants in classes that have not filled to see if they are able to move to another time. Still another alternative is to limit the size of a class that is in less demand to allow one instructor to move from that time to a time when a larger number of people want to participate.

If you don't deal with these problems before the first day of classes, you may end up inconveniencing participants and their families, making poor use of your staff time, and causing confusion. Taking care of problems ahead of time helps ensure a smooth, efficient operation.

Increasing Enrollments

If your classes are not full, or if you want to expand the number of classes you have scheduled, try some of these ideas:

- Evaluate your members and participants to see if your schedule is a barrier to participation. You may want to consider altering some class schedules and having the classes meet more than once a week at different session lengths, with each session still having the same number of classes. For example, one session could meet once a week for eight weeks, one could meet twice a week for four weeks, and one could meet four days a week for two weeks.

- Increase the number of instructors scheduled during class times and maximize your pool time. Good planning and organization of your classes will enable you to increase the number of classes in the pool.

- Expand your program using other community or neighborhood pool facilities.

- Offer swim lessons within your day camp and child care programs.

- Offer swim lessons to area child care centers.

- Offer swim lessons to public schools, private schools, churches, and home-school families.

- Find a new market for lessons, whether it's a new location, age group, or special ability group.

CLASS LEVELS

One of the difficult challenges in setting up swim classes is ensuring that participants are placed at the correct skill levels. Several methods can be used:

- Parents can register children for a specific level during registration by marking the appropriate space on the registration form. Front-desk staff may have information available to help them discuss levels with the parents, or such information may be included on the registration form. Work with front-desk staff before registration to tell them how to interpret the information for parents. You may want to use a skill level checklist such as the one shown in figure 3.4, or just provide a descriptive list of skills to help parents choose the appropriate level for their child. During peak registration times, you might consider having an aquatics instructor or coordinator available to answer parents' questions and to assist the front-desk staff member.

- Parents can sign up for a class time in which several different levels are taught. In this case, the parents only have to identify a range of levels that may be appropriate. For instance, the YMCA may have a class time during which the Polliwog, Guppy, and Minnow levels are offered together and one during which the Fish, Flying Fish, and Shark levels are available. Then, on the first day of class, the instructors can evaluate the skills of those children whose parents don't know what level is appropriate and place them in the proper level.

- You can schedule a special observation session during which parents can bring their children to the YMCA to have their swimming skills evaluated. The children can then be registered at the proper level.

Skills Mastered

This list does not include all the skills covered in each level; it contains those skills that may help parents determine the level at which their child should register.

Look at each level and determine whether your child can consistently perform ALL the skills within that level. If so, check the next level, and keep moving through the levels until you reach one for which your child cannot consistently perform ALL the skills. That probably is the right level for your child.

It is better to underestimate the child's ability than to overestimate it. It is much easier to move a child to a higher level than to move him or her down.

If you are still not sure of your child's level after looking at this list, talk to someone at the front desk or your YMCA's aquatics director to learn what methods your YMCA can use to assess children's readiness for each level.

Polliwog

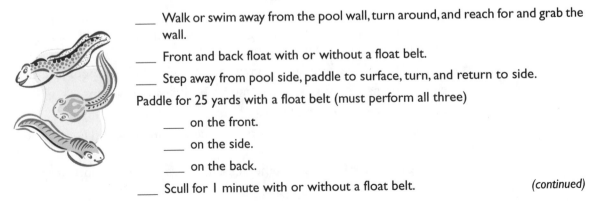

____ Walk or swim away from the pool wall, turn around, and reach for and grab the wall.

____ Front and back float with or without a float belt.

____ Step away from pool side, paddle to surface, turn, and return to side.

Paddle for 25 yards with a float belt (must perform all three)

    ____ on the front.

    ____ on the side.

    ____ on the back.

____ Scull for 1 minute with or without a float belt.

(continued)

Figure 3.4 Skill level checklist.

Guppy

____ Front and back float for 1 minute without a float belt.

____ Tread water for 20 to 30 seconds with or without a float belt.

____ Jump into deep water, paddle stroke 15 feet, roll to a back float for 10 seconds, then return to the side without a float belt.

____ Perform 10 bobs in deep water without a float belt.

Swim for 25 yards with or without a float belt

    ____ on the front with an alternating paddle, using rhythmic breathing.

    ____ on the front with a symmetrical paddle.

    ____ on the side with an alternating paddle.

    ____ on the back with an alternating paddle.

    ____ on the back with a symmetrical paddle.

____ Jump into deep water and swim up 5 to 7 feet.

____ Jump into water from a 1-meter board and swim to the side with or without a float belt. (Only if your YMCA has the appropriate water depth in the pool.)

____ Perform a kneeling dive with assistance, glide, then paddle 15 feet without a float belt. (Only if your YMCA has the appropriate water depth in the pool.)

Minnow

____ Tread water for 1 minute using a scissors kick.

Swim for 25 yards without a float belt

    ____ on the front with an alternating paddle. (crawl stroke)

    ____ on the front with a symmetrical paddle. (breaststroke)

    ____ on the side with an alternating paddle and a scissors kick. (sidestroke)

    ____ on the back with an alternating overarm stroke. (back crawl stroke)

    ____ on the back with a symmetrical paddle. (elementary backstroke)

____ Perform a stride dive. (Only if your YMCA has the appropriate water depth in the pool.)

____ Perform a standing dive. (Only if your YMCA has the appropriate water depth in the pool.)

____ Jump into the pool from a 1-meter board using an arm swing and swim to the side. (Only if your YMCA has the appropriate water depth in the pool.)

Fish

____ Float for 6 minutes with minimum movement on the front or back without a float belt.

____ Tread water in deep water for 3 minutes using a combination of single, double, and circle kicks.

Swim 50 yards

    ____ of the crawl stroke with rotary breathing and open turns.

    ____ of the breaststroke with a pull, kick, and glide with open turns.

Figure 3.4 *(continued)*

___ of the elementary backstroke with a glide.

___ of the back crawl with a roll and bent arm with open turns.

___ of the sidestroke with a regular scissors kick with a glide.

___ Swim 25 yards of the butterfly stroke.

___ Do headfirst and feetfirst sculling for 45 feet each.

___ Perform a standing dive from a 1-meter board. (Only if your YMCA has the appropriate water depth in the pool.)

___ Perform a headfirst and feetfirst surface dive and swim down 6 to 8 feet. (Only if your YMCA has the appropriate water depth in the pool.)

Flying Fish

___ Tread water for 6 minutes using all four kicks: single, double, circle, and rotary.

Swim 100 yards

___ of the crawl stroke with bilateral breathing and open turns.

___ of the breaststroke with open turns.

___ of the elementary backstroke with a glide.

___ of the back crawl with open turns.

___ of the sidestroke using the regular and inverted scissors kick.

___ Swim 15 yards of the butterfly stroke.

___ Perform a flip turn for the crawl stroke and back crawl stroke.

Shark

___ Swim 100 yards of the crawl stroke with a front start and front flip turn.

___ Swim 100 yards of the breaststroke with a pull-out.

___ Swim 50 yards of the inverted breaststroke.

___ Swim 100 yards of the back crawl, performing transitions with a dolphin kick and streamlining.

___ Swim 50 yards of the overarm sidestroke (25 yards on each side).

___ Swim 25 yards of the butterfly stroke, streamlined and using a push-off.

___ Swim 50 yards of the trudgen crawl.

___ Swim 200 yards of the individual medley: butterfly, backstroke, breaststroke, and front crawl stroke.

Figure 3.4   (continued)

• For children who have attended swim classes previously, instructors may indicate on students' progress reports what levels the children should take during the next session.

No matter which method you use, you will always have a few students on the first day of classes who either don't know in which level they belong or are in the wrong level. Before the first day of classes, determine a procedure for taking care of this situation. Make sure that children who must be moved to another level are treated tactfully. Be sensitive about students' feelings, and avoid making statements such as

"You're not good enough for this level," "We need to move you to a lower level," or "Don't you know what level you should be in?"

Also check to see if your YMCA's program registration forms or other parts of the registration system may create problems in assigning or recording information about levels. For example, some standard registration forms may not have a space in which parents can indicate their children's level.

Another problem might occur if front-desk staff have not been informed that children must be at least six years old to take part in the Youth and Adult program. They may then allow a child younger than six to sign up, leading to problems on the first day of class. Think through the registration process in terms of the information you need to give and the information you want to get.

CLASS ORGANIZATION

You should orchestrate or coordinate good class organization for effective program operation. Good organization and preplanning of your classes will make teaching easier for your instructors and learning more effective for your students. Use consistent procedures in organizing your classes, and make sure your instructors choose organizational patterns for practice that maximize students' opportunity to practice skills. Keep safety elements in mind, and consider how instructional flotation devices (IFDs) and games can enhance skill learning.

Organizing Pool Usage

Before lessons begin, talk with your instructors about the most efficient way to use the pool during each class period. By planning ahead of time, you can get the most use of the entire pool for a wide variety of activities and minimize the amount of confusion during instruction. YMCA swim classes should include 10 to 15 minutes each for a series swim, activities in the shallow end of the pool, and activities in the deep end (or another part) of the pool. You need to think about how the classes that are together during the same period can best use the different parts of the pool.

If you schedule the series swims for all classes for the same 15-minute period, instructors should make sure that all classes swim in the same direction. This minimizes the chances that swimmers will run into each other. Assign certain lanes to each class or level.

During the rest of the class, swimmers can swim widthwise so classes can be kept separate. Classes usually switch places at some point during the lesson, most often moving from the shallow to the deep end or vice versa. Figure 3.5 shows two diagrams of possible ways classes could be organized to best use the pool space.

Instructors should organize classes so students get the maximum amount of activity:

- They should select some simple and some challenging activities.
- They should encourage students to master all tasks but allow students to progress at their own pace.
- They should choose activities and games that the children like so as to stimulate interest and participation.
- They should use those organizational patterns that will allow the most practice while still being safe for students (see "Class Organizational Patterns"). Instructors should make sure they have a full view of the entire class throughout the activity, with no student being out of their direct view.

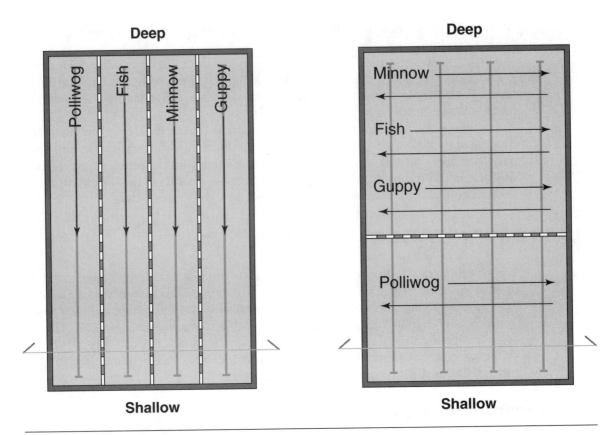

Figure 3.5 Possible pool use patterns.

Near the end of the session, instructors should evaluate their students, and the students (and their parents, if the students are children) will have the chance to evaluate the course. For children's classes, instructors should also keep parents involved throughout the course, beginning with a class orientation and continuing with periodic discussions of students' progress with the parents, as well as Family Huddle and Parent Handouts.

An important part of your job as a director is to provide a learning environment that is safe for participants. Having appropriate instructor/participant ratios and the help of an assistant makes it easier for instructors to watch over students. Giving new students an orientation to the pool area and setting up class rules can help prevent dangerous situations from arising.

Instructor/Participant Ratios

The ratio of instructor to participants should be based on several factors:

- The age of the participants
- The program being offered
- The size of the facility
- The other programs being held in the pool at the same time
- The number of assistants available
- The number of lifeguards on duty

However, the YMCA of the USA has set the following generally recommended ratios for swim classes in addition to having one or more lifeguards on deck:

Parent/child classes	1:10 to 12 pairs
Preschool classes	1:6
Youth classes:	
Polliwogs and Guppies	1:8
Minnows and up	1:10
Adult instructional classes (depending on the type of class and the skill level of the participants)	1:8 to 12
Water fitness	1:25
Lifeguard classes	1:20

Lesson Plans and Skill Sheets

Your instructors should all develop lesson plans for each session of whatever course they are teaching. Lesson plans are necessary to ensure that all of the following occur:

- Students are exposed to all important skills and concepts in the course of each session
- An appropriate balance of time is spent on each class component
- Class time is used efficiently, allowing maximum student participation
- A varied yet balanced mix of class organization patterns and creative learning techniques is used
- Safety is built into each component of the lesson

A good lesson plan keeps classes consistent, even when instructors are absent and someone else has to lead the class.

Instructors should also use skill sheets to keep track of participants' progress. Make sure that instructors consistently complete them, as the sheets are important for overall program management.

Refer to *YMCA Swim Lessons: Teaching Swimming Fundamentals* to learn about effective class management, student evaluation, and lesson and session planning. For water fitness classes, see *YMCA Water Fitness for Health*.

Class Organizational Patterns

Instructors can arrange students in a number of patterns or formations for practice and other class activities. Using a variety of class organizational patterns helps keep the class interesting and fun. However, some patterns are more appropriate than others for certain skills or ability levels. In this section, we'll discuss the advantages and disadvantages of various formations.

Encourage instructors to look at the flow of their classes when they plan lessons to determine which patterns to use. Suggest they consider the following factors in choosing a pattern:

- The task being worked on
- Class safety
- Students' skills
- The ability of all students to see and hear clearly

- The opportunity for personal instructor attention
- Maximum opportunity to practice

No matter what pattern they use, instructors must make sure they are positioned where they can see all of their students all the time. They should be close enough to see and hear each student and to be able to control or stop activity when necessary.

Here are some commonly used aquatics patterns or formations: the wave, the stagger, the corner swim, the short course and long course practice swims, the circle swim, and the single line pattern.

Wave

Level: Intermediate and advanced swimmers

Advantages: Effective for students working on skills with or without instructional flotation devices. Allows a large number of students a lot of practice.

To form the wave, the instructor divides the class into two or more groups. All members of the first group (referred to as a wave) start together and swim in a line abreast. The second group starts either after the first group has finished or far enough behind the first group (usually 3 to 10 seconds later) that they won't interfere with each other (see figure 3.6).

This formation allows instructors to give general comments to the class at the ends or sides of the pool, but they may need to move around to observe for individual evaluations. However, it is more difficult for instructors to provide individual attention to students without interrupting the flow of the pattern.

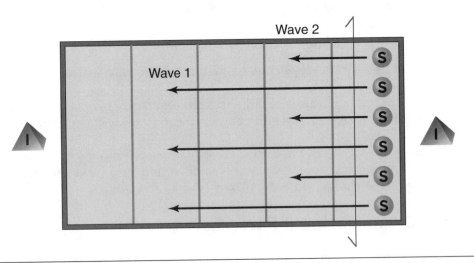

Figure 3.6 Wave formation.

Stagger

Level: Advanced beginners and up

Advantages: Provides practice time while observing individuals

The characteristics of this formation are similar to those of the wave. The instructor stands in the pool or on the side of the pool, and the swimmers line up on the deck or along the side. The first swimmer swims to a predetermined mark, at which time the instructor signals the next swimmer to start (see figure 3.7).

In this formation, as opposed to the wave, it's easier to provide students with individual attention as they reach the end or side of the pool.

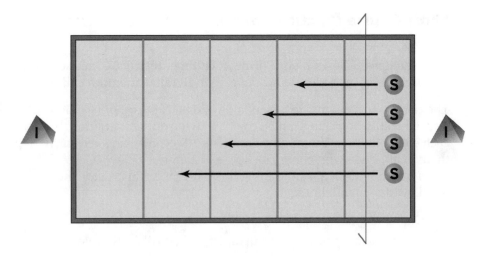

Figure 3.7 Stagger pattern.

Corner Swim

Level: All class levels

Advantages: Good for short distances for beginning and intermediate swimmers, as the size of the circle can be varied based on students' abilities. Instructor can see students easily at all times, primarily from the front and back. Students get individual attention and a fair amount of swim time.

Students line up along the pool wall, with the line ending in a corner of the pool. The student at the head of the line swims out from the corner to the instructor, then swims to the adjacent wall and continues swimming until she or he finishes at the end of the line in the corner. Meanwhile, the line has moved up so the next swimmer is in the starting position (see figure 3.8).

Instructors must space students so they can keep moving and not get stacked up. Students need to know where the beginning and ending points are and what objects are being used as markers (such as safety cones or kickboards) if they are swimming across the width of the pool.

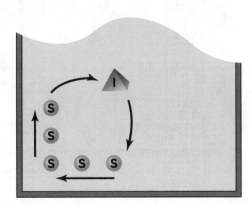

Figure 3.8 Corner swim pattern.

Short Course Practice Swim (Length Circle Swim)

Level: All levels

Advantages: Allows plenty of practice time. Instructor can see front, side, and back views of students and can give individual attention at the end of the pool.

The class swims down one lane or side and back the other (see figure 3.9). Students start by ability, so pacing can be controlled. In another variation, half the class is on each end of the lane. Swimmers allow 5 to 10 seconds between starts, depending on their ability, and swim either clockwise or counterclockwise.

Before students begin swimming this pattern, the instructor should remind them to follow these guidelines:

- Don't hang onto the side.
- When you are finished, line up against the wall on the last side.
- If you want to pass, tap the swimmer in front of you on the foot. Stay in the inside of the circle when you pass.
- If you have long hair, tie it back or wear a swim cap.
- You may want to wear goggles, which will help you see the others swimming around you. (*Note:* Don't allow students to wear goggles while diving from the deck, doing surface dives, or swimming underwater. The pressure differential between the inside and outside of the goggles could cause injury to the eyes.)

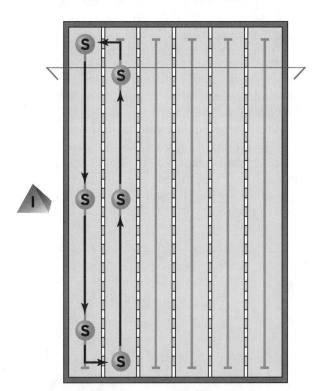

Figure 3.9   Short course practice swim pattern.

Long Course Practice Swim

Level: Intermediate and advanced swimmers

Advantages: Allows maximum amount of practice using the entire pool. Beneficial for those working on endurance.

The class swims down one lane and back the next until all lanes have been covered. Students try to swim at the same pace and keep a safe distance apart (see figure 3.10).

To correct individual swimmers, the instructor should stop them one at a time, then pace them so they can get back into the line smoothly.

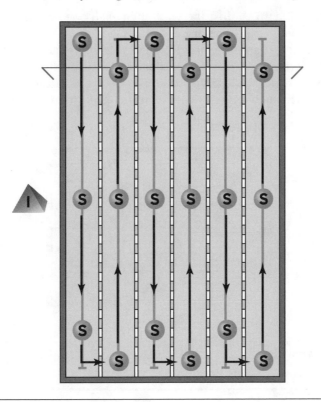

Figure 3.10   Long course practice swim pattern.

Circle Swim

Level: All levels

Advantages: Instructor can observe each student's performance.

Students line up along a pool wall. As the student at the head of the line swims out to the instructor, the rest of the students move up so the next swimmer is in the starting position. After that first student reaches the instructor, he or she swims back to the end of the line. The next student swims out as the first student swims back (see figure 3.11).

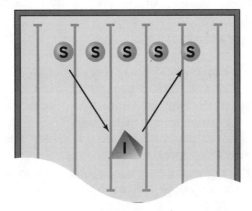

Figure 3.11   Circle swim pattern.

Single Line Pattern

Level: Beginners

Advantages: Good for teaching new skills. Best pattern for providing personal attention to students, although it shortens the amount of time spent practicing.

Students line up against the wall, then each one swims out to the instructor and back to the wall where she or he started (see figure 3.12).

The instructor can give individual correction as each student swims out and can watch students from the front and back to evaluate their performance. When possible, instructors should give students who are waiting to swim another task until it's their turn, such as practicing a flutter kick, rotary breathing, or arm circles in place.

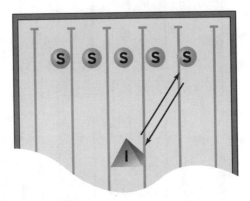

Figure 3.12   Single line pattern.

Other Patterns

Other organizational patterns can be used for class activities. Figure 3.13a shows some possible patterns for class demonstrations. The patterns shown in figure 3.13b can be used for water practice. The patterns shown in figure 3.13c are good for group discussions, and those in figure 3.13d are for series swimming and instruction.

First-Day Orientation

Holding an initial orientation for students and their parents is crucial for the safety and satisfaction of participants in aquatics classes. You can then reinforce your initial orientation and teach students and parents more about water safety and swimming skills through Family Huddles and Parent Handouts.

Student Orientation

The first day of a program can make any student anxious. Each student is meeting new people in what is perhaps an unfamiliar situation. Thus, all staff members need to be well aware of first-day procedures and know how to orient students to the pool, to basic safety rules, and to instruction. They also must do this in a way that is not too tedious for students who have previously attended swim classes and are already familiar with the procedures.

Orientation can be done either with all classes together or with classes individually. Instructors should check *Teaching Swimming Fundamentals, The Youth and Adult*

a. Class Demonstrations

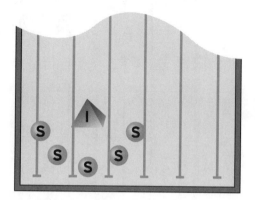

Half circle

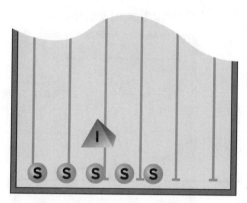

Single line formation

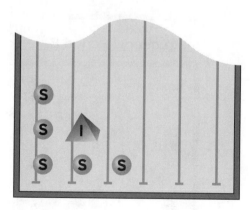

"L" formation

b. Water Practice:

(continued)

Figure 3.13 Other practice patterns.

c. Class Group Discussion

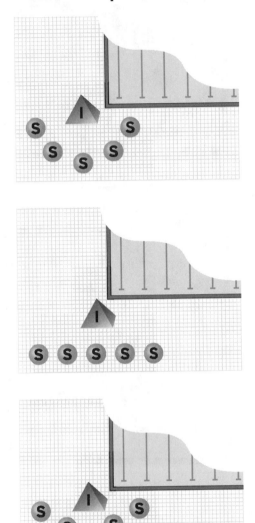

Key

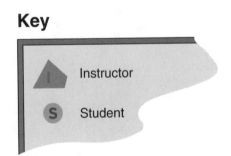

I — Instructor

S — Student

d. Series Swim

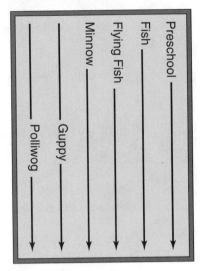

Instructional Period A

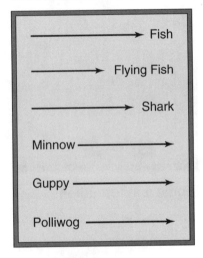

Instructional Period B

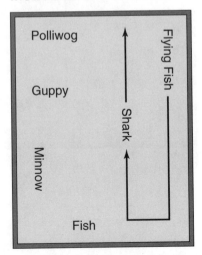

Figure 3.13 *(continued)*

Aquatic Program Manual, and *The Parent/Child and Preschool Aquatic Program Manual* for descriptions of how to do an initial orientation with students.

A thorough orientation on the first day of a session should cover the following information:

- Pool rules
- The need to stay with the instructor
- Where to wait or line up before or after class
- Expectations for behavior, including the following:
  - Listen to your instructor and classmates.
  - Obey the lifeguard's instructions.
  - Be honest about your feelings.
  - Respect others.
  - Be responsible for your own learning.
  - Enter the water only when a lifeguard is on duty and when told to do so by your instructor.
  - Throw away chewing gum before entering the pool.
- Hygiene, including the following:
  - Use the restroom prior to class.
  - Wear proper swimming apparel.
  - Take a soap shower and a warm rinse before entering the pool.
  - Wear nonslip water shoes on deck and in the locker room.
- Proper pool entry
- Pool tour

Parent Orientation

Many YMCAs have found it useful to hold a parent orientation at the beginning of each session. A good orientation will help parents understand what you are trying to achieve in your YMCA swimming program and your YMCA's policies on issues affecting their children. It will also help your class run more smoothly by ensuring that children bring whatever equipment they need to class. Some of the topics that should be included in a parent orientation include the following:

1. A welcome to the program
2. A statement of the program goals
3. Infant guidelines (for those in the Parent/Child program)
4. Viewing area policy
5. A communication phone number and contact person or persons
6. The name of the aquatics director or coordinator
7. The name and level for each instructor
8. Session dates, times
9. The YMCA's philosophy on progression through the levels, allowing children to work at their own pace
10. A first-time parent separation policy (what parents should do if young children are upset at being left alone in class)

11. Pool rules and showering rules
12. Progress reports and program evaluations at the end of the session
13. Family Huddles and Parent Education sheets
14. Registration and reenrollment policies
15. How character development is addressed in the program
16. Volunteer opportunities
17. Annual support campaign

Family Huddles and Parent Handouts

Family Huddles are handouts sent home with swim class participants that describe activities for the whole family. These handouts serve several functions:

- They reinforce what the child learned in class, improving student retention of learning.
- They educate students and their families about the YMCA.
- They help teach character development beyond the swim class itself.
- They provide an opportunity for students and their families to learn about water safety and to strengthen their relationships with each other.

Each level of the YMCA Swim Lessons Preschool and Youth programs has Family Huddles, which can be found in the *YMCA Swim Lessons Administrator's Manual.* Instructors should pass out Family Huddles at the end of each swim class and ask at the beginning of the following class whether the students completed the Huddle activities. They should have students share their experiences in doing the activities and answer any questions students may have.

The *YMCA Swim Lessons Administrator's Manual* also includes a set of Parent Handouts. These cover topics such as safety tips, ways to provide support to swim students, and orientation information.

CLASS SUPERVISION

Several methods can be used to run an aquatics program successfully. One option is suggested here, but you may need to modify it or develop one that better suits your needs. Many factors can affect how you choose to supervise your classes, including your registration methods, staffing patterns, facility layout, and budget constraints. Take time to think through what will be the best method for you and your YMCA.

In this suggested option, you, as the aquatics director (or the coordinator or head instructor), coordinate the classes on the first day. You meet class participants as they enter the pool deck, take roll, and verify that all participants are listed on the roster (figure 3.14 is a sample class roster form). If students are missing or participants are present who have not enrolled, take care of such problems with sensitivity. Also check with students to make sure they are enrolled at the correct level.

Once all this is done, assign the students to their instructors. You will have already told the instructors which levels they will be teaching during each of the time periods, preferably at least a week before the first lesson. Also make sure that the instructor-to-student ratio is appropriate (see page \bb\ in this chapter).

Introduce students to their instructors by calling out the names of the students who belong with that instructor based on the students' skill levels. Note on the roster the instructor to whom each student is assigned. If students don't know what

Class Roster

Program _____ Level _____

Starts _____ Ends _____ Meets _____ At _____

No. of sessions/programs _____ Limit (max. enrollment) _____

Fees: Member _____ Nonmember _____

Special Instructions:

Date	Name	Home/Business phone	M/F	Age	Member	Amt. Paid	Receipt No.	Level	1	2	3	4	5	6	7	8	9	10

	Male	Female	Total
Members			
Nonmembers			
TOTAL			

Figure 3.14 Sample class roster form.

level is appropriate for them, take them to an area of the pool where you or instructors who have not yet been assigned students can evaluate them. Then place those students in the appropriate classes.

As the instructors start their classes, giving students an orientation and pool rules review and checking students' skill levels, move from class to class writing the students' names on the instructors' skill sheets (discussed in the next session). Verify that all students are in the correct levels and double-check that the students' and instructors' names are correct on the roster, making adjustments as necessary.

Finally, give parents an orientation to the program and an orientation handout, present an overview of what is happening in classes, and answer any questions they may have. (A parent orientation may also be held before the first day.)

During subsequent lessons, meet students as they enter for class. Call them by name. Ask them if they remember who their instructor is and ask how they liked the prior class. Then announce that instructors should call their students together. Assist the instructors by putting flotation belts on students who need them, observing series swims, and announcing when the series swim time is over and instructors should move to their assigned positions in the pool.

As the instructors teach, walk around to each class, observe, and bring over any equipment needed for the lesson. Visit with parents who are present, answering their questions, and announce when it is time for classes to switch pool areas. At the end of the lesson, have Family Huddle handouts ready for instructors to distribute.

When the present class period is over, start preparations for the next period. Between lessons, meet with individual instructors periodically to review their lesson plans and session plan. Figure 3.15 is a sample session planning form; Figure 3.16 is a sample lesson planning form.

You also are responsible for seeing that class and student evaluations are carried out. In an eight-class session, for example, distribute class evaluation forms to parents during the fifth or sixth class. Pass out pencils, tell parents how to fill out the form, and let them know that you will be back in a few minutes to collect the forms. After reviewing the evaluations, you should also check that instructors are ready by the sixth or seventh class to hand out students' progress reports (see next section). This allows time during the same session to take corrective action when possible. Students who are passing to the next level should receive both a progress report and a recognition item such as a card or certificate.

STUDENT EVALUATION

The instructor evaluates each student following each class. He or she notes the student's progress on a skill sheet, a summary form that shows the skills covered at a given level (Polliwog, Guppy, and so on), the class roster and attendance, and the progress on each skill with specific comments for each student. An example of a skill sheet form is shown in figure 3.17.

The skill sheet results are then summarized near the end of the session in a progress report. Progress reports are given to students to show them and their parents their progress during that session. An example of a progress report form is shown in figure 3.18.

The progress report lists each of the skills and allows instructors to check off whether the student has completed (mastered) a skill or is still working on it and whether the student has a satisfactory attitude. Instructors should always include positive comments and suggestions in the "Instructor's Comments" section. Once the instructors have completed their progress reports, review the reports for accuracy, legibility, and proper use of grammar.

YMCA Swimming Session Planning Form

Level: _____ Number of students: _____ Session: _____ Instructor: _____

	Personal safety	Personal growth	Stroke development	Water sports and games	Rescue
#1					
#2					
#3					
#4					
#5					
#6					
#7					
#8					

Figure 3.15 Sample session planning form.

YMCA Swimming Lesson Planning Form

Instructor: _____   Day: _____   Date: _____

Class (level): _____   Session: _____   Class time: _____

Today's learning objectives: Safety considerations: Material/equipment:

1. _____   1. _____   1. _____

2. _____   2. _____   2. _____

3. _____   3. _____   3. _____

	Time	Description of activity/ method of teaching	Class organization pattern	Equipment needed	Notes or explanation
Greeting					
Warm-up/series swim					
Review					
Introduce new skills					
Practice					
Conclusion— fun activity					
At-home activity					

Figure 3.16   Sample lesson planning form.

82

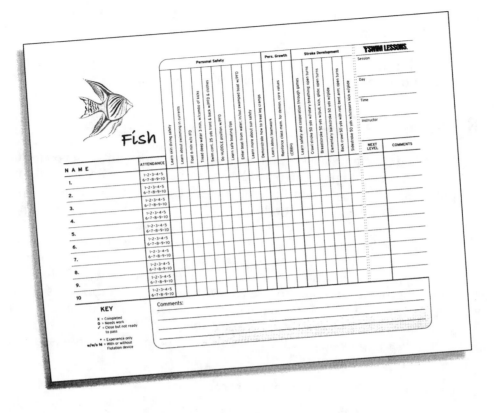

Figure 3.17 Sample skill sheet form.

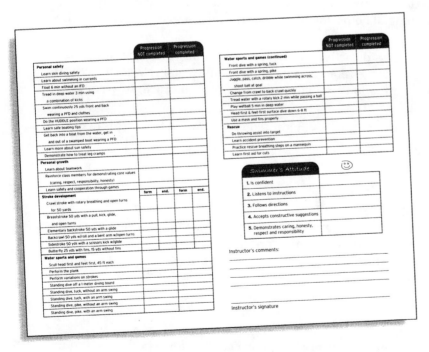

Figure 3.18 Sample progress report form.

Try to distribute the progress reports before the last day of class, then award students their recognition items on the last day. This helps parents who want to reregister their child for the next session by telling them in which level their child should be enrolled. They can register early to beat the last-day rush and, hopefully, get their child into the preferred class time before classes fill up.

PROGRAM STATISTICS

Recording program statistics at the end of each session will assist you in developing future budgets and program schedules. The easiest way to do this is to have a computer registration program that automatically compiles the information. You can also develop a basic spreadsheet that will help you work with the data; but if that is not possible, you can still do it in just a few minutes by hand.

Taking the time to do this at the end of each session will save you many hours of work when budget development time comes around, helping you to budget more efficiently and accurately. It also helps you monitor your annual progress for each aquatics program and can provide you with insight into fluctuations in the number of participants. This information will be most helpful to your program committee when they sit down to review your programs.

Here is a step-by-step method for collecting program statistics (see sample data collection forms in figures 3.19 and 3.20):

1. Collect the following data from each roster:

   - The number of members and nonmembers
   - The number of males and females

2. Total the rosters from the entire session for each type of program and compile them. Insert the number of members and nonmembers for each of the classes based on the days of the week that the class ran. This information is very useful for planning; it helps you maximize the next session's program schedule.

3. Summarize your session activity by program. List all your programs and the total participation by session, and run cumulative totals by session and by program. This summation can help you compare annual activity from year to year.

4. Add the annual information to your budget preparation form. This helps you budget much faster and more accurately.

SPECIAL EVENTS

If you want to maintain high interest in classes and attract new swim participants, try holding special events. They can bring variety and fun to your swim program. Five events that many YMCAs use are water shows, bring-a-friend days, a water carnival, open house demonstrations, or the weeklong Splash program.

Water Shows

Invite classes to participate in a water show. Each class or level performs a routine that they learned during class. The routine can include some of the synchronized swimming skills or games from the program. The show is between 30 to 45 minutes long and is followed by a recreational swim.

Program	January	February	March	April	May	June	July	August	September	October	November	December
Monday												
Tuesday												
Wednesday												
Thursday												
Friday												
Saturday												
Mon/Wed												
Tues/Thurs												
Mon/Wed/Fri												
Monday-Friday												
TOTAL												

Figure 3.19 Sample program statistics collection form.

Summary: Year-to-Date Enrollment

Year

Class	Jan.	Feb.	Mar.	Apr.	May	June	July	Aug.	Sep.	Oct.	Nov.	Dec.

Figure 3.20 Sample summary of program statistics form.

Bring-a-Friend Day

Designate a time when students can bring a friend to class. At this special time, students first demonstrate some of the skills they've learned in class. Then their friends join them to play a variety of games and activities. Additional staff might be needed to supervise the larger class sizes so the correct ratios can be maintained. If classes are full, an alternative might be to have friends come to observe and then distribute a family swim pass to each of them.

Water Carnival

Invite families of students to play games used in class and some special family games. Some of the activities may include practice of safety skills such as basic rescues, boating safety activities, or wacky relays based on safety skills. If you open up the carnival to YMCA members and people from the community during registration, you can offer to sign up new participants during the carnival.

Open House Demonstration

Invite students to the YMCA's Open House to demonstrate a variety of skills learned during their swim classes. The Open House allows spectators to see what the classes are like, the progression of skills in the program, and the skills required to complete each level.

YMCA Splash Program

The YMCA Splash program was developed by the YMCA of the USA as an introduction and orientation to swimming and water safety skills. It is aimed primarily at grade school children and their families, but it can also be modified for younger

children or adults. Most YMCAs offer it as a five-day pool or classroom program, but it is possible to offer a one-day specialty course on boating safety, backyard pool safety, or beach safety as well. The idea is to provide the program at little or no cost, in part as a service to the community in teaching water safety, as well as a way to attract new participants to regular YMCA swimming and boating safety programs.

A kit is available from the YMCA Program Store (Item no. 0-88011-742-7). See the description in chapter 14.

EXTENSION PROGRAMMING

Aquatics programs are logical ones to use for outreach into the community. Everyone needs to know something about water safety, and most children find learning to swim fun, challenging, and confidence building. Here are just a few extension program ideas:

- Hold YMCA Splash in schools or bring classes from schools to the YMCA
- Offer free swim clinics in conjunction with a family day held at area pools
- Hold pool safety clinics for backyard pool owners at area pool builder showrooms, in neighborhoods, or at community centers
- Offer swim lesson programs at apartment complexes or other community pools
- Hold water safety clinics at apartment complexes for residents
- Hold YMCA Splash safety programs for day care centers, Boys and Girls Clubs, Scout groups

In this section, we offer some suggestions on how to reach out to participants in low-income communities and to work in diverse communities. We also talk about the advantages of collaboration and how to collaborate successfully. As outreach may include offering programming in non-YMCA facilities, we next deal with tips for selecting and contracting for facilities outside your own YMCA. Finally, we provide some ideas for funding and equipment sources.

Reaching Out to Low-Income Communities

When your YMCA decides to reach out into low-income communities, you must be aware of the many challenges the children in these areas are facing—challenges that may affect their ability to focus on the activities you have designed for them. These children may be subjected to hunger, domestic violence, poverty, or the threat of street violence. We are not suggesting that these conditions are not present in predominantly middle-income areas. However, in low-income communities, children may be exposed to these conditions more frequently. You will need to create an environment for children that can help them develop to their fullest potential, despite these challenges (Leffert, Saito, Blyth, and Kroenke, 1996).

All children have four basic developmental needs: food and shelter; supportive, caring relationships; safe environments; and opportunities for growth. The needs in these areas vary and are influenced by children's physical, social, emotional, and intellectual development, as well as by their unique characteristics, history, and current life situations. The foundation on which children and youth develop comprises the places, opportunities, and relationships they experience in their families, schools, communities, youth programs, and religious congregations. If this foundation stimulates and supports development and provides appropriate boundaries and limitations, children will most likely grow into healthy and productive adults (Leffert, Saito, Blyth, and Kroenke, 1996).

We do not suggest that programs for children from low-income communities must be very different from those for children from middle- or high-income communities. Instead, such programs must emphasize what all children need: to develop the coping skills necessary to becoming resilient, successful adults. Resilient individuals can be successful despite the risks or adversities they may face.

The key to developing programs and staff to meet children's needs, particularly those of children from low-income homes, is to provide a consistent setting, one in which children can learn skills that will help them cope successfully in society and can develop their ability to make sound life decisions. We must also provide staff members who can serve as role models, individuals who exhibit positive behavior and provide a safe, stimulating environment for children.

A successful program will do the following:

- Hook students into the program by providing experiences that are fun and make them feel welcome.
- Create a safe environment.
- Teach values.
- Create a group identity so that the students feel there is something solid on which they can rely, giving them a sense of safety and control, as well as a consistent experience. Group identity is created by repetition of activities, games, and songs.
- Build social skills.
- Promote cultural pride by integrating culturally relevant activities, stories, and rituals. Such activities build understanding across ethnic and racial groups by promoting a sense of family and community and by exploring our similarities and learning about our differences.
- Build self-esteem by giving children a chance to recognize and use their talents, abilities, and skills, and to discover new strengths and gifts of which they may have been unaware.
- Achieve group and individual goals.
- Provide role models and teach leadership skills.
- Expose members to new experiences.

Although the focus of this section has been on children experiencing economic difficulties, children from all economic groups are at risk from many causes, including

- environmental conditions (e.g., dangerous neighborhood, domestic violence),
- poor education,
- lack of family support,
- traumatic experience (e.g., natural disasters, divorce, death),
- physical adversities (e.g., low birth weight, malnutrition, chronic illness), and
- psychological adversities (e.g., mental illness, drug and alcohol abuse).

Research tends not to isolate one cause from another; healthy child development is affected by all risk factors, alone and in combination.

Just as risk factors can affect children's development in all types of situations, so too can factors that build resilience in children and adolescents. Such factors include the following:

- Effective parenting
- Connections with other competent adults

- Problem-solving and critical thinking skills
- Achieving in areas of talent or accomplishment valued by self and others
- Self-efficacy, self-worth, and hopefulness
- Religious faith or religious affiliations
- Good schools and other community assets
- A safe, stimulating environment

Parents and mentors are also key factors in promoting a child's healthy development, and effective parents and mentors have a number of attributes and behaviors in common. These include

- making a person feel worthwhile and valuable through consistent nurturing behavior;
- modeling competent behavior;
- providing information and access to knowledge;
- coaching competent behavior;
- providing guidance and constructive feedback, steering children away from wasteful or dangerous pitfalls through advice and proactive buffering;
- supporting the undertaking of new challenges that they feel confident the young person could handle or could stretch to meet;
- functioning as advocates; and
- providing opportunities for competence- and confidence-building experiences.

YMCA staff and volunteers with these attributes can serve as mentors to children at risk.

YMCA aquatics programs can be successful in helping to build a foundation for children's resiliency. The presence of consistent and competent instructors can enhance the probability that children will withstand the effects of negative environments.

It is equally important to build a collaborative web to meet the needs of low-income children and their families in the community. Your YMCA cannot do it alone; you must work with others in the community to provide additional services to the children you serve. The manual entitled *YMCA Family Resource and Support Programs* (Item no. 0-7360-0774-1), available through the YMCA Program Store, provides additional information on how to support families in your communities.

You will have to give additional thought to how to fund your aquatics programs to serve children in low-income areas, as participants' families may not be able to pay the regular fees. You may have to turn to other income sources, such as sustaining dollars, grants, public (governmental) funding, or fundraising events with your collaborative partners. (See "Developmental Assets and Impact Research" in chapter 2 for measuring the impact of your work on youth, which can help you in fundraising.)

The YMCA of the USA offers many certification courses for working with youth. Refer to the "Youth and Community Development" section of the *YMCA of the USA Training Course Catalog*.

Working in Diverse Communities

YMCA aquatics programs are especially important for communities that have few opportunities to participate in water activities. Water safety is important lifesaving information that everyone should know. Before you start a swim program in a new community, however, talk to the people in the community to find out if they will support the program and will give you tips for succeeding.

Culture has a critical impact on the individuals and communities YMCAs seek to serve. Before you expand programming into new communities, you must try to understand the culture within that community so that you can show respect for it and work within the cultural parameters. Take the time to ask questions about cultural issues that may affect program design. Learning cultural expectations relating to time, context, parenting styles, nonverbal communication, privacy, emotion, and silence can provide you with insights that may help you succeed. By identifying and building on the community's cultural assets when designing and delivering programs, you will be able to better serve community members' needs and be more successful.

Some of us may never have had exposure to certain groups of people. Not everyone is raising children. Not everyone lives in a racially or ethnically diverse community. Not everyone lives in the city. If your YMCA doesn't have programs for young people, there won't be any chance for you to work with that group. If none of your staff speaks Spanish, chances are, you won't be able to communicate effectively with a Latino community. The same goes for seniors or people with disabilities. If the program isn't there and presented in a familiar way, the people won't be there either.

Negative images that are used to label entire groups of people reinforce people's fears and separation from each other. These negative perceptions are always incorrect; however, the way they came to be believed may or may not have been in the control of the person who holds those views. A person may have been raised with those beliefs. The important thing is to be able to identify prejudice when it occurs, question and tackle it, and then replace it with more appropriate responses. Additional training is available from the YMCA that will help you gain greater understanding of this issue.

Collaboration

According to the YMCA of the USA, collaboration "is the process of involving individuals, agencies, or organizations in efforts to accomplish a common task. Collaborations require shared decision making, with resources allocated so as to best achieve the common purpose."

The reason for collaborating is to consolidate resources to achieve goals that are larger than either organization could reach on its own. When YMCAs collaborate, they strengthen their communities and themselves. Collaborating helps ensure that services to families are coordinated, brings in more contributions, and fosters good publicity for the YMCA.

Collaboration can result in additional services, funding, resources, and volunteers for any project. Consider the following examples:

• Join with schools, churches, or nonprofits such as homeless shelters or housing projects to find children who can't afford swim lessons. Find sponsors, hold a joint fundraiser, and give more children a chance to swim.

• Work with local colleges, universities, and high schools to offer lifeguarding and YMCA Aquatic Specialty Instructor and other certification courses for students. Students studying these courses at the YMCA gain new skills and job training and are a potential source for future YMCA staff.

• Contact elementary schools, child care centers, churches, and home-schooling and family child care groups to arrange for swim lessons, recreational swims, or YMCA Splash.

• Go to parks and recreation departments, local schools, or Boys and Girls Clubs to offer YMCA swimming lessons in their pools, either providing instructors or offering instructor training to their staff.

• Work with local pool builders and pool equipment and supply stores to promote your YMCA swim program.

• Approach apartment complexes to offer swim lessons at their pools for their residents.

• Create intra-association collaborations with YMCAs without pools.

To help you in setting up a collaborative effort, you may want to use the following checklist:

• Is the collaboration supported by key leaders in all organizations involved?

• Has a collaboration mission statement been framed?

• Are the roles and understanding of those roles clear to all?

• Are the individuals being served by the collaboration also involved in the success of the program?

• Do collaborators share a common work ethic?

• Does the collaboration have a designated life span, and if so, are its goals reasonable and has a time frame been developed for accomplishing them?

• Does the commitment to the collaboration exist at all levels of the organization?

• Are there staff members dedicated to working for the collaboration? Should there be?

• Have the collaboration's needs, such as training and ongoing financial support, been addressed?

• Is there a plan for the collaboration's survival in the event that leadership changes?

• Have the collaborators worked out ways to achieve maximum productivity in light of busy schedules?

• Is the general agreement in writing?

• Is there a "family tree" among collaborators (i.e., do the collaborating organizations have common board members, donors, program participants)?

• Is a written diary kept, updated, and available to collaborators regarding the collaboration?

• Is a plan in place for evaluating the collaboration's effectiveness?

• Does a plan exist for communicating the work of the collaboration externally?

Using Non-YMCA Facilities

When you collaborate, or if you simply want to expand your program, you will sometimes have to use non-YMCA facilities. Potential places to house a YMCA aquatics program include the following:

• Backyard pools
• Community pools
• Neighborhood pools
• Apartment complex pools
• Hotel pools
• Pools at schools, colleges, or universities
• Water parks

In such cases, make sure that you check the facilities carefully and discuss your arrangements to ensure that the facilities will meet your program's needs and your aquatic policies can be followed. Look at the following areas:

- Facility cleanliness and maintenance
- Ease of participants in locating the facility and the entrance they should use
- Arrangements and procedures your participants must use to gain access to the facility
- Registration at the facility (or through the YMCA)
- Fees for facility residents or patrons to register in the YMCA program
- Whether non-YMCA members can participate at the facility
- Whether an on-site phone is available
- Equipment storage
- Pool maintenance procedures to ensure that the pool is in proper condition for use
- Emergency procedures
- Insurance and liability coverage
- Whether health department standards have been met in the past season and are currently being met
- Whether the pool has a current permit and electrical inspections

Once you have a site in mind, consider the following questions as you begin to negotiate an agreement:

- Can you barter for the use of the site? Are there services you could provide the site owners in exchange for use of their pool?
- Can the rent be a donation or a tax deduction?
- Can you share the site, using the facility only a portion of the day?
- If the site doesn't meet all your needs or your YMCA's requirements, who will make the necessary site changes?
- Who will be responsible for the expense of maintenance or repairs?
- Is adequate parking available?
- Are there any local zoning ordinances that would prohibit the program from operating?
- What insurance coverage is needed, and who pays for what portions of it?
- Who will provide the chemicals necessary to treat the water?

The agreement should include some of the following items, which may or may not be applicable to your site:

- Name and address of facility owner
- Facility name and address
- Brief description of the facilities
- Hours and dates of use by the YMCA
- Activities scheduled
- Dates of agreement
- Fees for use

- Services the owner will make available, such as phone service, storage, or bathrooms
- Location of emergency and safety equipment
- Safety standards
- Maintenance schedule and who has responsibility for it
- Right or responsibility of your YMCA to make physical modifications, improvements, or alterations to the facility
- Certification of insurance from the owner evidencing your YMCA as an Additional Insured under the general, auto, and umbrella policies
- Certificate of insurance from your YMCA to the owner
- Permission to display a YMCA sign
- Your YMCA's responsibility to recruit, schedule, and register all participants on site and at the YMCA office
- Your YMCA's responsibility to secure parent/guardian release or consent forms for each participant, with copies kept at the site and at the YMCA
- Your YMCA's responsibility to recruit, train, and supervise the staff and to maintain an appropriate ratio of instructors to students
- Your YMCA's right to prohibit smoking and the consumption of alcoholic beverages and illegal drugs during all YMCA-sponsored activities or, if negotiable, a liability release if alcohol is established as a primary cause of accident
- A "hold harmless" agreement

Figure 3.21 is a sample agreement for use of non-YMCA facilities. Before an agreement is signed, make sure it has been reviewed by legal counsel and that you have received appropriate approval from your executive director or your board. Figure 3.22 gives guidelines you should consider when renting facilities from outside vendors.

Third Parties Using YMCA Facilities

As part of a collaboration, or for outside groups wishing to use the YMCA facility for recreation, you may need to arrange for the use of YMCA facilities by non-YMCA members. Just as for the use of a non-YMCA site, you will need to create an agreement with the third party that wants to use the YMCA's facilities. That agreement should do the following:

- Specify that the lease is solely to be used for not-for-profit purposes
- State that the group leasing the YMCA properties agrees to hold the YMCA harmless, indemnify the YMCA, and defend it from any and all claims made against the YMCA relating to the group's use of the leased facilities
- Specify the starting and ending dates of the lease
- Specify the exact area or areas to be leased to the group
- Specify that the group will conduct itself in line with the YMCA's values during the term of the lease
- Specify that the group will comply with all applicable laws
- Get a certificate of insurance to protect the YMCA
- Specify the fees due to the YMCA related to the lease

Use of Non-YMCA Facilities Agreement

It is the policy of the _____ YMCA to expand and decentralize selected program activities and services through the use of community and/or privately owned sites and facilities. When this occurs, a written agreement will be executed.

Name of owner: _____

Address: _____

City: _____ State: _____ ZIP code: _____

The undersigned (owner) agrees to provide the YMCA (brief description of facilities)

_____

_____

to the _____ YMCA during the hours of _____
to the purpose of conducting (specify the activities, class, or group) in conformity with the policies of the _____ YMCA and compliance with applicable local, state, and federal laws and regulations. This agreement shall be in force from (__ / __ / 20__) to (__ / __ / 20__), with an option to renew for a period of _____.

It is agreed that _____ (Owner/Lessor) will provide or make available a telephone for emergencies, sanitary facilities, and storage space as follows: _____

The following space may be used for medical and emergency service:

_____

It is further agreed that there will be full Fire Code compliance by both the (Owner/Lessor) and the YMCA. Fire extinguishers are located as follows: _____
and will be maintained and serviced at least annually by the (Owner/Lessor).

The facilities will be cleaned daily and routine maintenance functions performed by:

_____

The YMCA has/has not the right or responsibility to make physical modifications, improvements, or alterations to the facility upon approval of _____

The _____ (Owner/Lessor) will provide the YMCA with a Certificate of Insurance naming the YMCA as additional insured on the property damage.

The _____ (Owner/Lessor) will permit the display of a sign, "_____ YMCA PROGRAM" while YMCA activities are in progress. (Name the activity or program.)

The YMCA will recruit, schedule, and register all participants, maintaining a roster with name, address, and telephone number of participants on site and at the YMCA Office.

The YMCA will provide the _____ (Owner/Lessor) a Certificate of General Liability Insurance naming the Owner/Lessor as additional insured for losses arising out of the negligence of the YMCA.

The YMCA will secure parent/guardian release/consent forms for each participant with copies maintained at the site and the YMCA.

(continued)

Figure 3.21 Sample use of non-YMCA facilities agreement.

The YMCA will recruit, train, and supervise program/activity leaders, instructors, and supervisors with a ratio of one per _____ participants.

The YMCA will prohibit smoking and the consumption of alcoholic beverages and/or illegal drugs during all YMCA-sponsored activities.

_____   _____
Executive Director for the YMCA   Owner/Agent

_____   _____
Name of YMCA   Date   Organization/Agent name   Date

(**Note:** Be sure to have your legal counsel and human resources staff review and modify forms to comply with state law and your association's requirements.)

Figure 3.21   *(continued)*

Guidelines for Renting Pools Belonging to Others

The following are some things YMCAs should consider when renting the use of a pool owned by others:

- When and for how long will the pool be used by the YMCA? Will the use be shared with others?
- What pool-cleaning procedures are in place, and who will be responsible for the maintenance and cleanliness of the pool?
- Who will provide the lifeguards? Do the lifeguards have YMCA certification?
- Are the backup, break, and relief schedules for lifeguards posted?
- Is there an AED (automatic external defibrillator) on the premises, and is someone trained in its proper use?
- Is first aid equipment and oxygen available?
- Who will provide and maintain pool equipment such as kickboards, lifejackets, etc.?
- Are the emergency procedures clear and readily available?
- Is the pool designed to accommodate persons with special needs?
- Will the pool accommodate parent/child and preschool swim programs as well as youth and adult programs?
- Is there an insurance policy which provides a minimum of 1 million dollars in coverage to the YMCA?
- Have all the terms been put in a written document that is signed by both parties?

Even though your YMCA does not own the pool, it can still be held liable for injuries that occur there. It is important that you have a written document that spells out what each party is responsible for with regard to use of the pool. If you would like help with drafting the document, or would like us to review the document once it is drafted, please call the Office of the General Counsel at 800-872-9622, Ext. 7529.

Figure 3.22   Guidelines for renting non-YMCA facilities.

- Make certain, if the pool is part of the leased property, that the group leasing the pool adheres to appropriate lifeguard requirements, program supervision requirements, and appropriate emergency rules and regulations based on your association operating policies

If your YMCA does not have an existing agreement form to use for this purpose, be sure to have your legal counsel review the agreement you draw up before you present it to the third party.

Funding and Equipment Sources

If your YMCA does not have the resources to purchase the equipment needed for you to have a top-notch aquatics program, you can still look to sources within your community for help. For example, for a boating program, you can ask for assistance from your local U.S. Coast Guard Auxiliary, from boating organizations or clubs, and from boating companies or marinas. Scuba shops or sporting goods stores may be willing to offer equipment, instruction, or both for skin diving programs. Pool builders and pool and spa supply companies may help out with equipment or labor as well. Finally, you can search for sponsorships from the following:

- Local stores or vendors
- National companies with local distributors, such as Coca-Cola or Pepsi
- Local service clubs such as the Rotary, Lions, or Kiwanis
- Previous or current contributors to your YMCA

Funding sources, including local United Ways, are calling for greater accountability for the outcomes of program participants. It can be difficult, however, to demonstrate an impact on selected outcomes within the time frame of your program. You need to establish a clear set of desired outcomes for the program that are realistic and measurable and that guide program development. For youth aquatics programs, we recommend that you claim to support only three or four developmental assets (see "Developmental Assets and Impact Research" in chapter 2). To measure the effectiveness of the program based on those assets, use the YMCA publication *YMCA Youth Programs: A Leadership, Advocacy, and Evaluation Kit*, available through the YMCA Program Store (Item no. 0-7360-0766-0). This guide contains information that can help you link YMCA programming efforts to the research that supports asset building.

Although the YMCA is a not-for-profit agency, we depend on participant fees to help maintain our services. We are committed to serving people regardless of their income level, but we expect participants to pay a fee based on their financial ability. Contingent on financial resources of the association and verification of application information, YMCA scholarships will be awarded to applicants.

BIBLIOGRAPHY

Leffert, Nancy, Rebecca N. Saito, Dale A. Blyth, and Candyce H. Kroenke. 1996. *Making the case: Measuring the impact of youth development programs* (a Search Institute report commissioned by the YMCA of the USA). Minneapolis: Search Institute.

Member Service and Involvement

Membership and your aquatics program are essential to one another. One builds on the other. A strong aquatics program helps build membership, and a strong membership builds a strong aquatics program. You need to understand this relationship to benefit both your aquatics program and the membership program.

We know through surveys that members are satisfied when the facilities are clean and have equipment that works and when they believe they get good value for their money. Poor service may cause members to leave, but excellent service will make members want to be part of the YMCA. In this chapter, we'll explain how you can improve program value and field member complaints.

We also know that YMCAs get new members by word of mouth (see chapter 8 for more on word-of-mouth promotion), by members bringing in new members, and by upgrading program participants to full members. Ultimately, we want members to move from being casual users of YMCA services to being advocates for the YMCA. The second half of this chapter describes methods for making this happen.

ADDED PROGRAM VALUE

One way to add value to programs is to teach your staff positive member service attitudes. Start by having your staff brainstorm what a positive aquatics experience would look and feel like, then have them generate ideas on how to deliver it. When staff members do something extraordinary for a member that is beyond a member's expectations, we have not only satisfied a need, but have also added value. Recognize staff for doing this.

To find ways to add value, ask yourself these questions about your program:

Staff courtesy

Are our staff and instructors polite? Do staff and instructors greet students and members as they enter and leave the pool area? Do they speak respectfully at all times? Do they speak positively, particularly when reminding people about rules? Have they validated members' concerns and suggestions?

Staff responsiveness	Are we being responsive to the needs of our members? If equipment is broken, is it replaced quickly? If there is a problem or conflict with classes, is it resolved quickly? Do we return calls quickly? Do we follow up with their concerns? Do we educate them?
Condition of facility	Is it clean? Is it well maintained? Are things broken for long periods of time? Is the temperature of the pool and shower areas comfortable?
Quality of programs	Do we offer top-quality programs? Are instructors prepared, and do they start/end classes on time? Is the program the best it could be?
Meeting the public's expectations	Did their class meet their expectations? Did the YMCA live up to, exceed, or fall short of being everything they thought it would be?

Another way to add program value is to find out what your members value most about your program through a survey, member intercept, or personal interviews. Make a list of words or phrases most frequently mentioned, and ask other members to prioritize that list to establish the five most valued areas. Then make sure these attributes are built into your program and all your communication efforts to assure members that the YMCA is putting what they value into action at no extra charge. Make changes that members perceive as important, and support your staff so they can deliver the value-added service that members want and expect.

Here are some suggestions for changes that might make your facility easier to use and more comfortable, as well as some ideas for new services to members. Meet with staff and members to come up with additional ideas.

Locker Rooms

- Add a special-needs locker room.
- Make entrances wider.
- Hold an orientation for little boys and girls using the adult locker rooms for the first time.
- Put changing tables or wall-mounted changing stations in the locker rooms.
- Install toilets that are the right size for children.
- Separate the adult and family/children's locker rooms.
- Install sinks in locker rooms that are low enough for children to turn the water on and off. Include some mirrors, hand/hair dryers, towel dispensers, and soap dispensers low enough for children to use. Toddler safety seats can also be helpful to parents in the locker room.
- Have hooks in the shower area to hold bags and belongings so they won't get wet.
- Install handicapped-accessible shower stalls.
- Install easy-to-use push-button showers for kids and seniors.
- Provide lock and towel services.
- Have stools available in the shower.
- Have water extractors for swimsuits in each locker room.

Pool Area

- Install towel bars or hooks in the pool area.
- Add rails for easy entry and exit on steps.
- Install new rails on the walls of the pool and in the pool area.
- Provide cubbyhole lockers for kids. These lockers should be low to the ground and without a front, if possible.
- Install a toilet near the pool deck so swimmers don't have to go all the way back to the locker room.
- Install a hydraulic lift in your pool.
- Add a portable entrance ramp.
- Paint nonslip footprints on the pool deck to direct traffic.
- Provide a basket of toys for the pool.
- Provide babysitting for swimmers with small children.
- Paint a colorful mural on the walls.
- Have a viewing area for parents.
- Post the lifeguards' names at the entrance.
- Add palm trees, patio tables, and lounge chairs to the pool area.
- Hang banners, mobiles, or water toys above the water during lessons.
- Devote one corner to toys and games.
- Have a "kiddie corral," a fenced-in area on the pool deck or in the observation area for toddlers.

- Improve lighting and acoustics in the pool area.
- Add a whirlpool and/or a sauna.
- Install an underwater sound system.
- Think about expanding an outdoor pool area with umbrellas for shade, lighting for after-dark activities, a sandbox and playground equipment, and room for sand volleyball and other sports.

New Services

- Start a collaboration with an outdoor facility that would allow your members to use the facility during the summertime.
- Play underwater music.
- Teach cross-training principles.
- Host a swim stroke clinic.
- Provide towel service on the deck.
- Create an aquatics fitness center with water exercise stations.
- Designate a few lanes for stretching and water walking so nonswimmers can enjoy the pool too.
- Provide timing of member strokes.
- Ask fitness staff to provide fitness evaluations for swimmers.
- Pass out workout plans, diet plans, or information on other types of exercise.
- Provide charts so members can track their mileage.
- Provide incentives for reaching mileage goals.
- Put a thought for the day on the bottom of the pool.
- Have kickboards, fins, or pull buoys for lap swimmers.
- Hold special thank-you activities or hand out gifts on a regular basis.
- Provide exercise mats for stretching in the locker rooms or on the pool deck.
- Provide plastic bags for swimsuits and towels.
- Provide toys or activities for young children who are waiting for their siblings.

See the checklist of good practices for member service.

DEALING WITH COMPLAINTS AND PROBLEM SOLVING

Whether in person or on the phone, the way we handle complaints is one of our greatest opportunities to create *raving fans*. Most dissatisfied people never complain because they don't believe that their complaints will change anything, and some may leave; however, if you empower your staff to fix problems and resolve members' issues, the majority of people will stay with you.

Help your staff create an atmosphere in which it is incredibly easy and inviting for people to complain. Make sure your staff is caring and responsive, and that they don't fix blame, but instead fix the problem—as soon as possible. Encourage them to exceed members' expectations.

Tell your staff to follow these few points when they deal with a complaint:

- Don't take it personally, and stay calm. Do not raise your voice.
- Listen closely, and show by your body language that you are listening.
- Be sincere, empathetic, and respectful. Try to understand the other side of the situation.

Leadership

- The YMCA management team has an obsession for improving quality.
- The YMCA has a system in place that regularly measures the quality of all YMCA operations.

Staff

- The YMCA has enough staff to give prompt attention to members.
- The reception or front desk staff greet all members and guests personally using their names, for example, "Hello, Mr. Orenstein."
- Staff members are clean, well groomed, and dressed according to the standards set by the YMCA (for example, black pants, gray shirt, name badge).
- All staff wear an identification name badge while on duty.
- All staff are identified as staff or volunteers. Staff apparel features the YMCA logo and national theme.
- All staff members have an "on-stage" mentality. They behave as if they are there to perform for members, and while they are on the floor they give their full attention and energy to their performance.
- All staff know how to use the values of caring, honesty, respect, and responsibility as tools when dealing with a difficult situation.
- The executive director is committed to developing high-quality contact point standards.
- The process for developing standards includes front-line staff representing different levels and functions in the YMCA.
- All staff show an interest in members. They are warm, friendly, and willing to help at all times. All staff are helpful even when members are impolite.
- All staff immediately recognize and help members and guests.
- There is minimal small talk among staff while members and guests are present.
- Staff are efficient and well informed.
- The executive director is visible in the operation and he or she is friendly and interested in members and staff members.
- The membership director and the staff member on duty schedule time to circulate throughout the facility and program areas.

Front Desk or Reception Area

- All point-of-contact areas are clean and free of clutter, including food, beverages, and staff belongings.
- The reception counter or front desk is used only by authorized staff.
- Staff have a back-up system they can use when the front desk gets busy.
- A sign listing the YMCA's commitment to service is prominently displayed in the main lobby.

Telephone

- The telephones for answering incoming calls are separated from the part of the front desk where staff greet and serve current and potential members.

(continued)

- Only experienced staff answer the phone.
- All incoming calls are taken by a person rather than an automated system.
- The phone is answered promptly, never past the third ring.
- The YMCA has a standard caller greeting.
- When leaving messages, callers are given a choice of voicemail or a written message, which is repeated back to the caller.
- The date, the time of the call, and the name of the person who took the call is recorded for all messages on a standard message form.
- The YMCA has a telephone answering procedure that is regularly monitored. Periodic trainings are held to upgrade skills for all contact phone staff.
- Callers on hold are checked back with every 15 seconds.
- Callers can dial management staff directly.

Fingertip Information

This section refers to information that should be easily accessible by all staff, especially front-line and reception area staff.

- The YMCA has a computerized or manual system for keeping up-to-date information near the phone and reception area.
- Management staff have a check-in and check-out system that the phone receptionist and front-desk staff can consult easily.
- YMCA management staff share the responsibility for continuously updating information.
- The YMCA has a procedure for recording changes in programs and operations.
- The fingertip information includes all YMCA brochures or flyers.
- The fingertip information includes news releases and other public information to which callers may refer.
- The fingertip information includes a current roster of all management staff, program instructors, and facility staff posted in appropriate locations (for example, fitness staff in the exercise area, management staff near the reception area).
- The YMCA has a written emergency procedure that is regularly reinforced with all staff and is posted in all staff rooms and appropriate member areas.
- Corporate YMCAs have a directory of all branches with addresses and phone numbers of key contacts.
- All staff have easy access to all emergency phone numbers as well as other agency phone numbers, for example, the homeless shelter, crisis center, and poison control unit.
- YMCA front-line or reception staff have information on meetings and events held in and out of the building, including contact phone numbers.
- A system exists for referring all membership inquiries to a membership associate, director, or staff member who can interview and schedule an appointment with the prospective member.
- A system exists for recording all membership inquiries and tracking conversions to interviews.

Facility Cleanliness

- All YMCA signs are visible and well maintained.
- Each sign features the YMCA logo and meets YMCA of the USA graphic standards.
- The atmosphere of the entire building is warm, friendly, neat, and clean.
- The YMCA has a sufficient number of janitorial and maintenance staff members to thoroughly clean the facility.
- The YMCA has a cleaning schedule for the custodial staff of hourly, daily, weekly, and monthly jobs.
- The YMCA makes its commitment to cleanliness obvious by posting the cleaning schedule so that it is visible to members, staff members, and guests.
- The responsibility for cleanliness is in every staff member's job description and daily duties.
- The building superintendent/property manager and the executive director make rounds during times of peak use to see what needs improvement and assign staff accordingly.
- The YMCA regularly audits its cleanliness through member satisfaction surveys.
- The YMCA provides towels and cleaning supplies in all exercise areas to wipe equipment off after each member's use.
- The building superintendent/property manager is at all staff meetings, including retreats, trainings, and celebrations.

Equipment

- The members' program equipment goes through a thorough and well-documented inspection every day.
- All equipment that cannot be fixed within 24 hours is removed from the floor and stored until it is repaired.
- The YMCA posts a sign on broken equipment indicating that the equipment will be fixed within 24 hours.
- The YMCA keeps spare parts for equipment on hand.
- The YMCA has an equipment maintenance policy that staff members understand and support.
- The YMCA has a planned and well-documented preventive maintenance program.
- The YMCA has a well-trained certified maintenance staff that monitors all equipment and can make routine repairs immediately.
- The YMCA assigns staff members to make and document regular inspections of the facility.
- All staff members report broken equipment to maintenance staff using a form of which a copy is given to the CEO/executive, building superintendent/property manager, and front desk supervisor.

Property

- The building superintendent/property manager budgets for the time, effort, and expense of buying and properly maintaining well-designed, well-made equipment.

(continued)

Good Practices for Member Service (continued)

- The parking lots (owned or rented) are well maintained, visibly striped, and free of potholes, debris, and cracks.
- All dumpsters are fenced in and not visible to the general public.
- All landscaping of YMCA facilities (owned or rented) is groomed, well-maintained, and free of weeds and trash.
- The outside of all YMCA facilities (owned or rented) is clean and well maintained.
- The parking lots (owned or rented) are well lit, safe, and secure.
- YMCA paid staff do not park close to the front entrance of the building.
- The YMCA has allocated the correct number of parking spaces for handicapped parking.

Interior Furnishings

- YMCA indoor facilities (owned or rented) are brightly lit.
- YMCA interior and exterior signage is uniform and adheres to the graphic standards set by the YMCA of the USA.
- Facility corridors and stairwells are not used for storage.
- The carpet is not worn with traffic patterns or spills or frayed areas anywhere in YMCA facilities (owned or rented).
- Uncarpeted areas such as tile are kept clean, including corners.
- All lockers are in working order and are free of scratches, dents, and graffiti.
- All locker rooms are well ventilated, clean, and well lit.
- The lobby is well maintained, with furniture that is not worn, torn, broken, or stained. It is furnished as a social place for members and guests.
- All doors and windows are clean and clear for open viewing.

- Ask questions to make sure you fully understand the problem; problems usually are more complicated than they appear.
- Restate the problem so the person knows you are listening and understand the situation.
- Take ownership of the situation. Do not blame someone else, and accept the complaint as a real problem.
- Apologize, then ask what you can do to fix the problem. Try to solve it immediately, and keep your promises.
- After you have fixed the problem, follow up. Check with the member to make sure the problem has been resolved.
- Take long-term corrective action. Find out the root cause of the problem and work to prevent future occurrences.

Follow-up is arguably the most important step in turning an upset participant or member into a raving fan. It is the extra step that leaves a lasting impression with the person who is complaining. That person may or may not remember the problem, but she or he will remember how you handled the situation.

Be sure you give your staff the tools they need to solve problems for members. Begin by listing problems that occur frequently in your department, such as classes being canceled or children ending up in the wrong swim class, and then design strategies to resolve them. Let everyone know that when "A" happens, "B" is a good solution. Train your staff in creative problem solving, and let them use their common sense! Discuss problems and problem solving during your staff meetings.

MEMBER INVOLVEMENT

Plain and simple, relationships are the key to membership development. Staff, volunteers, and even members themselves broaden and enrich the YMCA's work by building relationships with members, volunteers, and donors. If the YMCA were a business, it might be content with a simple transaction: A customer wants or needs something the YMCA has to offer, the customer pays, and the YMCA serves to the best of its ability and hopes the customer will tell his or her friends all about it. But the YMCA is not a business; it's an association of people. It survives and thrives only through long-term involvement.

Steps in the Member Involvement Continuum

To gain people's long-term involvement, we need to move members along a continuum from their first introduction to the YMCA to commitment to the association and the YMCA (see figure 4.1).

The Introduction

Members' relationships with the YMCA start the moment they first make contact, whether by phone, through the Internet, or in person. Maybe a promotional brochure or flyer pulled them in; maybe a friend referred them; or maybe the YMCA sign just caught their eye. Regardless of how they found your YMCA, this first contact should be prospective members' point of entry into the member involvement process.

One way to make people's first contact with your department positive is to communicate information about your department to the front-desk staff. They are the first point of contact for all questions about your programs. Stay in contact with them by attending their staff meetings on a quarterly basis to provide program information, explain registration concerns, and get their feedback from parents about the registration process. Allow time for a question-and-answer period. A joint meeting between the front-desk staff and your aquatics staff may also help lower barriers and eliminate misinformation about each other's jobs.

Most people join the YMCA to meet a personal need. They aren't thinking about what they can do for others, how they can build community, or how they can further the YMCA's mission. They become aware of and committed to the YMCA's "big picture" only through broader exposure over time. But it certainly helps to have the right kind of entry point—one in which the staff member or volunteer at hand is thinking, "What can I do to begin this person's involvement on a positive note?"

The Casual Relationship

Most often, members start out in a casual relationship with the YMCA. They are users of the association or short-term purchasers of services such as fitness or child care. They are "customers" who come in and use a program, service, or facility, then

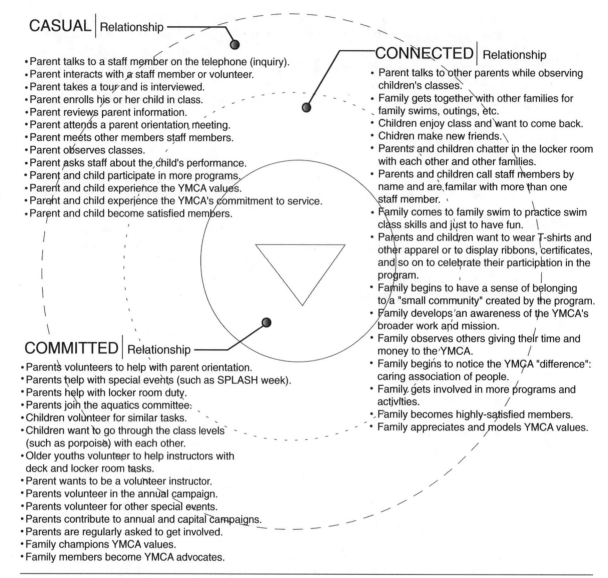

CASUAL | Relationship

- Parent talks to a staff member on the telephone (inquiry).
- Parent interacts with a staff member or volunteer.
- Parent takes a tour and is interviewed.
- Parent enrolls his or her child in class.
- Parent reviews parent information.
- Parent attends a parent orientation meeting.
- Parent meets other members staff members.
- Parent observes classes.
- Parent asks staff about the child's performance.
- Parent and child participate in more programs.
- Parent and child experience the YMCA values.
- Parent and child experience the YMCA's commitment to service.
- Parent and child become satisfied members.

CONNECTED | Relationship

- Parent talks to other parents while observing children's classes.
- Family gets together with other families for family swims, outings, etc.
- Children enjoy class and want to come back.
- Chidren make new friends.
- Parents and children chatter in the locker room with each other and other families.
- Parents and children call staff members by name and are familar with more than one staff member.
- Family comes to family swim to practice swim class skills and just to have fun.
- Parents and children want to wear T-shirts and other apparel or to display ribbons, certificates, and so on to celebrate their participation in the program.
- Family begins to have a sense of belonging to a "small community" created by the program.
- Family develops an awareness of the YMCA's broader work and mission.
- Family observes others giving their time and money to the YMCA.
- Family begins to notice the YMCA "difference": caring association of people.
- Family gets involved in more programs and activities.
- Family becomes highly-satisfied members.
- Family appreciates and models YMCA values.

COMMITTED | Relationship

- Parents volunteers to help with parent orientation.
- Parents help with special events (such as SPLASH week).
- Parents help with locker room duty.
- Parents join the aquatics committee.
- Children volunteer for similar tasks.
- Children want to go through the class levels (such as porpoise) with each other.
- Older youths volunteer to help instructors with deck and locker room tasks.
- Parent wants to be a volunteer instructor.
- Parents volunteer in the annual campaign.
- Parents volunteer for other special events.
- Parents contribute to annual and capital campaigns.
- Parents are regularly asked to get involved.
- Family champions YMCA values.
- Family members become YMCA advocates.

Figure 4.1   Member involvement circle for YMCA Swim Lessons.

leave. In a typical YMCA, about 70 percent of members have this casual relationship with the association.

There's nothing wrong with this type of relationship, and it's a great way to prepare a member for deeper involvement. Even within the "casual" phase, you can move a member through a continuum:

- Potential member steps into the YMCA or makes a telephone or Internet inquiry.
- Potential member interacts with a staff member or volunteer.
- Potential member takes a tour and is interviewed by the staff member or volunteer.
- Potential member enrolls in a program or joins as a member.
- New member participates in YMCA orientation.
- New member participates in program and membership offerings.
- Member meets staff as well as other members.

- Member gets a sense of the YMCA's values.
- Member benefits from the YMCA's commitment to service.
- Member becomes a satisfied member.

When a potential member tours the YMCA, the staff member or volunteer conducting the tour needs to find out what the prospective member's needs, wants, and goals are so that these can be matched with the right programs, facilities, and services. For example, the staff member might offer a learn-to-swim program and Leaders Club to a teen who wants to grow and make friends, or basketball and swimming to a family that wants to get off the couch but still be together. This doesn't have to be done through a formal sit-down interview; the staff member need only ask questions and get to know the potential member.

Once the prospect has enrolled as a member or program participant, staff members must track their every interaction with that member for the first year. This is the only way to get an intimate knowledge of the member's wants and needs, level of satisfaction, and level of participation. A national member retention study showed that the more frequently members participate in programs and activities, the more satisfied they are and the more likely they are to stick with the YMCA.

It's surprising how quickly a new member can learn about the YMCA's history, mission, and values, but only if staff and volunteers make an effort. Orientation is a good start, but the way members really get the message is by seeing caring, honesty, respect, and responsibility come alive in the behavior of every staff member and volunteer, even on difficult days.

New members may have ample opportunities to make friends with other members and with staff, but most of the time this won't happen unless staff members make it happen. Many YMCAs have had luck with ambassador, shepherd, and buddy programs that link members with other members, make them feel welcome, and help them meet practical needs, such as a workout or racquetball partner or someone with whom to car pool to and from the YMCA.

The Connected Relationship

Members move from casual to connected when they start to notice the YMCA "difference"—its emphasis on caring about others. As they get to know the staff and see members volunteering, they understand that there is more to the YMCA than just its facilities and programs.

Connected members will start to volunteer their time, perhaps through a community development project, as a YMCA Youth Super Sports coach, or as a greeter or ambassador for new members. They're no longer customers—they're contributors.

Connected members become word-of-mouth "marketers" for the YMCA. They tell their friends, neighbors, and relatives about the YMCA, indirectly recruiting new members. In a typical YMCA, 15 percent of members are in the connected stage.

As with the casual stage, connected members move through a continuum:

- Member makes friends.
- Member becomes part of a "small community" through a program or activity (more on that later!).
- Member develops a sense of belonging through that small community.
- Member becomes more aware of the YMCA's broader work and purpose.
- Member sees others giving their time and money to the YMCA.
- Member notices the YMCA "difference": a caring association of people.
- Member expands from one program to a variety of experiences.

- Member appreciates the YMCA's values (likely consistent with her or his own) and models them.
- Member goes from feeling satisfied to highly satisfied.

The Committed Relationship

The third level of YMCA involvement is the committed relationship. Committed members are no longer just users or even contributors; they are passionate advocates for the YMCA and "owners" of its mission. They belong to several small communities within the YMCA. They understand and can articulate the association's impact on the community. They show their support by giving their time, talent, and money. They contribute to the annual support campaign and take leadership roles on committees and task forces. They continue to tell everyone they know about the YMCA and help open doors to new opportunities for the association. These are the people who move the YMCA forward. In a typical YMCA, 15 percent of members, at most, are at this level of involvement.

The committed stage is the final part of the member involvement continuum:

- Member is asked regularly to get involved in the YMCA's work.
- Member champions the YMCA's values.
- Member volunteers regularly.
- Member contributes to the annual support and other campaigns.
- Member understands and articulates the YMCA's impact in the community.
- Member becomes a passionate YMCA advocate and "owner."

Here is an example of how members may move through the continuum for YMCA Swim Lessons. Think through other aquatics programs and determine ways to relate this model to them.

Introduction for YMCA Swim Lessons

- Parent talks to a staff member on the telephone (inquiry).
- Parent interacts with a staff member or volunteer.
- Parent takes a tour and is interviewed.
- Parent enrolls his or her child in class.

Casual Relationship for YMCA Swim Lessons

- Parent reviews parent information.
- Parent attends a parent orientation meeting.
- Parent meets other staff members.
- Parent observes classes.
- Parent asks staff about the child's performance.
- Parent and child participate in more programs.
- Parent and child experience the YMCA values.
- Parent and child experience the YMCA's commitment to service.
- Parent and child become satisfied members.

Connected Relationship for YMCA Swim Lessons

- Parent talks to other parents while observing children's classes.
- Family gets together with other families for family swims and outings.

- Children enjoy class and want to come back.
- Children make new friends.
- Parents and children chat in the locker room with each other and with other families.
- Parents and children call staff members by name and are familiar with more than one staff member.
- Family comes to family swim to practice swim class skills and just to have fun.
- Parents and children want to wear T-shirts and other apparel or to display ribbons, certificates, and so on, to celebrate their participation in the program.
- Family begins to have a sense of belonging to a "small community" created by the program.
- Family develops an awareness of the YMCA's broader work and mission.
- Family observes others giving their time and money to the YMCA.
- Family begins to notice the YMCA "difference": a caring association of people.
- Family gets involved in more programs and activities.
- Family becomes highly satisfied members.
- Family appreciates and models YMCA values.

Committed Relationship for YMCA Swim Lessons

- Parents volunteer to help with parent orientation.
- Parents help with special events (such as SPLASH Week).
- Parents help with locker room duty.
- Parents join the aquatics committee.
- Their children volunteer for similar tasks.
- Children want to go through the class levels (such as Porpoise) with each other.
- Older youths volunteer to help instructors and with other pool deck and locker room tasks.
- Parent wants to be a volunteer instructor.
- Parents volunteer in the annual campaign.
- Parents volunteer for other special events.
- Parents contribute to annual and capital campaigns.
- Parents are regularly asked to get involved.
- Family members champion YMCA values.
- Family members become YMCA advocates.

Staff's and Volunteers' Role in Member Involvement

All staff members—front-line, management, full- and part-time—and volunteers have a role to play in member involvement. Parents and others who interact with children talk about "teachable moments"—moments that the parent can seize to introduce or reinforce a value or a lesson. While members certainly shouldn't be treated like children (unless they are!), staff and volunteers can use a similar principle to get members involved. "Involvement moments" are chances for a staff member or volunteer to invite a member into a slightly deeper level of involvement with the YMCA. These moments may or may not involve actual enrollment in a program. And the member won't always say yes—but it's important to ask.

Here are some sample involvement moments:

- Ask a member who has learned a new skill in class to teach it to someone else.
- Ask a parent whose child is enrolled in classes to help with a special event.
- Ask a water fitness class member to greet new members or serve as group leader.
- Ask a swim team parent to volunteer as an assistant coach, lead a team warm-up, or join the parent "fan" club.
- Ask a parent to help score, officiate, or coach for a YMCA swim meet.
- Ask water fitness class members to check up, by phone, on others who haven't been to class.
- Ask a program participant to help raise funds for the program.
- Ask a member to help solve a problem she or he has complained about.
- Ask a member to be part of a group that will evaluate the YMCA's programs and services.

The important thing is to be personal—to customize the invitation to members' own interests and needs. A busy, employed mom may be more able, for now, to write a modest check than to attend committee meetings. An introverted member may appreciate being nudged to teach a skill to another member but probably would not feel comfortable jumping in as group leader the second week of class. The better the invitation fits the member, the more likely it is that the member will say yes.

Staff and volunteer responsibilities can be broken into six steps:

1. *Enrollment:* Staff and volunteers encourage potential members to enroll in programs and activities that meet their needs.

2. *Satisfaction:* Staff and volunteers continually ask members about their satisfaction with a program or activity, track responses, listen to suggestions, and respond promptly in a manner consistent with the values of caring, honesty, respect, and responsibility.

3. *Relationship building:* Staff and volunteers are open, friendly, and approachable to all YMCA members and participants. Staff and volunteers initiate interaction with and between members.

4. *Education and conversion:* Staff and volunteers know about and share their knowledge of the YMCA, its programs, its policies, its mission, its values, and how it benefits members and the community.

5. *Volunteerism and leadership:* Staff and volunteers create opportunities for members to volunteer in their areas of interest, and they ask members to do so whenever appropriate.

6. *Ownership:* Staff and volunteers encourage members to "own" the YMCA, using words such as "we," "us," and "our association" (and actions that match those words) to include members as well as staff and volunteers.

Here is a sample "Six Steps to Member Involvement" plan, from enrollment to ownership, for YMCA Swim Lessons. Such plans can also be developed for other YMCA aquatics programs.

Enrollment

- Understand who the YMCA is serving and not serving.
- Conduct formal and informal research about the intended (target) group.
- Evaluate the target group for potential enrollment.

- Create an offer valuable to the target group and matched to the group's needs and promote it to that group.
- Enroll the member in the YMCA.

Satisfaction

- Follow the uniform guidelines (for example, no wet swimsuits in public areas).
- Greet members.
- Introduce yourself and show interest and concern.
- Learn names and use them often.
- Ask "satisfaction questions" about progress and service.
- Listen to suggestions and respond promptly.
- Take care of complaints or concerns immediately.
- Anticipate needs and offer information and options.
- Be alert to facility and equipment repair needs.
- Always look for ways to improve performance.
- Emphasize fun—make the YMCA a happy place to come to.
- Plan lessons for each class.
- Write thoughtful progress reports for students.

Relationship Building

- Make members feel comfortable and at ease.
- Be open, friendly, and approachable to members.
- Initiate interaction with members.
- Be available before and after class to answer questions.
- Frequently ask if there is any way you can help.
- Ask about family, business, and hobbies—get to know the members personally.
- Introduce members to other members and staff.
- Invite members to participate in other classes or programs.
- Invite members to special events.
- Communicate progress and achievements to members, in person or with a note.
- Develop and maintain a member file for planned involvement.
- Encourage members to involve their family and friends in the program.
- Create relationship opportunities (such as social events and group activities).
- Be a friend and take personal care of members.
- Congratulate members on reaching their goals.

Education and Conversion

- Know YMCA aquatics inside and out and share that knowledge.
- Know all about the YMCA and its programs and policies and share that knowledge.
- Encourage participation in other programs and activities.
- Keep up-to-date on the latest information useful to members.
- Acquaint members with other YMCA programs and benefits.
- Be able to articulate the YMCA's mission, values, and benefits.

- Be prepared to present the case for and need for financial support.
- Create opportunities to talk about financial needs.
- Ask members to contribute to the annual campaign.
- Ask members to work in the annual campaign.

Volunteerism and Leadership

- Be able to articulate the role and importance of volunteers.
- Be informed about volunteer opportunities.
- Introduce members to others who are volunteers.
- Create new volunteer opportunities.
- Ask members to volunteer in their areas of interest.
- Ask members to get involved in minor volunteer roles first.
- Provide opportunities to welcome new members, plan events, and fulfill other volunteer roles.
- Encourage successful volunteers to step up their roles.
- Identify and help recruit campaigners and committee and board members.
- Find new ways to recognize and thank volunteers.
- Involve members in planning and decision making.

Ownership

- Use the terms "we," "us," and "our" when referring to the YMCA to give members a sense of ownership.
- Contribute to the annual support campaign.
- Find ways to put volunteers in leadership positions (such as committees and special events).
- Encourage those involved to recruit others as volunteers.
- Consider nurturing members' "ownership" of the YMCA a major part of your job.

Community Building

One of the best strategies for member involvement is to build small communities within the YMCA, then connect these to the larger community outside the YMCA. These small communities are groups of people gathered together because of common characteristics or interests. Here are some examples:

- Parents in the YMCA lobby, waiting for their children to finish a swim lesson
- A group of seniors enjoying a potluck after water fitness class
- A YMCA swim class
- The YMCA's aquatics staff working together on the annual support campaign
- The early-morning lap swimmers
- The swim team parents' advisory committee
- A group of staff members hanging out in the lobby after work

Some of the groups listed here are loosely connected; individuals within them may never have spoken more than a few words to each other. Others may know each other quite well; perhaps they've been together longer or have a more compelling reason to be together, or maybe the personalities in the group just mix better. Certain YMCA communities—YMCA swim teams, YMCA youth sports groups, and YMCA Guides groups—tend to be especially cohesive, probably because they have special cultures and purposes that are connected to the YMCA but have taken on a life of their own. But all these small communities represent an opportunity for the YMCA to build the kinds of relationships that keep members and program members coming back. Some may form on their own and need nurturing by YMCA volunteers and staff; other groups are brought together by design. They key is to recognize each of these groups for the opportunity they represent and to take advantage of that opportunity.

People may join the YMCA for its services, its convenience, its value, or its reputation. But they stay for the people. They stay because they have connected with others—with other members, with volunteers, and with staff—and with the organization's culture, values, and atmosphere. If a water fitness class participant connects only with the instructor, then if the instructor leaves, so does the participant. But if the participant becomes part of a cohesive small community of other participants, and if that person connects, not only with the instructor, but with the YMCA front-desk staff and the whole YMCA "feeling," he or she will probably stick around and try out other instructors, other classes, and other experiences.

These relationships move the casual purchaser of service—someone who buys an eight-week fitness class—to connected and committed YMCA members.

From Casual to Committed Group

The model we used to discuss member involvement works well for community building too. Small community members move along a continuum of involvement with one another, as shown in figure 4.2.

The casual group is a group of people who are just meeting each other, usually because they simply happen to be in the same place at the same time. Parents waiting for their children to finish a swim lesson may begin to chat; members of a cardiocycling class make small talk before the session begins. Here is a chance for a YMCA staff member or volunteer to introduce her- or himself and ask about satisfaction

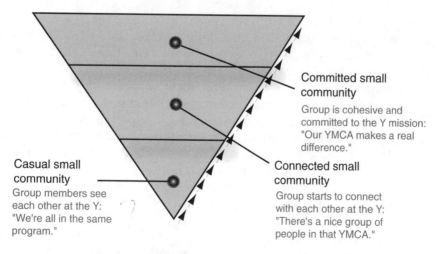

Committed small community

Group is cohesive and committed to the Y mission: "Our YMCA makes a real difference."

Casual small community

Group members see each other at the Y: "We're all in the same program."

Connected small community

Group starts to connect with each other at the Y: "There's a nice group of people in that YMCA."

Individual, Program Participant, Member

Figure 4.2 Building community: "Inside-out" model.

("Are you enjoying the water fitness class?" "How is your child doing in the pool?"). The staff member or volunteer can begin to introduce group members to each other if they're not doing this on their own. The group members start to acknowledge each other at each meeting with a warm greeting and casual conversation. They find commonalities—their children attend the same school, they belong to the same church, and so on. Staff and volunteers can promote this interaction and, in whatever ways are appropriate and feel natural for the group, can introduce the YMCA's values of caring, honesty, respect, and responsibility. Group members feel more and more at home with each other and with the YMCA.

In a connected group, individuals know each other better and call each other by name. If a YMCA staff member or volunteer presents a problem and asks for assistance, the group will rally to help. Staff members and volunteers can explore the YMCA's mission and values more deeply with the group and can ask members to begin to take leadership in a program area. Group members start to notice other group members giving their time, talent, and treasure to promote the YMCA's mission. Group members are modeling the four values and connecting, not just to each other, but also to the YMCA.

A committed group is one in which individuals work together to help the YMCA. They brainstorm ideas with staff and volunteers through volunteering, contributing, and campaigning. Group members understand the YMCA's impact on the community and feel that they are part of that impact. They become loyal partners and advocates for the organization.

Once YMCA staff and volunteers have met the first community-building challenge—turning groups into small communities that are at first casual, then connected, then committed—they face a second challenge: to take these wonderful small communities within the YMCA and connect them to the larger community.

A cohesive small community within the YMCA—a swim team, a group of child care parents, a staff department—can be a powerful force for strengthening the larger community. These groups can be enlisted in the YMCA's existing community development projects, such as tutoring children, mentoring teens, or helping to feed or clothe families in need. In Kansas City, for example, Seniors for Schools takes the YMCA's small community of active older adults and matches them with children who need help building reading skills. Volunteers commit to weekly tutoring sessions at the schools.

To promote collaboration, YMCAs can also connect their own small communities to other local organizations and alliances. In San Diego, the YMCA taps its small community of families in helping the county's Health and Human Services agency find adoptive homes for special-needs children.

Two national initiatives provide excellent ways for YMCAs to rally their small communities of members, program members, volunteers, and staff to fulfill the YMCA mission. The YMCA Strong Communities Agenda promotes YMCAs' work with low-income communities in urban, rural, small-town, and suburban areas nationwide. The YMCA Teen Action Agenda promotes YMCAs' work with teens and aims to empower the movement to involve one in every five teens nationwide (that's 4.8 million 12- to 17-year-olds) by the year 2005. For more information on these and other national initiatives, contact the YMCA of the USA's Association Resources department at 800-872-9622.

Here are some examples of how a group of people, brought together through YMCA Swim Lessons, might become a small community, moving from a casual to a connected to a committed group (Figure 4.3).

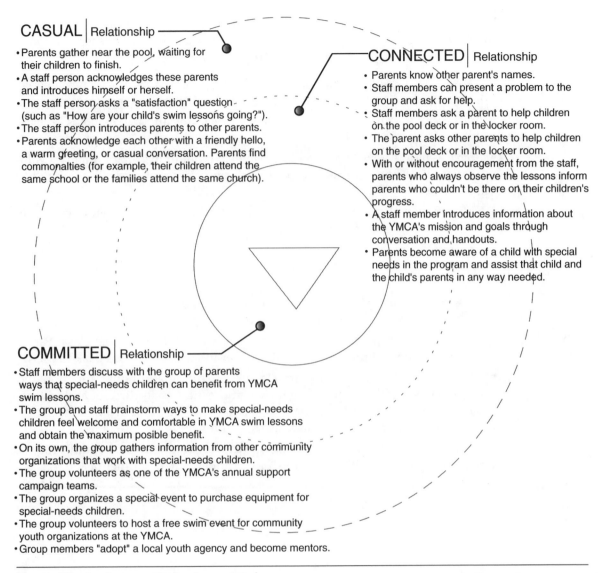

CASUAL | Relationship

- Parents gather near the pool, waiting for their children to finish.
- A staff person acknowledges these parents and introduces himself or herself.
- The staff person asks a "satisfaction" question (such as "How are your child's swim lessons going?").
- The staff person introduces parents to other parents.
- Parents acknowledge each other with a friendly hello, a warm greeting, or casual conversation. Parents find commonalties (for example, their children attend the same school or the families attend the same church).

CONNECTED | Relationship

- Parents know other parent's names.
- Staff members can present a problem to the group and ask for help.
- Staff members ask a parent to help children on the pool deck or in the locker room.
- The parent asks other parents to help children on the pool deck or in the locker room.
- With or without encouragement from the staff, parents who always observe the lessons inform parents who couldn't be there on their children's progress.
- A staff member introduces information about the YMCA's mission and goals through conversation and handouts.
- Parents become aware of a child with special needs in the program and assist that child and the child's parents in any way needed.

COMMITTED | Relationship

- Staff members discuss with the group of parents ways that special-needs children can benefit from YMCA swim lessons.
- The group and staff brainstorm ways to make special-needs children feel welcome and comfortable in YMCA swim lessons and obtain the maximum posible benefit.
- On its own, the group gathers information from other community organizations that work with special-needs children.
- The group volunteers as one of the YMCA's annual support campaign teams.
- The group organizes a special event to purchase equipment for special-needs children.
- The group volunteers to host a free swim event for community youth organizations at the YMCA.
- Group members "adopt" a local youth agency and become mentors.

Figure 4.3   Small community involvement circle.

Promoting Volunteerism Through Small Communities

Volunteerism is probably the best way to move members from casual to connected to committed. Nothing builds a sense of ownership and belonging like rolling up sleeves and getting to work on something that makes a difference for kids, families, and the community. Every successful YMCA has die-hard volunteers who, year after year, give their time and money to help their YMCA reach its potential. But most of these folks started small, and they started because someone asked them.

Members who become volunteers usually do so because they are part of a YMCA team, class, or committee made up of people who enjoy each other and because someone in that group asked them to volunteer. These teams, classes, and committees are the "small communities" that bind the YMCA into a caring association of people. Small-group work has always been the YMCA's strength, and it provides a perfect way to promote volunteerism.

Here is a list of possible volunteer roles for members of small communities within YMCA Swim Lessons. We hope this list will generate many more ideas for ways to give members a chance to belong, contribute, and grow.

- *Class greeter:* Greets members as they enter the pool area, especially new people, and introduces new participants to several "regulars" to make them feel welcome.
- *Class roster coordinator:* Takes attendance for classes and makes notes on class rosters.
- *Secret shopper:* Attends various classes to help monitor instructor quality; evaluates service to members. Listens to parents during classes and asks how they feel about the service.
- *Focus group participant:* Meets two to three times per year to help interpret results of surveys and recommend future adjustments to a program.
- *Aquatics advisory committee member:* At quarterly meetings, reviews program standards, satisfaction surveys, and secret shopper reports. Gives feedback for program development.
- *Class ambassador:* Calls members who have been absent for two weeks or more; looks out for the overall well-being of the class.
- *Potty runner:* Helps young children to the bathroom during swim class. Makes sure they get to the bathroom through the locker room, shower, and back to class.
- *Class aide:* Assists instructor with classes, providing additional attention and practice for class members. Helps organize equipment. Assists director and instructors with distribution of progress reports, Family Huddles, and evaluations. Helps maintain permanent record card database of swimmers.
- *Special event volunteer:* Helps run activities during water carnivals, family nights, or open houses. Assists with swim meets as a runner, timer, or other tasks.

Staff Development

Your staff enables you to accomplish your aquatics department goals. Thus, how well you find, hire, train and supervise your staff will make a great difference in whether you can achieve your goals. It all begins with how you envision your department structure; having a clear, written description of the responsibilities of each position and how it fits into the whole will guide your hiring and supervision. You will need to look continuously for good candidates to join your department, using many methods, and consider using both paid and volunteer staff. You'll also need to know how to interview candidates to choose the most promising ones and the steps to hiring once you've made your choice.

When you supervise your staff, you should have mutually agreed-on performance guidelines so both you and your employees know what your targets are. You can help them meet these guidelines through coaching and feedback and regular performance appraisals. For those who are having difficulty meeting guidelines, you will have to coach their performance and, in some cases, discipline them.

Ongoing responsibilities you will have for staff include training and scheduling. You also can help retain your staff through creating a supportive workplace, providing frequent recognition, and helping staff develop their careers.

For more information, see the YMCA of the USA People Management Resource Tool, available from the YMCA of the USA.

STRUCTURING POSITIONS

The first step is to determine what positions you need in your YMCA. For each position, you'll have to develop a job analysis and write a job description. Then all positions must be organized into a staffing structure, and each position must receive a pay grade and range within your YMCA's salary administration plan. Finally, you must set performance standards for each position.

Job Analysis

Before you write a job description, you should begin with a job analysis. Such an analysis should list the following:

- Duties and responsibilities of the position
- The skills, abilities, and knowledge needed to perform the job
- The mental or physical effort required of a person performing the job
- The working conditions under which the job is performed

When working on the analysis of a job, do the following:

- Review any current descriptions you have on file for the particular job.
- Obtain the supervisor's assessment of the job requirements and essential functions of the job.
- Interview current employees in the position to learn from them about the actual job requirements and what issues they see for effective performance of the job.
- Conduct an on-site visit and observe the job being done.
- Write the job description based on your observations and the input of others.
- Finalize the job description by having the supervisor and employee approve it.

Conducting a job analysis of your positions gives you the necessary information to evaluate whether a particular position is required. The information you gathered in the job analysis produces a job profile—a picture of what the job should look like. From the job profile you then develop the job specifications—those elements that are essential to the performance of that job, such as education, skills, and experience. These specifications form the basis for the development of the job description.

Job Descriptions

Having a good job description is essential to the process of recruiting the best staff. It provides the detailed functions and duties expected of a person in that position. A job description serves a variety of useful functions:

- Establishing hiring criteria
- Outlining job duties, which form the basis for performance standards and supervisory expectations
- Aiding supervisors in identifying training and development needs
- Providing a defense against charges of personnel or pay discrimination
- Establishing job content for rate setting and pay grade evaluations

The job description summarizes the job analysis and provides the basis for defensible job-related actions. It also serves employees by providing them with documentation from management that identifies and clarifies their jobs.

A typical job description contains several major parts: identification, general summary, essential functions and duties, job specifications, and disclaimer and approvals.

Identification

This section includes the job title, reporting relationships, and department/regional location; the date of analysis may be given. It may also include other information that is useful in tracking jobs and employees through a human resource information system (HRIS). Additional items commonly noted in the identification section are job code, pay grade, exempt/nonexempt status under the Fair Labor Standards Act (FLSA), and U.S. Equal Employment Opportunity Commission (EEOC) Classification (from EEO-1 form).

General Summary

This section is a concise statement of the general responsibilities and components that make this job different from others. It is preferably no longer than a paragraph.

Essential Functions and Duties

This section lists the essential functions and duties of the job. It contains clear, precise statements on the major tasks, duties, and responsibilities performed. Writing this section is the most time-consuming aspect of preparing job descriptions.

Job Specifications

This section gives the qualifications needed to perform the job satisfactorily. The job specifications typically are stated as (1) knowledge, skills, and abilities (KSAs), (2) education and experience, and (3) physical requirements and working conditions. The job specifications provide information necessary to determine what accommodations might and might not be possible under Americans With Disabilities Act (ADA) regulations.

Disclaimer and Approvals

This section is not always completed. A disclaimer allows employers to change employees' job duties or to request that employees perform duties not listed, so that the job description is not viewed as a "contract" between the employer and the employee.

You can see sample job descriptions on the YMCA of the USA Web site **www.ymcausa.org.** The ADA focused attention on the importance of well-written job descriptions. Legal compliance requires that they accurately represent the actual jobs. Following are guidelines for preparing legally satisfactory job descriptions.

Identifying titles: A job title should describe the job functions performed and should reflect the employee's relative responsibilities in the association. It also should be linked to the pay grade system.

Writing the general summary and essential functions and duties statements: It may be easier to write the general summary *after* the essential functions and duties statements have been completed. Otherwise, the general summary may be too long.

The general format for an essential functions and duties statement is as follows: (1) action verb, (2) to what applied, and (3) what/how/how often. There is a fine line between writing that is sufficiently descriptive and writing that is too detailed. Use precise action verbs that accurately describe the employee's tasks, duties, and responsibilities. For example, avoid the use of vague words such as "maintains," "handles," and "processes." Compare the statement "Processes expense vouchers" to "Reviews employee expense reports, verifies expense documentation, and submits to accounting for payment." The second statement more clearly describes the scope and nature of the duty performed. However, it is just as important to avoid the trap of writing a motion analysis. The statement "Walks to the filing cabinet, opens drawer, pulls out folder, and inserts material in correct folder" is an extreme example of a motion statement. The statement "Files correspondence and memoranda to maintain accurate customer policy records" is sufficiently descriptive without being overly detailed.

The language of the ADA stresses that the essential functions statements be organized in order of importance or "essentiality." If a description has eight statements, usually the last two or three duties described are less essential than the first two or three. Therefore, you should arrange job duties so that the most essential (the most critical and the ones taking most of the employee's time) are listed first and the supportive or marginal ones are listed later. Within that framework, group and arrange specific functional duties in some logical pattern. For instance, if a job requires an accounting supervisor to prepare several reports, the statements relating to the preparation of reports should be grouped together. A miscellaneous clause is typically included to ensure some managerial flexibility.

Some job descriptions contain sections about the materials or equipment used, working conditions, or special tools used. This information is often included in the specific duty statements or in comment sections.

Because executive and upper-management jobs encompass a wide range of duties and responsibilities, descriptions of these jobs often are written in more general terms than descriptions of jobs at lower levels.

In light of the ADA, you must clearly identify the physical and mental dimensions of each job. If lifting, seeing, hearing, talking, stooping, standing, walking, climbing, jumping, swimming, or crawling are required, note it. Also, specify weights to be lifted, along with specific visual and hearing requirements of jobs. These job specifications are the foundation for evaluating individuals with disabilities for employment.

Ask yourself the following questions as you develop a job description:

- Is this the minimum requirement to perform the job satisfactorily?
- Have I written essential functions statements that adequately describe the job?
- Are the statements in descending order of importance?
- Have I detailed the physical requirements of the position?

Here are a few resources you can use to help in creating job descriptions:

http://www.ijoa.org: The Institute for Job and Occupational Analysis facilitates research and application of job analysis and occupational analysis technologies.

http://www.jobdescription.com: This is an online service for creating individual, customized job descriptions. You can choose from their database and customize to meet your YMCA's unique requirements. There is a charge for their services.

http://www.oalj.dol.gov/libdot.htm: The Dictionary of Occupational Titles from the U.S. Department of Labor has a search function of approximately 12,000 job descriptions. This is an excellent start in writing a job description.

You can also purchase various off-the-shelf software applications to assist you in job profiling and writing job descriptions. You can build or retrieve a complete job profile to fit the position you are filling. Most of these applications can be customized.

On the Web site **(www.ymcausa.org)** are several sample aquatics job descriptions that you can use to start developing yours. You will need to modify the descriptions to meet your specific job requirements. The samples are for the following jobs:

- Lifeguard
- Head lifeguard
- Swim instructor
- Swim coach
- Water fitness instructor
- Instructional swim coordinator
- Pool manager
- Waterfront director
- Aquatics director

Staffing Structures

You can organize your department in many ways. Think of the functions that need to be performed, and develop a way to accomplish them through your work with your staff, both paid and unpaid. From your job analyses, you can develop job descriptions for these positions. Of course, the positions need to be properly budgeted and approved through the personnel policies of your YMCA.

Important things to remember in developing an organizational structure for your department include these:

- Form follows structure. Create a structure based on what jobs need to be performed, not on the people involved.
- Make sure there are clear lines of responsibility and authority.
- Communicate clearly.

Examples of common positions held in the aquatics department as part of the organizational structure are the following:

- Specialty instructors: instructors for YMCA Swim Lessons, Water Fitness.
- Aquatics assistants: volunteers or part-time paid assistants to the instructors.
- Head lifeguards: on-deck lead lifeguard who is responsible for coordinating rotations, making changes on the duty roster for duty periods, and serving as the lead rescuer in emergency situations.
- Aquatics coordinator: assists the aquatics director with department responsibilities. This person may have responsibility for a specific function, such as instruction

or lifeguarding, or a specific time, such as evenings or weekends. Aquatics coordinator may also be the job title used for nonexempt full- or part-time aquatics director positions in some YMCAs.

• Instruction coordinator: part- or full-time position of coordinating the instructional programs at the YMCA. Responsibilities may include screening job applicants and scheduling, supervising, and leading in-service training sessions.

• Lifeguard coordinator: part- or full-time position of coordinating lifeguarding at the YMCA. Responsibilities may include screening job applicants and scheduling, supervising, and leading in-service training sessions.

You may find that you want to use different titles or different combinations of tasks from those shown here.

All aquatics staff should be covered within the association's personnel policy as full-time, part-time, or volunteer staff. Individuals operating as independent contractors must meet IRS criteria to qualify as independent contractors. For information on the IRS criteria, see your human resources department or your executive director.

When you've determined the structure of your department, create an organizational chart showing to whom each employee reports.

Salary Administration

Although as an aquatics director you may not be directly involved in the process of salary administration, be aware that the salaries for your employees are part of the salary administration plan for your association. Most likely, the salary scale used for the positions in your department will be set through the top management of your organization, the personnel committee, and your human resources department.

The salary administration plan must be both externally competitive and internally equitable. One method by which your YMCA can establish the external equity of the plan is using Market Salary Surveys to establish that your wages are on a par with your competitors. Internal equity is how each position is valued relative to other positions within your association. By using a Job Evaluation/Pricing process, you can establish the relative worth of your positions and place them appropriately within your YMCA's salary structure. Ask your human resources department for assistance in this process.

With limited resources, YMCAs cannot rely strictly on the traditional base salary structure to effectively compensate their employees. YMCAs will most likely have to develop alternative supplements to cash-based compensation, not only to be competitive, but also to present employees with a complete and total compensation package. For more information on these processes, contact Human Resources Consulting in the Leadership Development Group at the YMCA of the USA and ask for the People Management Resource Tool.

The aquatics department has primarily part-time staff, and several certifications are required for positions. Therefore, when developing your salary structure, discuss with your human resources director the possibility of building in experience, returning from year to year, and YMCA certifications as determinants for base pay.

Performance Standards

Performance standards are statements describing how a specific job duty is to be performed. Each job segment should have one or more specific standards clearly defining the conditions that will prevail if a job is well done or expected results are achieved. These standards define and reflect the quality of the work, not the employee. They generally reflect the expectations of the supervisor. These standards are also linked to achievement of the organization's strategic plan, operating plan, and organizational goals. Such statements provide the basis for performance appraisals and the foundation of documentation in employee counseling statements. Once these standards are agreed on, they can be provided to staff members to ensure that each understands what is required to be successful.

Performance standards should be as follows:

- Specific
- Clear
- Reachable and challenging
- Job related
- Adjustable based on organization changes
- Not punitive
- Written
- Measurable

For example, for a lifeguard, performance standards might include the following:

- Keep physically fit.
- Be in uniform while on duty.
- Arrive on duty 10 minutes before the shift to check and prepare equipment.
- Enforce pool rules consistently.
- Practice association membership involvement standards consistently.

Establish checkpoints at which you discuss with staff how they are doing before performance appraisals. These are also times for discussing redirection of and changes that are to occur in goals or standards of performance. Determine the frequency of these meetings by the scope of the position and your needs and those of employees.

RECRUITING

The way we recruit staff members has a great impact on retention and turnover rates. Leaders today often use the same recruiting tactics and techniques they used many years ago. However, the times call for new, creative, and effective recruitment strategies. Having all YMCA supervisors do a thorough job of recruiting new staff would have a positive and profound impact on the YMCA and on its retention and staff turnover rates.

During times of low unemployment, competition is high for quality staff, most of whom are young adults. The number of water parks and specialty aquatics facilities has increased, along with the number of traditional pools, and water parks and specialty facilities require significantly more lifeguards than a traditional pool. This significantly affects the number of lifeguards available in a community. On top of this, the salary scale tends to be higher in these other centers than in YMCAs. And there are many good jobs outside of aquatics that pay much more and that have neither the responsibilities of lifeguarding nor the requirement for the same kind of intensive training.

The following actions will help you in recruiting:

- Anticipate turnover.
- Adopt a "we're always hiring" attitude. Don't let good candidates get away because you don't have a job for them.
- Begin measures to grow your own staff. Develop a recruiting strategy and an annual timeline. If your budget allows, hire a part-time recruiter. And if the money for a recruiter is not in the budget, it can be a great meaningful volunteer opportunity for someone.
- Engage volunteers (potential new staff members) such as members, college interns, senior center volunteers, and high school students (many of whom are required to do community service to graduate).
- Be creative—look beyond your current staff profile and recruit nontraditional YMCA staff members. Recruit older adults, new members, and former participants and staff. Remember that using the same sources and methods for recruiting will produce the same results.
- Be more aggressive and thorough in recruiting. Build relationships with students from local high schools, colleges and universities, technical schools, and other service provider organizations, as well as with club swim teams. Let them know about potential employment opportunities.
- "Sell" the YMCA—its values-based environment is a great place to work. Show how the YMCA is a unique, high-quality environment that provides great advancement opportunities and superior compensation, benefits, and working conditions.
- Get a group of staff together to generate new and innovative recruiting ideas.
- Conduct a focus group of new or potential staff members within a target age range to determine what recruitment strategies appeal to them. (See chapter 8 for more on focus groups.)
- Be creative with the tools you use to attract new staff, and learn how to "sell" the YMCA more effectively. Create recruiting videos and brochures (call the YMCA of the USA's Human Resources Consulting Team at 800-872-9622 for recruiting brochures and posters) that depict the YMCA's mission, character development focus, and wide range of career opportunities.
- Work with colleges and universities to incorporate YMCA training programs into their curricula, to increase intern involvement in YMCAs, and to develop stronger collaborations between the YMCAs and universities. This expands the pool of candidates.
- Participate in job recruitment fairs through high schools and colleges and universities.
- Publicize YMCA instructor-level courses in branch program brochures. Coordinate such training among branches.
- Break up long training courses so that they are offered in shorter blocks of time over a longer period. For example, instead of offering a 16-hour course over one weekend, offer it for 4 hours on each of four weekends. This not only makes it more convenient for people to attend (and thus increases your pool of eligible candidates), but it also increases retention of the subject matter.
- Consider hiring capable people of high character even if they are not currently certified and then offering them YMCA certification training at no cost. Develop

relationships with community organizations whose values are similar to the YMCA's (Scouts, 4-H, church groups).

- Keep in mind that the Fair Labor Standards Act requires payment for training required for employees to perform in their current position.

- Examine the costs and benefits of hiring a few full-time staffers rather than many part-time staffers. Turnover may be lower with full-time staffers (who may be more motivated to stay because of the benefits), thus making it less expensive in the long run than hiring many part-time staffers, who are generally believed to have higher turnover rates.

- Use a salary administration plan that includes opportunities for pay raises based on achievements such as the number of YMCA certifications obtained.

- Consider sharing the burden of staff and training costs with other YMCAs. More and more, YMCAs are sharing staff; for instance, two YMCAs may share a full-time aquatics director. Many are also collaborating to offer certification courses through shared trainers.

- Continuously work to identify, develop, and mentor future leaders. Make sure teens know about YMCA aquatics as a potential career. Develop a Teen Aquatic Leadership Program, an Aquatic Leaders Club, or a Porpoise Club. (However, when you hire teenagers, make sure your YMCA is in compliance with child labor laws.)

- Collaborate with other YMCA staffers, such as youth and teen program leaders, as well as other not-for-profits and places of worship, to identify potential staff members. Provide financial assistance for YMCA lifeguard courses for members in good standing of YMCA teen programs such as Black Achievers or Leaders Club.

- Recruit older adults and retired persons as staff members. Across the U.S., aging boomer retirees are taking part-time jobs as part of their wish to remain active and connected to their communities.

- Teach lifeguard classes and let students know about employment opportunities in area YMCAs.

Here are a few suggestions on where to advertise staff vacancies:

- Run a classified ad in local newspapers.
- Contact area high school and college swim team coaches and aquatics directors.
- Try college and university sport and physical education departments; see if they have a job board.
- Talk to area lifeguard classes about job opportunities.
- Put an article in your member newsletter.
- Talk to your members and class participants.
- Ask your staff for referrals.
- Ask through your YMCA Leaders Club or other teen programs at your YMCA and in your community (Junior Achievement, church groups, Scouts, 4-H).
- Try college job placement offices.
- Post an announcement on the job board at your YMCA or on your YMCA web site.
- Attend job fairs.

Unpaid Staff

Other staffing options are available besides paid staff. These include program volunteers, college interns or practicum students, and in-kind service staff.

Program Volunteers

A volunteer is one who provides services of his or her own free will. A YMCA volunteer is someone that has expertise, expects no monetary gain from the YMCA, is dedicated to the YMCA mission, and values the organization.

Sometimes staff tend to treat program volunteers differently, but volunteers should be treated just like any other staff members. Think of them as "unpaid staff." Treat volunteers as true members of the YMCA family; show them that they are one of us, that they are insiders. Work with them as you would work with paid staff members, using everything from job descriptions to a recruitment interview to a periodic performance appraisal. The training and qualifications for like roles do not change whether the person is paid or not. Volunteers have the right to

- be treated as coworkers,
- be given suitable assignments,
- know about the organization,
- obtain training,
- obtain continuing education,
- be given good direction and supervision,
- be promoted and given a variety of duties,
- be evaluated according to performance standards,
- be heard,
- be recognized, and
- have a place to work.

A volunteer program takes time, but it is well worth the investment. Good planning includes the development of goals and objectives with an established course of action for the volunteer. Think of all the things that you would like to do but do not have the time or resources to accomplish. Recruiting volunteers to accept these roles is a great way to fulfill your goals, and it gives volunteers an opportunity to feel needed and to give of themselves to help others. It also links a YMCA to its community.

Volunteers can perform many of the jobs in the aquatics department. Here are just a few positions:

- Swim instructor
- Lifeguard
- Lifeguard supervisor
- Instructor assistant
- Class coordinator (helps organize the kids before each class, takes attendance, and escorts them to the instructors; helps distribute class equipment and transfers it from instructor to instructor; assists children with putting on and taking off belts or lifejackets; assists children in the bathroom or locker room)
- Pool attendant (greets members, checks membership cards at the pool entrance, orients new members to the pool and explains pool rules)

- Swim team coach
- Assistant swim team coach
- Splash coordinator

Here are a few other functions that volunteers can perform:

- Time swim meets
- Present aquatic safety information to area community groups
- Teach aquatic safety to area youth groups
- Lead training sessions in staff meetings or in-service training
- Play a victim in emergency training sessions and lifeguard classes
- Make calls to past participants or prospective program participants
- Distribute flyers to area schools and vendors
- Call participants that have missed classes
- Recruit and organize additional program volunteers
- Lead new water fitness class member orientations
- Manage permanent record cards for swimmers
- Manage the aquatics department volunteer program

The recruitment technique you choose depends on the people you are targeting. Determine what they think about; what they read, watch, or listen to; where they live, work, and spend their free time. Get the word out about what you are looking for. Think about communicating information about your positions in member newsletters, program brochures, and press releases. Use a three-part recruitment message: (1) need or challenge, (2) how the volunteer can help, and (3) how the volunteer benefits.

Look at other groups in your community, such as the following:

- Civic groups
- Service clubs (Rotary, Lions, Kiwanis)
- Chamber of commerce
- Church groups
- Colleges and universities
- High schools
- Older adult groups

Contact these groups and talk to them or send them an announcement about your need for volunteers.

You can find volunteers just as you would find staff members, but the most effective way is by asking them or having someone else ask them. Research shows that people are three to four times more likely to volunteer if they are asked personally, as opposed to simply being exposed to signs, ads, and posters. And of those who are asked, the majority say yes. People who volunteer tend to volunteer for an organization they have a connection to or that a friend or family member benefits from. And, if they are already YMCA members, volunteering involves them more and gives them a greater understanding of the organization (see chapter 4 on "Member Service and Involvement").

Once you have recruited your volunteers, follow your YMCA's enlistment procedures. You should have a process established for the following:

- Applications
- Interviews
- Reference and criminal background checks
- Job descriptions
- Training plan
- Service records
- Performance standards
- Performance reviews
- Recognition for service

See the YMCA of the USA Web site for samples of the forms and procedures.

These are the keys to working with program volunteers:

- Recruit the right person for the right position, rather than recruiting at random.

- Involve the volunteers immediately. When people indicate an interest in volunteering, contact them quickly to set up a time for a talk or an interview. Once they have been recruited and placed, give volunteers specific assignments that they can act on immediately.

- Supervise volunteers and let them know how they're doing. The kind of supervision depends on the individual volunteer and the nature of the position. All volunteers deserve clear communication, coaching, and counseling.

- Provide them with leadership training.

For additional tips on working with program volunteers, take the Working With Program Volunteers course, available through the YMCA of the USA. Two other resources are *The Seven R's of Volunteer Development: A YMCA Resource Kit* (Item no. 0-87322-756-5) and *The Volunteer Champion Guide* (Item no. 0-7360-3378-5), available from the YMCA Program Store.

College Interns and Practicum Students

Some colleges have programs that require students to have certain on-the-job experiences relating to courses they are taking. Developing relationships with local college and university professors is the best way to recruit these students. Providing a good experience for these students is what these professors are seeking. Many times it can be a three-way win for all concerned. The professors have students learning how their classes apply in the "real world," students can see how the information they learned in classes works and may consider the YMCA as a career option, and the YMCA gains additional quality staff they may not have to pay for in dollars and another connection to the community.

The amount of time the students need to serve will vary from a few hours a week to 40 hours a week for a semester, depending on the program.

These students should be treated just like any other staff members. You need to tell them what is expected of them, give them thorough orientation and training, review their performance, and recognize successful task completion.

You may have to do the following as well:

- Provide information about the facility and program and the role the students will play.

- Interview or make site visits with the professor.

- Complete review information about the students' performance.

Members-in-Kind Service Staff

In-kind service staff are those that trade their service for something from the YMCA, such as a membership or program. Since they are receiving something of value for their time and expertise, they are no longer considered volunteers. Free and discounted memberships and programs are considered taxable compensation, and the YMCA may be required to report it as such on a 1099 income statement form, withhold income tax, pay FICA taxes, and be liable under worker's compensation and minimum wage laws. Make sure you talk to your human resources department or executive director about your association's policy regarding this type of staff. For more information about members-in-kind, contact the General Counsel's office at the YMCA of the USA.

Treat these staff members like any other staff members. Have a job description and written agreement that clearly states the understanding between them and the YMCA so there are no misunderstandings later on. Trade and report hours meticulously to comply with your agreement.

INTERVIEWING

A good interview is your tool for determining the best possible choice for a position you have open. The more skillful you become at interviewing, the better you will be able to meet the goals and objectives of your department.

An interview is a discussion, not an interrogation. This is the opportunity to make a good match between meeting the needs of the YMCA and those of the prospective employee. Both parties come to the interview with hopes and expectations; this discussion allows both to find out if they want to become partners in achieving the mission of the YMCA.

As an interviewer, you need to be a good listener and a sharp observer. You'll want to make this process as nonthreatening as possible and be friendly, courteous, and professional. Once prospective employees are at ease, they will be more likely to convey their true feelings, values, and expectations, as opposed to saying what they think you want to hear.

Posing good open-ended questions helps facilitate two-way communication. Frame the questions to bring out the information you need to judge the candidates' qualifications and to identify the knowledge, skills, behaviors, and experiences necessary for the position. Screen for appropriate staff. Ask questions that will encourage candidates to provide specific examples of times when they have used behaviors similar to those for each competency.

Prepare the questions you want to ask each candidate in advance. This not only helps you to be consistent from candidate to candidate, but it also helps guide your discussion so you don't skip any topics you wanted to cover. Keep questions objective and focused on job requirements and qualifications.

Review all the applications and choose to interview those applicants you believe most closely meet the job requirements and have the skills and knowledge to perform the job. A good rule of thumb to follow is to be certain you have more than one candidate in your applicant pool. For example, to avoid discrimination claims, do not conduct interviews with only one applicant for a position. Continue the recruiting process until you have obtained more candidates.

Before each interview, make notes about specific questions you need to ask or clarifications you want to make. Have the job application and job description with you during the interview.

Formulating Interview Questions

Federal and state laws make it illegal to discriminate in the hiring process. This process includes employer's advertising, application forms, and interview questions. These are the areas you are prohibited from inquiring about:

Race

Religion

Gender

Sexual orientation

Height and weight (unless there is a job-specific reason)

Age

Marital status

Arrest and conviction records (must establish business necessity)

National origin

Financial status (consumer credit reports must comply with the Fair Credit Reporting Act of 1970 and the Consumer Credit Reporting Reform Act of 1996)

Military record (type of discharge)

Physical or mental disability (unrelated to the job)

Table 5.1 is a list of illegal questions and a legal alternative for each. The following are some suggested questions for you to ask when you interview.

General Questions

- What certifications do you have?
- Tell me about your background in swimming. What specific strokes do you swim well?
- Tell me your definition of perseverance and how you have demonstrated it in your life.

Table 5.1   Illegal and Legal Interview Questions

Illegal	Legal
How many children do you have?	Is there anything that prevents you from working these hours?
What is your national origin?	Are you legally eligible for employment in the United States?
What type of military discharge did you receive?	What type of education, training, and work experience did you receive while in the military?
What clubs do you belong to?	What professional or trade groups do you belong to that you consider relevant to your ability to perform this job?
When did you graduate from high school?	Do you have a high school diploma or the equivalent?
What disabilities do you have?	Is there anything that prevents you from performing the essential functions of this job?
What is your maiden name?	Have you ever been known by another name? (If you need to contact former employers or references)

- Have you ever performed a water rescue (or lifesaving CPR or first aid)? Describe the situation and the actions you took.
- What are three of your areas of strength? What are three areas that need improvement?
- What did you do in your last job? What were your responsibilities?
- What aspects of your job did you like the best? The least?
- What disappointments did you experience in your previous jobs?
- In what areas did you need help or guidance from your boss?
- For what actions or qualities have your supervisors complimented you? Criticized you?
- Why did you leave your last position?
- If you could give one suggestion to management, what would it be?
- Describe the best boss you have had, and the worst.
- What about this job is appealing to you?
- These are the days and times for this lifeguard position you are applying for. I trust these terms and hours are acceptable to you?
- In what ways have your education and training prepared you to do this job?

Character

- What are your most important values? How did you acquire these? Why? What's most important to you in dealing with people?
- Tell me about a time when your values were challenged. What happened, and how did you handle it?
- Tell me your definition of responsibility and how you have demonstrated it in your life.
- Have you ever been in a role where you had the opportunity to affect someone's value development? Tell me about it.
- What is your definition of honesty?
- Describe an incident where retaining your value of honesty was uncomfortable or difficult.
- Who is the most honest person you know? How have you determined that this person is honest?

Teaching Skills

- Have you ever worked as a swim instructor? If so, where, when, and for whom?
- Why would you like a job as a swim instructor? Why do you think you would be good in the job?
- While teaching, how can you make sure your students are safe?
- How would you teach so children have fun in class and are motivated to learn new skills?
- How would you handle a person who is terrified of water?
- If you were teaching (name of stroke), how would you teach it?
- What age groups are you more comfortable with and why?
- What age groups would you like to teach and why?
- What do you think is the most important part of your job as a swim instructor?
- What are your favorite skills to teach?

Communication and Discipline

- What has your experience been in dealing with children?

- Have you had responsibility for discipline? How did you handle it? Be specific; for example, if a problem situation continued, how would you handle it?

- How would you discipline a child who is misbehaving? What would you do if, after being corrected, the child persisted in the misbehavior? What if the child's parent complained about how you handled the child?

- How would you handle a child who wanted to get out of the water before the lesson was over?

- If an emergency arose in the pool area, such as (give example), and you were the first one to notice it, what would you do? (This question is meant to see what interviewees' natural reaction would be, not just how they would implement standard procedures.)

Member Service

- How could you make your students feel special?

- How would you deal with parents who feel that their child has not progressed?

- What do you think good service is? How would you demonstrate good service to members and participants?

- How would you gain the trust and support of parents?

- Describe a situation in which you received good service.

- How would you exceed someone's expectations?

- How would you turn an angry member into a raving fan?

Organization

- What would you do to ensure the safety of your students?

- How would you make your class fun?

- How would you update records in your class?

- Give me an example of a project you were assigned with a deadline. How did you organize your time to meet the deadline?

Another set of very important questions to ask during an interview are those that may help you detect potential child abusers. Use the "Interview Questions" list from your Child Abuse Prevention training to select such questions.

Conducting the Interview

When you conduct the interview, the first step is to provide a comfortable environment without interruptions. Stand up and greet the applicant. Smile, shake hands, and introduce yourself. The next step is to provide the applicant with an overview of the interview format. Let the applicant know you will be asking questions, taking some notes, providing information about the YMCA, and asking for questions. Provide a time estimate to let the person know if you plan to meet for 30 minutes or two hours.

Next, ask your prepared questions. Make sure you have all candidates review the job description and ask them if they could perform all the duties and meet the qualifications as described. After asking your prepared questions, provide information about the YMCA, including the values and mission of the organization, child abuse prevention guidelines, the breadth of positions, and the benefits (intangible and tangible) of a career at the YMCA. Answer any questions, and let applicants know when you will be contacting them again.

Spend enough time in the interview process to get a good sense of each candidate's strengths and weaknesses. You may also want to plan for candidates to spend time in the work area, interacting with members and talking with other staff, so they can understand what the job entails.

Here are more tips on effective interviewing:

- Do the interviews in a room free of distractions and ask not to be disturbed by other staff or phone calls.

- Be attentive to applicants. Maintain eye contact and speak directly to them.

- Take notes during interviews. You will need these later so that you can recall each applicant when it is time to make the hiring decision. Be sure not to write subjective comments or personal opinions.

- Listen carefully and ask questions when you hear inconsistencies or are not quite sure you understood an applicant's answer.

- Use good active listening skills. Avoid jumping in and finishing the answer for the candidates.

- Don't indicate through verbal or body language approval or disapproval of an applicant's answers.

- Remember to explain to each candidate that you and your organization value the people in your care, take seriously the responsibility to protect all participants and employees, value all applicants and their willingness to take part, and seek to use all information appropriately (Stout and Backer, 1998).

- During the interviews, don't lead candidates to the conclusion that they will receive a job offer.

- Obtain a copy of each applicant's certification cards; assess the applicant's swimming, lifeguarding, and water safety skills by giving the applicant a practical skill assessment in the pool. Give all lifeguards and aquatics specialist instructor candidates a written test and a water skills examination. If an applicant is hired, put the results of the written and practical water skills exams in the applicant's personnel files, along with a copy of the certification cards.

Evaluating the Interview

Take time immediately after the interview to summarize your notes. If you are asking similar questions of each applicant, the process will be much more objective, and it will be easier for you to make a decision.

Review the YMCA child abuse prevention guidelines and determine if any "red flags" surfaced during the interview process. If any did, they indicate that you should examine the applicant more closely, look a bit deeper into the applicant's background, and take care when deciding whether or not to hire the applicant (Stout and Backer, 1998). (See appendix 2 for the YMCA's child abuse identification and prevention guidelines.)

Although there are no guarantees when it comes to hiring new employees, fairness, objectivity, realistic expectations, and honest communication will go a long way toward helping you hire the kind of employees you want and need.

Hiring Under the Americans With Disabilities Act (ADA)

When considering candidates who have a disability, you need to know what hiring practices are legally appropriate. This section provides general information on how to implement the Americans with Disabilities Act during hiring so that you can maintain compliance with the law. Discuss the issues described here with your branch executive or human resources department to ensure you are following your association's policies. If it is not clear what the correct rule is, contact an attorney.

Generally, you cannot conduct a medical examination or ask a job applicant whether he or she has a disability or inquire as to the nature or severity of a disability. This prohibition extends to interviews, application forms, inquiries by employment agencies, and inquiries during background and reference checks. However, after a conditional job offer has been made, you may conduct a medical exam or ask health-related questions provided that all applicants who receive a conditional job offer in the same job category are required to respond to the same inquiries. The prohibition against making any inquiries regarding disability during the application process protects qualified candidates from being screened out because of their disability before their actual ability to do the job has been evaluated. But, refraining from making such inquiries does not mean that you cannot obtain information regarding someone's qualifications for the job.

During the initial interview, you may ask questions about an applicant's ability to perform specific job functions or ask the applicant to describe or show how, with or without reasonable accommodation, he or she will be able to perform the functions of the job. However, you must not ask about a disability.

You must ask candidates questions in terms of their ability to perform the job duties, rather than asking them whether they have any impairment. Avoid questions such as "Do you have a disability?" "Do you suffer from vision or hearing loss?" or "Have you ever been treated for. . . ?" For example, you may ask whether the candidate would be able to see students demonstrating a technique during a class, but you cannot ask if the candidate has a visual impairment. As another example, you may ask whether an applicant can perform data entry if that is a function related to the job, but not whether the applicant has any physical limitations on the ability to type.

You may ask an applicant who has a known disability that would not interfere with performance of job functions to describe or demonstrate how he or she will perform a job function only if all other applicants are also asked to do so. You may ask an applicant who has a known disability that might interfere with or prevent performance of job functions to describe or demonstrate how these functions will be performed, with or without an accommodation, even if other applicants are not asked to do so.

Attaching a copy of the job description to the application form, or at least describing the essential job functions, physical demands, and work environment, is helpful. Then you may ask whether the applicant is able to perform these tasks with or without accommodation. If the applicant responds that she or he can perform the tasks and duties with accommodation, you may ask how the applicant would perform them and with what accommodation.

An employer need only attempt to implement a reasonable accommodation, not necessarily the preferred accommodation of the candidate. This should be done as a four-step process:

1. The employer analyzes the particular job involved to determine its purpose and essential functions.

2. The employer and the person with the disability work together to identify what barriers exist to the individual's performance of a particular job function. This analysis should include a review of the individual's abilities and limitations, as well as those factors in the work environment or those job tasks that pose difficulties for the individual.

3. The employer identifies a range of possible accommodations that could potentially remove the difficulties—either in the work environment or with respect to job tasks—and that would allow the individual to perform the essential functions of the job. The person with the disability may be able to supply the best choices.

4. Once the various possible accommodations are determined, the employer assesses the effectiveness of each one and the preferences of the individual to be accommodated. The employer then determines whether the various accommodations would pose an undue hardship on the employer.

This process should be documented.

To make sure you are using the proper procedures, follow these tips:

• Record the various reasonable accommodations that were considered and, where necessary, rejected. Keep detailed notes on all discussions with the person, outcomes of the discussions, investigations made, and so on.

• Standardize documentation. Create forms that a worker with a disability can use to apply for a reasonable accommodation, that the attending physician can complete, and upon which a cost–benefit analysis of reasonable accommodations may be proposed.

• Get assistance from your human resources department or from someone who is well trained in the ADA. Involve your immediate supervisor in the process. The presence of two employer representatives during the discussion with the candidate (you and either your supervisor or a human resources representative) will provide stronger documentation and evidence at a later stage if the reasonable accommodation is challenged. For additional information, contact the General Counsel's office at the YMCA of the USA.

• Get training in the ADA mandates concerning the employer's responsibilities, privacy concerns, and disability harassment issues.

• Involve your local legal counsel. Getting help and support on these issues is important. Legal counsel will be able to help you in developing policies and procedures for implementation of the ADA.

Reference and Background Checks

During the hiring process, you need to make a reasonable effort to learn about and verify the applicant's past. Conduct a thorough reference and criminal background check.

When you check applicants' references, you may not ask previous employers about a candidate's disabilities or illnesses or about anything that you, as a prospective employer, cannot ask of the applicant. You can ask the previous employers about the job the candidate held and his or her ability to perform those functions, the quality and quantity of work, how the candidate performed job functions with or without accommodations, and the person's attendance record.

You can also try getting written references if you obtain written permission from the applicant to check previous employers. You should send a copy of that permission statement along with your list of questions. Your questions must follow the same legal guidelines that apply to applications and interviews. Keep your questions relevant to the job.

Follow these tips on reference checks:

- Don't be surprised if some employers give out only dates worked and job title verification.
- Ask probing questions, not leading ones.
- Be a good listener; be sensitive to the tone of voice used and the willingness to give information.
- Clarify unclear statements or vague answers.
- Get the name of the individual you talked to and document all phases of the reference check process. Include who, when, and what.
- If a previous employer refuses to give out information, document the call and note it.

HIRING

Many factors help you determine whom you will hire:

- Applications
- Personal interviews
- References (personal/business)
- Certifications
- Previous work history
- Law enforcement record checks (when appropriate)
- Performance observation (and skill check)
- A trial performance period (probationary period)

Once you have decided to hire a candidate, follow all your association's procedures, and make sure that the candidate is added to the payroll properly. You and the candidate probably will need to complete several forms. If your YMCA has a probationary period for new employees, you should explain this to the new staff member. You should inform new employees that the hiring is conditional pending obtaining proof that the person is legally able to work in the United States (I-9 form) and, for some jobs, pending the outcome of a criminal history check, driving history check, and medical examination.

As you prepare the candidate to become a staff member, a statement of understanding such as the one shown in figure 5.1 helps guide both of you through the hiring process. (Have your legal counsel and human resources staff review and modify this and other forms to make sure they comply with your association's requirements and state law.)

Such statements show that the paid employee or volunteer has read, understood, and agreed to all matters relating to his or her job functions, which include the following:

- A position description, including environmental factors or specific abilities needed to perform the job
- Hours of work

YMCA Statement of Understanding

Staff member, _____, and the management of the _____ YMCA hereby agree to the following conditions of employment.

1. This is not an employment contract and may be terminated by either party at will, with or without cause.

2. The staff member has read and understands the job description relating to his/her position and agrees to fulfill the responsibilities as outlined.

3. The staff member understands that employment may be discontinued or hours changed due to insufficient program participation, enrollment, or his/her failure to fulfill responsibilities as outlined in his/her job description or training periods, or as deemed necessary due to budget cuts.

4. Employment is conditional until results of the staff member's driving record/criminal background have been checked and until information given by him/her has been verified.

5. The staff member will begin employment _____ and will end _____.

   The days and hours per week shall be _____.

6. Temporary seasonal employees _____
   _____.

   Season dates _____

7. Probation period for all employees is 90 days.

8. Pay dates shall be _____.

   Exceptions or comments _____

9. The staff member's rate of pay shall be _____.

Additional comments _____
_____
_____

_____   _____
Employee's signature   Date   Supervisor's signature   Date

_____ _____   _____
Date of Birth   Driver's license no.   Executive Director's signature

(**Note:** Be sure to have your legal counsel and human resources staff review and modify forms to comply with state law and your association's requirements.)

Figure 5.1 YMCA Statement of Understanding form.

- Responsibilities for enforcement of association rules and regulations
- Grievance/dismissal policy
- Performance appraisal
- Salary review*
- Vacations*
- Tardiness/absence policy
- Training opportunities
- Employee benefits
- Employee safety procedures
- Maintenance of certifications
- Attendance at orientation meeting and receipt of orientation materials

*For paid employees only, when applicable.

These agreements are kept on file.

You should also carefully review the job description with the employee and discuss the expected standards of performance. Then you should review the orientation process for the position.

Orienting New Staff

As new staff begin working at your YMCA, you need to make them feel a part of the YMCA team as soon as possible. You can make this happen either by holding an orientation meeting for new arrivals that covers the following topics or by meeting with them individually. In some associations, they may meet with the human resources staff. You may also break up your orientation into a number of meetings, some of which may be with other department staff members. Whatever method you choose for orienting your staff, you should cover the following topics:

About Your YMCA

- The YMCA mission statement
- Member involvement and service
- A brief history of your YMCA
- Staff organization structure
- Discussion of YMCA character development
- Review of the aquatics program, the YMCA program brochure, and the YMCA member handbook
- Member and nonmember benefits and privileges
- Role of volunteers at the YMCA
- A tour of the facility
- Where to park
- Age breakdowns of locker room usage (adults vs. youths)

Job Expectations, Compensation, and Benefits

- Job descriptions
- Personnel and payroll policies (time sheets and pay periods)
- Part-time and full-time benefits

- The need to reflect an attitude, image, and values consistent with national YMCA goals and philosophy
- Appropriate dress on the job (neat, professional-looking clothing, suitable for the activity, that identifies them as YMCA personnel)
- What personal belongings are and are not allowed in the locker room
- Duty schedules and procedures for substitutions
- Public relations
- Performance appraisals, counseling forms, and termination policies
- In-service training schedule and staff meetings
- Other training opportunities (mandatory and voluntary)

Teaching

- Class descriptions
- Teaching assignments and substitution policies
- Internship or practice teaching period with an experienced instructor
- Teaching techniques

Class Procedures

- Skill sheet and progress report procedures
- First-day and ongoing daily procedures
- Record-keeping responsibilities
- Lifeguarding procedures (if applicable)
- Child abuse prevention and reporting procedures

Pool Operations

- Pool maintenance and preventive maintenance procedures
- Pool opening and closing procedures
- Pool count or attendance procedures
- How to obtain and store equipment and supplies

Pool Safety and Emergency Procedures

- Pool rules and regulations
- Rules and procedures for class safety
- Emergency procedures and first aid
- Exposure control plan for blood-borne pathogens
- Occupational Safety and Health Administration (OSHA) standards and Material Safety Data Sheets (MSDSs)
- Child abuse prevention and reporting procedures
- Accident/incident reporting and worker's compensation reporting
- Personal safety issues (sun safety and chemical hazards)

Lifeguarding

- Rotations
- Zone coverage

- Lifeguard rescue skills
- In-service training

Provide written materials for new staff and volunteers in your YMCA's aquatics program operations manual. The manual should include at least the following:

1. All policies, standards, and operating procedures
2. Job description(s)
3. Statement of YMCA and program purpose, goals, and philosophy
4. Personnel policy, including plans for ongoing supervision, goal setting, performance review, training, and salary administration plan
5. Specific policies and procedures related to individual programs, such as health and safety (including information in this publication), emergency procedures, sun safety, transportation, OSHA rules regarding blood-borne pathogens, Material Safety Data Sheets, and child abuse prevention
6. Program description and fee structure
7. YMCA organizational chart with names
8. Lifeguard/staff conduct guidelines
9. Duty stations
10. Instructional program protocols
11. Substitution procedures
12. Accident reports/incident reports (see page 281)
13. Bathing code
14. Pool/diving rules
15. Procedures for enforcement of association rules and regulations

Document this with a signed acknowledgment of receipt of these materials and participation in orientation.

Here are a few additional things you can do for new staff to get them off on the right foot:

- Assign senior or veteran staff to new staff members.
- Have a "Know It All Checklist" for new employees (an overview of the YMCA; see sample on CD-ROM).
- Devise training plans for new employees.
- Check in with new employees after the first week and frequently thereafter to offer support.
- Evaluate new employees at the end of the introductory period and semiannually thereafter. If an employee only works seasonally, conduct an evaluation at the end of the working season.
- Require instructors to intern or practice teach a minimum of four hours with an experienced staff member before leading their own classes. Require lifeguards to intern with another experienced guard for at least one shift before being on duty on their own.

Make sure you allocate adequate time to orient and train new staff in their assigned duties. You can't assume that, just because you gave them staff manuals, they will automatically know how to perform all the procedures described in the manuals.

Setting Up New Personnel Files

Depending on your association's policies, you may or may not have to keep all personnel records in the human resources department (check with your human resources department). Even if they don't retain all records, your human resources department will keep most of the personnel files that are needed for employment laws. These would include the job application, W-2 forms, time sheets, and other hiring forms required by your association. You should also keep additional files for each active staff member (paid or volunteer). Once a staff member leaves or is terminated, you should give your files to your human resources department for them to determine what they need to include in the permanent files.

The information in your files should include the following:

- Name, address, phone number, alternative phone number, and emergency contact
- E-mail address
- Availability record
- Signed job description
- Signed orientation checklist
- Emergency procedures training
- Signed receipt of staff manual
- Copies of certification cards
- Copies of skill assessments
- Copies of performance evaluations
- Recognition ideas
- Training record
- Copies of counseling sessions

SUPERVISING

One of your important duties as aquatics director is to supervise staff so as to help you meet the organizational goals of your department. This involves performance management. The process you use will follow your association's compensation philosophy and policies and the procedures that have been developed.

Performance management is the ongoing process of setting performance expectations, providing feedback and coaching to reach those expectations, and reviewing and recognizing performance results.

Performance management systems must be linked or aligned with key areas such as strategic direction, objectives, values, and membership needs. Employees need to know what is expected of them and how their performance will be measured. Without this knowledge, employees will perform based on what they think is important or acceptable, which may not correlate with actual association objectives.

Done correctly, performance management can do the following:

- Connect the strategy, vision, and values of the YMCA to the work of teams and individuals
- Align team and individual skills and competencies with the association's core capabilities
- Translate vision and strategy into action
- Cascade goals throughout the association (divide development of the strategic/ operating plan among branches, departments, and specific programs so goals build on each other)
- Measure both *what* is done (goals) and *how* it is done (competencies)

Performance management can help employees understand the link between the association, their own growth and development, and the subsequent results and rewards by answering the following questions:

- What should I be doing?
- How am I doing?
- How can I grow?
- What's in it for me?
- What's next?

Individual and team performance has a direct correlation to your YMCA's overall performance. You need to explain to your staff the overall direction and work culture of your YMCA, and you should reward them for demonstrating behaviors and results that are in line with your YMCA's goals and objectives. This will ultimately lead to better performance and a more satisfied staff.

Performance Management Guidelines

Your performance management process should include the following:

- Goal setting and development planning
- Coaching and feedback
- Performance appraisal
- Rating approval and link to pay

Goal Setting and Development Planning

At the beginning of the performance year, meet with all staff to discuss upcoming goals and development needs to develop performance standards. Goals should follow the "SMART" criteria and be specific, measurable, achievable, realistic, and timed.

Feedback

Seek opportunities to provide feedback throughout the year, on at least a quarterly basis. Although providing feedback is an important first step, the overall goal is to get the employee to act—to either maintain or enhance positive performance or to change or correct negative performance. To achieve this goal, identify specific actions that the employee needs to take to achieve performance standards.

Performance Appraisal

At the end of the year, you should assess the employee's performance for the prior year and establish goals and development areas for the following year. A best practice is to ask the employee to first conduct a self-assessment. Using the goals set at the beginning of the performance year, review each one to see what was accomplished and what may have been obstacles to completion. If competencies are part of your review process, you and your employee should provide specific examples of demonstration of the competencies or the lack of them.

This is also an ideal time to discuss development plans for the next year, training plans, and career development opportunities. Do not discuss pay at this time, but rather at a later date, to keep the focus on the employee's performance.

Coaching and Feedback

Regularly observe your staff as they work, especially right after hiring, to ensure quality. Use a checklist such as the example in figure 5.2 to know what to watch for as you observe them. Then discuss with them the strengths and weaknesses you noted and methods for improving performance.

Besides evaluating your staff's teaching skills, you also should check their swimming skills on a regular basis. Improving their aquatic skills is valuable to them and develops their teaching or lifeguarding skills.

For example, you could ask instructors to perform four different strokes during a 400-yard swim, tread water, surface dive, underwater swim two to three body lengths, and front dive from a one-meter board. You might choose instead to have them demonstrate the prerequisite swims from the specialist instructor course they attended. Evaluate strokes using the stroke observation checklists from *Teaching Swimming Fundamentals*. Help staff improve their strokes by assigning stroke drills from *The Youth and Adult Aquatic Program Manual*.

Strongly encourage your staff to maintain a high level of swimming fitness. If you check on your staff on a regular basis, you will have documented the progress of their performance when performance appraisals come up.

Finally, talk to your staff informally on an individual ongoing basis, as well as during staff meetings and in-service training sessions. That way you can make them aware of any difficulties before they become serious problems and offer praise for those things they do well.

Instructor Observation Checklist

Name _____   Date _____

Observer _____

___ When talking, the instructor maintains eye contact with students and communicates in terms the students can understand.

___ The instructor keeps a balance between working with students individually and allowing students to practice and participate on their own.

___ The instructor can see all students at all times during the lesson.

___ The instructor uses a variety of organizational patterns, not just one or two.

___ The instructor keeps the class moving smoothly from one activity to another.

___ During class, the instructor smiles and has fun with the students.

___ Students seem to be having fun and are engaged in class activities.

___ The instructor recognizes and uses "teachable moments" to talk about character development.

___ The instructor teaches skills according to the program manual.

___ The instructor checks students' skill sheets regularly throughout the session.

___ The instructor starts and ends classes on time.

___ The instructor explains concepts to students clearly.

___ The instructor asks students questions to monitor their understanding.

___ The instructor provides students with feedback on their activities.

___ The instructor uses positive motivation techniques with students.

Other Comments:

_____

_____

_____

(**Note:** Be sure to have your legal counsel and human resources staff review and modify forms to comply with state law and your association's requirements.)

Figure 5.2   Sample Instructor Observation Checklist.

Performance Appraisal

A performance appraisal is the formal tool for evaluating an employee's performance. It is also the formal recognition system developed in your association. It includes the review of an employee's performance during the review period. The salary review meeting should be held separate from the performance appraisal. Improving performance should be the primary purpose of performance appraisals.

Performance appraisals are also a way to ensure that supervisors successfully coach their employees. Appraisals help both supervisors and employees improve their personal effectiveness and performance. In addition, they provide data for management decisions about salary increases, promotions, transfers, separations, and so on. This process also helps identify employees' developmental needs as a basis for creating individualized personal development plans that are congruent with the organization's needs. Finally, this process helps facilitate staff planning and teamwork.

You need to do a performance appraisal of each staff member according to the personnel policy of your association. The performance appraisal lets your employees know where they stand, recognizes good work, communicates directions for improvement, helps employees grow in their current jobs, develops and trains them for other jobs, and serves as an assessment record.

You need to document your dealings with personnel. Your documentation must be accurate, relying on objective and specific facts concerning actual on-the-job performances as they occur. It should be based on direct observation rather than "hearsay" reports from others.

You will need to have a standard form for evaluating all like positions. See figure 5.3 for a sample evaluation of part-time staff.

Performance appraisals should be based on performance standards that have been developed for each position within the organization. Those standards should be based on the written job description and should be reflected in the evaluation form for each position.

The most effective review is an employee's self-review, which is then compared to the predetermined criteria established in the performance standards. Once the employee reviews her- or himself, the review can be used as a guide for discussion with the supervisor. Where there is disagreement, further discussion is needed.

Hold reviews at regular intervals and on predetermined dates. Both you and your employee should plan for the review and be fully prepared to discuss progress on mutually accepted standards. Keep your questions and comments noncritical until you are certain you understand the situation from the employee's perspective. For every area where performance is below standard, establish and mutually agree on an action plan to improve performance. Revise and establish performance standards for the next review period. In addition, spend time talking with employees about how you can be a better coach and trainer as well as assist them in being successful.

Here are additional tips on performance appraisals:

- Use a "we" attitude when discussing problems. Don't place blame.
- Ask thought-provoking questions and then listen. Do more listening than talking.
- Function as a coach, not as an inspector. Provide feedback and recognition for positive performance.
- Make sure you explain your reasons for appraisals. Use specific examples and avoid generalities.

Swim Instructor Employee Evaluation

Employee's name _____ Position _____

Supervisor _____ Department _____

Rating scale: Outstanding (4); Above expectations (3); Meets expectations (2); Improvement needed (1); Does not meet expectations (0). An explanation needs to be included on any item marked with a (0) for "does not meet expectations." Circle one.

Major Duties

1. Teaching Skills

4 3 2 1 0   Creates a positive learning environment with a sufficient level of class control.

4 3 2 1 0   Knows names of students.

4 3 2 1 0   Uses positive reinforcement to accomplish goals.

4 3 2 1 0   Motivates participants.

4 3 2 1 0   Demonstrates correct water skill technique for each level.

4 3 2 1 0   Trains or assists with training.

4 3 2 1 0   Classes are organized and well planned.

4 3 2 1 0   Provides adequate skill instruction through a variety of teaching methods.

4 3 2 1 0   Spends the majority of the time in the water with the class.

4 3 2 1 0   Develops and uses lesson plans for each class.

2. Customer Service

4 3 2 1 0   Is courteous and respectful.

4 3 2 1 0   Promotes the YMCA and its programs.

4 3 2 1 0   Is able to answer questions for information or find a resource that does.

4 3 2 1 0   Follows up on repeated student absenteeism.

4 3 2 1 0   Maintains control of class.

3. Communication

4 3 2 1 0   Communicates rules and policies at the participant's level of comprehension.

4 3 2 1 0   Portrays positive image and concern.

4 3 2 1 0   Communicates skills at students' level of comprehension.

Consider the major duties and rate the employee in terms of the following factors:

1. Appearance and accuracy of work

4 3 2 1 0   Work is neat; rarely makes errors; rework is seldom required.

4 3 2 1 0   Maintains accurate records on skill sheets, progress reports, and permanent record cards.

4 3 2 1 0   Wears proper staff uniform.

4 3 2 1 0   Performs all administrative duties to ensure quality programs.

(continued)

Figure 5.3   Sample part-time staff evaluation form.

2. Volume/work pace:

4 3 2 1 0   Volume of work meets or exceeds that of an average worker.

4 3 2 1 0   Works at a steady pace.

4 3 2 1 0   Utilizes working time to the fullest.

4 3 2 1 0   Works in accordance with YMCA aquatics policy.

3. Organization or work:

4 3 2 1 0   Work is well organized; rarely misses deadlines.

4 3 2 1 0   Attends all staff meetings and trainings.

4 3 2 1 0   Keeps accurate records and distributes reports on time.

4 3 2 1 0   Locks and secures pool door when pool is closed (when assigned).

4. Job knowledge and initiative:

4 3 2 1 0   Well informed on most phases of the job.

4 3 2 1 0   Requires little or no assistance and instruction.

4 3 2 1 0   Acts independently in finding solutions to problems.

4 3 2 1 0   Is available as a community resource.

5. Judgment:

4 3 2 1 0   Decisions are very sound, practical, and well thought out.

4 3 2 1 0   Judgment is reliable.

4 3 2 1 0   Identifies hazards and tries to ensure the safety of participants and members.

4 3 2 1 0   Interprets and enforces pool rules and policies.

4 3 2 1 0   Analyzes students' abilities and assigns proper evaluation.

4 3 2 1 0   Adapts skills to students' abilities.

6. Work attitude:

4 3 2 1 0   Work attitude is positive.

4 3 2 1 0   Is very interested in work.

4 3 2 1 0   Is fully cooperative; goes the extra mile.

4 3 2 1 0   Acts with enthusiasm and creativity.

4 3 2 1 0   Is willing to accept a change of duty during shift.

7. People relationships:

4 3 2 1 0   Works well with coworkers; demonstrates an ability to respond positively to the complexities of interpersonal relationships.

4 3 2 1 0   Can communicate a child's progress to the parents in a positive manner.

4 3 2 1 0   Is able to work effectively with children/adults in a learning situation.

4 3 2 1 0   Recruits parents and volunteers to help in the program.

8. Adaptability:

4 3 2 1 0   Is very adaptable to new tasks or changing conditions if properly prepared and informed.

4 3 2 1 0   Willing to substitute for any other staff.

4 3 2 1 0   Willing to teach any class based on his or her ability.

Figure 5.3   *(continued)*

9. Punctuality:

4 3 2 1 0   Comes to work on time; is rarely late.

4 3 2 1 0   Is on deck prior to shift with class records and needed equipment.

4 3 2 1 0   Begins and ends class on time.

4 3 2 1 0   Is available to answer questions from parents and follow up on comments.

10. Attendance:

4 3 2 1 0   Is reliable.

4 3 2 1 0   Notifies supervisor in case of absence.

4 3 2 1 0   Is responsible for finding own qualified substitute based on procedures.

11. Supervision:

4 3 2 1 0   Requires very little direction or supervision.

4 3 2 1 0   Responds positively to criticism or suggestions from the supervisor.

4 3 2 1 0   Properly informs the supervisor of incidents that need follow-up.

Overall rating (determined by the majority number of ratings): _____

Objectives for the next rating period: _____

_____

Personal growth/training/career plan: _____

Recommendations of supervisor: _____

Employee comments: _____

_____

_____

Next review date: _____

_____   _____

Employee's signature   Date   Supervisor's signature   Date

Note: Be sure to have your legal counsel and human resources staff review and modify forms to comply with state law and your association's requirements.

_____

Figure 5.3   *(continued)*

- Give your honest ratings of performance. Don't be reluctant to rate performance adversely because it will have to be discussed with the employee.
- Use the entire rating period as a guide for your rating of performance. Don't overweigh a recent or single event.
- Use this process as your opportunity to communicate with employees, identify their training needs, and assist them with their personal and career development.
- Make your evaluation criteria objective and job related.
- Be consistent about how you evaluate all employees.
- Maintain written documentation of each appraisal, including recommendations and decisions.
- Do not let your appraisal be influenced by the employee's marital status, age, race, religion, ethnicity, disability, or sex.
- Nothing should come as a surprise to the employee. Any performance issues should be discussed throughout the review period.
- Close properly. Summarize and plan for improvements and changes. Write down the results and share them with the employee.

LEADING STAFF TO BETTER PERFORMANCE

No matter how good your hiring practices are, you may have employees whose performance is less than desired. Poor performance can usually be traced to employees

- not knowing what is expected,
- not knowing how they are doing,
- not being able to do the job because they do not know how,
- lacking organizational support and help from their supervisor, or
- having a poor working relationship with the organization and supervisor.

To overcome poor performance, try coaching your employees. Coaching is an attempt to help employees overcome performance weaknesses and build on their performance strengths. It involves identifying performance that can be improved, analyzing performance problems, correcting improper or dangerous practices, discussing work with employees from their point of view, and providing assistance and encouragement.

Coaching is not punishment or discipline. A good way to separate the two is to remember that performance is coached, whereas conduct is disciplined.

Coaching has the following characteristics:

- It involves face-to-face guidance and instruction.
- Its purpose is to improve job effectiveness and efficiency.
- It is based on the supervisor's job knowledge or on developmental opportunities he or she can provide.
- It requires a great amount of patience and energy.
- It ensures close attention to individual employees' needs.
- It happens daily rather than infrequently.

Remember, a good leader

- has a sincere interest in helping employees improve,
- has a thorough knowledge of position requirements and objectives,
- arranges for positive and progressive work to be approved and rewarded,
- operates from the sidelines (that is, does not try to do the job for employees, but supports them and gives them direction), and
- recognizes individual differences.

DISCIPLINING

Proper employee and volunteer conduct is essential for effective management of a YMCA. Thus, when employees or volunteers violate proper procedures or conduct, you must take disciplinary action in accordance with your YMCA's personnel policies. Use an appropriate counseling statement form to describe the problem and the changes you expect from the employee. Deal with situations with staff consistently and fairly, and do not delay or avoid dealing with incidents.

Write-ups on counseling statement forms—or immediate dismissal—can occur for any of the following reasons:

- Missing any work assignment without contacting the supervisor or providing a qualified substitute, or having different substitutes for the same class over a period of more than a few days
- Leaving the pool unattended while people are in the area
- Being dishonest, such as registering hours on the time card for time not worked
- Expiration of mandatory certifications
- Using profanity when communicating with or about patrons
- Socializing with members while on the job
- Excessive talking on the phone for personal reasons
- Showing a lack of respect for or insubordination to the supervisor
- Any evidence of drug or alcohol abuse
- Poor performance, when coaching is not working
- Rule violations
- Security breaches
- Criminal activity
- Health and safety threats
- Child abuse
- Dress code infractions
- Any other reason deemed serious by the employee's supervisor that directly conflicts with that employee's positive image as a YMCA aquatics staff member or with established safety procedures of the aquatics department

The keys to dealing effectively with someone who has to be disciplined are to

- do it immediately,
- make it memorable,
- review any applicable policies, and

- reach consensus on how the employee should act or perform in the future and agree on a time frame for improvement.

Meet with the employee in a private location without distractions. We recommend that you have another employee, preferably another supervisor or your supervisor, with you to verify what is said during the meeting. Do not try to hold these meetings when you are angry. It is helpful to develop a script for the meeting so you can be sure to say everything you intend to say.

Use your association's counseling forms to document the meeting. Document facts, not opinions. Identify the behavior or policy at issue, and summarize how the employee has failed to meet expectations and why this failure is important. Give the prior history, if applicable. Be sure to describe future expectations and a time frame for improvement. You and the employee should both sign and date a form that summarizes your joint discussion. The employee's signature is to verify that the form fairly represents what was said during the meeting. Have your immediate supervisor or another staff member witness the form as well. Keep the counseling form confidential, and place it in the employee's personnel file. An employee disciplinary report recording the warning can also be completed and filed (see sample in figure 5.4).

If you find you have to write up an employee for improper conduct three times, you should terminate the employee immediately after the third offense if that's consistent with your YMCA's personnel policy. However, before discharging an employee, ask yourself these important questions:

- Is the termination based on a specific final incident?
- Are there witnesses or is there documentation to support the case?
- Has the employee been confronted with the situation and given a chance to explain?
- Has the progressive disciplinary system in which the employee has previously been given warnings been followed?
- Has too much time passed since the final incident?
- Did the incident violate a known policy?

If you decide you have to terminate an employee, follow your association's policies. Check with your branch executive or human resources director to make sure everything is ready before you proceed, including having a complete personnel file. Have documented verbal warnings, as you should have given the employee feedback several times prior to the termination. Plan to have your supervisor and one other member of management or supervisory staff present during the termination.

Be prepared for the discussion with the employee who is to be terminated. Have your facts straight and give the employee a good reason for the termination. Provide a short, straightforward explanation for your action. Do not argue or apologize and, if you think that the employee may disagree, ask him or her for a release (ask your human resources department about this).

Allow the employee to talk about the situation, and take notes on what he or she says. Especially listen for comments that confirm your decision; they may be helpful if the employee brings a lawsuit against you. Immediately after the termination, write a report that includes the following:

- The date and time
- Who was present at the termination

Disciplinary Session

Employee's name _____

Supervisor's name _____

Date _____

Describe the problem.

Describe the history.

Describe the discussion.

Agreement

Follow-up

Employee's signature _____ Date _____

Supervisor's signature _____ Date _____

Figure 5.4 Sample disciplinary session sheet.

- What you said to the employee
- What the employee said or did not say

Have those who were in attendance sign and date the report, then give it to your human resources director or executive director.

Have someone from human resources or your branch executive give the employee an exit interview, using a form similar to that in figure 5.5. Such an interview allows the employee to have a say, as well as accurately documents the meeting. It may help identify problems in your employment practices, and it provides information to the terminated employee on his or her rights and benefits as a former employee.

Do not talk about the termination or the employee with anyone other than your supervisor or your human resource director. Direct any inquiries about the terminated employee to your human resources department.

See that the terminated employee receives any pay and benefits due him or her right away, and do not interfere with the employee's job search.

TRAINING

As a supervisor, part of your responsibility is to help good staff become even better. First, establish a training plan for each employee. Review the training plan with the employee and discuss when and where he or she should receive the training. Table 5.2 (on page 171) describes the prerequisites for YMCA certifications and topics for in-service training.

YMCA Certification Training

All aquatics staff and volunteers conducting YMCA programs and classes should be at least 16 years old (or have special approval of the director). See figure 5.6 for certification courses. They must also meet the following criteria for YMCA certification:

- They must be certified as YMCA Specialist Aquatics Instructors (including YMCA Scuba and Competitive Swimming programs) for the programs they are teaching or be so within six months of employment (for seasonal programs, 30 days). Noncertified staff are under the direct supervision of a person certified in that particular program until they receive their certification.

- They must hold current CPR (obstructed airway, adult, infant, and youth) and first aid automatic external defibrillator (AED), oxygen administration, and blood-borne pathogen certifications. See table 5.3 on page 181.

- They must have the necessary education or training in compliance with national guidelines or guidelines of the specific program and have been given an opportunity for continued education at least annually.

Remember the core principles relating to training, as described by Pike (2001). Training is done for the purpose of changing behavior or actions to get results. It is a process, not just an event. For training to be successful, it must be an active process between employees and supervisors. It starts long before the training begins and doesn't end until employees' performance improves. A certification means that the individual was able to meet the established criteria. It does not reflect on potential job performance.

Before the training begins, discuss with employees the purpose of the training and how it relates to their being able to perform their jobs well. Review with them what

Exit Interview

1. Were you satisfied with the following?

    a. Job held _____

    b. Wage rate _____

    c. Hours of work _____

    d. Opportunities for advancement _____

    e. Conditions of work _____

    f. Fringe benefits _____

2. Supervision

    a. Were instructions adequate? _____

    b. Were you given instruction or training? _____

    c. Comments _____

3. Do you have another job? _____

4. Reason for leaving:

    Domestic _____   Explain: _____

    Transportation _____   Explain: _____

    Other _____   Explain: _____

5. Was a transfer offered?

    To what department? _____

    Outcome _____

Comments by interviewer:

_____

_____

Comments by interviewee:

_____

_____

_____   _____   _____   _____
Interviewer's signature   Date   Interviewee's signature   Date

Note: Be sure to have your legal counsel and human resources staff review and modify forms to comply with state law and your association's requirements.

Figure 5.5 Sample exit interview form.

Aquatic Certification Courses

Instruction	Fitness	Lifeguard	Competitive	Management	Scuba
YMCA Swim Lessons Instructor: Youth and Adult, Parent/child, and Preschool	YMCA Water Fitness	YMCA Lifeguard	Principles of YMCA Competitive Swimming	YMCA Pool Operator on Location	YMCA Skin Diving/Snorkeling
YMCA Individuals With Disabilities Instructor	YMCA Active Older Adult Water Fitness	YMCA Aquatic Safety Assistant	YMCA Swim Official	YMCA Aquatic Management	YMCA Open Water Diver
YMCA Synchronized Swimming Instructor	Arthritis Foundation YMCA Aquatic Program (AFYAP)	YMCA Lifeguard Instructor	YMCA Swim Coach		YMCA Open Water Instructor
YMCA Water Polo/Wetball Instructor					

Figure 5.6 Aquatic certification training courses.

they need to bring and what they should expect when attending the course. Make sure they meet the course prerequisites and receive the manuals and precourse materials in plenty of time so they can be prepared for the course. Discuss what you will expect of them after the training experience.

While employees are attending training, their job is to fully participate in the training. After the course, take the time to talk to them about their experiences and help them to integrate the principles and concepts they learned into their jobs. Give them opportunities to use and demonstrate their new skills. This is an ongoing process, and the employees need your support and reinforcement. Try to review and reinforce the new skills at least six times in the first 30 days. This will greatly improve employees' retention of the material. Remember, training doesn't end until performance improves.

To certify your staff, you can either host a course or work with other YMCAs in your neighborhood to provide the course when you need it for your staff. If you want to offer the course at your facility, follow the standards for hosting a YMCA of the USA certification course (see the YMCA Web site **www.ymcausa.org** for "Standards for Hosting a YMCA of the USA Certification Course"). You should have one or more certified YMCA Specialist Aquatics Trainers on staff to train YMCA instructors according to YMCA of the USA Aquatics Guidelines. If you do not have a certified trainer on your staff for a particular course, recruit one. Contact the YMCA of

the USA certification department to locate certified trainers in your area. We also recommend that you invite surrounding YMCAs to participate whenever you offer a course. They may also have staff that need certification, and in this way you can support and work with your neighboring YMCAs, as well as sponsor a more cost-effective training event.

The instructor courses can be scheduled over a long weekend or offered in modules. Either way, participants must attend the entire course. For additional certification information, refer to the YMCA of the USA Training Course Catalog, which is published annually. To obtain a course catalog, call the YMCA of the USA certification department at 800-872-9622.

Staff In-Service Training

Staff training begins with certification and orientation, but it doesn't end there. Ongoing training for assistants and volunteers, as well as for instructors, helps keep the program coordinated and ensures that everyone is working to the best of their abilities.

In-service training is needed for every position. All employees need facility-specific training and emergency preparedness training, as well as specialized training based on their positions. One challenge is to make sure all staff members participate in the training. Part-time staff have other commitments, which makes it difficult for them to attend meetings. In addition, since the facility is open a lot and you need to staff the pool, it is hard to find a time when the entire staff can meet. So you need to be creative to make this happen. Make the in-service training program a combination of individual, paired, small group, and large group activities. Design them to be flexible to meet the scheduling needs of your staff. You can also have other staff members provide leadership for some of the training. Document completion of these activities and keep them on file.

See table 5.2 for recommendations as a guide for in-service training. If you have assistants and volunteers, include the following topics in their in-service training:

- An explanation of the YMCA's mission and character development goals
- An overview of the program in which they will assist
- A review of the components and skills of each level
- A description of the program's teaching techniques
- The role of the assistant in the program
- The role of volunteers in the YMCA
- Information on how to work with students
- Safety information
- Emergency procedures
- Program organization

See the "Orienting New Staff" section for a list of additional training topics. Volunteers who teach classes need to have the same certification and training that paid staff receive.

Finally, don't forget to get regular training yourself. You should have a written training plan and should participate in relevant training or continuous education each year (for example, YMCA of the USA aquatics training, university courses, and technical seminars).

You will want to make the training relevant to the needs of your staff and organization. If you attended the YMCA of the USA Program Training Orientation course, the principles you learned in that course will help you develop the training outlines you need. The YMCA of the USA's Web site has a sample training outline format you can use.

Staff Meetings

Hold required staff meetings on a regular basis. Regular meetings provide staff with an opportunity to meet and discuss how the program and department are going. They are a means to pass along new information and program updates and to coordinate efforts to maintain program consistency and quality. Meetings are also a time for team building and problem solving to improve the department and achieve goals. They allow frontline staff to share and give valuable feedback about the aquatics programs and about the ever-changing needs of the community.

Document meetings by recording meeting minutes and listing who attended, and make sure that absent or sick staff members get a copy of the minutes with a sign-off return sheet.

SCHEDULING

With the large number of part-time staff usually required in aquatics departments, staff scheduling can be a challenge. In addition, the schedules can change significantly based on seasons, sessions, and enrollment.

You can use a variety of methods to schedule your staff. You can purchase software that can assist you, but it tends to be expensive. You can also set up a chart to do the same thing.

On a chart, list the classes and activities, times, number of staff needed, and anticipated size of the program. Across the top of the chart in each column, list each staff member's name and availability. You now have all the information you need to complete the schedule. Figure 3.1 shows a sample staff scheduling.

Once you have completed the chart, evaluate it and check for the following:

• See that staff hours do not exceed the number of hours allowed for part-time staff.

• Balance the hours among staff based on availability. If you have six staff members that want as many hours as they can get, and you give significantly more hours to one or two and not the others, this can cause the others to become disgruntled.

• Make sure you think through staff rotations and breaks for lifeguards and instructors. For an indoor pool, don't schedule lifeguards for continuous duty periods longer than two hours without at least a 15-minute break. For an outdoor pool, in high temperatures and humidity, don't schedule lifeguards for a continuous duty period longer than an hour without a break.

• Make sure staff know the time they are to arrive. If in-service training is done weekly or daily, either solo or in teams, work those times into the schedule or note deadlines for the training requirement to be met.

Post the staff schedule so that all staff can review the chart and write down their schedules. Be sure to communicate with staff when new schedules are posted. If you notice days and times when you are short on staff, recruit and request staff for additional availability.

Two other issues you will need to consider related to scheduling are procedures for allowing staff to use a substitute so they can have time off and ways to deal with situations in which those who were scheduled to work do not show up.

Substituting Duty Schedules

If a staff member needs time off or wants a change after a schedule has been posted, you need to have in place procedures to make those changes that have been clearly communicated to staff.

Staff requesting time off should submit the request to you in writing two weeks or more ahead of time. You can either have them arrange for a substitute or find a substitute yourself. Once a substitute has agreed to work those hours, the employee originally scheduled should sign the substitution form, then ask for your approval, preferably in writing. (Figure 5.7 shows a sample staff substitution form.)

It is also handy to have a chart posted of staff that includes their names, contact information, availability, and certifications (figure 5.8). This list will be useful when looking for a substitute.

No Shows

At times, a staff member will not show up for work as scheduled. You need to have a backup plan to deal with these situations. If there are times during which this occurs often, you may want to consider having a staff member scheduled to be "on call" during those times. That person would not be on duty unless called in. The staff member would give you a phone number where she or he could be reached if needed. This is particularly helpful during recreational swim times if more than the normal number of members show up and the head lifeguard needs additional staff. Using an on-call process will get staff there faster than calling your entire staff roster to find a substitute.

(To be completed a minimum of two weeks prior to sub date)

Date: _____

Name: _____

Reason for sub: _____

Shift date and time: _____

Guarding/instructing: _____

If instructing, list levels of classes:_____

Subbing staff: _____   Phone:_____

Sub's signature:_____

Supervisor's signature: _____

Please make every effort to find your own sub. If you cannot find a sub, please list everyone you contacted and let me know as soon as possible. Thanks!

Figure 5.7 Staff substitution form.

Aquatic Staff

Regularly Scheduled Staff

Name	Phone #	Email	Positions certified in	Availability

Substitutes Only

Name	Phone #	Email	Positions certified in	Availability

Figure 5.8   Sample staff availability chart.

STAFF RETENTION

Most aquatics departments are staffed primarily with part-time workers and many young adults. Turnover is to be expected with these two work groups. Part-time workers are looking for a position that allows them to do other things that are important in their lives. They are available only limited times or days. Young adults in the workplace are still trying to find their niche and their desired career. They are working around school hours and other commitments. In addition, the aquatics department itself promotes the use of part-time workers because of the wide range of specialties involved, the hours those programs are offered, the seasonal nature of program participation, and the number of hours the facility is open. In most cases, very few full-time positions are available.

Staff turnover is a constant part of the aquatics director's world. It is worth the time and effort to do as much as you can to minimize turnover and keep your staff coming back season after season. Let's look at the costs involved in high staff turnover, both direct and indirect.

cost for loss of staff

First, what does it cost you directly each time one of your staff leaves for a better position? Take the following into consideration:

- Recruiting costs (advertisements)
- Cost of your time spent scheduling substitutes and replacements, communicating to parents, recruiting, interviewing, orienting, and training. Multiply the hourly rate by the number of hours it takes to do these tasks
- Loss of productivity on your part and the part of other staff
- Effect on quality (program development, program enrollment retention, relationships with members and participants, staff morale, parent support)
- Loss of revenue (cancellation of programs, program enrollment growth limited to ratios with remaining staff)
- Background/criminal history checks (time, costs)
- Human resources department staff time in processing and enrolling new staff members and terminating departing staff
- Orientation and training time and costs
- Staff medical examinations
- Other costs specific to your program and YMCA

Calculate your annual rate by taking the total costs from the previous list and multiplying them by the number of staff you replace each year. See the form for calculating staff turnover in figure 5.9.

Frequent staff turnover is a financial issue. Instead of spending money on replacing staff, try applying it up front to staff salaries and change the focus from replacing them to retaining them.

As for indirect costs, an important role for all our staff members is creating a positive environment for members. Having great YMCA people sets us apart from other organizations! And there is a strong connection between happy employees and happy members. Staff turnover affects members' attachment to the YMCA. When we lose a good employee, we also lose that person's "relationship equity"—all the energy that staff person has invested in getting to know members. Even the best replacement staff has to begin again at zero in getting to know people.

So, how do we retain employees? Here are a few suggestions:

- *Focus on the YMCA's mission.* YMCAs attract many employees because they believe the YMCA will be a good place to work. They may be drawn to the YMCA's Christian principles, core values, and mission. When those are only rhetoric and not reality, staff members will not stay, even if they enjoy their work—they can easily find another place to be paid more.

- *Create a supportive workplace.* Be fair, equitable, and consistent in your dealings with staff. Place employees in the positions they are best suited for and that best use their talents. Make sure all staff members know your expectations for their work, and see that they all have what they need to do their work. Administer a staff satisfaction survey, and interview voluntarily departing staff about their experiences at the YMCA.

- *Provide career development through training and leadership opportunities.* This can be done in many ways. Develop a career ladder for ambitious employees, and inform staff of national YMCA opportunities. Establish a mentoring program. Allow staff to attend workshops and training events. Provide opportunities to do special projects or sit on committees. Have teams of staff members do problem solving.

Calculating the Cost of Staff Turnover

Fees:

Employment advertisements (newspapers and other sources) ___
Phone charges (long distance charges in setting up interviews/reference checks) ___
Criminal background/history checks ___
Postage, printing costs (responding to applicants) ___
Training certification fees (required and optional) ___
Trainers' fees ___
Licenses/fees (e.g., chauffeurs' license) ___
Staff medical costs (physicals, immunizations, and TB tests) ___
Other costs specific to program ___

Subtotal: $__________

Director's Time (multiply total by hourly wage):

Writing and placing ads in paper or listing position openings elsewhere ___
Responding to inquiries ___
Scheduling interviews ___
Conducting interviews ___
Reference checks ___
Covering classrooms until vacancies are filled ___
Orientation ___
Training ___
Performance updates with new staff ___
Nurturing new staff and answering their questions ___
Other ___

Subtotal: $__________

Support Staff Time (multiply total by hourly wage):

Phone calls (responding to inquiries) ___
Processing new payroll records ___
Covering in classrooms until vacancies are filled ___
(differential only between staff wages and sub wages)
Other ___

Subtotal: $__________

Staff (multiply total by hourly wage):

Substitutes ___
Doubling up until new staff members are OK on their own ___
Other ___

Subtotal: $__________

(continued)

Figure 5.9 Calculating the cost of staff turnover.

New Hire Nonproductive Time (multiply total by hourly wage):

Orientation   ___
Training   ___
Salary before they begin the classroom and can be counted part of the ratio   ___
Other   ___

Subtotal: $_____

Indirect/Perceived Costs (try to affix a cost to the following):

Loss of director's productivity   ___
   (time spent interviewing, covering shift, experiencing the paralyzing effects of
   job stress, lack of time to raise money or follow through unfinished work)
Inability to move forward with initiatives when the staff keep changing   ___
Negative image from frequent turnover that might account for vacancies   ___
Frustrated staff and members   ___
Members who leave the YMCA   ___

Subtotal: $_____

Total Cost of Replacing One Employee   _____

Now that you have a sense of the full cost of turnover, it is time to see how this affects your annual budget. Begin by listing all staff employed on September 1 last year. Next list all staff employed on September 1 of the current year. How many new staff were hired to replace existing positions and how many positions were replaced more than once during the year? In the formula below, that number is A. B is the number pulled from the worksheet. C equals the estimated cost of turnover for all positions.

$A \times B = C$

For example, if you had six frontline positions turn over and the annual cost to the program was $800 per position, the combined turnover cost to your program is $4,800 per year.

Question to ponder: If you reallocated the money you spend on replacing staff and put it toward better staff salaries/benefits/working conditions/other benefits up front, would the staff you currently employ be more inclined to stay? Just imagine how much more productive you, the director, would be if they did.

Figure 5.9   *(continued)*

• *Increase pay or benefits.* Besides just giving raises, look at providing part-time staff with some benefits, such as health insurance, paid vacation, and personal days. Create more full-time positions or combine several part-time duties for more hours.

• *Show you are caring.* Show appreciation for the work staff members do and praise them often. Reward retention and longevity with gifts or other incentives. Care about each staff member as a person, and encourage his or her personal development. Learn what motivates each of them.

• *Have fun!* Sponsor fun events, such as a lifeguard competition or a water polo, softball, or volleyball team, where staff work together to represent the YMCA.

The better job you do in selecting, training, and supervising employees and maintaining a good work environment, the less time you'll have to spend on hiring.

In the next sections, we'll look in more detail at how to create a supportive workplace, how to recognize and reward staff, and how to provide career development for staff.

Create a Supportive Workplace

When we hire staff, we must communicate the YMCA difference. Mission must be at work in every YMCA, and mission is not for "members only." It must begin with how we treat our staff and volunteers. We should be role models for our caring philosophy in the way we treat new staff. We want to put them at ease, make them feel welcome, and give them our undivided, caring attention. We also need to emphasize mission and the relationship-building character of YMCA work right up front.

Based on 7,000 responses to surveys issued by more than 50 YMCAs, the most important things related to staff satisfaction are these beliefs:

- Promises by management are usually kept.
- People who do a good job are rewarded more than those who don't.
- I am rewarded for the quality of service I provide.
- I feel expectations for commitment to the YMCA are fair.
- Expectations for hours of work are reasonable.
- There are enough people in my department to get work done.
- I trust senior management will take my interests into account.

Many conditions can reduce people's motivation to work. Managers who say one thing but do another, who aren't clear about what they want workers to do, or who take workers for granted lose workers' confidence and interest. Having to perform tasks that are designed badly or being so rushed that the work ends up being poorly done also affects morale. Another negative factor can be a backstabbing atmosphere, in which no one trusts each other.

Your challenge is to minimize these demotivators. Staff morale has a powerful impact on the YMCA. If we do not treat our own staff family with the values of caring, honesty, respect, and responsibility, as well as the YMCA mission, we are being hypocritical. Hypocrisy saps motivation and eats away at your staff's morale. Your YMCA must practice what it preaches!

Your staff is critical to providing quality programs. If your staff members are happy and feel good about working with you, they are more apt to provide good service and do a good job for your members. To get a good idea of working conditions for your staff, give them a staff survey that addresses what it is like to work for you. This information also gives you an indication of the program quality. A sample survey is included as figure 5.10.

Be prepared to take action based on the survey responses you receive. To build a powerful and positive workplace, we suggest that you focus on four areas: staff member involvement, simple appreciation, fun and spirit, and making the mission and meaning connection for every job.

Staff member involvement is the place to begin. In chapter 4, we talked about moving members along a continuum of involvement from short-term purchasers of services to becoming partners and advocates of the YMCA. YMCA staff must become partners and advocates of the YMCA too.

When a new staff member is hired, that person probably will view her or his job as "just a job." When new staff members begin to connect with people and the YMCA's mission and values, their involvement deepens. They begin to notice that there is something different about working at the YMCA as opposed to the other jobs they have had.

Many new staff members never get beyond having a casual or connected relationship with the YMCA and their work to form a committed relationship (see figure 5.11). We should try to move all staff members along the continuum of involvement

YMCA Staff Survey

Listed below is a series of statements about your feelings about working at the YMCA. Please read each one carefully and circle the answer that best describes how you feel, thinking about the last three to four months.

Key: 1 Strongly agree   2 Agree   3 Disagree   4 Strongly disagree

A. Please tell us about your job:

The YMCA is better to work for than most organizations.	1 2 3 4
I like the kind of work I do.	1 2 3 4
My job makes good use of my skills and abilities.	1 2 3 4
My work gives me a feeling of personal accomplishment.	1 2 3 4
I feel encouraged to come up with new and better ways of doing things.	1 2 3 4
My job has sufficient variety to make it interesting and challenging.	1 2 3 4

B. Please tell us about the communication and direction you receive:

I have enough information to do my job well.	1 2 3 4
When I have more than I can handle, I know what my priorities are.	1 2 3 4
I am satisfied with the information I receive from management on what's going on in the organization.	1 2 3 4
I have a clear understanding of what we are trying to accomplish as an organization.	1 2 3 4
My goals and performance expectations are clear.	1 2 3 4
My most recent performance appraisal was consistent with the informal feedback I received during the year.	1 2 3 4

C. Please tell us about the teamwork within your branch and with other branches:

The people I work with cooperate to get the job done.	1 2 3 4
When I need it, I can get help from other departments at this branch.	1 2 3 4
Other departments keep us well informed about things that affect us.	1 2 3 4
I know who to call in other departments when I need help or information.	1 2 3 4
When I need it, I can get help from other branches.	1 2 3 4
The different branches cooperate well with one another.	1 2 3 4
At my branch, appropriate attention is given to planning.	1 2 3 4

(continued)

Figure 5.10 Sample staff survey.

D. Please tell us about the organization of your work:

My department has enough people to get the work done.	1	2	3	4
I am satisfied with my involvement in decisions that affect my work.	1	2	3	4
The physical working conditions are good at my branch.	1	2	3	4
It is clear to me when I should act on my own and when I should obtain my supervisor's approval.	1	2	3	4
If I need to make a decision or help with a problem, I can go directly to the right person.	1	2	3	4
I have received adequate training for my present job.	1	2	3	4
Other people in my department have the proper skills and training for their jobs.	1	2	3	4
I am able to work efficiently, without unnecessary paperwork, meetings, and so on.	1	2	3	4

E. Thinking about what's happened over the last 12 months, overall, how satisfied are you with your job? Please circle one answer.

1 Very satisfied   2 Satisfied   3 Dissatisfied   4 Very dissatisfied

Please explain why you responded the way you did above.

_____

_____

_____

Figure 5.10   (continued)

so that they become truly passionate advocates of the YMCA and its mission. We must do this by design, not by accident. It begins with the way we recruit and screen our potential staff members, and it continues with the hiring process and new staff orientation to the specific department training.

Getting staff involved sooner is better than later, because we need committed and passionate staff to serve and involve our members. Staff involvement is really about moving staff members' relationship from "it's a job" to "it's a calling." Doing this will make a significant difference in the culture of our workplace, as well as in the atmosphere and attitude that YMCA members experience when they come in contact with our staff.

Simple appreciation also goes a long way. Showing appreciation to our staff for the work that they do is important, and showing spontaneous everyday appreciation of each other is good too. We should notice and care not only about our employees' work, but about them as people as well. Remember, your work is about their work. With the many things you have on your mind as you go about your job, sometimes it's hard to remember to take notice and recognize their work. Give praise to your staff that is timely, specific, and sincere and is appropriate to the person involved.

Fun and spirit enliven the workplace and invigorate workers. There is real power in fun. It creates a contagious atmosphere that brings people together. It's time to lighten up at work and laugh more together.

Make the mission and meaning connection for every job—inspire them! The YMCA is a unique and special place to work because every single job connects to the mission. We are often so busy focusing on job skills, budget, equipment, facilities, and technology bells and whistles that we forget to connect employees' work with meaning. Making a real difference in people's lives is YMCA work.

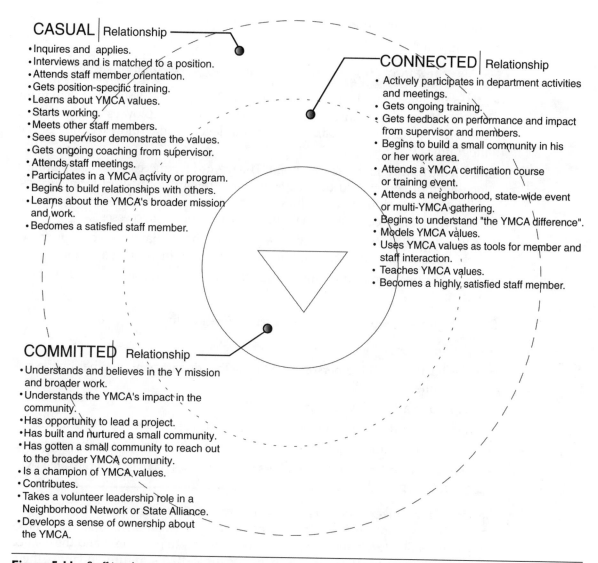

CASUAL | Relationship
- Inquires and applies.
- Interviews and is matched to a position.
- Attends staff member orientation.
- Gets position-specific training.
- Learns about YMCA values.
- Starts working.
- Meets other staff members.
- Sees supervisor demonstrate the values.
- Gets ongoing coaching from supervisor.
- Attends staff meetings.
- Participates in a YMCA activity or program.
- Begins to build relationships with others.
- Learns about the YMCA's broader mission and work.
- Becomes a satisfied staff member.

CONNECTED | Relationship
- Actively participates in department activities and meetings.
- Gets ongoing training.
- Gets feedback on performance and impact from supervisor and members.
- Begins to build a small community in his or her work area.
- Attends a YMCA certification course or training event.
- Attends a neighborhood, state-wide event or multi-YMCA gathering.
- Begins to understand "the YMCA difference".
- Models YMCA values.
- Uses YMCA values as tools for member and staff interaction.
- Teaches YMCA values.
- Becomes a highly satisfied staff member.

COMMITTED | Relationship
- Understands and believes in the Y mission and broader work.
- Understands the YMCA's impact in the community.
- Has opportunity to lead a project.
- Has built and nurtured a small community.
- Has gotten a small community to reach out to the broader YMCA community.
- Is a champion of YMCA values.
- Contributes.
- Takes a volunteer leadership role in a Neighborhood Network or State Alliance.
- Develops a sense of ownership about the YMCA.

Figure 5.11 Staff involvement continuum.

Recognize and Reward Staff

The YMCA is dedicated to developing the potential of its employees. We realize that no employee strives to be average. Creating an atmosphere in which excellence is rewarded is the key to providing excellent programs and service, so

- YMCAs should evaluate, recognize, and reward all employees on the basis of measurable performance standards (as described under "Performance Appraisal"), and

- YMCAs should design and implement recognition programs to recognize good performance and service.

A well-designed employee recognition program does the following:

- Reinforces the culture, goals, and values of the YMCA

- Vests each employee in the mission of the YMCA

- Motivates employees to perform their jobs in customer-focused ways that meet their standards of performance

- Improves staff retention
- Fosters a higher level of performance

Here are a few guidelines for creating an effective recognition program:

- Match the reward to the person. Survey employees to find out what they want so you can develop an incentive system that meets all employees' needs. Have a committee of employees participate in the development and execution of the program.
- Match the reward to the achievement. The reward for successfully completing a long-term project should be greater than the reward for a short-term success. Tailor the recognition to the achievement. Offer a variety of rewards, and provide progressive recognition that builds on a history of successes.
- Be timely and specific. Any incentive program should have a specific purpose, such as improving customer and member service or increasing attendance.
- Provide public recognition, and change the program often so people do not tire of it.

Some examples of possible awards for employees include these:

- A pat on the back for excellent member service
- A special award for the person who has held a department together over a period of time
- A smile and a "thank you" for a job well done
- A special award for someone who performs above and beyond the call of duty
- A free dinner for those staff members who have put in the most substitute hours
- A special award for the staff members whose classes have grown the most over a given time period

Be sure to recognize volunteers just as you do paid staff. One of the best forms of recognition for volunteers is to manage them the same as paid staff members, placing them in a suitable job and providing them with regular training and the chance to take on new assignments. Integrate them into the YMCA's culture, and make them feel part of the family. Include them in the fun, informal traditions that you have at your YMCA. For example, if you celebrate birthdays for the paid staff, do the same for your volunteers in similar assignments.

Other ways to recognize volunteers include these:

- Communicating with them regularly and honestly, making sure they understand the YMCA's structure and its lines of authority and communication
- Listening to volunteers, seeking their opinions, and responding to them
- Expressing appreciation informally (sending thank-you notes or buying them coffee)
- Using newsletters, bulletin boards, and other displays to highlight the work of your volunteers
- Holding recognition events that are fun, convenient, and meaningful

Staff Career Development

One of your roles as an aquatics director is to nurture staff, helping them to develop as people, just as we strive to help our participants grow. You can find many ways to help your staff grow beyond their present roles. This is an important, special way you can make a difference in their lives.

In your position, you must be a role model for your staff. You wear many hats:

Teacher	Teach staff skills relevant to their development in their positions.
Tutor	Provide staff with special help in specific areas to help them attain skills.
Coach	Work on your staff's performance; help them develop their skills and improve themselves.
Counselor	Advise and assist staff in making personal decisions.
Mentor	Foster a caring, sharing, and helping relationship with your staff while focusing on meeting their needs.

As a mentor, you should form one-on-one relationships with all members of your staff to encourage them to make beneficial changes in their lives. You should offer them your knowledge, insight, perspective, and wisdom in a supportive relationship that goes beyond duty or obligation. Also, if you are an experienced director, you can offer to be a mentor to a new director in your area (or, if you are new, perhaps you can find an experienced director who will mentor you).

Work with your YMCA to find ways to keep highly trained aquatics specialists by offering them opportunities that will not only increase their salaries, but also give them new tasks and challenges. One example would be for a senior aquatics professional to oversee a couple of other experienced aquatics professionals, who would in turn supervise coordinators and directors at multiple locations and YMCAs. For part-time positions, develop leadership positions within your department, such as instructional swim coordinator, head lifeguard, and trainer. These may not be full-time positions, but by giving those individuals additional hours to cover these responsibilities, you can give these staff members personal development opportunities.

Discuss career goals with staff and help them find ways to achieve those goals. If an aquatics director dreams of becoming an executive, find ways to provide opportunities for financial and volunteer development in the director's current position. If a lifeguard or swim instructor would like to advance into the position of aquatics director, then allow that person to help coordinate lifeguard or instructional programs or projects such as the parent orientation for YMCA Swim Lessons. Giving staff these types of opportunities helps them develop skills related to their career goals; it also allows them to see that working at the YMCA is more than a job and that their supervisor truly cares. Even if they move up in the organization, they are more likely to stay in an aquatics position longer. Also inform staff of career opportunities with the YMCA nationally. The YMCA is a large system with many national and international opportunities in a multitude of fields.

Allow staffers to work together as a team to solve departmental issues. For example, YMCAs might challenge their aquatics staffers with ways to improve member involvement and service in the association overall.

Consider collaborations among associations or a network of YMCAs to provide expanded leadership opportunities for current aquatics staff. These may include opportunities to lead a project or a committee among several YMCAs, workshops and events offered jointly by YMCAs, or shared aquatics staff recruitment campaigns.

Take time to find opportunities to help each member of your staff grow in spirit, mind, and body. To learn more about developing your staff and mentoring, contact the YMCA of the USA Leadership Development Group at 1-800-872-9622.

BIBLIOGRAPHY

Buckingham, Marcus, and Curt Coffman. 1999. *First, break all the rules: What the world's greatest managers do differently.* New York: Simon and Schuster.

Pike, Robert W. 2001. *Unlock the power to learn, unlock the power to perform.* Minneapolis: Bob Pike Group.

Stout, William T., and James K. Backer. 1998. *Staff screening guide.* Nexus Solutions, Inc. Copyright 1998, by Nexus Solutions, Inc. 999-639-8788 or e-mail **inq@nexus-solutions.com** or Great American at 800-722-3260 or **www.hsd.gaic.com**.

Table 5.2   Aquatic Positions, Minimum Recommendations, Training, and Certifications

Positions	Minimum certification recommendation for position		In-service emergency preparedness training	Ideas for specialized training topics for in-service training	Recommended frequency of in-service training
	Recommended age	Specialty certifications (in addition to certifications for all positions)			
Aquatic directors, coordinators, supervisors	Directors—at least 21 yrs Coord./supvr.—at least 18 yrs	• YMCA Pool Operator on Location • YMCA Aquatic Management • YMCA Program Trainer Orientation • Specialty Trainer Level in other YMCA aquatic programs	• Understanding of all aquatic emergency procedures & their role in training aquatic staff • Training with other departments on emergency procedures • Leading assessments and evaluations	• Leadership development • Scheduling • Time management • Problem solving • Negotiation skills • Customer service • Member involvement • Fiscal management • Hiring guidelines • Assessments • Team building	One hour per month
Pool maintenance coordinator/ staff	At least 18 yrs	• YMCA Pool Operator on Location • CPR • First aid	• Emergency procedures related to chemical handling and equipment operation • First aid procedures for chemical emergencies • Chemical clean up procedures	• Preventative maintenance plan and follow-up for equipment • Daily, weekly, monthly checklists • Chemical clean up procedures	Quarterly

(continued)

Table 5.2 (continued)

Positions	Minimum certification recommendation for position		In-service emergency preparedness training	Ideas for specialized training topics for in-service training	Recommended frequency of in-service training
	Recommended age	Specialty certifications (in addition to certifications for all positions)			
Lifeguard	At least 16 yrs	• YMCA Lifeguard	• Emergency procedures & reporting procedures • Rescue skills • CPR & first aid skills • Scanning & zone coverage skills • Victim recognition • Conditioning swim • Readiness drills	• Decision making • Problem solving • Rule enforcement • Crisis control • Pool management basics • Guarding individuals with disabilities • Communicating common terms in languages commonly used in our service area	At least two hours of "in-service" training per month during high season and at least one hour per month at other times of the year. Additional time would be needed for facilities that have play elements (e.g., slides, inflatables, interactive playgrounds, and zero depth entries) or open water (e.g., lakes and oceans), as these require other special procedures.
Swim lesson instructor – Parent/child	At least 16 yrs	• YMCA Fundamentals of Teaching YMCA Swimming • Parent/Child Swim Instructor • YMCA Lifeguard or YMCA Aquatic Safety Assistant	• Emergency procedures & scenarios during class (i.e., parent conducting inappropriate submerges)	• Pool activities & how they relate to child development • Songs & games • Class organization • Working with parents and children • Comfort hints and class problems • Use of parent handouts	One hour per session

| Swim lesson instructor – Preschool | At least 16 yrs | • YMCA Fundamentals of Teaching YMCA Swimming
• Preschool Swim Instructor
• YMCA Lifeguard or YMCA Aquatic Safety Assistant | • Emergency procedures & scenarios during class (i.e., parents late to pick up kids, kid letting go of the wall, bathroom procedures) | • Question Trees & other guided discovery activities
• Session and lesson planning
• Character development activities
• Member involvement
• Class management
• Working with special needs
• Class organization patterns
• Use of IFDs and toys
• Student-centered learning
• Family involvement, use of Family Huddles and parent handouts
• Developmental stages of swimming | One hour per session |
| | | | | • Educating parents on aquatic safety
• Program skill review and progression
• Water sports and games
• Personal safety and rescue
• Use of IFDS and toys
• Session and lesson planning
• Character development activities
• Member involvement
• Class management | |

(continued)

Table 5.2 (continued)

Positions	Minimum certification recommendation for position		In-service emergency preparedness training	Ideas for specialized training topics for in-service training	Recommended frequency of in-service training
	Recommended age	Specialty certifications (in addition to certifications for all positions)			
Swim lesson instructor – Preschool (continued)				• Working with parents and children • Comfort hints and class problems • Educating parents on aquatic safety • Stroke development • Working with 3-5 year olds • Personal growth activities • Personal safety skills • Water sports and games/songs • Rescue activities • Skill sheets and recognition	
Swim lesson instructor – Youth	At least 16 yrs	• YMCA Fundamentals of Teaching YMCA Swimming • Youth & Adult Swim Instructor • YMCA Lifeguard or YMCA Aquatic Safety Assistant	• Emergency procedures & scenarios during class (i.e., keeping eyes on all kids in class at all times)	• Stroke drills & technique improvement • Water sports & games • Session and lesson planning • Class organization • Class management • Discussion of progressing students to the next level	One hour per session

- Problem solving and sharing of ideas for helping students discover how to perform a skill
- Ideas on how to weave character development into the program
- Reviews of skills and development of instructors' swimming skills
- Emergency procedures and rescue skills
- Special events and activities planned for your Y
- Pool policies that prevent the transmission of disease
- YMCA of the USA aquatic guidelines
- Question Trees & other guided discovery activities
- Session and lesson planning
- Character development activities
- Member involvement
- Class management
- Working with special needs
- Class organization patterns
- Use of IFDs and toys
- Student-centered learning
- Family involvement and use of Family Huddles
- Plussing the program

(continued)

Table 5.2 *(continued)*

Positions	Minimum certification recommendation for position		In-service emergency preparedness training	Ideas for specialized training topics for in-service training	Recommended frequency of in-service training
	Recommended age	Specialty certifications (in addition to certifications for all positions)			
Swim lesson instructor – Youth (continued)				• Developmental stages of swimming • Educating parents on aquatic safety • Stroke development • Working with 6-14 year olds • Personal growth activities • Water sports and games/songs • Rescue activities • Personal safety skills • Skill sheets and recognition	
Swim lesson instructor – Adult	At least 16 yrs	• YMCA Fundamentals of Teaching YMCA Swimming • Youth & Adult Swim Instructor • YMCA Lifeguard or YMCA Aquatic Safety Assistant	• Emergency procedures & scenarios during class (i.e., adults panicking in deep water)	• Setting goals with adults • Helping adults to overcome fears • Member involvement • Skill progressions and modifications • Teaching adults aquatic safety and rescue skills	One hour per session

	Age	Prerequisites			Time
Swim lesson instructor **–** **Individuals with disabilities**	At least 16 yrs	• YMCA Fundamentals of Teaching YMCA Swimming • Individuals with Disabilities • YMCA Lifeguard or YMCA Aquatic Safety Assistant	• Emergency procedures & scenarios during class (i.e., student panicking in deep water)	• Overview of a variety of disabilities & teaching tips • Skill progressions and modifications • Motivation • Working with family and caregivers	One hour per session
Water fitness instructor	At least 16 yrs	• YMCA Water Fitness Instructor • YMCA Lifeguard or YMCA Aquatic Safety Assistant	• Emergency procedures & scenarios during class (i.e., practicing with the lifeguard, cardiac arrest, nonswimmer slipping into deep end)	• Use of equipment • Sharing of information and ideas between instructors • How to set up for classes, instructors' administrative duties • Reviewing anatomy and biomechanics through muscle charts, muscle cards, and the YMCA *Personal Training Instructor Manual* • Studying water fitness research and the physical laws and properties of water • Fundamentals skills and exercise design and specificity of training and training guidelines • Designing workouts using SWEAT. This can be both a classroom and a pool session. • Teaching responsively and using equipment. This can be both a classroom and a pool session. • Exercise modifications based on conditions • Member involvement	One hour per session

(continued)

Table 5.2 (continued)

Positions	Minimum certification recommendation for position		In-service emergency preparedness training	Ideas for specialized training topics for in-service training	Recommended frequency of in-service training
	Recommended age	Specialty certifications (in addition to certifications for all positions)			
Older adult water fitness instructor	At least 16 yrs	• YMCA Water Fitness Instructor • YMCA Active Older Adult Water Fitness Instructor • YMCA Lifeguard or YMCA Aquatic Safety Assistant	• Emergency procedures & scenarios during class (i.e., practicing with the lifeguard, cardiac arrest, non swimmer slipping into deep end)	• Use of equipment • Sharing of information and ideas between instructors • Reviewing anatomy and biomechanics through muscle charts, muscle cards, and the *YMCA Personal Training Instructor Manual* • Studying water fitness research and the physical laws and properties of water • Fundamentals skills and exercise design and specificity of training and training guidelines • Designing workouts using SWEAT. This can be both a classroom and a pool session. • Teaching responsively and using equipment. This can be both a classroom and a pool session. • Exercise modifications based on conditions • Fitness assessments • Journaling • Motivation techniques • Member involvement	One hour per session

	Age	Certifications	Emergency procedures	Content	Frequency
Swim coach	One coach at least 18 yrs Assistants— at least 16 yrs	• Principles of YMCA Competitive Swimming & Diving • YMCA Swim Coach • YMCA Advanced Swim Coach (recommended) • YMCA Lifeguard or YMCA Aquatic Safety Assistant	• Emergency procedures & scenarios during practice & meets (i.e., starting block supervision, meet supervision, appropriate & safe dry land training)	• Teaching tips for improving technique and effective propulsion • Daily workout ideas • Review and feedback on season plan	Quarterly
Springboard diving instructor/ coach	At least 16 yrs	• YMCA Spring-board Diving Instructor • YMCA Lifeguard or YMCA Aquatic Safety Assistant	• Emergency procedures & scenarios during practice & meets (i.e., diving board rules, safe spotting)	• Skill progressions • Spotting techniques • Class organization • Additional ideas in US Diving Dive Safe manual	Quarterly
Water polo instructor/ coach	At least 16 yrs	• YMCA Water Polo Instructor/ Coach • YMCA Lifeguard or YMCA Aquatic Safety Assistant	• Emergency procedures & scenarios during practice, games, tournaments (i.e. safe ball handling, wearing of caps, whistle signals)	• Drills & teaching tips for technique • Practice plan ideas • Conditioning drills & exercises • Additional ideas in *U.S. Water Polo Level 1 Coaches Manual* and *YSL Youth and Adult Instructor Manual*	Quarterly

(continued)

Table 5.2 (continued)

Positions	Minimum certification recommendation for position		In-service emergency preparedness training	Ideas for specialized training topics for in-service training	Recommended frequency of in-service training
	Recommended age	Specialty certifications (in addition to certifications for all positions)			
Synchronized swimming instructor	At least 16 yrs	• YMCA Synchronized Swimming Instructor • YMCA Lifeguard or YMCA Aquatic Safety Assistant	• Emergency procedures & scenarios during practice & meets (i.e.	• Teaching tips for technique • Review of synchronized swimming skills & choreography • Additional ideas in U.S. Synchronized Swimming's *Intro Synchro* and *YMCA Youth Swim Lesson Manual*	Quarterly
Scuba/skin diving instructor	At least 18 yrs	• YMCA SCUBA • YMCA SLAM • YMCA Dive Instructor	• Emergency procedures & scenarios during lessons & trips	• Equipment handling & safe operation	Quarterly

(Session is considered 6-8 weeks)

Table 5.3 **YMCA Certification and Training Recommendations for All Aquatic Positions**

Certification and Training	Frequency and Details
CPR-PRO Certification From one of the following national certifying agencies: • American Heart Association Healthcare Provider • American Red Cross CPR for the Professional Rescuer • National Safety Council Pro • American Safety and Health Institute CPR-Pro Course	Prior to Hiring and Certify Each Year Must include training for administering CPR to adults, children, and infants; obstructed airway maneuver; as well as additional training in two-rescuer CPR, modified jaw thrust, and use of resuscitation-mask and bag-valve-mask resuscitators.
AED Certification (effective 1-1-2003) From one of the following national certifying agencies: • American Heart Association • American Red Cross • National Safety Council • American Safety and Health Institute	Prior to Hiring and Certify Each Year Plus recommended training every 3 months.
Oxygen Administration (effective 1-1-2003) From one of the following national certifying agencies: • American Red Cross • National Safety Council • American Safety and Health Institute	Prior to Hiring and Certify Every 2-3 Years
First Aid Certification From one of the following national certify agencies: • American Red Cross First Aid • National Safety Council First Aid • American Safety and Health Institute Universal First Aid	Prior to Hiring and Certify Every 2-3 Years Must Include training in victim assessment; treatment for bleeding, shock, burns, specific body area injuries, bites, stings, poisoning, cold- and heat-related conditions, and bone, muscle, and joint injuries; and handling medical emergencies and rescues.
YMCA Lifeguard or YMCA Aquatic Safety Assistant (for instructors only) certificaton	Prior to Hiring and Certify Every 2 Years
Bloodborne Pathogen Training	One hour annually
Child Abuse Prevention and Reporting Training	Annual review
Aquatic Department Orientation	Upon hiring

(continued)

Table 5.3 *(continued)*

Certification and Training	Frequency and Details
Local YMCA Orientation	Upon hiring
YMCA Staff Aquatic Safety Training (from the YMCA of USA)	Annual review
Local YMCA Initiatives	As needed
Character Development	1-2 hrs annually
Member Service	One hour per session
Campaign	Annual review
Career Planning and Development	Annual review

Management and Professional Development Skills

Working as a YMCA aquatics director is a wonderful career. You get the opportunity every day to help others reach their potential in countless ways. You're out in your community, working with people of all ages and abilities. In a single day, you can be lifeguarding or teaching a swim class in the morning, counseling a staff member about a personal problem, giving a presentation at a service club at noon, helping an older adult member find assistance with transportation to the doctor, meeting with a prospective donor about giving a gift to the YMCA, and sharing a child's accomplishment with a parent. So many skills are needed in this profession, which requires lifelong learning and achievement. What could be any better than this?

But how do you make sure you are the professional you need to be? First, you need to look at yourself. Do you set a good example? Do you "walk the talk"? Do you follow the principles that you advocate to your members and community? Determine if your lifestyle is consistent with the goals and objectives that we promote through the YMCA. Second, look at your own personal skill development. Do you actively pursue improvement in the areas where you are weak? Do you take the time to learn the skills to improve? Third, evaluate what is needed in your programs and how you work with your staff and volunteers. What do they need to be better, and what are you doing to offer what they need?

Growth as a supervisor, as a professional, and as a person will not only help you, but will also benefit your staff and the organization. In this chapter, we talk about the "people skills" needed for supervision; the professional skills you need for your job, such as problem solving, negotiation, and time management; ideas for improving your interactions with others in the organization; and career development. Additional training and continual improvement in the areas discussed in this chapter will help you be a successful aquatics leader and professional. We've hit the basics on each of these topics, but many additional resources and training courses are available to help you in your own development.

STAFF SUPERVISION

Management is getting things done through the effort of other people. It is the development of people, not the direction of activities. People need to accomplish those

Most aquatic directors will come into an existing facility operation. If you are in such a situation, To assist you in your first ninety days, here are some tips to help you get you off to the right start in your first ninety days.

Get to Know Your Staff

- Have the previous director, current coordinator, or new supervisor provide you with a list of employees.

- Ask a number of individuals (previous director, coordinators, fellow professional directors at your branch who know your staff, executive staff, or current staff) to rate employees from 1 to what ever number of staff you have, with 1 being the best and the highest number being the worst. Group them into thirds. Have them explain why the top group is where they are, the middle group is where they are, and the low group is where they are.

- From this list establish goals for moving the bottom two-thirds into the top third.

- Provide a written evaluation to each staff member so that each one understands what your goals are.

- Set up a "getting-to-know-you" meeting with each staff person in the first 30 days. Spend 15 minutes with each employee and ask the employee about her or his job, the hours she or he works, her or his goals, where she or he would like to be at the end of the year, and describe your goals for the overall staff.

- Be very visible to the staff, and have an open door policy.

- Review all staff certifications on file.

- Review the last staff performance evaluation.

- Become familiar with the association's personnel policy.

Get to Know Your Budget

- Before starting, ask for a copy of your new budget.

- Review goals with your supervisor.

- Ask your supervisor what the growth goals were and what plans were made to reach those goals. (For more on budgeting, see chapter 7.)

- Highlight areas of concern in the budget.

- Keep these notes so that when budget season starts, you are ready.

Get to Know Your Facility

- Schedule a meeting between yourself and the other directors so that you understand how aquatics and all other programs relate to each other.

- Schedule a meeting between yourself and the building and grounds director. Establish who is responsible for cleaning, maintenance, and water testing. Check these responsibilities with your supervisor.

- Determine the danger areas in the pool.

- Establish where guards have problems guarding the pool.

- Review and rehearse emergency procedures.

- Get up to speed on any ongoing problems, concerns, incidents or legal situations.

Get to Know Your Schedules

- Ask for a list of regular meetings so you can enter them into your organizer.
- Ask when the last staff meeting was held for your staff. No matter what the time frame, hold a new staff meeting within the first 30 days.
- Review pool schedules. Check to make sure that pool and class schedules and class schedules reflect budget goals.
- Establish weekly meetings between yourself and your leadership staff.
- Establish weekly meetings between yourself and your supervisor.

Get to Know Your Goals

- From different meetings between you and the executive director, your supervisor, and your staff, list all goals.
- Prioritize this list by putting safety goals first, staff needs second, and systems goals third.
- Establish a timeline for each goal and give the completion dates to your supervisor for regular review.

Get to Know Your Program

- Review the staff orientation process.
- Review hiring procedures.
- Review the programs being offered to see whether they are YMCA programs.
- Review parent handbooks.
- Set up a parent listening session to hear about needs from the participants.
- Ask a number of individuals (previous director, coordinators, fellow professional directors at your branch who know your staff, executive staff, or current staff) to rate present programs from 1 to what ever number you have, with 1 being the best and the highest number being the worst. Group them into thirds. Have them explain why the top group is where they are, the middle group is where they are, and the low group is where they are.

Get to Know Yourself

- Obtain any necessary YMCA certifications, including YMCA Aquatic Management training.
- Set up your exercise schedule.
- Set up your personal goals statement.
- Schedule meetings with leaders in your community.
- List your personal and career goals for your supervisor.
- Establish a training plan for yourself.
- Find out how you get to meet and get to know the other aquatic directors in your area.

tasks that will achieve your purpose, goals, and objectives. However, this should be encouraged by striving for the maximum development and growth of each person within the organization. The success of any organization, including the YMCA, depends on having an adequate number of human beings in the right jobs, at the right time, all producing at their highest capacity.

As a leader of your staff, you are a team leader and should strive to help your team be successful. As a manager of others, you should think of yourself as a motivator and a coach. You are a facilitator who produces the results of your aquatics department with the help of your staff.

A team leader is

- a facilitator,
- a person skilled at helping your group solve problems,
- a model of what is expected,
- a person who works to help the team succeed, and
- a person who develops and motivates the team to perform at its best.

Supervision requires both organization skills and people skills. *Organization skills* relate to the structure, tools, and systems that need to be in place to manage the department and to work within an association. These include the organizational chart, job descriptions, performance standards, and performance appraisals. These impart a visible order to your association and clearly articulate the goals of the YMCA to all employees. These tools build the foundation you use to keep yourself honest with and fair to all employees. *People skills* are needed to motivate, coach, and develop the people in your department. We have described many ideas and tips in other chapters that relate to these skills. You can't have effective supervision without both people skills and organization skills; you need to apply both to be effective.

In chapter 5, we discussed organization skills. In this chapter, we'll talk about people skills. Once the structure is in place, the supervisor's job is to do all he or she can to help staff members reach or exceed their standards of performance. Being a supervisor is an active role. The supervisor has to support and motivate as well as evaluate. The supervisor should observe, participate, plan, direct, balance, and celebrate.

Some people skills you should have include knowing which supervisory style to use with which employees, intervening in employees' work positively and negatively, and monitoring the state of your department by observing activities on a regular, informal basis. You should also know how to provide leadership to your department. Finally, we give you some tips on how you and your staff can avoid burnout.

Supervisory Style

When dealing with staff, consider each staff member's situation when you communicate with her or him. For instance, think how differently you would deal with a new staff member teaching a class on the first day of the session and another staff member that has been with you for a few years. You probably could tell the tenured staff member to teach a Minnow class at 9:00 A.M., and that would be sufficient. That person would know how to get the skill sheet and develop a lesson plan without any help, although you would be there to answer any questions. On the other hand, you would want to show a new staff member where to find the skill sheets and the process you use in developing lesson plans, as well as help the person think through how to plan the session. You would also want to have that staff member observe some classes and assist another instructor, then talk with you about his or her observations and questions. Finally, you would want to observe the new staff member's first class, then spend some time talking with the person about how the class went and answer questions. You have to treat each staff member individually based on the task and the situation.

You can use any of four different supervisory styles with employees, choosing the one that is best suited to the situation:

- *Telling:* You direct staff in what to do and how to do the task. You closely monitor them for successful completion. "This is what I want you to do, this how I want you to do it. Go ahead."
- *Coaching:* You persuade the staff member to act. You continue to direct and closely monitor them. You also explain decisions, solicit suggestions, and support progress. "We've got the talent. We've got the plan. Are you ready? Let's do it."
- *Supporting:* You are supportive. You facilitate and support their efforts toward task accomplishment. You share responsibility for decision making with them. "I'm with you all the way. If you have questions, I'm here."
- *Assigning:* You let them go. You give them responsibility for decision making and problem solving. "This one's all yours. Just keep me informed as to how it's going from time to time."

How you treat a staff member is based in part on how "mature" the person is in performing that task in that situation. This relates to the staff member's knowledge, experience, skill, talent, ability, attitude, and willingness to perform the task. Even when assigning a new task to a staff member who has been with you a long time, that person would need additional support and direction from you to be successful.

The other factor involved in choosing the right style based on the situation is the employee's level of commitment and competence. For instance, a new employee may be an enthusiastic beginner in the job. She or he is ready and willing to learn but needs to know how and what to do. Another employee may already know what to do and may already believe in the organization. That person probably needs a different style (depending on the task or situation). As a supervisor, you need to be able to shift gears and apply different styles readily. You need to realize what style of supervision will be most effective based on the task, the situation, and the person involved.

Communicate to your staff that you want them to talk to you and let you know how they feel about the tasks they are given, as well as the direction you give them. You want to match the appropriate style of supervision to each staff member. Such open communication helps build a stronger relationship between you and staff and creates a stronger team.

For more information on situational leadership, see Blanchard (1985).

Intervention

One of the more difficult tasks for a supervisor is intervening in the work of an employee. Some supervisors may avoid intervention because they feel awkward or uncomfortable. It is tempting to save everything for the next performance appraisal, but frequent observation and intervention are very helpful to staff. People like to know when they are doing things right or wrong. A good working relationship means regular communication and intervention, which can be either positive or negative.

Use positive intervention often. Use these tips when performing a positive intervention:

- Catch the person doing things right.
- Praise the person immediately.
- Be specific.
- Tell the person how you feel about what he or she did right.
- Make appropriate physical contact to show support for the person.
- Do all this in less than 60 seconds.

If an employee does something wrong, use these tips for a negative intervention:

- Tell the person what she or he did wrong.
- Be specific.
- Tell the person that you know he or she does things right and is a valued employee.
- Make appropriate physical contact to show support for the person.
- Don't do this in public.
- Do all this in less than 60 seconds.

If you do this whenever you catch a staff member doing something wrong, and if support is part of the intervention, the impact is positive. It is much easier for the staff member to hear one quick, specific correction than to listen to a list of negative behaviors during the performance appraisal session.

If the negative behavior or infraction escalates to the need for a discussion that lasts longer than a minute but is not as formal as a performance review, sit down with the staff member to address the concern. Such a session is called a RAP session, which stands for review, analyze, and plan. Follow the agenda for this session in this order: Review the past behavior, analyze the present behavior, and plan and focus on the future behavior (see figure 6.1 for a RAP recording sheet). The key to effectiveness is to focus on planning for and agreeing on future behavior. Spend the least amount of time on the review (15 percent), a little more on analysis (25 percent), and most of the time on planning (60 percent).

Here's a sample RAP 20-minute discussion guide to help you:

- Review (2 minutes)
    - Describe the problem.
- Analyze (5 minutes)
    - What factors created the problem?
    - What needs to be done to correct the situation?
- Plan (12 minutes)
    - List the steps to solve the problem and expected behaviors.
    - Develop an action plan. Include specific actions to be taken by whom and by when.
- Follow-through (1 minute)
    - What follow-up will be done?

The key is to move quickly from stating the problem as you see it (the past) to analyzing the situation (the present) and to planning how the staff member is going to correct the situation (the future). If the staff member shows defensiveness or has a

Sample RAP Recording Sheet

Review—2 minutes

What is the problem?

Analyze—5 minutes

What needs to be done to correct the situation? What factors created the problem?

Plan—12 minutes

List steps to solve the problem and expected behaviors.

Implementation plan

Action   By whom?   By when?

Follow-through

What follow-up will be done?

Supervisee's signature _____   Date _____

Supervisor's signature _____   Date _____

Figure 6.1   Sample RAP recording sheet.

significantly different perspective, the cause is most likely to be different interpretations of the past. Get these perspectives out on the table, but don't dwell on them. The present is easier to deal with, even when you have a difference of opinion. By spending more time dealing with the future, both of you can plan effectively. Gain agreement on future behavior, identify what needs to be done, and agree on the plan.

Monitoring Your Department

Getting out of your office and walking around your department regularly and often is part of active supervision. Walking around allows you to gather information about programs and staff, break down barriers between staff and management, talk to members and participants, and send messages about what is important to the YMCA—the work with our members and participants. Talk with staff and members to clarify questions and hear new ideas. Get to know them and allow them to learn about you and what you care about. Create the feeling that we are all on the same team, and remember why you are in this job.

Monitoring involves good observation and listening. Watch the dynamics of what is going on, the interaction between staff and members, and how the programs are going, and think about how it could be better. Listen intently and without assumptions. Let people talk to you and tell you what they think. Ask probing questions such as "Why are we doing it this way? Any ideas on how we could do it better or differently? What are your biggest problems now? What can I do to improve things?" Don't ask vague questions, nitpick, or blame. This is an opportunity to tell staff how much you appreciate their hard work by using the one-minute positive intervention described on page 188.

By doing this regularly, staff will realize that you are out and about as a way to find out about program quality and safety. However, you must be prepared to take action based on what you discover. Follow up immediately on things that you say you will do.

Leadership

As an aquatic director, you are a leader of the staff that helps you achieve the goals of your department. You want the YMCA's mission for meeting people's potential to be as important for your staff members as it is for your members and program participants. Knowing and understanding leadership is important for you to help your staff succeed and in turn help the department and organization succeed. Your leadership style and philosophy and the culture you create within your department affects those that work with you.

In your role, it is helpful to have tools that help you to help others grow. Let's look at servant leadership as one of those tools.

Servant leadership is a practical philosophy that supports people who really want to serve others and who choose to lead in a way that truly serves. It encourages others to work together, to trust each other, to see a vision of what they could become, to listen to each other. It encourages the ethical use of power and empowerment of others. The real motivation for leading is first and foremost to serve others, not to have them serve you.

Ask yourself these questions to see if your actions are those of a servant leader:

- Do those I serve grow as persons?
- Do they, while being served by me, become healthier, wiser, freer, more confident people who are more likely to become servant leaders themselves?

- What is the effect of my actions on the least privileged of the people I serve; will they benefit from my actions, or at least not be further deprived as a result of those actions?

As a leader, you will need the support of your staff if you are to accomplish anything. To gain their support, you must show yourself to be worthy of their expectations. First, your staff will feel more comfortable following you if they know that you know what you are doing! Have the right qualifications for your position, and be as competent as you can be at your job. A leader with a proven record of successful accomplishments inspires confidence in staff. Next, your staff will also want to know that you are someone they can trust and identify with, someone they can rely on. You can demonstrate this by following the YMCA's core values of caring, honesty, respect, and responsibility. While no one is perfect, do your best to live up to your values.

One of the most important things you can offer your staff as a leader is a vision of what you want you and your staff to accomplish. Share that vision with your staff and show them how they can contribute to it. This can be very motivating. Be sure to express your belief in that vision and your confidence that it can be achieved. If you are hesitant to commit yourself to your vision, your staff will be too.

Another way you can be a good leader is to show your staff that you care about them and give them your support and trust. While you should try to figure out the specific needs of your staff members and how you can meet them, there are several things you can do that will work for most people. For example, almost everyone responds well to praise. Continuously look for staff members who are doing things right and compliment them immediately. Be specific about what they've done that you like, and make your praise genuine.

Show you care about your staff members by taking the time to really listen to them. Hear not only what they say, but also how they feel and what they believe. Ask them questions to make sure you understand them correctly. Don't judge them before you know the whole story, and give serious consideration to their ideas.

Another thing you can do is remind your staff of your vision—often. Show them how their efforts will help achieve that vision. This will encourage them to continue, even when their tasks become difficult.

Make the work more engaging by identifying staff members' talents and interests, then adjusting or changing their positions so they can best use their gifts. Encourage them to improve their skills in areas of interest to them.

A final way that you can be a good leader is to identify among your staff and potential new hires those who also can be leaders. They can help you achieve your vision if you give them opportunities to grow. Such people have a number of attributes in common. One significant one is that they tend to be active, rather than passive. They solve problems on their own, and they come up with innovative new ideas to improve the organization.

Another sign of potential leaders is that others look up to them. Staff members know that they are people who can be counted on for help and guidance. Potential leaders have demonstrated that they are true to the YMCA's core values and are trustworthy.

Still another asset of potential leaders is that they have a positive attitude and like helping others. They can overlook their own problems to take care of others' needs. Making people happy is important to them.

Trustworthiness is also characteristic of potential leaders. They follow through on what they promise. They almost always meet their own responsibilities, and they are willing to give an extra effort when needed. Even when things get bad, you can count on them. They will not quit or complain when the going gets tough, but will do what they can to get everyone through it.

Finally, potential leaders will support your vision. They will be willing to apply their skills however they are needed to achieve the common goal.

Avoiding Burnout

No matter how much you like your job, you know there will be some bad days, unpleasant tasks, and troublesome stretches because of situations or program seasons. But you always have a choice about how you do your work, even if you don't have a choice about the work itself. Apply these five principles to help you and your staff make the most of each day:

- *Decide to be positive.* Attitude is a choice we can make. As you work, decide to do your best.
- *Be here.* Be absorbed in the present, in the person you are talking to or the work you are trying to accomplish.
- *Show you care.* Be enthusiastic and caring with staff and members.
- *Really listen.* When you talk with others, don't just hear the words they say, but listen to find out how they feel and what they believe.
- *Have fun.* Try to make every day enjoyable.

PROFESSIONAL SKILLS

As part of management, you are expected to have certain professional skills that are tools you can use daily in your job. These include the ability to solve problems, negotiate, and manage your time wisely.

Problem Solving

One constant in the role of an aquatics director is solving problems. It can be said about the work we do that we have total responsibility for things we have little control over.

As an aquatics director, you need to develop the ability to solve problems and move on. Problem solving is a continuous, complex process. You need to be creative, logical, and able to see around obstacles, as well as know how to find out the facts. In some cases, you will want others, such as your staff or volunteer committees, to assist you in solving problems; in other cases, you will want to deal with them yourself. You can solve problems in many different ways, but the key is to find the most effective and efficient method for the problem.

Part of defining a problem is to think through the process you will want to use. It will help if you have an organized way to attack problems, so we're supplying a few models here that can help you make effective decisions. The models include PACA, problem analysis, scenario development, and interpersonal problem analysis. Before we describe these models, though, let's focus on the important initial step of problem definition.

Defining the Problem

In all the models, the first step is to define the problem. Defining the problem as clearly as possible is very important in getting to the best solution. Some of the obstacles in defining a problem include

- not having all the facts,
- having more than one interconnected problem or issue,
- poor or no communication,
- misinterpretation of the facts or issues,
- assumptions (often based on past experiences),
- inferences,
- attitudes and opinions,
- emotions,
- time, and
- perspective.

In a problem situation, ask yourself the following key questions to get specific answers:

- Who is involved in the problem?
- What exactly is wrong?
- Where is the problem taking place? Who does it affect?
- When did the problem begin?

- What is the extent of the problem?
- Is there a pattern to the problem?
- Is the problem with people? Is the problem within an individual's control?
- Does the problem involve a lack of skills, knowledge, or motivation?
- Is the problem related to a lack of information or resources?
- Is the problem covered in existing operating procedures or policies?
- Do I have the power or influence to affect the problem?

We tend to deal with the symptoms rather than the problem itself. When talking to people about what the problem is, try to see past the symptoms to the real problem.

PACA

We teach our lifeguards a problem-solving model called PACA. It is one that you can use for many of your own problems. PACA stands for four questions you must ask yourself when considering a problem:

P—What is the problem?

A—What are the alternatives?

C—What are the consequences?

A—What's the action?

There's an example in Table 6.1.

Problem Analysis

Here is a different system of examining a problem, developing a solution, and implementing and evaluating the results of that solution.

Examining a Problem

Once you've noticed a problem, your first task is to determine what the key issue really is. Although many things may seem to be wrong, try to narrow it down to one.

Table 6.1   Sample PACA Process

Problem	Alternatives	Consequences	Action
Can't find an early morning lifeguard for Wednesday mornings	1 I guard that shift.	1 I will be very tired.	
	2 I pay a higher wage for the shift to get someone to take it.	2 I will have to get approval for the money, which will put me over budget.	
	3 I recruit some members who swim early in the morning to become lifeguard certified.	3 I will have to run a lifeguarding course.	I will recruit people to become lifeguard certified who are willing to work the early morning Wednesday shift.

Then factually describe that issue; search for the necessary information, don't guess. Look for what may be causing it to happen, the factors that might play a part and the circumstances that surround the problem.

Diagnosing the problem is a process of elimination. For example, your registrations have declined for four months, and you realize that this coincides with the release of a new brochure through a new distribution method initiated five months ago. No similar decline has occurred at other association branches. This problem has several possible causes: Is it the brochure, the brochure's distribution method, or a combination of both that contributed to the registration decline? Are there other contributing variables?

Developing a Solution

Once you feel you've determined the causes of your problem, create some objectives for your solution. State them in terms of particular results, and decide in what order you want to tackle them.

Begin by thinking of all the alternatives you can, being as creative as possible. For each alternative, develop specific details as to what will be done, by whom, and by when.

Next, for each alternative, think about the possible consequences, both good and bad. How likely are those consequences to occur, and how significant would they be if they happened? Check that the alternatives work and are affordable. Make sure you haven't listed alternatives that are impossible due to circumstances beyond your control.

Finally, evaluate your solutions by asking yourself whether each solution will do the following:

- Be in accord with the needs, values, and experiences of those involved
- Seem to improve the situation for everyone
- Be easy to express, understand, and implement
- Permit an initial tryout before full implementation
- Have clear results

Implementing and Evaluating the Results of the Solution

Once you've chosen a solution to try, describe when something will be done, who will do it, and what you want to happen as a result. Be sure to consider the monetary costs of implementing the solution.

Implement the solution, then monitor the results and document what happens. Plan to evaluate the results of the solution by describing what you hope to accomplish with your solution and devising a method of comparing the results with what you wanted to achieve.

Scenario Development

This problem-solving method asks you to consider the present problem scenario, envision a better one, and come up with plans to improve the situation.

Step 1: Assess the current scenario (define the problem/opportunity).

What is the situation as I see it?

What don't I know?

What area of the problem should I work on first?

Step 2:   Visualize the preferred scenario (develop a goal).

What are all of the ways this situation could be better?

Which of these ways do I want as my goal?

How determined am I to achieve this goal? How will I overcome the obstacles?

Step 3:   Design the strategies (achieve a goal).

What are some of the ways I can meet the goals?

Which way is best?

Do it.

Interpersonal Problem Analysis

The system described here is best used for solving interpersonal problems. It focuses on what you feel or sense about the situation and how you might change your own behavior to help solve the problem.

1. Write down a simple statement of the problem. Include yourself in the problem statement.

2. What are your feelings about and reactions to the problem?

3. How did you help create or continue the problem?

4. What changes in your awareness or feelings about the problem do you see/feel now?

5. What changes in behavior (yours and others) would be appropriate?

6. Write how willing you are to actually try out these changes in behavior.

For staffing problems, see the models in chapter 5 on staff development.

Negotiating Skills

The ability to negotiate effectively is beneficial for everyone. We all negotiate with our peers and family regularly. However, it's when negotiations become formal that we begin to look for guidance on the best way to achieve our goals. It can be very helpful to know how to arrive at good agreements, especially when you are trying to collaborate with other organizations and agencies. You may be trying to obtain additional pool time in another community pool for your swim team, or to start a new program in an underserved area in your community using school facilities. The outcome of a successful negotiation should benefit all parties involved, as the terms of an agreement or relationship can be the foundation for future agreements.

Here are some basic tips to use when negotiating:

• *Make a plan.* Good planning is the first step. You need to understand the history behind the negotiation, both from your perspective and that of the other party. Your research will be well worth the time.

• *Determine your goals and objectives.* Know what you want to satisfy your needs. Determine what is the least you will accept in order to achieve an agreement. Focus on the objectives, not on the personalities of the individuals involved. As you plan, be sure you can state factually why you are interested in the terms that you propose. Your offer or terms should make sense in context and reflect firm, logical reasoning. This will help focus the discussion on solutions that can be proven to meet your underlying needs.

You should also identify your own worst possible outcome and the alternatives if an agreement cannot be made. This will help you maintain the right perspective and help you better evaluate the desirability of the various options on the table for discussion. The better you understand your options, the easier it will be to present your interests firmly during the negotiation.

Discuss your plan with your executive director and make sure you understand the process required for any agreement or contract approval. Your executive director may also want to be involved in this process, so you will want to know at what point he or she should be included.

- *Get to know them.* Develop a relationship with those you will be negotiating with so you can understand their issues. You will want to determine their objectives, what motivates them to come to an agreement, and the needs and interests they are trying to address. Find out what they have done in other agreements. See if you can determine what is the least they will accept to achieve an agreement. Also find out what process is needed to complete the agreement.

- *Collaborate and establish a cooperative environment.* Create an environment in which you work together to make the best agreement possible. Brainstorm on how you can work together to make the agreement effective. Use your active listening skills, and try to make sure you are being understood correctly. Discuss your concerns and desires surrounding the issue rather than jumping to the bottom line. Also, decide together on objective criteria by which a decision may be judged.

- *Come to an agreement.* When the options proposed acknowledge, validate, and address the needs of all involved, both sides are likely to reach agreement quickly. Moreover, negotiating to meet the needs of all can lay the foundation for positive ongoing relationships. Evaluate the decision to see if it truly is beneficial to and satisfies the needs of both parties.

Use the YMCA's four values of caring, honesty, respect, and responsibility to guide your discussions. Focus on what is in the best interest of your YMCA in both the long and short term in making agreements.

Time Management

As an aquatics director, you will need to be able to prioritize your work and personal activities based on their importance and urgency. You should also try to balance your work and personal time commitments. To do this, you'll require time management and priority-setting skills.

In a typical day, we spend eight hours sleeping, one hour on personal hygiene, three hours on eating and meal preparation, two hours commuting, and eight hours working. This leaves about two hours per day to do all the things that make life worth living! But it gets worse. By their own account, most people waste at least two hours every day—or one whole month a year.

Working smart and understanding effective time management skills can make an important difference—no matter what your position. Although we all have some external demands on how we use our time, many time-eaters can be controlled internally.

Here are four steps that you can use to take charge of your time:

- Become aware of how you are using your time. Make it a habit to be conscious of where your time is being spent and why you are doing what you are doing.

- Learn to make the best possible use of your time. Set priorities for what needs to be done first, what can wait, and what you may not be able to get done at all. Smart time managers don't take on more work than they can handle.

- Know what your time management enemies are and learn to win the battle. Don't procrastinate. Don't tolerate distractions. Don't waste time.

- Work smarter, not harder. Be creative about how to get things done. Find different ways to get help from others and to access information quickly and easily. Adopt a work plan that fits your job and your personality.

You can better manage your time by planning and organizing your work, establishing priorities, and balancing your work and personal time.

Planning and Organizing

Effective work habits start with careful planning and goal setting. An hour of planning can be worth two to four hours of hard work. Spending a little time planning before you actually start a project can increase your productivity considerably.

Here are some suggestions on how to organize your environment, use a "To Do" list, and make use of organization tools to help with your planning.

1. Organize your work area, streamlining it as much as possible. Try to set up specific locations for different tasks and items: incoming mail, things to be filed, pending work (for example, waiting for a return phone call or for someone else to give you a piece of information), calendar placement, placement of phone messages, and so on. Keep the items you need to refer to most often close to you.

2. Develop a "To Do" list. Developing a "To Do" list is a key component of any time management planning method. Here's how to do it:

- Make a list of all the tasks you need to complete in the next week.
- Prioritize the list (we'll be talking about prioritizing tips a little later).
- Include several headings: Calls to Make, People to See, Letters and Reports Due, Deadlines, Ongoing Assignments, and Top Priority Items.
- Cross off/erase items once they are completed.
- At the end of a week, start a new list, carrying items not accomplished from the previous list and adding new activities to be done.
- Keep your list short and allot more time than necessary for most tasks—allow extra time for the inevitable interruptions.
- Break large tasks into small ones. List the smaller tasks on your list, not the overwhelming title of the entire project.
- Recognize time-wasting tasks.
- If a task is continually carried over from one list to another without getting done, it probably wasn't important in the first place.

Organization Tools

To manage your time effectively, you have to use the right tools. Let's talk about some of them:

- *Calendar.* Choose a planner based on your needs.
- *Appointment book.* List all appointments in definite times and spaces to prevent schedule conflicts. Look for additional room to pencil in names, locations, and subjects for discussion. Include personal/family activities and appointments in the same appointment book.

- *To Be Done Today (action) list.* Record projects with deadlines, add any new projects, then prioritize those tasks. A note on deadlines: Do not set your goal for having it done on the same date your supervisor gave you. Instead, give yourself an earlier deadline. Then if you miss it, you will still have extra time before the "real" deadline.

- *Tickler reminder.* Enter reminder notes to yourself under the "To Be Done Today" section.

Know what your "prime time" is each day—the time of day when you have the most energy, concentration, and efficiency. Plan around those times accordingly. What times of day do you find to be the best work times for you? Why is that? How do you manage your time accordingly?

Establishing Priorities

The techniques of managing your time help you to make three decisions:

- What am I going to spend my time on; that is, what is on my list?
- When am I going to do it?
- How much time will I spend on it?

To set priorities, you've first got to identify which activities need to be accomplished and their respective importance and urgency. Start by making a list of all the activities you must perform. Include formal duties, special projects, responses to routine requests from coworkers, and other tasks. Then evaluate tasks for importance and urgency. Importance and urgency are not the same! Importance is determined by meaning, relevance, and a sense of purpose. Urgency is determined by how close to "now" the task must be completed.

First, rate each task according to its importance. For each activity, ask yourself these questions: Does it really matter? How much of an impact does it have on the goals I've agreed on with my supervisor? Assign it an importance number:

1. Very important—directly affects goals
2. Important—should be done
3. Important—useful but possibly not essential
4. Unimportant—not necessary to do

Then rate each activity according to its urgency. Not all important tasks are urgent ones. Assign an urgency number:

1. Very urgent—must be done immediately
2. Urgent—must be done soon
3. Not urgent—time is on your side
4. Time is not a factor

Table 6.2 shows the types of tasks that fall into these four categories, according to importance and urgency.

Also rate each activity according to its potential for being performed by others. Assign a sharing number:

1. Must be done by me—requires my personal skills or authority
2. Can be done by someone else—others who have the skills or time available

Table 6.2	Quadrant of Quality	
	Urgent	**Not urgent**
Important	*Quadrant I* Crisis Pressing problems Deadline-driven projects Meetings, preparations	*Quadrant II* Preparation Prevention Values clarification Planning Relationship building Needed relaxation Empowerment
Not Important	*Quadrant III* Needless interruptions Unnecessary reports Unimportant meetings, phone calls, mail Other people's minor issues Many popular activities	*Quadrant IV* Trivia, busywork Some phone calls Time-wasters "Escape" activities Irrelevant mail Excessive TV Excessive relaxation

Then reconstruct your list, arranging tasks in order of the value of their combined importance and urgency numbers, from lowest to highest. If you can, assign those tasks with a sharing number of 2 to other people.

Here are some time-tested ways of keeping your plans on schedule:

- *Implement your planned actions.* This will require initiative and persistence on your part. Maintain a chart of progress toward your goals, weekly and monthly. This will discourage backsliding.

- *Start early.* Beginning your workday a few minutes early will help you minimize many personal time problems.

- *Decide quickly on small things.* Most problems do not require a lot of time for a decision. A prompt yes or no saves time! Be decisive.

- *Control the telephone.* What starts as a brief exchange can drag out into 15 minutes of irrelevant dialogue. Calls can also interrupt important meetings. Limit call length and ask to return the call if you're in the middle of something.

- *Limit chitchat.* If someone wants to explain what happened over the weekend or some other nonessential matter, suggest talking at lunch or during a break.

Balancing Work and Personal Time

Until this point, we've focused primarily on the issue of managing our time at the workplace. We probably all feel that we have too much to do and not enough time to do it. But what about incorporating those work demands into our overall lives? How many of you feel that it's difficult to juggle your work and home life demands?

Three ways to see that you include personal time in your daily life are setting personal goals, finding ways to take care of yourself, and assessing your progress on personal matters.

Setting Personal Goals

The first step in organizing for the coming week is to connect with what's most important in your life as a whole. It helps to have a clear vision about the following:

What's most important?

What gives your life meaning?

What do you want to be and to do in your life?

This is your personal mission statement and is a good way to clarify these questions. But for now, you may get some feeling for what's important to you by doing one of the following:

- List the three or four things you would consider "first things" in your life.
- Consider any long-range goals you might have set.
- Think about the most important relationships in your life.
- Think about any contributions you'd like to make.
- Reaffirm the feelings you want to have in your life—peace, confidence, happiness, contribution, meaning.
- Think about how you might spend this week if you knew you only had six months to live.

Be sure to work your personal goals into your planning for each day.

Taking Care of Yourself

How often do you make time in your day to make sure *you're* doing okay? We usually don't invest a lot of energy in increasing our own physical, social, mental, and spiritual growth. When we get too busy doing our jobs—at work and at home—or producing results, we often neglect to take care of ourselves. We don't exercise; we ignore key relationships; we don't take walks or read books. We tend to think of these as indulgences, but we shouldn't neglect any part of what keeps us healthy and whole.

Take a minute to try to identify some of your personal needs (as opposed to your boss's, your kids', or the YMCA's). What would you like to be able to do to take care of your physical and social needs? Mental and spiritual growth? Here are some sample ideas:

- Take a yoga class.
- Make a lunch date with your kids.
- Ask your boss if you can leave early one afternoon and make it time for yourself—or your kids.
- Start swimming at the YMCA twice a week.

Assessing Your Progress

At the end of each week, before organizing the next week, pause to ask questions such as these:

- What goals did I achieve?
- What challenges did I encounter?
- In making decisions, did I keep first things first?

Time Management Tips and Tricks

- Know and wisely use your peak performance period.
- Control interruptions.
- Start up and wind down efficiently.
- Group telephone calls, both incoming and outgoing.
- Leave and request detailed messages.
- Let others know when you are available—and when you are not.
- Find a place to hide when you need to focus.
- Work when others are not around.
- Use your commute.
- Handle paper only once.
- Develop and share your schedule.

Fundraising

Fundraising enables YMCAs to support quality programs and to help those who can't afford program fees. At most YMCAs, fundraising will include the annual campaign, donations of equipment or funds, proposals for special projects, and grants. We also offer a few fundraising ideas that you might try at your association.

Annual Campaigns

Fundraising is a core knowledge and skill for YMCA professionals and an important part of an aquatics professional's career development. Thus, you should get involved with your association's annual campaign. If you are not asked to or it is not a part of your job description, volunteer to get involved. For example, you can do one of the following:

- Recruit volunteers to help in the campaign.
- Give suggestions for prospects.
- Be a staff aide to a campaign team captain or division leader.
- Coordinate a phone-a-thon.
- Coordinate the staff campaign.
- Help with campaign meetings (kickoff, report meetings, victory meetings).

Donations of Equipment/Funds

If you need equipment for your program, one option is to look for equipment donations from community businesses or from members. However, before searching for a prospective donor, inform your executive or financial development director about what you are planning to do and what you will be asking for. The financial development plan for an association is an organized effort. You will need to clear any prospects with your executive or financial development director before doing anything, as your needs may be able to be addressed in another proposal. A prospective donor may be annoyed by being called on by several staff members for a variety of needs; it is much better to have a coordinated approach.

Proposals (Development for Special Projects/Requests)

Your association may have allocated funds for special projects or new programs. To obtain these funds, you will need to follow a special process. Check with your executive for the proper procedures. In many cases, you will have to submit a program proposal or business plan. You can see a sample proposal on the YMCA intranet site.

Grants

You may fund projects you are considering by obtaining grants from foundations, organizations, and corporations. A wide variety of resources and training are available to assist you in locating potential grants to submit proposals and in grant writing. Check out the YMCA of the USA Web site (**www.ymcausa.org**) for some of these resources.

A proposal should reflect planning, research, and vision. The importance of research cannot be overemphasized, both in terms of the groups solicited and the types of funds requested. The appropriate format should be used, and the required attachments should be included.

The most successful proposals are those that clearly and concisely state the community's and organization's needs and are targeted to donors that fund that field, a reflection of careful planning and research.

In writing or evaluating a proposal, the following conclusions drawn from a University of Pennsylvania study may be useful. A study team investigated the criteria foundations and government agencies consider most important when reviewing proposals for community-based projects. They concluded that all funders consider these five factors "highly important":

- Project purpose
- Feasibility

- Community need for the project
- Applicant accountability
- Competence

Other factors also considered important include the following:

- Project logic
- Probable impact
- Language
- Money needed
- Community support

Fundraising Ideas for Program Support

Special fundraising events are a great way to get support for your programs and equipment purchases. However, you will have to follow your association's approval process before holding any fundraising event. Your branch executive, financial development director, or board need to consider several factors before granting approval for such events. Your YMCA may have agreed to blackout periods with the United Way or other organizations during which fundraising cannot occur. Also, you may not be aware of other scheduled local events, so this process reduces the likelihood that your event will conflict with such events.

You can plan several types of events, including the following:

- *Swimming marathons.* While these events can be organized in a variety of ways, essentially they are swims for which swimmers solicit donations for the number of laps or the length of time they swim during a certain period.
- *Fitness blasts.* A variety of special instructors come in and lead water workouts for a registration fee. The net over the expenses for the event supports a program or an equipment purchase.
- *Corporate or community challenges.* Teams are recruited to participate in a variety of events for awards. The fees charged to the teams, less expenses, are used to support designated programs or purchase equipment.

Other possibilities include invitational swim meets, water carnivals, water shows, and triathalons.

INTERACTION WITH OTHERS IN THE ORGANIZATION

In your role as aquatics director, you are one part of a much larger organization. You will have to interact smoothly and effectively with others in your YMCA to accomplish your goals for the department and the association. Here are some ideas for how to better work with your boss, how to run meetings effectively, and how to use storytelling to influence those within and outside of the YMCA.

Managing Up the Organization

You may have your hands full managing your programs and staff, but another, sometimes unrealized, part of your role is to "manage up the organization." What this means is becoming a valuable asset to your boss. If your boss feels good about you and your work, your department will benefit as well as you. Here are some tips to help you:

- Be a loyal team member.
- No surprises! Keep your boss informed. Tell her or him when you believe things are beginning to be a problem and what you are doing about it.
- Take the initiative and make an appointment with your boss for at least a few minutes every week or two to discuss current issues and needs in your department.
- If your supervisor doesn't have an aquatics background, make sure you describe your requests and needs clearly. Spend time on why something is needed or is important, especially if it is an aquatics issue.
- When you go to your boss with a problem or concern, come armed with possible solutions. Get your boss's feedback and direction.
- Exceed your boss's expectations and meet all deadlines.
- If you are working on a concern, issue, or problem and you believe that someone may ask your boss about it, describe it to your boss and explain what you are doing about it.
- Give honest and sincere input, ideas, and suggestions about the organization.
- Ask your boss to give you honest feedback on how you can improve.
- Invite your boss to some of your in-service training sessions and staff meetings and give him or her a role to play.
- Give your boss a one-minute positive intervention.
- Volunteer for or request to be included in additional assignments that will help you in your career plan or give you more experience. For example, you can coordinate a special event, help in the annual sustaining campaign, or be the staff liaison to a committee.

FACILITATING MEETINGS

In your role as an aquatics director, you will be organizing and planning all types of meetings. According to Rees (1991), facilitating an effective meeting is an important skill. In an effective meeting, all group members are involved. They are encouraged to be creative and to express different viewpoints, and they have time to analyze and solve difficult issues. Your role as a facilitator is to focus the group on the meeting's content by helping the members achieve clear objectives, encouraging high levels of involvement and participation, and leading them to consensus and closure.

In your Program Trainer Orientation course, you learned how to develop a training design. You can use the same format and principles, with minor modifications, for planning meetings.

Before calling a meeting, make sure you know the purpose of the meeting and if there is a real need for each individual to take the time to come. Everyone there should understand why their attendance is needed and should have the opportunity to share and discuss ideas or opinions during the meeting. Meetings should be dialogues.

Avoid meeting to discuss something that the group does not have the power or ability to change or for which the decision has already been made. Holding such meetings builds resentment when the members realize that they have wasted their time.

Determine if there is a real need for the meeting or if there is another way the information can be shared or obtained. Can holding a conference call, having an e-mail discussion group, or sending out a report result in the same outcome? You should identify specific expected outcomes of the meeting and allow an appropriate amount of time to complete the tasks and discussions involved.

If the meeting is about a report on earlier items, send out the information so people can read it before the meeting. Use the meeting time for discussion and action planning.

Organize the agenda items of the meeting in order of importance. According to Rees (1991), you should word the agenda items according to the objectives of the meeting, stating what needs to be accomplished. For example, a typical agenda item might read "Emergency procedures update"; a better wording would be "Review current emergency procedures and make necessary changes." This will help keep the discussion focused on the meeting objectives. Allocate adequate time for discussing or dealing with each item appropriately. Plan an adequate number of breaks, at least one every 90 minutes.

Rees (1991) also suggests that you encourage everyone to participate. Aim to achieve consensus and closure for each item on the agenda. For a meeting to be worthwhile, it needs to have an outcome and accomplish something.

The process used during the meeting is just as important as the content (Rees, 1991). Use the concepts you learned in the Program Trainer Orientation course to help you with facilitating effective meetings. The process you use can influence the quality of the decisions made at meetings and the commitment of the participants to carrying out those decisions (Rees, 1991).

Someone should be assigned to take minutes of meetings, whether it is a member of the group or a nonparticipant who is there only to take minutes. The minutes should reflect the discussion and outcomes for each agenda item. If individuals were assigned or agreed to certain responsibilities for action items, those should be noted. Include in the minutes the names of all members present, as well the time, date, and location of the meeting. Distribute the minutes to each of the members within a reasonable amount of time after the meeting.

STORYTELLING

Storytelling is a very powerful tool we can use to connect people. Storytelling has been used for years as a way of connecting the past, present, and future and can be used to connect people to others, as well as to the mission and the values of the YMCA. Thousands of stories exist in the YMCA, and if staff and volunteers all told stories, everyone would look at the YMCA differently. Stories could inspire, teach, comfort, and entertain everyone connected to the YMCA. People would truly see the "YMCA difference."

Storytelling can produce the following results:

- Promote the YMCA's mission
- Keep special things about the YMCA alive and ever present
- Communicate the YMCA's culture to staff members
- Enhance the YMCA's image and position in the community
- Get staff and volunteers to see "the big picture" and how their work and contributions are valued
- Underscore how and why rules and procedures should be followed

Storytelling can be used as a method of communicating information or ideas. Stories make information easier to remember and more believable. In stories, words create pictures in the minds of people that, combined with facts, create a powerful message. A great story will be repeated and remembered far more than any statistical, financial, or membership report. Stories confirm, modify, or change what we do, how we work, who we are, or who we want to be. They help connect people together into a small community that they can relate to and feel comfortable in.

Storytelling can be used as a management tool in training, such as using a business fable to teach staff about the concept of teamwork. Stories can have a powerful impact when you use them to reinforce why we have rules and regulations, why we want staff to be alert, or even how proud you feel when you save someone's life.

Take the time to listen and learn about stories developing every day around your YMCA, and think how you can tell them during meetings and trainings to reinforce a point that you want to make. If you think you don't have anything to tell a story about, try thinking about these topics:

- An individual feat or team accomplishment in the YMCA, yours and others
- What you are most proud of
- How the mission comes alive in your work area
- A member whose life has changed because of the YMCA
- Staff who have provided outstanding service
- Your heroes and your mentors in the YMCA
- Why the YMCA

Steps to Storytelling

Before telling any story, ask yourself three questions:

1. What do you want people to feel after they hear your story?
2. What do you want people to remember from your story?
3. What do you want people to believe as a result of hearing your story?

Once you know these three things, then you can begin to tell a memorable story. Seven parts contribute to the telling of a great story.

- *Plot.* Have one central plot in your story and keep it simple.
- *Characters.* Create interesting and fun characters. What do they look like? How do they sound? What are their mannerisms and motives? People need to be able to visualize the characters in the story.
- *Action.* People like action, lots of it. Suspense, not knowing what is going to happen next, is a particularly powerful form of action. The action (sometimes) must keep you on the edge of your seat.
- *Timing.* Keep your stories *short.* Most stories from folklore run five to seven minutes. In YMCA settings keep them shorter, one to two minutes at the most!
- *Fluency.* Practice telling the story several times first. Memorize the sequence of events. Do not memorize every word or you will lose your spontaneity.
- *Listening.* Listening to stories teaches you a great deal about the environment around you. This is one of the reasons walking around in your department regularly can be so effective. You hear stories as you talk to people.
- *Creative license.* Many stories have been changed to make them more colorful, but the key facts and messages should remain authentic.

Here are a few ideas:

- Include time for positive storytelling during meetings, for example, during board/committee or staff meetings.
- Promote informal get-togethers and encourage people to tell stories that have a positive message.
- For orientation activities for new staff and volunteers, have organization veterans tell stories to the newcomers.
- Incorporate staff and member stories into newsletters and brochures.
- Develop a "big" timeline to be displayed in the YMCA's lobby that incorporates YMCA stories and events that have happened and what happened in the world at that time.

For more information on storytelling, take the storytelling training course, YMCA Storytelling as a Management Tool, available from the YMCA of the USA.

CAREER DEVELOPMENT

Aquatics directors can take many career paths. You should take responsibility for determining what your path will be. Think through the career that you want to have and develop a plan for how to make it come true. Many opportunities are open to YMCA professionals on either program or management ladders.

Three possible elements of your career plan are training, experience, and mentoring. Take the time to develop a written career plan based on these elements, incorporating action items into your weekly planning lists.

Training Plan

One step in your career development is to develop a training plan. Figure 6.3 shows a typical training progression. See the "YMCA Resources" section for more training ideas.

Experience

Although training will help you, experience continues to be the primary criterion in getting your next YMCA position. When you decide you want to move to another position, factors that influence whether the doors will open include successful experience in the following:

- Program design and delivery
- Recruitment, retention, and management of staff and volunteers
- Staff development
- Pool management
- Budget preparation and accountability
- Development and delivery of training programs
- Supervision and responsibility for nonaquatic activities and staff
- Fundraising accountability
- Facility management
- Community development activities
- Ability to work with others, interpersonal skills

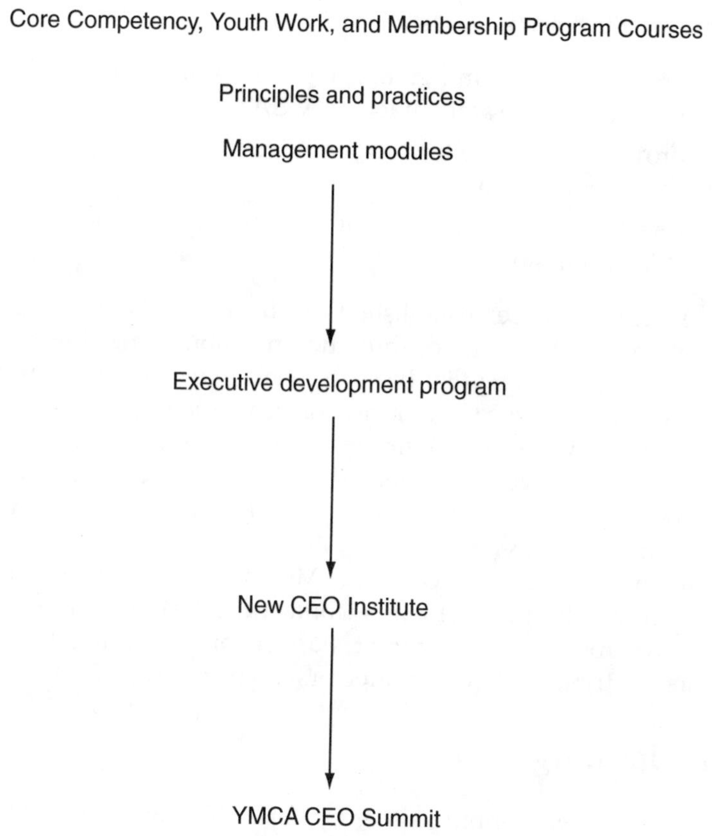

Core Competency, Youth Work, and Membership Program Courses

Principles and practices

Management modules

Executive development program

New CEO Institute

YMCA CEO Summit

Figure 6.3   Common training track for YMCA staff.

Here are other ways to promote your professional development:

- *Get involved.* Attend neighborhood and state aquatics meetings. Become a trainer in the YMCA of the USA training system. Volunteer for internal association committees. Join professional organizations such as the Association of Professional YMCA Directors (APD) or the American Alliance for Health, Physical Education and Dance (AAHPERD) Aquatic Council. Get to know other aquatics professionals in your community and state. Organize peer groups to meet and work on common goals.

- *Be informed.* Read aquatics-related materials in magazines such as *Aquatics International* or on aquatics-related Web sites. Write articles about programs and issues that you are passionate about and submit them for publication.

- *Develop yourself as a leader.* Read books and attend training and workshops on leadership, communication, team building, and time management.

- *Ask questions.* Get guidance and feedback. Call someone and get the answers you need.

- *Dress for success.* Your appearance should be professional and appropriate for the event.

Aquatics Director Mentoring Programs

Whether you are a new aquatics director or an experienced one, being involved in mentoring for professional development can be a good experience. Mentoring teams up new directors with experienced ones to help the new directors develop their skills and grow in the profession.

These are the objectives of such programs:

- To provide support and guidance to new aquatics professionals in order to enhance quality and safety at local YMCAs
- To provide an avenue for continuous training and learning opportunities, formally and informally
- To develop a strong network of high-quality aquatics professionals to further the YMCA mission

Once a team has been established, the team members should develop goals and expectations for their relationship and an action plan. The mentor should contact the new director on a regular basis to check on her or his progress.

Once you have selected your mentor, schedule regular meetings with her. Think about what you want to learn from your mentor and stay focused when she is teaching you. Take what you learn and adapt it to you and your situation. Let your mentor know when you've grown due to her assistance and show that you will stick with it until you succeed.

To get involved, contact your area Membership and Program Consultant. If you do not know who that person is, contact the YMCA of the USA to find out. If a mentoring program does not exist, start the process yourself. Develop a list of contacts and distribute it to other directors in your area.

Career Planning

You can do career planning either by yourself or with the help of your supervisor. Here are some definitions of different types of planning:

Career development: The outcome for an individual of personal or organizational career planning.

Career planning (individual employee): An active process in which an individual (with or without a supervisor's assistance) determines short- and long-term career goals specifically defined in terms of outcomes for the individual, rather than by job titles or positions within an organization.

Career pathing (the organization): An organizational process in which managers identify promotional possibilities and arrangement of current employees for (1) future succession possibilities (who might follow whom in key positions in the future), and (2) individual career planning, including training opportunities (where the employee might like to work next).

Career management (individual employee and the organization working together): Collaborative efforts between the individual and the organization that result in career development. This is an ongoing process actively pursued by employees, their supervisors, and the organization as a whole.

To do career planning, you must complete these tasks:

- Establish short- and long-range work *goals.*
- Identify the *resources* necessary to reach those goals.
- Set a *timetable* that can measure accomplishment of those goals.

Start by asking yourself these key questions:

- What knowledge and skills do I need to excel in my present job responsibilities? What new or different behaviors must I acquire for my performance to be rated as superior?

- What else do I need to understand about my YMCA—its history, organization, goals, finances, board governance, community impact, and so on? How would I systematically acquire this knowledge?

- What else do I need to understand about the nationwide/worldwide YMCA movement—its mission, structure, volunteerism, programmatic thrusts, and so on? How would I systematically acquire this knowledge?

- In addition to my specific job duties, what else do I need to do better to be a valuable contributor to my YMCA's operation: communicate with staff and members, make good decisions, solve problems, work with people in groups, train others, and so on? How would I systematically acquire these competencies?

Then use the worksheet in figure 6.4 to capture your thinking in response to these questions. For example, look at the first of the four key questions: What knowledge and skills do I need to excel in my present job responsibilities? What new or different behaviors must I acquire for my performance to be rated as "superior"?

First, identify the *what:* specific and concrete steps, actions, training courses, contacts, initiatives, or readings that you are committing to do.

Next, identify *by when:* by what specific date will the identified action occur?

Finally, describe *how well:* what new skills, beliefs, or behaviors will be evident—to you as well as to others—that will clearly demonstrate that you have successfully acquired new learnings and applied them in your work life.

Once you have completed your worksheet, transfer the action steps to your weekly/monthly planner. Then do this for each of the other three key questions as well.

As an example of how you might demonstrate new skills or behaviors, here are some observable ways to affect the financial health of your YMCA:

- Work in a productive, cost-efficient manner.
- Provide quality services/programs so that people will join the YMCA or retain their memberships.

Career Management Worksheet

My Career Plan		
What	By When	How Well . . .

Weekly/Monthly Planner

To Do:

To Call:

To Read:

Figure 6.4 Career management worksheet.

- Spread the good word about YMCA programs and the benefits of membership to increase membership and program participation.
- Share the YMCA's mission and "stories of success" so that people understand the importance of supporting YMCA programs and activities.
- Make your own personal contribution to your YMCA.
- Take good care of equipment and supplies so they last longer and can be used by others.
- Be resourceful. When you need an item or piece of equipment, look at alternatives to purchasing it new, such as getting it donated, buying a used one, or asking volunteers to make it.
- Don't be wasteful. Keep an up-to-date inventory of what you have and records on how and when it is used. This will enable you to order only what you need.
- Keep good records. Follow up on people who owe money.
- Start an employee contest for cost-cutting measures.

YMCA RESOURCES

Here are recommended core training and resources for aquatics directors.

Core Training

- Program Trainer Orientation
- YMCA Aquatic Management
- YMCA Pool Operator on Location
- YMCA Lifeguard and YMCA Lifeguard Instructor
- YMCA Swim Lessons Instructor and Trainer

Additional courses are recommended based on your interests and the needs of your association. See the YMCA of the USA Course Catalog for a list of all courses available.

Resources

- State and local bathing codes
- *YMCA Aquatic Management: A Guide to Effective Leadership*
- *Principles of YMCA Competitive Swimming*
- *YMCA of the USA Urgent Safety Bulletin* (July 1997)
- YMCA of the USA Medical Advisory Committee Statements
- *On the Guard II* (4th ed.)
- *YMCA Pool Operations Manual* (2nd ed.)
- *YMCA Swim Lessons Administrator's Manual*
- *YMCA Swim Lessons: Teaching Swimming Fundamentals*
- *YMCA Swim Lessons: The Parent/Child and Preschool Aquatic Program Manual*
- *YMCA Swim Lessons: The Youth and Adult Aquatic Program Manual*
- *Ready to Respond: Critical Issues in YMCA Aquatics in the 21st Century*
- *YMCA Water Fitness for Health*

Visit the YMCA of the USA Web site for regular updates about new materials and resources available. For site information, contact the YMCA of the USA at 800-872-9622.

BIBLIOGRAPHY

Blanchard, Kenneth. 1985. *Leadership and the One Minute Manager: Increasing Effectiveness Through Situational Leadership.* New York: William Morrow, Inc.

Rees, Fran. 1991. *How to lead work teams: Facilitation skills.* San Diego: Pfeiffer.

Fiscal Management

For fiscal purposes, local YMCAs are considered to be legal [501(c)(3) not-for-profit] entities. Fiscal management is the method by which the local YMCA manages its resources. It involves planning and control.

Planning is the act of detailing and articulating what the goals and objectives are for an upcoming fiscal period (usually a year). This planning process includes the details of the activities that are to take place and the resources that will be needed to support those activities. The sum of all the operating plans for the entire organization makes up the operating budget. Generally, the board of directors approves the annual operating budget.

In most organizations, the annual operating plan is an extension of a strategic plan that details long-term goals. The annual operating plan and budget should always be created so that it is in alignment with long-term strategies.

Control is overseeing actual expenditures and income to make them match the budget. Once the plan has been approved, the staff responsible for the individual budget areas enact the program or activity, incur expenses, raise money, and so on. The organization's accounting system then tracks the actual revenue and expenses and reports them *compared to the budget*. Where there are significant variances (actual minus budget), an explanation is required. Knowledge of variances helps the organization to know if there are changing conditions that could create a financial threat. The quicker we know there is a problem, the quicker we can react to it by making adjustments, changing plans or strategies to maintain our fiscal health.

In this chapter, we start by defining "operating plans" and "budgeting," then walk you through the process of creating a YMCA budget, starting with program budgets and going up to the association budget. We then tackle the procedures for creating a budget by reviewing the concepts of direct and indirect income, discussing break-even analysis, and describing possible income sources and expenses. We also talk about budget spreads and tips for good budgeting. After briefly discussing how to defend your budget, we finish with ideas for monitoring your budget and a description of the YMCA's system of accounting.

OPERATING PLAN

On completion of the strategic plan (as described in chapter 2), staff must prepare an operating plan for the upcoming year. An operating plan is a schedule of events and responsibilities that details the actions to be taken to accomplish the goals and objectives laid out in the strategic plan. A YMCA should have an annual operating plan that corresponds to its fiscal year for each major organizational unit. The plan ensures that all involved know what needs to be done, can coordinate their efforts when getting it done, and can keep close track of whether and how it got done. The operating plan includes the budget for all activities.

Imagine you were driving a car on a camping vacation. It would be important to have a destination in mind—your "long-range goal." Knowing the destination alone, however, would not be enough to get you there successfully. You would need to have detailed instructions about which roads to take and when to make turns, the estimated distance and time, where you could stop for food and gas, gauges that told you how much gas you had in your tank, and warning systems that told you if the engine overheated.

Now imagine that you were not driving the car alone, but instead you had 20 people doing different jobs simultaneously. Your organization's executive director would be at the steering wheel with a couple of board members looking over his or her shoulder; four others would be at each of the wheels making them spin; other people would be looking out each window, reporting what they saw to the driver; and someone else would be in the back making sandwiches. It would take an impressive plan to move this crew in the same direction.

This is the stuff of operating plans: which programs and management functions are going to do what, by when, and how much "gas" (money and person power) will it require. This level of detail is unnecessary in a strategic plan itself—in fact, it would clutter up the presentation of the long-range vision. The strategic plan focuses on the swimming hole at the camp you are going to, not on which gas station to stop at along the way.

A good operating plan has three important attributes:

- An appropriate level of detail—enough to guide the work, but not so much that it becomes overwhelming, confusing, or unnecessarily constrains creativity
- A format that allows for periodic reports on progress toward the specific goals and objectives
- A structure that coincides with the strategic plan—the goal statements for the strategic plan and the operating plan are one and the same; the objective statements for the strategic plan and the operating plan differ

Monthly financial statements often present a projected budget for revenues and expenses and then report actual figures for a given time period. Operating plans should allow for the same type of comparison. The plan declares the "budgeted" work in terms of goals and objectives for each program area and management function. The actual progress is reported by departments on a monthly or perhaps quarterly basis. Such a "budget-to-actual" report gives a clear reading on how the "trip" is going.

BUDGETING

Budgeting for YMCAs is a means to an end—the task of fulfilling human needs. Human need is a major factor in budgeting and goal setting. A budget is a human goal as well as a dollar goal. A budget is a plan expressed in numbers. It reflects the organizational priorities and program plans that are determined by the organizational and strategic plan.

A *budget* is a schedule of *anticipated* income and *authorized* expenditures. It is the *financial plan* on which the association is to operate during the year. The budget should be based not only on past performance, but also on projected growth expected for the year, taking into consideration *increased operating costs.*

A budget has built-in feedback that permits management to monitor, direct, and control the activities of the organization. It is a controlling instrument for financial operations in relation to actual income and expenditures. It is the goals adopted for effective financial management. A budget is an important "tracking" mechanism to help you see whether operations are going as planned and, if not, the reasons for the variances.

Each organization will have a different budgeting process because each organization plans differently, analyzes differently, and manages differently. Some core concepts and principles are common to many organizations, but there are differences. The budget process brings together many different kinds of decisions and information. Because they involve input from all parts of the organization, this often reflects both the strengths and weaknesses of the organization.

BUDGET PROCESS

Staff and volunteers formulate the budget together, but only the policy volunteers (the board of directors) may approve the budget. Depending on the size of your association or branch, this process varies, but the main concepts are consistent. Each department head is responsible for formulating her or his department's budget. With the help of key staff, each department head uses the individual program budgets to build her or his department's budget. Each department head should do the preliminary work and consult with the executive before submitting the budget. Once the branch budget has been completed, it is presented to the Branch Finance or Budget committee for consideration. Final approval of the budget is up to the board of directors of the association. In metropolitan associations, each branch board of management first approves the budget and then recommends it to the metropolitan board of directors for approval.

Each of these budgets builds on the next, as shown in figure 7.1.

Association budget branch or unit budget
↑
Department budget
(Aquatic, Health and Fitness, Administration, Child care, etc.)
↑
Program budget
(YMCA Swim lessons, Lifeguard, Water fitness, etc)

Figure 7.1 Budget sequence.

Program Budgets

Staff create program budgets for each of the main program areas for the association. In the aquatics department, this may include swim lessons and water fitness classes.

The number of program budgets included within a department varies by association.

Each program should be evaluated based on the number of sessions per year, the number of participants per session, and the related income/expense per session. If previous directors have kept good records, those records will provide a history of previous years for comparison.

The budget philosophy of each association will determine the degree of income over expenses needed to meet the percentage of department and association overhead to be distributed to each program.

Department Budgets

A *department budget* is the total income and expenses for a specific department. As an aquatics director, you must understand fiscal management and be involved with the budgeting process because you have specific and detailed knowledge of the aquatics department's programs and facilities. You know what is needed to make the department successful. Such knowledge is very important for developing a good budget. You are also responsible for making daily decisions that will affect the budget.

The budget will reflect how well your program is doing. It will be influenced by participation, scheduling, program quality, community needs, and many other factors. It will also reflect the quality of the decisions you make, as you will be the person making those decisions for the aquatics department. These decisions include the number of staff scheduled, the number of classes offered, whether or not to send staff home on a slow day, and how much time to spend on preventive maintenance and care of equipment. Finally, it will also reflect your problem-solving techniques. For instance, if the first session of swim lessons is short on participation, you will have to decide how to best make it up.

In preparing a department budget, do the following:

- Review carefully the budget preparation materials that you receive from your executive or finance department and make sure you understand them.
- Evaluate copies of last year's budget and budget preparation notes.
- Refer to program statistics by session and the budget history for the last three years.
- Understand the association's objectives for the year as they relate to the organizational priorities and strategic plan.
- Know what help or input will be needed and by when.
- Submit all pieces on or before the target date.
- Understand your association's method of assigning and determining overhead costs.
- The total of all the income line items becomes the department income budget, and the total of all expense items becomes the department expense budget.
- The amount by which the department income and expense budgets vary is a function of the association's budget philosophy.
- Keep a file of all your notes by line item so you can explain how you arrived at the figure.

Branch Budgets

Department budgets are combined to create the branch budget. It may need to be revised one or more times to achieve the desired result for the association.

Each association will have its own policy on how branch budgets are to be turned in to the association. Some will require that each branch balance, while others will have target surpluses and deficits so that, when combined, the association's budget will balance.

Association Budget

The association budget is the combination of all branch budgets. In a single-unit association, the department budgets are combined into an association budget.

After the association budget has been approved by the board, management should monitor it monthly looking for variances. Variances are favorable or unfavorable, not over or under. Variances can identify opportunities, define problems, aid decision making, and help coordinate efforts. Look for trends that require deeper examination and work to correct a problem or explore an opportunity.

The association budget should be realistic but should have some "reach" in it.

CREATING A BUDGET

To carry out their mission of service to members and the community on a long-term basis, YMCAs need to be not only "not-for-profit" organizations, but also "not-for-loss" organizations. YMCAs can provide programs and services only to the extent that they are able to obtain contributions and revenues to cover their costs. Analysis of program costs and revenues is needed to make sure that is happening and also to provide members, donors, funding agencies, and the public with clear evidence that funds provided to the YMCA are being used properly. Good intentions don't justify poor performance. We need to demonstrate good stewardship of the financial resources that are given to us.

A true picture of costs for a YMCA program must include an appropriate share of the cost of any building space it uses and of such shared support service activities as fundraising, accounting, personnel administration, and general management. Similarly, a true picture of revenues for a YMCA program must include its appropriate share of membership income, contributions, government contracts and grants, United Way funds, and other income.

We analyze program revenues and costs for the following reasons:

- To ensure that programs that are supposed to be carrying their own weight are actually doing so
- To see that programs that are supposed to be subsidized are actually being subsidized and by how much
- To base charges to members and program participants on a correct picture of actual program costs, subsidies, contributions, and other funding

A realistic understanding of program revenues and costs is also important in deciding which YMCA programs to expand, restructure, scale back, or eliminate in the future. Organizations that maintain and use such information on a regular basis are able to manage their programs better and to make a stronger case to funding agencies and donors than those who do not.

Let's start by describing the composition of the income and expense budgets for an association. Sources of earned income include the following:

- Membership
- Joiners' fees

- Program fees
- Facility rentals
- Sales of supplies

Sources of contributed income include these:

- Sustaining membership (annual campaigns)
- Special events
- United Way
- Foundation and grants
- Government contracts
- Special gifts
- Endowments
- Capital funds

Line items of expense include the following:

- Salaries
- Employee benefits
- Purchased, contracted, or donated services
- Supplies
- Telephone service
- Postage
- Rent and occupancy expenses
- Equipment cost (expendable or rented)
- Promotion and publications
- Travel and transportation expenses
- Conferences, meetings, and training
- Membership dues
- Awards and grants
- Insurance
- Miscellaneous

Costs related to salaries include these:

- Health benefits
- Retirement
- Unemployment compensation
- Worker's compensation
- FICA
- Training
- Vacation/holidays/sick days
- Liability insurance

When looking at the organization as a whole, we don't see any shared expenses that need to be added. However, when we look at particular program areas within the organization, we quickly recognize that several programs each share to some degree the costs and benefits of such items as the following:

- Building/occupancy expenses
- Liability insurance
- Operating debt
- Investment income
- Fundraising
- Membership
- General promotion
- Legal and accounting support
- General management
- Personnel administration

These shared costs and revenues must be properly allocated among the organization's various programs and added to the costs and revenues directly related to each program to determine the actual total costs and revenues of each program or activity. This brings us to the distinction between *direct* and *indirect* (or shared) income and expenses.

Direct vs. Indirect Income and Expenses

Direct income and expenses are those that are directly and exclusively related to a particular activity, product, service, program, location, or unit. Indirect income and expenses are those that are shared between two or more activities, locations, or units. For example, the cost of lifeguards, swimming instructors, pool chemicals and filter supplies, and water bills are clearly direct costs of a YMCA aquatics program. On the other hand, the cost of a facility executive, bookkeeper, telephone service, electrical service, and similar administrative and occupancy costs are indirect costs shared by aquatics and other activities operating in the facility.

Certain direct expenses are frequently incorrectly thought of as indirect expenses. In particular, payroll taxes and employee fringe benefit costs are often referred to as indirect expenses. However, payroll taxes and employee fringe benefit costs of employees working solely in a particular activity or location are direct expenses of that activity or location, not indirect expenses.

The difference between direct and indirect expenses is also sometimes confused with the difference between fixed and variable costs. However, both types of expenses may include both fixed and variable costs. *Fixed* and *variable* are terms that classify expenses on the basis of whether or not they vary with output. For example, the cost of keeping the swimming pool filled and properly conditioned is essentially fixed and does not vary with the number of swim classes conducted. However, the cost of swim instructor time is variable, as it can fluctuate with the number of classes conducted. Both are direct expenses of the aquatics program, as they are not shared with other departments.

The costs of shared support services are relatively fixed in the short run, similar to basics like rent and groceries for a family. The costs directly related to programs are relatively more variable in the short run and represent the activities that the organization can afford to purchase with funds left over after the basic support services have been paid for. The fixed costs of support services often equal or exceed the variable costs of total program activities. Therefore, programs must usually generate revenues (including contributions and other support) equal to two to three times their direct costs simply to break even, since both direct and indirect costs must be covered.

Accounting principles and federal contract regulations largely determine the allocation methods considered acceptable under specific circumstances. Your association will determine the methods of allocation to be used, and you should become aware of them for proper department planning.

This information is important to you because when you develop your budget, other calculations will be made to determine whether your program is showing a surplus or a deficit. The overall operation of the YMCA has expenses that will be allocated to every activity within the facility.

Here are some questions you should ask your supervisor when preparing your budget:

• Is the aquatics department responsible for all direct expenses relating to aquatics programming and facilities? For example, some associations may put all the pool chemical expenses into the property or administration budget.

• Are there income or expense items that lie in other departments' budgets that we need to prepare amounts for and submit to other departments? For instance, lifeguard salaries may be in the membership department budget; the aquatics department may have membership income allocations to the aquatics department budget; or the aquatics department may run a planned deficit and when the entire branch budget is pulled together, it balances.

Break-Even Analysis

Break-even analysis pinpoints where revenue equals total costs. The break-even analysis will help you determine how many participants or how much income you need to cover the direct expenses of that program. You may also add indirect expenses to the formula. Do a cost analysis before starting or canceling a program. This information will help you decide whether or not to begin or cancel the program or show that you need income from somewhere else to support it. It also can tell you how much the program can contribute to overhead.

To calculate your break-even point, determine the income based on participation and identify each cost as either fixed or variable. Fixed costs include items such as some staff costs, promotion, and equipment. Variable costs would include items such as supplies and equipment. Figure 7.2 is a cost-analysis form you can use to calculate the break-even point for a program.

Next we'll talk about sources of income and the many expenses that might come up in aquatics programs. Note that the discussion of budget items in this section includes direct program income and expenses but not overhead expenses such as utilities, insurance, or support payments.

Income

Income must cover expenses. Performing break-even analyses may help you to determine what the programs are likely to cost and thus what fees you should charge. Make sure that the fees you decide on will be sufficient and will meet your association's fee-setting objectives. You need to know what programs are included in your membership for no fee and the association's policies on setting different program fees for members and nonmembers.

Break down each of the dollar amounts on your budget to the number of participants of each program and the number of classes per session. This level of detail will help you manage the budget throughout the year. When you first come into a position and see the budget, you will want to find the detailed materials used to build

Program Cost Analysis Sheet

Branch _____

Date _____

Department _____

Income

_____ Members enrolled @ $ _____ fee for _____ sessions = _____

_____ Nonmembers enrolled @ $ _____ fee for _____ sessions = _____

Other income: 1400 — Merchandise sales net income   = _____

1700 — Miscellaneous income   = _____

Other: _____   = _____

TOTAL INCOME = _____

Direct Program Expenses

2120 — Program Salaries

Name or Position

_____ $ _____ × _____ hrs/session = _____

_____ $ _____ × _____ hrs/session = _____

_____ $ _____ × _____ hrs/session = _____

_____ $ _____ × _____ hrs/session = _____

_____ $ _____ × _____ hrs/session = _____

TOTAL SALARIES = _____

2200 - 2300 — Benefits/Taxes

Name or Position

_____ Full-time staff salaries x _____% = _____

_____ Part-time staff salaries x _____% = _____

TOTAL BENEFITS/TAXES = _____

2400 — Professional Fees: Persons or Companies

2500 — Supplies (items purchased specifically for this program)

Program equipment _____

_____ = _____

Awards/certificates _____ = _____

Office supplies (handouts, forms, etc.) _____ = _____

TOTAL SUPPLIES = _____

(continued)

Figure 7.2 Sample program cost-analysis form.

2700 — Postage

_____ = _____

2800 — Occupancy (rental of space or facilities)

Cost per hour/day/week $ _____ x no. of hours/days/weeks = _____

3100 — Promotion

Number of brochures/flyers _____ = _____

Distribution _____ = _____

Printing costs of brochures/flyers _____ = _____

Postage _____ = _____

Other (newspapers, radio, posters) _____ = _____

TOTAL PROMOTION = _____

3100 — Transportation

Mileage for staff _____ miles x _____ sessions = _____

Rental of vehicles _____ = _____

TOTAL TRANSPORTATION = _____

3200 — Conference and training

Instructor training: _____

Number of people _____ x fee $_____ = _____

Lifeguard training: _____

Number of people _____ x fee $_____ = _____

CPR and first-aid training: _____

Number of people _____ x fee $_____ = _____

Other: _____ = _____

TOTAL CONFERENCE AND TRAINING = _____

TOTAL DIRECT PROGRAM EXPENSES = _____

Indirect Expenses

Administrative overhead = total expense $ _____ x _____ % = _____
(include administration salaries and benefits, and all general office expenses such as utilities, insurance, etc.)

National dues and Metro support = expenses $ _____ x _____ % = _____

TOTAL INDIRECT EXPENSES = _____

TOTAL SURPLUS (OR DEFICIT) = _____

Figure 7.2 _(continued)_

the budget. If they aren't available, you will need to try to rebuild the budget so you have a clear idea of the expectations for each program.

Use the average number of participants per instructor to calculate your income from fees, and take into account your YMCA's policy on financial assistance and scholarships. Other possible sources of income include rentals of the pool to other organizations or donated income designated for scholarships or program support.

Track the number of individuals who participate at reduced rates, whether they are scholarships, in-kind employees, or credits for cancellation of prior programs. This affects your income calculations.

Expenses

Some of the main categories of expenses for an aquatics program are likely to be the following (the account numbers are ones commonly used by YMCAs):

- Salaries and benefits (account numbers 2100–2300)
- Equipment and supplies (account numbers 2500s)
- Rental of facilities and care of the pool (account numbers 2800s)
- Promotion (account numbers 3100s)
- Employees' expenses, such as mileage (account numbers 3200s)
- Training (account numbers 3300s)

Let's look at each one briefly.

Salaries and Benefits

The salaries for which you are most likely going to be responsible are those of the instructors, the lifeguards, the aquatics assistants, and yourself as the aquatics director. For all of these, remember to include the costs of taxes and benefits, using the current rates for payroll taxes, FICA, health benefits, and retirement. A current average percentage is 26 percent of the salary for part-time staff and 32 percent for full-time staff. Check with your director or human resources staff to determine what percentages you should use.

Staff Salaries and Benefits

To determine the cost of salaries for all your staff, you need to know the following:

- The number of classes per session
- The number of sessions per year
- The length of each class or program (usually 45 minutes for Youth and Adult programs and 30 minutes for Parent/Child and Preschool programs)
- All programs that will be operated during the year, including special events, day camp swims, rental groups, and birthday parties
- The number of instructors and assistants who will teach during each class period (for example, at some class periods you may have three instructors, at some six, and at some only two)
- The instructor/participant ratios (see pages 68-69 for the suggested ratios)
- The amount of time you require staff to be present before class starts or between classes or duty shifts
- Salaries paid for each staff member

- The training hours per year required for each staff member (for example, for instructors, 1 hour per session week for staff meetings plus 1 to 2 hours per session for instructor in-service training and 12 hours for orientation training) (See the chart in chapter 5 for the number of certification hours needed.)

See the program chapters in part II for information on other programs.

Lifeguards' Salaries and Benefits

Calculate the cost of lifeguards' salaries by determining the number of hours lifeguards will be needed per week and the number of lifeguards that will be needed to cover each program activity (classes, recreation, fitness, and competitive) scheduled. During the day, the number of lifeguards needed will change based on the activities scheduled. Once you know the number of lifeguard hours per week, multiply it by the total number of weeks the program operates during the year. This may change based on your sessions, so make adjustments.

You will also need to include hours for in-service training and certification per lifeguard position. For example, the training hours per year required for each lifeguard might be 1 hour a month for staff meetings; 2 hours a month for lifeguard in-service training for rescue readiness; 6 to 12 hours for certification renewal (CPR, first aid, AED, oxygen administration, lifeguard); and 12 hours for orientation training.

Other Situations

Here are some additional tips for special situations:

- If you plan to schedule special events that require staffing, be sure to add the appropriate number of hours for lifeguards or activity leaders.
- All or part of your aquatics director's salary may be allocated to the aquatics department or prorated to different program classifications (YMCA Swim Lessons, swim team) within the department. How much of it does depends on your other duties and your association's procedures for budgeting full-time staff. When staff spend their time working in more than one department, the salary, retirement, Social Security, and so on, may be prorated as a direct expense in the budget of each department.
- Nonexempt employees are full-time employees to whom overtime is paid. Make sure you allocate some dollars that may need to be paid for any authorized overtime worked by these employees.
- You may need to add to your expenses a line item relating to volunteer hours for things such as supplies and awards.

Equipment and Supplies

A number of different types of equipment and supplies are needed for running an aquatics program:

- Maintenance supplies (if not paid for as overhead).
- Medical supplies (if not paid for as overhead).
- Pool licenses (if not paid for as overhead).
- Program equipment and supplies. For example, for YMCA Swim Lessons, you will need instructional flotation devices (IFDs), personal flotation devices (PFDs) in various styles and sizes, youth masks and fins of various sizes, pencils (for parents to write up evaluations), an inflatable boat, toys, balls, a CPR mannequin, AED trainer, safety cones, rescue tubes, and backboards. Some of these may be used by other YMCA programs as well.

- Instructor and participant materials. For instance, for YMCA Swim Lessons, you will need skill sheets, progress reports, Family Huddles, parent education handouts, and progress cards (if not paid for as overhead).
- Training equipment and supplies, such as newsprint, markers, and overhead transparencies.
- Staff uniforms and supplies, such as hats, swimsuits, shirts, whistles, and sunscreen.

See the program chapters in part II for additional information for each type of program. Figure 7.3 is a sample equipment list based on three YMCA Swim Lessons classes (a total of 24 students and three instructors) operating at the same time.

Equipment List

✔ Kickboards   24

✔ Flotation belts   16

✔ Water logs   16

✔ Life jackets   (4 infant, 6 preschool, 8 youth, and 8 adult)

✔ Mask, fins, and snorkels (12 sets, a combination of youth and adult sizes)

✔ Balls   (4 sponge, playground, beach ball, and junior water polo)

✔ Rowboat or canoe and oars/paddles
  (an inflatable boat can also be used)

✔ Reaching pole

✔ Ring buoy

✔ Rescue tube

✔ Throw bags

✔ Toys

✔ CPR mannequin

✔ Resuscitation mask

Additional Equipment

✔ Hand paddles

✔ Pull buoys

✔ Foam flotation barbells

Note: If your equipment supply is low, as part of the planning of your pool organization, you may need to coordinate when each of the classes has access to the various equipment at different times during the class period.

Figure 7.3 Sample equipment list for YMCA swim lessons.

You have the responsibility for spending YMCA money wisely. When purchasing supplies and equipment, be concerned with quality, service, expedient delivery, and price. Get the best value for your money and time.

Before sending someone out to the local store for supplies and equipment, think through the best method for spending your dollars. Remember, there are costs for staff going to a store to make purchases, not only the dollar costs for their time, but also the costs for other things that are not getting done while they are gone. In addition, your YMCA may be exposed to liability if they are injured, cause injury to another person, or commit any act of negligence. A few trips may be unavoidable, but most staff shopping trips are not necessary with good planning.

Here are some tips for purchasing:

- Develop a list of common items you purchase and the quantities you typically use.
- Find a couple of vendors that will deliver to bid on those items. Choose the best vendor based on quality, delivery, service, and price.
- Develop an inventory log so you know when you are running low on supplies and equipment. This log should include the item description, quantity and date ordered, quantity and date received, quantity and date used, and quantity balance.
- Try to gain purchasing power by creating joint orders with other departments and YMCAs.

When you budget for equipment and supplies, use vendor catalogs to determine current prices. You can obtain the *YMCA Preferred Vendors Guide* with the names and phone numbers of vendors and *YMCA Purchasing Strategies for Saving Money and Time* from the YMCA of the USA Purchasing Department at 800-872-9622.

Postage

Use current bulk and first-class rates to budget mailing costs for promotional materials for programs.

Printing

These are the costs for printing brochures and flyers or program materials.

Rental of Facilities and Care of the Pool

If you rent facilities to operate your program, the rental fees go into this account. The expenses related to maintenance and operation of the pool, such as costs for pool chemicals, may be charged in full or in part to your aquatics department.

Promotion

The costs of promoting the programs may include paying for items such as the following, depending on your association policy on allocating promotional costs. Such costs may be assigned to one department, prorated to each department, or charged to a specific program when only that program is being promoted:

- Flyers
- Display ads
- Classified ads (for staff)
- A portion of the cost of a YMCA program brochure

- Posters
- Radio or TV ads
- Promotional giveaways

Employee Expenses

These expenses could include mileage and other expenses paid to employees relating to the programs. For instance, if the staff must drive to other locations, their mileage reimbursement is charged to this account.

Training

Under this category, include any costs from training events, such as registration fees, and related expenses, such as books and other printed materials. Typical types of training expenses are these:

- Specialty Aquatic Instructor certification (YMCA swim lessons, lifeguard, water fitness)
- Specialty Aquatic Trainer certification
- YMCA Lifeguard or Aquatic Safety Assistant certification
- Teaching YMCA Swimming certification
- Staff meetings and in-service training
- CPR/first aid training
- Other training and certification courses

Financial Aid

You should budget for financial aid given to participants. Many different methods are used to accomplish this; be sure you understand the procedures for your association. Often branches allocate a certain amount to a department for financial assistance to help keep overall costs down. They plan for a certain number of scholarships to be given to individuals who might receive financial aid in order to participate in programs and activities. These are tracked through the accounting system. In some cases, these are noted as a credit in a separate income account for financial assistance, while in others, they will be included in the program income account. This process is important for reporting to donors and the United Way, so check with your supervisor on how your YMCA handles this.

Budget Spreads

Once you have developed your annual budget and it has been approved, spread it over 12 months. This becomes your monthly budget. The association fiscal year varies among YMCAs. Some will follow the calendar year, while others may go from July to June, October to September, or November to October.

When you spread your budget over the 12 months, be as accurate as possible. Although some items can be divided by 12 and be fairly accurate, most need to be evaluated individually. Past year actuals can be helpful, but don't depend on them entirely. Consider changes in planned program schedules, session dates, new or eliminated programs, and peak times for staff needs, and make adjustments based on this information.

Tips for Good Budgeting

Here are some additional tips for good budgeting:

- Allocate the time needed to do it right. Doing the budget in sufficient detail in the development stage will save many hours throughout the year.
- Review budget comparisons and two-to-three-year comparisons of actuals if they are helpful in evaluating trends.
- Gather all the data needed and keep good records throughout the year. This will save countless time in budget development.
- There is a difference of opinion as to whether to budget income first or expenses first. We suggest that you develop earned income from programs as realistically as possible, then plan expenses for the programs.
- Document your numbers and be prepared to defend and justify your budget.
- Be aware of trends in the community and association priorities and make any necessary adjustments.
- Budget realistic wages; include projected raises, promotions, new hires, cutbacks, training hours, preparation and administrative time (if applicable).
- Use percentages and ratios to assist with performance analysis.
- Know the break-even points for your programs.
- Monitor program enrollments and make necessary adjustments right away.
- See that budget spreads reflect current-year plans.
- When projecting income and expenses, don't budget for full classes. Plan that some will and some won't be at capacity. For instance, for YMCA Swim Lessons preschool classes in which the instructor/student ratio is 1:6, if you planned on all classes being full, 2,400 preschoolers would be participating in your program for the year. That would be only 400 classes. However, it's unlikely that all classes will be full throughout the year, so use a modified ratio to make your expenses more realistic. For instance, using a 4.5:1 ratio would increase the number of classes to 533. By using 533 classes, your projection will be more realistic.
- Don't hesitate to ask for assistance. If you don't understand something related to fiscal management, find someone who will help you learn. Talk to your supervisor or someone in your finance department.
- Involve other staff and volunteers in the process.

DEFENDING AND JUSTIFYING YOUR BUDGET

After you complete your budget, you will probably be asked to present it to your supervisor or executive. You may even be asked to write a narrative about the primary components and key changes from the previous year. You will want to highlight the increased service to your members and community and any new programs, as well as how your budget directly affects the achievement of your association goals and priorities for the upcoming year.

After all the departments in your YMCA have submitted their budgets to the executive, it will be his or her responsibility to balance the overall budget. It is most likely that the executive will find the income does not match the expenses in the first round. The executive will then need to make decisions to cut expenses in order to balance. Most likely you will be asked to analyze your budget again and make recommendations on where you can cut expenses and make a case for why and where expenses cannot be cut. This is where difficult decisions need to be made.

Your careful preparation and knowledge of your budget can make a big difference in keeping it as intact as possible. If you can explain how your budget was based directly on participation and the staffing requirements for those participation numbers, and how those numbers are based directly on the regulations, operating policies, and priorities of the association, you can substantiate your case.

If you must cut expenses, you will also need to adjust your income projections; there should be a direct correlation between both areas. Remember, other department heads will want to keep their budgets intact just as much as you do. You just need to be ready to make the better case.

MONITORING AND MANAGING THE BUDGET

Once your budget has been approved, you will then be responsible for monitoring the budget and making it balance. In this section, we'll first tell you how YMCAs in general monitor their budgets, then give you some tips on how to keep tabs on your own budget, and finally describe the YMCA's system of accounting numbers.

Administration and Control of the Budget

The staff has primary responsibility for budget administration and control. The CEO/general director is responsible for working with the branch executives, metropolitan staff, and the Business and Finance Committee to keep all operations within budgetary limitations as much as possible.

Each branch executive, together with the branch board of management, is responsible for keeping the branch income and expenses within budgeted amounts. The branch executive sees that department heads in the branch keep their department operations within the department budgets, month by month.

Each department head should receive a copy of the budget and a monthly financial statement for the operations for which she or he is responsible. Effective management demands that each person know what is expected of him or her and what progress is being made toward performance goals.

The income budget is a goal of achievement for each department. It should be a standard of performance for which the department head is held accountable. Department heads and the executive should receive daily income reports that show the production of income to date in order to achieve monthly income goals.

The total association or branch budget should balance by the end of the fiscal year. However, monthly budgets may not balance because of the seasonal nature of the program.

Here are some helpful methods for monitoring budgets:

- Know your budgeted income and expenses for each month. Don't wait for the monthly statements because, if you need to make adjustments, this delays progress. Instead, monitor weekly income reports and track expenses as they are turned in for processing.

- Know your session enrollments for each program. Monitor registration for each session, and compare enrollment to previous years.

- Variance reporting is a good way to keep up with what is going on. Do midmonth and end-of-month variance reports. In a variance report, you evaluate each line item based on budget and last year's actuals. For any variance over/under $250 (or some other amount recommended by your executive), describe why you believe the variance has occurred, what you are doing to improve the variance, and project the variance for the next 15 days on midmonth reports.

• Develop contingency plans that you can quickly adopt if either unexpected funding comes in or anticipated levels of funding or program participation don't materialize. For programs relying on fees, identify benchmarks where, for example, the revenue must be at a certain level by a certain date or an alternative plan/budget must be adopted.

• If you notice that income is not coming in as projected, think of ways you can increase program participation. This may mean making phone calls to last-session participants, sending out flyers to current participants, contacting program participants in other departments (child care, Y-Guides, or youth sports), or submitting press releases to local newspapers. (See "Increasing Enrollments" in chapter 3.)

• If your expenses are higher than projected, prompt action is needed. Let your executive know right away; explain why it is happening and what you are going to do to improve the situation. However, never sacrifice safety to meet the budget.

• Excess expenditures often come up with salaries. Make sure staff are not clocking in earlier than scheduled or staying later. Carefully monitor class enrollment compared to the number of instructors teaching. Allowing classes to operate at very low ratios makes a significant impact on your salaries account, and most likely the income is not there to support it.

• Gather payroll estimates based on hours turned in after each payroll period.

• Charge income and expenses to the proper accounts so that you can really use the budget and reports as management tools. If you charge items to line accounts that have funds available rather than charging them to the proper accounts, it's more difficult to get good information about the programs and what is happening. If you charge to the wrong accounts, you will give yourself false information for future budgets.

• When the financial reports and general ledgers are ready for each month, evaluate them and make sure charges are being coded to the proper accounts. If some charges are not properly coded, track down where they should be going and submit proper journal entries.

• Indicate actual income and expenses on the monthly budget breakdowns after monthly financial reports are available. It will be helpful to you in creating budget breakdowns for the following year.

• Keep a file of what you want to change for next year.

• Keep track of equipment that needs to be replaced and in what month and year.

• For any grants you are awarded, make sure record keeping is up to date and receivables are coming in as scheduled.

• Try to earn more than you spend. It is good to have a surplus, which is not a profit. Since the YMCA is a tax-exempt organization, there is no such thing as a profit. There is only a surplus.

Account Numbers

This section describes the standard YMCA chart of accounts and the procedure involved in classifying and coding transactions uniformly. The chart of accounts is a systematic listing of transactions and fund balances by type. It is designed to provide you and others with the detailed information needed to prepare proper financial statements and to manage the organization effectively and efficiently.

In the standard YMCA chart of accounts, each type of transaction and fund balance is identified by name and numerical code. It also includes a systematic structure for identifying and classifying transactions and fund balances by fund, program or function, location, department, district, and corporate entity. Be sure that you refer to your chart of accounts and are careful to allocate income and expenses to the proper accounts. See table 7.1 for a sample chart of accounts commonly used in aquatic departments.

The standard YMCA chart of accounts includes three principal components, each of which may also have additional subcomponents:

- Fund/Classes Location (Branch/Division and Department)
- General Ledger Account (Major codes)
- Program Classification Structure (PCS codes)

The components and subcomponents are defined by a 16-digit coding system.

Classifying income and expenses by branch/division location and department is necessary to provide financial and operating information on program operations that can be analyzed to assess the performance of the unit or program. This is how the first component, Fund/Classes Location, is identified. The funds designation can be unrestricted, temporarily restricted (e.g., custodial or building and equipment), or permanently restricted (e.g., endowment or annuity funds). The location codes identify the branches or divisions.

The General Ledger Account numbers used are broken down by the major income and expense areas; from that, minor income and expense numbers are assigned. These are then used consistently across the association. This helps in managing and communicating about the budget. Here's an example:

2100s   Salaries

2110	Professional staff salaries
2120	Program staff salaries
2121	Aquatics program staff salaries

The Program Classification Structure (PCS) of the YMCA of the USA is used to identify and code the various activities carried out by YMCAs. PCS codes are divided into major and minor categories that are defined consistently and that satisfy both the accounting and reporting requirements of the United Way and other funding sources. This system also provides for uniformity and comparability of fiscal and statistical data related to YMCA programs to ensure better information for planning, reporting, evaluation, and decision making. For instance, codes can be assigned for specific programs and activities relating to aquatics, including water fitness, swim lessons, swim team.

02 (aquatics-program category)

0201 (aquatics-water fitness (program activity))

020134 (aquatics-water fitness-arthritis [AFYAP](specific program activity))

So the complete account number coding for AFYAP instructor salaries would be

01-1020-2121-020134

How income and expense transactions are reported directly determines how they are classified. In a YMCA standard financial system, income and expense transactions normally are classified in three different ways. First, a transaction is classified within the fund in which it is incurred, for example, unrestricted. Second, a transaction is classified by location, such as branch/division or department. Then it is classified as the general ledger account type, such as salaries or supplies. Finally, it is classified by the functional purpose (or program classification) for which it was expended. Therefore, a transaction can be classified and numerically coded through the following four-step process:

	Numeric code position
Fund classification	
Unrestricted fund	10
Location classification	
Central branch	10-20
Aquatics department	10-2030
General ledger account	
Aquatics program salaries	10-2030-2121
Program classification (PCS)	
Aquatics water fitness arthritis program	10-2030-2121-020134

Table 7.1 Chart of YMCA General Ledger Accounts Summary

Table of 4-digit "major" GL accounts commonly used by aquatic directors (other accounts are available: see *YMCA Financial Management; Guidelines for Accounting and Financial Activity* from YMCA of the USA)

Public Support and Revenue Accounts Public Support

_ Received Directly

0100 Contributions

  0110 Individuals and Businesses

  0120 Foundations and Trusts

  0130 Nonprivileged or Sustaining Memberships

  0140 Contributed Services and Materials

  0150 Other Contributions

0300 Special Events

  0301 Special Event "A"

  0302 Special Event "B"

0500 Legacies and Bequests

_ Received Indirectly

0700 Contributed by Associated Organizations

  0730 Swim Team

  0740 Unassigned

0800 Allocated by Federated Fund-Raising Organizations

  0810 United Way Regular Allocations

  0820 United Way Special Allocations

Table 7.1 *(continued)*

0900 Allocated by Unassociated and Nonfederated Fund-Raising Organizations

1000 Fees and Grants from Government Agencies

 1010 Purchase of Service Fees

 1050 Grants

 1080 Contracts (Note: The fourth digit could be used to denote city, state, or federal government.)

Revenue

1100 Membership Dues (11X9 Refunds for all Subdivisions)

 1180 Daily Fees (all)

 1189 Refunds Daily Fees

1300 Program Service Fees

1400 Sales of Supplies and Services

 1410 Sales of Supplies and Services to Local Member Units

 1450 Sales to Participants

1600 Miscellaneous Revenue

Expense Accounts Expenses

2100 Salaries and Wages

 2120 Program

 2160 Maintenance and custodial

2200 Employee Benefits

 2210 Medical, dental, and hospital plan premiums

 2220 Pension and retirement plan premiums

 2230 Group life insurance premiums

 2240 Disability insurance premiums

 2260 Supplemental payments to pensioned employees

2300 Payroll Taxes, Etc.

 2310 FICA payments (employer's share)

 2320 Unemployment insurance premiums

 2330 Worker's compensation insurance

 2340 Disability insurance premiums (State Mandated)

2400 Purchased, Contract or Donated Services

 2440 Contract service fees

 2441 Custodial

 2442 Pool Maintenance

 2490 Donated services

2500 Supplies

 2510 Office

 2520 Maintenance buildings and grounds

 2530 Medical

 2540 Recreational, vocational, and crafts

(continued)

Table 7.1 *(continued)*

2550 Food and beverages

    2560 Laundry, linen, and housekeeping

    2570 Merchandise purchased for resale

    2580 Subscriptions and periodicals

2600 Telephone

2700 Postage and Shipping

    2710 Postage and parcel post

    2720 Freight in or out (unless charged elsewhere)

    2730 Messenger Service

    2740 Bulk, Third Class

2800 Occupancy

    2810 Building rental

    2820 Licenses and permits

    2830 Utilities

        2831 Electric

        2832 Gas

        2833 Oil

        2834 Coal

        2835 Steam

        2836 Water and sewage

2840 Maintenance of buildings and grounds

        2841 Maintenance and repair materials

        2845 Maintenance and repair contract service

2900 Equipment: Cost Expendable or Rented

    2910 Equipment rental

    2920 Equipment licenses and permits

    2930 Expendable equipment purchases

    2940 Maintenance of equipment

        2941 Equipment maintenance and repair materials

        2945 Equipment maintenance and repair contract services

3100 Printing, Publications, and Promotions

    3110 Advertising

    3120 Preparation of Promotional Materials

    3130 Publications

    3140 Promotional Literature

    3150 General Promotions

3200 Travel and Transportation Expenses

    3210 Food and lodging

        3211 Food costs Out of Town

Table 7.1 *(continued)*

        3215 Lodging costs Out of Town

        3218 Food costs Local

    3220 Transportation fares

    3230 Local transportation

        3231 Bus and taxi fares

        3235 Mileage allowances

    3240 Other employee expenses

3300 Conferences, Conventions, and Meetings

    3310 Meeting space and equipment rental

    3320 Meeting supplies and related costs

    3340 Meeting food costs

    3350 Conferences

3400 Specific Assistance to Individuals

    3410 Materials and appliances: crafts, vocational, prosthetic

    3450 Transportation

3500 Membership Dues

    3510 Fair share support, National Council of YMCAs

    3520 Dues organizational

    3530 Dues individuals

3600 Awards and Grants

    3630 Scholarships and tuitions

3700 Financing Costs

3800 Other Insurance Premiums

3900 Miscellaneous

4000 Depreciation or Amortization

4800 Intra-YMCA Allocation of Expenses (contra to 1800)

5300 Current Budgeted Fixed Asset Purchases

    5350 Equipment

5800 Board Appropriations

5900 Other Changes in Fund Balances

    5951 Fixed-asset purchases

Communication and Program Promotion

An important part of your planning involves promoting your aquatics programs. Your primary role in marketing and promotion will be developing quality programs that bring members into your YMCA because they are fulfilling an identified need. However, knowing effective ways to promote your programs will help you and others at your YMCA to get the word out and highlight the key benefits your programs offer.

We start by getting you acquainted with two of the basic concepts for good communication and promotion: target audiences and key messages. Then we look at how you can improve your YMCA's image with members and in the community and the steps your YMCA can take to generate good word-of-mouth advertising about your facility and programs.

Next we talk about various ways to promote your aquatics programs. Some of those we discuss here are internal communication with members, printed pieces, public service announcements (PSAs), and stories in the media, including special events. This is followed by ideas and a worksheet on how to create a promotional plan. Finally, we discuss how you can get more information about how people view your YMCA and programs through focus groups or individual depth interviews.

Before we even talk about how to communicate about and promote programs, though, let's start with some basic communication concepts.

BASICS OF COMMUNICATION

When you want to let the public know about your YMCA and your programs, you first need to decide which groups of people would be most interested in what you are offering. This will be your target audience. Then you need to formulate a few key messages that succinctly describe the unique qualities and benefits of your YMCA or programs. You can use these key messages in whatever form of communication or promotion you choose, from one-on-one conversations to TV ads and printed flyers. This helps ensure that people hear a consistent message about the YMCA or program over and over again.

Target Audiences

One of the first few questions you need to ask yourself is which people you want to reach and whose behavior or thinking you need to influence. This helps you formulate your target audience. Aquatics programs can reach people of all ages and all abilities, so target audiences will differ based on which program you are promoting.

For each program, think through which groups of people you want to reach. Whose behavior or thinking do you need to influence in order to gain participants for your program? Think of who ultimately has the power to decide about participation. You may want to list all possible groups, then focus on those that are most significant. For instance, what you would highlight to motivate kids to participate in a program is different than what parents would look for.

Let's look at YMCA Swim Lessons as an example. Different audiences will be attracted to each of the three aquatics programs:

• The Parent/Child Aquatic Program for children under three years of age appeals mainly to parents of young children. Exposure to your program may be their first experience with your YMCA. A positive experience in this program can lead to parents' further investment and involvement in the YMCA as they trade in their program memberships for family memberships.

• The Preschool Aquatic Program is for children ages three to five years. This program is attractive to parents who want their young children to learn safety in and around the water.

• The Youth and Adult Aquatic Program appeals to parents who want to see progress in their children's swimming proficiency. They may hope their children will be able to join the swim team or participate in other aquatic sports someday (and the kids themselves may have similar aspirations). The parents are looking for a safe, caring environment for their kids; the kids are looking for fun. Adult candidates for this program may have developed a fear of the water as children, may never have had the opportunity to take lessons, or may be comfortable in water but interested in improving their skills.

Another target audience is the media. Helpful hints for working with television, print, and radio media are included later in this chapter. Be sure to designate a media spokesperson for your aquatics program. Find out the policy for your association for specific media contacts and procedures. The spokesperson should be able to answer questions about your aquatics programs, water safety, and related issues and trends. Be sure your spokesperson reviews all the appropriate materials in this manual, and give him or her copies of any material you send to the media. Make sure all your staff members know who the spokesperson is.

Key Messages

Develop key messages for your program before beginning any promotion. Evaluate the program and determine its benefits and features for the target market you are trying to attract. To do this, first think about the program features as "What are we selling or promoting?" Then, for each of those features, ask yourself "So what? What does this feature mean to the customer?"

As an example, here are some key messages for YMCA Swim Lessons:

• The YMCA Swim Lessons programs promote children's health and safety.

• The programs support parents and encourage their participation in teaching kids valuable life skills.

- YMCA Swim Lessons stress positive values and give kids the opportunity to practice them, promoting kids' growth in self-esteem and self-worth while they are having a great time.

- For the Parent/Child component of the program, stress the benefits of both parents and their babies spending time together, which helps them bond and grow closer. Making this point helps position the YMCA as an organization that strengthens families.

You might want to use focus groups to help you develop key messages for particular programs. See "Focus Groups/Individual Depth Interviews" for more on this process.

All promotional pieces should include the YMCA's national theme, "We build strong kids, strong families, strong communities," as supported by the following strategic positioning statement:

The YMCA movement is something different and special. We are particularly relevant to today's society because we fill a void in the community. We put Christian principles into practice. We welcome and support children and families and help build the values of caring, honesty, respect, and responsibility. We are for everyone—people of all ages, races, religions, incomes, and abilities. The YMCA builds community.

A positioning statement is a communications tool. Just as the consistent use of a logo gives communications pieces visual unity, the uniform use of a positioning statement gives such pieces a consistent tone. The statement should serve as a blueprint for all types of communication: one-on-one meetings, personal notes, newsletters, annual reports, fundraising pieces, program brochures, ads, and other pieces. This is true whether the communication is going to members, program members, board members and other volunteers, paid staff, donors, the media, community leaders, or the general public.

IMAGE

Image is the community's perception of you. Perception is reality when it comes to our image. Your task is to give them a positive feeling about your YMCA, but creating a positive image is an ongoing process. Factors involved in developing an image of the YMCA include the following:

- How the facility looks
- The YMCA's image in the community
- Staff behavior and attitudes
- Image-enhancing materials
- Consistency

How the facility looks includes its cleanliness, décor, and maintenance. The cleanliness of the facility reflects on the YMCA's image. How well the staff cares for it gives members and participants certain perceptions and feelings. Are the facility, locker rooms, and pool deck clean and orderly? Are the grounds well maintained? Is the facility well maintained, with fresh paint in pleasing or energizing colors? Do the pictures and other decorations reflect what you want people to feel about the YMCA? Are the YMCA of the USA's purpose, goals, and mission statement visibly posted and included in program guides? The YMCA's national theme is "We build strong kids, strong families, and strong communities." When your members walk into your YMCA, will they have that perception? These are questions you should

ask yourself, and you should do your part to see that they can be answered positively.

Community image relates to the roles the YMCA plays in the community. Is the YMCA involved in improving the community, and is it a partner in solving community problems? Does the YMCA participate in community events such as "Community Days," blood drives, or disaster shelter location? Do all members of the community feel welcome at the YMCA—people of all ages, ethnic and economic groups, and abilities—or is it seen as a place for only a small segment of the community? Does the YMCA get involved with community issues like offering after-prom parties, health fairs, or aquatics and boating safety activities? Does the YMCA partner with local hospitals, schools, and park districts on programs instead of viewing them as competition? Do staff regularly give presentations to community groups on what the YMCA is doing? Do they plan collaborative events and activities with other community organizations?

The quality of the staff working in and around a YMCA also affects the quality of the experience for our members and program participants. Do staff members dress professionally, whether in a uniform or street clothes? Are staff members recognizable and available to meet and address participants' and members' questions and needs? Do staff members have the qualifications and training needed to perform their job functions appropriately? Is customer service a priority for all staff? How are members and program participants treated when they register? What kind of information are they given, and how much time is taken to make sure they choose programs that will meet their needs? People will also respond to staff behavior such as the following:

- The amount of personal attention they get from class instructors
- Whether problems and complaints are handled courteously and in a timely manner
- Whether phone and written inquiries are answered promptly and correctly
- When volunteers and employees talk enthusiastically and positively about the YMCA to friends and neighbors
- When employees are courteous and positive in their informal interactions with each other and with members

The appearance of materials such as YMCA business cards, stationery, promotional materials, letters, bulletin boards, brochure racks, and interior and exterior signage affects people's image of the YMCA. These materials should have a clean, professional look.

Consistency in all the areas we just touched on should help you project the desired image of the YMCA. Someone should coordinate these efforts, and enhancing the YMCA's image should be a priority for all staff and volunteers.

WORD-OF-MOUTH PROMOTION

Personal communications are almost always more effective than mass media or the written word. One person talking directly to another has much more impact. So it is important to understand word-of-mouth advertising and to concentrate on how to maximize those efforts. We will also discuss the other methods and how to use them as effectively as possible, but don't forget the most important one.

According to the YMCA of the USA's Research and Planning Department, more than 60 percent of the people who join your YMCA have been referred by a friend, neighbor, colleague, or acquaintance. Word of mouth is the YMCA's most powerful membership and program recruitment tool. Advertising builds awareness so when consumers are ready to purchase, a product or service will be at the top of their mind. Word of mouth encourages action.

The following excerpt is taken from the California YMCAs' *Image Development Guide*, written by Dave Cason and Larry Rosen for the YMCA of Metropolitan Los Angeles:

> *The most elaborate advertising campaign cannot buy what word of mouth offers— credibility. Consumers are sophisticated about advertising and skeptical of it. That's why most of those who contact the YMCA do so because of a referral from a friend or associate. Research shows that people rely most heavily on the judgment of others when evaluating products and services. Some 40 percent say that other people are their most reliable source of information for making buying decisions, while only 6 percent rely on advertising. Word-of-mouth advertising works because most consumers prefer not to experiment. They would rather buy what has been tested and accepted by others— especially by those they trust. Ultimately, the opinions of others minimize risk.*

Cason and Rosen also say that word-of-mouth advertising campaign can be very effective, and given that large resources may not be available for paid advertising, it should be your first consideration in developing a promotion plan. Here are 10 steps they suggest you consider in designing a word-of-mouth campaign for your YMCA:

1. **Present high-quality programs.** The success of word of mouth ultimately depends on the quality of members' experiences and their perception of that quality. The aquatics programs offered at your YMCA must be congruent with the needs and expectations of the participants. When we meet or, preferably, exceed the expectations of members, they will on average enthusiastically tell four or five others. Conversely, dissatisfied members are twice as likely to communicate their concerns and will communicate their dissatisfaction to an average of 26 people.

2. **Be congruent.** For example, YMCAs that aim to serve families must recognize the importance of ensuring that programs, scheduling, staff systems, facilities, and equipment— the whole YMCA "environment"—are congruent with the needs and characteristics of the families in their area. Basic to the idea that a satisfied parent will attract other parents to the YMCA is the fundamental requirement that the parent immediately and consistently identify that everything about the YMCA "feels right for me."

3. **Do more than serve people; involve them.** From the first moment of contact with a new member or program participant, everyone who works at the YMCA should make it a primary goal to promote that person's expanded involvement in the YMCA. Providing quality service merely sets up the conditions that increase the likelihood that a person will welcome broader involvement; quality service is a means to a more important end, not an objective in itself. People who are "served" are cast in the roles of buyers and users; people who are involved as co-owners in what the YMCA delivers come to see themselves as partners and advocates. Partners and advocates actively invite others to join them in the membership experience.

4. **Encourage people.** The most important part of word-of-mouth advertising is to get people talking about your YMCA. One of the best ways to do this is through sampling. Guest visits and one-week trial memberships provide opportunities for prospective members to sample programs. Sampling opportunities can be presented in many ways, such as guest passes, open houses, demonstrations, and special events. For the aquatics program, offering the YMCA Splash program (see pages 86-87) and holding open houses with class demonstrations are sampling opportunities.

5. **Promote good internal communications.** Well-informed staff and members should be able to communicate effectively to others about our offerings and their value. An internal communications program should include a newsletter with valuable information items, educational articles, and profiles of members whose experiences have been exceptionally positive. Training for frontline staff and volunteers—desk staff, fitness instructors, lifeguards, swim instructors—in how to interpret our work is vital, since most people's impressions about the YMCA result from interactions with them. They should routinely talk to members and participants about service opportunities and involvement with the YMCA. Displaying messages on posters and bulletin boards inside facilities are also useful ways to reinforce or communicate new messages to members.

For your aquatics program, work with your membership and marketing staff to publicize stories about participants in your program. Be an advocate for your aquatics program; tell stories about your participants and how aquatics has made a difference in their lives. Find spaces near the pool, such as bulletin boards in high-traffic areas, in which to communicate messages.

6. **Create champions.** Work at catching staff and members saying good things about your YMCA. Reward and recognize them immediately when it happens. Some YMCAs display members' pictures and written profiles about them on bulletin boards. This and other personal recognition programs encourage positive "insider" talk.

7. **Run a "no hassle" program.** Eliminate as many irritations to participants as possible. Simplify forms and provide easy-to-understand explanations and instructions. Offering an unconditional service guarantee assures members that we are committed to seeing that they are satisfied. This can be very effective in building confidence with members and frontline staff.

With your aquatics program, fine tune your program schedules to make classes as convenient as possible for families with multiple children. Offer different combinations of levels and have multiple instructors.

The number of pool hours scheduled for classes and programs vs. the number of hours for lap swimming and recreation is a constant issue in most aquatics departments. Set priorities for facility scheduling, but seek out alternative locations and use creative scheduling to try to accommodate members' needs.

8. **Seek out members' complaints.** Of all our members, 96 percent are unlikely to tell us their concerns. We know that when members' concerns are resolved satisfactorily, they tend to be more loyal and more likely to say positive things about the YMCA. So an essential element of a word-of-mouth advertising program is actively

soliciting complaints and practicing recovery—problem solving and putting things right when they go wrong. Member forums and telephone hotlines can be effective ways of eliciting feedback from members.

In your aquatics program, your involvement and presence during class times can be helpful in building a rapport with the parents in your program. As you build a relationship with them, they will feel more comfortable about talking to you about their concerns, big and little. Also consider using evaluation forms during each session and asking questions that will give you insight into your program from their perspective.

9. **Be role models.** YMCA leaders must model the behavior that they seek from staff, volunteers, and members. They must communicate a clear, consistent, and positive message, knowing that others will emulate them.

10. **Strive for consistency.** All external communications should be consistent with what staff and members are saying about your YMCA. Ideally, what we communicate to the public will reinforce the messages that are conveyed internally.

A word-of-mouth advertising program consists of thousands of little steps that lead to a powerful method of communicating our work to the community. It is an ongoing process that is best managed through careful planning. More important, no amount of promotion can substitute for the previous guidelines, nor can it overcome deficiencies in these areas. Until your YMCA has made significant and substantive strides in each of these 10 areas, external communication could actually do you more harm than good. Many successful companies enjoy robust health and steadily increasing sales by concentrating solely on these 10 areas while doing no mass advertising whatsoever.

PROGRAM PROMOTION

Many methods are available to you for promoting your aquatics programs. Consider those listed here and think about which of them will reach your identified target audience best at the lowest cost:

- Bulletin boards
- Mall displays
- Yellow pages
- Brochures
- Posters
- Direct mail
- Video/slide presentations
- Billboards
- Display ads in newspapers and magazines
- Newspaper or magazine articles
- Cooperative promotions with community businesses or organizations
- Radio ads or appearances on talk shows
- TV ads or appearances on talk shows

These methods may be used to reach members and participants or to communicate with those in the larger community. Methods to reach the community may include print pieces, publicity through other organizations, public service announcements, media features, and special events.

Communications With Members/Participants

Promote aquatics programs in any internal communications tools you might have, such as well-placed bulletin boards in high-traffic areas and employee, volunteer, and member newsletters. Try to communicate with your members at least eight times per year. You also can promote programs on your YMCA's Web site home page. Use artwork to give your articles and displays a fun look. Photos of kids having a great time in the water are always good for catching people's attention. Choose photos that are representative of your community and reflect member involvement.

If you are recruiting volunteers, include a "Wanted: Caring Adults" notice with a brief job description. Remember to state the need or problem to be solved, what the volunteer can do to help fill the need or solve the problem, and what the volunteer will get out of it. For instance, your notice might read, "Sometimes kids are afraid of the water, so they don't get the chance to learn how to swim. You can help them overcome their fears as a Parent/Child and Preschool program volunteer. You'll never forget the look of pride on a preschooler's face when she's learned to float all by herself."

Because children involved in other YMCA programs are a key target market for the Swim Lessons programs, you will need to cross-promote. You might send postcards or flyers promoting the swim program to parents of children who are in child care, youth sports, and other programs. You could also give take-home flyers to children in these programs. Certainly, if you were offering a YMCA Splash learn-to-swim program during YMCA Splash month in May, you'd want to take that opportunity to promote the YMCA Swim Lessons program too. You also could send postcards or flyers to everyone who had a family membership. Cross-marketing between your programs is very effective.

If your YMCA is a branch of a metro YMCA or you are collaborating with other associations to publicize aquatics programs, consider having a central office develop all the brochures and aquatics progress reports for your group.

Print Communications

Printed pieces are one of the most common tools used by YMCAs to promote programs. These may include flyers, posters, and brochures.

In the aquatics section of program brochures or program guides, write the copy based on the benefits and features of each of the programs and focus on the target market you are trying to attract. Tie benefits to the features of each program (see "Key Messages"), and promote the benefits more than the features. Describe the program benefits in terms of what the target market may be buying. Include what makes your program unique compared to others in your community.

Use this checklist to maximize the effectiveness of your brochures:

- Did we complete the communication worksheet before deciding that a brochure was the best solution to our communications problem? (See pages 256-257.)

- Is the brochure written from the target audience's perspective? Does it feature key messages in the headlines and subheads? Are the supporting points in the copy?

- Are the photos in the brochure representative of the individuals you are trying to attract?

- Does the brochure conflict with any other long-term organizational or communication goals?

- Does the brochure contain a statement of your YMCA's mission or purpose?

- Does it contain a statement on the availability of financial assistance?
- Is the design of the brochure appropriate to its purpose? A flyer that will be thrown away in a week does not need to be printed on heavy stock.
- Did we check on all the details—correct times, dates, and addresses? The spelling of people's names? Did we call the phone numbers printed in the brochure to be sure that they are right?
- Did we show the copy and layout of the brochure to a neighbor or member of the target audience to see that the brochure is easy to understand and that it accomplishes its purposes?
- Did someone proofread the brochure—preferably someone who never laid eyes on it before?
- Did we nail down the quantities, format, number of colors, and type of paper to be used for the brochure?
- Did we include program costs for each activity and the length of each session for each entry?
- Does the logo meet graphic standards? (See the sidebar.)

If a segment of a community in your service area uses a different language, you may want to consider developing materials in that language. This can help tell your story to that group.

Graphics Standards

The YMCA of the USA has set graphics standards for the use of some of their national symbols. Three of the most commonly used symbols are the YMCA logo, the national theme, and the mission statement.

The logo: Whenever you use the YMCA logo in print or audiovisual materials or signs, only three colors are allowed:

- All black
- Black with the triangle in red (PMS 185)
- Reversed out (white) from a colored background

The national theme: The national theme can be used with the YMCA logo in any configuration as long as the name YMCA appears somewhere else on the same page. The wording of the theme, which is "We build strong kids, strong families, strong communities," cannot be changed in any way.

The mission statement: If your YMCA chooses to use the YMCA mission statement or it is used descriptively in copy, you must use the words "spirit, mind, and body" in that particular order. The mission statement should read as follows:

YMCA mission: To put Christian principles into practice through programs that build healthy spirit, mind, and body for all.

YMCA
We build strong kids,
strong families, strong communities.

You can also use the program identity logo developed for your aquatics program. The YMCA of the USA has created a uniform look and graphics standard for use with all YMCA programs. The aquatics program identity logos can be found at the YMCA of the USA Web site (www.ymcausa.org).

By using these logos, we are simply identifying YMCA programming by combining one of America's most recognizable symbols with clean, crisp, clear names for what we do each and every day from coast to coast. This will help all YMCA aquatics programs across the United States to support each other's promotional efforts. It is also useful in a society where people move often.

Use of the YMCA logo attached to the program name is appropriate in all black, or the logo can be in PMS 185 (red) for the triangle and black. When referring to a program in text, you should not abbreviate the "YMCA" to the "Y"; rather, refer to the program using YMCA, such as "YMCA Swim Lessons."

Although in their graphics standard set in January 1997, the YMCA of the USA did prohibit the use of the YMCA logo with other elements, this use of the logo as part of the program identity logo is permitted.

For more information on graphics standards related to the YMCA, contact Association Advancement at 800-872-9622 or the YMCA of the USA Web site. Many community agencies and businesses may be willing to help you publicize your aquatics programs. Think of all the ways you can get flyers out to the public:

- Post them on bulletin boards at grocery stores, discount department stores, post offices, drugstores, and schools.
- Place them in grocery stores that have kiosks for free handouts.
- Ask your local family restaurant or family-oriented video rental outlet to put some out by the cash register.
- Give them to retailers to use as shopping bag stuffers.
- Ask utilities, banks, or credit card companies to include them as envelope stuffers along with bills or statements.
- Ask local family physicians, pediatricians, and obstetricians—especially those on your board—if they would be willing to put out flyers in their waiting rooms.
- Provide them to libraries, play groups, child care centers, nursery schools, real estate agents, and Welcome Wagons.

Flyers aren't the only way to catch people's attention; here are a few alternative suggestions:

- Give local restaurants paper place mats or tray liners for kids to color in, featuring program artwork and registration dates and locations.
- Ask your local groceries or drugstores to print artwork and basic program information on their bags. (They could print a child safety message and list the YMCA as a resource.)
- Request space on electronic billboards—usually found along urban expressways and on or near banks, car dealerships, or fast-food restaurants—for an aquatics program message.
- If you are part of a metro YMCA or a collaborative group of associations, try putting your collective message on a billboard.

Publicity Through Other Organizations

Check whether schools will consider handing out your flyers to kids to take home. If the schools have newsletters, you can provide them with a news release and ask them to run an item on YMCA aquatics programs. You could also place your spokesperson on the agenda of a PTA or school board meeting to discuss children's safety and how aquatics can help promote children's health and self-esteem. You may want to inform other civic, social service, and health organizations about your programs as well.

Public Service Announcements (PSAs)

PSAs are a vital marketing resource for all not-for-profit organizations. PSAs allow not-for-profits, typically working with very limited budgets, to get their messages heard on radio and television while sparing them the enormous costs associated with broadcast advertising. Expressing the mission of your YMCA and its position as an integral provider of aquatic safety and family services helps you gain placement of PSAs in support of your programs.

Follow these hints for effective use of PSAs:

• Contact public service directors (for radio and television stations) and community bulletin board editors (for cable television stations) at least three months in advance to determine their requirements for accepting and airing PSAs. Consider arranging a meeting with the director in person to discuss the objectives of your aquatics program and the importance of airing the PSAs. If the director cannot meet in person, make an appointment to speak with him or her over the phone at a convenient time.

• Local radio stations might air only preproduced (canned) spots. In this case, perhaps one station can help you produce them and also make copies for use by other stations. (You will probably have to pay a fee.) Generally, 45 words create a 15-second spot and 75 words create a 30-second spot.

• Try to get your local community access television station(s) to run a PSA as a community bulletin board announcement. Send releases to the community service news at local cable stations and to The Weather Channel.

• For tracking purposes, provide stations with a feedback sheet to complete that will tell whether or not they used a PSA, how often it aired, and over how many weeks it aired. If you include a self-addressed, stamped envelope, the station staff will be more likely to return this information.

You can find 15- and 30-second PSAs in the "Promotion Samples" section on the YMCA web site. You will need to edit these sample spots to reflect your YMCA's plans and the requirements of the stations. In doing PSAs, you could include your spokesperson, a local celebrity, or a local sponsor.

For clarification on the many uses of PSAs, call the Media Relations staff at the YMCA of the USA at 800-872-9622.

Media Features

Getting the media to do a story on your program or special event will take more effort than getting a PSA aired, but it will give you a chance to tell people much more than you can squeeze into a 15- to 30-second spot. Working from a media list you've compiled, approach the media and make editors, reporters, and talk show hosts aware of your programs or special events. Be sure to time your approach properly, and give them plenty of lead time, usually two to four weeks.

Compiling a Media List

Read the newspapers, watch television news and talk shows, and listen to radio programs to decide whom to place on your media list. Be informed about the reporters you are going to approach; know the topics and issues they frequently cover. This will save you time when deciding whom to approach to pitch a story on a specific YMCA program or issue. You'll want to target reporters and writers who cover health and lifestyle issues or handle light (entertainment) features.

The media tends to be more receptive if you pitch your story from a national perspective or trend. For example, state "The CDC has reported that children are x percent less active than 10 years ago. The YMCA is going to do something about it."

Your list should include any columnists who write about local concerns and issues. You'll also want to target the following individuals:

- For daily newspapers, the city/metro editor, features editor, calendar editor, photo desk editor, and editor of the editorial page
- For weekly newspapers, the managing editor and editorial page editor
- For television news, the health and lifestyle reporter, assignment editor, and weekend assignment editor
- For radio stations, the news director
- For local wire services, the daybook editor
- For Web sites that cover local news/events, look for contact information on the site's home page

Because of the transient nature of news reporting, update your media lists frequently, at least semiannually.

Pitching Your Story

In addition to sending written materials such as calendar announcements, news releases, media alerts, and background materials to the media, you should also use more direct approaches. Pitching story ideas to the media establishes relationships and shows them that you are vested in helping your programs succeed and achieving your mission. Here are some helpful hints:

- *Train a spokesperson.* An eloquent, informed spokesperson is an asset to any media campaign. News directors are often looking for relevant topics to introduce to their audiences. The proper spokesperson can translate an organization's message to this constituency.

Consider placing your spokesperson, possibly along with the spokesperson of a collaborating organization or sponsor, on local television and radio news shows and programs that cover health and fitness, family, and lifestyle issues.

The YMCA of the USA can help you personalize your approach to include your best practices and highlight the strengths of your spokesperson. Call the Media Relations staff at 800-872-9622 for assistance.

- *Get the media involved.* If a local media personality likes the YMCA or focuses on kids' issues, try to get her or him personally involved in your aquatics program. Getting the reporter to invest personal time in the program might help guarantee publicity for the program and your YMCA. You might want to try to involve her or him as a volunteer on a board or committee.

- *Make a phone call before sending a pitch letter.* Sending a pitch letter to introduce your concept or programs is a fine way to introduce yourself and your idea to a reporter. It might be more effective, however, if you contacted the reporter by phone to discuss your story idea before sending the letter and background materials. Include in your background materials as much of the following as possible: a news release, an advisory memo giving the specifics of the programs (what, why, where, when), and a fact sheet. We have provided you with samples of a pitch letter and a general news release on the web site.

When you write a news release, include the most important facts of who, what, where, when, and why in your lead paragraph. Put the second most important facts supporting the information listed earlier in the next paragraph(s). Then add information in descending order of importance. Use short sentences, short paragraphs, and simple words. You'll gain more notice if you connect your information to part of a larger story or trend.

Mail, rather than fax, your news release to smaller weekly or community newspapers, where they will often scan in the information verbatim. Staff at these papers may not have the ability to scan a fax into a computer.

Whether you make your initial contact via mail or phone, you'll want to follow up with a phone call about a week later to see if the reporter is interested in writing a story or setting up an interview. When you call, do the following:

- *Mention collaborations.* If your YMCA is collaborating with schools or other organizations, be sure to mention that aspect in your pitch letter or follow-up. This point serves as a value-added "hook" to entice the media to cover your programs by making them more valid.

- *Cite statistics.* Statistical figures will substantiate position statements. Emphasize that the programs meet an important community need, and support that position with relevant research data.

- *Point out photo opportunities.* If your program will draw in lots of kids, point out that the program will provide a strong visual or photo opportunity.

- *Package the program with other programs or stories.* If the media does not express interest in covering your program as a single story, try to package the program with other relevant programs currently running at your YMCA or position the program as part of a larger story on trends in water safety or child development. The story does not have to focus solely on the YMCA, but the YMCA should receive premium attention as a valued resource, an expert in aquatic safety as well as child safety and healthy development.

If the media wants more material, you can offer expert spokespeople or background materials (facts, statistics) and any information you have on your aquatics programs, character development, or other related programs.

Timing Your Media Approach

Part of the trick to getting media coverage of your programs is catching media reporters or producers at the right time. What constitutes the right timing differs among newspapers, talk shows, and radio and television news. You may also want to send information about your programs to the media periodically for continuing coverage after registration. Here are some timing suggestions:

- *Calendar announcements.* Provide calendar editors at local newspapers with the time, date, location, cost, and contact information for your event at least one month in advance.

- *Newspaper features and radio and television talk shows.* Start pitching the story to these outlets at least a month before your targeted hit date (the date on which you'd like to see the publicity run or air). For talk shows, do your homework—find out the lead time for booking guests, which will vary from show to show. At, or preferably before, the interview, provide the interviewer with a handout that includes an introductory paragraph about your program.

• *Radio and television news.* Wait until two weeks before your desired publicity hit date. Reporters and producers work on tight schedules. When you call them, check first to make certain they aren't working on a deadline. If they are, ask them when would be a convenient time for you to call back. Don't be surprised if they don't decide to cover your program on the spot.

When you approach a television news reporter, the item you are presenting to the reporter should have vibrant visual appeal. Hold off on contacting television news unless you have a special event or photo opportunity to highlight.

• *Ongoing coverage.* Because YMCA aquatics programs run year-round, you can showcase the benefits of your programs to the community and gain publicity for those programs beyond their registration periods. Send periodic news releases and photos from the individual programs to your local news sources. Time them to coincide with similar topics currently appearing in the news.

Finally, if you are placing any paid advertising, you may want to time your pitching around the run dates of the advertising. Typically, you will not have control over when a pitched story will appear, but being informed can help you control peaks and valleys in the success of your media campaign. Don't mention that you purchased an ad when pitching an editorial. It implies that you think a story has been bought. Editors and advertising salespeople are two separate groups.

Note that it is okay to ask a reporter, editor, or producer when a story will run; however, never demand or even strongly suggest a date for placement. You often can obtain desired placement by stressing important dates relevant to your programs. For example, say "Registration for the Parent/Child and Preschool and the Youth and Adult programs begins (date) and the programs run from (date) to (date)," or "It's important that you know that registration for the programs expires (date)."

To summarize, remember that these are the three most important things for you to do to get the media to promote your programs:

• Contact the media with the appropriate lead time.

• Follow up with phone calls and additional materials.

• Be flexible! The key to any successful media campaign is flexibility. Remember that you are seeking assistance from the media to promote your programs. Do your best to accommodate their changing schedules, provide them with comprehensive information in a timely manner, and thank them for their support.

If you follow these guidelines, you'll have a good chance of drawing attendance to your programs while bringing public attention to how your programs benefit the community.

Special Events

"A special event is a key message disguised as a good time," said one longtime YMCA professional. A special event related to one or more of your aquatics programs could communicate the message that the YMCA is an expert and a community leader in water safety and promoting children's healthy development. Holding a special event to announce your programs can provide your YMCA with an opportunity to showcase them to new and existing members and gain media attention in the process.

The media is often attracted to special events that help publicize the kickoff or a second phase of a program. Such events can provide multiple photo opportunities in an informal setting. They also can provide the media with one-on-one interview opportunities with YMCA spokespersons and YMCA members. If you are expecting

Broadcast Public Services Announcements (PSA's)

Use these sample PSAs with local broadcast media. Note that you can edit these PSAs according to the directions you receive from the station. You will need to tailor them to your YMCA and add the missing information (in boldface here).

15 sec.	Learning to swim can boost a kid's self-esteem a mile high. YMCA Swim Lessons—a series of programs offered by the **name of YMCA**—can give *YOUR* child that great feeling. Registrations are being held at **location** on **date(s)**. Call **phone number of YMCA.**
30 sec.	Swimming is one of the best ways to stay healthy. And it's something you never outgrow. Come to the **name of YMCA** for YMCA Swim Lessons—a series of programs for kids and adults. Registration will be held at **location** on **date(s)**. YMCA Swim Lessons offer enjoyable ways to learn swimming and water safety skills, too. Call **phone number of YMCA** for details.

Program Brochure Copy

YMCA Swim Lessons: Swim Instruction for Everyone

There is a reason why the YMCA is referred to as America's Favorite Swim Instructor. In YMCA Swim Lessons, not only are students taught how to swim, but they also learn about themselves, about aquatic and boating safety and rescue skills, and about water activities they can enjoy for a lifetime of fitness. Best of all, it makes them feel proud of what they have accomplished.

Instruction is caring and personalized, run by certified staff. A variety of classes is available to meet your family's needs: mornings, afternoons, evenings, and Saturdays. Class size is determined by considering safety factors and the age of the participants, making sure classes don't get too big to be comfortable.

Class fees are **fee** per session for each child. Scholarships are available for those with limited incomes. Call **name** at **phone number** to find out more about applying for a scholarship.

Please be sure to attend our parent orientation meeting held the week before each session begins. See the **insert the place meeting information is printed or posted** for details. During the meeting, we will give you an overview of the program, tips for supporting your child, and ways to reinforce the activities learned during class. We look forward to seeing you at this meeting.

Here are descriptions of the swim classes that we offer. Choose the ones that will work best for you and your family. If you need financial assistance, contact **name** at **this YMCA**. And remember, at the YMCA, we build a healthy spirit, mind, and body for all.

Parent/Child

This 30-minute class is for children six to 36 months and their parents. The primary objective is to get both the parent and child comfortable in the water. The child will become aware of the differences between moving through water and on dry land, while the parent will become aware of how to teach his or her child to be safer in and around the water. Classes are designed to allow the child to have fun in the water while the parent guides him or her to learn aquatic skills. The child will be exposed to games that use basic movements in the water such as kicking, arm strokes, and breath control. Activities are based on the developmental abilities of the child.

The Parent-Child program has four levels, all determined by age.

Shrimps	This is an introduction to the aquatic environment for parents and their infants age 6—8 months. Parents are encouraged to develop appropriate expectations for their children's performance in the water. They learn basic aquatic safety and have a positive experience with their children that can help them grow closer.

(continued)

Kippers	This level continues to provide positive aquatic experiences for parents and 9- to 12-month-old infants. The infants learn basic water skills and have fun playing with toys and flotation devices. Parents review and learn more about basic aquatic safety.
Inias	Children 13 to 18 months do more independent exploration of the aquatic environment with help from parents. The parents again review and learn additional information about aquatic safety. The program provides opportunities for parent-child teams to socialize with each other.
Perch	Children 19 to 36 months start moving more independently through the water under their parents' guidance. Parents learn more about aquatic and boating safety, and children begin to learn something about these topics as well. At this point the instructor begins to prepare the children to work directly with an instructor on their own.

Preschool

This program is designed for children ages three to five. This is a child's first experience in the pool without parental assistance. The children are taught the basic skills that are the building blocks of swimming. They also learn about pool safety, boating safety, and the use of personal flotation devices. The 30-minute class is taught by a caring, certified YMCA Swim Lessons instructor. Class participants are divided into skill levels, and class size is such that the instructor can provide children with individual attention.

Pikes	At this level, children usually begin attending classes without their parents. This level helps children develop safe pool behavior, adjust to the water, and develop independent movement in the water. It is designed for new swimmers, teaching basic paddle stroke and kicking skills, pool safety, and comfort in holding the faces in the water while blowing bubbles and swimming.
Eels	This advanced beginner level reinforces Pike skills. It is for children who are comfortable in the water. They are taught to flutter kick, dive, float, and perform the progressive paddle stroke. Children can swim across the pool without assistance by the end of this level.
Rays	At this level children review previous skills, improve stroke skills, build endurance by swimming on their front and back, and learn to tread water and perform more progressive diving skills. Children can swim across the pool on their front and back without assistance by the end of this level.
Starfish	Children at this level review previously learned skills and refine their crawl and back strokes and floating skills. They also learn underwater swimming skills. Children can swim a length of the pool on the front and back at the end of this level.

Youth

This program is for children ages six to eleven. Each skill level builds upon the preceding level, with seven levels covering all the strokes, diving fundamentals, and safety skills.

Polliwog	This is the beginning level for school-age children. It gets children acquainted with the pool, the use of flotation devices, and front and back floating. By the end of this level, they should know the front paddlestroke, side and back paddle, and some synchronized swimming and wetball (the lead-up game to water polo) movements.

(continued)

Guppy	The children continue to practice and build upon basic skills, now performing more skills without the aid of a flotation device. They are introduced to lead-up strokes to the front and back crawl, sidestroke, breaststroke, and elementary backstroke. More synchronized swimming and wetball skills are taught, as well as some diving skills.
Minnow	This is the initial intermediate level. The children further refine the lead-up strokes they have learned as their skills become more like those normally used in swimming. They learn still more synchronized swimming, wetball, and diving skills.
Fish	At this point, students work to perform the crawl stroke, elementary backstroke, back crawl stroke, and sidestroke, with turns. They are introduced to the butterfly stroke. They continue learning additional synchronized swimming movements, wetball skills, and diving skills, and are introduced to the use of mask and fins.
Flying Fish	At this advanced level, students work on refining their strokes and increasing their endurance. They develop the ability to perform more complex combinations of synchronized swimming movements, learn to dive off a one-meter board, and develop better wetball playing skills. They are also introduced to the use of a snorkel.
Shark	The students at this level continue to improve their strokes, with starts and turns, and are introduced to the inverted breaststroke, the crawl, and the overarm sidestroke. Opportunities are provided for further work on synchronized swimming, wetball, and skin diving.
Porpoise	At this final level, students are exposed to a wide range of aquatic experiences through a class and club format. In class these advanced swimmers learn new strokes and rescue skills, as well as develop volunteerism and leadership skills. Through the club, they try various aquatic sports and games, with club members forming smaller groups to explore different aquatic pursuits in more depth.

Teens

In the Swim of Things	This class is for teens age 12 to 17 who have not had swimming lessons before or who are not comfortable in the water. Basic swimming and water safety skills are taught in a relaxed, fun way.

Adult

Adult classes are for individuals ages 18 and older.

Fear No More	This is a special class for those who are afraid of water. Instructors work with students in a small group to help them overcome their fears and begin to develop basic swim skills.
Beginner	This class is for adults who don't feel at ease in the water or who have never participated in swimming lessons. Nonswimmers are taught basic swimming skills and water safety.
Intermediate/Advanced	This is a class for adults who are comfortable in the water and who would like to work on stroke development and endurance. It is perfect for those who have limited swimming skills and who would like to improve their techniques.

a local celebrity or speaker to participate in the event, be sure to inform the media. If the event is unique enough, or if you believe it is large enough to warrant such coverage, you might want to approach a radio station whose audience matches yours to broadcast live from the event.

PROMOTIONAL PLAN

To do a good job of promoting your aquatics programs, you should have a promotional plan. A promotional plan details what needs to be done when and the costs involved. Such planning not only helps you in scheduling, but also in including an adequate amount of dollars in the budget.

Using the communication worksheet in figure 8.1 will help you formulate your promotional plan.

Communication Worksheet

What is our communication objective?

What are we trying to accomplish? What kind of results do we seek? What do we want people to do, think, or feel? Can we quantify our objective: How many people? What percent increase? *The result should be clear, attainable, and stated in 10 words or less, such as "Get 2,500 kids to participate in youth swim classes."*

What environment are we operating in?

What is the current situation in our service area? How strong is the economy? Are there other providers of the same service, other organizations with similar goals?

Who is our target audience?

Who are the people we want to reach? Whose behavior or thinking do we need to influence? *Think of who ultimately has the power to make decisions that will affect your objective. It helps to list all possible groups of people on a separate sheet, then decide on the one or two that are most important. For instance, what would motivate kids to participate in a program is different than what parents would look for. When the promotional plan is determined, you need to direct the piece to those whom you are trying to influence.*

What does our target audience currently believe?

What perceptions, both good or bad, will encourage or discourage these people from taking the action that will achieve our objective? *List negative and positive perceptions on a sheet of paper.*

What are the key messages?

Based on the target audience's perceptions, what key thoughts do we need to communicate to them to reach our objective? What will fill in their knowledge gaps, overcome their negative beliefs, and accentuate their positive ones? What are the essential ideas? *Your messages may be based on the ideas in the positive column that you generated in the previous question. Key messages should be stated in 10 words or less. Here's an example: "YMCA Swim Lessons are led by caring, trained instructors."*

(continued)

Figure 8.1   Communication worksheet.

What are three points that support each message?

What facts, statistics, quotes from authorities or experts, analogies, or examples from personal experience will prove the truth of the message?

Which communication tools and techniques will be the most effective?

What will get the message across most efficiently? Will personal communication solve the problem? Which kinds of publications, shows, media, or people have influence with the target audience? Does something already exist that can solve the problem? Do we need more than one tool? Possibilities include the following:

- Face-to-face talks *(between whom, when, where, how many?)*
- Small group discussions or meetings *(between whom, when, where, how many?)*
- Phone calls *(by whom, when, where, how many?)*
- Personal notes *(by whom, when, where, how many?)*
- Speeches *(by whom, when, where, how many?)*
- Audiovisuals *(what kind, to show when and where, how many?)*
- Special events *(for whom, when, where, how many?)*
- Mass-produced letters *(from whom, when, where, how many?)*
- Brochures, schedules, posters, and other printed pieces *(distributed when, where, how many?)*
- Newsletters *(which issues, how many readers?)*
- News in the media *(when, which ones: paper, magazines, radio, cable TV, broadcast TV?)*
- Advertising *(when, which ones: paper, magazines, radio, cable TV, broadcast TV?)*
- Others *(what, when, where, how many?)*

Who's responsible?

Who—volunteers, staff members, or both—will handle which parts of the task?

When's the deadline? What's the schedule for completion? When must the talks, discussions, speeches, or special events take place? When must the piece be in the hands of the targeted audience? When will it be shown (if audiovisual)?

What's the budget? How much money will it take to accomplish the objective? Is there a local or corporate partner identified to help support the program?

Figure 8.1 *(continued)*

FOCUS GROUPS/INDIVIDUAL DEPTH INTERVIEWS

Holding planned, focused discussions with either groups or individuals can assist you in developing programs, solving problems, and enhancing program service. Such discussions are known as focus groups or individual depth interviews. Each of these is better used in some situations than in others, so here are some suggestions on how to choose between these two options (YMCA of the USA, 1997).

Use focus groups when

- interaction of respondents may stimulate a richer response or new and valuable thoughts;

- group or peer pressure will be valuable in challenging the thinking of respondents and illuminating conflicting opinions;
- the subject matter is not so sensitive that respondents will temper responses or withhold information;
- the topic is such that most respondents can say all that is relevant or all that they know in less than 10 minutes;
- the volume of stimulus is not extensive;
- a single subject area is to be examined in depth and strings of behavior are less relevant;
- enough is known to establish a meaningful topic guide;
- key decisions makers can and want to observe "firsthand" consumer information;
- an acceptable number of target respondents can be assembled in one location;
- quick turnaround is critical and funds are limited.

If possible, have one interviewer conduct the research; working with several groups will not fatigue or bore the interviewer.

Use individual depth interviews when

- group interaction is likely to be limited or nonproductive;
- group or peer pressure would inhibit responses and cloud the meaning of results;
- the subject matter is so sensitive that respondents would be unwilling to talk openly in a group;
- the topic is such that a greater depth of response per individual is desirable, as with complex subject matter or very knowledgeable respondents;
- a large amount of stimulus material must be evaluated;
- it is necessary to understand how attitudes and behaviors link together on an individual pattern basis;
- it may be necessary to develop the interview guide by altering it after each of the initial interviews;
- "firsthand" consumer information is not critical or observation is not logistically possible;
- respondents are geographically dispersed or not easily assembled for other reasons;
- quick turnaround is not critical, and the budget will permit higher cost.

For individual depth interviews, have numerous interviewers on the project. One interviewer would become fatigued or bored doing all the interviews.

If you choose to conduct a focus group, here are step-by-step instructions on implementation:

Preparing for the Focus Group
- Identify the need (member satisfaction, adding value to membership offer, program discovery) to conduct a focus group. Tie the need to a specific marketing, long range, or operational goal.
- Write a specific measurable goal for the focus group.
- Determine the budget (rental fee for site, food, mailing of invitations, participant thank-you gifts) for conducting the focus group.

- Set a specific date for the focus group and work backward.
- Plan to moderate the focus group or secure a moderator.
- Secure a recorder for conducting the focus group.
- Determine with management what outcomes are expected.
- Determine the site for the focus group.
- Three months before the focus group, select a random sample of 15 members, former members, or individuals who do not belong to the YMCA.
- Two months before the focus group, mail invitations to the participants. Follow up with a personal phone call to every participant. Explain the reason for the focus group and emphasize that their participation will be a valuable asset to the YMCA.
- One month prior, prepare a set of questions with management that will help the YMCA accomplish its objective and goal for conducting the focus group.
- Three weeks prior, reconfirm participants' attendance using a follow-up letter summarizing what you have discussed with them over the phone.
- Two weeks prior, reconfirm the site, moderator, and recorder. Set a date with management to review and evaluate the feedback from the focus group.
- One week prior, purchase, rent, or secure the items needed for the focus group.
- One week prior, reconfirm the focus group questions with management.

Meeting With the Focus Group

- The morning of the focus group, walk through and visualize each step of the focus group.
- Start the focus group by greeting participants and setting the tone and atmosphere.
- Discuss how the focus group will aid the YMCA in its decision making.
- Indicate to the participants that whatever is shared in the room will remain confidential.
- Tell participants that you will be asking them a series of questions (direct, open-ended).
- Conduct the focus group.
- Check in with the recorder periodically.
- Thank participants for their valuable input and present each one with a gift (sweatshirt, gym bag).

Following Up After the Focus Group

- The moderator and recorder review the focus group feedback.
- The moderator shares the information with management and their staff teams.
- Management evaluates the feedback as to its findings and measures how well the focus group met its goal and objective.
- Management decides how best to utilize the information provided and the next steps for implementation, including budget, staff, and volunteer implications.
- Handwritten thank-you notes are mailed to each participant, the moderator (if not yourself), and the recorder.
- Management follows through on each of the next steps set for implementation and evaluates staff performance on meeting those goals and objectives.
- Management evaluates the contribution and return on investment.

Here are some sample types of questions that might be asked of YMCA or community members in a focus group:

- Building the relevant context information: What are the experiences or issues surrounding YMCA programs or membership that influence how it is viewed?
- Top-of-mind associations: What's the first thing that comes to mind when I say YMCA swim programs? YMCA facility? YMCA membership?
- Constructing images: Who are the people who purchase YMCA memberships? What do they look like? What are their lives about? What are they looking for?
- Querying the meaning of the obvious: What does "family time" mean to you? What does "West Family YMCA" mean to you?
- Establishing conceptual maps of a program: How would you group the different YMCA programs? How do they go together for you? How are the groups similar or different?
- Image matching: Here are pictures of 10 different situations or people. Which go with this program and which do not? Why?
- "Man from the moon" routine: I'm from the moon; I've never heard of the YMCA. Describe it to me. Why would I want to join? Convince me.
- Chain of questions: Why do you enroll in fitness programs? Why is that important? Why does that make a difference to you? Would it ever not be important?
- Benefit chain: The YMCA offers a child care program. What's the benefit of that?
- Sentence completions: The best YMCA is one that . . . The best thing about being a member is . . . Taking swimming lessons makes me feel . . .
- Role playing: Okay, now you're the executive director. What would you do?
- Best of all possible worlds scenario: Forget about reality. What would you like the YMCA to be?

Here are some sample types of questions that might be asked of YMCA staff members during a focus group:

- What is it like working for the YMCA?
- What do you like best about your job?
- What do you like least about your job?
- What tools do you need to do your job better?
- Are you rewarded for a job well done? How?
- How do you feel about how you are compensated?
- Who do you feel you can go to if you have a problem?
- Do you feel the four values of caring, honesty, respect, and responsibility are evident in the YMCA workplace?
- Do you feel you contribute to or are an integral part of the YMCA's mission and the work that it does in the community?
- Would you recommend the YMCA to your best friend? Why or why not?
- Use this as an ending question: If you had to use one word (or a maximum of three words) to describe why you continue to work for the YMCA, what would it (they) be?

BIBLIOGRAPHY

YMCA of the USA. 1997. Resource information regarding focus groups and in-depth interviews. YMCA of the USA Web site.

Emergency and Risk Management

One of the most serious duties of an aquatics director is taking responsibility for the health and safety of patrons and staff. Besides your moral duty to keep your facility safe and to have procedures for dealing with all types of emergencies, there are also legal issues involved.

We begin by explaining the concept of risk management, the types of emergencies that you should prepare to handle, ways to identify hazards, and insurance. Next we talk about the procedures for preparing for emergencies, creating policy, and developing emergency plans. Other relevant topics include record keeping and crisis management. Finally, we'll give you an introduction to the legal process, aquatics liability and defenses, and record keeping related to legal requirements.

WHAT IS RISK MANAGEMENT?

Risk can be considered to be anything that threatens the ability of a not-for-profit to accomplish its mission. *Risk management* is a discipline that enables people and organizations to cope with uncertainty by taking steps to protect their vital assets and resources. *The risk management process provides a framework for identifying hazards and associated risks and deciding what to do about them.* Of course, just making a laundry list of all possible risks is not enough. It is easy to quickly become overwhelmed by the huge list of risks an organization faces.

But not all risks are created equal. Risk management is not just about identifying risks; it is about learning to weigh various risks and making decisions about which risks deserve immediate attention.

Risk management is not a task to be completed and shelved. It is an ongoing process that, once understood, should be integrated into all aspects of your organization's management. Your association should have a risk management policy and procedures in place. You need to know what these are and to understand your role in implementing them. It also will help you to have an understanding of how they are established. Let's take a closer look at how this process works.

- *Establish the context.* Begin a risk management program by setting goals and identifying any potential barriers or impediments to the implementation of the program. Ask the question: "What are we trying to accomplish by integrating risk management into our operations?" Some common goals for not-for-profit risk management efforts include reducing injuries, avoiding costly claims, preserving the not-for-profit's reputation in the community, freeing up resources for mission-critical activities, and ensuring adequate risk financing.

- *Acknowledge and identify risks.* There are many ways to undertake risk identification; the key is using a framework or strategy that allows you to identify all major risks facing your not-for-profit.

- *Evaluate and prioritize risks.* The third step in the process is to keep things in perspective and establish a list of action items in priority order. The risk of an asteroid crashing into your organization's annual Black Tie event is remote, so it probably makes more sense to work on a more likely risk—that someone could slip and hurt him- or herself on a wet pool deck.

- *Select appropriate risk management strategies and implement your plan.* Four risk management techniques (described next) can be used individually or in combination to address virtually every risk facing your not-for-profit.

- *Monitor and update the risk management program.* Not-for-profits are dynamic organizations that constantly face new challenges and opportunities. Risk management techniques and plans should be reviewed periodically to make certain that they remain the most appropriate strategy given the organization's needs and circumstances.

Four basic risk management techniques are avoidance, modification, retention, and sharing.

1. *Avoidance:* Whenever an organization cannot ensure a high degree of safety for a service it offers, it should choose avoidance as a risk management technique. Do not offer programs that pose too great a risk. In some cases, avoidance is the most appropriate technique because a not-for-profit simply doesn't have the financial resources required to fund adequate training, supervision, equipment, or other safety measures. Always ask yourself "Is there something we could do to deliver this program/conduct this activity safely?" If you answer yes, risk modification may be the more practical technique.

2. *Modification:* Modification is simply changing an activity to make it safer for all involved. Policies and procedures are examples of risk modification. An organization concerned about the risk of using unsafe drivers may add Division of Motor Vehicles record checks to its screening process, or an annual road test for all drivers. An organization concerned about the lack of male and female chaperones for an overnight camping trip may decide to host a day-long hike and picnic instead. A pool with glare from a window in the deep end in the afternoon can alter the location of the activity or move the lifeguard chair during this time period.

3. *Retention.* There are two ways to retain risk: by design or unintentionally. A not-for-profit may decide that other available techniques aren't suitable and will therefore choose to retain the risk of harm or loss. Not-for-profits make conscious decisions to retain risk every day. For example, when a not-for-profit purchases liability insurance and elects a $1,000 deductible or self-insured retention, it's retaining risk. This can be a rational and appropriate approach to managing risk. Where organizations get into trouble is when risk is retained unintentionally. The unintentional retention of risk can be the result of failing to understand the exclusions of an insurance policy, insufficient understanding of the scope of risk an organization faces, or simply a lack of time to consider the risk and how it can be addressed.

4. *Sharing.* This technique involves sharing risk with another organization through a contract. Two common examples are insurance contracts that require an insurer to pay for claims expenses and losses under certain circumstances and service con-

tracts whereby a provider (such as a transportation service or caterer) agrees to perform a service and assume liability for potential harm occurring in the delivery of the service.

Regular risk assessments, effective policy formulation, and appropriate insurance coverage are three important risk management tools that serve the best interests of YMCAs. When it comes to safety and risk management related to your association's programs, these key systems and procedures should be in place:

- Your YMCA has a documented safety and risk management policy.
- Each staff member has "safety" job requirements in her or his job description.
- Appropriate staff have performance standards on claims. They are expected to try to reduce the occurrence of specific types of accidents.
- Written policies exist and are implemented relating to

  a. aquatics,

  b. child care,

  c. employee safety,

  d. personnel, and

  e. transportation.

- Written emergency procedures exist.
- Each new employee and volunteer receives orientation and training on the YMCA's policies and procedures for the prevention of child abuse.
- Each new employee and volunteer is given an orientation on the safety requirements of the YMCA. The general orientation includes legally required trainings such as those mandated by OSHA.
- Each new employee and volunteer is given safety training for the specific program and the safety requirements and hazards of his or her position.
- Facility and equipment inspections are performed regularly (daily, weekly, monthly) to identify potential hazards. These inspections are documented, and corrective actions are taken. The inspection documents are retained.
- Each program has a written safety and risk management program plan that is available to every staff person.
- Periodic (weekly, monthly) practice drills are held for medical emergencies, severe weather, missing persons, vehicle evacuation, and other emergencies. There is a record of drills and they are retained.
- All accidents (members, participants, employees) are reported and accident reports are written. Supervisors review these reports. Accident statistics are presented to and reviewed by management annually (or more frequently).
- A safety and risk management plan exists for field trips and off-site programs that addresses

  a. communication,

  b. emergency assistance such as first aid,

  c. supervision (ratios, location),

  d. transportation,

  e. site inspection and identification of hazards and risks,

  f. security, and

  g. equipment.

TYPES OF EMERGENCIES

Many different types of emergencies can arise at your aquatics facility: medical, water, missing persons, environmental, chemical, mechanical, facility, and facility security. Your facility should have written emergency plans for likely emergencies in each of these categories, including facility evacuation if needed.

Medical Emergencies

Medical emergencies can be divided into two general situations: life-threatening and potentially life-threatening. In life-threatening emergencies, death probably will occur if no action is taken. Such emergencies require immediate advanced first aid, such as CPR, and transportation to a medical facility. In potentially life-threatening emergencies, death is less certain, but such conditions still require immediate action. Outside emergency medical assistance may still be needed, including transport to a medical facility. Here are some examples of life-threatening and potentially life-threatening emergencies:

Life-Threatening Emergencies

- Cardiac arrest
- Drowning/near-drowning
- Uncontrolled bleeding
- Poisoning
- Cessation of breathing

Potentially Life-Threatening Emergencies

- Seizure
- Heart attack or angina
- Spinal injury
- Loss of consciousness
- Fracture
- Reaction to extreme heat or cold

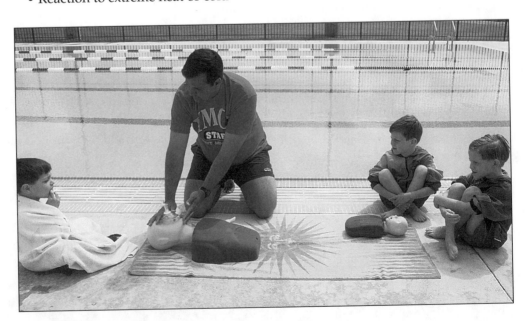

- Obstructed airway or respiratory emergency
- Allergic reaction
- Asthma attack
- Diabetes or insulin shock
- Cut or laceration

Undoubtedly you could list other medical emergencies. Your staff should discuss how to handle such emergencies at your facility, including OSHA regulations for avoiding blood-borne pathogens.

Water Emergencies

Through in-service training, the staff at your facility should collaborate to develop the emergency procedures needed to react effectively and efficiently. Be sure you have plans to cover

- drownings and near-drownings,
- severe injury in the water and spinal injury in the water,
- cardiac or respiratory emergencies in the water, and
- multiple-victim rescues with more than one victim or more than one lifeguard.

Contact your local emergency medical system (EMS) as to their needs and what assistance they will require so you can integrate these things into your emergency procedures.

Missing Persons

If a missing person is believed to be in the water, the situation is life threatening. If the person is believed to be out of the water, the situation is less critical. In any case, your staff must make efforts to locate the missing person. Possible scenarios include these:

- Last seen in the water (immediately life threatening)
- Whereabouts unknown (potentially life threatening)
- Lost child

Environmental Emergencies

Facility personnel must know the policy and procedures for a variety of weather-related situations:

- Thunderstorms and lightning
- Hurricanes
- Tornadoes and high winds
- Heavy rain, floods, and hailstorms
- High and low temperatures
- Reduced visibility (because of fog, haze, dust, blowing debris, or other causes)
- Earth tremors or earthquakes
- Waves or currents (open water area)
- Floods

Chemical Emergencies

Pool operators should be very careful in handling the chemicals used to keep the water properly balanced for their swimming facilities. Unfortunately, accidents occur that can create potentially hazardous conditions. Each facility should have procedures for handling a variety of chemical emergencies:

- Liquid or gaseous chlorine leaks from tank ruptures, leaks, or spills resulting in serious or fatal injuries
- Pool-acid spills resulting in caustic vapors and skin irritations
- Explosion of flammable chemicals (for example, granular or tablet chlorine or bromine sticks)
- Imbalance in water chemistry (for example, cloudiness or improper pH or chlorine level, irritating swimmers' skin or eyes)

Mechanical Emergencies

Various potential mechanical hazards exist depending on the type of facility you have. Your facility should have procedures to handle the following:

- Structural failure
- Filtration system failure
- Lighting failure
- Equipment malfunctions (slides, wave pools, and diving boards)

Facility Emergencies

Not all emergency situations that affect your facility will occur within the pool area. Be sure your facility has provisions for handling a variety of emergency situations:

- Structural fire on the grounds
- Brushfire on the grounds
- Bomb threats
- Violent threats by firearms
- Electrical outages
- Chemical explosion on the grounds or nearby, presenting danger from fire or fumes
- Fire nearby, presenting danger from flames or smoke
- Communication failures (radio or telephone)
- Equipment failures, such as failure of lifesaving equipment requiring replacement, an empty oxygen tank, a broken backboard, or an AED battery outage

Facility Security Emergencies

All facilities should have a plan to ensure the security of the facility when closing between activities or for the day (see "Sample Pool Closing and Security Procedure, page 278). Maintenance personnel or night security staff may implement these plans. You also need procedures for dealing with situations such as the following:

- Breach of facility security
- Facility closing
- Breaking and entering
- A trespasser in distress in the water
- Maintenance of security during and after a drowning
- Crowd control
- Reductions, restrictions, or expansions of facility water space as a result of reno-vations
- Water safety check
- Law enforcement
- Riot
- Theft
- Assault
- Indecent exposure

HAZARD IDENTIFICATION AND ANALYSIS

As an aquatics director, you are responsible for risk control for the swimming facil-ity and all aquatics programs. But before you can choose one of the four methods of controlling risk—avoidance, modification, retention, or sharing—you must first iden-tify the risks in your area.

Let's begin by defining a few terms:

Hazard: a source of danger

Hazardous: a condition exposing a person to risk or injury

Risk: a dangerous element or factor that presents the possibility of injury

Table 9.1 shows a variety of aquatic hazards and their related possible risks.

You need to have risk control systems in place to minimize and manage aquatic hazards. The following lists will give you an idea of the kinds of systems that can help you manage and control the risks involved in aquatics programs.

Facility Control Systems

Planned hazard identification and risk analysis

Proper safety equipment

Attention to water chemistry and filtration

Attention to remedial and preventive maintenance

Opening and closing procedures (including documentation)

Staff and Program Control Systems

Management training

Proper verification of certifications and a filing system, including YMCA Lifeguard, CPR, first aid, and instructor certifications—AED, oxygen administration, blood borne pathogens

Proper supervision

In-service staff training

Location and coverage by lifeguards

Table 9.1	Hazards and Risks in Swimming	
	Hazards	**Risks**
Program (aquatic)	Swimming and diving connected with instruction, competitive swimming, and fitness or recreational swimming	Drowning Neck fractures Anoxia Fractures Contusions Lacerations Abrasions Insect stings
Equipment	Mechanical and electrical equipment, including vacuum cleaners, automatic timers, filters, chemical feeders, audiovisual equipment, and underwater lights. Chemicals, including disinfectants, cleaning agents, pH modifiers, algaecides, and other chemicals needed for proper water balance.	Mechanical and electrical: Electrical shock Contusions Sprains Chemical: Noxious gases Fire Explosion Chemical burns Spills
Facility	Design hazards, including hopper or spoon pool bottoms, the slope of the bottom of the pool, entrance locations, steps or gutters. Fixed equipment, including starting blocks, diving boards, ladders, water attractions, drains, lifeguard chairs, and bulkheads. Surfaces that can be hazards are the pool bottom, decks, and showers and locker rooms. Other equipment on the pool deck, including deck chairs, storage lockers, lane lines, etc.	Drowning Neck fractures Anoxia Contusions Lacerations Abrasions Fractures Insect stings

Written and rehearsed emergency and accident management procedures
Public relations
Instructors' lesson plans and coaches' training plans
Safe teaching and coaching methods

Facility Information Control Systems

Job descriptions
Employment applications
Preemployment exams, both written and practical
Staff evaluations
Accident and incident reports
Staff meeting minutes
Risk recognition forms (agreement to participate, waiver, and release forms)
Maintenance records
Pool logs
Safety inspection checklists
Orientation and staff handbook receipt from employees

Your aquatics facility should have a risk management plan that is part of an overall facility plan. Your role as director includes the following:

• *Identification of risks.* Inspect the aquatics facility and determine the risks involved with the program and facility. Think about all the potential accidents and emergency situations that could occur. Review state and local laws and codes applicable to the facility. Consult the YMCA of the USA's Aquatic Guidelines (appendix 4) and develop your own association policy guidelines. (See more on this in chapter 2 or contact YMCA Services Corporation.)

• *Evaluation of the severity and occurrence of risks.* Review your facility's records of accidents, past emergencies, and injury charts. Review staff responses to these situations and the outcomes of their actions.

• *Management of risks.* Based on the information you have compiled, determine what needs to be communicated to members and participants about safety. Determine methods you can use to educate them on safety in your facility. This would include how you can educate parents and participants before beginning a program and how you can remind them about safety throughout your program. This is an important part of accident prevention.

Develop an action plan for what needs to be done when any accident or emergency occurs. This plan should include specific procedures explaining who does what and in what order. These plans must be specific to your facility.

Some risks can be minimized by retaining or transferring them. These methods can involve retaining and controlling some risks through having deductible insurance, so that part of the loss is paid for by the sponsor, or transferring the risk by signing the entire monetary risk over to an insurance company. You will need to communicate with your association's risk manager about these methods.

Having qualified personnel is one of the most important methods for controlling risks. You can greatly reduce or eliminate risks by hiring qualified staff and providing a comprehensive in-service training program. The program should include skill development (especially rescue skills), policy reinforcement, emergency drills and procedures, and leadership opportunities. Budget for this, and follow through.

Providing safe facilities, equipment, and environment is an important part of managing risk. You may not be able to alter facilities once they are built, but you can do other things to help minimize the risks created by the facilities. For instance, if you have a shallow-water pool, you can create and enforce no-diving rules for participants. Thoughtful development of facility and equipment rules can be a major step in minimizing accidents. Also see that your aquatics facility is maintained properly. Make sure that staff check the facility and equipment for safety regularly and document such checks. Staff should report any hazards found during those checks, and the hazards should be attended to immediately or closed off from patrons.

Finally, make safety a priority for your program. Ask your executive to meet with you quarterly to review only aquatic safety issues. Also stay current on updated YMCA Aquatics Guidelines and new research on safety issues such as spa drowning or protective measures for blood-borne pathogens. Be aware of relevant program and equipment issues, and know where to obtain resources related to these issues:

a. YMCA aquatics manuals and other YMCA publications

b. Reputable Web sites

c. Aquatics industry magazines

d. State and local bathing codes

e. Pool design manuals

f. YMCA Services Corporation

• *Administration of risk management plan.* Make sure all staff know their roles in risk management; use flow charts to explain lines of communication. Their responsibilities include rehearsal of emergency procedures and enforcement of rules. You can make the plan work by hiring quality staff and providing them with a comprehensive orientation program, ongoing in-service training, and good supervision.

You should also have a good reporting system in place for accidents. You should take the time to analyze previous accidents and responses so you can evaluate your emergency procedures and make necessary modifications.

• *Assessment of risk management plan.* A final but important step is to check to make sure you are operating as well as you think you are. You can do this by assessing your program in the following ways:

   a. In-house assessment that includes staff and policy reviews regularly throughout each year

   b. Association/peer assessments, including staff and policy reviews, performed by staff from other departments or other YMCAs at least annually

   c. YMCA aquatics program assessment provided as a fee-for-service program through YMCA Services at least every five years

These are general guidelines for the amount of time between each of these assessments; perform them more often if staff turnover or the number of incidents increases. (See chapter 2 for more on program assessment.)

As the aquatics director, you are one of the key people in your YMCA's management who is most in touch with emergency preparation needs. As such, you may want to take a lead role in developing and instituting emergency action plans for the entire YMCA. You can share your knowledge with other supervisors and guide them. Be the advocate for safety at your facility.

INSURANCE

Your YMCA will have a comprehensive insurance package that is reviewed at least annually by insurance advisers and legal counsel. It should include, where applicable, the following items:

• Comprehensive liability
• Property coverage
• Accident coverage
• Employer's nonownership liability
• Hired and leased vehicle coverage
• Fire, theft, and catastrophe coverage
• Motor vehicle coverage
• Worker's compensation
• Directors' and officers' liability coverage

Your insurance package should cover your aquatics programs and facilities and the staff and volunteers involved in program delivery. The coverage should meet the requirements of state and local laws and should be coordinated with your YMCA's insurance coverage. You should understand the basic types of insurance coverage used in aquatics programs and facilities. The three categories of protection are property, social, and liability. Most claims originate from building and grounds hazards, transporting individuals, program activities, and performance of duties by employees.

EMERGENCY AND ACCIDENT MANAGEMENT PROCEDURES

An *aquatic emergency* is a sudden occurrence in an aquatics facility that, if not attended to with a quick, planned response, may result in injury or death. An *aquatics accident* is an incident or accident in an aquatics facility in which an injury or death has occurred.

Because even the best risk management plan can't eliminate all risks, you must be ready to deal with emergencies and accidents at your facility. You need to prepare for emergencies by determining what is needed to respond, setting policy guidelines, and developing emergency plans for a number of different scenarios.

Preparing for Emergencies

The most successful emergency responses are the result of effective teamwork, reducing the risks for both lifeguards and patrons and increasing the speed and efficiency with which an emergency situation can be handled. Formulate plans and an in-service training program for handling a variety of emergencies. Also evaluate your staff's performance after an emergency to help them identify hazardous areas and refine their responses, as well as to highlight their successes.

Your emergency team includes not only lifeguards, but also other key staff members, law enforcement officials, fire department personnel, emergency medical staff, civil defense officials, and the members of a variety of other local organizations. Involving each group in your plans makes those plans more efficient and more effective.

All facility staff should have some aquatic safety training. Branch directors, facility supervisors, and other managers must participate in the Staff Aquatic Safety Training (SAST), available from the YMCA Program Store, once a year as a refresher (it should be mandatory for any new branch director, facility supervisor, or manager as part of their orientation). They may also participate in the YMCA Aquatic Safety Assistant (YASA) certification course. These trainings can help managers and staff identify issues that may need to be addressed so that their YMCAs can be prepared for emergencies. You should also meet regularly with your aquatics staff and participate in regular training and drills related to safety.

Anyone responsible for supervising a facility should be fully prepared to

- assist a lifeguard in an emergency,
- supervise the pool area, and
- support the work of the lifeguards.

These skills and related best practices are taught in the safety trainings referred to earlier.

Other ways you can prepare for emergencies are to examine the facility's layout for the best emergency routes, assess whether additional rescue equipment is needed, and make sure all staff know the emergency medical procedures.

Facility Layout

Another key to quick and successful emergency response is knowing the layout of your facility. That may sound simple enough, but knowing the easiest way for medical personnel to reach each area is vital in an emergency. Plan for emergency access—don't leave finding the best route for emergency personnel to chance! Determine ahead of time the shortest and safest routes for paramedics to reach all locations at your facility.

Consider the following factors:

- The length and width of the backboard and ambulance gurney
- Stairs
- Sharp corners and narrow hallways
- Locked doors or other obstacles

Once you have planned the shortest and safest access routes for emergency personnel, make sure that these routes are kept clear at all times. The excitement of an emergency situation may make clearing the routes difficult when it is most important.

Arrange in-service training sessions with outside emergency personnel to practice your procedures. During these practice sessions, you can determine whether you have selected appropriate access routes and, when possible, what the best location is for them to enter the building. Post those routes, along with the locations of fire alarms, fire extinguishers, telephones, first aid areas, and tornado areas, for all staff and patrons.

Also make sure that exits, and especially emergency doors, are marked clearly from the pool area and that lightbulbs are replaced in lighted signs. Patrons should have easy access to emergency doors in case evacuation of the pool area is necessary. Prominently post near the pool and locker rooms a participant accident and emergency evacuation plan with clear, precise directions.

Equipment Assessment List

Make sure your equipment and supplies are examined and checked off every day as part of your opening procedure. Every facility should have a variety of lifeguarding and emergency medical equipment available within easy access of lifeguard stations at all times, including an adequate supply of the following:

- Shepherd's crooks or reaching poles
- Soft ring buoys 15 to 18 inches in diameter, attached securely to a length of line sufficient to reach across the width of the pool
- Rescue tubes or buoys (one for each lifeguard)
- Backboards with straps (a minimum of three), head immobilizers, and a complete set of cervical collars (three adult and three child)
- Telephones and posted emergency telephone numbers
- First aid kits completely stocked to treat all common pool emergencies (including resuscitation masks, mechanical suction devices, protective glasses, rubber gloves, and gowns)
- Blankets
- Oxygen (recommended)
- AEDs (recommended)

Every locale has different codes specifying the requirements for the equipment needs of recreational facilities. Contact your state, county, and local health departments for lists of the apparatus they require.

Emergency and rescue equipment that is broken, in poor repair, or locked in a room is of little use in an emergency. All equipment should be in good working condition, available for use at all times, and should be inspected regularly.

Place first aid kits and equipment throughout your facility, and post signs showing their location. Inventory first aid materials and equipment monthly, and replace and update supplies on a regular basis. Keep a record of all inspections on file.

Emergency equipment is valuable only if all staff members know where it is stored and how to use it. Post signs showing the location of emergency equipment. Schedule regular staff in-service training sessions to ensure that lifeguards can react effectively to a variety of emergency situations within their zone of responsibility.

Emergency Medical Procedures

All personnel should be aware of the needs and procedures of the EMS personnel who respond to emergencies. Ignorance or misunderstanding of these needs and procedures may cause increased danger for the injured individual and may expose the facility to increased legal liability.

All your staff should know how to contact the EMS in your area. In many areas of the country, emergency medical assistance can be summoned by dialing 911. Check to see if your community uses this system. If not, prominently post emergency phone numbers near all telephones at your facility. Make sure an accessible phone or emergency alarm system is in the immediate pool area, with procedures and emergency numbers posted next to it.

If the lifeguard who first notices an emergency doesn't make the call to the EMS, she or he should delegate that task to another lifeguard or to a responsible adult. The caller has a crucial role in providing information to the medical team being dispatched. Post a script next to the phone with these guidelines for communicating with the EMS operator:

- Give your name, location, and telephone number to initiate the conversation.
- Explain what type of accident has occurred, what types of injuries victims have sustained, and where in the facility it occurred.
- Describe each victim's condition and what first aid has been provided.
- Answer honestly any questions asked of you. If you don't know an answer, say so. Do not guess! Someone's life is at stake.
- Ask the EMS operator to repeat your message back to you, especially if you have multiple facilities.
- Wait for the EMS operator to tell you to hang up the phone, then wait until the operator has disconnected before you do hang up. This will ensure that the EMS has gotten all of the information needed from you before you are disconnected.
- Wait by the phone momentarily to see whether a follow-up call is made.

Lifeguards should never transport a victim; they should wait for the EMS. If a victim's condition were to worsen while en route to the hospital in a car, a guard couldn't provide the necessary assistance, but paramedics could. The YMCA will also be protected from potential legal action regarding transportation by using emergency medical services rather than a private vehicle. In a remote area, exceptions may be necessary depending on the type of emergency. Lifeguards should follow the emergency plan set up previously.

Emergency Policy Guidelines

The YMCA encourages the management of all facilities to document emergency procedures before any emergency occurs. Having trained, knowledgeable personnel

can only enhance the quality and safety of your aquatics program. Establish the following steps:

1. Develop a plan.

   - Obtain copies of local and state regulations.
   - Analyze all past incident and accident reports.
   - Identify every potential emergency and accident that could possibly occur in your facility.
   - Establish an action plan for each situation deemed important. Break the plan down by what must be accomplished in the first 5 minutes, within 20 minutes, within the hour, within 5 hours, and within 24 hours.
   - Define the area that would be affected by the emergency and identify all personnel, equipment, and facilities that could be involved in any emergency or accident.
   - Identify and analyze all equipment and personnel needs in your facility.

2. Create a chain of command.

   - Specify a chain of command.
   - Specify an emergency team leader and define this leader's responsibilities and limitations.
   - Specify the personnel who should be involved in an emergency response and assign specific duties.

3. Write up procedures.

   - Establish a sequence of emergency steps.
   - Define the procedures for moving and transporting victims.
   - List emergency phone numbers. Prepare a written script for calling in emergencies and post it by the phone. (You may also want to have an emergency button for guards to call for assistance.)
   - Post accident and emergency procedures.

4. Plan training.

- Establish programs for the recruitment and training of your personnel.
- Develop and implement an in-service training program.
- Schedule regular safety rules and emergency procedure trainings and emergency procedure practice sessions for staff and volunteers. Rehearse procedures every two weeks during periods of peak facility use and at least once a month during other periods. Run drills at all times of the day that include the whole staff, not just the pool staff. Document these trainings and practice sessions.
- Annually involve an ambulance call to see how and where the paramedics respond. Work this out in advance with the EMS manager.

5. File reports.

- Develop an accident report and an accident report system.
- Instruct lifeguards in the importance of and procedures for completing accident and incident reports (described later in this chapter).

6. Prepare for public relations.

- Select one spokesperson for the facility and direct all questions to that person.
- Establish policies for providing information to the media, police, and other designated persons.
- Develop and implement a community relations program.

Have staff practice emergency procedures frequently and systematically. Present both planned practices with scenarios and unannounced drills. Only through practice will reactions be refined and procedures fully understood. Practice also makes the emergency situation less stressful, as all team members become familiar with their responsibilities. The more comfortable team members are when responding to their duties during an emergency, the more effective and efficient they will be.

When staff members practice emergency action plans, evaluate their performance with them and identify areas for improvement. Document all practices and keep them on file.

Developing Emergency Plans

Emergency plans include these fundamental steps, for which procedures should be clearly documented and understood by all related personnel:

- Initial reaction and assessment
- Initiation of the primary response by the lifeguard, including calling EMS
- Initiation of any necessary secondary response by other team members leading to resolution of the emergency (including providing first aid)
- Notification of designated personnel (Staff should be instructed not to comment on the emergency situation to any witness, bystander, or reporter. Only those specified in the chain of command should be given information.)
- Completion of the necessary incident or accident report
- Investigation of the incident
- Media statement by designated person
- Evaluation of the procedures utilized

The manner in which each of these steps is completed varies with the specific situation. You must determine which guards perform which duties. If you have a single-guard facility at certain times, you must establish a procedure for the lone lifeguard to signal for immediate assistance from other support staff and teach the lifeguard how to recruit assistance from adult patrons, if necessary. Under those circumstances, carefully define the responsibilities for the guard and be sure he or she can obtain the necessary assistance when needed. Make sure your facility has written procedures for handling emergencies. Be sure your staff members are familiar with the procedures and their responsibilities. Have the lifeguard in a single-guard facility practice coaching specific procedures such as a spinal cord injury where he or she may have to use members in the procedures. In-service training and practice sessions will help them feel comfortable in responding. Post major emergency procedures as a reminder to staff.

Also establish accident and emergency procedures for each off-site location in cooperation with the lessee or contracting organization. Write up these procedures and include them in your YMCA's aquatics program operations manual.

Below are some examples of emergency plans for pool evacuation, a life-threatening medical emergency, a near-drowning, and a missing person, plus a sample pool closing and security procedure.

Sample Pool Evacuation Plan

Each facility must have a plan for evacuating the pool area. In all emergencies, quick and organized action is important. This plan is appropriate for a weather emergency.

1. If you are the first guard to respond, signal other lifeguards to initiate the evacuation plan.

2. Signal swimmers to clear the pool.

3. Remain on post until all swimmers have left the water.

4. Assist other staff in directing patrons to a shelter or designated area.

5. Reassure patrons of their safety.

6. Report to management for further instruction or assignment.

7. Assist as necessary.

8. Assist in completion of the incident report form.

Sample Emergency Plan for a Life-Threatening Medical Emergency

This is a procedure for providing first aid for a heart attack victim requiring prompt attention:

1. Signal another guard to cover your area while you initiate first aid. If you are the only lifeguard, call for assistance using your preplanned emergency signal.

2. Assess the situation, call for EMS assistance, and provide the emergency first aid necessary.

3. Notify those in the chain of command.

4. Complete an accident report and file it with the appropriate person before returning to duty.

5. Review your actions with the manager.

Sample Emergency Plan for a Near-Drowning

A procedure for handling a water rescue situation at a multiguard facility is outlined here. Figure 9.1 illustrates one way that responsibilities can be divided.

1. Guard #1—Signals an emergency and initiates rescue and/or first aid.

2. Guard #2—Clears the pool and sends everyone into the locker rooms, then circles the pool to be sure no one was left behind. At this point Guard #2 begins to assist Guard #1.

3. Guard #3—Communicates with Guard #1 on the condition of the victim, then calls the EMS to explain the victim's condition. Guard #3 then goes to the emergency access door to make sure the EMS can gain access to area where the victim is located. Then Guard #1 calmly notifies those on the chain of command of the accident; they in turn notify emergency contacts (relatives or other designated individuals).

4. Guard #1 should complete and file an accident report, and all guards should return to duty as soon as possible.

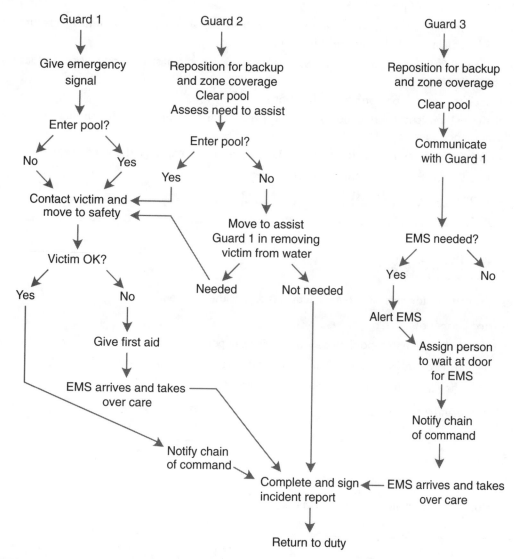

Figure 9.1   Multiguard emergency plan flowchart.

Sample Emergency Plan for a Missing Person

Have an emergency plan for finding a missing person and have your staff practice it. A variety of different search and rescue techniques can be used for open water areas; see *On the Guard II* (4th ed.) for more details.

Here are steps for a missing person search at a pool:

1. Signal the other guards to initiate missing person procedures.
2. Signal an immediate pool check.
3. Clear the pool.
4. Get an accurate description of the missing person, including age, race, height, weight, color of hair, color of clothing, and where he or she was last seen. Keep the person giving this description in a designated area to be available whenever necessary.
5. Do a visual search as quickly as possible.
6. If the missing person has become a drowning victim, complete the rescue and begin emergency first aid immediately. Arrange for EMS assistance.
7. If it is determined that the missing person is not a drowning victim, allow swimmers to return to the water while taking the following steps in order:
   a. Check all facilities, including washrooms, locker rooms, gymnasiums, and any related facility on the grounds.
   b. Check the missing person's home by phone.
   c. If the person is not found, notify those on the chain of command, who should in turn notify emergency contacts.
   d. Notify law enforcement officials. This is the duty of the manager or the head lifeguard.
8. Complete the necessary accident or incident report.
9. Return to duty as soon as possible.

Sample Pool Closing and Security Procedure

Use these procedures for closing between activities and at the day's end.

1. Lifeguard clears pool.
2. Lifeguard circles the entire pool, closely observing the pool bottom to be sure no one is left behind.
3. Another lifeguard, staff member, or Y member witnesses the lifeguard circling the pool.
4. Lifeguard who circled the pool signs the pool log as follows:

Pool closed and locked by:

_____   _____   _____
Lifeguard signature   Date   Time

5. Witness signs the log as follows:

Pool closure and locking procedure witnessed by:

_____   _____   _____
Witness signature   Date   Time

6. When an outdoor pool is closed and heavy rain has obscured the bottom, the lifeguard should make a thorough underwater search before signing the log.

Self-Assessment of Emergency Preparedness

To see how well you have prepared your facility and staff to handle aquatic emergencies, use the checklist in figure 9.4 (page 285) for assessment.

RECORD KEEPING

Good records are an important component of risk management and emergency planning. Accurate records are needed for the following purposes:

- Budget development
- Consistency in hiring practices
- Compliance with state regulations
- Documentation of completed maintenance
- Documentation of safety inspections
- Staff evaluation for promotion and termination
- Verification of attention to health and sanitation
- Verification that your risk management plan is functioning
- Liability purposes
- Tracking injuries

You will need to keep several types of records:

Employment records: applications, job descriptions, written tests, payroll, staff evaluation, manager's report. Some of these records may be filed in the personnel office and others in the aquatics director's office.

Maintenance records: pool log, remedial maintenance, inventory control

Safety: hazard analysis, safety inspections, risk control reports, in-service training, staff meeting minutes

Accidents: accident and incident reports, injury charts

You must store and organize your records properly. Different departments within your organization may have responsibility for maintaining some of these types of records for the whole association. Determining who is responsible for maintaining each of these records is important. To be sure you turn in or maintain the proper records, ask your executive.

Try to keep records such as medical release forms and emergency information accessible to staff. Your staff won't need to see these records often, but access may be crucial in an emergency situation.

Let's look at two documents that can be used to record the details of accidents and incidents and analyze them to prevent future occurrences: accident and incident reports and injury charts.

Accident and Incident Reports

As professionals, your staff members are responsible for their decisions. In the case of an emergency, completing accident and incident reports is often the only way to substantiate your facility's procedures and your staff's actions if they are ever questioned. An accident report is used any time first aid is required; an incident report is used for any other situation, usually one in which a lifeguard, staff member, or outside agency is called into action (such as discipline problems or theft).

Establish procedures for reporting and recording an accident or emergency, and explain them to your staff. Insist that staff complete the reports carefully as soon after the emergency as possible, as accurate detail is critical. Make sure that copies of the forms are readily available.

Once a staff member has filled out a form, make and send copies of this report to the appropriate authorities, as well as to the supervisor and the executive director for review and follow-up. Also give the staff person who filled out the form a copy for her or his own records. Keep the original form on file.

A sample Accident Report Form is shown in figure 9.2. This sample should serve as a guide; amend it to meet the unique needs of your facility. From the form or other records, the following information should be provided:

- Names, titles, employment numbers, years of experience, locations of assignments, hours on duty, and lunch periods of employees involved
- Date, type, and amount of training for each employee involved
- Time, location, and nature of the accident
- Number of persons involved in the accident
- Weather and water conditions
- Number of people present at the pool or beach where the accident occurred
- General comments of importance in evaluating the situation
- Plan or sketch of the area showing any unusual conditions and assignment of personnel if deemed necessary (should be prepared by the supervisor and the lifeguard)
- Names, addresses, and phone numbers of witnesses to the accident
- Social security number and birth date of the victim

These questions should also be answered:

- How did the employee become aware of the accident?
- How soon did the employee respond to the emergency situation?
- What did the employee do in response to the emergency situation?
- Did the guard have to enter the water to effect a rescue?
- How far did the guard have to swim?
- What action did the guard take to help the victim?
- What rescue equipment did the guard use?
- What did the guard observe about the victim's condition?
- Did the guard observe signs of spinal injury? If so, what were they?
- Did the guard need assistance with the rescue?
- Did anything interfere with the rescue?
- Did the guard do everything possible to help revive the victim?
- Was the victim identified? By whom?
- What were the factors contributing to the accident?
- What was the victim doing at the time of distress?
- Could the victim swim?
- Had the victim disregarded rules or orders given by the lifeguard?
- What first aid was administered?
- Was CPR necessary? Was effective circulation noted in carotid pulse or skin color?

- Were police, emergency squad, and ambulance called? At what time?
- How soon did they respond?
- What action did they take?
- Was rescue breathing continued? By whom?
- When did the EMS personnel or doctor take over?
- When did the EMS personnel or doctor make a declaration of the victim's condition?
- Was the victim removed from the beach or pool area? At what time?

Sample Accident Report Form

Date of report: _____

Name of injured person: _____ Age: _____ Sex: _____

Address: _____

Date of accident: _____ Time: _____ Number of people in water: _____

Water condition: _____ Weather condition: _____

Describe the accident. Include where the accident occurred, what happened, and how many people were involved in the accident.

List the names of those involved in the accident and comment on their swimming skills if such skills contributed to the accident.

Did those involved disregard rules or orders of the lifeguard? _____ If so, explain.

Identify who, if anyone, was injured and describe the injuries.

Describe the first aid given.

Was CPR used? _____ For how long? _____

Were law enforcement or EMS squads called? _____ What time did they arrive? _____

Was additional medical attention required? _____ If so, indicate where individuals were taken, who provided treatment, and what treatment was given.

(continued)

Figure 9.2 Sample accident report form.

Blood-Borne Pathogen Program Exposure Incident

Employee name: _____ Soc. Sec. no.: _____

Was the source the injured person listed above? _____ Yes _____ No

If not, give source's name: _____

Address: _____ Phone no.: _____

Document route of exposure: (mucous membrane, puncture, etc.) _____

_____

Was protective equipment used? _____ Yes   Describe equipment. _____

_____

_____

Was protective equipment used? _____ No   Give reason it was not used. _____

_____

_____

Describe postexposure cleanup procedures that were used: _____

_____

Lifeguard Information

Name: _____ Position: _____

Years of experience: _____ Assignment location: _____ Hours on/off duty: _____

List names, addresses, and phone numbers of at least two witnesses on the back of this sheet.

Sketch the area of the accident, showing unusual conditions (if any) and assignments of personnel.

General comments of employees:

Signature: _____ Date: _____

Figure 9.2 *(continued)*

Because some incidents require less emergency action, your facility may not have a form for reporting them. Minor incidents, such as a patron running on the deck, do not require a report. If staff have asked a patron to leave the facility or if an outside agency has been contacted, have staff prepare a report describing the situation, those involved, and the actions taken. Define for staff when these forms need to be completed.

Injury Chart

One way to improve your ability to prevent and react to injury situations is to determine what injuries occur and where. An injury chart can be an effective tool for gathering that information. The chart is a diagram of the supervised area, complete with all pieces of equipment, diving boards, ladders, lifelines, depth markings, lifeguard stations, fences, recreation areas, and auxiliary facilities. Each time an accident occurs, it is noted on the chart with a code. (See sample chart in figure 9.3.)

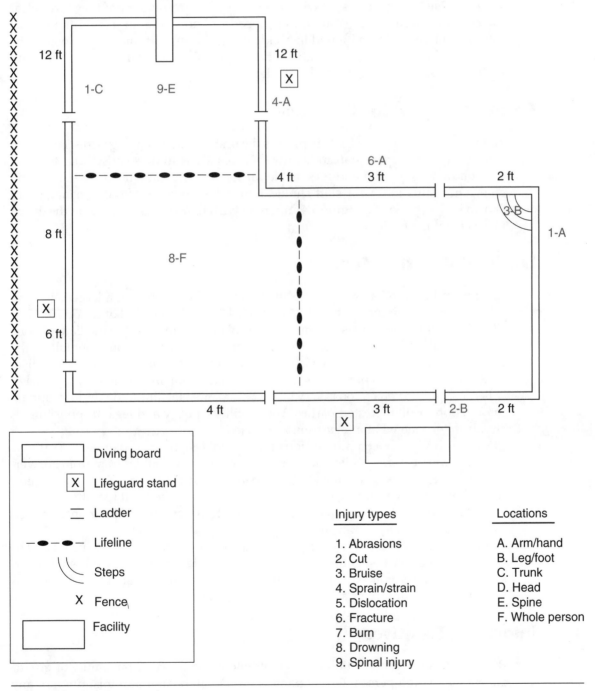

Figure 9.3 Sample injury chart.

Your facility may have a code system for listing all the types of injuries sustained. A letter, number, or symbol may be assigned to each injury. From this chart, you and your staff can learn about the common accidents and injuries at the facility and where they are likely to occur. You can then plan actions to be taken to prevent future accidents: establish new rules, repair equipment, install additional safety equipment, reposition lifeguards, add additional staff, or limit access to an area.

CRISIS MANAGEMENT

When a crisis arises, your staff will do a better job of resolving it if they have clear directions on what to do. You will also need to know how to handle the media, inform relatives of those injured in accidents, and transport injured persons to the hospital. After the crisis, you will want to help your staff deal with any posttraumatic distress that results from the incident.

Crisis Management Checklist

Having emergency procedures in place is the first step in managing crises. However, it also helps to prepare staff to handle their reactions to those crises and to think about how to stay calm and reasonable during stressful situations. To handle any emergency situation, your staff should know the elements of crisis management shown in the checklist in figure 9.4. You may wish to post this checklist in the guard room and at the front desk.

Dealing With the Media

Be prepared for media involvement in any emergency involving a large facility or when an accident or incident has been reported to EMS personnel or the police. Your YMCA should have a crisis communication plan for handling the media.Only one person should be the media contact—all other YMCA people should not talk to the press. Although most reporters wish you and your facility no ill will, sensationalism sells news, so it is good practice to use care in making statements about emergencies.

Because public perception is very important to most facilities, convey appropriate information to all interested parties. Your facility's policy and legal responsibilities should determine what information is released.

Your facility's crisis communication plan should designate a spokesperson to make all media contacts and public statements. All other staff should refrain from answering questions or making comments. Some patrons may ask seemingly innocent questions about events at the facility or about the situation itself. All too often the "patron" turns out to be a media or legal representative trying to obtain information that may or may not be relevant to the incident.

It may be helpful to have a standard statement that staff can use, such as: "The accident is under investigation, and a statement will be released by our spokesperson shortly. Thank you. Now I must return to my job." Instruct staff to move on and answer no more questions after making this statement.

Informing Relatives

Part of your emergency action plan should include contacting the family or guardians of the injured person. Notify parents immediately after administration of any first aid treatment to children. If the injury is severe and the staff is attending to the

Checklist for Crisis Management

Be Prepared

Know your facility's emergency procedures, including how to fill out an incident report, and review them regularly. Make sure phone numbers are available for the following people or agencies:

    Supervisor/manager:

    Police/sheriff:

    Fire:

    Ambulance:

    Poison control center:

    Chemical accident hotline:

    Health department:

Maintain Order

Confusion and fear can make a bad situation worse. Stay calm and act with authority. Follow procedures as you have practiced them. Make sure that everyone present is in a safe place and unharmed before continuing with emergency plans.

Notify the Chain of Command

Report the incident to your supervisor or another designated manager as soon as possible. If necessary, call for emergency personnel or information.

Protect Your Facility

Make no statements to anyone about the incident; only the media spokesperson should discuss it publicly. File your incident report as soon as you can, using your facility's standard form. Include separate documentation of witnesses' statements.

Return to Your Post

Resume regular operations as soon as possible. This helps calm patrons and staff and reduces negative speculation about the event.

Learn From the Experience

With other staff, review how the incident was handled. Discuss the event, determine the causes, evaluate your responses, and consider what other actions you could have taken. This lets you offer ideas for improving safety, express your emotions about the occurrence, and help improve emergency procedures.

Figure 9.4 Crisis management checklist.

injury until EMS arrives, notify the parents as soon as possible after EMS assumes control of treatment. Depending on the policies established, your executive or other appointed director will be the one to call the family. The information given to the family will vary according to the severity of the injury.

The following information will be helpful to the family:

- Give your name.
- Explain that there has been an accident.
- Give a brief explanation of the accident.
- Inform them of who was contacted (EMS, doctor, hospital).
- Identify the hospital where the injured person was taken.
- Give the phone number where the director can be contacted.

Answer any additional questions the family may have relating to the accident. Families will appreciate information about the injury and the transport of their family member to a medical facility. Try to be calm and reassuring when reporting the incident to the family.

Transporting Victims to a Hospital

A YMCA representative, usually the aquatics director or another professional staff member, should accompany an injured child or member to a medical facility and stay until the family arrives. This may involve comforting the injured person or being present while he or she is being cared for before the arrival of the family. As part of good emergency planning, discuss what the YMCA representative can and cannot say to the family and others, and make sure he or she is clear about this long before any accident occurs.

STAFF POSTTRAUMATIC STRESS

Any time staff are involved in a rescue, they are subject to great stress as a result of their duty to react to the emergency and the danger faced in doing so. Well-trained professionals generally can respond to emergencies without stress interfering with rescue efforts. It is vital that staff remain calm while carrying out emergency procedures. That is why practice is so important.

After the emergency is over, however, especially one in which a severe injury or death occurred, staff may experience posttraumatic stress disorder. Psychological trauma can occur in the wake of an unexpected event that a person has experienced intimately and forcefully. Many levels of trauma are possible, but typically the more intensely the person experienced the event, the greater the trauma may be.

People have a variety of responses to experiencing or seeing a severe injury. Victims may have no memory of the event. Some may eventually remember what happened, while others may never recall it. As losing a block of time can be very frightening, some people may need help in accepting this loss; others may feel relieved that they don't remember.

Many perceptual distortions may also have occurred during the traumatic incident. Time may have seemed changed so that seconds seemed to last for minutes. A trauma victim's sense of time is almost never accurate. Loud sounds may have been muted to popping noises. Traumatized people rarely feel the full pain of their injury as it occurs or immediately after. Later, they also may be ashamed and disgusted about what they did.

Responses to a traumatic incident might include recurrent upsetting emotions or memories such as the following:

- Attacks of anxious arousal
- Fear of losing control over impulses and drives
- Fear that painful intrusive elements of trauma will not cease
- Fear that grief will result in ceaseless crying and uncontrollable emotional turbulence
- Fear of total breakdown
- Guilt over specific behaviors enacted during the event
- Guilt over specific actions during the event
- Anger/rage toward authorities, persons, and institutions
- Guilt over presumed lost opportunity to effect a less tragic outcome

Traumatized people may experience recurrent nightmares, which could be described as "dreams of incomplete, unconsummated action." In those dreams, they may feel the following:

- An inability to complete an important action that would facilitate survival at the moment
- A sense of being fettered and totally frozen by fear and catastrophic expectations
- A sense of vulnerability
- A feeling of being a victim of dangerous, menacing forces with intent to do harm
- An inability to escape from menacing pursuit

Other symptoms that may occur include the following:

- Undue, prolonged anxiety; state of constant tension and fear.
- An inability to fall asleep.
- Irritability and aggressive outbursts.
- Self-blame.
- Dissociation from reality through illusions, hallucinations, or flashbacks. The person has an inner sense of fragmentation, of things crumbling or falling apart. Fear and rage are walled off.
- Prolonged or severe depression characterized by

    a. feelings of inadequacy, helplessness, hopelessness, undue pessimism, and loss of confidence;

    b. changes in behavior patterns;

    c. withdrawal from friends and loved ones whom the individual normally enjoys and from occupations and hobbies that usually give the person pleasure; or

    d. low energy, chronic fatigue, and decreased effectiveness.

- Abrupt changes in mood and behavior, with serious alterations in the individual's normal habits or ways of thinking.
- Physical symptoms caused by tension, such as a daily headache, a tension-induced migraine, or nausea.

As the aquatics director, you need to know how to handle staff's or victims' trauma. The first step is to recognize that it can happen. Organize a written plan for dealing with the possibility, and include psychological professionals as you develop your plan. Incorporate it into your emergency action plan.

As an immediate response to a traumatic situation, do the following:

- Oversee the emergency action plan.
- Close the facility, if necessary.
- Debrief staff using an approved statement. Give them as much factual information as possible about the incident and the condition of the injured party. (This also helps avoid misinformation.)
- Show genuine concern. A sensitive approach by you may influence how quickly and thoroughly a staff member recovers. Keep in mind that people's emotions will range from numbness to fear or anger; those directly involved may be in a state of shock.
- Provide nonjudgmental moral support to others directly involved.
- Follow up with phone calls to staff and members.
- Have a counselor on call for staff to discuss feelings, either in person or by phone.

After you have taken care of immediate concerns, be prepared to offer your staff support and assistance with their reactions to the event. Set aside time within 24 to 72 hours of the incident for staff to discuss and work through their feelings. Offer professional services to facilitate the discussion. Have separate discussion groups for those who were directly involved and those who were indirectly involved. Invite others who witnessed the traumatic event to participate in counseling.

If some staff members show symptoms of trauma but are not willing to participate in discussion, do not force them to do so. Approach them privately and sensitively talk to them about the symptoms you've observed. Let them know that you can refer them to an individual counselor.

Encourage your staff's recovery by giving them the following suggestions:

- Think through what you did during the incident and emphasize those things you did well.
- Be aware that authorities are not trying to assess blame as they gather information about the accident; their questions are just part of the necessary "system." Be as objective as possible.
- Don't isolate yourself. Talk with supportive others in a safe environment. Remember to support others who are in similar situations.
- Eat a healthy, balanced diet to significantly improve your ability to cope (National Safety Council, 1997).
- Try to maintain a normal life schedule, including schoolwork, socializing, and lifeguarding.

ACCIDENT INVESTIGATION

Part of preparing for emergencies is planning for accident investigations. After an accident or injury, you can do a number of things to help in the investigation of the incident. Knowing what needs to be done will help you plan the most effective way to complete the investigation so you can then move forward with your program operations. Be sure you review with your executive the steps you plan to take to be sure they agree with your association's procedures, your legal counsel's advice, and the insurance agents. Taking prompt action to compile information and obtain the facts relating to the case can also assist you in educating your defense counsel. Your association may want to seek additional advice from an aquatics liability expert as well. The amount of your personal involvement in accident investigation will be determined by your association's procedures, but you need to know what will happen after a major accident.

The accident reports should be factual, describing everything that happened and relating how staff and others responded. Do not release any accident reports or related records to unauthorized persons. We've already discussed completing accident reports. Other actions will include the following:

Obtaining witness statements. Witness statements should be done by the YMCA lawyer if at all possible. There should be clear communication as to your involvement as executive, the lawyers, and the insurance company.

Creating an accident chronology and timeline from witness statements.

Preparing for meetings with supervisors, police, the coroner, and the health department.

Taking pictures or videotape of the pool area and signage.

Implementing necessary sanitation procedures.

Making copies of all reports for your attorney and insurance company.

Filing claims and incident reports with the appropriate insurance companies, child welfare agencies, health department, OSHA, and state and local agencies.

Data compilation will include many pieces. Your record keeping will be important in the efficient retrieval and review of relevant files. These may include the following, depending on the type of accident:

Accident-related reports (EMS, police, autopsy, accident, weather, daily pool log, emergency room admission, photographs and videotape)

Witness data such as name, address, Social Security number, birth date, and phone number

Personnel data, including job descriptions, application forms, evaluations, certifications, reprimands and commendations

Media records, including newspaper articles and television news video

Copies of current state and local codes, design manuals and health department directives

Rescue equipment inventory, including type of rescue items, number of each, and condition of the equipment (rescue tubes, rescue buoys, backboards, cervical collars, suction kits, oxygen cylinder and AEDs)

Facility policies, including your lifeguard manual, operations manual, and pool rules and warnings

Design data, including depth markers, transition slope, under- and above-water lighting levels, and blueprints and architect specifications (specs and what was actually built)

Operations data, including testing and recording of the Langelier Saturation Index, disinfectant level, turbidity, TDS (total dissolved solids), water and air temperature, filter gauge pressure, flow meter reading, number of bathers, and bacteria test

Inspections, including electrical and health department, and safety checklists, lab reports, and permits to operate

Staff records, including lesson plans, instructor manuals, skill sheets, coaches' workouts, course outlines, written tests, and performance records

You may be asked to help educate your defense counsel about the facts so that they can present your case most effectively. Some of the topics and information that you may want to review include these:

Pool operations manual

Facility lifeguard orientation and in-service training program

Accident emergency procedures

Lifeguard evaluations and certifications

Lifeguard, CPR, and first aid manuals

Bathing codes and design manuals

Discuss the materials in your files and assist with interrogatories and depositions.

THE LEGAL PROCESS

After any accident, there is a possibility that the victim or a relative of the victim will initiate legal action against the aquatics facility and the lifeguards on duty at the time of the accident. The process usually follows the general path illustrated in figure 9.5.

In our society, a lawsuit can be brought against anyone for any reason, so the filing of a complaint doesn't mean a facility or lifeguard is guilty of any wrongdoing. Rather,

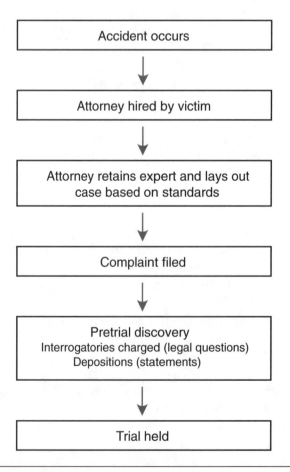

Figure 9.5   The lawsuit process.

it means that the plaintiff's attorney has gathered information on the case and that the plaintiff is willing to present the case to a court for a decision.

Before a trial, attorneys for the plaintiff and for the defense continue to gather information and to secure sworn testimony from experts on the standard of care for the particular situation under examination. This is called pretrial discovery. The plaintiff must prove that the defendant's actions caused the injury sustained and that the injury was foreseeable and therefore preventable.

Such court cases may be heard by a jury or by a judge alone. In either situation, both sides of the case are presented. After a deliberation or discussion period, the judge or jury decides whether the defendant is guilty of the charges and, if so, what damages should be awarded.

Aquatics Liability

Most lawsuits concerning aquatic activities involve a perceived wrong. Liability arises when an injury results from a swimmer's failure to observe proper aquatic technique. Most lawsuits filed against aquatics facilities focus on two elements that give rise to liability: negligence and nuisance. Because specific laws regarding aquatics liability vary from state to state, we will consider general principles in this section. Check with the appropriate departments in your local government to learn about the laws governing aquatics facilities in your area.

Negligence

In the law of negligence, the person bringing suit—the plaintiff—must prove

- that the defendant owed a duty to the plaintiff,
- that the defendant breached that duty,
- that the plaintiff suffered some injury or loss, and
- that the injury or loss was caused by the defendant's breach (proximate cause).

All four elements must be proved for the lawsuit to advance.

Negligence can take many forms. *Willful negligence* is performing an action intended to cause someone harm. Unintentional acts of negligence that cause harm are considered *slight, ordinary,* or *gross negligence,* depending on their severity. Examples of unintentional negligence include failure to foresee a potential hazard, carelessness, poor judgment, excitement, inattention to duty, inexperience, ignorance, stupidity, and forgetfulness.

Lifeguards assume a legal duty to provide the services they were trained to provide to each patron of your facility while they are on duty. That doesn't mean that they ensure the safety of patrons. Rather, it means that if an accident occurs while a lifeguard is on duty, he or she must function competently. In other words, a lifeguard must respond by providing the standard of care outlined by the organization that certified him or her and the care that is expected of professional lifeguards. If a lifeguard performed according to those standards, he or she should not be found negligent.

Two common types of negligence are not responding to constructive notice and not fulfilling the ordinary standard of care.

The facility management should know of any potentially dangerous conditions that may exist, regardless of whether or not they have actual knowledge or actual notice of those conditions. In other words, if an employee or a patron sees a hazardous condition but fails to report it to the owner, the owner is considered to have *constructive notice* because she or he should have been aware of the condition. If an injury occurs because of this hazardous condition, the owner can be held liable because of negligence.

In any pool facility, the management must ensure the following conditions:

- Chemicals are stored safely and used properly.
- Rescue equipment is in good working condition and readily available.
- Ladders and diving structures are safe and in good repair.
- Lighting, including underwater lighting, is safe and adequate for intended use.
- Pool water is disinfected and pH levels are correctly adjusted according to local or state regulations.
- Water is clear enough to see the drains at the deep end.
- Water depth is clearly and accurately marked at all places, especially in shallow and deep water.
- Regular checks are made for hazards such as broken glass, equipment that has not been put away, or cracked cement around posts supporting the diving structure and lifeguard chairs.

A lifeguard also can be found negligent if he or she does not fulfill the *ordinary standard of care* owed a patron; a lifeguard is obligated to use the care that circumstances would indicate to a prudent and careful person. Negligence would be based on the plaintiff's demonstrating that the lifeguard's actions fell below what could be expected of other similarly trained individuals in similar circumstances.

Attractive Nuisance

An attractive nuisance is not the same as negligence. Rather, in the legal sense, it is something that attracts people to it and causes harm, inconvenience, annoyance, or damage. The operation of a swimming facility is not by itself a nuisance if it is done without disturbing the surroundings. Large floodlights, loud music, and inadequate parking, however, could be judged nuisances. An attractive nuisance may also include parts of an association facility such as playground apparatus, a ropes course, a bicycle path, trampoline, or a spray pool.

Liability Defenses

To avoid legal liability, you must exercise reasonable care. Although there are numerous ways to be held liable for an injury, the only sure way to avoid liability is to see that an injury doesn't occur. By taking the appropriate actions to ensure the safety of your patrons and by adhering to state and local regulations for aquatics facilities, you will be doing as much as you can to prevent accidents.

Many organizations suggest that lifeguards obtain liability insurance for their lifeguarding activities. Most facilities have liability insurance to protect themselves and their employees, and many personal general liability insurance policies include such liability coverage.

If a liability suit against an aquatics facility should come to trial, the following are some types of defenses that the defendants might use.

Governmental or Sovereign Immunity

In some states, government employees involved in liability actions can claim immunity because of their positions as "agents" of the state.

Charitable Immunity

In the charitable immunity defense, or a cap on assessable damages, immunity is granted by law to organizations that are deemed charities. In some states, this defense is available to YMCAs. In other states it is not. Check with a lawyer in your state to determine if the defense is available.

Assumption of Risk

In the assumption-of-risk defense, the defendant combats the plaintiff's charges by claiming that the plaintiff assumed or accepted a certain level of risk by entering the aquatics facility and by participating in the activity that led to the injury. For example, a patron who dove from the diving board and hit her or his head on the end of the board could be said to have assumed that risk by deciding to attempt a dive.

Last Clear Chance

In many accidents, the injured party could have stopped some action before the injury occurred. If the plaintiff had a clear chance to avoid the accident and did not, the lifeguard and/or facilities might not be found negligent.

Importance of Accurate Records

In many facilities, patrons must sign waivers of liability. By signing such forms, they agree that they will not hold the facility liable for injuries they receive while participating in specific activities. These waivers do not remove liability resulting from faulty or damaged equipment or any intentional or willful negligence by staff. Such waivers are not effective with minors, who are not legally able to waive their rights.

Other records that may be of use in aquatics facilities include staff manuals, emergency plans, posted rules governing the facility, accident and incident reports, and chemical safety logs. These records can establish the standard of care that your facility provides, and they include information that will be vital to your defense in the event of a lawsuit. Be sure you and your staff complete these records systematically and file them carefully. If you usually keep excellent records but cannot provide them for a particular situation, you would appear to have failed to have met the standards your organization has set. It is not generally necessary to keep records for longer than five years.

BIBLIOGRAPHY

Everstine, D., and Everstine, L. 1993. *The trauma response.* New York: W.W. Norton.

National Safety Council. 1997. *First aid and CPR standard.* Sudbury, MA: Jones and Bartlett.

Wison, J., and Kahana, B. (Eds.) 1988. *Human adaptation to extreme stress.* New York: Plenum Press.

Wolman, B., and Stricker, G. (Eds.). 1994. *Anxiety and related disorders.* New York: John Wiley & Sons.

Rules and Regulations

To prevent aquatic accidents, you need to be familiar with your state's bathing code, your swimming facility, and the hazards within your facility. You then can establish rules that minimize danger and see that they are enforced consistently.

If your facility has water recreation attractions, such as slides or wave pools, or inflatables, you will need to have additional special rules and regulations to ensure patrons' safety. And finally, you need to prepare your guards to handle situations that may include patrons' breaking the law or threatening others.

ESTABLISHING AND COMMUNICATING RULES

You, as the aquatics director, will be the prime staff person involved in the development, communication, and enforcement of the rules of your aquatics facility. In most facilities, the management tries to keep the number of rules for patrons to a minimum to keep the atmosphere as enjoyable as possible. When you find that additional rules are needed, consider both the safety and enjoyment of patrons when you design those rules. Set rules that are realistic, specific, and understandable.

To add a rule based on your evaluation of the incidents and accidents at your facility, draft a statement of how you want to deal with the situation and include your rationale for the rule. Then share it with your executive director to gain his or her support. Finally, submit it to your program/aquatics committee for discussion and for recommendation to the board for final approval. Once the rule is approved, it is your responsibility to communicate it to the members and patrons of the facility, lifeguards, and other staff members. After the rules are established, the lifeguards must enforce the rules consistently among patrons.

The first step in enforcing the rules is communicating them. The most logical way to inform the users of a facility of the rules is to post them in the swimming area. Fences at pool entrances, lifeguard stands, and diving mounts are all appropriate spots to mount signs. (Refer to the American National Standards Institute sign standards for suggestions on creating readable signs.) Copies of the rules can be handed out with pool passes or perhaps listed in a facility newsletter.

COMMON RULES FOR HIGH-RISK LOCATIONS

Certain areas of any aquatics environment can be more dangerous than others. Lifeguards must closely supervise the areas where accidents occur most frequently (see figure 10.1). In the following section, each area's potential dangers are described, along with some suggested safety rules. (For more on safety and water play elements, see chapter 12.)

Entrance

Wanting to get into the water as quickly as possible often leads swimmers to run at the entrance to the pool. A wet and slippery deck poses a high risk, and one swimmer can easily collide with another.

Pool Deck

Running and rough play are the primary concerns on the pool deck. Many falls are the result of runners sliding or bumping into other patrons. Nonswimmers also can be knocked into the water by people running on the deck. Good-natured rough play often escalates, causing participants or bystanders to be pushed or knocked to the ground or into the water. This behavior detracts from the enjoyment of others at your facility.

Guards should also check the deck when the pool opens to make sure that equipment or other obstructions are not on the deck where patrons might trip or fall on them.

Suggested rule:

Pushing and rough play are prohibited.

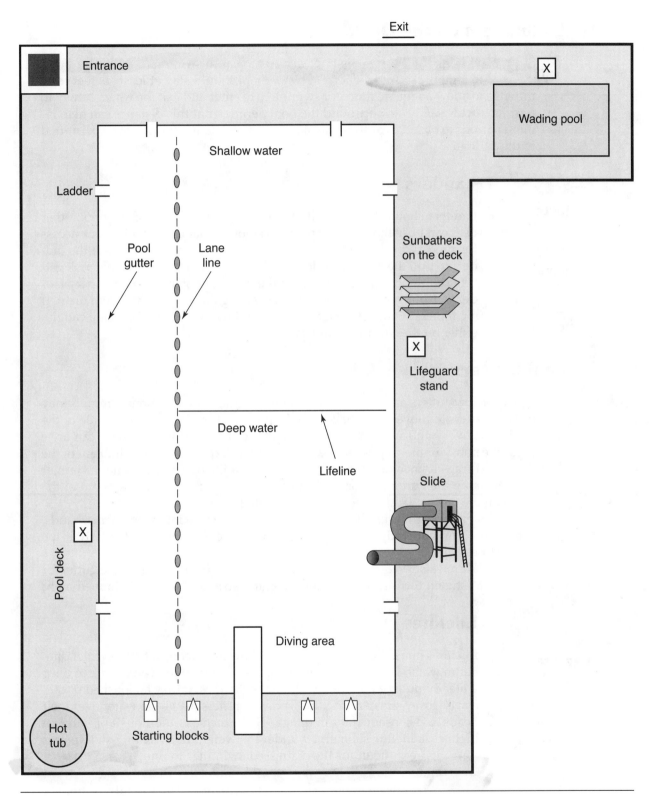

Figure 10.1 High-risk areas in a swimming facility.

Sunbathers on the Deck

Sunbathers lying too close to the pool's edge can cause swimmers walking around the pool to stumble or trip. Generally, sunbathers should stay at least six feet from the edge to allow adequate room for swimmers to enter and exit the water. A two- to four-inch-wide safety stripe around the pool perimeter at this distance can help remind patrons to observe this rule. Breakable or metal items should not be permitted in the deck area.

Ladders

Suggested rule:

- Only one swimmer on the ladder at a time.

Ladders should be used only for getting into and out of the pool; other uses can pose hazards. People who sit on the ladders to talk block access for tired swimmers. Other dangers include swimmers who use the ladders to pull themselves underwater and back to the surface; they risk getting caught in a rung, shoved off the ladder, or stepped on. Slippery ladders are dangerous when swimmers swing on them or dive from them. If swimmers swim between the ladder and the wall, they risk being caught, either on the surface or underwater.

Pool Gutters

Pool overflow gutters or troughs pose several potential dangers. Nonswimmers may use the gutters to move from shallow to deep water, traveling along the side of the pool hand over hand when the guard is looking the other way. Danger can arise when the nonswimmer is pushed away from the wall or attempts to climb out of the water and traps a knee or elbow in the gutter. If a lifeguard spots a nonswimmer moving along the gutter, she or he should have the nonswimmer climb out of the water on the nearest ladder and walk back to shallow water.

Prohibit patrons from standing on the gutters or climbing into them. Arms, hands, legs, or feet can get wedged in the gutter and cause an injury, particularly if the patron loses balance.

Small children also enjoy jumping into the water and turning to grab the gutter for support. Mistimed turns result in many cut chins, so stop this activity immediately.

Lifelines

Suggested rules:

- Keep off the lifelines.
- Use lifelines only for temporary support.

Lifelines mark the break between shallow and deep water. The chief danger to watch for is small children or weak swimmers who edge into deep water by pulling themselves along the lifelines. If they are pushed or otherwise lose a grasp on the lines, nonswimmers may be in water over their heads and consequently in danger. Swimmers should not sit or hang on lifelines; a lifeline submerged under the weight of a chatting swimmer is much more difficult for the distressed swimmer to find. Be sure to keep the lifelines strung tightly enough to be visible and to support panicky swimmers. They should be strong enough and strung tightly enough to support an adult with his or her head above water, with the rope not submerging more than a foot.

The Water

Any water area is potentially hazardous if swimmers are not careful. Flotation devices such as inner tubes and plastic toys can be dangerous if a nonswimming user floats into deep water or the device deflates and traps the person in it. If someone tries to get out of a flotation device, she or he may experience difficulty. These swimming aids are even more dangerous on crowded days when swimmers may accidentally bump into them, causing the user to fall away from the flotation device. They also obstruct the lifeguard's view of the bottom of the pool.

Many parents buy swimming aids for their children and perhaps gain a false sense of security from them. Parents must supervise their children at all times, whether or not the children are using swimming aids. But lifeguards must keep in mind that parental vigilance doesn't mean that they don't have to keep watch on those children as well.

A second general concern in any aquatics facility is patrons who enter the water at an unsafe depth. Consider a nonswimmer going down a ladder unknowingly into deep water or a skilled swimmer diving at a steep angle into the shallow end of the pool. Lifeguards can decrease the probability that someone will enter the water not knowing the depth by pointing out depth markers to patrons.

Depth markers should appear on the vertical wall of the pool and on the deck or coping. In some pools, a contour depth line shows all swimmers exactly how deep the water is in relation to their height. The contour line, a reverse image of the pool bottom, generally on a fence or wall, provides a profile of the pool bottom and depths. Patrons can easily stand next to the contour line to determine the point in the pool where it is safe for them to enter.

A third general concern is underwater swimming and other breath-holding activities. Underwater swimmers may be jumped on, possibly receiving back injuries. Another common problem for underwater swimmers is blacking out from breath holding and hyperventilation. Swimmers may take a series of deep breaths before swimming across the pool underwater. This decreases the amount of carbon dioxide in the blood, and because carbon dioxide tells the brain when to breathe, the reduction interferes with the breathing process. In effect, a swimmer can black out—and possibly drown—because he or she doesn't breathe when necessary.

Tell lifeguards if they suspect that swimmers are unable to swim underwater properly, they should not allow those swimmers to swim long distances or repeat swims at the surface or underwater during recreational periods while holding their breath. If a lifeguard sees someone performing these activities, she or he should intervene and stop the activity. Such activities might include the following:

- Hyperventilation
- Hypoxic breathing (a dangerous activity used by some swimming coaches that has little, if any, training value)
- Swimming multiple lengths or widths underwater or on the surface
- Performing multiple sprints without taking breaths between strokes
- Breath-holding games or contests
- Free-diving static apnea

Suggested rules:

- Coast Guard-approved PFDs only.
- Adult supervision required.

Shallow Water

The primary dangers in shallow water are diving and dunking. Even an experienced diver may hit the bottom, causing injuries to the fingers, hands, head, neck, or back. Depths should be clearly marked at regular intervals and at changes in water depth and contour to alert divers to the conditions. Standing front dives should be performed in no less than nine feet of water. (For YMCA guidelines on diving and diving water depth, see "Risk Management Involving Starting Blocks or Platforms, Water Depth, Deep Diving Starts, and Supervision" on the YMCA intranet web site.)

Post a warning sign to indicate that diving is not allowed in shallow water, such as "Danger! Shallow water. Diving prohibited. Paralysis or death may occur." You may want to use a universal warning sign that can be more easily understood by sight- or hearing-impaired individuals or by multilingual patrons.

Dunking is also a common activity for playful children and adults. The unsuspecting swimmer may ingest water and become scared or be injured hitting the side or bottom of the pool.

Suggested rules:

- Diving allowed only in marked areas.
- No dunking or rough play.

Deep Water

Those who are most in danger in deep water are nonswimmers and underwater swimmers. The nonswimmers can be spotted moving to the deep water along the gutter, on the deck, or from the diving board. Before entering the water, they may look very apprehensive and usually have their arms folded or wrapped around themselves. Lifeguards should prevent nonswimmers from getting into deep water.

Patrons should take a swimming test before being allowed to swim in deep water. A common swim test is to ask those patrons who want to swim in deep water to first swim across the shallow end to the wall, using any style. Those who can do this successfully are then escorted to the deep water, where they are asked to jump in, surface, swim 40 feet on their front, and stop. Then they must turn over, tread water for 10 to 15 seconds, then turn onto their back and return to the starting position, either on their front or on their back. Another swim test is to ask them to swim 75 feet.

Masks, fins, and snorkels may lure poor swimmers into deep water by providing false security. Warn lifeguards to keep a close watch on anyone using such equipment (if your facility allows it). Goggles, while safe in water up to five feet deep, should not be worn at greater depths. The pressure on the eyes may cause discomfort or injury.

Allow diving from the deck only where the water is more than nine feet deep.

Starting Blocks and Platforms

Starting blocks and platforms pose a significant hazard, especially to the inexperienced swimmer. No one should be allowed to dive from a starting block or platform of any height except in a competitive program. Check local and state bathing codes for guidelines on placement of the blocks and the water depth required. Also check with your insurance carrier regarding the regulations that carrier requires. The YMCA of the USA recommends that diving blocks be placed in the deep end, with a water depth of at least five feet. Swim coaches or YMCA Swim Lessons instructors should not teach or allow a pike dive, dive in the hole, or shoot start to be made unless the depth under the block is at least nine feet.

If starting blocks or platforms cannot be removed during recreational swims, the YMCA suggests they be capped and that warning signs be posted to stop patrons from using them. (See "Risk Management Involving Starting Blocks or Platforms, Water Depth, Deep Diving Starts, and Supervision" on the YMCA intranet web site.)

Slides

Slides, which continue to become more popular in swimming facilities and water parks, are another high-risk area. Pools with slides should have at least one lifeguard whose main responsibility is the slide area.

All sliders should enter the water feetfirst in a sitting position to avoid head injuries. Lifeguards should watch carefully that each slider returns to the surface and clears the area before the next person begins. The area at the bottom of the slide must be kept open to avoid injuries from swimmers being hit by sliders. Also be aware that outdoor slides can get hot enough to cause burns, particularly on hot days. All slides should have a water spray to keep sliders safe. See chapter 12 for more on slides and other aquatics attractions.

Recreational Springboard Diving Areas

Diving off a one-meter board may be done either in a separate well or in an area of the pool that is at least 11 feet, 6 inches deep for a consistent 16 feet in front of the board. In either case, lifeguards need to give these diving areas special attention. Post the rules for the type of diving allowed prominently, and encourage guards to enforce the rules consistently. An alert lifeguard can prevent many accidents associated with diving. Some of the many causes for diving accidents include the condition and arrangement of the equipment and diving areas, the visibility into the water, numerous weather factors, and the depth and distance to the upslope of the pool bottom.

Have lifeguards check the diving boards regularly throughout the day. Tell them to restrict the fulcrum setting to keep the board "stiff" for recreational use. Lifeguards should watch each diver return to the surface and exit the diving area before another diver approaches. They should also watch for rough play on and around the boards.

For YMCA guidelines on diving and diving water depth, see "Risk Management Involving Starting Blocks or Platforms, Water Depth, Deep Diving Starts, and Supervision" on the YMCA of the USA Web site.

We recommend that your facility follow the safe diving practices put forth by United States Diving. For competitive programs, follow current state and local codes and national governing bodies' regulations for the sport.

Do not allow recreational use of a three-meter board or tower. Such equipment should be used only by participants in a supervised program with specially trained diving instructors.

Lifeguard Towers and Equipment

Lifeguard towers and stands present a hazard because they attract young swimmers, who often gather at the foot of a stand, potentially obscuring the lifeguard's view. Lifeguards should be sure to scan the water under and around towers in their range of vision. Older patrons may enjoy socializing with the lifeguards, but the lifeguards need to keep their conversations brief and continue to scan their areas while talking.

Ring buoys and other safety devices may prove equally attractive and dangerous. A ring buoy, like any flotation device, could prove dangerous as a floating aid to a foolhardy nonswimmer. Such equipment is to be used only by trained personnel.

Wading Pools and Zero-Depth-Entry Pools

The reason most facilities decide to add wading pools or zero-depth-entry pools is to provide a safe haven for nonswimmers to enjoy the water. Parents often supervise their nonswimming children in these areas, but sometimes they become involved in conversation and don't notice that a child is experiencing difficulty. Lifeguards should not be lulled into thinking that their responsibility is covered by parents' supervision of their children.

Suggested rules:

- No running or rough play.
- Adult supervision required.
- No diving.

Wading pool or zero-depth-entry pool accidents are typically the result of rough play by older siblings or nonswimmers who are old enough to be in the main pool. They run and splash, creating an environment in which people can be knocked under the water or onto the deck, and lifeguards should warn them to stop.

Others who frequent wading pools or zero-depth-entry pools are adults who want to sit in shallow water or to watch the children play. On very hot days, such pools may become congested, and a wet deck combined with crowded conditions makes slipping and falling into the pools or on the surrounding deck a real danger.

Spas and Whirlpools

Spas are relatively new additions to aquatics facilities. If your facility has one, you'll need to learn your state's codes for it and add this area to your list of danger zones. The most common physical hazards of a spa area are drowning, falling, medical conditions, and electrocution. The drownings and falls are often attributed to medical conditions or to the use of alcohol in the area. Electrocutions result from the use of electrical devices in the area.

When people who are overheated from vigorous exercise or have just used a sauna get into a spa, the danger of heat-related illness increases greatly. People should cool down properly after exercising before they enter the spa, and vigorous exercise should not be allowed in the spa.

Spas attract even people who know they should stay away, such as people with epilepsy or diabetes. Be sure that you post the rules of the whirlpool or spa prominently, assign a lifeguard to watch the spa area, and have that guard enforce the rules rigidly.

For additional information about whirlpool or spa management, see the *YMCA Pool Operations Manual* (2nd ed.).

Suggested Rules for Spas:
• Do not use the spa alone. • Spa use is not recommended immediately after intense physical activity or after sauna use.

- Aerobic exercise in the spa is prohibited.
- Enter and exit the spa slowly and cautiously.
- Pregnant women, patrons with cardiovascular or respiratory problems or epilepsy, and children under five should avoid using the spa.
- Older children must be accompanied and supervised by a responsible adult.
- Limit use to 10 minutes.
- Diving or jumping are prohibited.
- Underwater submersion is prohibited.
- Food or drink are not allowed in the spa area.
- Shower before entering the spa.
- Body lotions, oils, or suntan products are not allowed in the spa.
- Keep hair away from drain/suction by wearing a cap or pinning hair on top of head.

WATER RECREATION ATTRACTIONS SAFETY

If you are planning a new pool or renovations of an existing one, you may well be considering adding one or more water recreation attractions. In most of these attractions, water helps control the speed of the rider, reduce friction between the rider and the activity surface, and restrain or cushion the rider in a landing area at the end of the ride.

To assign lifeguards appropriately to water recreation attractions, you need to understand the main causes of accidents on attractions. You also need to learn the characteristics of some specific attractions, the most common accidents on those attractions, and where lifeguards should be stationed on each. We will also give you some fundamental operational safety standards to follow for water recreation attractions, as well as information on how to communicate rules and safety concerns to patrons using signs or taped messages.

Causes of Accidents at Water Recreation Attractions

Over the past 20 years, enough information has been acquired to provide a clear picture of the primary causes of accidents at water recreation attractions, which include the following:

1. *Unsafe design:* Many attractions are manufactured and put into use without proper safety testing that uses appropriate research design and experimental testing.

2. *Facility operations:* After attractions have been installed on site, some owners and operators do not operate them properly. Sometimes owners and operators increase water flow rates or fail to maintain proper water depths for slides, run-outs, and catch pools. Maintenance may also be substandard.

3. *Poor supervision:* Lifeguards are sometimes inattentive to their dispatcher and ride supervision, rule enforcement, and catch pool duties.

4. *Patron behavior.* Water recreation area patrons who come to have fun may have medical problems, such as a heart condition, that may affect their safety on

attractions. Many patrons also are first-time visitors, unfamiliar with the rules or the attraction's characteristics. In their excitement, they often fail to read signs or listen to recorded announcements. Some patrons also choose to disobey rules.

5. *Poor communication by management:* Often patrons fail to read signs at attractions because of the large number of signs or improper signage. Signs may be difficult to read because of the color of the letters or numbers, the background colors, or the height, thickness, or style of the font used. Placing signs where they are hard to read, failing to provide pictorial and bilingual signs, or failing to consistently use signal words such as "Danger," "Warning," and "Caution" often render a sign ineffective; in other words, such signs simply do not communicate properly. Recorded statements played while patrons wait in line may also fail to communicate because the tape wears out, the message is too long or is played too frequently, or the words are not clear.

Lifeguarding Tips for Individual Attractions

Each attraction has its own specific hazards. As an aquatics director, you need to know the characteristics of each attraction, those situations likely to lead to accidents, and where lifeguards should be stationed. The attractions covered here include wave pools, deep-water activity pools, free-fall and speed slides, serpentine slides and rapids, coaster rides, lazy or winding rivers, and interactive playgrounds.

Wave Pools

Waves in wave pools (see figure 10.2) are created by one of two methods: compressed air or moving paddles.

In the compressed air method, air is simultaneously forced into half of the water chambers (the odd-numbered ones) located within the end wall, pushing the water out through the bottom of the chambers. After the water has escaped from the odd-numbered chambers, it is then released from the even-numbered chambers.

Figure 10.2 Wave pool.

In the paddle-operated method, a large, mechanically operated paddle moves in a chamber in which a cascade of water is released from the back wall to displace water in a filled chamber.

A wave pool may produce waves on a cycle of small waves for 20 minutes followed by a 20-minute off-cycle period or one large wave every 5 to 10 minutes.

Wave pool hazards relate directly to the size and frequency of waves, as well as the cement bottom of the pool. Common wave pool accidents include the following:

- Swimmers in the four- to five-foot depth zone who are knocked over by waves
- Swimmers or nonswimmers who become buoyant as a wave lifts them off the bottom, causing them to panic
- Swimmers who are injured when waves push them into recessed wall ladders in the deep end
- Patrons in shallow water who are knocked down by people riding the waves on inflatable rafts
- Swimmers floating on inner tubes in deep water who fall off the tube, submerge, and cannot return to the surface because of the number of tubes covering the surface
- Swimmers hanging onto pool railings because they are not strong enough to swim safely through the waves to shallow water

Patrons who suffer impact injuries from contact with the bottom or who are struck by other patrons riding on rafts may bleed and have an increased risk of spinal injuries. Lifeguards should be trained in and prepared to follow precautions for blood-borne pathogens.

Some rules that might help prevent accidents in wave pools are these (Lifesaving Society, 1993):

- Do not allow swimmers to hold onto one another in the deep zone (to minimize collisions).
- Restrict parents who are holding children to the shallow zone.
- Require swimmers to keep a safe distance from the walls (to prevent collisions with the walls).
- Do not allow body surfing or diving in shallow water.
- Limit the size of the waves (to avoid injuries resulting from collisions between swimmers and waves).
- Because flotation mattresses and tubes may interfere with the lifeguards' ability to see, divide the pool into two sections: one for swimmers and one for patrons with flotation devices. Another possibility is to limit the number of flotation devices allowed in the pool.
- Allow only those flotation devices that are provided by the facility (World Waterpark Association, 1989).
- Require patrons to enter the wave pool from the beach area only, not the sides (World Waterpark Association, 1989).

According to the Royal Life Saving Society Canada (Lifesaving Society, 1993), when a rescue is necessary, lifeguards should stop the waves but not evacuate the wave pool, as in a regular swimming pool (figure 10.3). Rescues usually can be completed with just local crowd control. However, when a total evacuation of the pool is necessary, as when bad weather hits, guards should use a more detailed crowd control plan. They should stop the waves, signal the patrons to leave, and supervise the departure of the swimmers.

Figure 10.3 When a rescue is needed in a wave pool, stop the waves.

The number of sitting lifeguards and standing lifeguards depends on the size of the pool and the number of patrons in the water. Place lifeguard chairs only near water depths over five feet along the sides of the pool (figure 10.4). Place standing or moving guards between chairs, along the back wall, and in shallow water. Additional guards may be in the water with tubes. The seated guards should handle communication. Teamwork is essential, as overlapping zone coverage should be used in wave pools (Lifesaving Society, 1993).

Deep-Water Activity Pools

Deep-water activity pools are associated with a variety of attractions. Sometimes they are used as a landing area for patrons exiting from a "shotgun slide" five to six feet above the surface of the water. They also provide entry areas for diving boards, diving platforms, cable or rope swings, zip lines, nets, or rings on cables, along with inflatables or walking and play surfaces anchored to the bottom. Depending on the activity, the water depth may vary from 11.5 to 18 feet.

Accidents in this type of pool are related to entries. Entries from objects high above the water are sometimes unplanned falls or sudden drops, and impact with the water can be painful. Accidents common to deep-water pools are the following:

- An injured or weak swimmer suddenly entering deep water
- A person losing consciousness who ends up lying facedown in the water from impact with the water, another person, or some part of the attraction

Lifeguards should be ready to use blood-borne pathogen procedures with impact injuries.

The number of lifeguards and their locations should be determined by the activity:

- For shotgun slides, post a lifeguard dispatcher at the top of the slide. Station another lifeguard near the drop zone where patrons enter the water.

Figure 10.4 Lifeguard chairs should be placed along the sides of the pool.

- For pools with 7.5- and 10-meter platforms, water depths will range from 15 to 18 feet. In case they have to rescue a submerged victim, lifeguards should have mask, fins, and snorkel handy. They should receive in-service training on how to use this equipment in victim recovery from the bottom and practice rescue procedures regularly.

For most of these deep-water activities, a lifeguard must be stationed near the entry point. Other lifeguards should be situated where they have an unobstructed view of the sides.

Free-Fall and Speed Slides

Free-fall and speed slides are similar in design. Free-fall slides are long slides with very steep drops. Some are so steep that the top of the slide is enclosed, giving the rider the sensation of falling straight down. Speed slides have a more gentle slope and sometimes have a bump halfway down. These slides may end in a catch pool or a long run-out, which is generally where accidents occur.

Because of the speeds attained on these slides, riders should stay in a position in which their legs are crossed at the ankles and their arms are folded across their chest (figure 10.5). Injuries on these attractions usually result from a combination of speed and improper body position, as in these situations:

- Soft tissue injuries, such as strains and sprains affecting the limbs, can occur.
- Serious internal injuries can occur from entering the catch pool or run-out with legs apart.
- Broken bones or dislocated joints can occur from impact with the slide after becoming airborne from sliding over a speed bump. Hitting water in the catch

Figure 10.5 A rider of a free-fall slide should stay in a position in which the legs are crossed at the ankles and the arms are folded across the chest.

pool or hitting the wall or steps at the end of a slide run-out or catch pool that is too short can produce similar injuries.

Station lifeguards for free-fall and speed slides at the top of the slide to control the dispatch of riders and at the bottom in the run-out area or adjacent to the catch pool.

Serpentine Slides and Rapids

Serpentine slides are generally long slides that wind their way down a hillside or superstructure much like a roller coaster (see figure 10.6). They are constructed of fiberglass or cement. Riders slide on mats or in one- or two-person tubes, or they body-slide feetfirst with arms and legs crossed (as when using a speed slide). Rapids-type rides simulate tubing in a creek or river. Such rides wind downhill and may have one or two catch basins at points between the top and bottom where the ride funnels riders into a cave or to the next drop level.

When you install a slide, follow these guidelines:

- Follow the manufacturer's recommendations on water depth for a serpentine slide with a low-grade discharge (a 10 percent grade is recommended). Slides that do not have a safe deceleration to near zero velocity at the point of discharge should have a minimum depth of nine feet and would preferably meet one-meter board guidelines for water depth (figure 10.7).

- Some catch pool areas have a pad to help absorb any impact from the landing. Check with your manufacturer on their recommendation based on the slide you are considering.

- Follow the same guideline for pool depth at the mouth of a drop slide as you would use for a one-meter board.

Figure 10.6 A serpentine slide.

Figure 10.7 A low-grade discharge at the end of the slide is recommended.

- Install closed steps with landings instead of ladders (according to industry standards).
- Have permanently enclosed sides on the platform.
- Make sure that there is plenty of empty space (at least nine feet) above the platform.
- Make sure that deck obstructions meet codes.

- If the pool has a diving board and a slide in the deep end, make sure there is a space at least 10 feet wide between them.
- Post signs to identify assumption of risk for riders. We recommend you require parental releases before allowing those under 18 years of age to use the equipment.

Accidents may occur anywhere from the top to the bottom of these slides. Common accidents include the following:

- Falling off a mat and losing body control, producing soft tissue injuries, broken bones, or head injuries.
- Stopping on the way down and blocking the following riders, causing impact injuries.
- Riding in one- or two-person tubes and hitting the walls of the slide with the head, arms, or feet. The rider cannot control the tube as it spins and turns on its downhill course.
- Sliding and getting caught in a hydraulic formed at the end of the ride. Hydraulics are the result of water cascading from the slide into the catch pool, which forms a waterfall effect that produces a reverse circular current. A hydraulic can make it extremely difficult to stand up, especially for young children or weak swimmers, and may even hold a person on the bottom.
- An excessive number of tubes collecting in a rapids' catch basin where some tubes may be overturned, causing injury or even drowning.

To help prevent accidents on serpentine slides, follow these guidelines:

- Be aware of conditions in the catch pool, such as currents created from the water flow.
- Require the lifeguards stationed in the catch pool to always have their rescue tubes (see figure 10.8). It is also helpful for them to wear deck shoes to minimize slipping.
- Have written emergency procedures for this area and have staff rehearse them. When possible, have EMS personnel participate in these rehearsals.
- Station lifeguards at the top and bottom of the slide. The guard at the top has dispatching duties, and the guard at the bottom supervises proper exiting of the participants.
- Don't allow children on the equipment if they are shorter than 48 inches (four feet). It is recommended that children be six inches taller than the water depth in the catch pool, or other modifications should be in place (e.g., deep-water swim test, use of lifejackets, or a guard in the catch pool). Be sure to discuss this with the manufacturer to ensure that the slide will be properly positioned so that the groups you want to serve will exit into the appropriate water depth.
- Heed weight limits established by the manufacturers. A weight limit used by some manufacturers is about 250 pounds for a basic serpentine slide.
- Don't use members as safety testers. A staff member should test the slide first thing each day as part of the daily inspection.
- Stop water flow and the dispatch of participants during a major rescue (such as when multiple guards are involved in the assistance and care of an injured swimmer). Have a water shutoff button close by so the guard can stop water flow quickly.

Figure 10.8 Lifeguards in the catch pool should have rescue tubes.

- Allow only feetfirst sliding.
- Have staff perform a safety inspection before opening each day.
- Have staff keep a detailed log of any maintenance and safety inspections.
- Review and analyze an injury chart and incident reports for any corrective measures that can be taken to reduce the possibility of repeat occurrences. Note and date any actions taken.

Riders may need assistance or rescue at any point from the top of the ride to the catch pool. Station standing lifeguards at the dispatch positions, the catch pool, and appropriate locations in between. The lifeguard positioned at the bottom of the slide should be in the water with a tube (figure 10.9). Two guards on deck should be available for communication with the guards at the dispatch position.

Coaster Ride

Coaster rides are similar to, but shorter than, speed slides. They are often constructed in pairs. Riders sit on plastic sleds that glide down on small metal rollers or water-lubricated surfaces. When the rider and sled leave the slide, they skim along the surface of a long catch pool, gradually slowing down until coming to a stop.

Accidents common to coaster rides include the following:

- Collisions between two sleds discharged simultaneously
- Sleds flipping over, resulting in a rider hitting a side wall or the bottom

Position lifeguards assigned to coaster rides at the top of the slide to dispatch riders and adjacent to or in the catch pool to assist injured or disoriented riders. Lifeguards in the catch pool should be ready to use blood-borne pathogen protocols.

Figure 10.9   The lifeguard at the bottom of the slide should be in the water.

Lazy or Winding Rivers

The paths of lazy or winding rivers may be oval in shape or they may wind their way through a water recreation area, sometimes encompassing the entire area. They generally are three to four feet in depth and float patrons along on inner tubes at two to three miles per hour (see figure 10.10).

Figure 10.10   A lazy or winding river.

Lazy or winding rivers generally have a low incidence of accidents. Those that do occur are often the following:

- Patrons slipping or falling at the point of entrance or exit
- Patrons injuring themselves by getting out of the river and then jumping or diving back in
- Patrons hitting their heads after falling from an overturned tube as the result of horseplay
- Patrons blocking the progress of other riders

Station lifeguards at the entrance and exit points to assist riders in getting into and out of tubes. They also must be positioned sitting or standing along the river so that no part of the river is out of the sight of a lifeguard at any time (figure 10.11).

Interactive Playground

Interactive playgrounds (figure 10.12) combine equipment for water fun such as water slides with playground elements such as climbing nets. Often the equipment is designed to follow a theme. The equipment is in water that ranges from zero depth to 18 inches.

Your facility should follow these safety precautions for interactive playgrounds:

- Post the rules by each piece of aquatics equipment and at pool entrances (figure 10.13).
- Make sure that the rules are clearly written and easily understood by all.
- Instruct adults to closely supervise their children, and lay out the park so it is easy for them to do so (World Waterpark Association, 1989).
- Have special guarding policies in writing for each piece of equipment.

Figure 10.11   Lifeguards should be stationed along the river.

Figure 10.12   An interactive playground.

Figure 10.13   Post the rules next to pool entrances and equipment.

- Tell lifeguards to strictly enforce all policies and rules, especially those related to running and horseplay.
- Station an additional lifeguard on a play structure to monitor slides and potentially hazardous play.
- Have smooth surfaces on all objects (walls and pipes).
- Have contour lines to show increases in depth.

- Make sure it's clear that the playground is intended for children under four feet tall.
- Make sure slides have an open tube at the end of the slide so visibility is clear (figure 10.14).
- Ensure that the angle and exit of slides are not dangerous and conform to Consumer Product Safety Commission standards.

Figure 10.14   Slides should have open tubes at the end to help visibility.

Operational Safety Guidelines for Lifeguards

As water recreation areas have many different types of activities, ensure that each attraction is supervised and guarded according to its individual characteristics. We recommend the following operational safety guidelines for water recreation attractions:

- Always emphasize accident prevention.
- Provide lifeguards with orientation and in-service training specific to each attraction.
- Provide lifeguards with some means of communication and signaling, such as an intercom system, FM radio, public address system, signal lights, radio telephones, cell phones, walkie-talkies, CB radios, air horns, or whistles.
- Have staff completely inspect and test each attraction according to manufacturer's instructions each day before use. They should then fill out a daily checklist specific to the attraction to record findings. After inspection and testing, have a lifeguard ride the attraction as it would normally be used by patrons. If maintenance needs to be performed, have it done before the attraction is opened for use or close the attraction until the required maintenance can be completed. Make sure all maintenance procedures are recorded in the log.

- Have staff inspect first aid, safety, and rescue equipment, including first aid kits, HIV precautionary kits, and resuscitation masks, and record the results of the inspection in a log.
- You or a staff member should test and adjust the water chemistry balance each time the filters are cleaned and test and adjust the disinfectant levels hourly.
- Develop written emergency and accident management procedures (which should be practiced) specific to each attraction, as well as an emergency procedure for an unplanned shutdown of each attraction.
- Remember that the keys to accident prevention are for lifeguards to

  a. maintain a high level of physical conditioning,

  b. pay constant attention to scanning and lifeguard duties, and

  c. consistently enforce rules.

- Lifeguards should use their victim recognition skills and be ready to respond quickly when they see a patron

  a. slip and fall;

  b. collide with another rider, side wall, end wall, or bottom;

  c. lose body control on an attraction;

  d. fall from an attraction;

  e. become airborne and hit a hard surface;

  f. fail to read signs or listen to recorded messages and warnings;

  g. act as if he or she is under the influence of drugs or alcohol;

  h. appear to be suffering from a medical condition, such as a heart attack, epilepsy, diabetes, or heat exhaustion;

  i. fail to heed warnings such as height, weight, or age restrictions; or

  j. act disoriented or unstable.

Communication at Water Recreation Attractions

Lifeguards must communicate often and clearly with all coworkers and patrons, especially patrons who are visiting for the first time, as they are more likely to be injured than those who frequent the attractions regularly. Lifeguards must keep in mind that patrons are excited and eager to ride as many attractions as possible, so they sometimes don't read the rules and warning signs or listen carefully to recorded messages. Some children may also be unsupervised by an adult. Lifeguards may have to repeat warnings and rules verbally in a dispatch area, even though patrons have been presented with signs and recorded messages along the way into or up to an attraction.

Table 10.1 represents general areas of concern for which you should develop warning and safety rules. Lifeguards should communicate and enforce these rules. (Warning signs relating to the activities or behaviors identified in this list should be matched to specific park attractions.)

As mentioned, besides posting signs, you may want to have recorded messages on warnings and rules announced over loudspeakers located along entrance paths and stairs. When you have such a message recorded, make sure the person recording it does the following:

- Speaks clearly and slowly
- Uses inflections, avoiding a monotone

Table 10.1	Warning and Safety Rules Areas of Concern

WARNING SIGNS

Personal Health
- Fear of heights or sudden immersion
- Fatigue and exhaustion
- Heart problems

Proper Use of Equipment
- Tubes, rafts, mats, sleds, and PFDs

Slowing and Stopping
- Extending arms and legs to slow
- Extending arms and legs to stop
- Holding on to wave pool rails

Rider Behavior
- Changing body positions
- Multiple riders, trains
- Weaving back and forth

Activity Use Prohibited
- For people on certain prescription drugs or those using recreational drugs or alcohol

Water Depth
- At entrance and exit of attractions
- On the coping of all pools

General Warnings
- Failure to follow the rules or instructions can result in paralysis or serious or fatal injury.
- Lifeguards must always be obeyed.
- Failure to obey can result in dismissal.

SAFETY SIGNS

Bathing and Personal Attire
- Bathing suits
- Clothing—T-shirts
- Glasses, sunglasses
- Jewelry
- Dentures, hearing aids
- Prosthetics

Patron Limitations
- Age
- Height
- Weight or overweight
- Height and weight for large patrons

Body Position
- Headfirst
- Feetfirst
- Prone position
- Supine position
- Sitting position

Entry Positions
- Jumping
- Diving
- Running
- Swinging
- Pushing off

Exit Rules
- Approved behavior
- Where exit is allowed

Special Rules
- Unique to special attractions

- Makes the message brief and concise
- Uses language that everyone can understand
- Uses positive messages, avoiding sarcasm and profanity

Consider having multilingual messages in languages that are consistent with the languages and nationalities of those who frequent your facility, such as Spanish, French, German, and Japanese.

Be sure the message is loud enough to be heard but not obnoxiously loud.

INFLATABLE SAFETY

Inflatables are a popular addition to pools these days, and many YMCAs have used them successfully to increase participation during recreational swims. Inflatables are large objects or animals usually made of a reinforced polyvinyl chloride (PVC) fabric with a tough polyester mesh bonded between two layers of PVC to allow for stretching and flexing. Inflatables come in many models, shapes, and sizes. They range in price and are available from a number of vendors.

Inflatables can be put into your pool or taken out with relative ease. They can add a new look and provide great fun for your members and participants. Some associations have bought more than one inflatable, then shared them among their branches. If you decide to buy one, be sure you know what age group you are targeting before you decide which kind to buy.

Be sure you purchase one that is the appropriate size for your pool and can be put in the appropriate depth. Have the manufacturer confirm that the particular play structure you want to purchase will fit your YMCA's intended use, pool size, and depth.

Inflatables come in two types:

• Sealed inflatables are play structures that can support one or more persons above the surface of the water (figure 10.15). They are capped once they are filled with air. Many different designs are available.

• Constant-blow inflatables such as aqua fun runs and inflatable water slides have an air blower permanently connected and running constantly while the inflatable is in use. These tend to be used differently than sealed inflatables. For example, participants try to run the length of aqua fun runs and use them as obstacle courses.

As always, it is the YMCA's responsibility to ensure the safety of users of this equipment. When using inflatables, consider the following precautions in addition to the manufacturer's safety recommendations and applicable state and local codes. Also consider these factors in your cost analysis before buying an inflatable.

Figure 10.15   A sealed inflatable.

Sealed Inflatables

Figure 10.16 shows how a sealed inflatable should normally be anchored. No matter what inflatable is used, it should cover a continuous area of no more than one square meter (39 square inches) of water and should be no more than one meter in height above the water's surface. Wherever possible, the depth should be consistent on all sides of the inflatable.

Limited product safety research is available on the appropriate depth at which inflatables should be placed. Because of the variety of activities for which inflatables can be used, a minimum of five feet is recommended for sealed inflatables (and an even greater depth would be preferable). As new research becomes available, this depth should be adjusted.

Because of the five-foot depth recommendation, we suggest that you require all swimmers to take a deep-water swim test before allowing them to play on the structure. We recommend that children or adults who cannot swim not be

1 Minimum distance: 8 ft.

2 Minimum depth: 5 ft.
   (deeper is preferred for larger inflatables)

3 Anchor lines to be smooth, nonabrasive, and highly visible

Figure 10.16   Normal method for anchoring a sealed inflatable.

allowed to use these play structures. If your YMCA chooses to allow young children and their parents who are not proficient swimmers to play on the structure, make parents aware that accidental falls can be frightening for children, possibly causing them to acquire a fear of the water. In such situations, you may want to consider requiring children to wear life jackets and establishing a separate play period for parents and their young children.

Figure 10.17 shows the bottom method for anchoring a sealed inflatable.

When installing a sealed inflatable, your staff should take the following precautions:

• Inspect the inflatable before each use. Pay particular attention to seams, anchorage points, and other potential areas of weakness. Record these checks in a log book.

• Before using an electric blower for inflation or deflation, check the blower for safety. Look for any damage to cables, plugs, sockets, and switches and make sure that the mesh guards over the air inlet and outlets are secure. Then plug it into an outlet with ground fault circuit interrupters.

• When you fill the inflatable with air, do not let it obstruct the movement of people onto the pool

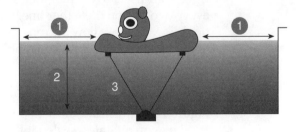

1 Minimum distance: 8 ft.

2 Minimum depth: 5 ft.
   (deeper is preferred for larger inflatables)

3 Anchor lines to be smooth, nonabrasive, and highly visible

Figure 10.17   Bottom method for anchoring a sealed inflatable.

deck or block emergency exits. Choose a location convenient for safe inflating and deflating. See that electrical cords do not cross traffic areas.

• If on-duty guards are the ones inflating or deflating the inflatable, close the pool while this is being done.

• Transport the inflatable carefully. Carry it, rather than dragging it along the pool deck (figure 10.18). The life span of inflatables varies according to their care, use, and storage, but on average is three years. With care, they will last longer.

Figure 10.18   Transport inflatables by carrying them.

• Use nylon or other water-resistant tether lines with a minimum diameter of three-eighths inch to tether all pool inflatables. Place five-inch "lock-on" rope floats every two feet on the tether line, with a brass swivel clip on one end to attach to the pool side. Do not allow patrons to pull on or play with the tether lines or to use the tether lines to climb on the inflatable. Use anchor lines that are smooth, nonabrasive, and highly visible.

• Leave a minimum clearance of eight feet on all sides of the sealed inflatable.

Figure 10.19 illustrates how to position a sealed inflatable.

When you operate a sealed inflatable, station at least one lifeguard on the deck on each side of the inflatable structure. Use additional guards if needed to help supervise in the water, depending on the number, age, and abilities of the swimmers using the inflatable. This does not include the general-duty guards for other swimmers using the pool.

Allow only a small age range to play on the inflatable at one time (for example, 10- to 12-year-olds should not play at the same time as 5- to 7-year-olds). Recommended playing time for each group is between 15 and 20 minutes.

Develop an emergency plan and train staff to use it for the following: dealing with unruly behavior, collapse or partial collapse of the inflatable, failure of the tether ropes, or serious injury of a swimmer.

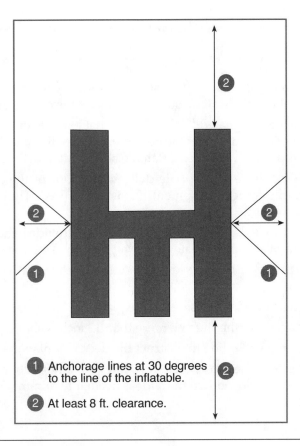

1 Anchorage lines at 30 degrees to the line of the inflatable.

2 At least 8 ft. clearance.

Figure 10.19 Positioning a sealed inflatable.

We suggest you set the following rules for use of the sealed inflatable, to be enforced by lifeguards:

- Headfirst dismounts are not allowed.
- Standing on the inflatable is not allowed (unless it is specifically designed for this use).
- Swimmers are not allowed to push or throw each other onto or off of the inflatable.
- Swimmers are not allowed to deliberately swim under the inflatable or to lift it to try to knock others from the inflatable.
- Swinging, hanging, or pulling on the anchor ropes is not allowed.
- Swimsuit pins or sharp objects are not allowed near the inflatable.

Also consider setting an age minimum, depending on the size of the inflatable you purchase.

Constant-Blow Inflatables

Two common types of constant-blow inflatables are inflatable slides and aqua runs.

Inflatable Slides

The inflatable slide is attached to a three-meter diving platform or a customized frame. The active sliding length is about 26 feet. The air blower works continuously so that the proper air pressure is delivered, and the user safely slides between two large air-filled side tubes. The positioning of an inflatable water slide is shown in figure 10.20.

When your YMCA installs an inflatable slide, follow these precautions:

- Use a constant-blower-filled slide that is secured to a platform or frame three meters above the water's surface to ensure the correct angle of descent.

- Establish a designated "splash area" that extends out at least 15 feet from the bottom of the slide. Form the boundary lines of the splash or nonswimming area using ropes with floats or inflatable booms attached every two feet.

- Have staff make appropriate daily inspections of the slide, supporting structure, and electrical equipment if it is being used. They should log and report them properly.

- Use stairs with landings instead of ladders. Provide handrails of a diameter and height that are appropriate for the age group using the slide.

- Leave plenty of empty space above the platform (at least eight feet of ceiling clearance).

- Completely enclose all sides of the platform.

- Place the exit of the slide no more than 12 inches above the surface of the water.

- Do not allow the slide to obstruct the deck in violation of state or local codes.

- If water is needed to operate the slide, put a hose attachment in place. An adequate water flow down the slide is needed to minimize friction burns to users.

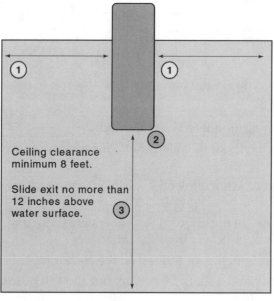

Ceiling clearance minimum 8 feet.

Slide exit no more than 12 inches above water surface.

(1) Minimum clearance from pool side, 6 feet (more is preferred).

(2) Minimum landing depth, 9 feet.

(3) Minimum distance from base of slide to edge of landing area, 15 feet.

(4) Splash area partitioned by ropes or inflatable boom.

Figure 10.20   Positioning of an inflatable water slide.

- Provide at least 6 feet of clearance on either side of the pool tank (10 feet is preferable).
- Place the slide in a pool depth of at least 9 feet (2.8 meters), and leave 15 feet of clearance in front of the exit point of the slide. Use lifelines to mark this area. Limited research is available on the appropriate depth in which to place inflatable slides. As new research becomes available, adjust this depth.
- Be aware that the sliding surface will wear out with use and require patching and repairing. Some slides have a replaceable sliding surface, which should be inspected and patched or replaced as needed. This can increase the life span of the slide.

We suggest you set the following rules for use of the inflatable slide, to be enforced by lifeguards:

- To use the slide, a patron must be within the weight limits recommended by the manufacturer.
- Patrons who are less than four feet tall are not allowed to use the slide.
- Only one person is allowed down the slide at a time.
- Patrons must slide in the feetfirst sliding position only.
- Running or jumping on the slide are not allowed.

Position one guard at the top of the slide to make sure the rider is in the proper slide position. This guard can also control the flow of participants using the slide and climbing the stairs. Station another guard on the deck to supervise the exit point of the slide and the swimmers' clearance of the splash area.

Aqua Fun Runs

Aqua fun runs are constant-blow structures that run up to 40 feet in length and are a maximum of 4 feet, 9 inches wide. Aqua fun runs raise many safety concerns. For instance, fun runs that cover more than 39 square inches (one square meter) of water surface area shouldn't be used because of the increased risk that someone could become trapped underneath. The play elements of the structure should be no more than one meter in height of playable surface above the water. A number of aqua fun runs do meet these recommendations.

The purpose of aqua fun runs is for swimmers to traverse (walk or run) the structure like an obstacle course. We recognize that some facilities may choose to use the structure as a sealed inflatable instead of as a fun run. In this case, you will need to establish different operating procedures and rules, and you should follow the recommendations for sealed inflatables. A word of caution: Having two sets of rules can confuse your swimmers and make rule enforcement more difficult.

Check your pool carefully before buying an aqua fun run. Some pools won't be able to accommodate the safety recommendations for this type of inflatable.

The proper anchoring for an aqua fun run (constant-blow inflatable) is shown in figure 10.21.

When your YMCA installs an aqua fun run, follow these precautions:

- Purchase an inflatable appropriate to the depths and dimensions of the pool.
- Place the structure in deep water (at least nine feet) where there will be no other users around the structure.
- Provide at least 12 feet of clearance from the finish to the edge of the pool.

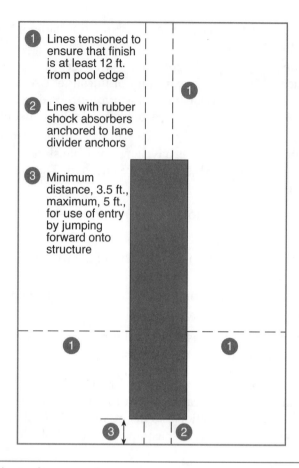

① Lines tensioned to ensure that finish is at least 12 ft. from pool edge

② Lines with rubber shock absorbers anchored to lane divider anchors

③ Minimum distance, 3.5 ft., maximum, 5 ft., for use of entry by jumping forward onto structure

Figure 10.21   Proper anchoring for an aqua fun run.

- Provide at least 12 feet of clearance on each side of the pool. The end of the run should allow participants to exit into the deep end of the pool.
- Keep the air blower in constant operation while the structure is in use. Be in full compliance with electrical codes and regulations.
- Clear the pool area when the inflatable is being put in or taken out.

Rules of operation for aqua fun runs are similar to those for sealed inflatables, plus the following:

- Assign at least two guards to the aqua fun run—one to dispatch swimmers and supervise their getting on, the other to supervise the run and dismount and clear the dismount area.
- Have lifeguards control the flow of participants. Tell them to dispatch only one participant onto the inflatable at a time.
- No substantive research has been done on the best entry of swimmers onto the run. Until more research is completed, use your best judgment as to how your swimmers should get onto the structure. Two methods are possible:
  1. Station a lifeguard at the beginning of the run, with its starting point against the edge of the pool. That lifeguard should help users step carefully onto the structure before they traverse the obstacle course.
  2. Have a lifeguard closely supervise the swimmers as they jump onto the unit (rather than step onto it) to ensure forward projection and to reduce the dan-

ger of falling back and hitting the pool side. The unit is placed so there is a minimum clearance of 3.5 feet and a maximum clearance of 5 feet from the edge of the pool to the start of the structure.

- Instruct lifeguards to tell swimmers that, once they reach the far end, they must slide off feetfirst and then swim to the nearest side.

- Instruct lifeguards to tell swimmers that, if they lose their balance, they should fall off the fun run, not try to dive off it.

- If the aqua fun run is being used as a sealed inflatable (for play and not as a run), then do not allow participants to stand on it, but only to crawl on it. Post rules about the type of play allowable on the inflatable that can be understood by swimmers and enforced by lifeguards.

BIBLIOGRAPHY

American Red Cross. 1995. *Head lifeguard.* St. Louis: Mosby Lifeline.

Lifesaving Society. 1993. *Alert: Lifeguarding in action.* North York, Ontario, Canada: The Royal Life Saving Society Canada.

World Waterpark Association. 1989. *Considerations for operating safety.* Lenexa, KS: World Waterpark Association.

Lifeguarding Procedures

Lifeguarding is a difficult job. First, guards are responsible for seeing that people follow the rules, and even for stopping rule violations before they occur. They have to know how to be tactful, yet firm. We provide some guides for you to use in training your lifeguards to accomplish this task.

Second, guards have to be constantly vigilant while they are on duty. You can help them do this by ensuring that all guards know which areas they are to cover and how to scan. Install a regular rotation system to help them stay alert, and assign them to appropriate guarding locations. Institute whatever communication systems are needed to allow guards to coordinate their efforts, and create group swimming safety checks so guards can easily keep track of all swimmers.

Finally, your guards may run into some special types of guarding situations while working at the YMCA, such as guarding classes or children from other programs, or guarding at competitive events or for rental groups. It also is likely that at some time they may have to deal with language barriers between themselves and patrons, or with people who have disabilities. We have some suggestions for handling these situations.

ENFORCING THE RULES

Rule enforcement is always difficult. No one likes to play watchdog, and no one likes to be corrected. But lifeguards must enforce the rules to meet their responsibility of providing a safe environment in which patrons can have enjoyable aquatics experiences.

To help you train lifeguards to enforce rules reasonably without offending patrons, we have some guidelines you can use for rule enforcement and a system lifeguards can use when enforcing rules called Q-1-2.

Guidelines for Rule Enforcement

Discipline is needed whenever someone's behavior

- could result in injury to self or others,
- could result in damage to property, or
- infringes on the comfort and enjoyment of others in the area.

A few guidelines will help your lifeguards and staff enforce the rules at your facility:

• Know all rules and the procedures for enforcing them.

• Use a short blast of your whistle to get patrons' attention. (Management should provide shirts and whistles for all lifeguards.)

• Be consistent, enforcing the same rule in the same way for everyone. Don't make exceptions for friends, fellow employees, or adults. Also, enforce the rules in the same way each and every day.

• React immediately. Blow your whistle as soon as you detect a rule being broken. The patron will know what behavior has drawn your attention.

• Be specific. If there is a question over what behavior is prohibited, be specific in describing your concern. For example, you may say, "I saw you running on the deck. As you know, that is against the rules because you may run into another swimmer and knock someone down." You have pointed out the incorrect behavior and indicated why it was a problem.

• Provide alternative behaviors if you can. You might encourage the runner on the deck to take a group to the grassy recreation area, where there is room for such activities.

By following these guidelines, your lifeguards should be able to gain the respect and cooperation of those who use your swimming facility. Each time they enforce the rules, they gain experience in how to deal with people successfully.

Remind your lifeguards that their primary responsibility is to scan their areas, and that enforcing rules is just one part of their duties. They must never stop scanning the water. Tell them that if a rule enforcement discussion becomes lengthy or takes their attention away from their assigned areas, they should signal for assistance.

Q-1-2 Accident Prevention System

Lifeguards are always watching for potential problems in order to act on them before they become emergencies. But intervening over and over again becomes annoying to both the lifeguard and the patrons. So how can guards enforce the rules without blowing their whistles constantly?

One solution is to learn to use the Q-1-2 system, which works with children and adults alike. There are three advantages to using this system:

- It helps lifeguards be consistent and fair.
- It reduces the stress and emotion of enforcing rules.
- It allows lifeguards to remain focused on their assigned areas.

Let's look at each step of this three-part system.

Q: Question

The process begins before someone actually violates a rule or does something potentially dangerous. Lifeguards will frequently notice people who appear to be preparing to do something that might put them or someone else in danger. For example:

- A person walks very tentatively to the edge of the diving board or deep end.
- A swimmer starts across the pool but then returns, struggling and gasping for air.
- Someone floats a kickboard a few feet from the deck and appears to be preparing to jump onto or over it.
- A patron on the deck says to another, "Race you to the deep end."

Although no one in these situations has violated a rule or done anything dangerous, the potential is clear. The first step, Q, is to ask the person a question. The lifeguard asks the person to come stand beside her or him, then asks a question without looking away from the assigned area or having to shout.

Questions are used, not to accuse, but to help make sure people have enough information about the situations they are in. The following questions might be useful in the scenarios just described:

- Have you ever jumped off the board before? Can you swim across the pool? Would you show me?
- Have you ever had swimming lessons? Can you stand up in that depth?
- Were you going to jump on the kickboard? Do you know what would happen if you landed on it?
- How are you going to race? In the water? On the deck?

Sometimes the question itself gets the point across. However, be sure you listen to the answer. If it does not indicate that the person is aware of the potential problem, give more information or instructions:

- You need to be able to swim across the swimming pool before jumping off the diving board. Wait until the break, and I'll let you try.
- Maybe you should swim in the shallow end for now.
- Do not jump on or over the kickboard.
- There seem to be too many people in the pool for you to race now.

1: Warning

The second step of the system is used when the lifeguard sees someone do something unsafe or against pool rules. First, the guard calls the person to his or her side to avoid having to shout or look away from the water. Next, the guard tells the person what he or she saw. This may sound silly; what the guard saw might have been obvious. But people sometimes don't realize what they have just done. Also, the guard wants to be certain the person knows what he or she is being warned about.

Because this will be the offender's one and only warning, the lifeguard should use simple, direct statements using this format.

- I saw . . .
- That is . . .
- Please . . .

Here are some examples of how this would work:

- *I saw* you jump off the side of the diving board. *That is* dangerous because it is too near the deck. *Please* jump off the end of the board.
- *I saw* you running. *That is* unsafe because the deck is wet. *Please* walk.
- *I saw* you dive into shallow water. *That is* very dangerous because you may hit your head and injure your neck. *Please* dive only in the deep end.
- *I saw* you enter the pool without taking a shower. *That is* against our pool rules because it makes the water dirty. *Please* shower before entering the pool.

Lifeguards should always make simple, direct statements, without emotion. These are all statements of fact and do not call for discussion. People often will want to argue in their defense, but guards should try to avoid long discussions. They can listen but maintain their focus on the water. They must make it clear to the person being given the warning that if the undesirable behavior is repeated, they will have to ask the person to leave or to take a time-out (see next section).

2: Time-Out

If an adult repeats the behavior the guard has warned about, the guard should request that someone in management ask the patron to leave the pool area (see next section). With children, the lifeguard should direct them to take a time-out from the pool instead. Giving a time-out means removing the child from the water and from the company of others to a chair for a short period. (Whether a lifeguard should give a teen a time-out depends on your facility's guidelines and the lifeguard's own judgment.)

Again, the lifeguard should call the offender to her or his side. Then, without emotion, the guard should say, "I saw you run (push, jump off the side of the board) again. Please go to the time-out chair for five minutes. Then come back to see me."

The purpose of a time-out is not public humiliation but to have the child think about proper behavior. The time-out chair should be away from the edge of the pool and out of the sun but in sight of a lifeguard or other staff member. Post the rules in the time-out area so the offender can think about what he or she should be doing more than what was done wrong.

The child should keep track of the time, not the lifeguard. An easy way to do this is to give the youngster an inexpensive plastic stopwatch or kitchen timer. The guard starts the watch or timer and hands it to the child with instructions to bring it back when it says 5:00 (or whatever time you choose).

When the child returns to the lifeguard from the time-out chair, the lifeguard asks the child for a description of what to do in the future in the same situation. The lifeguard should ask why the recommended way is better. (Basically, the guard is asking for a repeat of the warning given.) If the person cannot answer appropriately, the guard should explain the warning and ask for it to be repeated.

Asking a Patron to Leave

If an adult performs an undesirable behavior after a warning, or if a child does so after one or more time-outs, the lifeguard should inform management so the head guard, manager, or assistant manager can meet with the patron and ask her or him to leave the premises voluntarily. If a minor is involved, the parent or guardian should be contacted. Afterward, the guard should file an incident report. To ensure consistency among lifeguards and the support of management, discuss the issue of dismissing people from the facility and determine procedures at staff meetings. (See YMCA Services on the YMCA of the USA Web site for a sample program policy for expulsion of patrons.)

What if a child repeats the same behavior after a time-out? Every facility will have different rules, so lifeguards should know the steps your facility has established to enforce rules consistently. However, unlike before, every repeated behavior need not be treated the same way. Not showering before swimming may earn a time-out; dangerous behavior may merit removal from the area.

Exceptions

The Q-1-2 system is designed to be fair and consistent, but exceptions will arise. The system is only a tool—lifeguards should use it, not allow it or swimmers to use them. The lifeguard's judgment should always overrule the system when warranted.

For example, a swimmer may do several different things that merit warnings but never repeat the same behavior to earn a time-out. In such a case, the lifeguard should explain to the child that he or she has seen the several offenses and wants the child to take a time-out. After the child returns from the time-out, the guard should ask for a list of the things that have caused warnings.

A regular young patron who receives a warning one day and repeats the behavior the next day should go to time-out without a new warning. A lifeguard may reasonably hold higher expectations for those who use a facility regularly.

Regardless of what occurs, lifeguards should maintain a professional attitude. They should treat patrons courteously and focus on the behavior to be corrected, not on the individual. Lifeguards should *never* shout or use abusive language or physical violence.

SETTING UP GUARDING PROCEDURES

The quality of any facility is due in large part to the commitment management makes to its patrons and staff. You should be committed to providing a safe and fun environment for patrons, ensuring that

- there are enough lifeguards on duty to serve the patrons,
- the lifeguards are certified, and
- the lifeguards are positioned at waterside to assist swimmers.

The capacity of the facility is important in determining the number of lifeguards needed on duty. Each facility should have a minimum of one certified lifeguard on duty when it is open, including during skill instruction classes and swim team activities. Beyond that, state and local ordinances prescribe supervision requirements, and many facilities set their own stricter standards.

These standards should be based on the following conditions:

- Size and shape of the pool
- Equipment in the pool areas (slides, inflatable objects)
- Bather load
- Skill level of swimmers
- Activity or activities in the pool area (on deck and in the water)
- Changes in glare from the sun
- Number of high-use or high-risk areas
- Ability to handle emergencies properly and effectively
- Meeting or exceeding compliance with applicable state and local codes

As the appropriate number of lifeguards depends on those conditions just listed, carefully consider the situational factors before setting a specific number. As a rule of thumb, begin your consideration with a ratio of 1:25. One lifeguard isn't always adequate to supervise the pool and to implement emergency procedures effectively. You should also consider having at least one of the lifeguards on duty be a minimum of 18 years of age and have at least one person over the age of 21 in or near the pool area who is trained in aquatic emergency procedures and can support their implementation. Write up and include standards in the facility's lifeguard manual or administrator's manual.

Divide the facility into zones for particular activities, such as diving, wading, and perhaps ball playing. These zones help both patrons and lifeguards know what behavior is appropriate for each area.

To guard effectively, lifeguards must follow a system for scanning and know how to scan. They also need a rotation system that helps them stay alert. Whether they sit in chairs or guard poolside, they should understand the benefits and limitations of their guarding locations. They also will need a communication system to coordinate themselves as a team. Finally, the YMCA may present them with some special guarding situations for which they will need preparation.

Supervision Systems

All lifeguards must know what area of the facility they are responsible for at all times. If just one person on a large staff neglects her or his area, a serious accident may result.

Several factors influence what is considered a proper supervision system:

- Size and shape of the facility
- Demographics of the population using the facility
- Number of people in the water
- Number of lifeguards available
- Aquatics experience of swimmers and guards
- Environmental conditions
- Lighting conditions
- Types of activities
- Positioning of guards
- Placement of lifeguard chairs or towers

The most common systems are entire-area coverage and zone coverage. You should also formulate an emergency coverage plan.

Entire-Area Coverage

In entire-area coverage, a single lifeguard supervises the entire swimming area. The system works best when the swimming area is small and there are few swimmers. Entire-area coverage has both advantages and disadvantages:

Advantages

Only one lifeguard is required.

The lifeguard understands his or her responsibilities.

Disadvantages

The lifeguard may be responsible for a large area and will likely be unable to comply with a 10 × 10 response.

The lifeguard tends to concentrate on boundaries rather than the entire swimming area.

The lifeguard gets little change of pace.

Although entire-area coverage is suitable for small pool settings with no obstructions, it would be difficult to use in a large, complex facility. If it becomes necessary to cover a large swimming area in this manner, consider closing some sections of the facility and concentrating the swimmers in a manageable area. When a single guard is on duty, additional trained staff need to be available to assist in emergency situations.

Zone Coverage

In zone coverage, the swimming area is broken into smaller units, or zones, with one lifeguard responsible for each. The zones should overlap to ensure complete coverage (see figure 11.1 for examples).

Consider several factors in designating zones for a facility:

- Zones should not require a lifeguard to scan more than 180 degrees. Some state codes are more restrictive, limiting guards to scanning 90 degrees or less.
- Zones should minimize blind spots.
- High-risk areas should overlap into the areas of responsibility for two guard positions, ensuring double coverage.

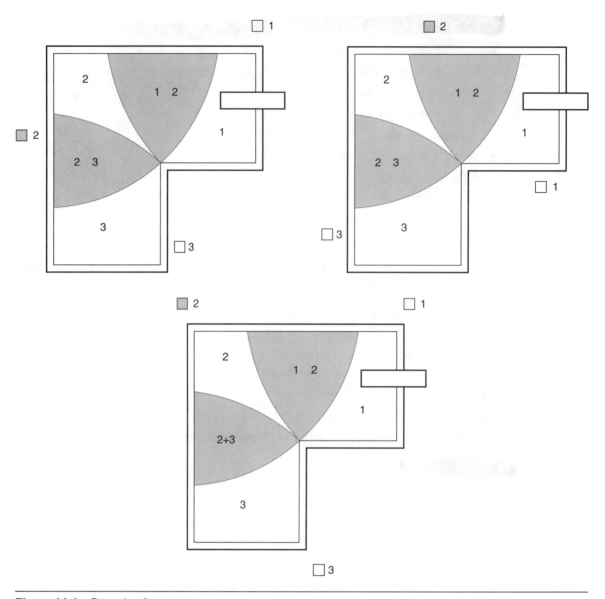

Figure 11.1 Example of zone coverage.

- Each zone should be set up so it's possible for a lifeguard to both scan the area within 10 seconds and reach any point in the zone within 10 seconds.

Zone coverage is usually accompanied by a rotation system, discussed later in this section. Zone coverage has its own advantages and disadvantages:

Advantages

Guards concentrate on limited areas.

There is double coverage in overlap areas.

Rotation keeps lifeguards refreshed.

Guards can interact with patrons more easily.

Disadvantages

More lifeguards are required.

Confusion about areas of responsibility may result in areas being unguarded.

This system allows the greatest flexibility for management and the greatest definition of area for lifeguards.

Emergency Coverage

Every facility needs an emergency coverage plan. Whenever there are two or more lifeguards and one must enter the water, the other lifeguards on duty must shift their responsibilities to cover larger areas. The guards remaining out of the water will probably have to move to new positions to cover the pool or waterfront effectively and to perform emergency procedures. If your facility uses entire-area coverage, assistance must be nearby so the lifeguard can call for help in an emergency.

All lifeguards should know the procedures for emergency coverage. You are responsible for seeing that all staff are aware of their responsibilities and for posting an emergency coverage diagram. Encourage lifeguards who are unsure of their responsibilities to ask. Their preparation could prevent an injury or accident.

Scanning

According to Fenner, Leahy, Buhk, and Dawes (1999), the ability to scan for long time periods is a lifeguard's most valuable contribution to drowning prevention. *Scanning* here means observing, recording, and assessing the condition of the patrons in the areas assigned. Scanning must be constant, vigilant, and systematic. Lifeguards should have no other duties while they are guarding.

Lifeguards should be positioned where they have a clear, unobstructed view of their assigned areas (Lifesaving Society, 1993). If your facility is using zone coverage, each guard must know the area assigned to every lifeguard station in the facility. Post a diagram of the zone coverage system so lifeguards can learn the zones and any accompanying high-risk areas or blind spots. Tell guards to pay extra attention to the high-risk areas (see pages 296-302 for common high-risk areas); their vigilance will pay off. If guards have a blind spot in their areas, they should ask their supervisors if they may adjust their positions to make that section more visible. If that is not possible, they should ask the manager about making additional coverage arrangements. Guards should also conduct a complete inspection of the pool area and pool bottom immediately after each class or recreational swim period.

Schedule regular in-service training to help lifeguards improve their scanning techniques. [For more information on scanning, refer to *On the Guard II* (4th ed.).]

According to Fenner, Leahy, Buhk, and Dawes (1999), fatigue can cause scanning ability to deteriorate. Many of the conditions under which guarding is done can fatigue lifeguards, such as dehydration, physical and mental fatigue, eyestrain, hunger, and exposure to sun and wind. Guards should come to work well rested and should avoid medications (prescription and nonprescription) that affect their alertness. Observe your guards for signs of fatigue. Check that they do the following:

- Drink enough water.
- Maintain good posture.
- Use adequate protection against the sun and wind.
- Rotate tasks or areas so they get sufficient breaks from being on duty.
- Adjust their positions to offset glare, whether they are indoors or outdoors. They should wear polarized sunglasses that allow clear peripheral vision.

In single-guard facilities at which the guard is not able to rotate, make sure that the guard receives the support needed to stay alert.

Rotation Systems

When there are two or more lifeguards, they should rotate regularly. Rotation relieves the boredom of watching the same area for an entire day, which keeps guards alert. It also makes it easier to shift zone responsibilities when necessary. In addition, rotation distributes the most and least enjoyable areas among all guards.

Most rotation systems are set up on a time schedule. A lifeguard returning from break usually initiates the rotation, temporarily putting one extra guard on duty until the rotation is complete. Between rotation cycles, the guard who rotates off duty gets a short break. In some facilities, the guard may be rotated, not to a break, but to another task, such as picking up trash or checking chemical levels. Generally, rotations should occur every 20 minutes; however, your facility, weather conditions, or bather load may affect the length of time you choose for your rotation schedule.

Staff also may be rotated at a prearranged signal. This type of rotation is usually set in motion by a change in the number of swimmers in an area. Only the head lifeguard or another guard assigned to that duty should give the signal; an individual guard should not make such a rotation decision.

Rotation systems can be designed in different ways. Figure 11.2 illustrates a generic approach to rotation triggered by a guard returning from a break.

If your facility uses elevated lifeguard stands, one guard replacing another on a stand must scan as the second guard climbs down. Once on the ground, that guard must scan the assigned area until the new guard is in position on the elevated stand.

If there are not enough lifeguards on duty to provide an extra guard for the rotation, guards should exchange positions in a prearranged order, watching the zones as they switch. One guard would move to replace another, and the guards would

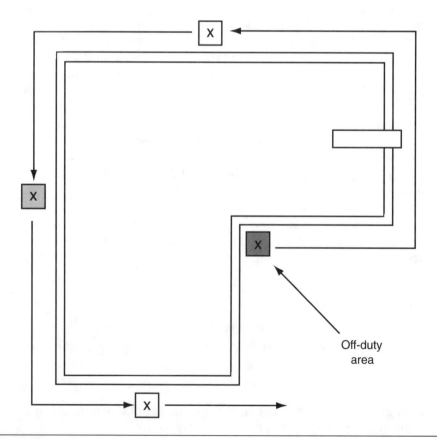

Off-duty
area

Figure 11.2   Example of a rotation system.

exchange any necessary information about the potential hazards. The relieved guard would then move to the next assigned position, and so on.

Whatever system is in operation at your facility, the following guidelines for rotation are important:

- Rotate regularly.
- Rotate systematically.
- Move the lifeguard from the most demanding position to either a break period or a less demanding spot.
- As they rotate, lifeguards should remain alert to potential problems and patron needs.

Lifeguarding Locations

Where lifeguards stand, sit, or rove is as important as determining the areas that they supervise. Locations govern how well guards can see their assigned areas and how quickly they can react to an emergency. Guards should be positioned so they have a full view of their assigned areas, above and below the water's surface. It should be impossible for anyone to enter the pool area without being observed by a lifeguard.

Lifeguards may be stationed either in elevated chairs (or towers) or on the ground as roving lifeguards. Each position has different advantages. For example, from an elevated area, the guard can see what is going on in the pool much better than from the ground. At ground level, waves or other swimmers may obscure some patrons. It's also more difficult at ground level to see distressed or actively drowning victims, who may be changing from a horizontal to a vertical position and making little progress in moving toward the edge of the pool. However, on the ground, guards are closer to patrons, making it easier to give them advice, cautions, or reprimands.

The location of the sun and the placement of windows at an indoor facility have a definite effect on where lifeguards and lifeguard stands should be placed. Consider whether glare from outdoors or reflecting up from the water will keep guards from seeing the pool clearly at certain times of the day.

Towers and Elevated Chairs

Both towers and elevated chairs (five to six feet high) will give lifeguards a better viewing point than a station on the ground. Elevated lifeguard stands are the best for supervising the swimming area, but guards must be sure to scan the areas next to and beneath the chair, which are blind spots where accidents can happen.

Place chairs or towers appropriately so guards are able to scan effectively (see page 336. Locate lifeguarding chairs at poolside and facing all entrances. Place them according to the zone coverages used. The height of the chairs should be appropriate for effective vision, usually five feet above the water's surface. This height is better because the lifeguard's field of vision enables her or him to observe the vertical position of an active drowning victim and eliminates the possibility of a patron standing or walking in front of chairs that are only two to three feet high. If a chair is not placed properly, the guard can take a roving position until the chair can be moved. Check your state bathing code to see if you are in compliance with the regulations in place regarding lifeguarding chairs.

On a tower or chair, lifeguards should keep all equipment within easy reach in case of an emergency. Rather than storing it on the ground, they should mount it on the tower or the elevated chair. The guards should have a rescue tube or buoy with them at all times. They need to protect the extra line from the rescue tube or buoy so it doesn't get tangled on either the guard's body or the chair.

Guards will also need to practice getting down from the station. Depending on the height of the station and the depth of the water, guards may jump or climb down. When jumping from any height, guards should look before they leap! Guards should never jump directly onto a deck or dock from a station.

Lifeguards should check the area beneath them to avoid landing on a patron or injuring themselves. When they do jump, they should tightly grasp any equipment they are taking with them, being careful of lines that can get caught. They need to maintain control of their rescue equipment at all times. Finally, guards should bend their knees when they land; landing with locked knees can be very painful and can cause serious injury to the knees and back. Have guards practice getting down from the tower or chair until they can do it fluidly. Every second counts in an emergency.

If lifeguards intend to jump directly into the water, they must know that the water is deep enough for jumping safely. In traditional pools, that should be easy. In a wave pool, guards must time their jumps so they hit the water at the peak of the swell. In a river, the depth and speed of the water change with rainfall or drought. Lifeguards should know the conditions in their area before jumping into the water from a tower or an elevated chair.

Roving Lifeguards

Lifeguards who patrol the area by walking around the perimeter find it easier to handle public relations and to discipline patrons courteously. They are also able to provide educational tips to patrons because they are more accessible. Many times, roving guards are assigned to shallow-water areas so they can carefully supervise the water and the surrounding deck or beach. Roving guards must carry a rescue tube or buoy so that it is ready for use. These guards may also serve as a communication link between lifeguard towers, particularly at beaches.

As aquatics director, you should make regular unannounced visits to the swimming area to see how well the lifeguards are performing their duties. You should observe at different times of the day and on each of the days of the week that the swimming area is open. Evaluate your lifeguards' performances on a regular basis.

Guard Communication Systems

Communication is very important to your lifeguards' success. Not only do they need to communicate well with the patrons of your facility, but they must be able to do the same with the other members of their lifeguarding team. Several communication systems exist for lifeguards:

- Whistle signals
- Hand signals
- Rescue equipment signals
- Flags
- Radios
- Telephones
- Megaphones
- CB radios
- Signal lights
- Handheld public address devices with sirens
- Air horns
- Radio telephones (single band)

Select one or more of these systems and familiarize all lifeguards with them.

Whistle Signals

Patterns of whistle blows can be used to signal particular situations. One common signal system is the following:

- One short blast—used to get swimmers' attention
- Two short blasts—used to get other lifeguards' attention
- One long blast—used to initiate emergency procedures

Hand Signals

Lifeguards frequently use hand signals to communicate with patrons and other lifeguards. Some examples are illustrated in figure 11.3. These signals are frequently accompanied by whistle signals. Tell guards to always hold the signal for a few seconds to be sure it has been seen.

Figure 11.3 Common hand signals.

Rescue Equipment Signals

Some signals can be made using a rescue tube or buoy (see figure 11.4). Rescue equipment held vertically and moved from side to side means assistance is needed. Rescue equipment held horizontally over the head means the situation is under control.

Flags

Flags are not used in most swimming pools, but they are used at some waterfront areas and are common at water slides and water parks. Waving a red flag means danger or stop sending water sliders down the slide. Waving a green flag indicates that all is well.

Radios

Two-way and CB radios are most frequently used in large waterfront areas where visual contact is more difficult. These radios are for lifeguarding business only, not socializing.

Telephones

Phones are important for use in emergencies. Emergency numbers should be listed on or posted near the telephones. If cell or cordless phones are used, a standard phone also should be available in case the cell or cordless phones do not work. Restrict phone use to business or emergency use only.

Megaphones

A *megaphone* is a cone-shaped device used to intensify and direct the voice. Using a megaphone can be helpful when a facility is crowded.

Figure 11.4   Rescue equipment signals.

Group Swimming Safety Check Systems

Most camps and youth organizations use one or more safety check systems to account for all individuals quickly. These systems keep lifeguards aware of the number and location of swimmers in the water; they are especially useful in lake or river environments where visibility is limited. Failure to enforce the system undermines its value.

Four of the most common safety check systems are the buddy system, the tag board (or roll call) system, the cap system, and the pool check. Each is useful for a different purpose; ask lifeguards for input on which systems to use. And for any system to work, lifeguards must inform the swimmers of the procedures.

Buddy System

In the buddy system, every swimmer is assigned a "buddy" of similar ability. If there is an uneven number of swimmers, one set of buddies may be a triad. Buddies are required to stay close to each other at all times. Then, if one buddy is having difficulty, the other buddy can signal for help.

At a predetermined signal, different from all other signals used by the staff, swimmers "buddy up"—they stop, join hands with their buddies, raise their arms high, and remain stationary. Such positioning lets staff members count groups and account for all swimmers. At a second sounding of the signal, buddies may drop hands and continue their activities.

Lifeguards should test this system frequently so that partners remain close together. If any buddies have strayed too far apart when the lifeguard signals to "buddy up," the guard should warn the violators that another instance of being away from a buddy will result in time out of the water (see page 330). Consistent enforcement of the system rules, along with other swimming rules, will make the buddy system work.

Tag Board and Roll Call Systems

The tag board and roll call systems both work in the same way—swimmers are accounted for before they enter the water and after their swimming period is over. With the tag board system, each person gets a tag with his or her name on it. Swimmers hang their tags on a pegboard as they enter the water and remove them when they leave the water, both under the watchful eye of a lifeguard or camp staff member. A variation of this system uses color-coded tags with a different color on each side. One color indicates swimmers are in the water, the other that they are out. At the end of each swimming period, the group leader can easily check to see that all swimmers have left the water.

If a tag is unaccounted for, staff members start a search immediately. For the safety of all swimmers, the group leader must enforce the rule that each individual is responsible for her or his own tag. Lifeguards should spot-check swimmers to test whether they are following the rules and placing their tags correctly on the board as they enter the water. They should identify a swimmer and look to see that the swimmer's tag is displayed appropriately. If it is not, they should summon the swimmer and discuss the rules.

The roll call system operates on the same principle of checking attendance before and after the swimming session, but no equipment is necessary. The group leader simply takes attendance by calling names aloud before the swimmers enter the water and immediately after they exit. If someone doesn't respond, staff starts a search immediately. One drawback of the roll call system is that the time between roll calls could be the time during which a swimmer becomes missing.

Cap System

This system allows lifeguards, staff, and swimmers to differentiate among different swimming skill levels by looking at what color bathing cap, headband, or wristband a swimmer is wearing. The system can be used with either of the other safety check systems. The following color coding is widely used:

- Nonswimmers and beginners wear red.
- Intermediate swimmers wear yellow.
- Advanced swimmers wear blue or green.
- Leaders and lifeguards wear white.

The advantage of this system is that a lifeguard can easily spot red or yellow in an area reserved for advanced swimmers and can act quickly to move that person to a safer area.

Pool Check

The widely used pool check system is designed for busy periods when lifeguards want to be sure that they can account for all swimmers. On a specified signal, all swimmers are asked to leave the water or sit on the edge of the pool. This system allows the lifeguards to check periodically that no one is on the pool bottom and provides the swimmers with a rest period.

Pool checks can be annoying to patrons if overused; however, if they are necessary to ensure safety, carry them out. To make checks less objectionable, consider coupling them with announcements for all patrons, brief swimming tips, or the beginning of special activities.

HANDLING OFFENSIVE OR DANGEROUS SITUATIONS

Although every facility has rules of conduct, some patrons inevitably try to test those rules. Lifeguards are responsible for ensuring that a patron doesn't endanger the safety or well-being of others. This section is designed to help them handle those situations. Post emergency contact phone numbers in the pool office in case lifeguards should need additional assistance.

Crowd Control

If an accident occurs, a lifeguard may be put in charge of moving the patrons from the accident area. Moving the patrons will allow staff to deal with the situation without onlookers. The lifeguard should stay composed and be respectful as he or she moves patrons to a prearranged area, such as a locker room or another part of the facility or grounds. The lifeguard should remind everyone to remain calm, as the situation is being taken care of by the facility's trained staff.

If you have single-guard situations, create an emergency plan for the lifeguard to obtain assistance with crowd control immediately when it is needed.

Theft

Post conspicuous notices stating that the YMCA is not responsible for lost or stolen personal property. However, lifeguards should be alert to any theft. If an incident is reported to a lifeguard, he or she should follow the emergency procedures in place. A staff member should call law enforcement officials.

The guard should not accuse a person of theft. He or she should present the evidence to the law enforcement authorities and let them make any charges. Otherwise, the guard and the YMCA could be charged with making a false accusation if he or she acted hastily and had no proof of the claim. Make sure the guard fills out the appropriate incident report form and obtains statements from witnesses before they leave the scene.

Sexual Activity

Do not permit inappropriate sexual behavior in your facility. Guards should diplomatically control these situations from the start of the swimming season.

Indecent Exposure

Exposing oneself in public is a crime in most areas. If someone indecently exposes her- or himself, the lifeguard should suggest that the person cover up immediately. If the request is ignored or the behavior is repeated, the guard should contact the management and police.

Disregard for Lifeguard Authority

Lifeguards who work at a facility that their friends frequent can put themselves and their friends in an awkward situation. The lifeguard is duty-bound to enforce the rules of the facility, no matter who violates them. It may help if lifeguards explain that to their friends if the friends are causing problems.

Anyone who disregards a lifeguard's authority is creating a risk, and lifeguards must not allow patrons to ignore their instructions. Lifeguards should summon the manager or assistant manager with a prearranged signal, such as a raised, clenched fist, to assist them in these instances. Repeated disregard for authority is grounds for banning offenders from the facility. If necessary, the supervisor or the aquatics director should contact local authorities to escort a troublemaker from the scene.

Conflicts or Disturbances

Lifeguards can use their customer relations skills when situations arise. In a conflict, they can use the PACA problem-solving process (see page 194) to find solutions and get needs met, as long as people communicate honestly and listen to one another. When they are trying to resolve such situations, they should keep the following guidelines in mind:

- Keep your emotions in check and stay calm. Remember that the conflict is not about you, and don't take it personally.
- Listen actively and acknowledge what is being said. Use "I" statements, and restate what was said to be sure you understood it correctly.
- Be respectful.
- Speak for a purpose; don't talk just to hear yourself talk.
- Ask each party to state the problem, their feelings, and what they want.
- Maintain control of the situation and the process of resolution.

Lifeguards may be able to resolve a situation in one of the following ways (American Red Cross, 1995):

- Allow one party to decide that the argument is not worth the trouble and "give in" to the other person's position.
- Have both parties apologize without necessarily implying that they did or said anything wrong, or have them take equal responsibility for the conflict.
- Have each party consent to give up something to resolve the conflict.
- Reduce tension surrounding the conflict by making light of the situation in ways that do not offend those involved.
- Use a technique that relies on chance to resolve the issue, such as flipping a coin or choosing a number between 1 and 10.
- Get the parties to agree to wait for a better time in which to discuss and resolve the conflict.

If a situation arises between patrons in the pool or pool area and a lifeguard cannot resolve it quickly, he or she should call for an off-duty lifeguard or a supervisor, who can either deal with the patrons or change places with the lifeguard involved. Establish a prearranged signal a lifeguard can use to alert other lifeguards or the supervisor of such situations so that his or her zone in the pool remains covered.

If the lifeguard is having difficulty getting patrons to resolve their dispute, he or she should involve the head lifeguard or supervisor. The head lifeguard or supervisor should separate the two individuals and ask them to move to different areas, then talk with each of them separately. If the situation escalates, contact the police for assistance.

The lifeguard should complete an incident report form after any disturbance.

Violence

The first step in dealing with violence in the pool area is to create a plan to minimize the chances of violence occurring and put that plan in place. One part of the plan should be to influence patrons' behavior by having staff members who appear and behave professionally. Lifeguards should command authority in the facility. Their attitude, behavior, and appearance will all affect patrons' perception of their authority.

Another part of the plan should be to post the rules and see that they are enforced consistently and effectively. Everyone who enters your facility should know the rules. Place signs listing the rules at the facility's entrance and in multiple locations within the facility. Your staff should be able to explain to patrons why the rules exist.

Your facility's emergency plan should include procedures for preventing or dealing with violent acts. Staff should know and practice these procedures, just as they do other emergency procedures.

Tell staff that if they suspect a violent act may occur, they should notify their supervisors right away. If a violent act clearly is about to happen, they should contact their supervisors and the authorities immediately. Staff should not intervene or confront those involved, and they should not approach anyone with a weapon; instead, they should retreat and follow the facility's procedures. Their priority should be the safety of your patrons, as well as their own.

Once authorities arrive, staff should listen to the authorities' instructions and let them take charge. Staff should identify those who were involved in the violence, and the aquatics director or the manager on duty should inform those people that they are either not allowed back in the pool at all or only after a certain time period.

After a violent incident, staff members should reopen the pool only when guards are mentally prepared to resume their duties.

Substance Abuse

People who are abusing substances such as alcohol or other drugs should not be in or around aquatics areas; their lack of judgment and reduced physical abilities could easily endanger both them and other patrons. Tell lifeguards to watch for signs or behavior patterns that are characteristic of substance abuse:

- Unusual tiredness
- The odor of alcohol, tobacco, or other drugs
- Unsteadiness and lack of coordination
- Unusual detachment from the group
- Unusual changes in mood or attitude
- Unexplained lack of interest in normal activities
- Unusual giddiness
- Preoccupation with drug-related clothing, signs, or other paraphernalia
- Obvious slurring of words
- Public use of alcohol, tobacco, or other drugs

If a lifeguard suspects that a patron in her or his area is under the influence of alcohol or other drugs, that lifeguard should watch the patron carefully and request that the manager or head lifeguard join in observing the patron. If the manager agrees that the patron is acting suspiciously, the manager should ask the patron to leave. The manager should encourage the patron to have someone take him or her home and not drive, and may authorize calling a taxi or providing other transportation assistance. If the person will not leave, the manager or aquatics director should contact the police. Once the person has left, the lifeguard should document the behavior on an incident report form. The manager may inform the parents of youthful abusers.

Concern for Younger Patrons

If lifeguards think they see signs of child abuse or neglect or of drug abuse in children, they should notify their manager or the appropriate staff member and explain what they have observed. That staff person can then document the signs, contact the child's parents, and take whatever steps are deemed appropriate and necessary by state and local codes, including referrals to agencies and services. (See "Child Abuse Identification and Prevention: Recommended Guidelines for YMCAs" in appendix 2.)

Problems Unique to Your Facility

Although the previous section may provide some basis for decision making, each facility has its own unique difficulties and its own rules. To a great extent, lifeguards must make their own decisions about what constitutes a potentially dangerous situation. Study the layout of your facility and the rules that have been made to govern it. If you see potential problem areas, establish additional rules that will preserve a safe and fun environment.

SPECIAL GUARDING SITUATIONS

YMCAs present many different types of lifeguarding situations, some more common than others. Have your lifeguards consider how to react to each of the following situations and to seek additional training if they need it.

Keep in mind that if other departments in your YMCA are going to use the pool for their programs, you must see that your staff trains them in appropriate aquatic safety skills before they bring participants to the pool.

Classes

When guards are assigned to lifeguard during a class, their role is simply to provide lifeguarding services. In any class situation, guards should watch every swimmer, just as they would during a free-swim period. They should assess the comfort and skill level of each swimmer and use that information to guide their attention. Guards should keep all class members grouped together with the instructor's help. Swimmers need to hear instructions, and the guards need to know where the swimmers are and that the swimmers are practicing the skills for their class.

Day Camps and Day Care

In day camp and day care situations, when possible, guards should give children a skill test and divide them into groups by skill level for swimming activity. Lifeguarding will be a little easier when guards know that the swimmers are of similar abilities. A common swim test is to ask those children who want to swim in deep water to first swim across the shallow end to the wall, using any style. Those children who can do this successfully are then escorted to the deep water, where they are asked to jump in, surface, swim 40 feet on their front, and stop. They then must turn over, tread water for 10 to 15 seconds, then turn onto their back and return to the starting position, either on their front or on their back. Another swim test is to ask them to swim 75 feet.

If the group is not divided, it might be a perfect chance to institute one of the group-swimming safety check systems just described. Guards should select the one that will let them keep track of swimmers most easily.

Working with young swimmers is an excellent opportunity to teach them water safety. Lifeguards should review the rules frequently with children; repetition will help the children learn and understand the rules. Guards should train camp or day care staff to assist them in teaching the rules and watching their groups. They also should be sure that staff members have learned the rules and know the facility's emergency system. However, lifeguards must make it clear to staff that they, as lifeguards, are in charge of the swimming activity.

Guards should clear the water periodically. While the water is empty, they should scan the pool bottom. In a waterfront situation, they should check attendance carefully. These "out of the water" checks are good teaching opportunities and give swimmers a chance to rest.

In working with a group of only young children, lifeguards might find it useful to stand on the deck near the children. The guards will then be closer should anyone become frightened or need help in the water, and they'll be close enough to begin teaching these young swimmers the rules. Lifeguards should always check with the facility manager before independently changing their positions based on the group using the area.

For guidelines for aquatics in day camps and day care, see the YMCA Aquatics Guidelines in appendix 4.

Competitive Events

The most common activities lifeguards at a competitive event will become involved in are assisting distressed swimmers or divers, controlling crowds, maintaining safety, and responding to potential spinal injuries. Guards should establish communication with the meet director so that any incident is handled effectively.

Although lifeguards may feel that there is no possibility of having to go into the water to assist a swimmer during a swim meet, they must be prepared. They should arrive at such an assignment dressed as they would for a shift at a crowded pool. They'll still need rescue equipment available in the usual places. If an incident does occur, they want to be able to react efficiently and effectively. The guards must stay alert and be ready to respond.

Rental Groups

Groups that rent a facility for a party need special attention. Some patrons assume that the rules are relaxed because they are the only ones at the facility.

With any rental group, have a signed agreement that clearly states the rules and enforcement policy and procedures. Have guards enforce these rules just as they do during a regular swim session. Tell guards about any special agreements you might have made with the group.

When the group arrives at your facility, the guards should learn who is in charge. That person will be their contact should any incidents occur. Next, guards should review the rules with the group and remind them that the purpose of the rules is to ensure their safety. If the group doesn't follow the rules, they will be asked to leave and risk not being able to use the facility in the future.

If a group brings their own lifeguards to your facility, have those lifeguards meet with the facility guards to discuss facility rules, emergency procedures, and hazards specific to your facility. Conversely, if a group from your YMCA is visiting another facility and brings lifeguards, your lifeguards should learn that facility's rules, emergency procedures, and hazards before anyone enters the water.

Language Barriers

Guards may face a situation in which a swimmer doesn't speak their language. With our country becoming more ethnically diverse, another lifeguard or patron may be able to translate. Encourage guards to get to know those around them who can help. If there is no one to translate, guards can use common hand signals to communicate.

People With Disabilities

Under the Americans With Disabilities Act, people with disabilities must have access to all facilities and must receive equal opportunity to use them. Furthermore, they must be treated according to the same standards as other patrons. Those with disabilities are people first! You and your guards must determine how to work with each person with a disability.

Disabilities can be categorized in many ways. Perhaps the most common divisions are

- sensory disabilities (blindness, deafness);
- physical disabilities;
- developmental disabilities (may be either physical or mental); and
- mental disabilities.

People with sensory disabilities rely on their nondisabled senses to receive communication. For example, people who cannot see rely on their hearing, and those who cannot hear rely on sight. Have your guards practice giving instructions using just their hands and no words. Then have them try doing it just speaking, with no hand signals. If your facility has deaf patrons, consider having your guards develop a vocabulary of sign language signals and making a board available to write on.

Swimming is a common therapeutic activity for people with physical and developmental disabilities. Some of these individuals may have difficulties communicating or moving that could place them in danger. So they can participate in aquatic activities safely, your guards need to learn how to handle emergencies involving people with disabilities.

People with physical disabilities may not have sufficient buoyancy, strength, flexibility, or agility to navigate certain areas of your facility safely. Ask guards to give these individuals a little extra attention, especially if these people are moving into areas requiring more skill.

People with developmental disabilities may have excellent physical skills. The guards' obligation with these patrons is to help them understand and follow the rules of the facility. People with communication deficits may have no trouble swimming or understanding the rules. However, they may have difficulty understanding what a guard is trying to communicate because of impaired senses, or they may have difficulty expressing their questions or concerns to a guard.

So what can your guards do to be effective in these situations? First, ask them to be alert enough to notice anyone with a disability who is at your facility. Medic alert tags may indicate those who have disabilities. Suggest that guards talk with disabled patrons about the facility and about their needs. Most people with disabilities are happy to discuss their situation if someone approaches them in a supportive, professional manner. Tell your lifeguards that they should be sure that people with a developmental or communication disability understand the rules and policies of the facility. The guards should work with them and their companions to ensure that they understand. If someone with a disability asks a guard a question, the guard should work hard to understand it and should provide an answer that the person can understand.

Lifeguards can use the same rescue techniques they were taught in their certification course to provide assistance to people with disabilities, but they must be flexible and somewhat inventive. If a swimmer does not have a right arm for the guard to grab, the guard will have to perform the rescue using the person's left arm. Or a swimmer may not be able to see the equipment the guard is extending—how can the guard get the swimmer to grab it? Once guards are aware of a patron with a specific disability, they should think through how they would assist that person should the need arise. Guards should plan ahead and use whatever works!

For more on guarding people with disabilities, see *On the Guard II* (4th ed.) and *Teaching Swimming Fundamentals*.

BIBLIOGRAPHY

American Red Cross. 1995. *Head lifeguard*. St. Louis: Mosby Lifeline.

Fenner, P. Leahy, S., Buhk, A., and Dawes, P. 1999. Prevention of drowning: Visual scanning and attention span in lifeguards. *The journal of occupational health and safety—Australia and New Zealand*, 15(1), 61-66.

Lifesaving Society. 1993. *Alert: Lifeguarding in action*. North York, Ontario, Canada: The Royal Life Saving Society Canada.

Aquatics Facility Management

Facility operation is one of your core responsibilities as an aquatics director. Whether primary responsibility for pool operation belongs to you or the property management department, you need to have the skills and knowledge to be a critical member of the pool operation team. You will be part of discussions, planning, and implementation relating to

- compliance with state and local regulations and scheduling of maintenance and inspections;
- safe and sanitary operation of the pool;
- pool chemistry, water testing, and common water problems;
- development of or consulting about new facilities; and
- enhancement of current facilities.

We strongly encourage you to obtain the YMCA Pool Operator on Location (POOL) certification. This comprehensive course covers the safe operation of pools. It includes training in filtration; swimming pool chemistry and common water problems; safe handling, use, and disposal of pool chemicals; disinfection systems; water testing; spa and hot tub operation; hazard identification and risk control; pool maintenance; and winterization, energy conservation, and cost-effective operation. The *YMCA Pool Operations Manual* is available from the YMCA Program Store at 800-747-0089.

POOL MAINTENANCE

One of your first steps to effective pool maintenance will be developing a detailed aquatics facility management plan. A well-thought-out plan will best use staff and financial resources to preserve the integrity and safety of your pool while meeting state and local regulations.

You also need to be familiar with safety and sanitation precautions, diving safety, signage requirements, pool filtration, pool chemistry, water testing, and how to solve common water problems. Although you may not take care of these things directly, you are responsible for them. Finally, you need to keep good records of pool maintenance and operations.

Aquatics Facility Management Plan

We encourage you to develop a written aquatics facility management plan for your facility. Such a plan will help you improve preventive maintenance and communicate more easily about maintenance, and will serve as a record of essential information about the facility for the directors who may follow you.

Begin by checking that all administrative policies, procedures, and practices are in accordance with your state and local regulations (where applicable), including the following:

- Licensing requirements and operating permits (be aware of when you must renew licenses and schedule pre-renewal inspection in advance so you have time for any needed repairs)
- Fire and building codes
- Local or state swimming pool and bathing codes
- Zoning laws
- Transportation regulations
- Electrical inspection codes (if not part of the swimming pool and bathing code) (Check that you have the most current version of codes.)
- ADA requirements
- Documented and current lifeguard and CPR certifications
- YMCA policies above and beyond local and state requirements
- OSHA regulations (Right-to-Know, personal protection, emergency response, and others)
- Other regulations

Ensure that your YMCA has assigned someone to be in charge of and give priority to maintaining governmental compliance records, licenses, and pool operation records and to ensure that all certifications are up to date. Promptly obtain any records that are missing or code information that is not on hand from the proper regulatory authority.

This person should also ensure that all staff who are involved with the operation and use of the pool and its mechanical equipment and natatorium space are properly trained. Many of the government OSHA standards and life safety certifications such as CPR training require annual certification.

Obtain a copy of your local and state bathing codes. Keep it on file, review it with your staff, and if required, post it for the public to see. If you are not now in compliance with local and state regulations, give priority to becoming compliant.

Based on regulations, manufacturers' recommendations, and the best practices for maintenance, create a schedule for inspecting all parts of the pool facility and for performing regular maintenance functions. This would include the following:

- Inspecting all aquatics facilities and equipment for safety regularly (daily, weekly, monthly, or annually, depending on the area of the facility inspected) and judging them suitable for use. (Keep records of inspections for at least five years.)
- Performing preventive maintenance for all facilities and equipment and documenting when it was performed, who performed it, and that it was approved.
- Testing the pool area emergency lighting system monthly.
- Inspecting the emergency lighting, regular pool lighting, and mechanical, ventilation, and plumbing systems periodically and keeping them in good working condition. (Keep a schedule of inspections and a written report on file.)

• Maintaining and backwashing pool filters in accordance with the manufacturer's instructions.

• Cleaning and disinfecting all floor and deck surfaces and equipment on a regular basis, as well as checking to make sure they are free of unsafe or hazardous conditions. (Keep proof of maintenance on file.)

• Measuring water and air temperature, chemical levels, humidity, pool clarity, and bather load every hour during pool operation, and measuring the Langelier Saturation Index water balance weekly. (Record these measurements in a pool log; keep it on file for at least five years, or longer if the documentation is relevant to pending litigation.)

• Having a licensed structural engineer inspect the roof and ceiling for structural safety and signs of corrosion at least every five years. (*Note:* Suspended ceilings are not recommended for pools.)

Have a YMCA POOL–certified operator on staff to monitor and maintain the disinfection, filtration, and mechanical operation of each pool to ensure that state and local health department standards are being met. Keep records on file as proof of this function, and send copies to the state health department as required.

Most inspections cover not only the pool or the waterfront, but also any structures on the facility grounds, and the results should be reported to the managers of the facility. As a general guideline, the following areas should be checked:

Bottom	Diving area
Water clarity	Diving boards
Chemical readings	Diving stands
Air and water temperature	Radio or phone system
Deck	Entry and exit areas
Ladders	Shower and locker room areas
Lifelines and lane lines	Water fountains
First aid and safety equipment	Deck chairs or furniture
Lights	Drain areas
Filtration system	Main drain (once a year when pool is drained; visually each day)

If a problem is noted in any of these areas, you must do the necessary maintenance. You must remove the risk associated with the conditions to try to ensure the safety of patrons and to protect your facility from legal action in the event of a related injury. Do not allow patrons to enter problem areas until the hazards are removed or fixed.

See sample pool maintenance and safety checklists to include daily inspections (checklists), weekly checks (checklists), and other types of checks (equipment safety checks, program-specific safety checks, facility safety checks) on the YMCA of the USA Web site.

File the inspection forms, together with maintenance reports indicating when and how the noted safety problems were handled, in a secure location. Keep them for at least five years.

Finally, check to see if all sites and facilities are appropriate for the class activities held, including equipment and supplies of sufficient quality, quantity, and variety that are developmentally appropriate for the participants' ages, abilities, disabilities, and the size of the group. (See "Designing Facilities for Programs" on pages 375-379 for recommended facility requirements and each program chapter for recommended supplies and equipment.)

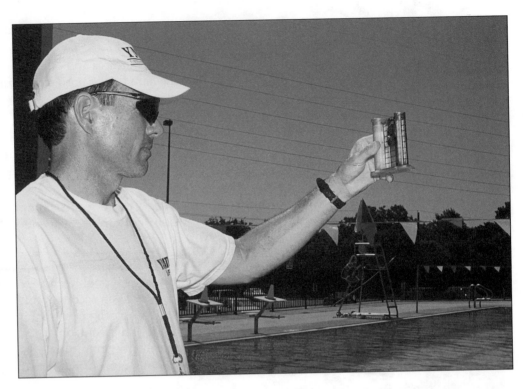

Beyond the YMCA POOL certification course, YMCA custodians and supervisors can receive training and certification in cleaning and sanitation procedures by attending the Custodial Technician Training program. For more information, contact the Building and Furnishings Service (BFS)/Property Management department or attend a YMCA Program School.

Safety and Sanitation Precautions

Pool chemical safety, electrical safety, starting block safety, and maintenance of non-slip surfaces are all areas of concern in pool management. Pools must also be kept clear of fecal contamination, which can spread many different diseases. Finally, security is necessary to protect patrons and the facility from unauthorized entries.

Chemical Safety

In some associations, the aquatics director may not be solely responsible for the management of pool chemistry, but you must understand it. You must be aware of the potential dangers of pool chemicals; mishandling them is hazardous.

So that all staff better understand the dangers and proper handling of the chemicals used at your facility, be sure copies of the Material Safety Data Sheets for those chemicals are available to them. According to OSHA Right-to-Know standards, these informational sheets must be available; the YMCA of the USA recommends they be posted in the room or readily available where the chemicals are used and copies be available at a central location in the event of an emergency. Train staff in the safe handling of pool chemicals before they work with such chemicals. Be aware of the Right-to-Know standard, which states that employees have the right to know if they are working with hazardous materials and have been given the information they need to protect themselves. Have all staff sign off that they have read and know the hazardous material information and know where to find it for the first aid information.

Make sure that chemicals are clearly identified and stored properly. Post a warning sign on the outside of the door where chemicals are stored.

For more on hazardous material storage and cleanup in case of spills, check the *YMCA Pool Operations Manual* and OSHA regulations.

Electrical Safety

Any pool environment poses the potential for electrical shock because electrical outlets and fixtures in this area often come in contact with water. For your protection, the National Electrical Code has established stringent requirements for the location of electrical fixtures in pool areas. Outlets in all wet areas are typically required to have covers and ground fault circuit interrupters (GFCIs). The pool and all fixed equipment should be inspected by a licensed electrician to be certified as bonded and grounded.

Your facility must meet safety requirements, but your staff must also exercise caution and common sense in preventing electrical accidents. Don't allow them to use tape recorders, video cameras, or other electronic devices near the water's edge, and warn them not to stand in water as they reach into the electrical box of the pool filter compartment.

Another area related to electrical safety is properly securing the electrical and mechanical systems during unexpected power failures. Create procedures for staff to follow once power has been restored to ensure that the pool mechanical equipment is operating properly, the lights are all on, the chemicals in the water are balanced, and the chemical feeders are working. Do not reopen the pool for use until everything has been checked and is running properly.

Finally, your pool lighting should meet certain standards. For indoor pools, you should have a minimum illumination of 30 foot-candles at the water's surface when underwater lighting is on. Without underwater lighting, you should have a minimum illumination of 50 foot-candles. Underwater lighting should provide 100 foot-candles of illumination as measured at the surface. For outdoor pools, underwater lighting should provide 60 foot-candles of illumination as measured at the surface.

Starting Block Safety

Competitive swim teams often dive into the water from starting blocks. Allow only swim team members to use starting blocks with proper supervision and safety instruction, and post safety warnings that prohibit starting block use by other swimmers. Place starting blocks only in the deep end of the pool in no less than five feet of water. Remove or cap starting blocks to avoid unintended use, and if the starting blocks are in the shallow end, remove them.

Nonslip Surface Maintenance

One task that is frequently performed incorrectly, and that could cause an accident, is the cleaning of nonslip surfaces. Such surfaces can be found on places such as decks, springboards, diving mount steps, starting block surfaces and steps, lifeguard chair steps, steps leading to water slides and flumes, and steps to diving platforms. At outdoor facilities where these surfaces are constantly wet and are shaded, green algae can cause the surface to become slippery. In indoor pools, especially those with high humidity or poor air handling, or in which the air handling system is turned off overnight (which is improper), black mildew may form on these surfaces, which can also cause slipperiness.

In an effort to clean these surfaces, personnel may scrub the surface with detergent and a stiff-bristled brush. However, frequent scrubbing with such a brush will loosen the silica in the paint or loosen the sand put on top of the wet paint (as is done in homemade resurfacing). If the gritty material is removed by scrubbing, the surfaces become smooth and slippery when wet and are then hazardous.

A better way to clean nonslip surfaces is to apply household bleach, full strength, to the entire surface to be cleaned. After letting it stand for up to five minutes, rinse off the bleach with a hose. This type of cleaning removes the slime while leaving the grit material in place. It also takes less effort than scrubbing!

Fecal Contamination of Pool Water

Fecal matter in the water can transmit many different bacteria, viruses, and parasites, including blood-borne pathogens, to others. This is why your staff must take immediate action if they see feces in the pool. Establish a written facility cleanup policy for staff to follow (see the Center for Disease Control's recommendations on their Web page if your health department does not have recommendations).

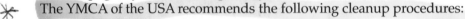

The YMCA of the USA recommends the following cleanup procedures:

• If the feces are solid and the free chlorine level is above 1.5 parts per million (ppm), clear the pool, remove the fecal matter, and check the free chlorine level in three different locations. Take samples from shallow, transitional, and deep water, and not from water in front of inlets. Close the pool for 30 minutes.

• If the feces are solid and the free chlorine level is below 1.5 ppm, follow the same steps as in the previous example. However, in this case, close the pool and treat the water until the free chlorine residual is 2.0 ppm in three different locations. Do not reopen the pool until 30 minutes after the free chlorine residual has reached 2.0 ppm.

• If the feces are liquid and include particulates, the person who had the fecal accident has had diarrhea in the last two weeks, or your health department has identified your pool as the source of cryptosporidium, use more extensive procedures (detailed in the YMCA Medical Advisory Committee's statement on feces cleanup on the YMCA of the USA Web site).

You can reduce the occurrence of fecal accidents in several ways. One action you can take is to help parents get their children to the bathroom by scheduling an hourly break for disinfectant testing and bathroom use. Have staff let patrons know that this break provides optimal timing for bathroom use. To prevent transmission of germs and get people to use the facilities, make sure that the bathrooms are clean and located a convenient distance from the pool to ensure their use, stock the bathrooms with toilet paper, and make sure there is ample soap for hand washing.

Also, consider posting a sign in a conspicuous location before pool entry that states the following:

• Don't swim when you have diarrhea.
• Don't swallow the pool water.
• Wash your hands with soap and water after using the rest room or changing diapers.
• Take your kids to the bathroom often.
• Change diapers in the bathroom and not at poolside.
• Wash your child thoroughly (especially the rear end) with soap and water before swimming.

Encourage swimmers to shower with soap and water before entering the pool. This could reduce the risk of pool contamination by removing invisible fecal matter from their bottoms. A quick rinsing over a swimsuit with cold water will not do much good. Try to make hot water available in swimmers' shower facilities.

Keep the chemical feed equipment and chemicals at optimal levels within state and local government regulations. Be sure to monitor chlorine regularly where the chlorine is needed—at poolside. Also monitor pH regularly, as poor pH control can compromise chlorine's effectiveness as a disinfectant. Prevent water parks, pools, or hot tubs from running out of chlorine through regular monitoring and pumphouse and systems checks.

If your kiddie pool filtration system is connected with other pools, this increases the chance that fecal contamination can be dispersed from the kiddie pool to the other pools. You might consider keeping diaper/toddler-aged children in pools specifically designated for them. It pays to be proactive.

For more information on the prevention and control of fecal contamination in swimming pools, check the YMCA of the USA web site.

Swim Diapers: A False Sense of Security

The use of swim diapers and swim pants may give many parents and pool staff a false sense of security regarding fecal contamination. No published scientific information exists on how well these diapers and pants are able to keep feces or infection-causing germs from leaking into the pool. However, it is unlikely that swim diapers and pants are able to keep diarrheal stools, which are at high risk for containing germs, from leaking into the pool. Swim diapers and swim pants are not a solution for a child with diarrhea or a substitute for frequent diaper changing.

Security

Every facility needs regular procedures for opening and closing. You should create a list of actions staff must take to prepare the facility to open and to close it at night. Two people should sign off on this list to verify that all the proper procedures were followed.

Your facility should be fitted with the appropriate devices to make it secure. Entrances and exits to the pool should have self-closing and lockable doors or gates so the area can be secured against unauthorized access. All windows should be secured against opening and entry from the outside.

Also formulate procedures for lifeguards and staff to follow if they have to shut down the facility because of bad weather (such as thunderstorms) or other emergencies. The procedures should describe the steps to be taken, who should perform them, and how to evacuate the pool or facility quickly and safely.

Springboard Diving Safety

A variety of injuries can occur at diving facilities. These include cuts, abrasions, severe lacerations, contusions, swelling, broken bones, concussions, fractured skulls, broken eardrums, sinus squeeze, and head or neck injuries. Such injuries may be caused by a diver striking the diving board or platform, falling from the diving board onto the deck, landing flat on the surface of the water, slipping and falling on the diving board or platform, stumbling on the ladder to the board or platform, or descending into the water.

Have diving coaches and lifeguards review the signs and symptoms of these injuries and practice first aid treatment for them. Develop an emergency action plan for the diving facility and have staff practice this plan on a regular basis. Include coaches, other divers, lifeguards, and EMS in practice sessions. Practice will familiarize all involved with rescue procedures and will contribute to quick and decisive action during an emergency.

Include all diving policies in staff in-service training. Brief lifeguards on what types of injuries occur, diving rules and regulations, their authority to enforce rules and regulations for safety, and rescue procedures. By informing lifeguards of potential risk factors, you can help create a less risky environment.

In this section, we discuss specific ways to reduce diving risk related to spinal injuries, the pool bottom, platforms, and diving apparatuses.

Spinal Injuries

Spinal injuries have not occurred in diving facilities that meet NCAA, FINA, and high school regulations for minimum dimensions (Gabriel, 1988). This type of injury occurs primarily in backyard, hotel/motel, and apartment complex pools. The injuries at these facilities result from divers hitting the upslope of the bottom in front of the diving board. Victims of these spinal injuries strike the bottom in four to six feet of water (Gabrielsen, 1991).

Although spinal injuries are extremely rare in deep pools, you still need to prepare your lifeguards and coaches for this type of injury and practice spinal injury management procedures for deep-water pools. Each pool has characteristics that should be taken into account when developing emergency protocol and spinal injury management procedures. See *On the Guard II* (4th ed.) for further information on diving injuries. (For minimum depth information, see "Risk Management Involving Starting Blocks or Platforms, Water Depth, Deep Diving Starts, and Supervision" on the YMCA of the USA Web site.)

Pool Bottom Visibility

Some diving facilities have a dark-colored bottom, which makes it difficult to see people on the bottom, especially people of color. If your pool has such a bottom, tell lifeguards and coaches to watch for each diver to return to the surface after completing a dive.

Water agitation on the surface may also make it difficult to see the pool bottom. Tell your lifeguards and coaches to position themselves wherever their view of the bottom is best. Do not allow swimmers in the diving pool during diving activities.

Platforms and Three-Meter Boards

Severe injuries may result when unqualified divers jump or dive from a height of three meters or more. Thus, you should restrict the use of 3-meter diving boards and 3-, 5-, 7.5-, and 10-meter platforms to competitive divers under the direct supervision of a qualified diving coach or instructor. Close off such apparatuses for recreational use at all times.

If your facility has platforms, develop, in cooperation with the diving coach, a procedure for use of the diving tower (if a procedure is not already in place). In facilities with 3-, 5-, 7.5- and 10-meter platforms, you can reduce risks by having the coach designate at which level and when a dive may be attempted. This is necessary because divers have difficulty seeing when other divers are going to attempt a dive from another platform. Allow only one diver at a time to attempt a dive from a platform. For example, the diving coach can designate the level by yelling "five." This means the next dive should be attempted from the five-meter platform. No other dives should be attempted from any other level until the coach yells the next level. This procedure eliminates the risk of divers colliding in the air or landing on top of each other in the water.

Whatever procedures you develop, make sure all coaches and divers are familiar with them and strictly enforce them. Before competitions, you or the diving coach should mail a copy of the policies and procedures to all coaches who will be using the facility. Post signs at the diving tower that specify rules, regulations, and procedures. This will help you maintain consistent enforcement and safety no matter which coaches and diving teams are using the facility.

Diving apparatuses include diving boards and stands, diving platforms, dry-land diving pits, and trampolines. These can be a source of safety risks, but proper maintenance and inspection can reduce such risks. Have staff inspect each apparatus for safety on a daily or weekly basis. Here are some maintenance procedures you can follow for diving boards, diving stands, and diving platforms that will reduce risk.

- *Diving boards:* Diving boards will last a long time if properly maintained. See that diving boards are inspected weekly.

Inspect the surface of the board to determine if the abrasive surface is worn, as a worn surface will cause the board to be slippery. The board will most likely be worn at the tip end where divers land in preparation for a spring into the air. If the surface is slippery, replace the board or have it resurfaced by the manufacturer.

Sometimes the tip end of the board is slippery from an accumulation of dust, body oils, and suntan lotions. Clean the board by wetting it and sprinkling calcium hypochlorite (granular chlorine) on the board. Let it stand for about 20 to 30 minutes, then rinse it off. This process will help kill any algae forming on the board, as well as clean off some of the oil and dirt.

Make sure all fulcrum padding is in place. Absence of a rubber strip on a competitive board can eventually cause a weakness in the board and may cause stress fractures in the aluminum ribs beneath the board. Replace missing rubber strips with new ones purchased from the manufacturer.

Through continual use, competitive boards will eventually warp, causing a downward slant toward the tip end of the board. This downward slant can change the angle of trajectory of a diver, causing the diver to angle out and away from the board. This could become a hazard if not corrected. Replace the board or send it to the manufacturer to have it straightened and stress tested.

Inspect the underside of the board. On competitive boards, check the aluminum ribs for stress fractures. If fractures are found, remove the board and replace it. Stress fractures indicate a weakness in the integrity of the board and cannot be repaired, so the board must be replaced.

Check the rivets that hold the supportive structure to the underside of a competitive board. The rivets can be seen on the top side of the board, running in two rows along most of the length of the board. If the paint and surfacing around a rivet have cracked and a dark residue has formed around it, the rivet is loose. This will affect the integrity of the board. Generally, a loose rivet will appear in the fulcrum area, which is a high-stress area, and it is possible the board will break when a diver bounces on it. Remove the board and replace it or send it to the manufacturer for repair.

- *Diving stand:* The diving stand is an integral part of the diving equipment. A good stand can make a difference in the height attainable when diving from the diving board. A daily inspection of the bolts that hold the board on the stand will ensure the safety of the diver. Some stands have a rigid bar to which the board is bolted. Other stands have hinged plates to which the board is bolted. Both types of anchors present specific problems.

A rigid bar will be torqued every time the board is bounced, which creates several problems. When the bar is torqued, so are other sections of the stand; the bolts holding the stand together, the anchor bar, and metal tubing on the stand will be weakened. The solid bar also places a lot of stress on the bolts that hold the board to the anchor bar. The bolts will gradually bend, which increases the chances of a bolt breaking on this type of stand. Periodically tighten the nuts on the stand to maintain a more rigid support for the board. Inspect the bolts that anchor the board to the stand periodically and replace them if they are bent. Tighten the bolts on a regular basis to maintain a stable anchor of the board to the stand.

Stands with hinges pose a different problem. This type of stand eliminates torque on the bolts, anchor points, and stand, but the hinges have a pin that holds the two pieces of the hinge together. Inspect the hinge pins weekly to make sure they are in place and not slipping out. As hinges can be purchased separately from the manufacturer, replace the hinges if any damage is evident. Oil the hinges weekly to reduce wear and prolong the life of the pin. Observe the hinges, bolts, and stand when a diver bounces off the board to identify problem areas because of loose fittings.

Also inspect the areas where the stand is anchored to the deck. If the stand is not solidly connected to the deck when a diver bounces off the board, tighten the bolts that anchor the stand. If this does not stabilize the stand, prohibit diving from that apparatus and have the anchor professionally repaired. A loose anchor can result in a severe injury to the diver or bystanders. Black residue around a hinge, bolt, or rivet is an indication of a loose fitting. Items in such condition must be tightened, replaced, or repaired.

Railings on either side of diving stands should extend to the edge of the pool. This safety feature prevents divers from falling onto the deck and also requires divers to exit the board at one end or the other. Railings or an enclosure should be on the stand that is sufficient to prevent falling. Test railings for stability. If they are unstable, tighten all bolts connected to the rail structure.

On one popular type of competitive stand, rails are secured to the diving stand by metal straps. Competitive divers often sit on the rails while waiting to dive, which, along with stand vibration, eventually weakens the metal straps. Check all metal straps and replace cracked or broken ones. Metal straps may be purchased separately from the manufacturer.

The ladder should slant at an angle toward the back end of the diving board. Inspect the steps leading up to the diving board weekly. Test the steps to make sure they are solidly anchored to the ladder frame. Steps should have a nonskid surface . Clean steps in the same manner as previously described for cleaning the diving board.

A fulcrum is the section of the stand on which the board rests. Each model of stand has a fulcrum unique to the stand. Some fulcrums are stationary and some are movable.

If a stationary fulcrum is attached to a stand with bolts, rivets, or welds, inspect them weekly. Tighten any loose bolts and repair any damaged welds or rivets. Prohibit use of a diving apparatus until repairs are made.

Inspect movable fulcrums on a weekly basis. Check the fulcrum wheel to make sure it is adequately secured to the fulcrum, and make sure the fulcrum runs perpendicular to the board. An angled fulcrum will create torque on the board that could cause a diver to travel at a sideways angle off the board rather than directly in front of the board. The torque also causes structural stress on the board. If the fulcrum is not perpendicular to the board, adjust it. Follow the manufacturer's directions for greasing movable parts.

Recreational divers rarely have the technical knowledge to set a movable fulcrum to the proper position. Some injuries can be avoided if the movable fulcrum is locked in one position during recreational swimming. This will also reduce maintenance and repair costs.

For all diving boards, make sure they are level. An upward slant will cause a diver to land close to the end of the board, and a downward slant will cast the diver too far forward of the board.

- *Diving platforms (towers):* Give special attention to facilities with a diving tower. Routine inspections of the tower will ensure the safety of anyone utilizing the apparatus.

Platforms have a variety of nonskid surfaces. Inspect these surfaces for wear and slipperiness. Replace worn matting. Scrub slippery surfaces in the same manner as previously described for diving boards. Clean platforms on a regular basis, as a slippery surface could result in a severe injury.

Make sure the guardrails surrounding each platform and stairway are securely anchored to the tower. Repair any loose railings immediately. If they can't be repaired immediately, close the tower apparatus for use until they are.

Other diving apparatuses, including dry-land diving pits, trampolines, and spotting rigs, also need to be inspected on a regular basis. If your facility has such apparatuses, develop a safety checklist for their regular inspection and repair.

Signage

Along with adequate safety inspections, every aquatics facility should have signs with rules and regulations; procedures for use of the pool, locker rooms, and diving areas; and warnings and information about water depth and other potential hazards. These signs should be permanently mounted in visible locations in either the pool or locker room areas as appropriate, and they should be large enough to be read from a distance. They should be written in language that is easy to understand and positive. Where possible, use universal symbols, and in multilingual areas, use multilingual signs. Rules should be reviewed with members and participants when they join or when they first come to the pool.

All depth markings should be at least four inches high and be posted in both feet and meters. They must appear on the pool deck and on the vertical wall at or above the water's surface, and they must be of a contrasting color with the background.

Filtration

Each aquatics facility has its own system and procedures for maintaining the water environment. Although these systems vary, all should meet the standards set by the appropriate local and state public health and safety organizations. Obtain more information from your pool manager, or receive additional training through the YMCA POOL (Pool Operator on Location) course. Be sure to follow manufacturer's instructions relating to care and use of the equipment.

Filtration Equipment

In general, the filtration system in a pool is designed to recirculate the water continuously, keeping it clean, safe, and enjoyable for all swimmers. The system serves several important functions:

- Removes hair, lint, leaves, and other items that would otherwise interfere with the water treatment process
- Adds fresh water to replace water lost through leakage, splashing, evaporation, cleaning, and skimming

- Recirculates water so that all pool water is filtered every six to eight hours (check your state code on required filtration rate)
- Adds chlorine or bromine to disinfect the water
- Adds soda ash or acid when necessary to maintain the appropriate pH level
- Filters out any materials suspended in the water
- Cleans itself with a backwash system

The catcher that removes foreign matter from the water protects the pumping unit. Having debris flow through the system would cause unnecessary wear and reduce the pump's effectiveness.

Repairs on the pumps and motors that run the filtration system should always be made by competent technicians who are familiar with the manufacturers' instructions for the equipment. Normal maintenance consists of

- protecting the pumps and motors against water and chemical corrosion;
- lubricating the pumps and motors; and
- adjusting the pump packing to ensure a slight water leak, thus avoiding overtightening the adjustment bolts.

Dirt and other suspended particles must be removed from pool water to provide maximum clarity. Most pools use one of two types of filtration systems: sand-and-gravel or diatomaceous earth.

- *Sand-and-gravel filtration systems:* There are three common types of sand-and-gravel filters:
  - Vacuum sand filters consist of a bed of several layers of gravel topped with sand in an open tank. Water flows through the layers of sand and gravel, which trap the dirt, and is recirculated by a combination of gravity and vacuum forces.
  - Pressure sand filters are closed filter tanks containing several layers of sand and gravel. Water is forced through the layers, which trap the dirt, usually in the first layer of sand.
  - High-pressure sand filters combine two or more small, closed filter tanks, usually consisting of a few feet of sand. This setup is used to speed the filtration. Dirt particles are removed throughout the entire bed of sand as the water moves through the filter from top to bottom.

- *Diatomaceous earth filtration systems:* These filters also remove small particles from the water, but diatomaceous earth differs from sand in that it is made up of fossilized marine plant life, or diatoms. When diatomaceous earth is applied to the system's filter elements, water passes through and around the tiny spaces in the diatoms, which trap the dirt particles. Because of the size of their individual particles, diatomaceous earth filters can remove smaller particles than sand-and-gravel filters.

Cleaning the Pool Bottom

Filters remove the fine dirt that is suspended in the water, but a certain amount of matter settles to the pool bottom. Removing this residue takes some of the strain off the filters and makes for a more attractive pool.

The extra dirt can be picked up by a pool vacuum. Three common types are a portable pump and motor, which can be rolled to the edge of the pool, a vacuum line hooked directly to the filter system, and the automatic pool vacuum.

The vacuum line is perhaps the most popular method because it operates without any loss of water. Connections to the vacuum hose are made at various points around the pool via outlets a few inches under the surface.

The best time to vacuum is in the morning when no one is in the pool, after the sediment has settled overnight. In smaller pools, the operation can be done from the deck by using a long pole with a vacuum head attached to a vacuum along the bottom of the pool. In larger pools, automatic vacuums move across the pool bottom. If the pool is being cleaned with an automatic vacuum, keep the pool closed and locked to swimmers (unless otherwise required by local fire codes), as should be done whenever pool maintenance is being performed.

Pool Chemistry

Maintaining safe, clean water for swimming requires the use of chemicals to kill bacteria and to keep the proper pH balance. The correct balance helps ensure that water isn't irritating to swimmers and, in outdoor pools, that algae won't form in the water and on pool surfaces. The amount of chemicals to be used is determined by the chemical make-up of the potable fill water, the number of swimmers, and other factors that introduce dirt and bacteria into the pool water.

Disinfecting Water

Chlorine is the most common water disinfectant, although bromine has become more popular recently. They work in similar ways. For our purposes, we'll consider how chlorine functions. If your facility uses bromine, ask about proper testing procedures.

Chlorine acts quickly and can be maintained in the water to provide for continuous disinfection. Although chlorine can be corrosive and poisonous, when used properly, it poses no great difficulty in distribution or handling.

Water can be chlorinated in several ways. A common method of chlorination is using hypochlorites in liquid, granular, or powder form. Such substances are applied by a chemical feeder that must operate constantly to maintain a steady amount of chlorine, or a residual, suspended in the water.

Water must be tested for the residual value of chlorine; it is considered safe if a minimal value of 0.5 ppm can be maintained. The recommended minimum level is 1.5 ppm. The acceptable level of chlorine residual varies among states, so check with your health department to learn about local standards.

One common method used to test residual chlorine is the colorimeter test. A sample of water to be tested is mixed with the test solution in a test tube, and the coloring immediately produced indicates the amount of residual chlorine present. By comparing the color to a fixed scale, you can make an accurate reading in seconds. Another test uses a test strip, whose coloration is also compared to a fixed scale.

Acid-Base Balance

Water molecules are constantly breaking up into positive and negative ions. An excess of positive ions makes the water more acid, which can cause skin irritation and corrode metal surfaces. An excess of negative ions makes the water more basic, which can lead to cloudy water and form scale on filters and plumbing. Thus, a proper balance of acid to base is sought for effective filtration, for effective use of chlorine, and for swimmers' comfort.

This balance is maintained by testing for pH, a measurement of how basic or acid the water is. A pH test is used to monitor the water. You can determine the pH with a colorimeter test or test strips: A rating below 7.0 is considered acidic; above 7.0, basic. The recommended pH range is 7.4 to 7.6. At this level, the water is suitably alkaline (basic) for the filtration system to operate. Soda ash (sodium carbonate), added through a chemical feeder, is the generally accepted material used to raise the pH level when necessary.

Algae Control

Algae is slimy-looking green or brown plant life that makes pools look and smell uncared for. Because wind and rain can introduce algae to water, growth of algae is more of a problem in outdoor than indoor pools. If conditions are right, algae can multiply enough within 24 to 48 hours to grow on the pool walls and make the water appear green or brown.

Warm water encourages the growth of algae as well as bacteria. Control of algae has been a perplexing problem for outdoor pool operators. The best method for controlling algae is to prevent its growth. Once algae begins its growth cycle, the chief method for control is superchlorinating the water. During this procedure, which must be done when the pool is not in use, the chlorine residual is raised to 3.0 ppm, three times the recommended amount of residual.

Pool Volume

Whatever chemical is to be applied, the pool volume (sometimes known as facility capacity) is an important determinant of the amount to be used. A variety of formulas exist for determining the volume of water in the pool. Once you know the capacity, check the manufacturer's instructions for proper chemical application.

In general, you can determine the volume of a rectangular pool by using the following formula:

$$\text{Volume in gallons} = (\text{length} \times \text{width} \times \text{average depth}) \times 7.5$$

where 7.5 is the number of gallons in a cubic foot of water.

Water Testing

It is vital that the water in any aquatics facility be tested systematically. Faulty procedures or lack of adherence to standards can increase the risk of spreading communicable diseases, damaging the filtration system, and promoting algae growth. Your facility should have a commercial-grade testing kit available for testing disinfectant levels, pH, alkalinity, and calcium hardness (hard water). The facility should also test for the amount of total dissolved solids in the water—the sweat, body lotion, hair spray, disinfectant, and other solids that would be left if all of the pool water evaporated. If the chemicals used in testing the water are over one year old (six months for phenol red), they should be replaced; they must be fresh to ensure valid testing. In fact, chemicals stored incorrectly may not last even two weeks.

Your facility procedures should call for the water to be tested at regular intervals during the day. The need for more frequent testing depends on the number of swimmers, the temperature, and numerous other factors.

Table 12.1 identifies six tests that should be conducted, what tests should be used, and acceptable levels for each.

You may also calculate the Langelier Saturation Index weekly to ensure pH balance at a specific pool temperature. This index is important because the pH can af-

Table 12.1	**Water Quality Tests**	
Element tested	**Type of test**	**Appropriate level**
Residual chlorine	Colorimeter or test strip	1.5 ppm
Residual chlorine	Colorimeter or test strip*	2.0 ppm
pH	Chemical tests or test strips	7.4-7.6
Alkalinity	Chemical test kit	80-100 ppm
Calcium hardness	Chemical test kit	80-200 ppm
Total dissolved solids	Chemical test kit	200-600 ppm

*You can also use chlorine colorimeters and test strips to determine the amount of residual bromine by doubling the chlorine reading.

fect both patron comfort and the pool system. Ideally, the Langelier Saturation Index should equal zero. A positive index means that a deposit may form on the valves, pipes, and pumps. A negative index means that the water may begin to corrode metal surfaces. Both circumstances can be corrected by adding corrective chemicals: muriatic acid or sodium bisulfate for positive readings and soda ash, bicarbonate of soda, or calcium chloride for negative readings.

The Langelier Saturation Index uses five variables to calculate water balance: pH, temperature, calcium hardness, alkalinity, and total dissolved solids. Temperature, calcium hardness, and alkalinity must be converted to factor weightings for use in the formula. Factor information is presented in table 12.2. Simply look up your test scores and use the related factor weighting in the formula.

$$\text{Saturation index} = \text{pH} + \text{temperature factor} + \text{calcium hardness factor} + \text{alkalinity factor} - \text{total dissolved solids}$$

For additional information about the Saturation index, consult the *YMCA Pool Operations Manual*.

Table 12.2	**Langelier Saturation Index**				
Section 1		**Section 2**		**Section 3**	
Temperature (°F)	**Temperature factor**	**Calcium hardness (ppm)**	**Calcium factor**	**Total alkalinity (ppm)**	**Alkalinity factor**
32	0.0	5	0.3	5	0.7
37	0.1	25	1.0	25	1.4
46	0.2	50	1.3	50	1.7
53	0.3	75	1.5	75	1.9
60	0.4	100	1.6	100	2.0
66	0.5	150	1.8	150	2.2
76	0.6	200	1.9	200	2.3
84	0.7	300	2.1	300	2.5
94	0.8	400	2.2	400	2.6
105	0.9	800	2.5	800	2.9
128	1.0	1,000	2.6	1,000	3.0

Common Water Problems

Water problems begin when the water is not tested systematically and adjusted to maintain proper disinfectant levels. When the water chemistry becomes unbalanced, the following problems may result:

Low levels of disinfectant

Algae growth

Turbidity or cloudiness

Colored water

Hard water

The first letters of each of these problems make up the acronym LATCH.

Low Levels of Disinfectant

You must maintain an appropriate level of disinfectant in the water. The amount of free residual chlorine or bromine in the water may decline for several reasons:

- Increased bather load
- Old chlorine or bromine being used (check manufacturer's shelf life recommendations)
- Slow circulation at the end of the filter cycle
- Sunlight and air temperature increases
- Wave and water action from pool activities
- Backwash
- Lack of showers
- Swimming in street clothes that are dirty

Algae Growth

Although algae themselves are not life-threatening, they should be eliminated immediately to avoid odors, slippery surfaces, decreased visibility, and a stale taste to the water. Good pool maintenance—routine superchlorination and meticulous attention to filtration and vacuuming—will reduce the likelihood of developing algae problems.

Turbidity

Pool water must be clear enough at all times to permit guards to see the bottom of the pool. Cloudy water means that impurities have not been filtered out. The problem may be caused by water contamination, a malfunctioning filter, or unbalanced water chemistry. The best solution is to prevent turbidity in the first place. If it does occur, check to see that you have maintained the pool according to the recommended water chemistry values. Here are the steps to preventing and overcoming cloudy water:

- Maintain appropriate water chemistry levels (see the "Water Testing" section on pages 362-363).
- Maintain the appropriate water level.
- Backwash filters on a systematic schedule.
- Keep pool entrances and deck areas clean.
- Avoid channeling of sand filters.

Colored Water

Colored water is caused by the presence of metallic ions. Each metal produces a different color; for example, copper makes the water appear more blue, and iron gives a reddish-brown tint. You can remove the coloration by adjusting the pH to the appropriate level, superchlorinating, vacuuming the pool, cleaning the filter system, and readjusting the residual chlorine levels.

Hard Water

In many areas of the United States, hard water—water high in calcium—is a typical complaint. Although hard water doesn't negatively affect patrons, it damages plumbing and filtration systems. You can avert hard water problems easily by treating the water with sodium hexametaphosphate or a water softener when the pool is filled.

Spas

Hot tubs and whirlpools, which are becoming increasingly popular at many aquatics facilities, pose some hazards—electrocution, drowning, and the transmission of disease seem to be the most common. A few rules and common sense will help make spas safe for patrons to enjoy. Review the rules listed on page 302 for some suggestions to make the spa at your facility hazard-free.

The health-related problems associated with spas can be reduced if you

- maintain the spa at a temperature between 98 degrees and 104 degrees Fahrenheit,
- keep the water chemistry balanced,
- test for the presence of bacteria and treat the water as necessary, and
- log spa temperature and chemical readings as you do for your pool.

Record Keeping

You must maintain proper records relating to aquatics facility maintenance and operation, including the following:

- Current copies of state laws and regulations related to swimming pools (available on file to all aquatics staff)
- State pool operation and bacteriological reports (If required, these are submitted to the state on a regular basis, with copies kept on file.)
- All maintenance service and requests
- Daily pool activity and chemical logs
- Accident/incident reports
- State bathing codes
- OSHA guidelines

DEVELOPING AND IMPROVING YOUR FACILITY

Besides being responsible for the maintenance of your facility, you are also expected to develop and improve your facility over time to better fit your programs and your members' needs. If you are contemplating making changes, we explain how to do a step-by-step analysis to determine what's really needed. If you think a new facility is necessary, we offer further analysis and some suggestions on what your facility might include. You may also decide that major renovations are not needed, but still want to add some elements that will enhance your facility and programs; we have some recommendations. Finally, we have a list of guidelines for what facility features are needed to make each of a number of YMCA aquatics programs safe and successful.

Analyzing Your Facility

If you are considering major renovations, review the following six steps to determine if you should proceed, build a new pool, or utilize an existing community pool through a collaboration or rental. Additional information is also available from the YMCA of the USA BFS/Property Management department.

Step 1: Compare It to Program Goals

Determine your program development goals and apply them to the proposed facility. This will determine what kind of facility you need. Decide whether you need multiple pools on one site or pools at several sites in the community. Also decide whether you need indoor or outdoor pools. Most important, determine if a new facility would meet the needs of the YMCA and the community.

Step 2: Tie It to Needs

Determine what needs you are addressing with the proposed project. Will the new facility do the following:

- Provide new activities and interests?
- Change the pool configuration?
- Increase attendance by providing more pool time for popular activities?
- Increase member satisfaction?

Think about the impact on your association:

- Will this result in shortages of parking or available space?
- Will we have adequate utilities?
- Will we have a bathhouse and locker rooms that are big enough and in good condition?
- Will the facility conform to the Americans With Disabilities Act?
- Will the facility be designed so that the new area can be adequately supervised?

Step 3: Evaluate Your Existing Pool

Examine your existing pool:

- What is its condition?
- Are there extraordinary subsurface conditions?
- How much of the existing facility could be reused?
- What is the long-term cost difference between renovating the old facility and building a new one?

Step 4: Evaluate Your Assets

Do a physical analysis of the facility. Evaluate the condition of the pool, locker rooms, and mechanical areas. Consider the life expectancy of the equipment and the age of

the facility. Look at the new building codes and ADA regulations to determine how much upgrading will be needed to keep your old facility in compliance with the new regulations. Determine if you want to invest in this part of the community or if there is another area in which you need to expand. Evaluate your current site access and space use. Is adequate parking available? Will subsurface conditions handle the elements of an aquatics center? Consider the use of a professional aquatics consultant.

Step 5: Check Your Master Plan

Make sure that you are working within your association's master plan. (See item one, "Start with a plan," in the next section.)

Step 6: Decide

Make a decision. Look at the special features your pool should have and the size it should be, based on your research and the programs you are operating now and will be operating in the future. If you need a new facility, do you have the resources to build it? And even if you do, will you have the resources to run a new facility once it's finished?

Creating a New Aquatics Facility

The first step in creating a new facility will be deciding if it is affordable and fits with your YMCA's master plan. If the decision is made in favor of a new facility and your YMCA has the money and requires it, you can even consider building two pools or a family aquatics center. Also, if your new facility includes water recreation attractions, you will need to know how to operate them safely.

Deciding on the Feasibility of a New Facility

If you think a new facility will be the best solution to your YMCA's needs, you should then look seriously at your YMCA's master plan, have a feasibility study done, and consider whether you will be better off with an outdoor or an indoor pool.

1. **Start with a plan.** Successful YMCAs have master plans for facility development. These plans result from a process that combines skills from the specialties of architecture, program planning, and research. The result is a master plan—your guide to future development.

The master plan establishes your YMCA's priorities, programs, and total facility needs; estimates the cost of building and operating new facilities; and if necessary, divides the building program into phases. It should be reviewed from time to time with the board to ensure that it still fits the current and future goals of the YMCA. There can be different kinds of master plans, all of which should be coordinated in the development of a new facility:

- *A programmatic master plan:* This plan will map out the services you want to offer.
- *A fiscal master plan:* This plan will cover how much you will need to spend to build and safely operate a new facility.
- *A facility and evaluation master plan:* This plan is usually graphic in nature, showing the actual layout.

2. **Do your homework.** Before a YMCA commits itself to building a major facility, it should contract with someone to do a feasibility study. A feasibility study will provide development guidelines, a basis for marketing strategies, and a financial analysis of the project. In essence, it answers the question "If we build it, will they come?" In most cases, a consultant is hired to conduct a feasibility study. The cost of a study is usually about 3 percent of the project cost.

The study should include the following:

- Demographics and psychographics for the target market
- Marketing suggestions
- An estimate of the total staff base necessary to run the new facility (instructional, lifeguarding, competitive, housekeeping, maintenance, administration)
- Information on sources of competition for recreation dollars
- Information on how difficult or expensive it would be to expand the facility (Currently, building a pool costs about $135 per square foot.)
- Data on traffic flow and patterns around the facility's location
- Information on the municipal water supply and disposal system serving the facility
- A list of contractors/designers/aquatics consultants/architects/engineers familiar with bathing, health, and building codes
- Information on weather patterns (such as the number of anticipated sunny days) and the length of the summer season (This is particularly important for outdoor facilities.)
- Projected attendance levels and patterns for the first five years of operation
- Design suggestions for support facilities (such as food service areas, the bathhouse, parking lots, and special attractions)
- Recommendations for rate schedules (for season passes, multiday passes)
- Projected operating costs (Currently, indoor pool operation costs about $10 per square foot annually.)
- The need for a warm-water (84 to 90 degrees) or cool-water pool (78 to 83 degrees)

3. **Choose an indoor or an outdoor pool.** If part of your decision is whether to build your pool indoors or outdoors, here are a few factors to keep in mind.

Indoor Pool

- Indoor pools operate year-round, which increases both operating costs and participation. Expect participation levels to have seasonal highs and lows.
- Indoor pools create a strong base for membership generation.
- Broader program opportunities are available for an indoor pool.
- Indoor pools tend to be designed for multiple-use groups. That means there will be competition for pool time, especially during peak periods.
- Hours of operation for indoor pools are usually longer than for outdoor pools. They can be as long as 5:30 A.M. to 10:00 P.M. This would probably result in increased staffing requirements.
- Indoor facilities are usually smaller than outdoor facilities because of construction and operating costs.
- Construction costs are significantly higher for indoor pools.
- Indoor pools have less available space for building, deck, HVAC, materials, and operations.
- Leisure time is reduced. People tend not to lounge as much in indoor pool areas.
- Most swimmers will tend to change clothes at the indoor pool, so larger locker rooms are needed to provide changing space for all swimmers.

Outdoor Pool

- Outdoor pools operate seasonally.
- People often come to outdoor pools in their suits, then leave. Fewer locker room amenities and facilities are needed.
- Outdoor facilities tend to be larger than indoor facilities.
- Outdoor facilities are less expensive to build and operate.
- Deck space is more expensive, especially if you need lawn chairs and picnic and concession areas.
- Shaded areas will be needed to help protect participants and staff from the sun.
- Security is more difficult to maintain.
- Programming is more difficult to plan and control because of weather.

The decision finally comes down to whom you're trying to serve, your goals, and what programs you need to offer.

Deciding on Two Pools

If having more than one pool is an option, look at your program plan to determine what features the second pool should have. A second pool gives you a chance to diversify your programming and increase participants' comfort by having both a cold- and warm-water pool. You can consider a number of basic pool types:

- A competitive pool
- A shallow instructional pool
- A deep-water pool
- A zero-depth-entry pool

- A family/instructional pool
- A wave pool
- A warm-water pool
- A flume/slide
- A spa/whirlpool
- A "lazy river"
- A diving tank

Some of these types can be combined in one pool. For instance, a warm-water pool (84 to 90 degrees) could be designed to include an instructional pool, a zero-depth and interactive play area, a flume slide with a barrier, and a spa.

Creating a YMCA Family Aquatics Center

One of the most ambitious building projects a YMCA can undertake is the construction of a family aquatics center. These centers are often worth the extra effort it takes to create them. They can

- encourage more youth, adult, and family participation;
- increase attendance and be financially self-supporting;
- satisfy a broad range of aquatic interests for all ages; and
- provide attractive, exciting, and safe recreational opportunities.

Most family aquatics centers are located outdoors, requiring between five and eight acres of land, and they can serve between 1,500 and 2,000 visitors a day. Although most YMCAs can't build a complete family aquatics center of that size, they can combine some of the elements or attractions of these centers to design a facility that meets the needs of their community.

Some of the elements of a family aquatics center are the following:

- *Zero-depth-entry pools:* Families (especially those with young children) enjoy the shallow water during their leisure time. In a typical water park, 60 percent of the water is less than 3.5 feet deep. Families congregate in the zero-depth and wading areas.

- *Water in motion:* This can take the form of "rain," mushrooms, or sprays.

- *Water slides:* A variety of slides are available, including children's flumes, standard ride flumes, corkscrew slides, speed slides, inner tube rides (both chute and pool types), rampage rides, and drop slides. They are usually made of fiberglass or concrete.

- *Wave pools:* A wave pool produces waves of various heights, intervals, or patterns. These have been around for 25 years, but they are expensive to build.

- *Lazy rivers:* These areas are usually long, winding channels where water flows in a path through the water park or pool area.

- *Whirlpools:* These are not necessary for a center to be successful, but they are popular, especially with adults.

Family aquatics centers sometimes have traditional features such as these:

- *Competitive pools:* Not every pool needs to be a competitive pool. You have to look at the market and the level of participation you want.

- *Diving pools:* These deep-water pools serve diving board and some platform diving participants. They may also be used for Scuba, snorkeling, kayaking, synchronized swimming, water polo, and lifeguard training. Three-meter platforms can also be used for inflatable slides (see the "Inflatables" section in chapter 10).

• *Lap swimming pools:* There is an increasing need for these pools for competition and fitness swimming.

• *Instructional or warm-water pools:* These are used for many purposes, such as swimming lessons, water exercise classes, and therapy and rehabilitation programs. Some designs include interactive family play areas.

These casual leisure features can be found most often in outdoor facilities:

• *Sand turf areas:* Larger deck and turf areas are needed.

• *Sand play:* Sand playgrounds and sand volleyball areas are very popular. Sand play areas are one of the top five elements at successful family aquatics centers. Having sand will increase maintenance costs, however.

• *Adult sun and shade areas:* Such an area can be very appealing to some members.

• *Concessions:* Try to have a nice selection of food and a nice picnic area.

Maintenance costs increase with these types of facilities. One person with a hose will no longer be sufficient.

These special features can also contribute to a successful family aquatics center:

• Landscaping and natural features
• Artificial stone
• Decorative fencing and barriers in addition to the standard fencing requirements

Making the Most of an Existing Facility

If your YMCA doesn't need or can't afford a new facility or renovation, you can still make improvements to your present facility. These may consist of changes in the look of the pool or programming additions, or you may choose to purchase new equipment. Work with your staff to come up with new ideas for updating your pool facility.

Updating Changes

You may find that some inexpensive changes will work wonders. For example, sometimes you can draw more people into your pool by giving it a more fresh, up-to-date look. Consider adding one or more of the following:

New paint

Posters

Interactive or creative water play areas

Wall graphics

New signage

Bulletin boards

Conversation areas

New equipment

Improved lighting

Acoustics

Replacement of damaged or corroded elements

It's important to remember that the best ideas don't always require a lot of money. Improving your pool area and your recreational swims might depend more on creative thinking from your staff than on your budget. Creative changes to program and staff training or inexpensive amenities added to an existing facility can make a big difference.

Equipment

Equipment can make a big difference in a YMCA pool. The new products available, such as an inflatable or aqua fun run, create an instant atmosphere of fun. But before buying any equipment, think carefully about the impact the equipment might have. Establish a meticulous evaluation process before you purchase anything. Taking the following steps can help you through this process before you decide to purchase the equipment:

1. Make sure your target audience is clearly identified and will truly benefit from the new equipment.
2. Ensure that the new equipment will be consistent with your aquatics plan and goals.
3. Discuss the purchase with your aquatics and maintenance staffs.
4. Discuss the purchase with other aquatics professionals and visit facilities with that equipment, if possible.
5. Check references by obtaining the names and phone numbers of other YMCAs, agencies, or businesses that have purchased the product.
6. Contact these other agencies or businesses and ask about costs that resulted from the use of the product, problems, successes, impact on membership, participation, maintenance, programming, staffing, and risk management.
7. Contact the Consumer Product Safety Commission. Request a safety information bulletin, if one is available and can be received in time for the review, related to the commercial use of the product.
8. Request complete product information from the manufacturer or distributor, especially regarding operating instructions, warnings, warranties, and product liability coverage. Request a certificate of insurance evidencing coverage.
9. Contact your insurance agent to verify coverage of the new product.
10. Contact the health department to find out if the applicable health or pool codes will have any effect on the product.
11. Check building and fire codes in your area to ensure that product installation is compatible with the codes.
12. Ensure that you have the appropriate infrastructure, such as size and type of deck, electrical supply, and additional storage for the product.
13. Conduct a risk analysis related to the product. This process should examine eight factors: installation, intended use, foreseeable use, supervision and warnings, injury potential, security and storage, warranties, and impact on the aquatics program. Your evaluation should include a process that will give you answers to the following questions.

Installation and Maintenance

- Will the product be permanently or semipermanently installed?
- Will the product be placed, installed, or anchored in shallow or deep water?
- If anchored, how will the product be anchored—with ropes or wires?

- Will ropes or wires be covered with material that will prevent abrasions or friction burns?
- To what will the product be anchored—the walls, the pool bottom, or the ceiling structure?
- Will installation interfere with other activities?
- How will repairs be completed? Are the materials available? Who is authorized to make repairs—you or a company representative?
- How many people need to be available to install the product, maintain it, and take it down?
- How will staff be trained to install and maintain the product and take it down?
- How will the weather affect the product's installation and use? Would extreme heat have an effect? Wind? Sun?
- How long will the product hold up in chlorinated water?
- How much time will be needed for maintenance?
- How frequently will the product need cleaning?
- Will special chemicals or equipment be needed for cleaning?
- How do pool chemicals affect the product?
- What is the impact on the budget?

Intended Use

- How do you get on/mount the product?
- How do you get off/dismount the product?
- What happens when you are on it?
- Is human behavior predictable during use of the product?
- Is the ability to swim necessary for someone to use the product?

Foreseeable Use

- Can the product be misused? How?
- Are there abnormal or unintended uses?
- Could someone run on the pool deck and jump or dive onto the product?
- What injuries could result from use or misuse of the product?
- Can entrapment occur below or behind the product?
- Can participants dive from the device?

Supervision and Warnings

- Does the product require supervision?
- How many staff and lifeguards would be required to adequately supervise? What is the budget impact? What special or additional training is needed, including how to respond to any emergency?
- How often would the product need to be inspected? Repaired?
- Does the manufacturer provide warnings about use of the product or prohibit certain uses?
- What safety research has the manufacturer done? Will the manufacturer share the results of this research?
- Signage and warnings are often needed. If this product needs them, where should they be placed? Would they be seen and understood by swimmers?

- Can you visualize where lifeguards will need to be stationed so that all sides of the product (including underneath it) will be adequately supervised?
- What is the maximum number of swimmers the lifeguards will be able to supervise adequately at one time?
- Is there anyone who should not be allowed to use the product? Is it appropriate for all ages? For people with disabilities?
- Would additional emergency procedures need to be developed for use of the product? What types? Is there a written policy and procedures that tell staff what to do in the event there aren't enough guards available for the number of people using the product?
- Should swimmers be segregated according to age groups, or can a mixture of age groups safely use the equipment at the same time?

Injury Potential

- If someone falls off the product, will that person land in the pool, on the deck, or on other people? Could a person jump or vault off the product out of control? Is supervision necessary to prevent person-to-person collisions?
- Is the surface of the product rough or slippery? Will it cause bruises or abrasions?
- Is injury possible from impact with the product?
- Can lifeguards see participants on all sides of the device?
- Does the product make use of ropes or wires? Is entanglement possible in or under the product?
- What is the body position and speed as a participant comes off the product?
- What is the possibility of deflation or entrapment?

Security and Storage

- How can misuse be prevented if the product is left in place (e.g., starting blocks must be removed when not in use)?
- Will inflatables have to be deflated? How will they be moved or inflated?
- What are the possibilities of vandalism? (Is the pool indoor or outdoor?)
- How much space is needed for storage? Are there any special storage needs?
- How would weather affect the product during storage if it were outdoors (e.g., sun, rain, heat, cold)? Can it be left outside over the winter in a cold climate?

Warranties

- What is the product warranted against?
- What is the life expectancy of the product?
- Where was the product made? Does the manufacturer provide information on how to control the inherent risks in using the product?
- Who is the U.S. distributor, and will it provide a warranty?
- What can you do if the product is broken or defective? Are repair parts or chemicals available in the U.S.?
- Will the manufacturer provide a certificate of insurance demonstrating product liability coverage?

Aquatics Program Impact

- What impact will the product have on programs and activities? Will it affect the water surface for aquatics exercise, competitive swimming and diving, lap swimming, or classes?

- How much deck space will be used?
- Will installation of hooks, wires, ropes, stanchions, and so on, have an effect on other activities?
- Will the product increase pool use by children and reduce pool use by adults?
- How will use of the equipment and its setup/takedown time affect the pool schedule and the balance of recreational swims, swim classes, and swim team practices?
- Is it a member or a nonmember activity?
- Will it be available for use for YMCA special events?
- Will it be available for use for pool rentals? If so, are procedures in place for securing a certificate of insurance and hold harmless agreement from the contracted group with the YMCA named as additional insured?
- How much will the product increase participation?
- Do you have the appropriate staff and budget to cover the additional supervision?

Your final step before purchasing equipment is to do a cost–benefit analysis and make an educated decision on the purchase. The costs you'll want to consider include purchase price; installation costs; maintenance costs, including repair and replacement of parts; replacement costs when the equipment wears out; and additional staff costs and supervision resulting from setup, takedown, repair, training, and usage. Base your calculations on the expected life span of the product. Finally, be prepared for increased electrical, water, and chemical expenses from pumping water on the equipment and from increased evaporation rates.

For additional information on purchasing, contact the YMCA of the USA Purchasing department for a copy of "YMCA Purchasing Strategies for Saving Time and Money."

You should time the construction or completion of installation so that you can benefit from a full season of activity; otherwise, you need to make appropriate downward budget adjustments. Consult your architect for a schedule that includes planning, design, construction documents, bidding, construction permits, start-up, punch lists, and estimated move-in. Keep in mind that just adding a slide will not necessarily give you long-term participation growth. You will find it necessary to make continual improvements to the pool areas to maintain a positive growth rate after your initial investment. It's the same with YMCA fitness centers: One new machine won't make a long-term difference in membership, but regular additions to the fitness area will. No matter how ambitious you want to be for your aquatics center, a good plan with comprehensive research will help you build it successfully.

Designing Facilities for Programs

When you think about your pool, start with its functions. What programs do you want to offer now and in the future? Who are you trying to serve? Because form follows function, here are some recommended facility requirements for popular YMCA aquatics programs to consider.

If you are intending to operate:	Consider the following:
YMCA Swim Lessons	Access to an area with a minimum water depth of 9 feet for at least 10 feet ahead of the wall is needed for teaching diving off the deck. The recommendation of constant depth

is to avoid injuries from the use of hopper and spoon-shaped bottom pools in teaching diving.

Youth and Adult Swim Lessons

The shallow end should be 3.5 to 4 feet deep for beginners.

An off-deck viewing area should be available.

Parent/Child and Preschool Swim Lessons

Access to an area with a minimum water depth of 9 feet for at least 10 feet ahead of the wall is needed for teaching diving off the side. The recommendation of constant depth is to avoid injuries from the use of hopper and spoon-shaped bottom pools in teaching diving.

Having a 2.5- to 3-foot area or zero-depth entry pool is helpful for young children.

A separate warm-water instructional pool 2.5 to 4 inches deep is helpful.

The recommended water temperature is 85 degrees, with a minimum of 82 degrees. The air temperature should be 2 to 4 degrees higher.

An off-deck viewing area should be available.

Competitive Swim Program
(Youth and Masters)

Access to an area with a minimum water depth of 9 feet for at least 10 feet ahead of the wall is needed for teaching starts off the deck. The recommendation of constant depth is to avoid injuries from the use of hopper and spoon-shaped bottom pools in teaching diving.

Starting blocks should be placed in the deep end of the pool with a minimum depth of no less than five feet. Swimmers should perform starts in this area only when they are proficient and with proper supervision and safety instruction. Check with your state code, as some states require a greater depth of six feet or more.

The shallow end must have a minimum depth of four feet for turns.

For starting blocks, backstroke flags, or false start ropes, sleeves or stanchions should be installed during construction.

If you think you might want a timing system in the future, conduit and electrical service can be installed during construction.

Typically, YMCAs use a seven-foot lane width. Determine the number of lanes based on your projection of program growth and the variety of programs you will schedule at the same time in the pool.

Follow current NCAA pool regulations if you want your pool competition events to qualify.

The recommended water temperature is 79 to 81 degrees.

An off-deck viewing or spectator seating area is needed for swim meets. Add spectator seating on deck only if you expect to host meets regularly. Deck space is very expensive; the current price averages more than $150 a square foot for indoor pools.

Water Polo/Wetball

Instructional/recreational play	Program and rules can be adapted to the pool using shallow or deep water.
	Water polo stanchions or sleeves can be added during construction, with goals added at a later date.
Competitive programs	Follow the USA Water Polo Official Playing Rules specifications.

Synchronized Swimming

Instructional/recreational play	Program and rules can be adapted to the pool using shallow or deep water.
	An underwater sound system is extremely helpful. Systems are available that can be added externally.
Competitive programs	You need a minimum area of 40 by 40 feet that is no less than nine inches deep.
	The pool must be 25 yards long and not less than 40 feet wide.
	Follow United States Synchronized Swimming Official Rules specifications.

Springboard Diving

Recreational	See Medical Advisory Statement No. 13, Diving Board Guidelines. (Recommendations of the YMCA of the USA Medical Advisory Committee are available from the YMCA of the USA Program Development department.)
Competitive	See the NCAA rule book for specifications and follow YMCA of the USA Medical Advisory Committee Statement No. 13.

YMCA Scuba Program — An six-foot minimum depth is recommended.

Water Fitness programs — Both shallow- and deep-end programs are popular. You will need a large area of 3.5- to 5-foot depth for shallow-end classes and 8- to 10-foot depth for deep-end classes.

The recommended temperature is 80 to 86 degrees (up to 88 degrees for arthritic classes).

For classes where participants primarily stay in one place, you will need an average of 25 square feet per person.

Lifeguard program

For teaching and staff drills: Access to an area with a minimum water depth of 9 feet for at least 10 feet ahead of the wall is needed for teaching. This minimum depth is needed for teaching entries, recovery of a submerged victim, and deep-water backboarding.

A constant depth of 9 feet or 10 feet should prevent potential diving accidents.

Programs for People With Disabilities

Instructional and recreational

For entry into the pool, have stairs into the shallow end for ambulatory participants and a pool ramp, pool lift, or transfer tiers for nonambulatory participants.

The ideal temperature varies with the type of disability the participants have. Many need warmer water (83 to 88 degrees), whereas some (e.g., those with multiple sclerosis) need cool water (80 to 83 degrees).

Fitness swimming

A depth of 3.5 to 4 feet is needed in the shallow end for turns.

A minimum water depth of 9 feet for at least 10 feet ahead of the wall is needed if you allow swimmers to dive into the water.

Recreational swims

For sealed inflatables, the water depth should be five feet.

For constant-blow inflatables, the water depth should be nine feet.

For inflatable slides, the water depth should be nine feet.

The water depth for permanent slides should meet the manufacturer's recommendation.

See pages 318-325 in chapter 10 for more information on inflatables.

The most highly used area in the pool is the shallow end. Families and young children will use a zero-depth-entry pool a lot.

Here are more suggestions about pools in general:

• Determine the amount of deck space according to the programs you offer, keeping in mind that deck space is expensive. Consider that classes will have deck discussions and demonstrations and will practice some skills on deck first before trying them in the water. Decide if you want spectators to be on deck or to observe through an off-deck viewing area.

• Given the relatively high costs associated with operating air handling systems for natatoriums, keep the cubic feet of the natatorium to a minimum. Determine the size based on the space requirements for the programs you have planned. For instance, if your program does not require a 24-foot ceiling or a large spectator area, don't allocate that type of space.

• Most YMCAs have a pool vessel (tank) that is 75 feet long.

• Choose your pool width according to the number of lanes you need. Base it on the volume of users, current and projected, and the variety of programs offered in the pool at the same time (pool schedule). Most YMCAs use seven-foot lanes.

• For indoor pools, indirect artificial lighting is preferred because it helps minimize glare on the pool water surface.

• Make sure you have sufficient storage areas for pool equipment (e.g., kickboards, belts, rescue equipment) and program supplies (toys, program materials, skills sheets, inspection reports, first aid kit and supplies, accident/incident reports, biohazard kit and containers, testing kit, clipboards).

• Make sure that pool staff members have a storage area where they can store personal items and materials (class lesson plans and records, reference materials).

• Place the locker room entries to the natatorium at the shallow end of the pool.

• Have an emergency communication system (e.g., phone, call button) linking the natatorium/pool staff to the front desk or emergency support services.

• Have proper signage notifying swimmers of pool rules.

If your program warrants it and funding is available, you may want to add one or more of these amenities:

• A family or special-needs changing area
• Portable guard chairs
• An audio system with underwater capability
• An acoustical/sound abatement system or treatment on the walls
• A spa/whirlpool in the pool area with a deck shower

ADDITIONAL RESOURCES

If you have questions about pool construction, aquatics programming, YMCA trends, or pool-related products, you can contact these YMCA of the USA departments:

• BFS/Property Management is the YMCA's architectural consulting department, which provides local YMCAs with assistance in facility renovations and new construction. Its staff of architects works with associations to help produce facilities that meet program needs, are cost-effective, and can be maintained affordably.

• Program Development develops and supports local YMCA program activities. It tracks trends, discovers models and innovations, develops programs and training, and identifies key issues.

• The YMCA Purchasing Service establishes national contracts with preferred vendors to provide YMCAs with equipment and supplies at reduced prices. These contracts help YMCAs get the most for their money in high-quality products and services.

• Research and Planning distributes information important to YMCAs in their own planning, research, and evaluation. This includes internal studies of YMCA operations and analyses of social trends that might affect YMCAs.

All of these departments can be reached by calling the YMCA of the USA's national headquarters at 800-872-9622.

• Y Services Corporation (YSC) is a wholly owned for-profit subsidiary of the National Council of YMCAs of the United States. YSC provides risk management consultation, training, and oversight of YMCAs' property, casualty, and health insurance programs. Risk consultations, claims management, loss prevention, and insurance development are four key areas of activity. The primary focus of YSC is to enhance the interest and ability of YMCAs to minimize the adverse effects of accidental losses through proactive risk management practices specifically designed for YMCAs.

BIBLIOGRAPHY

Gabriel, J.L. (Ed.) (1988). *Diving safety. A position paper.* Indianapolis, IN: United States Diving Inc.

Gabrielsen, M.A. (Ed.) (1987). *Swimming pools: A guide to their planning, design, and operation.* Champaign, IL: Human Kinetics.

YMCA Aquatics Programs

The YMCA's many aquatics programs, most of which are described in Part II, can be broadly categorized as instructional activities or sports and recreational activities. Let's briefly look at the programs in each of these categories, as well as some other aquatic activities that YMCAs might offer.

YMCA INSTRUCTIONAL AQUATICS PROGRAMS

The YMCA offers a broad range of instructional programs for people of all ages and ability levels. Trained and certified instructors lead all programs, and all programs have corresponding instructors' manuals. Some programs also have participant resources. (We recommend that you use YMCA certifications, materials, and standards except in those program areas not covered by the YMCA of the USA.)

We expect instructors to show respect for the uniqueness of each student and to teach using student-centered methods. Their instruction should help develop each student's potential, teach safety in all aspects of the program, and improve skills. They evaluate students using a system of achievement, skill monitoring, and recognition rather than formal testing to determine passing or failing (except for lifeguarding classes).

The following program descriptions provide a quick reference to the variety of programs offered.

YMCA Swim Lessons

The YMCA Swim Lessons (chapter 13) series includes three programs:

- the Parent/Child program for parents and their children under three years of age;
- the Preschool program for children ages three to five years; and
- the Youth and Adult program, which may be offered and marketed separately for youth, teens, and adults.

All three programs are marketed under the name "YMCA Swim Lessons."

The Parent/Child Aquatic Program

The Parent/Child Aquatic Program is for children from six months up to three years of age. It consists of water enrichment and aquatics readiness activities for children. In this program, children must be accompanied by a parent or trusted adult at all times for the safety and comfort of each child.

In these classes, parents learn to respect the value of games and play for the young child. Also, by following the instructor's example, parents discover that the best way to guide a child toward learning is through positive reinforcement and appropriate praise. Play makes the learning experience positive, and sharing the experience reinforces trust between the parent and child.

Instructional flotation devices such as float belts, bubbles, or cubes are used in all infant and preschool programs to help children gain confidence and comfort in the water. The instructor must emphasize, however, that just because small children have self-confidence in the water does not mean that they are "water safe."

Preschool Aquatic Program

The Preschool Aquatic Program teaches water adjustment and basic swimming skills for children from three to five years of age. In this program, parents' presence is optional. YMCAs may choose to hold separate classes for children older than three years with parents and for children alone.

The Preschool Aquatic Program stresses enjoyment, development of children's confidence, and safety. Each class emphasizes mental and spiritual growth, as well as physical development. The children (and their parents, if included) develop beginning swimming skills and learn about water and boating safety, emergency situations, use of personal flotation devices, and nonswimming rescues. Parents of participating children receive an orientation as part of the first class.

Activities are centered around five main components: personal safety, personal growth, stroke development, water sports and games, and rescue. The emphasis is on learning, using a student-centered and developmentally appropriate approach to teaching.

The preschool program is a lead-in to the youth program, as the skills and activities taught in the four levels of the preschool program are similar to those of the first two levels of the youth program.

The Youth and Adult Aquatic Program

The YMCA Youth and Adult Aquatic Program is designed for participants six years of age and up. The classes are participant-centered and use a problem-solving, guided-discovery teaching approach.

The emphasis is on learning, not on passing or failing. Each developmental level is divided into five components, which include personal safety, personal growth, stroke development, water games and sports, and rescue. In each of the levels, the skills and activities promote health and fitness. Instructors organize classes by peer grouping within each level to utilize the entire pool and to maximize class participation. Instructional flotation devices are provided to help participants gain confidence in the water and see progress quickly. Series swimming is also incorporated into the classes to increase endurance and strength.

Porpoise Level/YMCA Aquatic Leadership

The highest level of the YMCA Youth and Adult Aquatic Program, the Porpoise level, can be offered as either a regular class or an Aquatic Leadership club (for young people 11 to 15). The club format is more flexible, and it allows older children and teens the opportunity to develop a program that fits their interests. Under adult leadership, club members are allowed to initiate and lead activities of their choosing. These might include sailing, skin diving and snorkeling, Scuba, competitive swimming, water polo, water skiing, or aquatic leadership and instruction. Other nonaquatic activities might be service projects or social activities. Many clubs also have recognition systems in which members earn points to obtain awards.

Aquatic Safety Programs

The YMCA Aquatic Safety Programs (chapter 14) include YMCA Splash, as well as the Aquatic Safety, Aquatic Personal Safety and Survival, Aquatic Safety Assistant, and Lifeguard courses.

YMCA Splash

A community-based learn-to-swim program many YMCAs use is YMCA Splash. This five-day program teaches children and families basic swimming skills and water safety practices. It also may include short one-day courses on beach safety, backyard pool safety, and safe boating.

Aquatic Safety Course

Both nonswimmers and swimmers are welcome in this course on basic water safety. This short course includes the history and philosophy of YMCA aquatic safety and lifeguard training, personal aquatic safety information, accident prevention, basic first aid and rescue breathing, and nonswimming rescues.

Aquatic Personal Safety and Survival Course

This course for swimmers includes most of the topics covered in the Aquatic Safety Course, plus general aquatics information and basic survival skills and principles.

YMCA Aquatic Safety Assistant Course

This course prepares swimmers to become assistants to lifeguards and provides an aquatic safety foundation for coaches and instructor candidates. It includes topics such as accident prevention, recognition of potential hazards, use and care of equipment, child abuse prevention, lifeguard assistance, recognition of distressed swimmers and rescue techniques, and personal safety.

YMCA Lifeguard

The YMCA Lifeguard course is designed to prepare the participants with the knowledge and skills needed to be a lifeguard. The course provides certification for two years. YMCA Lifeguard certification is recognized and accepted by many organizations and in state codes.

The comprehensive course provides information on the basic skills and knowledge for lifeguarding in pool, lake, river, ocean, and water park environments. It offers up-to-date information on how to guard, anticipating and preventing problems before they occur, and taking action to help those in danger when necessary.

YMCA Water Fitness for Health

The purpose of the YMCA Water Fitness for Health (chapter 16) program is to encourage people of all ages to utilize the buoyant qualities of water to enhance their physical fitness through exercises. Water can make some movements possible that would be very difficult on land. It's an ideal form of exercise for all ages and increases physical strength and endurance without putting stress and strain on joints, as in land-based exercise. Swimmers and nonswimmers alike can take part in this type of exercise to reduce emotional stress and tension, improve health and physical appearance, and encourage and improve feelings of well-being and self-esteem.

Another water fitness program is Active Older Adults Water Fitness. This functional fitness program is for active older adults who want to have a better life on land through exercise in the water. Instructors for this program learn about the aging process, exercise modifications, and functional fitness assessments.

Arthritis Foundation/YMCA Aquatic Program

The Arthritis Foundation/YMCA Aquatic Program (chapters 16 and 18) provides people with arthritis the opportunity to participate in a recreational group activity and have a positive experience in the water. This program was developed in collaboration with the National Arthritis Foundation for persons with arthritis. It should complement, not substitute for, a doctor's prescribed exercises.

The program emphasizes good body mechanics, keeping joints in a stable and functional position, and reducing the effort required to do activities. The strongest or largest muscle groups are used to reduce stress on the bones and joints. Participants are instructed to distribute their weight evenly over several joints. Class structure may vary depending on the group of participants. Normally, classes begin with five minutes of warm-up exercises in the water, then proceed through the approved range of exercises.

YMCA Swim Lessons: Individuals With Disabilities

The purpose of the YMCA Swim Lessons: Individuals with Disabilities program (chapter 18) is to teach individuals with disabilities swimming skills and exercises that can build strength, increase fitness levels, and improve self-esteem. For some, the buoyancy of water allows freer movement and an opportunity to walk and move unaided. These programs are highly specific to the type and level of disability. Participants may have physical disabilities, mental impairment, visual impairment, be deaf or have hearing impairment, or have learning disabilities.

Participant skills are broken into sequential progressions, including periods of skill development, repetition, and relaxation. Movement exploration activities include adjustment to water, breath control, actions in the water, space and body awareness, and locomotion. Using visual, verbal, and abstract stimuli in a multisensory approach is often helpful. Tasks are divided into small, easily manageable, sequential steps so students can experience success often. Games provide a fun opportunity for water adjustment and skills mastery. Once students have mastered basic swimming skills, class sessions may include synchronized swimming, basic rescue skills, and safe boating activities.

YMCA AQUATIC SPORTS AND RECREATIONAL ACTIVITIES

In addition to the instructional programs conducted by the YMCA, a variety of additional activities may complement and round out the aquatic interests of different age groups. Once participants have mastered the techniques of swimming and water safety, they should be encouraged to use their skills by enjoying aquatic sports and activities.

Many YMCAs offer programs in competitive and masters swimming, springboard diving, skin diving and Scuba, synchronized swimming, and wetball or water polo. Many YMCA campsites also have waterfront facilities. Each program offers a challenge for every age and ability. This section provides descriptions of each program and the program resources available.

YMCA Competitive Swimming

The purpose of the competitive swimming program (chapter 17) is to train individuals of all ages to compete in YMCA league programs and potentially in neighborhood, state, and national championships. Some YMCA teams compete in USA Swimming-sponsored competitions.

A complete program includes training, competitive events, personal growth activities, and social events to ensure that competitive swimming fulfills all the objectives of YMCA programs for individuals.

Competition is organized by age groups: 8 and under, 10 and under, 11-12, 13-14, 15-19 (provided participants are still in high school), and senior (12 and over). Each age group competes in freestyle, backstroke, breaststroke, butterfly, individual medley, medley relay, and freestyle relay. The distances vary according to the age group. All events are officiated by YMCA-certified officials.

YMCA Masters Swimming

Masters swimming (chapter 17) is an age-grouped competitive aquatics program for adults beginning at age 19. Groups are divided into five-year spans, such as 19-24, 25-29, and 30-34.

A national championship is conducted annually, and local and regional competitions are available in some areas. The National YMCA Competitive Swimming and Diving Committee governs the national championship, and local YMCAs bid to host the competitions.

YMCAs may register with United States Masters Swimming and represent the YMCA in regional and national competitions. Because US Masters Swimming is the United States' governing body for masters swimming, athletes may qualify for national and international competition and have an additional opportunity to further their talents while reflecting accomplishment on their YMCA programs.

YMCA Springboard Diving

Springboard diving (chapter 17) is a good complement to the YMCA Swim Lessons program. The YMCA approach emphasizes diving safety, and the recommended guidelines for pool depths and board heights should be carefully followed. As with all YMCA programs, improving self-confidence is emphasized. Participants of all ages can learn the diving groups (forward, reverse, and so on) and positions (tuck, pike, and so on). Other program components include takeoffs, rules, safety, and training.

YMCA Camp Waterfront

Many YMCAs have campsites near rivers or lakes. Although no official course is offered at this time just on waterfront administration, the information in this manual provides the basics to help any waterfront or aquatics director to select a safe beach, outfit and organize it properly, design a well-rounded program, and provide a safe and clean aquatics recreation area for all campers. See chapter 19 for this information.

YMCA Skin Diving

The YMCA has developed a YMCA Skin Diving program. Swimmers who are interested in expanding their aquatics knowledge find skin diving enjoyable and challenging. Skin diving is growing in popularity worldwide, and the YMCA wants to provide a safe and enjoyable skin diving experience. Participants for skin diving must be at least 10 years old and swim competently or at the Shark level of the YMCA Swim Lessons program.

A mask, fins, and a snorkel are used extensively. Participants learn to clear the mask and snorkel using several different techniques. They review the purpose, use, and care of a mask, fins, and snorkel. Instruction also includes a variety of headfirst and feetfirst dives and various kicks such as the flutter, dolphin, and back kicks.

YMCA Scuba

The YMCA Scuba Program (chapter 20) is a natural progression of the YMCA aquatics program. It consists of a progressive development system from the basic "I Tried Scuba" through levels of training up to professional YMCA Scuba instructor. The YMCA Scuba Program is the only scuba training program that develops safe and confident divers while emphasizing the YMCA philosophy of spirit, mind, and body. A YMCA Scuba instructor is a highly trained and dedicated professional with much to offer your scuba students and your YMCA facility.

Many specialty certification courses are available through YMCA Scuba. Each of these individual certifications has specific requirements and procedures for training. The YMCA Scuba Program is significantly different from other scuba agencies because the YMCA mission and membership are promoted in the training curriculum. The YMCA Scuba Program builds self-confidence, not just equipment dependence. YMCA Scuba also offers courses that cover material comprehensively, rather than presenting it in tiny increments, as commercial agencies do. These differences are the reason that the YMCA Scuba Program has an outstanding safety record.

YMCA Synchronized Swimming

The synchronized swimming program (chapter 21) is an excellent alternative or complement to the YMCA Swim Lessons program and is suitable for people of all ages. Some swimming skills are usually required to enter the program, including satisfactory performance of the crawl stroke and backstroke at the Minnow level (YMCA Swim Lessons). Greater skills develop as the learner progresses. Some classes and special activities are available for nonswimmers.

YMCA Synchronized Swimming program components include skill development, personal safety, and personal growth. The program objectives are to develop watermanship (body control, agility, breath control, endurance, and so on), to enable participants to swim with others to a rhythmic accompaniment, and to provide an arena for creative expression and performance. To stimulate creative thinking, students should be encouraged to choreograph and perform simple routines.

Synchronized swimming can be presented as a stand-alone class or as a competitive program. Each synchronized swimming skill is presented in a logical sequence. Instruction highlights body position and the method of execution, using a step-by-step approach to each skill, and then concludes with a swimming sequence put to music that integrates the skills. Demonstrations and water shows may be an integral part of the course. Students can progress from this general instruction in synchronized swimming to the competitive or art forms. The YMCA has developed a liaison with United States Synchronized Swimming to provide further opportunities for YMCA program participants.

YMCA Wetball (Water Polo)

Water polo (chapter 22) is the fastest growing aquatic sport in the United States. This energetic sport emphasizes swimming ability, conditioning, ball skills, and teamwork. It is a game that is both fun and safe for people of all ages.

YMCA Wetball is a three-level progressive program to learn the game of water polo. The program is designed so that it can be used for swimmers and nonswimmers. The objectives of the program are to introduce basic skills of water polo, teach correct positioning, and prepare the player for play. These objectives are met through basic drills, game-type activities, and lots of encouragement. Adaptations are made based on the age and skill levels of the participants. Once players have progressed through the three levels, they are ready for more advanced water polo play. Such play is available through participation in leagues sponsored by the YMCA and U.S. Water Polo.

OTHER YMCA AQUATICS PROGRAMS

Almost all YMCAs offer recreational swimming, although it is not an official program. Also, the YMCA provides two other aquatics courses for those who manage pools.

Recreational Swimming

A well-rounded aquatics program includes lap swimming, recreational swim time for youth, family, and other YMCA groups (Y-Guides and Y-Princesses, day camp, older adults), specialty aquatic sports such as inner tube water polo and kayaking, and special aquatics events such as a water carnival. See chapter 15 for more information.

Pool Operator on Location (POOL)

The YMCA Pool Operator on Location course covers the essentials of filtration and disinfection, pool water chemistry, pool area maintenance and safety, safe handling of pool chemicals, and daily operations. The course is for individuals who are responsible for maintaining a swimming pool and supervisors who need to understand water chemistry, disinfection systems, water testing, and safe pool operation.

YMCA Aquatic Management: A Guide to Effective Leadership

The YMCA Aquatic Management course is for individuals who are responsible for the management and operation of an aquatics program. This course includes topics such as YMCA organization and development, communications, fiscal management, staffing, program development and management, administration of aquatics programs, risk management, and problem solving. It is designed for aquatics directors as well as other program directors or executive directors who are responsible for supervising the aquatics program area.

YMCA Swim Lessons Programs

In this chapter we will discuss basic information about the programs, how to transition your current program to YMCA Swim Lessons, and program promotion. Examples of how to manage the programs were included in earlier chapters. The YMCA Swim Lessons series includes three programs:

- the Parent/Child program for parents and their children under three years of age;
- the Preschool program for children ages three to five years old; and
- the Youth and Adult program, which may be offered and marketed separately for youth, teens, and adults.

All three programs are marketed under one name: "YMCA Swim Lessons." Recommended class lengths are 30 minutes for Parent/Child classes, 30-45 minutes for Preschool classes, and 45 minutes for Youth and Adult classes. Session lengths vary among associations, with most being six to eight weeks per session or eight classes to a session.

The new programs are based on the latest research on teaching *and* on asset-based youth development. They include components that parents are seeking in programs—character development, family involvement, safety education, and volunteerism.

The new programs were created with the help of a group of YMCA aquatics experts who pooled their knowledge (pun intended!). They were then field-tested at YMCAs across the country and adjusted to be as effective as possible. This gives local instructors well-thought-out, tested programs and skill progressions for teaching all levels of swimming.

In addition, the programs include training for instructors so they can provide the best possible instruction for their students. Through participation in the YMCA Swim Lessons instructor training and certification program, instructor candidates learn how to develop lesson plans for each of their classes.

The combination of YMCA nationally certified swimming programs with the YMCA of the USA's instructor training system gives every YMCA access to the same high-quality programs. This can be useful in promoting the programs to parents, especially those who move or change YMCAs. They will expect to find the same high-quality instruction in each YMCA Swim Lessons program.

PROGRAM LEVELS

Each program has several levels. This allows instructors to group children with similar skills and abilities, facilitating instruction.

In the Parent/Child program, pairs are grouped by the age of the child. Children in the preschool and youth programs are grouped according to their developmental abilities, which may or may not correspond to their chronological age. This division allows children to learn with others at their own level and emphasizes the learning process rather than what they know or don't know at a certain age. Table 13.1 is a general guide for the recommended groupings.

PROGRAM CONTENT

The same five components are used throughout all three YMCA Swim Lessons programs: personal safety, personal growth, stroke development, water sports and games, and rescue. The activities within each component are developmentally appropriate and are progressive relative to each of the components in each level.

The programs include information and skill training not only in swimming, but also in aquatic sports and activities such as skin diving, synchronized swimming, springboard diving, and wetball. This encourages students to develop a lifelong interest in aquatics.

Teaching boating safety is emphasized in the Parent/Child, Preschool, and Youth and Adult programs. Boating is an increasingly popular activity, with more than 76 million Americans enjoying the open water. The vast majority of accidents while boating are preventable. By expanding people's knowledge of boating safety principles, we can help prevent needless accidents and save lives.

Finally, students are encouraged to develop the YMCA's four core values of caring, honesty, respect, and responsibility. Within each of the levels are age-appropri-

Table 13.1	Swim Lessons Program Levels	
Level	**Age**	**Ability**
Shrimps	6 to 8 months	Child can control the head and sit with support from the hands.
Kippers	9 to 12 months	Child can sit without hand support and stand with support from the hands.
Inias	13 to 18 months	Child can stand without support and walk with or without support or aid.
Perch	19 to 36 months	Child can run and jump.
Preschool program:		
Pike	Beginner I	
Eel	Beginner II	
Ray	Advanced Beginner I	
Starfish	Advanced Beginner II	
Youth and Adult program:		
Polliwog	Introductory level	
Guppy	Beginning skill level	
Minnow	Intermediate skill level	
Fish	Swimmer level	
Flying Fish	Advanced swimmer	
Shark	Beginning leadership level	
Porpoise	A class or club program	

ate activities that allow the instructor and students to define, demonstrate, and celebrate the core values. At the Shark and Porpoise levels, students are given opportunities to help others by volunteering.

TEACHING METHODS

The YMCA Swim Lessons programs promote enjoyment of learning and follow the philosophy that success breeds success. Children will like YMCA Swim Lessons because they start with those skills they are ready to learn. They will be able to succeed often and build self-confidence. Instruction is delivered in a student-centered, caring atmosphere with well-trained instructors who can give personalized attention. Lessons are developmentally appropriate and designed to quickly and effectively teach skills. Finally, as always, safety is a high priority.

Research has helped us match our instruction and delivery of the programs with what we know to be the normal development and learning process for children and adults. For example:

- Motor learning research shows that the stages of learning a motor skill move from an awkward, step-by-step movement at the conscious stage to more rapid, automatic movement at the motor stage.

• Motor control research demonstrates that movement skill performance is best conceived of as a system comprising the primary factors of person, task, and environment.

• Motor development research shows that the progressions of change result from the interactions among the person, the task, and the environment. Specifically, the principles associated with teaching progressions relate to changes in the task, going from simple to complex.

• Child development research shows that developmentally appropriate practices are those tasks, skills, and learning activities that best fit a child's age, fitness, skill level, and experience.

Our teaching is now geared even more to how we know children and adults learn. For example, we know people learn new motor skills best by the "whole" method of teaching. In YMCA Swim Lessons, this means we teach whole strokes in each level. Beginning at the Pike level in the Preschool program, students must swim a certain distance to complete that level. However, in these earlier levels, strokes may be basic or rudimentary. As students advance, they must show increasing coordination, comfort, and endurance with their strokes (and they usually do so quite naturally). Using this teaching method provides students with a solid foundation for refining their strokes as they progress through the programs.

Another plus is that instructors learn to teach using movement exploration principles. The programs allow children to learn how to move in the water effectively and efficiently at their own pace *and* in their own way. As they progress through each level, instructors encourage students to explore movements so they can understand the best way to move effectively. As the students build strength and endurance, they master the familiar swimming strokes.

PROGRAM BENEFITS

YMCA Swim Lessons programs benefit YMCAs by helping them

• meet the mission and program objectives of the YMCA,
• incorporate YMCA character development into swimming lessons,
• involve families,
• teach lifesaving and survival skills,
• address community issues of safety in and around the water,
• help participants develop leadership skills, and
• encourage volunteerism.

Parents will like that

• students are taught swimming and water safety skills in a student-centered, caring atmosphere;
• instructors are well-trained and can give students personalized attention;
• lessons are developmentally appropriate and designed to teach skills quickly and effectively;
• safety is a high priority;
• lessons include information and skill training in other aquatic sports and activities, such as competitive swimming, skin diving, springboard diving, synchronized swimming, and wetball;

- instructors encourage students to develop a lifelong interest in aquatics; and
- instructors promote and reinforce the character development values of caring, honesty, respect, and responsibility.

Children will like that they

- start with those skills they are ready to learn;
- are able to succeed often;
- can build self-confidence;
- have fun learning swimming, water safety, and water sports skills; and
- make new friends!

PROGRAM MATERIALS

The following certification courses related to YMCA Swim Lessons are available:

Fundamentals of Teaching YMCA Swim Lessons

YMCA Swim Lessons: Preschool Instructor

YMCA Swim Lessons: Parent-Child Instructor

YMCA Preschool and Parent-Child Swimming Trainer

YMCA Swim Lessons: Youth and Adult Swim Instructor I (first three levels only)

YMCA Swim Lessons: Youth and Adult Swim Instructor II (all seven levels)

YMCA Youth and Adult Swimming Trainer

Instructor manuals available include these:

YMCA Swim Lessons: Teaching Swimming Fundamentals

YMCA Swim Lessons: The Parent/Child and Preschool Aquatic Program Manual

YMCA Swim Lessons: The Youth and Adult Aquatic Program Manual

The *YMCA Swim Lessons Administrator's Manual* helps aquatics directors manage and administer the programs more effectively. Ready-to-photocopy master pages include progress reports, skill sheets, stroke observation sheets, Parent Handouts, and Family Huddles. Family Huddles are worksheets that students take home with them. The worksheets were developed to help children continue learning beyond the class by sharing what they learn with family members.

A variety of promotional products are also available:

- A certificate for the Parent/Child program (the level is written on the certificate)
- Certificates for each level of the Preschool program (Pike, Eel, Ray, Starfish levels)
- Stickers for each level of the Preschool program and the first four levels of the Youth and Adult program
- Ribbons for each level of the Youth and Adult program
- Patches for each level of the Youth and Adult program
- Certificates for each level of the Youth and Adult program

The program manuals and promotional products are available from the YMCA Program Store.

PROGRAM EQUIPMENT

Have a wide variety of instructional flotation devices and other program equipment in good condition for participants and instructors to use during classes. The equipment adds to the students' experience in the water. Just as we continue to add new equipment to our fitness centers, it is important to do the same for our aquatics programs. Although most YMCAs will have most of this equipment already, if you don't have some of the following items, you should consider adding these to your inventory:

- Boat/canoe (an inflatable one is acceptable)
- Life jackets for infants, preschoolers, youth, and adults
- Instructional flotation devices (e.g., belts, water logs, kickboards)
- Balls of various sizes (foam balls, playground balls, junior water polo balls)
- Masks, fins, and snorkels for youth and adults
- Water polo goals or cones to mark off a goal area

PARENT ORIENTATION

Hold an orientation to help parents understand what you are trying to achieve in your YMCA Swim Lessons programs and what your YMCA's policies are on issues affecting their children. Such an orientation will also help your classes run more smoothly by ensuring that children bring whatever equipment they need to class. Some of the topics that should be included in a parent orientation are the following:

- A welcome
- A statement of the goals of the programs (use the news release for talking points)
- Infant guidelines (for those in the Parent/Child program)
- Viewing area policy
- A communication phone number and contact person or persons
- The name of the aquatics director or coordinator

- The name and level for each instructor
- Session dates and times
- The YMCA's philosophy on progression through the levels, allowing children to work *at their own* pace
- A first-time parent separation policy (what parents ought to do if young children are upset at being left alone in class)
- Pool and showering rules
- Progress reports and program evaluations at the end of the session
- Family Huddles and Parent Handout sheets
- Registration and reenrollment policies
- Membership information
- How character development is addressed in the programs
- Volunteer opportunities
- The annual support campaign

Hold an orientation meeting either a week before the session or on the first day of the session. You may also hand out the information in written form when parents register their children for class.

After an initial orientation, provide parents with additional, more specific information about class activities through the Family Huddles and about parenting through Parent Handouts (see the *YMCA Swim Lessons Administrator's Manual*).

TRANSITIONING TO YMCA SWIM LESSONS

If your YMCA is not currently operating the YMCA Swim Lessons programs, here are some tips on how to transition to them. Proper planning will ensure a smooth transition to the new programs.

One of the first things to decide is in which session you will convert to the new programs. A branch should convert all of its classes at the same time. Similarly, in metropolitan associations, there are marketing and promotional benefits to having all branches convert at the same time.

Table 13.2 is a planning checklist for making the transition from your programs to the new YMCA Swim Lessons programs.

PROGRAM PROMOTION

Here is some basic promotional information for each of the Swim Lessons programs. For more help with promotion, contact YMCA of the USA Association Advancement department (see chapter 8). See if your YMCA has a copy of the *YMCA Communications Handbook*, a comprehensive guide to communications, available from the YMCA Program Store.

Also, before you begin any promotional campaign, make sure everyone involved—from the front-desk staff to the lifeguards—is familiar with the promotional information.

Promotional Information

This should give you a start on writing promotional material for the infant, preschool, youth, and adult aquatics programs. For each program, there is a customer profile, benefits to promote, and suggested promotional tools.

Table 13.2	Planning Checklist for Transition to YMCA Swim Lessons Programs

Time	Key action steps
6 months before	☐ Inform other management staff of the upcoming changes and plan their roles in the transition. ☐ Describe why you are changing programs. ☐ Schedule a meeting with supervisors and volunteers about the new programs. ☐ Review budgeting, equipment, and training needs, as well as opportunities for membership growth and promotional planning. Review new equipment needs and joint purchasing opportunities. ☐ Discuss promotional planning opportunities with your association (such as Healthy Kids Day celebration events). ☐ Schedule instructor training and recruit a trainer for the courses.
5 months before	☐ Inform all staff about the upcoming program change. ☐ Schedule association training events.
4 months before	☐ For current participants, let them know what session they will be in with the new program. ☐ Discuss program changes with the aquatics staff. ☐ Purchase new equipment and participant materials (ribbons, stickers, patches). ☐ Begin training front desk staff about the new programs. ☐ Tell current participants and their parents when the new programs will begin and that (in most cases) they will remain in their current levels.
3 months before	☐ Get staff trained in the YMCA Swim Lessons programs. ☐ Put posters up in the YMCA announcing the new programs.
2 months before	☐ Have trainers provide crossover training for instructors in the new programs. ☐ Add new program material to program brochure material. ☐ Have the member newsletter announce the new programs and their benefits.
1 month before	☐ Have skill sheets, progress reports, Family Huddles, and parent handouts printed and ready for the new programs. ☐ Discuss how you will transition into the new programs with your current participants. ☐ Have trainers continue crossover training for instructors in the new programs. ☐ Schedule Parents' Orientation. ☐ Begin open registration. ☐ Make parent information sheets about the programs available. ☐ Contact newspapers and radio and TV stations according to your promotional plan.

New programs begin

☐ Begin the new programs.

☐ Schedule additional Parent Orientations.

☐ Discuss with participants how the new programs affect what they do during lessons.

☐ During the first few sessions of the new programs, have instructors spend some time teaching participants the skills they haven't learned from the earlier levels in the new programs.

☐ Be more available than usual to talk to parents during classes and to provide additional information.

Infant Programs

Young first-time parents are most enthusiastic about these parent-child programs. A large percentage of new parents may be new to the community because the decision to have children follows the big decision to buy a home. Exposure to your program is often their first experience with your YMCA. These parents are also program members. A positive experience in these first classes will lead to further investment in your YMCA as they trade in their program memberships for family memberships. These classes are also very popular with working parents or when a new baby joins the family and can be promoted as a way to give the older child "special" time.

Some benefits you can use to promote infant programs include:

- A warm pool
- A safe program
- Enthusiastic, caring, mature instructors who work well with babies and parents
- A way for parents to learn water safety and help teach their children develop basic swimming and water safety skills
- A positive, fun program that fosters the parent-child relationship
- The YMCA mission and the availability of financial aid

Several kinds of promotional tools are available to use for this program: general YMCA program brochure, press releases, cable TV announcements, church bulletins, and flyers to obstetricians' and pediatricians' offices, libraries, play groups and day care centers, and to realtors and Welcome Wagon personnel.

Preschool Programs

Parents of children in beginner levels have high anxiety about their children accidentally drowning and thus feel it's necessary for their children to learn to swim. The children in the beginner levels may be either dangerously fearless or fretful and clingy. In either case, safety and a caring instructor who understands young children are very important.

Parents at the more advanced levels may begin to have swim team aspirations for their children and want to see them learn and become proficient at skills. An instructor who knows how to correct a child's stroke while preserving the child's self-esteem and yet be developmentally appropriate is very important. Using songs and games to teach skills is very motivational for this age group.

Some benefits you can use to promote the program include:

- Program safety—promote the certifications of your staff and lifeguards.
- If you adhere to all national guidelines and policies, promote this fact.
- Caring instructors, improvement of self-esteem, and the long-term fitness benefits of participation.
- Character development.
- Water safety activities.
- The YMCA mission and the availability of financial aid.

Again, several kinds of promotional tools are available: YMCA program brochure, press releases (ask the local paper to do a feature on preschool classes), cable TV announcements, church bulletins, flyers to libraries, pediatricians' offices, nursery schools and day care centers, and to realtors and Welcome Wagon personnel.

YMCA Swim Lessons—Youth Ages 6-18

The YMCA stands in the forefront of swimming instruction for children. Through the teacher's guidance and easy-to-follow steps, young people learn the proper techniques for swimming, water sports, and boating and water safety.

Parents of beginner-level children may still worry about their children accidentally drowning, while others want their children to progress through the program, learning to swim and to appreciate and respect the water. Children may have aspirations to become lifeguards or join a swim team. Parental concerns continue to be safety, the qualifications of instructors, and measurable progress.

Children range from weepy and clingy or dangerously fearless beginners to students who may or may not be motivated to press on. All children develop at different rates, so the instructor must make sure to teach safely in a caring, fun manner that enhances children's self-esteem. This group can become easily bored or discouraged. As children learn the basics of swimming and the skills within all the core components of the program, the instructor should give children opportunities to use these skills to reduce boredom, improve retention, and enrich the program.

Some benefits you can use to promote the program include:

- Staff certifications
- Safety, including adherence to national guidelines and your association policy

- Measurable results (Track the number of children taught to swim or that graduate to the next levels.)
- Lifetime fitness, sports, and recreational benefits
- Safe, caring, competent, and fun instructors
- Developing children's appreciation of aquatic sports
- Character development activities

  Some promotional messages and slogans include:

- Swimming is a Lifetime Sport—Start Your Child Now!
- Swimming—Safety—Fitness—Fun!
- Come Swim With Us . . . at (your name) YMCA!
- Get In the Swim . . . at (your name) YMCA!
- Catch the Wave . . . at (your name) YMCA!
- Take the Plunge . . . at (your name) YMCA!
- Learn to swim well at (your name) YMCA!

Other ideas include: Press releases or feature stories on children in the program, the YMCA program brochure, announcements on cable TV, and flyers to physicians' and orthodontists' offices, libraries, and elementary schools. Special events to get children or their parents interested in YMCA swim programs include a beach party, Healthy Kids activities, and the YMCA Splash program. Invite Boy and Girl Scout Troops to "Book Your Badge," taking swim courses to meet their aquatics badge or pin requirements.

Adult Swim Lessons

Adults who do not know how to swim fall into two categories: those who were traumatized or developed a fear of water as children and never went near the water again, and those who never had the opportunity to take swim lessons. With fearful adults, instructors must take great care to show respect, caring, and competence. Building trust is very important.

Adults who are comfortable in water want to improve their strokes and techniques. Their skills range from beginner to advanced, including triathletes who would enjoy a sophisticated adult stroke clinic or a masters program.

Some benefits you can use to promote the program include:

- Certified, caring staff trained to handle fearful swimmers
- Safety aspects of learning to swim
- Fitness and self-esteem benefits of swimming
- The opportunity to spice up lap swimming with different strokes
- The YMCA mission and the availability of financial aid

 The following are some promotional tools, ideas, and messages you can use:

- More than a million people learn to swim at the YMCA each year.
- The YMCA has more than 110 years of experience teaching people to swim.
- It's never too late to learn!

Promote through the YMCA program brochure, church bulletins, libraries, and physicians' offices. Use cable TV announcements, a special adult learn-to-swim week, press releases, or feature stories.

Aquatic Safety Programs

The YMCA is uniquely suited to meet communities' need for a resource for teaching water safety. Today, many Americans do not know how to swim, even though water recreation activities are on the increase and thousands of people drown annually. Offering education in water skills and safety is even more important now that public schools have cut back on physical education and aquatics course offerings.

Your YMCA can offer the week-long YMCA Splash program to the public, particularly children, at least annually. This is a good program for introducing kids to some of the basics of swimming and aquatic safety, and for educating their parents as well.

Other YMCA basic aquatic safety programs are available for teens and adults: the Aquatic Safety Course and the Aquatic Personal Safety and Survival Course. These focus on teaching fundamental aquatic safety and survival techniques to both non-swimmers and swimmers.

More technical training is available through the YMCA Aquatic Safety Assistant Course, which certifies individuals to assist lifeguards, and the YMCA lifeguarding courses. Certification courses are available for Lifeguard, Lifeguard Instructor, and Lifeguard Trainer.

YMCA SPLASH

The primary purpose of the YMCA Splash program is to help people of all ages, especially children and families, learn basic swimming skills and water safety practices. It also provides opportunities to consider the four character development characteristics of caring, honesty, respect, and responsibility.

YMCA Splash was designed to be adaptable to many situations so it can meet the needs of the community. It can be presented as

- a five-day pool program,
- a five-day classroom program (when a pool is not available), or
- a one-day specialty course covering either boating safety, backyard pool safety, or beach safety.

The five-day program, which has a 30- to 45-minute lesson each day, includes the following:

- Basic swimming skills
- Beach safety
- Pool safety
- Boating safety
- Backyard pool safety
- Character development
- Family activities
- Parent education

The five-day pool program is designed primarily for grade school children but can be modified for use with children of any age or adults. The five-day classroom program is best used with children in the second to fourth grades, and the one-day specialty courses are more suitable for older children and adults.

An optional Parents' Presentation can be used with either of the five-day programs to instruct parents on the same topics covered in the classes. This will both convey information about water safety to parents and enable them to support their children's learning during the course. Outlines in the Splash kit support this program component. While the classes are going on in the pool, you or a volunteer can use these outlines to give a 10- to 15-minute presentation to parents about what is happening in class today. Each outline covers the theme of the day and includes parent tips on supporting what is being taught. For the concluding YMCA Program Highlight of the Day, ask one of the YMCA department heads to tell the parents about the programs in that department. A different program area is highlighted each day.

YMCAs may also feel free to condense or use only parts of the five-day program if their time is limited. A two- or three-day program can be conducted using the same content.

For program materials, get a YMCA Splash kit. It includes an administrator's manual and an instructor's manual; a copyable Tips for Parents booklet, activity book, and handouts for the classroom and pool; a video; promotional materials; and copyable participant certificate and evaluation forms. It's available through the YMCA Program Store at 800-747-0089.

Finally, remember that YMCA Splash can be offered in collaboration with schools, parks and recreation departments, and other community-based organizations. By collaborating and building community awareness, YMCAs can extend the program to children and families they have not traditionally reached, especially those in low-income neighborhoods.

Here are some ideas for planning and promoting a YMCA Splash program.

Planning

If you think you would like your YMCA to run a YMCA Splash program, you can begin planning. The following section covers how to assess community needs and what key steps to take as you plan, and it provides a sample timeline for carrying out program tasks.

Assessing Community Needs

As a first step in planning, you'll need to assess your community's needs to decide whether to offer YMCA Splash and, if so, to choose the form in which to offer it as well as other community water safety programs. This assessment is a good opportunity to discover what types of aquatics programs are needed and which members of the community are not currently being served. Through communication and collaboration with other agencies, you may also become aware of other community needs your YMCA can try to meet.

Two objectives for local YMCAs in sponsoring a YMCA Splash program are to raise community awareness of the need for effective, ongoing education on water safety and to offer a program that meets community needs. Performing a community assessment before proceeding with the program helps achieve both these objectives.

The two questions you must focus on in your assessment are what services are needed and who needs them. After you've decided who needs them, you can determine what other agencies can reach those groups and whether you wish to collaborate with them.

To see whether a YMCA Splash program is necessary, organize a committee to address the water safety issues in your community. Include both YMCA and community leaders. Through collaboration, you can be more successful in addressing these issues.

Evaluate local trends relating to aquatic activities and accident rates and find out what other agencies offer aquatics training. Some questions you will want to answer for your community include the following:

What is your local drowning and near-drowning rate? Can you break the statistics down by age, gender, and race?

Are there any other drowning-prevention organizations in your community?

Are there many lakes, rivers, or beaches in your community?

How many boating accidents occur in your area?

Are there any other boating safety organizations in your community?

What types of aquatics-related accidents have the local EMS, police, and fire departments been responding to?

What types of aquatic accidents have area hospitals, paramedics, and doctors been treating?

Would any other local agencies or organizations, such as sailing clubs, the local Coast Guard, or the Army Corps of Engineers, have information on accident rates?

How many backyard pools are in your community?

What concerns do community apartment complex managers and city officials have about their swimming pools?

Does your school system offer a water safety program?

Does your school system have a swimming proficiency requirement?

Once you determine that YMCA Splash is relevant to your community, evaluate which areas in the community should be offered the YMCA Splash program:

- Determine which areas are already well served by other aquatics programs and organizations.
- Survey YMCA and community leaders on who needs aquatics training.
- Check with the local United Way or the city government for any recent community assessments done by others.
- Use focus groups and surveys to assess the need in different areas of your community.

Planning Steps

Once you've decided to have a YMCA Splash program, take the following steps to help organize it.

Review all materials in the YMCA Splash kit. Be familiar with all aspects of the program and disseminate the materials to those who need them.

Designate a staff person or volunteer to chair your YMCA Splash program. The key to a successful program is coordinating the many departments, community organizations, and staff members involved in the process. Choose one person to facilitate planning meetings and to take responsibility for the overall management and coordination of the program and its evaluation.

Assign staff members to the YMCA Splash committee. Choose department heads and others who can give creative input to the planning process, and recruit other staff members and volunteers to assist with the event. Assign committee members specific activities or responsibilities for the YMCA Splash program, and create a timetable with appropriate deadlines for those tasks.

If you are in a metropolitan YMCA, make sure you have a representative from each branch to ensure consistency and communication. Each branch should have a committee of its own that represents the community it serves.

Recruit key community volunteers and community organization leaders to be part of your committee. Get these people and organizations involved early in the process so as to get their ideas and support for the event.

Develop your YMCA's goal for YMCA Splash. Determine your purpose in providing the program and the end results you want for your YMCA. Your desired outcomes could be to enhance your image in the community as a provider of aquatics training, to bring new people and nonmembers to your facility, to increase the use of water safety practices, to strengthen community collaboration, or similar goals.

Determine the type of YMCA Splash program you will conduct and the resources you will need. Planning these aspects early in the process allows for effective promotion of the program and accurate budgeting. It also permits staff members and volunteers to begin gathering the needed materials and resources. Be sure to keep the instructor-to-student and lifeguard-to-student ratios at a safe and effective level.

A key question to consider is what age group you want to serve with YMCA Splash. The five-day pool program is designed for grade school children, but the lesson plans can be adapted to preschool children, teens, adults, and families, or to a classroom environment. The specialty courses work best with older children and adults.

Once you have determined the type of program your YMCA will offer, think of ways to collaborate with other community organizations. Collaboration may be particularly important if you will be expanding into new parts of your community or if your YMCA does not have the resources to deliver the program effectively. Branches of metropolitan YMCAs can save money by pooling budgets for things such as printing and promotional items.

Develop your plan. Questions that should be answered in your planning process include the following:

- *Will YMCA Splash be sponsored solely by your YMCA, or will you collaborate with other community agencies and organizations?* Think about possible partners such as the following:

  - Hospitals
  - Parks and recreation department
  - The local United Way

- Service clubs
- Elementary and high schools, PTAs, and universities
- Drowning prevention groups
- Local businesses and corporations
- Boating safety groups
  a. The local United States Coast Guard
  b. The local United States Lifesaving Association (USLA)

- *Will the schools be involved in YMCA Splash? If so, how?* Check to see whether your YMCA can provide this program to a certain grade within the school system. Keep in mind that the program also can be adapted for classroom use, if needed.

- *Where will the YMCA Splash program be held? Are there other areas in the community you can serve through this program?* Most YMCAs hold YMCA Splash at their own facilities, but it can also be held at other community facilities such as community, school, or apartment complex pools, day or after-school care centers, and scout troop or Y-Guide gatherings. It can be effective in either a pool or a classroom. Evaluate your YMCA's goals and choose the sites that will best help you achieve those goals.

- *When do you want to hold the program?* The YMCA of the USA recommends holding it in May to coordinate with national promotion of the program. You might also consider holding it during National Safe Boating Week, which is usually held in the latter part of May. For more information, contact the National Safe Boating Council at 606-244-8242.

- *What times are best for holding the program?* Try to run a two- to three-hour block in the morning, afternoon, and evening. This will increase community awareness of YMCA programs and open new opportunities for increased on-site and off-site community programs for the YMCA.

- *How can you get your members and program participants involved?* Announcing YMCA Splash to all program participants, mentioning it in the YMCA member newsletter, or sending brochures to members are some ways to achieve this goal. (See "Promotion" later in this chapter for more ideas.)

- *How can you involve volunteers in the program?* Volunteers can help in many ways. For instance, they can assist with classes, supervise in the locker rooms, recruit participants, talk to community groups about the program, help with promotion and fundraising, and serve on the site selection committee.

- *How can you promote the event and draw in the community?* See "Promotion" later in this chapter for more information on promoting YMCA Splash.

Determine the need for a sponsor. Sponsors can offset the expenses of operating this program. Consider local corporations and businesses, service clubs, newspapers, TV stations, and hospitals as potential sponsors. See the sample solicitation letter in the YMCA Splash kit for an example of how to approach sponsors.

Designate a staff person to coordinate publicity. Ask this person to read the "Promotion" section of this chapter. With the committee's assistance, he or she should plan a promotion schedule.

In a metropolitan YMCA, this person may be the marketing director. In such a situation, the branches involved should have a similar objective and some similar activities so as to coordinate the metrowide effort effectively.

Train staff to run the program. Meet with staff to explain the program and review the instructor's manual from the Splash kit with them. Make sure they are ready to teach by the beginning of the program. Meet with them again after the program to make plans for improving the program for the following year.

Conduct a postprogram evaluation. Gather evaluations from parents and all collaborating organizations, and then plan an evaluation meeting for the week after the program ends. At that meeting, see whether you achieved your goal and note all comments for next year. After gathering all the input, complete and send in the YMCA Splash Staff Evaluation form from the YMCA Splash kit to the YMCA of the USA (see form for address).

Planning Timetable

Implementing a new program requires adequate time to carry out all the necessary tasks. To help you in scheduling, look over the following sample planning timetable. Adjust it to your circumstances as needed.

Six to Nine Months Before the Registration Deadline

Perform a community assessment.

Recruit committee members, schedule meetings, and assign tasks to committee members.

Develop your YMCA's goal for the program.

Determine the type of program you want and what program equipment and supplies or resources will be required.

Develop a budget. See the administrator's manual in the Splash kit for needed equipment and supplies, and also include staffing costs; gifts for volunteers; copying costs for children's certificates, handouts, and booklets; and promotional costs.

Consider collaborating with other community organizations.

Create a plan that includes the organizations that will sponsor the program, site(s), dates, and methods to involve YMCA members, volunteers, and the community.

Determine the need for sponsors and secure them if needed.

Order needed equipment and supplies.

Assign a staff member to prepare a promotional plan.

Three Months Before the Registration Deadline

Design and print promotional pieces.

Update and then prepare other printed materials (handouts, booklets). Schedule training meetings for staff and volunteers.

Acquaint the contact point staff with the program and the registration procedures.

Begin recruiting and scheduling instructors and lifeguards to implement the program.

Four to Six Weeks Before the Registration Deadline

Contact newspapers and radio and TV stations according to the promotional plan.

Distribute your promotional piece internally to YMCA program participants and members and externally to schools, businesses, and community groups as identified in the promotional plan.

Begin registration.

Two to Three Weeks Before the Registration Deadline

Develop and print additional resource materials for instructors, such as rosters and skill sheets.

Complete scheduling of instructors and lifeguards for the program.

Hold a staff orientation meeting.

Hold a volunteer orientation meeting.

After the Registration Deadline

Make up the class rosters.

Schedule media coverage as determined in the promotional plan.

Keep the contact point staff informed of any changes.

During the YMCA Splash Program

Post signs to guide participants to the program.

Have staff or volunteers available to greet participants and direct traffic. An on-deck supervisor can be helpful for working with parents and children.

Have instructors distribute the handouts to participants.

Stay close to what's happening. Observe the instructors in action, and talk to parents and participants.

At the end of each day, review with staff the successes achieved and the issues that arose, and come up with needed solutions for the next day.

Take time to get to know participants' parents.

On the last day of the five-day program, have instructors distribute the YMCA Splash booklets to parents and children and the evaluation forms to parents.

After the Program

Share program evaluations with the instructors and the committee.

Compile the evaluations and summarize the proposed changes for next year's program.

Inventory the remaining equipment and supplies.

Have a "thank you" celebration for staff and volunteers.

Make sure all participants have been added to the YMCA mailing list for future contacts.

Promotion

One of the most important parts of your planning will be promoting your YMCA Splash program. Although YMCA Splash is probably more of a program than a special event, it certainly fits this description. It is an ideal way to position your YMCA as an organization that

- promotes children's healthy, successful development and cares about their safety;
- helps children (and adults, too) grow in self-esteem and self-worth; and
- supports parents and eases their worries by teaching children valuable life skills.

Assign a staff member or form a YMCA Splash promotion committee to coordinate the campaign and create a promotion plan. A committee might include the executive director, aquatics director, communications director, and volunteers from your program and communications committees. If you're collaborating with other organizations, they should have representatives on the committee.

You also will need to designate someone as your event spokesperson, probably you or another program director. The spokesperson should be able to answer questions about your YMCA Splash plans, your aquatics programs, water safety, and related issues and trends. Be sure your spokesperson reviews all the appropriate materials from the Splash kit after you've revised them and added new information. You should also provide your spokesperson with copies of the material you send to the media. If you are collaborating with the school system or another group, it might be a good idea for your spokesperson to work with a spokesperson from that group so as to keep messages consistent, maximize results, and promote cooperation.

Make sure everyone involved in publicity is familiar with the promotional information in the YMCA Splash kit. Many sample promotional items are included, but only the most basic shells are provided. This is because YMCA Splash dates, locations, duration, and curriculum can vary across YMCAs. Customize the pieces carefully, incorporating the specific details of your program, and retype them on your own letterhead. Camera-ready ads, a proclamation, and logos, as well as clip art and a poster design, are also available in your YMCA Splash kit. These items were produced as loose pieces so you could easily take them to a printer or designer.

Your promotional plans should include ideas for both internal and external communications.

Internal Communications

To build excitement among your members, staff, and volunteers, create a YMCA Splash bulletin board. Some of the material provided in the Splash kit can be displayed on the board. If you have held learn-to-swim programs before, you might want to include photos or kids' drawings from these events. Any special flyers or other information you create could also be posted.

Promote YMCA Splash in any internal communications tools you might have, such as employee, volunteer, and member newsletters. Use the camera-ready logo in the kit and perhaps some of the clip art to give your articles a fun look. If you are recruiting volunteers, include a "Wanted: Caring Adults" notice with a brief job description. Remember to state the need or problem to be solved, what the volunteer can do to help fill the need or solve the problem, and what the volunteer will get out of it. For instance, the first sentence might be "You'll never forget the look of pride on a child's face when she's learned to float all by herself."

Send letters to parents of children who are in YMCA child care (see a sample letter in the YMCA Splash kit or other YMCA children's programs). You could also give take-home flyers to children in these programs. (See the sample flyer in the YMCA Splash kit.)

The week before YMCA Splash, you could place a banner at the entrance to your lobby and decorate your front desk with balloons—or maybe a mobile with an aquatics theme (such as clip art fish colored in with crayons) made by kids in your programs. You could have stickers, buttons, and flyers at your front desk throughout the month before your event kicks off.

These are just some of the possible ideas. Have your committee brainstorm other ways to create a fun, exciting atmosphere around YMCA Splash.

External Communications

Consider creating a special postcard or flyer to mail to the parents of all the kids in your youth sports and child care programs. You could send postcards or flyers to everyone who has a family membership.

If you're collaborating with schools or other organizations, see whether they will consider mailing a postcard or flyer to parents or members or handing it out to kids to take home. If they have newsletters, you can provide the news release and see if they could include in their newsletter an item promoting YMCA Splash.

Schools also might be willing to add the event to their calendars or to allow you to display an exhibit in schools using the YMCA Splash logo and art. Your spokesperson could be placed on the agenda of a PTA or school board meeting to discuss children's safety and how aquatics can help build their self-esteem and to ask for support for YMCA Splash.

You may want to inform other civic, social service, and health organizations about YMCA Splash even if you're not collaborating with them. You might give a presentation at one of their meetings (see the sample presentation in the Splash kit). If you have corporate sponsors, they may run an item about YMCA Splash in their internal newsletters, pay for an ad to run in a local newspaper or magazine, or cover the cost of printing flyers. (See chapter 8 on promotion for more ideas.)

You will also probably want to get a proclamation issued by your legislature, mayor, city council, county board, or school board. (A camera-ready copy is in your YMCA Splash kit.) Whether or not it's issued with a signing ceremony, it is a popular way to validate and gain publicity for a special event or campaign such as YMCA Splash.

Administrative Tips

To help your YMCA Splash program run smoothly, first be prepared to answer some of the parents' common questions about this program:

- Do I have to be a member for my child to participate?
- Will my child know how to swim at the end of this program?
- Where does my child go when he or she gets here?
- What facilities are open to my child?
- Where should I wait for my child?
- How can I sign my child up for additional classes?

Also be prepared to handle situations that often crop up, such as people just showing up on the first day of the program without having registered, not having enough available spaces in classes, having a shortage of staff, or dealing with children who don't want to be involved.

Additional program resources for YMCA Splash include the *YMCA Swim Lessons Administrator's Guide* (also available through the YMCA Program Store) and a Spanish version of all the YMCA Splash kit handouts, which is online at the YMCA of the USA web site. For more information, contact the YMCA of the USA at 800-872-9622.

OTHER YMCA AQUATIC SAFETY COURSES

The YMCA has several aquatic safety courses that you can offer in your community. These are mainly meant for teens and adults, and they give swimmers and non-swimmers alike a chance to learn more about how to be safe around the water. The courses include the Aquatic Safety Course, the Aquatic Personal Safety and Survival Course, and the YMCA Aquatic Safety Assistant Course. The Aquatic Safety Assistant Course prepares individuals to help lifeguards, but does not qualify them to substitute for lifeguards.

Aquatic Safety Course

This introduction to water safety requires no previous training. It is designed to be adapted to the needs of individuals in different aquatic settings, from a corporate fitness program to family backyard pool safety. Nonswimmers are encouraged to enroll and participate, to the extent that they are able, so they can learn about basic water safety.

This is an excellent program for Boy Scout and Girl Scout troops to help them complete badge requirements. School groups also can use this program for water safety instruction.

The Aquatic Safety Course should be taught by a certified YMCA Lifeguard Instructor or YMCA Swim Lessons Instructor (instructor-to-student ratio should be 1:8.). It consists of four to six hours of classroom and water sessions and includes discussions of these topics:

- History and philosophy of the YMCA aquatic safety and lifeguard training programs
- Personal aquatic safety information
- Accident prevention principles
- Basic first aid and rescue breathing
- Nonswimming rescues

Oral or written tests are administered by the local YMCA. The training outline is located in the Instructor Manual for *On the Guard II* (4th ed.). Recognition cards are available from the YMCA Program Store.

Aquatic Personal Safety and Survival Course

This eight-hour course trains participants in personal safety and survival skills in and around aquatic environments. Classroom and pool sessions address these topics:

- The history and philosophy of YMCA aquatic safety
- Accident prevention principles
- General aquatics information
- Personal aquatic safety information
- Basic survival skills and principles
- Nonswimming rescues
- Basic first aid and rescue breathing

To take the course, candidates must meet the following prerequisites:

- Be at least 11 years old
- Be able to complete the following swimming test:
    1. Swim 300 yards, including 50 yards each of front crawl, breaststroke, elementary backstroke, inverted breaststroke (legs only), sidestroke left, and sidestroke right
    2. Tread water for two minutes
    3. Perform headfirst and feetfirst surface dives

The Aquatic Safety Course should be taught by a certified YMCA Lifeguard Instructor or YMCA Swim Lessons Instructor (instructor-to-student ratio should be

1:8). To receive a certificate of course completion, participants must score at least 80 percent on a written or oral knowledge test and demonstrate all skills on a performance test. The local YMCA issues a certificate of successful completion for participation in the course.

YMCA Aquatic Safety Assistant Course

The purpose of the YMCA Aquatic Safety Assistant Course is to present the knowledge and skills an individual needs to recognize and prevent aquatic risks and to assist a lifeguard in responding to an emergency such as an accident or injury. This 16-hour course trains assistants, coaches, and instructor candidates to perform these skills:

- Recognize potential accidents or incidents and prevent them while teaching a class or leading a program.
- Recognize potential hazards related to the program and facility and eliminate them or communicate to someone in authority about them.
- Use and care for equipment properly.
- Recognize and report suspected child abuse.
- Assist lifeguards in keeping aquatic activities safe and in following their YMCA's emergency action plan and procedures, including managing the scene of an accident.
- Recognize distressed swimmers and try to help them with basic rescue techniques using swimming assists.
- Communicate the need for assistance for themselves or others as necessary.
- Protect themselves from personal injury while teaching.
- Serve as a good role model of Christian values and safe behavior.

This certification does *not* include training in lifeguarding, so having an aquatic safety assistant in a program or class does *not* meet the requirement of having a certified lifeguard on duty. The certification only allows the person to assist a lifeguard during an emergency. Certification as an aquatic safety assistant also does not include instruction in how to teach or lead swimming or exercise classes. Such instruction must come through YMCA aquatics specialist instructor courses, for which the Aquatic Safety Assistant Course is a prerequisite.

To take the Aquatic Safety Assistant Course, candidates must meet the following prerequisites:

- Be at least 14 years old
- Be able to complete the following swimming test:

    1. Swim 100 yards, any stroke
    2. Tread water for two minutes
    3. Perform a headfirst or feetfirst surface dive in four to six feet of water or submerge and touch the hand on the bottom of the pool in five feet of water

- Have and maintain current CPR and first aid certifications (same as lifeguard prerequisites)
- Have the strength and maturity to assist in backboarding procedures

The YMCA Aquatic Safety Assistant Course is conducted by a certified YMCA Lifeguard Instructor (instructor-to-student ratio should be 1:15). To become certified as an aquatic safety assistant, participants must complete the course, score 80 percent or better on a written or oral knowledge test, and successfully perform all the skills in a practical skills test. Certification may also depend on the instructor's subjective judgment about participants' maturity, attitude, and classroom participation as shown during the course.

To keep this certification current, individuals must renew it every two years and keep their CPR and first aid certifications current. To renew the Aquatic Safety Assistant certification, participants must take the written and practical skills tests from a currently certified YMCA Lifeguard Instructor.

Summary

Table 14.1 summarizes the purpose, age levels, course hours, and renewal intervals for the YMCA's water safety programs.

Table 14.1   Summary of YMCA Water Safety Programs

Course	Purpose	Age	Course hours	Renewal
Aquatic safety	Safety for non-teens and swimmers	Adults	4-6 hours	N/A
Aquatic personal safety and survival	Safety for swimmers	Age 11 and up	8 hours	N/A
Aquatic safety assistant	Assisting lifeguards	Age 14 and up	16 hours	Every 2 years

No matter which of these programs you offer at your YMCA, they provide a valuable service to your community, enhancing and educating the community about aquatic safety. Expand these programs to your community through other agencies, schools, and apartment complexes.

YMCA LIFEGUARDING

In keeping with the seriousness of lifesaving, the YMCA has created a system for thorough training of lifeguards. All training leads to certification, and you will need to find well-trained instructors to teach your lifeguarding classes. You will also need to gather the necessary equipment and to budget for program expenses. Finally, you will have to promote your lifeguard training program. This section ends with some lifeguard training administrative tips on handling program problems and making your program better.

Certifications

The YMCA Lifeguarding program has three levels of certification: Lifeguard, Lifeguard Instructor, and Lifeguard Trainer.

YMCA Lifeguard

The YMCA has developed a unique program to prepare skilled lifeguards for a demanding profession. A *lifeguard* by definition has a legal duty to protect the safety of people in an assigned area. Lifeguards have a moral and professional obligation to prevent potential accident situations by enforcing the rules and regulations of their aquatic setting and to react to any emergencies that occur. Lifeguards have a legal duty to respond only if they are on duty at their facility. Should a lifeguard be involved in an accident while off duty, she or he is covered by Good Samaritan laws. These laws can't prevent lawsuits, but they do ensure that the lifeguard's actions are compared to the actions expected of others in similar rescue situations with similar training and certification.

The YMCA's research-based lifeguard training program provides a comprehensive education centered on preventing accidents in aquatics environments. It focuses on the practical aspects of what lifeguards need to know and on lifeguard and patron safety. Lifeguard training enables students to learn and apply safety principles in their own lives, develop leadership skills, learn how to maintain a healthy lifestyle, and improve their decision-making skills.

Besides being advanced-level swimmers, candidates to become YMCA lifeguards should be caring, strong, quick to respond, confident, fit, and intelligent, with good interpersonal skills. The YMCA strives to include all people in its programs, but the hazardous duty of a lifeguard may disqualify some candidates with certain physical or mental conditions from becoming certified. To become certified as a YMCA lifeguard, an individual must be able to accomplish these tasks:

- Remain alert, with no lapses in consciousness
- Sit for extended periods, including in an elevated chair
- Move to various locations, including in and around an elevated chair
- Communicate verbally, including projecting the voice across distances, and communicate swiftly and effectively with emergency personnel over the telephone and in person

- Hear noises and distress signals in an aquatics environment, including in water, understanding that significant background noise exists in aquatics environments
- Observe all assigned sections of the water area
- Perform all needed rescues and survival skills
- Think in the abstract, solve problems, make decisions, instruct, evaluate, supervise, and remember
- Operate alone as a lifeguard, without other lifeguards for support

To participate in the lifeguard training program, an individual must meet the following prerequisites:

- Be at least 16 years old by the last day of the scheduled course. Parental consent is required for those under 18.
- Have and maintain current cardiopulmonary resuscitation (CPR) and first aid certifications. CPR certification must include training for administering CPR to adults, children, and infants, as well as additional training in two-rescuer CPR, modified jaw thrust, and use of resuscitation mask and bag-valve-mask resuscitators. First aid certification must include training in victim assessment; treatment for bleeding, shock, burns, specific body area injuries, bites, stings, poisoning, cold- and heat-related conditions, and bone, muscle, and joint injuries; and handling medical emergencies and rescues. For YMCA of the USA courses that require CPR or first aid certifications as a prerequisite, the YMCA of the USA will accept appropriate certifications from the following nationally recognized organizations: American Heart Association (Health Care Provider course for Basic Life Support only), American Red Cross, CPR-Pro National Safety Council, and CPR-Pro American Safety and Health Institute (CPR-Pro Course and Universal First Aid).
- Pass the following swimming test:
    a. Perform a long, shallow front dive, then swim 500 yards, including 100 yards each of sidestroke, front crawl, breaststroke, sidestroke kick with one arm forward, and inverted breaststroke kick with arms on the stomach.
    b. Tread water for at least two minutes with legs only.
    c. Surface-dive headfirst and feetfirst in 8 to 10 feet of water and swim underwater for 15 feet.
- Have and maintain current certification in oxygen administration
- Have and maintain current certification in automatic external defibrillation (AED)

The individual must also complete the course and fulfill all certification requirements. Medical clearance before participation may also be required.

The lifeguard training course includes 30 hours of classroom and pool sessions, plus a two-hour practical experience, that cover these topics:

- The importance of aquatic safety
- Personal safety survival skills and swimming strokes
- Aquatics environments and aquatic science
- Aquatic rescues, including situation assessment, use of a rescue tube or buoy (required for rescue) and other rescue equipment, nonswimming assists, and swimming rescues
- How to handle special situations, such as spinal injuries, rescue breathing, scuba rescue, open-water guarding and rescue, search-and-recovery operations, and first aid procedures specific to the aquatics environment

- Lifeguard responsibilities and administration, including duties, rules, legal responsibilities, emergency procedures, reports, and pool maintenance
- Lifeguarding techniques
- Personal health and safety of lifeguards
- Job searches and additional training opportunities

The required course text is *On the Guard II* (4th ed.).

Lifeguard certification is conducted by a certified YMCA Lifeguard Instructor (instructor-to-student ratio of 1:20). To be certified, a candidate must complete the course, score 80 percent or better on each section of a written or oral knowledge test, and correctly perform all skills in a practical skills test. Certification may also include the instructor's subjective judgment about the maturity, attitude, and classroom participation the candidate demonstrated during the course.

Certification is reported to YMCA of the USA Program Certifications, 101 N. Wacker Dr., Chicago, IL 60606. The certification, which is renewable every two years through the individual's local YMCA, is valid only if the individual keeps his or her certifications in CPR, AED, oxygen administration, and first aid current.

YMCA Lifeguard Instructor

Certification as a YMCA Lifeguard Instructor allows individuals to provide the training necessary for people to become lifeguards and aquatic safety assistants. They must take the 18-hour YMCA Lifeguard Instructor course to become certified. The course is based on the content of the *Instructor Manual for On the Guard II* (4th ed.) and *On the Guard II* (4th ed.).

To participate in the Lifeguard Instructor course, an individual must meet the following prerequisites:

- Be at least 18 years old before certification.
- Have and maintain current certification as a YMCA lifeguard (including current certification in CPR, oxygen administration, AED, and first aid).
- Have taken one of the following courses: Principles of YMCA Aquatic Leadership, Basic Aquatic Leadership Course, Fundamentals of Teaching YMCA Swimming, or YMCA Water Fitness Instructor.
- Have attended the Program Trainer Orientation course.

To be certified, a candidate must successfully pass a written or oral knowledge test and correctly perform all skills in a practical skills test. Certification is reported to YMCA of the USA Program Certifications, 101 N. Wacker Dr., Chicago, IL 60606. The certification is renewable every three years through the individual's local YMCA. Completion of this course does *not* automatically renew YMCA Lifeguard certification.

YMCA Lifeguard Instructors are also certified to teach the Aquatic Safety Course; the Aquatic Personal Safety and Survival Course; the YMCA Aquatic Safety Assistant Course; the Crossover ARC *(Lifeguarding Today)* to YMCA *(On the Guard II, 4th ed.)* Course; and the Basic Water Safety for Police, EMS, and Fire Protection Services Course.

YMCA Lifeguard Trainer

Certification as a YMCA Lifeguard Trainer prepares individuals to teach staff and volunteers the certification courses for Principles of YMCA Aquatic Leadership, YMCA Lifeguard Instructor, and YMCA Aquatic Safety Assistant. A 23-hour certification course is based on the *Instructor Manual for On the Guard II* (4th ed.) and *On the Guard II* (4th ed.).

To participate in the lifeguard trainer course, an individual must meet the following prerequisites:

- Be at least 21 years old before certification.
- Have and maintain current certification as a YMCA lifeguard (including current certification in CPR, oxygen administration, AED, and first aid).
- Have and maintain current certification as a YMCA Lifeguard Instructor and have experience teaching the present lifeguarding program after becoming a certified instructor.
- Have taken one of the following courses: Principles of YMCA Aquatic Leadership, Basic Aquatic Leadership Course, Teaching YMCA Swimming Fundamentals, or Water Fitness Instructor.
- Have attended a Program Trainer Orientation.
- Have and maintain current certification as a Program Trainer Orientation Trainer (this certification may be obtained after the Lifeguard Trainer course).
- Complete a program trainer candidate application. It should include a statement from the individual's executive director verifying that she or he has taught 300 hours of aquatics, with at least 50 hours of teaching YMCA Lifeguard as a certified YMCA Lifeguard Instructor.

To be certified, candidates must successfully pass a written or oral knowledge test and correctly perform all skills in a practical skills test. Candidates' teaching skills will also be observed and evaluated. Certification is reported to YMCA of the USA Program Certifications, 101 N. Wacker Dr., Chicago, IL 60606. Successful completion of this course automatically renews the individual's YMCA Lifeguard Instructor certification. Although there is no renewal for YMCA Lifeguard Trainer certification, individuals must continue to keep their YMCA Lifeguard and YMCA Lifeguard Instructor certifications current.

Summary

Table 14.2 summarizes the purpose, age levels, course hours, and renewal intervals for the YMCA's lifeguarding programs.

If someone on your staff is interested in becoming a YMCA Lifeguard Instructor or a Lifeguard Trainer, consult your local YMCA staff or YMCA of the USA Program Development (800-USA-YMCA).

Table 14.2 YMCA Lifeguarding Courses Summary

Course	Purpose	Age	Course hours	Renewal
Lifeguard	Become a lifeguard	Age 16 and up	31 hours	Every 2 years
Lifeguard Instructor	Train and certify lifeguards	Age 18 and up	18 hours	Every 3 years
Lifeguard Trainer	Train and certify lifeguard instructors	Age 21 and up	23 hours	N/A

Staff

As you search for YMCA Lifeguard Instructors for your lifeguard training program, look for those who have these qualities:

- Excellent performance as a lifeguard
- Demonstrated leadership skills in working as a team
- Demonstrated desire to teach and lead others
- Professionalism
- Mentoring ability with young or new staff
- Maturity
- Swim instructor skills
- Ability to complete paperwork by deadlines
- Ability to perform the skills he or she asks students to complete
- An understanding of the seriousness of the program he or she is teaching
- Ability to follow a training design
- Flexibility
- Ability to be firm, fair, and tactful

Besides asking Lifeguard Instructor candidates the general interview questions in chapter 5, also ask some of these specific interview questions:

- What does a good lifeguard look like? How would you work with your class to bring your vision of a good guard about?
- What does good customer service in a lifeguard class look like?
- What do you do when a student isn't keeping up with the assignments?
- How do you deal with a student who shows up without the necessary skills?
- How do you incorporate character development into your lifeguard class?
- What questions would you ask yourself before certifying a guard to determine your confidence in her or his abilities?

Once lifeguard classes are under way, monitor staff for quality and development by sitting in on one or more classes. Ask instructors for their agendas for the observed classes, and regularly check on their progression through the program. Ask yourself these questions as you observe:

- Does the class look active?
- Is the training design being followed?
- Does the instructor look organized, and is he or she having fun?
- Are the skills the instructor is teaching those you want to see?

Be sure to give instructors regular practice on lifeguarding skills and review of the training design.

Equipment Needs

Here is the equipment necessary for teaching a lifeguard class:

Classroom Equipment

Newsprint

Markers (at least one per table group)

Three-by-five cards or notes

Masking tape

Scissors (at least one pair per table group)

Water test kit

Paper

Pencils

On the Guard II (4th ed.) manuals

First aid kit

Biohazard kit

Cervical collar

Resuscitation mask, bag-valve mask, and suction devices

Foam ball or other soft ball (optional)

Pool Equipment

If you do not have the minimum equipment listed, you will need to add more time to your course schedule.

Rescue tubes (1:6 students is recommended as minimum)

Rescue buoys (1:6 students is recommended as minimum)

Ring buoys

Poles

Shepherd's crooks

Lifejackets

Backboards/straps, including head immobilizer and set of cervical collars (1:6 students is recommended as minimum)

Resuscitation masks

Bag-valve mask

Gloves

Manual suction device (aspirator)

Oxygen tank

Automated external defibrillator trainer

Paddleboards

Inflatable rescue tubes

Whistles

Towels

Masks

Fins

Snorkels

Scuba equipment [tank, buoyancy compensator (BC), weight belt]

Diving bricks

Assortment of instructional flotation devices: kickboards, water logs, barbells

Stopwatch (optional)

Balls (optional)

Audiovisual Equipment

Overhead projector and screen (if using transparencies for overheads)

LCD Projector and the CD-ROM from the *Instructor Manual* (if using PowerPoint presentations for overheads)

TV and VCR

Video: *Instructor Manual for On the Guard II, 4th Edition* (ISBN 0-7360-4089-7), YMCA Program Store, 800-747-0089

Budget

When you budget for this course, take the following costs into account:

- The equipment listed previously
- Prep time for the instructor
- Class time for the instructor
- Final paperwork time for the instructor
- Certification fee for national ($8)
- Copies of course handouts
- Manuals for participants

Promotion

Begin thinking about promotion by identifying your audience. Those who attend lifeguard certification classes are usually young, between 16 and their early twenties. Young participants want to work as lifeguards. For many, it will be their first job after babysitting or fast-food restaurants.

Adults who participate may be fulfilling certification or recertification requirements to become scout leaders or YMCA swim coaches or instructors. Another group of adults could be home owners with backyard pools or parents wanting to know how to protect their families on the water.

Older adults may be anxious about completing the physical components of the course. Younger participants may not have the maturity to successfully complete the course.

Here are some key points to use in your promotion for lifeguard classes:

- Get your first job. *Or* Get ready for summer employment.
- Be prepared to pursue training for other positions within the YMCA, such as swim instructor or coach.
- Save a life—learn CPR, first aid, and lifeguarding.
- Get certified for that volunteer scout position.
- Save a life, be a hero.
- The program supports the YMCA mission.
- Financial aid is available for participants.

- (For parents) YMCA lifeguards must be at least 16 years old, so they are mature enough to take on responsibility for people's lives.
- (For parents) YMCA lifeguards must be recertified every two years so they are always aware of the latest information on lifeguarding.
- Recruit people for lifeguard classes all the time. Get connected with high schools and colleges, swim teams, recreation departments, and parent groups. Contact church groups, Boy Scout/Girl Scout troops, teachers, and swim coaches.
- At your YMCA, talk to lap swimmers, regular masters swimmers, or parents of young children about whether they'd like to become guards. Mail notices of lifeguard training to your membership. Advertise in your YMCA's program brochure and newsletter.
- If you create a flyer, use the program descriptions found in *On the Guard II* (4th ed.). Send flyers to local scouting chapters, high schools, youth groups, and doctors' and dentists' offices.
- Finally, for publicity, use cable TV announcements, PSAs, and press releases. Enroll your lifeguards in a local or regional competition and seek press coverage of the results.

Administrative Tips

Here are some common questions asked by those who want to participate in the lifeguard training and by parents:

- Where can I work when I'm done?
- How can I recertify?
- How long is this training good for?
- Do I have to know how to swim?
- (From parent) If my child takes this class, will she or he automatically pass?
- (From parent) How many classes can my child miss and still pass the class?
- (From parent) If my child turns 16 during the session, can he or she take the class?

These are some common problems that arise in lifeguard classes:

- Parents are upset when their child doesn't pass.
- Participants insist they must pass because they've already been offered a job.
- Members are upset because of the pool time required for lifeguard instruction.
- The instructor is unclear about her or his expectations for students.

Finally, here are some signs of trouble with your lifeguard certification program:

- Not very many students are passing.
- Students want refunds.
- The instructor is not following the training design.
- The number of students per instructor is too high.
- Not enough scenarios are practiced.
- Not enough equipment is available for practice.
- There's not enough time or space in the pool for practice.

- Students don't understand how YMCA lifeguard certification differs from certifications by other organizations.
- Non-YMCA pool administrators say they cannot accept YMCA lifeguard certification.

Here are some ways you can help make your aquatic safety programs successful:

- Communicate with staff leadership regularly. Be able to answer questions about their classes and programs.
- Observe the classes regularly. Make sure the instructors are teaching according to program standards. Provide regular feedback to the instructors.
- Review the class agenda and make sure the required course components are included. See that instructors follow the Program Trainer Orientation training design.
- Have an evaluation program in place.
- Warn instructors to be alert to students who are having difficulty and to deal with them early.
- Keep costs down to encourage participation. Offer lifeguard classes at no cost to future employees.
- Choose a Lifeguard Instructor who is CPR and first aid instructor certified and offer those courses before the lifeguard classes.
- Teach AED and oxygen administration.
- Take the programs to the site and target markets in which you are working.
- Recruit the necessary staff before the start.
- Have all appropriate forms and handouts ready for classes.
- Listen during class for issues that might arise.
- Plan room spaces early. Make sure that the rooms and supplies are available.
- Remain supportive during the class.
- Provide paid prep time for the class.
- Order books on time.
- Process in-house check requests and other paperwork in a timely fashion.
- Obtain volunteers from the community for some parts of the course. For example, ask a local attorney to talk about lifeguards' liability; ask a scuba instructor to teach the basics of scuba; or ask a local doctor to talk about spinal injury management and blood-borne pathogens. Be sure to schedule additional course time for these presentations.

Recreational Swimming and Special Situations

Most YMCAs make some type of recreational swimming available to their members. This may be lap swimming or other types of swims or fitness activities. You should consider this to be a program, just as you would swim lessons or water fitness.

It's also likely that your pool may be rented by private groups, that your YMCA may have family nights, or that the pool will be made available to children in the YMCA child care or day camp programs. You will need to prepare for these special situations as well.

RECREATIONAL SWIMMING

Many different types of programs can be included in your recreational swimming program area, including these:

- Specialty swims such as swim around the world or the 10,000-mile club
- Adult lap or open lap swims
- Family swims
- Swims in which people may use flotation devices and inflatables
- Teen swims
- Water walking
- Daily workouts, with a "thought for the day" posted
- Stroke technique coaching once a month
- Flick and Float (watching a movie while floating in the pool)

One way to ensure that lap swims run smoothly is to post lap swimming etiquette rules. This is especially effective if you designate each lane to be for slow, medium, or fast swimmers and have the lifeguard help swimmers determine which type of lane to use. Put medium and slow lanes against the walls and fast lanes toward the center of the pool to keep participants from crossing the fast lane to get to the slower lane. If you only have two lanes available, designate each one for a different speed, and think about what two speeds would be best for your swimmers. (Fast and medium are usually good.) Try to have at least one lap swim during prime time, as members expect to be able to swim during that time period.

Here are some examples of etiquette rules:

- Swim on the right side of the lane, counterclockwise.
- Choose the lane that matches your ability. If you are constantly passing or being passed, switch to a more appropriate lane.
- Pass slower swimmers within five yards of the wall to avoid midlane collisions.
- Lightly touch the foot of a slower swimmer as a signal that you want to pass.
- If you are the slower swimmer and your foot is touched, stay at the wall and wait to be passed.
- Do not stand in the middle of lane when you are at the wall. Instead, rest by the corners so other swimmers can continue to do flip turns.
- Use common sense, and remember our core values of caring, honesty, respect, and responsibility.

Here are few tips for running a successful recreational swimming program:

- Post signs to designate usage areas in your pool (e.g., classes, lap, recreation)
- Treat lap and recreational swimming as a program.
- Tell lifeguards to perform a water test for children before allowing them to enter the deep end (see a description in chapter 11).
- Make sure lifeguards know the zones for which they are responsible.
- Include a clear description for each swim in your program brochure. Explain them in as few words as possible.
- Post schedules in your program brochure and make them readily available to members.
- Keep your schedule consistent and avoid making many changes. If a change in schedule is needed, give members enough warning.

Help your staff to do a better job with recreational swims by doing the following:

- Give staff good responses for common complaints.
- Get to know the regulars and introduce them to new staff.
- Support staff on the decisions they make.
- Have good systems in place for dealing with those who regularly break the rules.

Try some of these in-service training ideas with your staff:

- Discuss how to deal with the regular complainer.
- Discuss how to work with members in a positive manner when they break a rule.
- Require staff to lap swim during lap swim times so that they have an understanding of what patrons are experiencing. (Do not do this while they are on duty.)
- Describe your YMCA's guidelines for inflatables, if you have this equipment.
- Discuss how to use values to guide decisions.

Equipment you should consider for recreational swims includes these items:

- Lane lines
- Lifelines
- Kickboards

- Pull buoys
- Fins
- Paddles
- PFDs
- Signs to mark lane speeds

When you budget for recreational programs, include the cost of equipment plus regular staffing costs. Keep in mind you may have to add more staff during large swims. Track participation levels to determine when you may need to schedule more staff.

Here are some common questions that members or parents have about the recreational programs. Prepare answers to these questions and share them with your aquatics and front-desk staff.

- Why is the pool so hot/cold?
- Why do you keep taking my time away?
- Why do you only allow this group to swim at this time?
- What do you mean that my water walking is in the way?
- Why do I have to stay with my kids during family swim?
- What equipment can I use during this time? Can I use my inner tube or inflatable mattress, inflatable arm bands, or other inflatables?

If you notice any of the following situations occurring, take action by talking to members and staff to see how they can be resolved:

- Members trying to make their own schedules by requesting special times for their interests

- Frequent comments from staff that members are not following the rules
- Children being separated from their parents during recreational swim times

Such situations can be indicators of other issues that need to be addressed.

Finally, here are some good ideas to increase participation in recreational programs:

- For lap swimmers, use regular incentive programs such as mileage programs that include prizes and recognition.
- Periodically schedule a staff member to help lap swimmers improve their strokes and design workout plans.
- Have equipment readily available for members to retrieve.
- Plan family games and activities for family nights, teen activities for teen nights, or childrens' games for Y-Guides swims. You can also use such activities periodically during recreational swims.
- Post your pool schedule whenever it is updated.
- Encourage staff to help members meet other members that come during the same time (see chapter 4 on member involvement).
- Encourage staff to have short, positive interactions with members.
- Take action to resolve members' regular complaints.
- Encourage staff to learn regular participants' names and to greet them as they enter the pool area.

SPECIAL SITUATIONS

A number of special situations can arise at your pool. Your YMCA may allow private groups to rent your pool, especially for birthday parties, and it may also hold special family events. It is also likely that your child care and day camp programs may include either swim lessons or recreational swimming as part of their overall programming.

Here are some ideas on how to best handle such situations:

- *Pool rentals and birthday parties.* Advertise in your YMCA's brochure, with community groups and churches, on bulletin boards, and with special flyers at the front desk. Having inflatables may increase interest in rentals and birthday parties. Make sure a written agreement has been filled out and signed ahead of time and that all fees have been paid. The agreement should include information such as the name and phone number of the group's representative, the exact times of the rental and setup/cleanup, the pool rules and emergency procedures, expectations, the role of the lifeguard, the expected number of swimmers and the ratio of adults to kids, and a waiver of liability. (See chapter 3 for more detail on how to develop a rental agreement.) Have in place a system for updating any changes in the number of participants. Follow all rules that would be in place for any other YMCA activity; for example, do swim tests to decide who should swim in the deep end. Have a designated staff person as the contact on the day of the party/rental. Offer facility tours to parents that attend the pool rental or birthday party.

- *Family events.* Advertise family events in your membership newsletter, brochure, and throughout the YMCA. Have a system in place for sign-up before the event so that you know the number of people expected. Ask for help from other branch departments. Make family events a part of the program or aquatics committee's responsibilities. Involve volunteers in the planning and operation of these events.

- *Child care and day camp swim lessons.* Mention swim lessons in the child care and day camp advertisements. Promote swim lessons during child care and day camp sign-up. Go to the child care or day camp site and speak to the kids. Educate the program directors as to the objectives of the lessons and develop a rapport with them to gain their support for the swim lessons program. Ask them to review their licensing agency's codes regarding the swim lessons activity and ratios. Encourage child care and day camp staff to assist aquatics instructors with lessons.

- *Child care and day camp recreational swimming.* Maintain all rules and regulations that would apply to any recreational swimming activity. Develop an effective and efficient system for reviewing rules and swimming ability and for getting participants into and out of the pool. Utilize child care and day camp staff to watch the children and to handle discipline problems.

For all these special situations, maintain the same ratios of lifeguard to participants or instructor to participants as for regular programming. If anything, you may want to add staff for these situations, as sometimes giving the swim tests and beginning activities may take longer than usual. Be sure to add the appropriate number of staff when using inflatables. For more information, see chapter 19 on camp waterfronts and the YMCA of the USA Aquatics Guidelines in appendix 4.

Support your staff when they handle special situations by doing the following:

- Build a good relationship between the child care/day camp staff and the aquatics staff. Have them meet each other before the group comes to swim for the first time.
- Train staff on the challenges of working with different groups and other staff.
- Be visible at special events, and have a supervisor at all such events.

Here are some in-service training ideas for your staff:

- Practice scenarios and procedures related to special situations.
- Ask participants to evaluate the events or programs. Then review and read the evaluations at the in-service training after the event or program.
- Train staff on the setup and use of inflatables.

Finally, here are some situations that might occur that should alert you to problems:

- *Pool rentals and birthday parties.* Rental agreements are not signed or paid for before use. Participants want special treatment and don't want to follow pool rules. The group shows up early or late. Group members are using alcohol or illegal drugs. The group has a lot of young children and few adults.
- *Family events.* Too many participants show up.
- *Child care and day camp swim lessons.* Child care or day camp staff are not present.
- *Child care and day camp recreational swimming.* Child care or day camp staff are not maintaining the normal operating ratio. Staff members are not following rules. Staff members spend too much time playing in the water rather than monitoring swimmers.

Plan with your staff what to do if any of these situations should occur.

YMCA Water Fitness

YMCA Water Fitness is water exercise, but that doesn't mean it's just a light exercise program for elderly ladies. In fact, water fitness can provide heavy duty workouts for athletes and can build muscles as well as cardiorespiratory endurance. It can also help people with medical conditions or disabilities to get a more vigorous workout than they could on land. The great thing about water fitness is that it is accessible to almost everyone of every age, with no swimming skills needed, but it is effective only if instructors know how to program exercise in the water as opposed to on land.

In this chapter, we start by explaining why water fitness is needed and in what ways water exercise is better than exercise on land. We give you a list of possible types of programs, then describe the instructor training available in this area. Next we discuss staffing, as well as how you can cross-train staff from both aquatics and health and fitness departments to lead water fitness classes. This is followed by some ideas you can give your instructors on how to encourage program participation and be responsive to participants' needs. Then we move to special sections on personal training and instructor safety. Facility and equipment needs are next, with a bit on budgeting, followed by some ways to promote your water fitness programs effectively. The chapter ends with some administrative tips to help you avoid problems and improve your programs.

WHO NEEDS A WATER FITNESS PROGRAM?

Approximately 70 to 80 percent of Americans do *not* engage in physical activity regularly, leading to higher health care costs and a poorer quality of life (Satcher, 2001). Low fitness caused by inactivity is as harmful as having diabetes, smoking cigars, or having high blood pressure and high cholesterol (Blair, 2001). Americans are also becoming fatter. According to Kyle J. McInnis, Sc.D. (2001), associate professor at the University of Massachusetts-Boston, "one of every two adults in the USA is overweight or obese." In a report by the American Council on Exercise (1999), the estimated cost of obesity in the United States is $238 billion, with lack of exercise being the number-one cause of the current 22.4 percent rate of obesity.

Inactivity and obesity are only some of the conditions affecting a healthy lifestyle; others include stress, high blood pressure, and smoking. Our members, who are more diverse than ever, seek new health goals to prevent or manage such conditions, which may lead to dysfunction. The health of people in the United States depends in part on fitness professionals who can respond to a wide range of needs and objectives. YMCAs have the opportunity to set the standard for responding to and caring for members with diverse programs that target a lifetime of activity.

America's population is also aging. People over 55 look forward to a long journey through life, one full of enriching moments. A good quality of life will mean not just physical functioning, but an active life, one full of purpose and meaning. According to Waneen Spirduso (1995), the mix includes the following:

- Health and fitness, including physical function, energy, vitality, and general health
- Cognitive health, feelings of well-being, life satisfaction, and emotional and cognitive functioning
- Social functioning and recreational activities
- Economic status

Offering fun and effective activities in our facilities can keep people out of the doctor's office and change unfit people into happier, more active members. Facilities that do not market to and "care for" the new diverse market of sedentary or overweight people and those needing special programs could be in financial trouble.

Linking of exercise programs with health care professionals may grow as physician training evolves to include counseling on lifestyle activities. Physicians typically are trained to refer patients to community programs and hope that facilities can provide the proper guidance in nutrition, exercise, and healthy lifestyles. YMCAs should be ready to respond to these referrals by delivering programs that meet the objectives recommended by physicians, produce positive effects, and are so much fun that participants make a lifetime commitment to a healthy lifestyle.

With new health and fitness trainings, including the YMCA Water Fitness for Health program, YMCAs have an opportunity to be leaders in lifestyle health and to help make a difference in this country. Comprehensive lifestyle education for the wide diversity of people attending our facilities requires good education for staff and a wide variety of activity choices that encompass individual needs. Water exercise is an important component of a health program that allows people to work within their abilities within the health care continuum (figure 16.1), even as their health needs change during their lives.

YMCA Water Fitness targets both the apparently healthy and those with health challenges who have been cleared by their health care providers to participate in a community program. Water's properties provide a broad range of intensity options, so participants are taught how to take charge of their own exercise by using simple progressions. Participants assume the responsibility to individualize exercise intensity according to where they are on the continuum.

Ill................Not ill (sedentary)	Physically active..........Physically fit........Athletes
(*Physicians*)	(*Fitness educators*)

Figure 16.1   The health care continuum.

WHY DO WATER EXERCISE?

Water provides a liquid weight machine that offers resistance work in functional ranges of motion for daily living, while the support of buoyancy cushions impact against joints. As participants age or experience physical changes from conditions such as injury or pregnancy, they can modify their training programs for comfort and safety.

Simply dropping land exercises into the pool will not ensure effective training results. Instructors must design exercises to take into account the properties of water and their effect against the body. The YMCA Water Fitness for Health program teaches instructors how to design water-specific exercises for best results. People who are unable or unwilling to exercise on land may be able to meet their health objectives by training in the pool using purposeful exercises that produce results. Those results can then be quantified using simple field assessments included in the program.

According to IDEA Fitness Program Surveys (1999), the use of water programs is growing. Between 1996 and 1997, managers of fitness facilities responding to IDEA's surveys reported an increase of 12 percent in water fitness activities, with 46 percent of all health facilities now offering classes. The age range of participants has also changed, with an increase of 23 percent in facilities reporting participants 56 years old and older. Water fitness classes rank sixth as the most frequently appearing programs on facility schedules (five days a week).

Water exercise has some unique benefits:

• *Lifetime skills:* Water provides a private and safe environment in which lifetime exercise skills are developed and can be performed as the body changes over time. Swimming skills are not necessary with vertical water exercise; however, participants must develop specific exercise skills to ensure safe body mechanics as they train in the "liquid weight machine" of the pool.

- *Impact:* Impact can be personally adjusted from about 50 percent of body weight at waist depth to zero in deep water, making the exercises comfortable. Beginning exercisers, participants with balance problems, or those who need to limit impact can easily adjust according to their needs.

- *Buoyancy:* Buoyancy encourages freedom of movement without the fear of falling down. Participants can practice large ranges of motion and challenge both balance and recovery to stand skills with ease and support. Higher intensity jump training can be practiced with a lower risk of injury (Sanders, 2000).

- *Balance:* Balance in the water may be at the hips, the chest, or points in between based on water depth, body buoyancy, equipment used, and body position (vertical, tilted, or horizontal). Participants can challenge their core stabilizers to respond during the entire workout differently than on land.

- *Hydrostatic pressure:* Hydrostatic pressure pushes against the chest and body. This helps strengthen the breathing system so breathing on land becomes easier (Becker and Cole, 1997). Hydrostatic pressure aids venous circulation and contributes to reduction in edema or swelling, which is especially helpful for prenatal participants.

- *Functional rehabilitation:* Aquatics therapy has been documented to be beneficial for functional rehabilitation (Koury, 1996). However, participants shouldn't wait until they are injured to hit the pool; they should learn how to work the water to prevent injury. Then, if they do need rehabilitation, their water skills will be developed so they can work through rehab and continue their exercise program, using the gentle buoyancy of water to modify and protect the affected area.

- *Improved performance:* Water training has been documented to improve or maintain land performance for a wide variety of people, including recreational and competitive runners and older adults who want to improve their activities of daily living on land, such as stair climbing, speed walking, agility, sit to stand, and balance (Bushman et al., 1997; Morrow, Jensen, and Peace, 1996; Sanders, Constantino, Rippee, et al., 1997; Simmons and Hansen, 1996).

- *Resisted movement:* Liquid resistance surrounds the body, providing on-demand work in many planes of movement, overloading and mimicking real-life movements. The resistance of movement performed at an average speed is estimated to be about 12 to 15 times that of air, based on water's being about 800 times more dense than air (DiPrampero, 1986). As all movements can be resisted in the water, muscular conditioning can be completed efficiently. For example, biceps and triceps can be overloaded concentrically during the same exercise.

Combined cardiorespiratory and strength classes is one of the top fitness trends, with water able to target both muscular and cardiorespiratory endurance effectively and efficiently. Group resistance training is popular, and the "liquid weight machine" of water, along with a variety of equipment for overloading, allows students to individualize resistance work while working out as a group.

- *Progressions:* Intensity progressions can be individualized, and intensity can be regulated by participants "on demand" by using variations in speed, surface area, and water currents. After the basic skills are developed, participants can adjust their own intensity and still work with the group.

- *Equipment to get eccentric:* Most resistance work performed in water targets muscular endurance and concentric work. Water-specific equipment must be added to expand the range of resistance available to progress an exercise and provide the opportunity for eccentric contractions.

The use of group exercise equipment is increasing, with one of the largest increases being in water fitness (IDEA Fitness Program Surveys, 1999). Between 1996 and 1997, the number of facilities that use water fitness equipment in group exercise increased by 20 percent. To provide a progressive program, facilities will need to invest in equipment or modify existing equipment for special needs so participants can progress along the health care continuum.

- *Compound movements:* Compound movements such as lifting a load while jogging can be safely overloaded at slower speeds (one-half to one-third compared to land) for training proper biomechanics during functional living patterns such as walking and lifting a load onto a shelf.

- *Weight management:* Water's resistance can provide an effective environment for weight management, as is shown in several studies. Walking in water at xiphoid level at two miles per hour required greater energy expenditure when compared to walking at the same speed on a treadmill (Napoletan and Hicks, 1995). Water-specific jumping jax performed in the pool using an aquatic step elicited a higher $\dot{V}O_2$max when compared to a basic step jax move performed on land (Evans and Cureton, 1998). Deep-water running at 76 percent of maximum heart rate compared favorably to running on land at a nine-minute-mile pace, with both estimated at 11.5 kilocalories (kcal) per minute (Michaud et al., 1995). A 30-minute water running session could "cost" your members approximately 345 kcal without the impact of land. The American College of Sports Medicine (1995) recommends that intensity be high enough to expend approximately 300 kcal per session with a three-day-per-week program.

- *Intensity and volume without risks:* By using buoyancy and resistance, participants may be able to pace themselves as they gradually increase the volume and intensity of training, while working more comfortably with less impact and without increasing the risk of orthopedic injury.

- *Abdominals always:* Water currents work against the body to constantly challenge the trunk core muscles to maintain proper alignment as participants stop, start, and change directions during a movement. They work their abs the entire time, functionally—and vertically!

- *Purpose play:* People of a wide variety of ages, fitness levels, and abilities can put water resistance and buoyancy to work during many fun sports play drills that allow their bodies to keep up with the athletes they are in their minds! They can run, jump, and ski moguls safely while buoyancy and resistance support and slow movements to both protect and train their bodies.

PROGRAM TYPES

Many types of water exercise programs are possible; here are a few:

- *Shallow-water workout:* This full-body workout is a combination of cardiorespiratory endurance, muscle conditioning, and interval training. A variety of equipment is used, including gloves, bands, and balls.

- *Deep-water workout:* This full-body workout, a combination of cardiorespiratory endurance, muscle conditioning, and interval training, is conducted in the deep end of the pool. Equipment used may include fins, gloves, and belts. Participants can achieve an increased range of motion using nonimpact movements.

- *Combo workout:* The combo workout combines shallow- and deep-water components.

- *Sports conditioning workout:* Such a workout will typically involve high- and low-intensity combinations of sets for designated time periods. Movements may be specific to particular sports.

• *Active Older Adults (AOA) Water Fitness Workout:* This workout is designed for Active Older Adults. It may include components of shallow- or deep-water workouts.

• *Arthritis Foundation YMCA Aquatic Program:* The warmth, buoyancy, and resistive property of water can help decrease pain and stiffness and improve or maintain joint flexibility for those with arthritis. All participants must have signed medical release forms from their doctors.

• *Arthritis Foundation YMCA Aquatic Program Plus:* This class provides an enjoyable and safe recreational water exercise program that includes exercises and activities designed to promote functional endurance as well as musculoskeletal flexibility and strength for individuals with arthritis.

Participants should (1) have functional and relatively comfortable shoulder and elbow motion; (2) be able to tolerate a 5-minute aquatics endurance component or 15 minutes of standing or walking on land without excessive pain, fatigue, or shortness of breath; (3) require no more than minimal assistance to enter or exit the pool; (4) feel comfortable and confident in water; and (5) have signed medical release forms from their doctors.

• *Personal Training:* This is one-on-one training utilizing water fitness principles. (See later section on "Personal Training.")

• *Skills and Drills:* This is a basic skill class that meets once a week. The class format is up to the participants. Basic water fitness skills and use of equipment are taught and practiced in a group that is smaller than a regular class, with more one-on-one attention.

• *Water Fitness Workout:* This workout is a 45-minute "all depths" workout in which participants learn not only the fundamentals skills of working out in the water, but also how to target their health and fitness objectives with safe, effective, and water-specific exercises. They learn how to improve their skills and increase their intensity to get the most out of their workouts. This class is for apparently healthy people of all skill and fitness levels.

• *Water Fitness Challenge:* The 45-minute "challenge class" is for skilled and fit participants. It offers an opportunity to "turn up the intensity" of their workouts. This class targets health and fitness objectives by combining a variety of teaching methods and equipment to help maximize training. Participants "gear up" with interval sets, work the circuit course, "flip and wave" with fins, and "jump train" with steps.

• *Buddy Classes:* Parents and kids team up for a workout—kids are in buoyancy devices so parents can move them around as their "resistance" devices.

• *Group Personal Training:* These are specialty classes for groups such as overweight individuals or those with multiple sclerosis or Parkinson's disease.

In all courses, try to maintain an instructor-to-student ratio of 1:25, although you may have to vary it depending on the pool and the type of class. Always have an appropriate number of lifeguards on duty during water fitness classes.

INSTRUCTOR TRAINING

With the addition of the YMCA Water Fitness for Health and Active Older Adult Water Fitness courses, the YMCA has the opportunity to set the standard in the industry for a health-targeted, responsive water program. Currently, no water exercise certification is available in the United States that meets national standards and criteria for certification.

YMCAs could open these certification courses to non-YMCA professionals by advertising courses locally and by making the prerequisite classes easily available to non-YMCA professionals. Recruiting fitness instructors from outside the YMCAs would hopefully grow your team of professionals.

Note: WaterFit™/Wave Aerobics® offers ACE/AEA-approved professional certificate of training courses, and they are the foundation for the new YMCA certifications. After successful completion of these courses—WaterFit/Speedo Aquatic Fitness System Instructor Training Course and The Golden Waves, Functional Water Fitness Training Courses—candidates are eligible for YMCA certification by completing the YMCA prerequisites and paying the certification fee.

Prerequisites for YMCA certification include the following:

YMCA Water Fitness Instructor (YWFI)

Be at least 16 years old

Hold a current YMCA Lifeguard or YMCA Aquatic Safety Assistant (YASA) certification

Hold current CPR (including adult, child, infant, and two-rescuer CPR and obstructed airway maneuver) and first-aid certifications

YMCA Active Older Adults Water Fitness Instructor

Be at least 18 years old

Hold a current YMCA Lifeguard or YMCA Aquatic Safety Assistant certification

Hold current CPR (including adult, child, infant, and two-rescuer CPR and obstructed airway maneuver) and first-aid certifications

(Recommended) Working with Active Older Adults certification

The YMCA Water Fitness for Health program and text are designed to bring participants the most current information about water exercise, bridging science and research to pool exercise, using water-specific progressions that maximize the properties of water for better living on land. The text was written by a group of fitness and medical professionals who also work as health educators.

Both courses, YMCA Water Fitness for Health Instructor and Active Older Adult Water Fitness Instructor, are comprehensive and challenging. Candidates are expected to learn basic exercise science, physiology, and muscle and joint actions, as well as how to apply exercise training principles to the water environment using research-based information. The Active Older Adults course examines functional water fitness progressions and modifications for about 15 medical conditions. Both courses require instructors to learn how to perform exercises as technical skills, then learn how to teach and coach students so they too master those skills.

YMCA Water Fitness for Health should be the basis for all water fitness programs in your pools, as it incorporates the YMCA mission and objectives. This manual should be a resource for you and your instructors as you develop, manage, and grow your water fitness programs:

• Chapters 1-12 are for the water fitness program for healthy adults, covering workouts with specific guidelines, leadership, safety, fitness principles, research, physical laws of water, use of equipment, and teaching responsively.

• Chapters 13-16 discuss functional training for those with special considerations. Besides older adults, these populations include people with orthopedic, neurological, or cardiovascular conditions or general medical conditions such as pregnancy, obesity, diabetes, or mastectomy recovery. This is truly an exciting new way that YMCAs throughout the country can meet their communities' needs.

Water Fitness Instructor is a 20-hour training. It is best held in modules, like a lifeguard course, perhaps once per week for six or seven weeks or twice a week for three weeks or on a Friday evening and all day Saturday for two weekends. Breaking this training up into small parts helps participants process and remember the material. *Before attending the training,* all instructors must have read their manuals and completed the study guide. Stress to your staff that the course will be difficult to follow for those who have not prepared properly. Videos are also available to review during class or on an individual basis. If you are not able to hold the training at your facility, get your staff training through Program Schools. Contact the YMCA of the USA for information on schools in your area.

A motivated, properly trained instructor will help motivate your staff. Ideally, one of your instructors will become a Water Fitness Trainer. If that is not possible, check to see if a trainer is available from a nearby branch or association.

Use *YMCA Water Fitness for Health* for your staff meetings and in-service training sessions. All instructors should have access to the manual to read chapters 1 through 12. You might try holding monthly or quarterly meetings to review different parts of the book; for example, you could schedule the following:

- *Meeting 1.* Chapters 1-3, including a pool tour and discussion of how to set up for classes, instructors' administrative duties, and emergency procedures for staff.

- *Meeting 2.* Chapters 4-5, reviewing anatomy and biomechanics through muscle charts, muscle cards, and the *YMCA Personal Training Instructor Manual.*

- *Meeting 3.* Chapters 6-7, studying water fitness research and the physical laws and properties of water. This can be combined with a pool session using some of the technical drills from chapter 7. Have each instructor explain one of the principles and present drills in the pool.

- *Meeting 4.* Chapters 8-9, covering fundamental skills and exercise design and specificity of training and training guidelines.

- *Meeting 5.* Chapter 10, designing workouts using SWEAT. This can be both a classroom and a pool session.

- *Meeting 6.* Chapters 11-12 on teaching responsively and using equipment. This can be both a classroom and a pool session.

Once your instructors have been certified as YMCA Water Fitness Instructors, those who are interested should start learning the functional training portion of the book (chapters 13-16). They really need to understand the material in chapters 1-12 before progressing to the rest of the manual. Once you have a core group of instructors interested in the functional training, schedule a YMCA trainer to hold the Active Older Adult Water Fitness Instructor Certification. This 16-hour class can also be taught in modules. Topics include functional training, exercise considerations for older adults, guidelines for working with special populations, and administration of activities of daily living (ADL) assessments.

Your staff should review the manual periodically and take the renewal courses to stay certified and continue their knowledge of water fitness. The manual includes program forms, workouts, cue cards, and assessments of ADLs that will enhance your water fitness classes.

The scope and breadth of the information in the manual can be overwhelming. It needs to be introduced gradually to the members as instructors themselves absorb the materials and become comfortable with the new concepts. Support your staff with reference materials such as videos that provide underwater footage and workouts that complement the training and text. The videos, along with continuing education workshops, conferences, and new equipment, will help your program progress and keep your staff responsive to your members' needs.

YMCA Water Fitness for Health includes information for advanced programs that can be taught during continuing education workshops. Each of the 27 special conditions included in the book could be offered as an advanced training. For example, you could hold classes that target specific medical conditions such as multiple sclerosis, fibromyalgia, back pain, Parkinson's disease, or pregnancy. These small-group or personal training programs could be used to respond to the needs of your community and to work with health care providers. To provide advanced fitness training (which relates to participants' skill level as well as fitness level) and training for competitive athletes, create "challenge" classes that target very fit members. Offer kids' and "buddy" training classes, which can bring families together in the pool for fitness, enhance your swim and land fitness programs, and provide more multigenerational programs.

Since water fitness can successfully meet the objectives of a wide range of members, a water fitness program based on health, fun, and lifetime skills can increase participation. A water fitness program for health that dovetails with land programs increases choices and offers variety for better adherence. The "one size fits all" concept of a fitness program simply doesn't apply here, and the more choices you offer members, the more successful you will be at providing opportunities for lifetime participation.

STAFF

Having knowledgeable and enthusiastic water fitness staff is crucial to the quality of your water fitness programs. Here are the qualifications you should look for in candidates, some suggested interview questions and auditioning methods, and ideas for monitoring and evaluating staff once they've been hired.

Characteristics and Qualifications

As you search for water fitness instructors, look for candidates who

- are trained and certified in YMCA Water Fitness;
- work well with adults (or the water fitness population);
- are able to follow up on participant attendance and progress;
- are able to give specific feedback to participants regarding water fitness techniques and health and fitness principles;
- are able to develop, organize, and coordinate special events;
- care about students first, rather than their own workouts;
- stay current on fitness information;
- are open to learning from other instructors; and
- are open to cross-training using water and land skills.

We recommend that instructors have the following training or certifications:

- Current CPR and first aid
- YMCA Aquatic Safety Assistant or YMCA Lifeguard

Instructors who plan to teach water fitness, older adult, or arthritis classes should also have these certifications:

- YMCA Water Fitness Instructor or YMCA AOA Water Fitness Instructor
- Arthritis Foundation/YMCA Aquatic Program Instructor

You can view a sample job description for a water fitness instructor on the YMCA of the USA Web site.

Because in YMCAs, water fitness programs are generally separate from group exercise programs, you can extend an invitation to land instructors who may be interested in expanding their teaching skills to include water fitness. In such cases, you can observe the land instructors' classes to assess their overall interpersonal communication skills, class atmosphere, attention to safety, and overall teaching ability. You can then offer a structured water fitness training program for land instructors that takes their knowledge base into account and focuses on specific water fitness principles and teaching techniques.

Interviewing Instructor Candidates

While general interviewing questions can be found in chapter 5, here are some more specific ones you might use when talking to water fitness instructor candidates:

- Describe a typical class.
- What types of equipment do you use during water fitness classes?
- What continuing education workshops have you attended within the past year?
- What makes a good water fitness instructor?
- How do you motivate participants?
- How can you demonstrate character development in your class?
- Where and when did you receive your water fitness information and training?
- What fitness magazines or books have you read recently?
- Do you know the American College of Sports Medicine (ACSM) guidelines for working out?
- What is your current fitness workout?
- Explain proper body alignment.
- When did you last participate in a group exercise class? Explain the components of the class and the traits of the instructor.
- What are the components of a water fitness class?
- How does exercising in the water differ from exercising on land?
- Name ways to protect yourself from injury while teaching on deck.
- Name some ways to offer specific feedback to class participants.
- How do you find out the goals of your class participants?
- Who was the last instructor to give you feedback on classes? What were her or his comments?
- What are your goals as a water fitness instructor?
- What is the next course/training you would like to attend?
- Name some ways to educate your class about the YMCA and healthy lifestyles.
- How can your class participants have fun during class?

Besides interviewing candidates, you may want to have a fitness class audition. Many facilities ask potential instructors to perform a short routine on deck or in the water for a make-believe group of participants. However, you may also choose one of the following options:

- Gather a small group of participants at the end of a class and offer them an incentive (such as complementary guest passes) for staying in the water so the candidate can lead them through a short workout.

- Ask the candidate for a videotape of his or her most popular class. The tape will allow you to see the instructor in his or her natural environment and let you better observe the instructor's teaching skills and interaction with participants.

Monitoring and Evaluating Staff

When you have new instructors, pair them up with other successful water exercise instructors. Assign them to observe the veteran instructors' classes and ask them to document three new things they learned and three skills they need to work on. After a few weeks of observation, allow the new instructors to present the class warm-up or some other small class segment. Finally, have the instructors schedule mock classes using their friends as participants, and videotape them teaching these "classes." Review the tapes with them to identify their strengths and areas for improvement.

Periodically attend or audit water fitness classes so you can give instructors feedback on a regular basis. Do not tie your evaluations to merit raises, as this may make staff overly anxious. However, do take into account how well instructors implement your suggestions for improvements. (*Note:* If possible, teach water fitness classes yourself on a regular basis. This helps instructors respect your knowledge and accept your feedback.)

See that all water fitness class participants know how to scull, how to recover to a stand from a horizontal position, how to maintain proper body alignment, and how to keep themselves warm. They should also know how to monitor their own exercise intensity. Participants should be allowed to exercise at their own pace—not on a beat. Finally, the instructor should teach participants progressions and modifications as needed.

A quick way to evaluate classes is to use a "went well/do differently" format. For example, for an experienced instructor, you may need to focus on only three points in each area. Figure 16.2 shows an example.

For a more formal evaluation, use a form similar to the one in figure 16.3 to help you when you observe classes. Share your observations with instructors, and help them improve their teaching skills when necessary.

You also should evaluate the exercises used in classes using the following questions:

- What is the purpose of the exercise or workout?
- Does it meet the exercise training objective according to physiological criteria?
- What properties of water create the work?
- Can the body stay warm?
- Is the movement safe, effective, and functional?
- Can it done differently or better?

Went Well/Do Differently

1. **Excellent movement progression and use of pool.** Rework the cool-down part of the class to include a re-warm-up in order to avoid a drop in participants' body temperature.

2. **Super enthusiasm and individual coaching/attention.** If you'd set out some of the equipment ahead of time, there wouldn't be as much time spent on set up in the middle of class.

3. **Explanation of muscle groups and attention to proper posture.** I'm not sure what you meant about working the deltoids on the shoulder raises. As buoyancy is assisting the deltoids, most of the work is done by the lats. Let's chat about that tomorrow.

Figure 16.2   Sample evaluation using the "went well/do differently" format.

YMCA Water Fitness Instructor Evaluation

Name: _____

Date: _____

Evaluated by: _____

Legend:

+ = Proficient   / = Adequate   − = Needs improvement   NA= Not applicable

Instructor Considerations

___ Wears appropriate attire.

___ Wears protective/supportive footwear.

___ Uses teaching aids.

___ Can be seen by students.

___ Acknowledges class participants before beginning.

Deck Demos

___ Executes moves safely, with low impact.

___ Uses proper body alignment.

___ Performs deck demo at water speed.

___ Performs a water-specific demo.

___ Manages class well.

___ Class understands and follows demo moves.

___ Has appropriate transition timing.

Communication

___ Uses safe and effective vocal cueing.

___ Inflection, pitch, and enunciation are good.

___ Projects, rather than screaming.

___ Keeps eye contact with participants and uses their names.

___ Interacts with and shows interest in the class.

___ Describes exercises and movements well.

___ Is enthusiastic and motivates.

___ Gives specific correctional feedback.

___ Gives participants tips on performing exercises and on health and fitness.

General Criteria

___ Uses and explains how to apply properties of water for good quality of movement.

___ Teaches at least two intensity options for every exercise.

___ Explains how to create and encourages use of an individually challenging pace.

___ Explains and monitors exercise intensity.

___ Balances rebound moves with neutral and suspended moves.

(continued)

Figure 16.3   Sample water fitness instructor evaluation form.

___ Uses water as the primary environment for the workout.

___ Uses and demonstrates equipment properly.

___ Makes sure students keep warm.

___ Provides a multi-dimensionally balanced workout.

___ Shows creativity and variety in workouts.

___ Uses S.W.E.A.T. to develop moves.

___ Uses basic moves.

___ Uses clear verbal directions and appropriate music volume.

___ Promotes participant interaction and emphasizes fun.

___ Manages the group, especially in varying water depths.

___ Keeps movement speed appropriate.

___ Uses appropriate music.

___ Gives participants feedback in an appropriate manner.

Warm-up/Stretch Segment

___ Uses demo speed appropriate for the movement.

___ Keeps students warm and comfortable by the movements presented (e.g., shoulder shrugs).

___ Uses music tempo appropriate for the movements.

___ Increases the range of motion gradually.

Cardio Segment

___ Increases exercise intensity gradually.

___ Explains an effective method of moderating intensity and sees that participants use it.

___ Uses a variety of muscle groups (especially the abductors and hamstrings).

___ Uses traveling moves appropriately.

___ Balances rebound moves off the bottom with resistance moves through the water.

___ Decreases exercise intensity gradually at the end of the segment.

Muscular Strength/Endurance Segment

___ Considers muscle balance.

___ Executes movements in and out of the water at the proper speed to eliminate uncontrolled momentum in the air.

___ If equipment is used (including the wall), teaches proper use of the equipment for a variety of fitness levels.

___ Demonstrates and encourages use of good body mechanics during exercise.

___ Stretches tight muscles, strengthens weak muscles.

Comments

_____

_____

_____

_____

_____

Figure 16.3 *(continued)*

It's also good to have staff evaluate each other periodically, when possible. This requires that instructors trust each other and be able to give feedback openly and constructively. An instructor can visit another's class and give both the teaching instructor and the aquatics director a copy of her or his "went well/do differently" list. You should budget money to pay the observing instructors for their time and provide additional incentives for the process to take place on an ongoing basis.

Finally, give the instructors a chance to evaluate you as well. This will be important in helping you assess your management effectiveness. They should evaluate you on communication, role clarification, direction, and overall satisfaction. Be sure you read and respond to their comments positively, making changes as needed, so instructors know that what they say will be heeded.

Training Staff

You will want to give your new staff the operations manual for water fitness programs. Operations manuals are discussed in chapter 5, but here are some additional topics you might want to add to your water fitness manual:

- Policies on what attire is appropriate for participants
- Policies on equipment use
- Staff resources such as a music or video library
- In-service training
- Procedures for finding substitutes
- A calendar of all the eduational and YMCA-related events that staff are required to attend (staff meetings, trainings, open house or other YMCA events)

To help your instructors improve their teaching, try these ideas:

- Develop incentive programs for continued education.
- Encourage instructors to share ideas.
- Ask participants and instructors to evaluate the program.
- Coordinate in-service and master classes for instructors.

Here are some ideas you can use for instructors' in-service training:

- Share exercises, music, and other class materials.
- Share ideas for use of equipment.
- Attend each other's classes and then discuss specific ideas and offer each other feedback.
- Practice rescue skills with lifeguards
- Practice scenarios that are likely to occur in these classes.
- Co-teach classes with other instructors; afterward, offer each other specific feedback. (This can also be done with instructors in other branches or YMCAs in the area.)
- Hold joint land and water fitness instructor meetings to review fitness principles, muscles, and joint action. One goal might be to cross-train instructors so they can teach both in the pool and on land. This in turn would encourage your members to cross-train and become healthier.

COMBINING LAND AND WATER FITNESS PROGRAMS

Combining both land and water programs to target health objectives can provide participants with a lifetime of balanced exercise options. Market your water and land programs together as healthy lifestyle activities that complement each other.

Cross-train your instructors so they can teach on both land and water effectively. Be sure instructors understand the benefits of each mode and help members choose a balanced program of activity based on their position on the health care continuum.

Offer orientation "splash" workshops in the pool for your land participants and a land-based dry-side demo (stability balls, resistance tubing, free weights) for water participants. Help them cross the bridge to discover the wet and dry sides of exercise.

In YMCAs, water fitness classes may be managed by either the aquatics director or the health and fitness director. In either case, a close working relationship between the two departments will help management, instructors, and participants. Staff should feel they are part of both departments, which will require teamwork between the leaders of both departments.

WORKING WITH PARTICIPANTS

The challenge of every exercise professional is to encourage people to participate in a lifetime exercise plan. When programs are more purposeful, class participants are more willing to change their patterns of behavior so activity (attending classes or engaging in self-directed activity) becomes a natural part of their daily routine. Here are two leadership ideas that can bring a personal sense of purpose to water fitness exercise classes.

Encouraging Participation

In the Project Prime study conducted at the Cooper Institute (Boldt, 1999), it was suggested that both cognitive and behavior processes should be addressed during exercise programs to optimize adherence. The activity level targeted during the study was 150 minutes per week or 30 minutes per day, five days a week, of physical activity. To help study participants successfully reach their objectives, some were coached in the following areas, which your instructors could coach as well:

Cognitive

1. Increase participants' knowledge about exercise. For example, what skills do they need to know or what influence might their past exercise and physical activity have on current and future patterns.

2. Be sure they understand the risks of inactivity. For example, not maintaining a program of regular physical activity carries the same relative risk as having high blood pressure and high cholesterol.

3. Encourage them to care about the consequences of their inactivity. For example, talk about what kind of behaviors parents would want to encourage in their children.

4. So they comprehend the benefits of activity, personalize the benefits; for example, explain how taking time to walk and talk with their spouse or children benefits their families.

5. Increase their awareness of opportunities in the community to participate in all types of activities, such as a local walking or cycling club or walking in malls that offer indoor walking space if the weather is bad.

Behavior

1. Suggest that they substitute more active alternatives to current lifestyle patterns. For example, suggest that participants could do short 10-minute walks at their workplace or, instead of sitting in the stands at the kids' soccer game, walk around the field to see the game from all angles.

2. Encourage them to enlist social support from friends, trainers, instructors, or family. For example, family members might share home responsibilities to encourage each other's activity.

3. Tell them to give themselves appropriate rewards for achieving short- and long-term goals.

4. Have them commit to being active by developing very specific short- and long-term goals, for example, walking to the park with the kids and flying a kite on Saturday morning.

5. Suggest that they establish reminders to be active. For example, they can keep their gym clothes and walking shoes handy or use a step counter to keep track of how much activity they are getting.

To attract new participants to a program, these topics can be included in press releases and in public health talks to community groups, schools, community living centers, and church groups. New YMCA members could be offered this education as part of their orientation. During classes, integrate the information into sessions to offer students the best opportunity for activity success.

Becoming Responsive Instructors

Train your instructors to look for clues to poor nutrition or stress in participants and to try a variety of ways to communicate with participants about these issues. Responsive teaching is key to helping people make real and lasting changes in their lifestyles that enhance the quality of their lives.

Great teaching takes work, practice, and time to develop people's skills and understanding (Siebert, 1991). Here are a few ideas that your instructors can use with their students.

Show That You Care

Greet students with a warm smile and sincere eye contact. Give them your time. Offer to spend time before or after class to answer questions.

Observe students as they walk into class. Notice their body language, posture, gait, and movement quality. Slumping shoulders may be a clue that someone is stressed or eating poorly. Make time to ask them what is going on. For example, if the poor posture is from sitting for hours at a computer, you might recommend postural exercises.

Listen carefully. Learn to be an active listener, and check whether you understand by saying "I understand that you . . ." and repeating the question or point your participant is sharing. Effective communication requires a combination of skills that take practice.

Carol Kennedy, M.S., fitness/wellness program director at the University of Indiana, uses this simple and fun exercise to help her staff develop good communication skills:

1. She has each staff member choose a partner. One becomes the teacher, the other is the student.

2. She assigns the teacher a simple activity to teach the student, such as walking up a set of stairs and opening a door. The teacher can use verbal cues only. (Time allowed: two minutes.)

3. Teacher and student then switch roles, and the teacher is instructed to communicate a different task, but this time without speaking, using demonstration only. (Time allowed: two minutes.)

4. She then has the group discuss the task. What did they learn? How did they feel? They talk about the importance of using a variety of methods for effective communication.

Kennedy points out that it is also valuable for the staff to discuss the challenges of participants who have sensory limitations. Simple health histories are a good way to identify special needs. You can provide some time before class for a private discussion with a participant, or you might want to have a trained staff member take a report and share it with you. Questions are best when they are simple and open-ended.

Ask Participants to Record Activities

A powerful tool can be to read journals that participants keep of their physical activity. Once in a while, for at least four weeks, have participants record their activities and feelings about their own wellness. Their responses can help you understand them so you can tailor the program in response. If you write a response in a journal, be sure that it is within your scope of practice. Motivational comments (cheering them for their accomplishments) help with adherence, and practical tips on regulating intensity or modifying specific exercises can help make the program more effective and comfortable. With athletes, journals can help you identify burnout, overtraining, and other problems that may be affecting performance. Any abnormal responses to the program should be discussed with the participant, who may have to be encouraged to modify his or her training plan or see his or her health care provider.

Use Five-Minute Tickers

Tatiana Kolovou, M.B.A., director of Team Performance, suggests using five-minute tickers or surveys with one or two action questions to learn about your participants. Here are some examples: What are your personal fitness goals? What would you like to be able to do better? What activities have gotten easier (or harder)? List activities that you have added to your life . . . any you'd like to add? You can use the information to plan classes and create a team training. For example, if you know that Ed wants to improve his skiing, include a simple "ski" progression during class just for Ed, and let the class know "we're working on Ed's skiing now."

Write Down Participants' Goals

Another method of discovering participants' goals is to ask the class as a whole. Have each instructor post a large piece of newsprint before a water fitness class that says "What is your goal for taking this class?" Provide a marker for participants to use to write answers before or after class. The instructor should record the information from each class and compare what the different classes said. The answers can then be used to plan future classes.

A different question that could be used this way is "What are your fitness goals?" Four categories should appear after the question:

Cardiorespiratory fitness	Muscular fitness
Flexibility fitness	Weight management

Participants mark an X under each category in which they are interested. Again, the instructor can use this to plan classes.

Praise Each Participant Separately

Barry A. Franklin, Ph.D., FACSM, recently wrote a wonderful article called "The Power of Praise" (Franklin, 2000) about the effect that kindness and recognition can have on people. This is a good message to keep in mind. Participants want to be with instructors who recognize even the slightest achievement, even if it's only showing up for class.

Positive, specific, corrective feedback is a type of praise that will empower participants to learn. This type of feedback provides them with encouraging, positive messages that are specifically directed to the task. During the exchange, the participant receives some information that corrects or makes the exercise or task more effective, safer, or more comfortable (Sanders, 2000). For example, "Carol, your body alignment is good, with shoulders over hips (positive). Now try to walk using larger steps (corrective and specific) and feel how your body allows you to enlarge the move with better balance!" Participants who are praised for their efforts and proficiency will feel good about their progress and are likely to take charge of their own workouts.

To summarize, no two participants come to class with identical needs and wants. It takes effort on the part of the instructor to identify individual characteristics, but it can be well worth the effort for the participant and for the instructor. By using their ears, eyes, and a few devices for getting to know their participants, instructors can help participants enjoy the experience and successfully achieve their physical fitness goals.

PERSONAL TRAINING

If your YMCA offers personal training as part of your overall water fitness program, here are some tips for working with your personal trainers and helping them work with your members.

Personal training instructors should recognize that both muscular conditioning and cardiorespiratory training can be achieved in the aquatics environment. Aerobic water exercise can consist of either the "vertical" exercise typically found in water fitness classes or "horizontal" exercise such as lap swimming. Muscular development can also be achieved in the water by using the water's resistance, often with the help of exercise equipment such as webbed gloves, fins, kickboards, Styrofoam dumbbells, belts, and "noodles." By including water fitness as a component of exercise programs, personal training instructors provide participants with another choice of activities to achieve training results. Participants develop lifetime skills that they can modify as their exercise needs develop and change over time (Sanders, 1999b).

Many healthy adults who enjoy the water will want to use it to cross-train for new challenges and variety; however, the water is particularly conducive to exercise for those with specific health conditions and concerns. Personal training instructors can work with physicians and other health professionals to develop appropriate exercise programs for the following types of individuals:

- Athletes who want to decrease impact and to overload patterns of movement in the safety of the water (Sanders, 1999a)

- Obese participants who need to decrease impact and increase exercise duration while enjoying the added benefit of the privacy water exercise affords (Sanders, 1999a)

- Participants with orthopedic conditions such as arthritis, total hip or knee replacement, postrehabilitation from knee and shoulder surgery, low back pain, fibromyalgia, and osteoporosis (Sanders and Maloney-Hills, 1998)

- Participants suffering from neurological conditions such as multiple sclerosis, stroke, and Parkinson's disease who may benefit from the support of water (Sanders and Maloney-Hills, 1998)

- Participants who need to carefully regulate exercise intensity due to cardiorespiratory conditions such as cardiovascular disease, pulmonary disease, and hypertension (Sanders and Maloney-Hills, 1998)

- Those with general medical conditions such as pregnancy, diabetes mellitus, and recovery from mastectomy (Sanders and Maloney-Hills, 1998)

The following are some guidelines for teaching water exercise effectively:

1. Account for land and water differences. Understanding water's effect on the body is essential: Water provides continuous resistance to movement. A biceps

curl performed on land utilizes gravity and a weight to provide concentric muscular work, whereas the same movement performed in the water with a buoyant dumbbell works the triceps eccentrically (Kennedy and Sanders, 1995).

2. Teach participants personal balance, stabilization, and safety. Participants need to develop basic skills for moving through the water safely and effectively. These skills include sculling to enhance balance, recovering to a stand, and keeping good body alignment. When working in a YMCA pool with lifeguards, know your responsibilities as a member of the emergency response team. An emergency action plan must be in place and must be understood by all parties at all times (Sanders, 1999b).

3. Teach proper technique. Those interested in horizontal fitness swimming should have a qualified person assess their stroke techniques in the water. If stroke work is needed, include some swim instruction during workout time or have participants register for swim lessons. For additional help in developing an effective workout for lap swimmers, consult with a YMCA aquatics director, swim instructor, or swim team coach.

4. Choose a water depth. Participants can work in three water depths: shallow (navel to nipple), transitional (nipple to neck), and deep (armpit depth or deeper, feet touch bottom lightly or not at all). The depth depends on the facility, the objective of the workout, the availability of equipment, and the skill level of the participant. A person who needs to reduce impact may want to work out in deep water using a buoyancy belt for support, whereas someone who wants to improve a functional skill such as speed walking might choose shallow water (Sanders, 1999b).

5. Monitor water temperature. The temperature of the water affects exercise design. Competitive athletic training conducted at a high intensity (above 4.2 METs) should be performed in water 80 to 83 degrees Fahrenheit, whereas vigorous aerobics (4.2 METs) or moderate-intensity activity (below 4.2 METs) should be performed in water 83 to 86 degrees Fahrenheit (Sanders, 2000).

6. Teach participants how to regulate exercise intensity. Participants will need to learn to feel the water and to discover their own resistance levels by practicing movements through progressions. Speed, surface area, water currents, and buoyancy all need to be managed to achieve appropriate levels of work and rest. Equipment may need to be added to appropriately overload different muscle groups. For example, webbed gloves may provide sufficient overload for triceps work, whereas the biceps may require the larger surface area of a fitness paddle (Kennedy and Sanders, 1995).

7. Use equipment effectively. In water, iron dumbbells are replaced by foam ones. The surface area or buoyancy of equipment moving through the water is used to provide resistance. Many types of water exercise equipment are available, and you will need to understand how using various equipment affects both exercise design and safety. Teach participants the skills unique to using each piece of equipment (Kennedy and Sanders, 1995).

For additional information on water fitness, refer to the *YMCA Water Fitness for Health* manual available from the YMCA Program Store.

INSTRUCTOR SAFETY

For their safety and to reduce injuries, tell your instructors to do the following:

- Wear well-cushioned, nonslip, supportive shoes.
- Work on a mat, and limit your moves to low-impact demonstration exercises.
- Use stools or chairs to assist with your demonstrations and to provide a resting place.
- Use visual and verbal cues and teach the skills.
- Never communicate by yelling. Instead, use a microphone, turn off the music, or teach small groups in the water.
- Limit your own exercise intensity. Also, limit the number of classes you teach, and take a break from the exercises to coach.
- Check your stance; stand tall and centered.
- Wear sun protection, glasses, a hat, and sunscreen to minimize sun exposure dangers.
- Layer on apparel that encourages either heat loss in hot conditions or heat retention in cool situations.
- Shower with clear water after immersion, and apply lotion while your body is still wet.
- Drink water to help your body thermoregulate in any temperature.
- Be sure the facility has good ventilation. If you detect a strong chemical smell, check immediately with the pool manager.
- If you are injured or become ill, take care of the condition and rest to ensure recovery.
- If you are "burned out" or feel like you can't face another class with enthusiasm, try these ideas: Take a break, attend someone else's class, do something else, buy a new water exercise video for ideas, attend a conference, or ask your supervisor to help you get recharged.

FACILITY AND EQUIPMENT NEEDS

As you plan for water fitness classes, you'll need to consider how much and what parts of the pool must be reserved, what the pool temperature needs to be, and what equipment will be required.

Using the Facility

Depending on your facility, members, and staffing, you may offer a variety of classes that target low- to high-intensity training. For each class, try to have enough space so each participant can move comfortably, about six to eight feet per person. Determine what areas of the pool you will need at what times. Here are the three recommended water depths:

Shallow	For an individual standing on the bottom of the pool, water should be navel to nipple depth.
Transitional	An individual's feet can touch the bottom and her or his lungs are submerged, with water nipple to neck depth.
Deep	An individual "stands" in a vertical position with the lungs submerged, with water usually about armpit depth or deeper. Feet may be touching the bottom lightly or not at all.

While instructors can run classes in which people are at more than one depth, they must pay additional attention so as to provide effective feedback and exercise modifications for the different depths. If mixed depths are used, instructors should have students wear buoyancy devices to maximize the time they spend suspended (budget for the necessary equipment).

When scheduling classes, consider these conditions:

- Pool dimensions (shallow/deep water)
- Pool temperature
- Indoor/outdoor facility
- Availability of equipment
- Facility proximity to the local bus route
- Day care hours

You may want to consider offering multiple classes at the same time so different family members can participate simultaneously. For example, you could offer YMCA Swim Lessons in one area of the pool and water fitness in another area. However, make sure that the types of classes offered at the same time will not interfere with each other.

Here are some suggestions for ways to keep classes on schedule:

- Develop an ongoing voicemail line listing class changes and updates daily.
- Reward staff (through an incentive program) who maintain a high attendance record with their classes.
- Work on each schedule at least two months in advance to allow for alternative plans and troubleshooting. Always ask staff for their availability and a wish list of their favorite classes.
- Have an effective substitution system for instructors.
- Cross-train staff to avoid having class instructors who can never be out sick.

Pool Temperature

The YMCA of the USA recommends the following water temperatures for the comfort of your participants, taking exercise intensity into account:

Competitive athletic training at high intensity	80-83 degrees Fahrenheit
Fitness classes	83-86 degrees Fahrenheit
Functional fitness	83-86 degrees Fahrenheit
Arthritis classes (depends on intensity)	83-88 degrees Fahrenheit

The water temperature may affect which classes you schedule at the same time.

Equipment

Equipment changes the way water acts against the body. It can increase the quality and safety of a water fitness program and offer participants an opportunity to advance their training individually by increasing exercise intensity. To use equipment properly, instructors must understand the purpose of each piece of equipment they use and design movements with that equipment based on the properties of water and exercise science. Instructors must evaluate the function and safety of each exercise with equipment before using it in class.

Equipment can

- add variety to the class,
- increase (or decrease) the intensity of the workout,
- provide buoyancy support,
- add resistance to movements to create greater work while training, and
- give participants the opportunity to advance their exercise.

Here's more on the types of equipment available and how to evaluate them.

Equipment Categories

Water-specific equipment falls into three categories: surface area, buoyancy, and land/ water integration.

- *Surface area equipment* expands the surface area to be worked, increasing drag without providing any buoyancy. Such equipment includes webbed gloves, nonbuoyant dumbbells, fitness paddles, swim fins, and water parachutes.

- *Buoyancy equipment* floats enough to provide flotation support for an arm, a leg, or the entire body. This increased buoyancy provides resistance to downward movements against buoyancy's upward force. The amount of buoyancy overload depends on the type of equipment and the individual's body composition. Buoyancy equipment includes whole-body devices such as foam or inflatable belts; arm and leg devices such as dumbbells or cuffs (foam or inflatable); and free-floating devices such as noodles, logs, or kickboards.

- *Land/water integration equipment* includes pieces of equipment that are either the same or similar to ones used on land. Most provide an opportunity to bridge from land to water training by permitting modification of land exercises for the water. This equipment includes aquatic steps, tethers, resistance bands, and balls.

Equipment Evaluation

Before an instructor adds equipment to an exercise, he or she should ask these questions:

- What is the purpose of the equipment?
- What are the fitness benefits of using the equipment? Does it effectively meet the exercise objectives?
- Can it be used at a number of intensity levels?
- What basic skills are required to use it functionally and safely?
- Will it provide safe and progressive work?
- Is the equipment safe, durable, and comfortable to use? Is the product easy to fit onto the body?
- What is the cost of the equipment? Will it fit into the budget? Is it worth it compared to the benefits?

Here is a suggested list of basic equipment for getting started:

- *Soft webbed gloves* help participants stabilize themselves so they can use larger movements. Gloves also offer progressive upper-body overload for effective muscular training. Offer these for sale at the front desk if you don't have enough money in the budget to supply them to class members.

• *Buoyancy belts* are worn around the waist. They are necessary for participants to work in deep water, even those who are swimmers, to ensure a balanced muscular workout.

• *Water shoes* make walking in and around the pool safe. They provide good traction as participants move in the shallow end of the pool, which is important for balance and an effective workout.

• *Swimsuits* should have good support; if not, participants can wear jog bras under their suits. Participants can also wear T-shirts or tights or leggings into the pool for warmth and comfort.

• *A sound system with a microphone* (not simply a boom box) is necessary so the instructor can give clear verbal cues.

Optional equipment you might consider purchasing includes nonbuoyant dumbbells, fitness paddles, swim fins, water parachutes, foam barbells, noodles, kickboards, aquatic steps, tethers, resistance bands, and balls.

BUDGETING

When you put together a budget for your water fitness classes, include the following costs:

• Adequate supply of equipment for 20 participants (see previous lists of suggested equipment)
• Instructor hours for teaching classes
• Planning time for instructors
• In-service training (about one hour per session or per month)
• Certification costs (new or renewal of CPR, first aid, YASA or Lifeguard, YMCA Instructor)

PROMOTION AND COMMUNICATION

Begin any promotion by identifying your audience. Water fitness participants may be mildly to severely overweight and may be self-conscious about their appearance. Some will want to participate without getting their hair or faces wet. Participants often are female, and they range from the 30-something to 70-plus age groups. They join because they can no longer keep up with traditional land aerobics classes without injury, because they haven't exercised for some time, or because they are postpartum or are suffering from some type of injury (e.g., knees, back). Another growing group is those who want to cross-train from land exercise programs, as well as those who need sports conditioning or who receive personal training.

Keep in mind that, although music is an exceptional motivator, older participants tend to dislike rap music or excessive volume levels, and they enjoy the social aspects of carrying on conversations while exercising.

Some benefits of water fitness that you can promote include the following:

• Water exercises put less stress on joints than land exercises because the effects of gravity are minimized.
• The joints tend to have a greater range of motion underwater.

- Working against water resistance improves muscle strength and tone and cardiorespiratory endurance.
- Water fitness is a safe and effective method for improving flexibility and general fitness levels.
- Water currents massage the muscles and improve circulation.
- Water fitness is a refreshing and cool way to get fit.
- Swimming skills are not needed for participation.
- Participants can make friends and have the support of the class.
- The program supports the YMCA mission.
- Financial aid is available for participants.

Some promotional messages you might use include these:

- Exercise, Socialize, and Energize!
- Stay Cool—Work Out in the Pool
- Aquatic Fitness: The Wave of the Future
- Are you ready for the beach?

Write class descriptions with the potential participant in mind. How classes are named and described can make a big difference in how members perceive them. Be sure that your descriptions are factual and professional. For example, you can describe a deep-water exercise class as providing a "focused abdominal workout," but don't promise the "six-pack" look. A shallow-water class can be promoted as a "liquid sculpting" session, as the water provides a combination of cardiorespiratory and resistance training. However, don't mention fat-burning zones or body composition effects. Benefits will vary with each individual and can be influenced by a number of circumstances.

If you decide to create a flyer on your water fitness programs, be sure you use the water fitness program identity logo. Make the flyers available in doctors', obstetricians', and dentists' offices, at weight loss centers, and in libraries.

At the YMCA, advertise in your YMCA program brochure and newsletter. See that all class schedules list both land and water fitness programs together. Hang water fitness posters on the walls. Give away or sell T-shirts with the water fitness program identity logo and the name of your YMCA.

Get mentions of your programs in church and school bulletins. Use cable TV announcements, PSAs on the radio (figure 16.4 shows sample PSAs), and news releases (figure 16.5 is a sample news release).

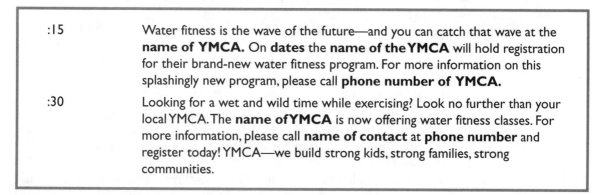

Figure 16.4   Sample PSAs for water fitness.

Name of YMCA Launches New Program

New YMCA Water Fitness Program Makes a Big Splash!

Town (date)—Looking for a way to get fit but don't want the same old exercise routine? The **name of YMCA** is now offering a new program—YMCA Water Fitness. This water exercise program can benefit individuals who are just starting to exercise, as well as those who would like a more intense workout. The **name of YMCA** announced today that registration for YMCA Water Fitness will take place **dates** at **location.**

With more and more individuals taking water fitness classes, the advantages of the YMCA Water Fitness Program are apparent in the pool and in daily life as well. In YMCA Water Fitness, participants perform movements and specific exercises that will cross over and provide benefits in day-to-day activities. **Name of Y spokesperson and title** says, "As in all YMCA programs, the ultimate goal of the YMCA Water Fitness Program is to develop the whole person spiritually, mentally, and physically." The program works to reinforce the values of caring, honesty, respect, and responsibility that should be a part of the relationship between participants and instructors. Guidance and development of goals are part of the program. Physical fitness helps build participants' self-confidence, and YMCA Water Fitness instructors help participants create a workout that achieves their goals.

The **name of the YMCA** offers different water fitness classes such as **list specific classes** that are based on various skills and fitness levels. **Name** adds, "The YMCA Water Fitness Program is a great and different way for people to get involved in physical activity. They can find the class that suits their needs and get the most of their workout."

Registration for the new YMCA Water Fitness Program is open **date** through **date. State costs.** For additional information, call **name of contact** at **phone number.**

For more than 110 years, the YMCA has been a leader in aquatics and water safety. About 2,300 YMCAs can be found in communities across the United States. YMCAs serve around 16 million people, including 8 million youth. To find the YMCA nearest you, call toll-free 888-333-YMCA or visit the YMCA of the USA Web site at www.ymca.net.

Figure 16.5   Sample news release.

Approach assisted-living homes, community centers, and churches about offering water fitness to their members. Connect with doctors in the community and let them know about your water fitness classes, especially those who serve pregnant women and mothers with young children, people who are overweight, or seniors. Go to schools and offer to do a wet track practice or a water workout for their physical education classes or sports teams, or present water fitness as an after-school program.

Attract people to try water fitness by offering sample classes to participants in other aquatics programs, such as swim team, masters swimmers, and youth swim classes. Ask water fitness participants to bring a friend or family member to class for a day. Hold advanced master workshop classes or water fitness class challenges. Have special classes for families, summer camp children, or staff.

To promote volunteerism within your classes and get more recognition for your program, ask participants to do things such as raise funds for the YMCA's Annual Fund, hold a water fitness marathon to raise money for charity, or establish a water exercise committee.

You can use these sample PSAs with local broadcast media. Edit them according to the directions you receive from the station. Tailor them to your YMCA and add the missing information.

ADMINISTRATIVE TIPS

To help you develop your water fitness programs, let's look at a few common problems that can arise and some ideas for making your programs successful.

Here are some questions commonly asked by members about water fitness programs:

- What is the difference between land and water exercise?
- Do I have to know how to swim?
- Do I have to get my hair wet?
- How can I get a more advanced workout?
- Describe the differences in the water exercise classes.
- What is the minimum age for the classes?

Have answers for these questions, and review them with your front-desk staff and other aquatics staff members.

Common problems that arise during water exercise classes include the following:

- *Participants are not happy with the water temperature.* The water temperature should be set to accommodate all the different activities that are held in the pool. See if the water temperature can be adjusted; if not, have instructors encourage participants who are too cold to wear water fitness wear into the pool.

- *Participants are unhappy with the music used in class.* Get a feel for whether most participants are unhappy, or just a few. Encourage instructors to use a variety of music. Have instructors explain to participants that they attempt to use a variety of music to appeal to as many people as possible.

- *Participants won't stop talking during class, frustrating the instructor.* Encourage the instructor to vary the workout and keep the participants engaged and moving. Help the instructor understand that the social aspects of the class are important also, and suggest that she or he should not be too bothered by the talking.

- *The instructor is more interested in her or his own workout than in leading/educating the class at the level the participants need.* Explain to the instructor what her or his role is in meeting participants' needs. Suggest that the instructor work out alone at another time.

The following are some things to look for that should alert you to problems with the program:

- Instructors doing the same workout each time
- Decreases in attendance
- Locker room "grumbling"
- Instructors feeling that they are not part of the aquatics department or the health and fitness department
- A lack of enthusiasm from instructors and class participants
- Member complaints (If these occur, listen to what participants have to say and observe the class.)
- A highly choreographed class in which everyone is on the same beat (not individualized)
- A class in which the instructor counts and the students hold onto the wall during most of the class (assuming they are not people with disabilities)

- An instructor who is talking excessively during class or no interaction among students
- Deep-water classes in which the instructor is in the water and students can't follow the moves
- Students who aren't having fun
- Students who are getting cold

Finally, here are some tips for running a successful water exercise program:

- To attract participants, provide handouts on the benefits of water training and offer water fitness orientations to members. Play water fitness videos in the lobby.
- Use only trained and certified instructors, and provide them with ongoing workshops and continuing education.
- Have a good music system and use a variety of music.
- Have up-to-date equipment: gloves, belts, fins, balls, bands, tethers, steps, power buoys, etc.
- Hold special events for participants, such as nutrition workshops or brown-bag lunches with fitness topics.
- Include fitness assessments so members can track their progress and staff can report how fit the program is making members! Offer a new-member fitness consultation (including body composition, flexibility, and strength testing) and continue with 3-, 6-, and 12-month follow-ups.
- Sell basic gear such as gloves at the front desk.
- Keep an accurate headcount of each class meeting and compare daily attendance to class registrations and water temperature fluctuations.
- Provide ongoing incentives to class participants, either for attendance in your class or in conjunction with other YMCA departments. For instance, as an incentive, if a participant attends 10 YMCA classes in March, he or she gets a free T-shirt.
- Have instructors contact any class member who misses more than two weeks of class.
- Give class members options if they have to miss their scheduled classes, either by recommending other class sessions they can attend during the week or by supplying them with individual fitness routines they can do at home.

Here are some additional programming tips:

- Offer a variety of classes at different times. Match programming to the demographic use of your facility.
- Target professionals with early-morning and after-work classes.
- Match weekday morning classes with day care use.
- Arrange for local retirement facilities to bus their participants to your facility for a midday class.
- Offer sports-related/cross-conditioning theme classes to complement popular land exercise. For example, offer boxing on Tuesdays and Thursdays at 6:00 P.M. and Sports Splash on Wednesdays at 6:00 P.M.
- Before putting them on the schedule, try new equipment-related offerings or new ideas as specially promoted master classes at a special time.
- Schedule regular Fresh Splash "playouts" that introduce three new progressions or a new piece of equipment. Communicate with the fitness personal training program and offer one-on-one or small-group training water fitness options.
- Design special occasion/holiday classes (Halloween, New Year's Eve).

BIBLIOGRAPHY

American College of Sports Medicine. 1995. *ACSM's guidelines for exercise testing and prescription* (5th ed.). Baltimore: Williams & Wilkins.

American Council on Exercise. 1999. Lewin Group Health Report, *ACE Fitness Matters*. Nov./Dec.

Becker, B., and A. Cole. 1997. *Comprehensive aquatic therapy*. Boston: Butterworth-Heinemann.

Blair, S. 2001. Fitness, fatness and health. Lecture at International Health Promotion and Aerobic Convention, Taipei, Taiwan, August 16-19.

Boldt, L.G. 1999. *The Tao of abundance*. New York: Penguin.

Brick, V.C., Cingle, L. 1996. *Fitness management*. San Diego, CA: IDEA, Inc.

Bushman, B., M. Flynn, F. Andres, C. Lambert, M. Taylor, and W. Braun. 1997. Effect of 4 weeks of deep water run training on running performance. *Medicine and Science in Sports and Exercise*, 29:5, 694-699.

DiPrampero, P.E. 1986. The energy cost of human locomotion on land and in water. *International Journal of Sports Medicine*, 7 (2): 55-72.

Evans, E., and K. Cureton. 1998. Metabolic, circulatory and perceptual responses to bench stepping in water. *Journal of Strength and Conditioning Research*, Summer.

Franklin, B. 2000. The power of praise. *Sports Medicine Bulletin*, 35(1): 3.

Grantham, W.C., Patton, R.W., York, T.D., Winick, M.L. 1998. *Health fitness management*. Champaign, IL: Human Kinetics.

IDEA Fitness Program Surveys. 1999. *IDEA Fitness Manager*, October, 11:5.

IDEA, The Health & Fitness Source. 1998. *Program director*. San Diego, CA: IDEA, Inc.

IDEA, The Health & Fitness Source. 1998. *Successful program development*. San Diego, CA: IDEA, Inc.

Kennedy, C., and M. Sanders. (1995). Strength training gets wet. *IDEA Today*, 13(5): 24-30.

Koury, J. 1996. *Aquatic therapy programming guidelines for orthopedic rehabilitation*. Champaign, IL:Human Kinetics.

LaForge, R. 1995. Exercise associated mood alterations: A review of interactive neurobiologic mechanisms. *Medicine, Exercise, Nutrition, and Health*, 4: 17-32.

LaForge, R. 1996. The science and application of mind-body fitness. Presentation at the YMCA of the USA Healthy People Conference, October 10–13, Orlando, FL.

Mathis, R.L., & Jackson, J.H. 1994. *Human resource management*. St. Paul, MN: West Publishing Corporation.

McInnis, K.J. 2001. Speech at ACSM National Meeting, Baltimore, MD, May 30-June 3.

Michaud, T., J. Rodriguez-Zayas, F. Andres, M. Flynn, and C. Lambert. 1995. Comparative exercise responses of deep-water and treadmill running. *Journal of Strength and Conditioning*, 9:2, 104-109.

Morrow, M.J., R.L. Jensen, and C.R.Peace. 1996. Physiological adaptations to deep water and land based running training programs. *Medicine and Science in Sports and Exercise*, 28(5), Abstract 1252.

Napoletan, J.C., and R.W. Hicks. 1995. The metabolic effects of underwater treadmill exercise at two departments. *APTR*, 3(2): 9-14.

Patton, R.W., Grantham, W.C., Gerson, R.F., Gettmen, L.R. 1989. *Developing and managing health/fitness facilities*. Champaign, IL: Human Kinetics.

Peter, J.P., & Donnelly, Jr. J.H. 1994. *A preface to marketing management*. Chicago, IL: Irwin.

Rikli, R.E., and C.J. Jones. 1999. Development and validation of a functional fitness test for community-residing older adults. *Journal of Aging and Physical Activity*, 7(2): 129-161.

Sanders, M., Ed. 2000. *YMCA water fitness for health*. Champaign, IL: Human Kinetics for YMCA of the USA.

Sanders, M.E. 1999a. Cross over to the water. *IDEA, Health and Fitness Source*, 17(3): 53-58.

Sanders, M.E. 1999b. *WaterFit™ Instructor training and Speedo® aquatic fitness system, 2nd edition*. Reno, NV: WaterFit™/Wave Aerobics®.

Sanders, M., and C. Maloney-Hills. 1998. *The golden waves functional water training for health program* and *The golden waves functional water training for health, leadership program.* Sanford Center for Aging: University of Nevada, Reno, NV. Videocassettes.

Sanders, M.E., N.L. Constantino, N.E. Rippee, A.L. Barret, D. Griffin, P. Krumpe, and R. Fredericks. 1997. Comparison of results of functional water training on field and laboratory measures in older women (Abstract). *Supplement to Medicine and Science in Sports and Exercise,* 29(5): S110.

Sanders, M. & Rippee N. 1993. *Speedo® aquatic fitness instructor manual.* London: Speedo International.

Satcher, D. 2001. Keynote address at the ACSM Health and Fitness Summit Conference, Las Vegas, NV, April 17-20.

Siebert, G. 1991. How do you become a really great teacher? *Fitness Management,* February, p. 17.

Simmons, V., and P. Hansen. 1996. Effectiveness of water exercise on postural mobility in the well elderly: An experimental study on balance enhancement. *Journal of Gerentology: Medical Sciences,* 51 A(5): M 233–M238.

Spirduso, W. 1995. *Physical dimensions of aging.* Champaign, IL: Human Kinetics.

Swim Team Programs

The purpose of this chapter is to help you organize and develop a new swim team. Thorough planning is the key ingredient in offering a quality program. The plan we describe here applies mainly to first-year teams, but it can help more established programs as well. Specific parts of this chapter should help you determine what type of swim team program you want to develop and the steps you should take to meet your goals.

We explain the benefits of a swim team program and how to research the resources that you'll need to start one. We outline the different types of teams possible, then describe how to look for team coaches and program participants. This is followed by information on scheduling pool time and practice recommendations.

We then give you an idea of the start-up costs, describing potential income sources and probable expenses. We follow this with ideas for promoting your program and a description of the types of competitions your team is likely to participate in. Program evaluation completes this section.

Other topics we cover include how to organize a swim team advisory committee of swimmers' parents, how to integrate character development into your program, and how to host competitions, along with suggestions on communicating and on developing a team handbook. We end the chapter with ideas for a masters program and a diving program, as well as some administrative tips.

By following the guidelines in this chapter, you will develop a vision for your team and a plan for your team's growth and development. By studying this chapter, you have already taken the most important step toward developing a quality program.

For additional information about managing and developing competitive swim programs, read *Principles of YMCA Competitive Swimming and Diving* (2nd ed.) (Item no. 0-7360-3452-8). This resource manual is available from the YMCA Program Store, 800-747-0089.

STARTING YOUR SWIM TEAM FROM SCRATCH

Swim team programs grow from many sources. Often individuals with past competitive swimming experience are the leaders in forming a swim team organization. Swim team programs are a natural extension of local community summer swim league programs or swim lessons at local YMCAs or community centers and are an excellent organized fitness activity for youth.

Regardless of the impetus for your new team, several key ingredients must exist before you can get started. In developing a year-round or seasonal program, ask yourself the following questions regarding feasibility:

What is our vision for the program?

How can we involve our parent volunteers in the initial planning stages?

Who will lead the program?

Where will the participants come from?

Is pool time available?

What will our start-up costs be?

How will we promote the program?

With whom will the team compete?

What is the recommended season length?

How can we encourage diversity?

How can we emphasize YMCA values?

What other swim team programs are available in the community?

The question "What is our vision for the program?" is the most important issue you must address. Can you visualize what your program will look like, sound like, and even feel like once you're up and swimming? How will you know if you have successfully met your goal? Goal setting is an important ingredient in developing your vision. If you think of it as a directional map, planning will be much easier.

You will notice that the word *program* is used often in place of *team*. Remember that programming time, space, personnel, and a philosophy is much more effective than offering only an activity. Is it enough to just offer access to a facility, or is it better to offer activities, instruction, and motivation to shape a child's life on a daily basis? The YMCA was founded for those sharing interests to meet and exchange support and ideals. In all YMCA sports programs, everyone should be involved, and all children should have the opportunity to be the best they can be.

Program Benefits

What are the primary benefits of a competitive swimming program? Sport physiologists have always recommended swimming as an excellent lifetime aerobic activity. Sport psychologists have stressed the benefits of team sports and the life lessons learned from competition. Through participation in sports, children can learn to set goals, develop new skills, work as a team, and treat others fairly.

All sports give parents the opportunity to take an active role in their children's activities. Operation of the sport of swimming is dependent on the participation of parent volunteers. The YMCA promotes family-child programming, and swimming is one of the best activities for family participation. Interaction with other families will help children develop their social skills and provide an excellent opportunity for parents to share experiences.

One very important but often overlooked benefit of the sport is that swimming is fun! Children prefer activities that they enjoy and perceive as being fun. Several years ago, the Institute for the Study of Youth Sports at Michigan State University conducted a study on why young people in grades 7 through 12 participate in sports (Horn, 1982). The findings indicated that the number-one reason for participating was to have fun. Other reasons included

- to improve skills,
- to stay in shape,
- for team spirit,
- for the excitement of competition,
- to be physically fit, and
- for the challenge.

Even among the most dedicated athletes, winning took a backseat to self-improvement and competition.

Be sure to look at other programs in your area and strive to be different. Think of creative types of activities, such as team trips, parent-child swim meets, community swim clinics, or exhibitions during swim lessons.

Program Resources

Now that you have determined your program goals and vision, you need to find the resources to make your dream a reality.

Start by reviewing the "Rules That Govern YMCA Competitive Sports" and the "Technical Assistance Paper on YMCA Competitive Swimming Programs" on the YMCA of the USA Web site. These documents deal with the expected conduct of your program. In addition, they contain detailed information regarding the eligibility of individuals and associations, as well as the rules for the conduct of championships and definitions of types of competitions.

Other competitive swimming programs, such as other YMCA programs in your area, club swimming teams, high school teams, masters swimming programs, or community summer league teams, will be able to help you with the background information you need to get started. Using ideas from other programs will help you shape your swim team. Consult with people running at least three other types of swim team programs, including at least one YMCA program, to help develop your plan. Your YMCA of the USA program consultant can also provide assistance.

Parents will play an important role in the program's operation and growth. Set up a committee of interested parent volunteers to help with the early planning stages. Have the committee develop a plan to research the following areas:

- Facilities available
- Cost of staff
- Cost of training equipment
- Meet and travel expenses
- Other swim teams in the area and how they operate
- Cost of administrative work and overhead
- Access to schools as a source of participants
- Contacts with summer league community pools as a source of participants

Team Characteristics

You will have several decisions to make about your new team. Will team members have membership in both the YMCA and USA Swimming? (USA Swimming is the governing body for the sport of swimming in the United States.) What type of team will it be? Will you aim to create a small, medium, or large team?

Participation in Swimming for Other Organizations

You may wish to have your team participate in both YMCA and USA Swimming competition. To compete in this arrangement, your team must be chartered as a YMCA team with your YMCA's name. Membership in USA Swimming is offered to team members.

The greatest benefit of participation in USA Swimming is the increased competitive opportunities your team will have for each level of your program. As your program grows in both size and diversity, the additional competitive outlets will sustain your more competitive athletes' interest.

Be sure to check how the rules that apply to dual representation affect your team. Programs such as high school or summer league community swimming are closed competitions, so swimmers from those programs are generally unaffected if they swim for the YMCA as well. However, their participation in other programs may affect your USA Swimming involvement. Check with your local USA Swimming committee and high school athletic association before finalizing your representation plans.

If you have an adult competitive team, you may have to consider whether they can swim in both YMCA and United States Masters Swimming events.

Team Types

Depending on your situation, you may want to have a competitive team year-round or in the summer only. Other possibilities are a recreational league swim team or a masters competitive swim team.

You may also find competitive swimmers in the following types of classes:

- Precompetitive stroke instruction classes
- Adult fitness swimming classes
- Triathlon training classes

Finally, besides having teams, you might consider holding camps and clinics such as these:

- *Competitive clinic:* A special competitive swim class that focuses on all four strokes, starts, turns, and competitive technique. It is usually taught by a swim team coach or the head coach. It might include videotaping and critiquing of performance.

- *Stroke clinic:* Invite college coaches to conduct an upper-level stroke clinic in the evenings after the winter swim team season ends. That clinic should lead swimmers right up to the start of your summer swim team.

- *Swim camp:* After the winter swim team season ends, conduct a swim camp on Saturdays. Invite children 10 and under to attend and learn about competitive swimming (it's best to do this before baseball season begins in April). Offer T-shirts, a pizza party, and lots of swimming, instruction, and fun! Invite all participating swimmers to join your summer swim team.

These additional swim instruction activities keep swimmers in shape and attract new participants for your regular swim team.

Team Profiles

By size, teams seem to fall into the following profiles:

Small Team (fewer than 50 swimmers)

- Limited pool time
- Volunteer, part-time coach or YMCA director with additional YMCA responsibilities
- Little or no administrative help at the association level
- Small team budget (under $25,000)
- Limited training equipment
- All meets open to all team members at local level
- Low-key, fun introductory approach
- Accepts beginners and experienced swimmers
- Character development component

Medium Team (50 to 100 swimmers)

- Recognized YMCA program with adequate pool time
- Multilevel opportunities for swimmers of varying ages and abilities
- Parents' organization
- Full-time staff member or YMCA director with additional YMCA responsibilities (such as the aquatics director)
- Part-time assistant coaches
- Budget income from the YMCA as well as from fundraising projects ($25,000 to $75,000)
- Most meets open to all team members at the local, state, and possibly regional levels
- Character development component

Large Team (over 100 swimmers)
- Full-time YMCA coach or director devoted exclusively to the swim team
- Multiple practice groups with progressive levels
- Large budget (over $75,000)
- Complete equipment plus replacement program
- Possible use of multiple sites
- Strong, active parents' organization
- May involve tryouts
- Complete meet schedule, including dual meets, regional invitationals, and national competitions to serve all ability levels
- Individualized dryland, drill, and workout schedule
- Year-round involvement, with possible participation in both YMCA and USA Swimming competition
- National-level swimmers
- Possible full- or part-time age group coach (for example, a coach who works with swimmers 12 years old and younger)
- Three or more part-time assistant coaches and clerical staff
- Character development component

Table 17.1 shows YMCA recommended coach-to-swimmer ratios for different types of programs. With summer-only teams, swimmers may practice more frequently because of the shorter season.

Table 17.1   Recommended Coach-to-Swimmer Ratios

Ability level	Ages	Ratio
Novice precompetitive	5 to 9	1: 8 to 1:11
First and second year competitive	7 to 10	1:12 to 1:16
Advanced 12 and under	9 to 12	1:12 to 1:16
Novice precompetitive	10 to 18	1:10 to 1:14
First and second year competitive	10 to 18	1:12 to 1:16
Advanced 13 and older	13 to 18	1:18 to 1:22

Leadership

Having developed a vision for your swim team program, the next question is "Who will lead the program?" Finding personnel to serve as swim coaches will be a critical step in determining the short-term direction of the program. Experience, attitude, and organizational skills are the qualities you should look for in a coach.

Here are some ideas on how to look for possible candidates, interview and hire them, and monitor them once they're hired.

Seeking Candidates

Before you begin your search, develop a position description. Follow the same procedures as described in chapter 5.

To search for volunteers or part-time coaches, try these methods:

- Find out if any of your staff have competitive coaching or swimming backgrounds. It will be important for the coach to have some knowledge of the sport.
- If high school swimming exists in your area, check with local coaches to see if they might be available or if they know of potential candidates. Also, schoolteachers may be available to work part-time.
- If there are local community summer swim league programs in your area, ask their coaches if they are available. Most will be college age and perfect for a new, start-up position.
- If your association is located near a college, contact its job placement office or physical education department, or place an ad in the student newspaper.
- Consider retired people or those with flexible work schedules as potential part-time coaches.
- Post notices of volunteer opportunities in the YMCA program brochure and in your YMCA's locker rooms.

To look for candidates for full-time positions, these options may help:

- The American Swimming Coaches Association (ASCA) Job Service is an excellent resource for finding and placing coaches. Their staff will work directly with you to find candidates who best meet your team profile. You may contact ASCA at 800-356-2722.
- Consider advertising in *Swimming World,* the leading periodical on competitive swimming. You may contact *Swimming World* classifieds at 310-607-9956.
- The National YMCA Job Vacancy list is another tool for locating possible coaches. You may contact the National YMCA Job Vacancy list at 800-872-9622.
- The Internet can also be used to post information about paid and volunteer positions. For more help on recruitment, visit the YMCA of the USA Web site.

Remember that in your first year, you will probably have to consider volunteers or part-time coaches. You will have a limited budget, with a subsidy required from your association. Search for someone who will be enthusiastic, patient, and a good teacher. Administrative skills will be important, but volunteer parents can assist in this area.

As for assistant coaches, individuals with strong aquatics teaching backgrounds or even your more experienced senior swimmers will be ideal. Parents with competitive swimming experience may also be willing to offer some deck time. Be creative and persistent in your search for enthusiastic coaches who can share your program dreams.

Look for candidates with these attributes:

- Experience either swimming on a swim team or coaching a swim team
- Stroke technique and swim training knowledge
- Understanding of the swim team's role in the YMCA
- Positive manner of offering feedback to swimmers
- Ability to recruit swimmers and coaches

- Ability to work with the swim team advisory committee (see page 479)
- A willingness to become a member of the American Swimming Coaches Association and to continue to develop in knowledge
- Availability for swim meets

Interviewing for Coaching Positions

You will want to carefully interview each candidate you consider for swim team coaching positions. For information on how to interview YMCA staff in general, see chapter 5. Here are some interview questions specific to swim team coaches that you may want to use:

- Describe how you would teach a swimmer the (butterfly, front flip turn, competitive dive start).
- Describe your coaching philosophy.
- On a scale of 1 to 5, how important is winning?
- How can you teach healthy competition?
- What do you think about swim team advisory committees?
- How would you lead the swim team advisory committee? What are some of the roles parents could hold on a committee?
- Describe a sample workout.
- How would you coach several lanes of differing abilities at the same time?
- How do you help motivate swimmers?
- Have you ever run a swim meet before? Describe the process.
- What are some safety guidelines that you would use during practice? Specifically, what are guidelines to use when swimmers are diving from starting blocks?
- If the lifeguard does not show up, what do you do?

Monitoring Staff

Once you've hired the staff for your competitive swim program, here are some ways that you can monitor them for quality programming and development:

- Meet with the swim team coach frequently, at least twice a month.
- Depending on team size, you may want to give the swim team coach some responsibility for the swim team budget and make sure he or she understands how to monitor it.
- Help coaches understand the administrative aspects of their jobs, and follow up to make sure they are performing those duties properly.
- Observe swim team practices.
- Attend home and away swim meets.
- Evaluate whether appropriate coach-to-swimmer and lifeguard-to-swimmer ratios are being met at practices and meets.
- Include the swim team coach in aquatics staff meetings.
- Attend swim team advisory committee meetings.
- Set up a swim team comment box.

• Review the season plan (which should include season, phase, weekly, and daily plans) and check to see whether it is followed.

Offer educational opportunities to all levels of your staff, from the part-time coach to your full-time staff. For your part-time staff, your best resource will be the head coach. The staff should have regular meetings to cover topics that would make each coach more effective during the practice sessions. Training might include practicing with the lifeguards who normally guard during swim practices or working with program volunteers. It's a good idea to practice specific scenarios that may happen during the program, such as the following:

• Slips and falls on the deck
• Starting block use
• Swimmer collisions in the lane
• Swimmers getting lost at an away meet
• Bad weather conditions at meets
• A swimmer who is not picked up after practice
• Diving
• Meet warm-up procedures
• A parent who becomes violent

Swim team coaches should hold certifications in CPR, first aid, YMCA Lifeguard or YMCA Aquatic Safety Assistant, YMCA Principles of Competitive Swimming and Diving, and YMCA Swim Coach. However, you should encourage them to seek further YMCA of the USA training and certifications such as these:

• YMCA Advanced Swim Coach
• YMCA Level I Swim Official
• YMCA Personal Fitness (if using weight training for swimmers)
• Working with Program Volunteers
• Volunteerism Leadership Training Program module

One professional organization that can open many educational doors for your staff is the American Swimming Coaches Association. The ASCA offers many resources, including an annual clinic. These can serve as excellent supplements to the YMCA's certifications for swimming and advanced swimming coaches. The ASCA can certify your coaches at one of five levels based on knowledge, experience, and competitive achievements. For more information on the ASCA, visit their Web site at **www.swimmingcoach.org.**

In addition, USA Swimming has a vast library of information to help your coaches develop a season plan and to improve such skills as communication and marketing. For more information on USA Swimming, visit their Web site at **www.usswim.org.** Local clinics may be available at a reasonable cost, or your coaches may consider brainstorming with other coaches in your area.

Finally, you might suggest that your coaches read *USA Swimming* and *Swimming Technique.* These two periodicals address the technical aspects of competitive swimming.

Program Participants

You must have willing participants for any type of sports program. You can find possible swim team members from a variety of areas. Consider the following:

• Where do swimmers in your association's Swim Lessons program go once they have completed the top level of the program? What about swim team? You may want to have your coaches teach the upper-level youth classes.

• Any local organized swim leagues are ideal feeder programs for year-round swim teams. Develop a brochure and presentation and then contact the league organizers for the opportunity to introduce your program to the membership. Be active, available, and in attendance at league meets and functions. Offer a free stroke clinic for local community teams. This is an excellent way to introduce your program and help the league at the same time. Consider hosting a league relay or championship meet.

• Another feeder program can be a "Little Swim Team" program for children who are eight and under. The children swim twice a week for 45 minutes during a regular lesson time. The emphasis is on low coach-to-swimmer ratios and improving swimming skills and technique. Minimeets and dual meets are held, and all swimmers wear team suits during competition and attend a banquet at the end of the season. Parents and children love it; kids get a taste of competitive swimming and improve their skills, but they aren't overwhelmed during the school year.

• Encourage high school swimmers to continue their season with your YMCA team after the conclusion of the high school season.

• Offer YMCA Swim Lessons to schools in your area. This will be a way to identify talented swimmers and introduce them to competitive swimming.

• Once you're up and swimming, have a bring-a-friend day when team members can bring a friend to practice. You also can ask team members if they have siblings who might be interested in joining the team.

Shape your program to the needs of the community. Most kids just want to have fun in an organized activity such as a swim team. Parents want a sport in which their children will learn basic skills and improve interpersonal communication. Couple benefits to both children and parents with a YMCA membership and you have a winning combination for family involvement.

Pool Time

A swim team will require one important ingredient to be successful—pool time! Unlike sports such as soccer, softball, and other outdoor activities in which an open field will suffice, swimming requires specialized facilities.

The biggest obstacle facing all YMCA swim teams is the competition for pool time. Every YMCA with a pool faces the constant challenge of trying to offer space and programming for all of its members. Swim team practice time, swim lessons, family swim time, lap swimming, scuba, diving, and general free swim space are just some of the pool's many uses.

You may have to turn to outside facilities to meet your program needs or team expansion. In most cases, you will incur some type of facility use charge or lane rental fee. Be aware that most facilities may require insurance coverage for your team members. Check to be sure that your YMCA has this liability coverage in its insurance policy.

Consider the following facility opportunities:

- *City-owned or municipal facilities.* These facilities are likely choices because they are encouraged to address the needs of all taxpayers, which probably includes most members of your program. In most cases, these facilities are accessible and well maintained, and their staff is experienced in working with outside groups.

- *Community centers.* These may include facilities owned by service organizations such as the Kiwanis, Jaycees, Elks, or other similar groups.

- *Private health clubs.* Many health clubs offer full-service facilities for their membership, which may include lap swim pools. For your more experienced swimmers, access to the weight or exercise room may also be available.

- *Local schools or colleges.* Schools and colleges are often in need of reciprocal help. This type of arrangement may include the YMCA coach helping the local high school or working with local college swimmers during the off-season.

- *Private clubs or neighborhood pools.* Obviously, YMCAs in warm climates could benefit from the large number of neighborhood swimming pools. Some other regional areas have pools with seasonal (winterized) coverings such as bubbles or temporary buildings.

Practice Recommendations

In developing your practice structure, consider the recommended minimum guidelines shown in Table 17.2 for the various ages and levels of experience of your swimmers.

Being creative with your pool time and space will be an important tool in your program's short- and long-term development. Effective use of pool time will accomplish several goals of your program:

- *Serving the needs of swimmers at all levels.* Several groups may need to practice at the same time. Think of the types of things that novice and advanced swimmers could do together. Remember, they will often be competing together as teammates.

Table 17.2 **Recommended Minimum Guidelines for Practice**

Ability level	Ages	Practices per week	Pool time (hours per practice)
Novice precompetitive	5 to 9	3	3/4 to 1
First and second year competitive	7 to 10	3 to 4	1 to 1 1/2
Advanced 12 and under	9 to 12	4 to 5	1 to 2
Novice precompetitive	10 to 18	4	1 to 1 1/4
First and second year competitive	10 to 18	4 to 5	1 to 2
Advanced 13 and older	13 to 18	5 to 8*	1 1/2 to 2 1/2

*Includes two practices per day. Morning practices before school may serve as the primary or additional training opportunity.

- *Program growth.* By maximizing the available pool space at your YMCA and off-site locations, you will increase enrollment and revenue. Increased revenue in your budget helps pay for staff and training equipment and will ultimately help you attain your vision.

Any water space is usable. Let's say that the only pool available is a 20-yard pool. Even though competitions are typically held in pools of 25-yard, 25-meter, or 50-meter lengths, effective training can occur anywhere. If your pool is shaped with a separate deep end, be creative in using that area to teach dives or practice turns.

Start-Up Costs

Let's consider the start-up costs for your new swim team program. Your YMCA will help greatly in this area. Most YMCAs subsidize youth sports programs, including swim teams. The majority of this support applies to staff salaries, training equipment, and pool usage. However, you should strive to meet your direct (actual) costs, as well as indirect costs such as pool usage, utilities, administrative support, office supplies, insurance, and other expenses shared by departments at the YMCA.

A budget will be an important fiscal management tool in planning for your swim team season. Include the following line items when establishing your start-up budget:

Income

> Program fees
> Hosted swim meets
> Fundraising
> Resale swim team store
> Seasonal clinics or workshops
> Sponsorships

Expenses

> Staff salaries
> Pool rental fees
> Program supplies
> Swim meet entry fees
> Office supplies
> Awards

Income

Program fees are the primary source of income for all programs at the YMCA. In most cases, plan on program fees accounting for over 60 percent of the budgeted income. Fees should vary by practice groups according to the amount of practice time available.

Whenever your swimmers compete at another facility, a per-event or per-meet charge usually applies. Consider including the meet entry fees in your overall program fees. This will accomplish three goals:

1. You will be encouraging team members to participate in competitions, since they have already paid for the meets.

2. Most families would prefer not to be "nickled and dimed" for each meet their child attends.

3. You have income up front without the need to bill after a meet.

If this option does not appeal to you, plan to collect meet fees before competition.

Hosting swim meets is an excellent way to increase income for your program. It will require heavy volunteer involvement, but it spares families the cost of travel. Entry fees could be charged per event or per swimmer. Swim meet income should generate about 15 percent of your budget.

Consider setting up a concession table with drinks and snacks provided by your team's families. What about selling a meet program or heat sheet or obtaining paid ads for it?

Fundraising is a major source of income for nonprofit organizations like the YMCA. Plan on at least 20 percent of your established budget income coming from fundraising projects. As a start-up program, you will probably need to generate closer to 50 percent of your income from fundraising activities. However, be sure to coordinate your fundraising efforts with other fundraising activities conducted by your YMCA so that they do not compete or conflict with one another.

The key to effective fundraising is the way you present the project to your membership. Consider the phrase "fun-raising" as a description of your team activities. Be clear on how the money will be used. After all, you will be striving to involve swimmers and parents in a common interest. The types of fundraising activities you choose should be simple and painless, yet effective. Choose activities that require primarily a time commitment from the swimmers and parents.

Concentrate on large projects that can involve the entire team. Since car washes, bake sales, and yard sales typically produce a small income, many must be conducted. Consider selling poinsettias during the Thanksgiving or Christmas holidays. Contact a local nursery for availability and quantity discounts. One team sold more than 1,500 plants for $4,500 profit one year. For more ideas on fundraising, go to the YMCA Web site.

A resale swim team store is another income source for your team. Team T-shirts, sweats, hats, swim caps, goggles, team suits, equipment bags, and more can be purchased for sale to your membership. Mark up the items so that you generate some income from each sale. Set up a table at practices, staffed by parents waiting for their children. Contact a local screen printer and aquatics store for merchandise. A swim store may generate only 5 percent of total income, but the store is an excellent service for your families.

Preorder all items to limit inventory. Have parents pay at the time of ordering and order only what has been prepaid. Most screen printers and aquatics stores will be able to provide you with samples.

Swim clinics and workshops are a way of attracting new members and earning money at the same time. Much will depend on available pool time and staff. Preseason and postseason are the best times to offer clinics and workshops. Invite swimmers from local summer clubs to a one-week workshop before the summer season.

Finally, you may want to seek sponsorships from local businesses. Community involvement will take the financial pressure off you and your families and introduce the value of your program to the entire community.

Expenses

Staff salaries will be the largest expense of your program, accounting for almost 50 percent of your budget. Initially, you may have to depend on volunteers and part-time staff to help your program get off the ground. A benefits package of health and life insurance and possibly a YMCA retirement plan could be included in this line item.

You should pay head coaches an annual (full-time), seasonal, or hourly (part-time) salary. When determining salaries, consider experience, tenure, pay rates at other local programs, and other YMCA responsibilities.

Until your program is well established, your assistant coaches will most likely be volunteers or part-time employees of the team who are paid an hourly salary. Consider starting at minimum wage with an increase for safety certifications and experience.

Some swim meets will require travel to another facility. You should compensate paid coaches for their mileage or airfare, any hotel costs, meals, and miscellaneous expenses incurred as a direct result of attending the meet as a paid staff member. Develop an expense report for your coach to complete, and require receipts. Most YMCAs will have a basic expense report form.

Pool rental fees will primarily involve usage of off-site facilities. Most facilities will charge a per-hour or per-lane fee for outside groups. These charges will vary from $15 to $50 per hour or from $2 to $5 per lane per hour. In some cases, you may also be asked to pay lifeguarding and equipment rental costs. When renting a facility for a swim meet, you will usually encounter a one-time meet charge that could range from $100 to $6,000, depending on the facility and length of rental.

You may be required to submit proof of liability insurance coverage with your contract. Your YMCA should have a blanket coverage policy; check with the association program director for a copy.

You may need a storage bin for your equipment, as well as a message board or mailbox system. Be sure to include those requests in your contractual agreement. In addition, you may need to use the facility deck space for dryland exercises or stretching. Include these time and space needs with your request. (See figure 3.22, page 95 for guidelines on contracting for off-site space.)

You will also need to purchase program equipment for a start-up program. You will not need to provide each piece of equipment for all swimmers, but you should have enough of each item to serve one-third of your team. For a new team (fewer than 75 members), essential items would be 25 kickboards at $5 each and one pace clock at $125.

Certainly, your facility will need lane ropes, backstroke flags, and starting blocks. Top-of-the-line lane ropes cost approximately $250 each. You will need one less rope than the total number of lanes you have. Backstroke flags can be relatively inexpensive, at a cost of $30 per flag. As you grow, consider buying custom flags with your team name imprinted across the flags. Starting blocks will be an important addition to your facility, especially if you will be hosting meets.

For more established programs, several other types of training equipment and meet supplies would be helpful:

Pull buoys at $5 each

Swim fins at $20 per pair

Hand paddles at $10 per pair

Stopwatches at $15 each

Lap counters at $35 each

Swim Team Software and Swim Meet Software

Several other expenses may apply to your team. First, if your team is part of a swim league or your club has a dual membership with USA Swimming, there will probably be registration or league fees for each team member. The USA Swimming registration fee for individual swimmers is around $25 per swimmer and includes secondary insurance coverage. Check with USA Swimming and US Masters for the team registration fees.

- Fees for invitationals and other swim meets must be submitted with your meet entries. Swimmers should have paid the fees on registration for the meet.
- Basic office supplies will be important tools in administering your program. Telephone, postage, printing, paper, and other administrative services are essential. The association should be able to provide what you need.
- Awards such as ribbons are excellent incentives and rewards for your swimmers' efforts. You can buy these from award retailers.

Keep these thoughts in mind as you formulate your budget:

- Let people and programs drive the budget, not vice versa.
- Always underestimate your income and overestimate expenses.
- Be as detailed as possible in outlining income and expenses.
- Strive to meet at least your direct budget; that is, your direct program expenses.

Remember that your association is paying for indirect costs such as pool maintenance, utilities, administrative salaries, benefits, and all costs shared by the departments in your association.

Promotion

Promoting your program is another step in establishing your YMCA's swim team. We have touched on several promotional areas in our search for new swim team members. Several proven methods of promoting your program are word of mouth, community contacts, clinics and workshops, and a team brochure. You may also want to try to gain publicity through the media. For more information on promotion and communications, go to the YMCA Web site.

Word of Mouth

The most positive and economical promotional tool you will have will be the participants in the program. If the families in your program are pleased and enthusiastic about the team, their comments will spread like wildfire through schools, churches, workplaces, and social settings. The majority of new swimmers will have heard about your team from other families. Never underestimate the value of a satisfied parent!

Make YMCA members aware of the presence of the swim team by displaying swim team banners or having a swim team trophy case. Create a team bulletin board that displays the latest news about the team.

Community Contacts

High-profile coaches will also help promote your swim team. Your coaches should regularly attend high school swim meets, as well as community summer league meets, so families can put a face to a name. Ask coaches who attend meets to wear a T-shirt printed with your team name or logo, to be accessible for any questions, and to avoid voicing support for just one team. Remember, you are selling not only your YMCA team, but the sport of swimming as well.

In addition, think about offering a YMCA team cap or T-shirt to team members. In that way, current team members who may be competing for a high school or summer club team will be recognized as YMCA team members as well. Keep in mind that some high school and summer league coaches may have their own team outfits, so be careful not to ruffle any feathers.

Clinics and Workshops

We reiterate how effective it is to offer a free clinic or workshop for local high school or summer league teams. This is free publicity except for the cost of your coaches' time. Here are a few hints for running an effective clinic:

- Take several of your better swimmers to demonstrate techniques. Kids will relate positively to members of their peer group.
- Design a stroke correction checklist or handout for all participants.
- Involve the host team coach. Coaches will appreciate the opportunity to give and receive pointers on teaching stroke technique.
- Make it simple, concise, and most important, fun!
- Don't compare your program to other competitive teams in the area.
- Try to learn the names of the clinic participants. You will likely run into several swimmers later in the year, and hopefully they will recognize you.
- Promote the benefits of competitive swimming and your team.
- As a YMCA team, expect and present a high ethical level, which is one of the characteristics that makes us different.

Team Brochure

The best written form of promotion for your program will be a brochure or flyer. Whether a simple one-page typed piece or a full-color brochure, any written communication should include answers to the basic questions of who, what, when, where, and—in the case of your team—how much. Include a short statement on YMCA values and philosophy.

Be sure to include the following information in your team brochure or information sheet:

- *Minimum requirements to participate in your program.* Remember that you are guiding a swim team, not a begin-to-swim program. You may want to require swimmers to pass a specific level in the YMCA Swim Lessons program before permitting them to join the swim team. We recommend a minimum age of five years old for the precompetitive program and eight years old for the competitive program. As for skill level, consider Guppy level in YMCA Swim Lessons or the following skill level requirements:
  - Deep-water safe
  - Able to complete 25 yards without stopping
  - Able to swim freestyle, breathing to the side (rotary breathing)
  - Knowledge of one other competitive stroke

- *Descriptions of practice groups.* Offer the basic guidelines and age levels for each group. Parents will need to know which group their child would practice with.

- *Coaching staff backgrounds.* Identify team coaches and their swimming and coaching experience. If possible, indicate the practice groups and age groups with whom they will be working.

- *Practice schedule and expectations.* You may need to insert this item later, since practice schedules may change during the season. Many younger team members may participate in other sports, and parents will need to know how often you expect their child to be at practice.

• *Program uniqueness.* Why are you different? Highlight the things you do to make your YMCA swim team program different from other local teams or other youth sports programs. Be sure to include the character development component. If you have room, include testimonials from participants.

• *Cost.* Be clear about the payment plan and policies. Estimate additional costs such as swim meet fees, registration fees, and any other special costs.

• *Contact information.* Include a phone number and address for any questions. Remember that a question is an important opportunity for you to sell the program. Be accessible!

Distribute your brochure in YMCA Swim Lesson classes and other aquatics instruction classes. If your school system allows it, visit local schools to tell kids about the program and hand out your brochure there. Making it available to swimmers in summer leagues is another possibility. You can also ask physicians, orthodontists, and librarians if they will allow you to leave copies of your brochure in their offices or buildings.

Media Coverage

You can also spread the word about your swim team through the media. Use cable TV announcements and press releases to announce tryouts or registration. Try to get the media to do feature stories on the team or news coverage of meets or other special swim team events. See chapter 8 for more on how to contact the media for promotion.

Competitions

Now that you've got a swim team, you will want your swimmers to compete with other teams. You'll have to choose which types of meets to participate in and how often. Leagues offer many competitive opportunities, so you may want to join or form one. You will also need to develop procedures for deciding who enters which competitions and a plan for paying entry fees.

Types of Meets

There are several types of competition for swimmers:

• Intrasquad
• Local
• YMCA league
• Invitational
• District, state, or regional YMCA meets
• National meets

As you are starting a new team, and thus are introducing swimmers and parents to the sport, consider keeping meet travel to a minimum. Remember that in all levels of competition, you should set up your swimmers to be successful. Do not emphasize the winning aspect of competition as the most important success. Stress that doing one's best is a winning effort.

Intrasquad meets are informal meets involving only your team. These are excellent practice opportunities for volunteers and provide a low-pressure atmosphere for your swimmers. Try to furnish awards and recognition, even if only participant ribbons, for all swimmers. The best news is that your team will go undefeated!

Local meets can be arranged with other YMCAs or club teams in your area. These meets can include a variety of formats and create some exciting competitions. It is always fun to compete against classmates from school or friends who compete for another team. Travel time is minimized, and you might even waive the entry fee depending on where the meet is held. Local competitions will provide additional experience for your volunteers, and several volunteers may even pursue officiating swim meets.

Participation in a YMCA league is an excellent way to organize your competitive schedule, compete against teams with similar backgrounds, and offer consistency to your competitive program. We have found that a significant enrollment increase typically follows a team's involvement in a league format. Most meets will involve one or two other teams, which will help with the length of the meet and allow all team members to compete as one team. All competitions will follow basically the same format and rules.

Invitationals are meets that you are invited to attend, and they normally include from 6 to 20 other teams in a one- to three-day format. In some cases, entries may be limited to swimmers who have achieved particular time standards. A uniform set of time standards is established annually by USA Swimming based on average times from across the country.

Invitationals may be open to only YMCA teams or may include club teams who are members of USA Swimming. Participation in USA Swimming–sanctioned meets will require USA Swimming membership for members of your team.

If you have many YMCA programs in your area, you may also compete with other YMCA programs on district, state, and regional levels. In some cases, these competitions will not involve league members, so be sure to check with your area consultant to see if your team members are allowed to participate in them.

At the national level, the National YMCA Swimming and Diving Championships are offered for your most competitive swimmers between the ages of 12 and 21. Participants are required to have achieved a minimum qualifying time to enter each event. There is a short-course (25-yard pool) competition in April and a long-course (50-meter pool) competition in August.

Your swim meet schedule develops the swimmers in your program, both competitively and emotionally. Make every effort to offer a balanced schedule that effectively satisfies the needs of all participants on your team. You should include a series of low-key developmental meets, which will typically involve over 75 percent of your swimmers. Dual meets and intrasquad meets are the best competitions to serve the needs of inexperienced swimmers. For your more competitive swimmers, opportunities in a league will open more doors and expose the swimmers to a higher level of competition.

Plan on developing your meet schedule for the winter season as early as August. Try to identify competitions that will serve the needs and ability levels of all team members equally. If none exist, develop a meet yourself to ensure an opportunity for all swimmers to compete.

Joining or Forming a League

A YMCA league is an excellent way to involve all swimmers in your program. Most leagues set up a series of dual meets and conclude with a league or state championship meet. The dual meet against a team with a similar philosophy is a can't-miss arrangement. A league most likely exists in your area, and most leagues are more than willing to expand to accommodate new YMCA teams. Join an existing YMCA league if possible. If there is no YMCA league in your area, consider starting your own. Your program consultant can help you make contact with other teams in your area.

Remember, requirements for national-level YMCA competitions will include participation in three interassociation meets as well as a sanctioned YMCA championship meet. Make your YMCA swim team program a bona fide YMCA program by maintaining involvement with other YMCA teams. Each YMCA league has its own set of rules and guidelines in conjunction with the national YMCA rules for competitive swimming and diving. Your commitment to the league may be minimal in some cases or exclusive in others. Be sure to choose the arrangement that best fits your vision and goals for long-term growth.

If attempts to locate other YMCAs in your area are futile, you may want to contact other local or regional club teams. A league can be developed with any number of participating teams. Local travel, shortened time frames, and the competitive spirit of a dual meet will energize your swimmers and help inject the most important element of our sport—fun—into your swim team program.

If your association has multiple sites, create some in-town rivalries by scheduling a series of meets within your association. You may consider setting up meets for your older swimmers with local high school teams or even masters programs.

The goal in scheduling is to find other programs that have similar goals and philosophies. That way, your competitions will be spirited but kept in perspective.

Entering Meets

Teams and swimmers enter different types of meets in different ways. In dual-meet competition (that is, a meet between two associations), the coach will enter swimmers from her or his team in that meet's slated events while keeping in mind that total participation is the primary goal.

For invitational swim meets, to which many teams are invited and in which participation by teams is not limited to an exact number of participants per event, program organizers use one of three methods for entry: individual swimmer selection, coach's selection, and modified coach's selection.

Under the individual swimmer selection method, the swimmer elects to participate in a swim meet that is endorsed by the program. The meet entry may be submitted

- individually by each swimmer,
- as a team through the coaching staff, or
- as a team through an entry process that is administered by a parent or volunteer.

In all cases, the head coach should receive a copy of the entry so he or she can assign a coach to attend.

Using the coach's selection method, a coach designates the invitational meets that the team will attend. The coach also determines which swimmers will attend those meets and what events they will swim.

Some programs are administered through a modified coach's selection method, which is a combination of the first two methods. Some meets are designated as team meets in which the coach enters all swimmers, and some meets may be entered by swimmers individually.

Regardless of the entry method, the coach must help the swimmers select appropriate meets. The swim coach is the expert whom swimmers and parents look to for advice about a swimmer's readiness to participate in a given event. Just when is an age grouper ready to compete in a 100 or 200 of her or his stroke? Only the coach knows.

Since entry into invitational meets usually involves a fee, collecting, tracking, and disbursing the money can be a major headache. Rather than dealing with payments for each meet, with cash casually passed in envelopes, many program organizers have elected to use an escrow method of fee collection and disbursement. Under this system, each swimmer pays an agreed-on sum before the season for his or her meet entry fees. These fees are allocated to individual meet entry accounts. As the swimmers enter meets throughout the season, their individual accounts are debited for each meet's entry fees. At the end of the season, any unused escrow fees are returned to the swimmers. Swimmers who exceed the escrow amount are billed for the amount owed.

Evaluations

Evaluations are an excellent tool for listening to your membership. For year-round swim teams, consider doing evaluations at midyear (January), at the end of the indoor season (April), and at the end of the outdoor season (July).

Keep the evaluations simple for the best response. Encourage comments with open-ended questions. Consider the following simple format:

1. On a scale of 1 to 10, 10 being the highest, please rate the overall swim team season for your child.
2. What things can we do (or could we have done) to make this season a perfect 10 for you and your swimmer?
3. If you could make one suggestion that would greatly improve our program, what would it be?

If possible, hand deliver the evaluations; you'll obtain the highest response rate. Include a cover letter that encourages families to complete the form. Remember that a low response will mean one of two things—people are very happy or people are very unhappy. The problem is, you'll never know which unless you receive an adequate number of completed evaluations.

Consider developing a special form for the swimmers. You will be surprised at the insight of swimmers of all ages. They know what they want from the program. Listen carefully to their opinions.

Finally, be sure to follow up on some of the better suggestions and indicate that the follow-up was in response to the evaluations. Never forget that the program participants make the program, and you cannot ignore their opinions.

For more help on evaluation, see chapter 2.

Self-evaluation is also important. At the end of the season, the coaching staff should meet to review all facets of the program. Consider questions such as these:

- Was there a documented season plan for the program? If so, did we follow this plan?
- Were weekly and daily plans written, and were they followed?
- What are some external factors that may affect the program in the future, such as the opening and closing of competing area clubs?
- How effective was the program's marketing strategy?

The head coach should evaluate individually all coaching staff members (paid staff and volunteers). Along with these individual evaluations, the coaching staff should discuss as a group their effectiveness, considering the following items:

- Their collective strengths and weaknesses.
- The coach-to-swimmer ratio at practices and meets.
- The availability of coaching candidates for the future.
- Training needed for the future for coaches.
- Team goal evaluations.
- Objective, open discussion of parental evaluations. This should include an item-by-item discussion and an action plan for each.
- Adherence to safety standards in all team activities.
- Equipment and teaching aids needed for the future.

At the conclusion of the meeting, the group should adopt and document clearly defined, measurable goals for the coming season. Copies of these goals should be distributed to all coaches.

ORGANIZING A SWIM TEAM ADVISORY COMMITTEE

Getting help from parent volunteers will be critical in offering the type of swim team program you desire. You should already have identified key volunteers to help you research the background information noted earlier in the "Starting Your Team From Scratch" section. We recommend converting this group into a swim team advisory committee of team parents. Several ingredients will be essential:

- Have the coach and program supervisor select potential members. Include parents of swimmers from all groups and levels, especially those with strong business contacts in the community. Be sure that those chosen will be willing to offer adequate volunteer time to the committee.
- Have the group report to you or to the head swimming coach if she or he is a professional director in the association.
- Have this committee be a subcommittee within your YMCA board/committee structure.
- Identify areas in which subcommittees can be developed and in which committee members can enlist other parents to help.

Potential subcommittees may include the following:

- Transportation and out-of-town meets
- Swim meet management
- Club publicity
- Fundraising
- Social
- Concessions and meet hospitality
- Officials
- Awards

- Membership
- Sunshine and spirit
- Records
- Registration
- Swim store
- Newsletter

If you have parents whose children have been on swim teams where the parents were responsible for supervising the coaches and team, be sure to make it clear to them that at the YMCA, parents serve in an advisory capacity only. Their role is to assist the coaches. YMCA staff is responsible for overseeing the coaches and team.

Make it your goal to involve every parent in your program in some capacity. Ask each parent to volunteer for a minimum of eight hours per year. With 50 families in your program, you will have 400 volunteer hours that can help you offer the best program possible for the children.

The recommended committee structure is the perfect way to introduce new parents to the team. Pair new parents with more experienced swim team parents and seek early involvement. Remember, almost any parent can start and stop a stopwatch—it's a great way to start. Most important, the parents are actively supporting and investing in their children's program. Unlike the stock market, a positive return is guaranteed.

Begin to form a parent advisory committee by first developing operating guidelines for the group. These should describe the parent organization as a support group whose function is to assist the head swimming coach or aquatics director by enhancing the overall program. Figure 17.2 shows sample guidelines.

Recommended Committee Responsibilities

Although committee responsibilities will vary from club to club, here are some basic tasks to consider for the subcommittees identified earlier:

- *Transportation and out-of-town meets committee.* Makes travel arrangements for out-of-town meets.
- *Swim meet management committee.* Coordinates swim meets hosted by the club; recruits meet volunteers and officials.
- *Club publicity committee.* Promotes swimmer achievements and activities through newspaper and television coverage.
- *Fundraising committee.* Coordinates various fundraising activities; may develop subcommittees for each activity. May also be involved in general YMCA fundraising.
- *Social committee.* Plans family and team social activities and banquets.
- *Concessions and meet hospitality committee.* Directs swim meet concessions for hosted meets; organizes hospitality room for coaches and officials.
- *Officials committee.* Organizes team volunteers who may be interested in officiating; assists with officials' clinics and volunteer certifications.
- *Awards committee.* Plans year-end awards banquet; recommends awards criteria.
- *Membership committee.* Oversees program promotion to new members; acts as liaison between general membership and advisory group.

General Commission

The swim team advisory committee is responsible for assisting the YMCA swim team program supervisor and swim team coach in matters pertaining to the smooth functioning of a competitive swimming and diving program within the framework of the association's values, purpose, policies, and objectives.

Appointment and Composition

1. The swim team advisory committee is sanctioned annually by the YMCA swim team program supervisor.

2. One or two individuals shall be elected by the members committee to serve as members of the program (aquatic or branch advisory) committee.

3. The swim team advisory committee shall be composed of the aquatic director and/or head swimming coach, parents, swimmers' representatives, and other interested individuals.

4. The program supervisor serves as the chair of the swim team advisory committee.

Responsibilities

1. To assist in maintaining a cooperative swim team program

2. To choose from its membership committee chairpersons to oversee designated responsibilities

3. To report regularly to the program supervisor, including written minutes of all meetings

4. To raise funds to supplement income of the swim team

5. To provide, train, and help certify YMCA officials for hosted swim meets

6. To help recommend ways to incorporate character development into the club's program

7. To recommend ways to increase family activity in the club's programs

8. To conduct annual meetings of team membership

Figure 17.2 Sample swim team advisory committee guidelines.

- *Sunshine and spirit committee.* Sends cards or gifts to swimmers who are sick, which may involve family outreach; sends birthday greetings from the swim team; recognizes other family achievements or special events.
- *Records committee.* Maintains team records, as well as current times book.
- *Registration committee.* Oversees team and USA Swimming registrations of new and returning swimmers.
- *Swim store committee.* Organizes retail store selling team apparel and gifts.
- *Newsletter committee.* Assists with development, preparation, and distribution.

For more information on working with volunteers, see "The Seven Rs of Volunteer Development," available from the YMCA Program Store, or go to the YMCA Web site at **www.ymcausa.org.**

INTEGRATING CHARACTER DEVELOPMENT INTO YOUR PROGRAM

Character development is an integral part of the national YMCA program. The YMCA competitive swimming and diving program offers some wonderful moments in which participants can develop personal values that will affect them for a lifetime. The program is an excellent opportunity to teach the values of caring, honesty, responsibility, and respect.

You can ask your staff to emphasize these values in your program in the following ways:

- Communicate to team members that sporting behavior is an important part of the program.
- Teach the four values to team members so they know what those values mean. Give them examples.
- Consistently model those values in your behavior so team members can see what those values look like in action.
- Celebrate those values and hold them up to team members as what is right; this helps them learn to believe in the values.
- Ask team members to practice the values, over and over again.
- Consistently reinforce and reward behaviors that support the values, using the specific value word that is relevant: "Chris, thanks for helping LaKeisha find the practice equipment. That shows *caring*."
- Consistently confront team members whose behavior is inconsistent with the values, but do so in a way that does not devalue them.

Character development is essential to the YMCA sports philosophy. Both children and parents need to be included in this effort, and you and other YMCA staff must serve as resource persons to help them.

Character development can take place in competitive swimming and diving in many ways. First, coaches can teach values such as the following, based on the concept of fair play and the YMCA's historical concern for human values:

- Respect for oneself and others
- Putting winning in proper perspective
- Concern about personal fitness and lifetime sports involvement

- Responsibilities of team members and development of leadership
- Concern about the family and the role of parents

Second, coaches can help swimmers and their parents think about and determine their values—and link these values to behavior. They should find time for open discussions of important issues, in which the questions are often more important than the answers. Such issues might include the following:

- Personal goals and the steps toward achieving them
- Responsibilities to family and community
- Personal health issues such as diet and the use of drugs, alcohol, and tobacco
- Academic goals and school problems

You may want to have swimmers, parents, and coaches sign a code of ethics that includes YMCA character development.

Volunteer service projects are an excellent way for the athletes to put YMCA values into practice. For more information, contact the associate director for service-learning at the YMCA of the USA (800-872-9622) and ask for the *YMCA Service Learning Guide.*

Finally, character development should be an integral part of your staff's coaching style and practice—of how they relate to team members and conduct workouts. They need to involve swimmers in developing a team philosophy and team goals. When a values-related situation comes up during practice or events, or when a conflict develops between people, coaches can use it as a time to examine values. Such teachable moments may come

- as part of workout sessions,
- in the locker room,
- on bus trips,
- in one-on-one situations,
- during team meetings, or
- during meets.

Teachable moments can be triggered by either good or bad actions; coaches can praise individuals' or groups' supportive, fair behavior or can stop an activity briefly to talk about negative behavior. Here are some examples:

- If one team member yells at another for a mistake, the coach can talk to that team member about respect.
- If a team member does something dangerous during practice, the coach can have a brief discussion with that person about responsibility and caring for others.
- If one team member helps another who is injured, the coach can praise the person who helped for caring.
- If a team member admits to a false start that wasn't called, the coach can congratulate him or her for being honest.

Coaches should try to balance positive and negative instances, not use just negative situations.

Teachable moments are occasions when coaches can hold up the right value and explain why it is the acceptable thing to do. Doing this illustrates to team members what values look like beyond the words and how values are a part of our everyday lives.

For more information, discuss character development with your YMCA staff and plan to make it happen. See the *Principles of YMCA Competitive Swimming* manual and other YMCA character development resources available from the YMCA Program Store.

HOSTING COMPETITIONS

One of the best family components of your program will be the involvement of volunteers in hosting competitions. Being a swim meet host has many benefits, including

- providing the opportunity to display your YMCA philosophy in action,
- saving families money and time by competing closer to home,
- producing income for your general budget, and
- involving family members as participants or volunteers.

You will need volunteers to serve as swim meet director and swim meet management committee members. The swim meet management committee plans and coordinates the swim meets hosted by your club. A few subcommittees can probably handle smaller dual meets, while you may need many subcommittees for the large invitationals.

The responsibilities of your swim meet management committee and meet director should be as follows:

1. Establish the dates, location, and times for the meet.

2. Schedule facilities and secure the needed space and equipment for conducting the meet: locker rooms, spectator areas (temporary bleacher seating), starting blocks, lane lines, timing systems with starter unit or pistol, backstroke flags, diving boards and flash cards (if diving competition), recall rope, meet office, public address system, first aid equipment, and adequate tables and chairs, as well as supplies such as pencils, clipboards, three stopwatches per lane, and other related meet items.

3. Prepare and have all meet information sanctioned. Contact your competitive swimming field coordinator for proper forms and approval.

4. Distribute meet information to participating teams, including the following:

- Date, time, and site of meet (include directions).
- Pool description (i.e., water depth, number of lanes). Identify separate warm-up areas.
- For diving: types of diving boards, height of boards, depth of water.
- Order of events, timeline, and warm-up schedule.
- Eligibility and qualifying times.
- Meet format.
- Awards.
- Entry procedure, including entry fees and deadline for receipt of entries.
- List of hotels and restaurants.

5. Secure YMCA-certified technical officials. The host team should provide the meet referee. Contact visiting teams for potential officials, including stroke and turn judges and starters, as well as related diving officials.

6. Locate a hospitality room for coaches and officials, a place to post results, and concession areas.

7. Order awards (ribbons, medals, or trophies).
8. Plan the conduct of the meet:

   - National anthem
   - Pre-session devotion
   - Awards ceremonies

9. Establish a meet budget.
10. Advertise.

Here are some organizational tips for successful meets:

- Preplan and develop detailed descriptions of committee and coordinator responsibilities.
- Involve the head swimming coach in all aspects of the planning process.
- Pay attention to details. Follow up with regular committee meetings or contact with coordinators. Delegating the responsibility does not ensure completion of the task.
- Be creative in your meet approach. Ask how you can make the meet a memorable one that visitors will want to return to year after year.
- Be efficient in the conduct of the meet. Move at a constant yet balanced pace.
- Do not accept more entrants than you can handle. Quality always succeeds above quantity.
- Decorate your facility to welcome your guests.
- Double-check all entries, heat sheets, and score sheets for accuracy.
- Never forget to put the YMCA mission into action.

Meets can be organized differently depending on their size. Following are suggested schemes for intrasquad, dual, or three-team meets; midsized (four or more teams) or invitational meets; and championship meets.

Intrasquad, Dual, or Three-Team Meets

For meets of this size, consider forming the following subcommittees:

Meet director

Officials coordinator (technical roles)

Volunteer coordinator (administrative roles)

Head timer (coordinates volunteer timers)

Coach liaison

Concessions and hospitality coordinator

The meet director may be the host team coach or a parent volunteer. Follow this outline for organizing such meets:

1. Determine date, site, times, and meet format.
2. Schedule facility and reserve equipment.
3. Provide complete meet information to visiting teams. Identify any special arrangements or considerations.
4. Secure at least four Level II YMCA officials. One should serve as the meet referee, one as the starter, and two as stroke and turn judges. You will also need place judges, a head timer, three timers per lane, scorers, ribbon writers,

runners, clerk of course personnel, and other people for administrative responsibilities.

5. Provide all administrative supplies such as score sheets, disqualification slips, and entry cards. Be prepared to provide each team with results at the conclusion of the meet.

Midsized Meets (Four or More Teams) or Invitationals

These subcommittees will be helpful in supporting a midsized or invitational meet:

Meet director

Officials coordinator (technical roles)

Concessions and hospitality coordinator

Sales coordinator (T-shirt and program sales)

Head timer (coordinates volunteer timers)

Coach liaison

Facilities coordinator

Setup and cleanup

Awards committee

Meet office and computer personnel

Use this outline for planning a midsized meet:

1. Determine the date, site, times, and meet format. Make sure you receive a league or YMCA sanction.
2. Secure a facility to adequately handle expected participants. Be sure to have all equipment and supplies on hand.
3. Send required meet information to visiting teams.
4. Prepare a press release.
5. Order awards.
6. Recruit at least the recommended minimum number of meet officials:
   - One referee
   - One starter
   - Two stroke and turn judges
   - One announcer
   - Two runners
   - Three timers per lane (visiting teams may provide timers)
   - One head timer
   - Four place judges, two on each side (one to record, one to place)
   - Two clerk of course volunteers
   - Two scorers per team
   - Other meet personnel
7. Establish meet budget and set visiting team entry fees. Be sure to cover all direct expense costs.
8. Prepare master score sheet or heat sheet before the meet.
9. Prepare postmeet summary of results to distribute to participating teams.
10. Send press release of results.

Championship Meets

The following subcommittees are recommended for championship meets:

Meet director

Officials coordinator (technical roles)

Concessions and hospitality coordinator

Sales coordinator (T-shirt and program sales)

Head timer (coordinates volunteer timers)

Coach liaison

Facilities coordinator

Setup and cleanup

Awards committee

Meet office and computer personnel

Here is the outline for holding a championship meet:

1. Schedule facilities, secure necessary equipment, print heat sheet and meet program, and secure advertising and donations.
2. Develop a planning calendar starting at least nine months before the meet and establish timelines for task completion.
3. Develop a meet budget of income and expenses. Be sure to underestimate income and overestimate expenses.
4. Borrow or rent necessary office equipment such as computers and calculators. Plan for equipment to be in place several days before the competition.
5. Distribute printed registration information for coaches on their arrival at the meet.
6. Secure technical meet officials.
7. Develop a plan for printing results, heat sheets, and other printed forms or information.
8. Identify site space restrictions for competitors, coaches, and meet officials.
9. Order awards.
10. Contact retailers for swim supplies and aids to be in attendance at the meet. Make arrangements for display booths.
11. Contact local media before and after competition.
12. Develop a meet evaluation process to make suggestions for future competitions.

COMMUNICATING

No need in sports is overlooked as much as communication. Every moment of every day provides an opportunity for coaches to communicate, whether it be with swimmers, parents, or the community. Communication is education! By answering a question from a swimmer or parent, a coach is educating that swimmer or parent on your program philosophy.

The most important goal will be to communicate the YMCA philosophy. As in other youth sports, coaching competitive swimming and diving calls for teaching the fundamentals properly, developing basic team concepts, working on fair play values, and encouraging all swimmers and divers to participate and enjoy the sport.

The relationship between the coach and the team will be the critical ingredient in your team's success. The coach must be a leader, role model, teacher, and friend. This relationship is far more significant than the results of your competitions.

A good way for coaches to start improving communication is to follow the three ground rules of good communication:

- Speak for yourself. Say what and how you feel.
- Listen to others. Accept what they say and their right to say it. Hear what they say; don't just listen.
- Avoid put-downs. Be positive.

Coaches should also work on developing these three essential communication skills:

- *Asking open-ended questions.* Any question that has an obvious answer does not stimulate discussion or thinking. Coaches should always ask open-ended questions starting with phrases like "What do you think about . . . ?" or "How did you feel when . . . ?"

- *Listening.* Being a good listener is an art form. It is important to good communication and probably a little more important than talking. Everyone wants the coach to listen to them. It will take concentration. The coach may have to listen to a lot of things that may seem nonsensical, unfair, off the wall, or generally uninformative. However, by acknowledging others' comments, the coach will have a more open dialogue and receive more meaningful comments.

- *Giving positive reinforcement.* Any form of learning benefits from the appropriate use of positive reinforcement and acknowledgment. Reinforcement can be verbal, such as encouraging words, or nonverbal, such as smiles, pats on the back, eye contact, and overall body language. Coaches should recognize everyone's contributions and ideas with positive reinforcement.

Coaches will need to communicate with swimmers and parents both verbally and through a regular newsletter.

Verbal Communication

Most often a coach will communicate with an athlete verbally. Teaching proper technique and race strategy relies heavily on verbal communication.

Answering questions from parents or interested team members over the telephone depends totally on verbal communication. On the phone, coaches must be professional, patient, and good listeners. They should follow up on all phone messages within 24 hours, if possible.

Newsletter

Written communication highlighting current events and team achievements can be done through a team newsletter. Newsletters can take a detailed professional form or can be one-page handouts that contain essential information for your parents and swimmers.

Try to include the following items in your newsletters and other written communication to swimmers and parents:

- Event calendar and upcoming event descriptions
- Specific dates, times, and locations
- Directions, if needed
- Emergency phone numbers

- What to bring to an activity
- Transportation arrangements for activities
- Participation eligibility
- Meal and housing arrangements
- Room assignments
- Social items
- Rule changes
- Team policies and procedures
- Recognition of team achievements
- Birthday wishes
- Swimmers of the day, week, or month

Try to recognize all swimmers in some way in the newsletter. Do not favor your more competitive team members. Highlight out-of-team accomplishments (school honor rolls, Boy Scout and Girl Scout achievements, other sports highlights).

Finally, consider including some type of quotation, Bible verse, or motivational message in keeping with your overall YMCA philosophy. Never miss a chance to remind families of the uniqueness of your YMCA affiliation.

DEVELOPING A TEAM HANDBOOK

One important and beneficial communication tool you can use in your program is a team handbook. Your team handbook should serve as a policy manual for your team. In addition, a handbook can help educate your families about the sport of swimming and how your team fits into the overall scheme of the sport. Make it simple, direct, fun, and readable.

Try to arrange the information from broader topics, including team philosophy, to more specific concerns of the various practice levels in your program. A loose-leaf binder is ideal, as pages can be added or replaced as changes occur during the season. You could also consider posting the team handbook on your YMCA's Internet site, making it accessible with a password.

As a guide, consider including the following information:

Introduction
- Welcome or welcome back letter
- New parent orientation
- Mission statement and vision
- YMCA affiliation and relationship
- YMCA goals, Christian emphasis, and character development
- Team philosophy and objectives
- Code of conduct
- Brief history of the program
- Organizational chart and responsibilities
- Coaching staff profiles and staff office hours
- Practice schedules and site directions
- Team roster, including parents' names, swimmers' birthdays, schools, and grade levels
- Sources of club communication

Meets

- Information about USA Swimming (if applicable)
- Current meet schedule
- Eligibility for meets
- Sample swim meet information
- Team registration procedure
- How to enter swim meets
- Fee structure
- Billing policy and sample billing
- Team records
- Time standards

Practice

- Practice groups and requirements
- Practice attendance guidelines and policies
- Practice equipment descriptions

Health and Fitness

- Health concerns, such as asthma (recommended inhaler doses), swimmer's ear, and other special health needs and treatment
- Nutrition section
- Strength training program
- Dryland training program

Clinics

- Officials' clinics
- Special clinics and workshops

Swim Basics

- Glossary of swimming terms
- Basic stroke mechanics
- General rules of the sport

Volunteer Opportunities

- Parent and volunteer roles at practices and meets
- Committees and descriptions
- Fundraising goals and descriptions

The possibilities are virtually endless. What you choose to include should reflect the details of your program. Obviously, a thorough summary of your program could develop into a small book. It is important to be concise; be careful about overloading families, especially parents new to your program. Although the team handbook will probably serve as the primary resource guide for your families, regular communication and updates will be the key to keeping your families well informed.

A team handbook can be a fun and exciting project that helps define your program. Use parent volunteers, if possible, and make sure that the coach, swim team advisory committee, and YMCA review and approve the material before distribution.

Begin each season with a parent orientation meeting. Use the meeting to introduce the coaches, distribute the team handbook, discuss team philosophies and season goals, and review the previous season. This meeting might also be a good time to establish a team telephone tree. Each family can be responsible for contacting another family on the team about sudden schedule changes or special activities. This form of communication will serve two purposes: (1) communicate the change or activity, and (2) provide the opportunity for families to talk with others who have a common interest.

We recommend a series of introductory meetings for families new to the sport of swimming. Try to pair new families with more experienced families from your program. Regardless, a monthly meeting for the parents of each practice group would be an excellent way to reinforce the team handbook contents and answer questions.

ADMINISTRATIVE TIPS

No other YMCA aquatics program has greater opportunity to create "a tempest in a teapot" than the swim team. Pool space is often limited, and overzealous parents may not understand the YMCA's mission or youth sports philosophy. As the aquatics director, you'll need to educate parents in these areas.

Swim team parents invest considerable time and effort bringing their children to hours of practice while juggling their children's other needs and activities. This means that unhappy swim team parents can be an incredible source of bad YMCA public relations. To avoid such problems, try to establish a good working relationship among the swim team advisory committee, the head coach, and yourself to ensure good communications and a smoothly running program.

Keep an eye out for any of the following problems that might crop up with your competitive swim team:

- Parents meeting without the YMCA's knowledge
- Parents making policy decisions
- Parents hiring coaches
- Coaches and parents not understanding the big picture of the YMCA, seeing the swim team as an entity separate from the YMCA
- Not having enough meetings with your swim team coach to know what's going on
- Parents trying to coach
- Coaches speaking to swimmers negatively
- Coaches pushing swimmers to extremes in terms of training, eating habits, and dedication to swimming only

On the positive side, though, here are some key ideas to remember when working with your swim team:

- *Have a long-term vision for your program.* Share your vision with others, and your investment will multiply. Always keep the short-term picture in mind, but strive to improve in every area of your program.
- *Involve your volunteers.* Your volunteers can handle much of the administrative responsibility of your program, leaving the coaches to do what they do best—coaching.

- *You're different; you're a YMCA program!* Always strive to offer something different. Listen to your swimmers and parents—they should determine the program content. It is their program, and they will know what they want out of it. Focus on the YMCA mission and character development.

- *Building winners for life.* The YMCA Youth Super Sports motto is an excellent way to keep your overall program in focus. Be the best you can be against yourself and you will always be a winner.

- *Communicate.* Be sure your staff listens and uses every opportunity to promote your philosophy. Remind them that they have an awesome responsibility. With their swimmers, every moment is a teachable one. They can help prepare kids for life's challenges.

- *Stay hungry.* Never be satisfied with your personal growth or your program growth. Stay current on technical issues by joining professional organizations such as the American Swimming Coaches Association.

- *Let your program drive your budget.* Offer a good, solid program, and the budget will take care of itself. Underestimate your income and overestimate your expenses.

- *Host competitions with a flair.* Healthy competition is a strength of the YMCA. Attend a YMCA Nationals competition, and our entire sport will take on a different look. Local competitions should always include a devotion and a commitment to recognize all efforts as positive.

- *Make it fun!*

THE YMCA MASTERS SWIMMING PROGRAM

Masters swimming within the YMCA is probably the best-kept secret in America today. Thousands of YMCA members presently compete in United States Masters Swimming (USMS) meets throughout the country. The YMCA competitive swimming program includes thousands of former YMCA, high school, and collegiate swimmers who have stuck with lap swimming as adults as the easiest way to exercise and to maintain fitness.

This section describes the benefits to participants of a masters program, provides suggestions for starting a team and finding a coach, explains what activities team members might engage in, and offers some tips for coaching masters swimmers.

Benefits to Participants

Masters swimming should be regarded as an excellent physical conditioning program that fits into the YMCA's concept of physical fitness for adults. Its objective should be to maintain and improve health through participation in a continuing program that provides for aerobic and anaerobic swimming on a regular basis. Those who have participated in masters swimming over the years have reaped many health benefits; increased fitness, as evidenced by a lower resting pulse rate and lower blood pressure, is just one of them.

Before beginning any physical activity, each member should get a complete physical examination from her or his physician. Swimmers should gradually increase the length of their workouts before beginning competition. The pace of the individual's progress depends on the age of the swimmer and her or his past swimming experience.

Masters competition has rules regarding participants' sensory limitations (loss of hearing, eyesight) and the use of starting blocks. These rules may differ from the other levels of the competitive swimming program and should be consulted before organizing competitions.

Sources for Program Participants

You can find interested participants in several ways. First, the national YMCA aquatics program has trained many swimmers over the years, some of them competitors from the 1920s and 1930s. These former swimmers are everywhere, and they can provide an excellent foundation for the formation of a local masters group. Many are no longer active physically and need to be prodded and encouraged to get back into the water. But when they do become active, most are surprised and delighted with the results—mentally, spiritually, and of course, physically. This vast resource of past members can yield great volunteers and devoted new members.

Another source is those who already swim during lap swimming hours, those non-prime-time hours during which the pool is open to all. Many of these swimmers have not been in a structured program, and many are eager to participate. This is an untapped pool of talent. All they need is encouragement.

A Masters Swim Team Club

A successful masters swim team club must have regular, informal meetings during which members can share experiences and exchange ideas. These meetings create friendship and fellowship and forge the team into a viable group. Husbands, wives, boyfriends, and girlfriends should be encouraged to join the club. They may eventually get into masters swimming for fitness or competition, but they are also a ready source of support for other YMCA activities.

The first work of a new club might include the following:

1. Agreeing on the amount to charge for dues
2. Naming the team club
3. Outlining responsibilities
4. Electing officers and appointing committees
5. Registering with USMS (*Note:* If your YMCA team is planning to swim only in YMCA closed competition, it is not necessary to register with USMS.)
6. Deciding how to communicate with members by newsletter, bulletin board, or other means

Selecting a Team Coach

Good coaching is one of the main reasons to join or start a masters swim program. Swimmers become more motivated and stay committed when a good coach is running the show. When selecting a coach, prepare an announcement describing the club and its expectations of a coach. Include information about the club (including size), workout hours, what experience is necessary, and approximate salary and any additional benefits. If you presently have a swim program at your YMCA, starting a masters program could help pay the salary of the head coach or one of the assistant coaches.

Masters Swim Meets and Other Fitness Activities

Three types of masters swim meets are held:

• Dual meets arranged between associations are fun and are an excellent way for an association to get a masters team started. Coaches usually decide events, distances, and age groups before the meet.

• Open invitational meets attract a greater number of swimmers from a wider area. The meet usually offers most or all events and maybe some relays. Preregistration is usually required, but some meets allow deck entries. A $5 to $10 meet entry fee is charged to cover costs such as pool rental and awards. Most of these meets require participants to be members of USMS.

• The YMCA Masters National Swimming Championships are held under sanction by the National YMCA Competitive Swimming Committee. They are conducted annually in early April to mid-May by a host association. Entry information is mailed to all eligible YMCAs, usually in January of each year. Participants must hold a full-privilege membership with the association represented for at least 90 days before the meet, must not have competed for another YMCA during the previous four months, and must show membership cards on registration at the meet.

Swimming for fitness rather than competition is an integral part of the masters swimming program, and those who don't wish to compete in meets should be encouraged to participate in team activities.

Swim Training for Masters

When coaches develop a training program for your masters program, tell them to keep the following points in mind:

• Proceed with caution to carry out the program safely. Urge each participant to undergo a complete physical before embarking on any fitness program.

• Expect masters swimmers to have varying degrees of ability. They will also differ widely in age and include both men and women.

• Provide masters swimmers with the opportunity to work out at least three times a week. Daily workouts are preferable to achieve the maximum level of fitness. Most YMCAs have daily lap swims that can be used for masters swim team programs.

• Offer practice times early in the morning or later in the evening. Because of family and work commitments, most masters swimmers prefer those times. Ideal times for masters practices are 5:15 to 6:30 A.M., before open lap swimming in the morning, and 7:00 to 8:30 in the evening after other YMCA aquatics programs are done.

• To develop swimmers' endurance and stamina, move them toward controlled distance work, repeats, and intervals.

Teaching Stroke Mechanics

Stroke techniques have changed a lot over the years, so if your coaches work with a group of swimmers that span a wide range of ages, they will see a veritable parade of stroke forms—some good, some very bad. Your coaches may have some difficulty introducing stroke changes to swimmers at first, but when they realize the ease of modern mechanics—stressing natural movements and proper leverages—and see how the new techniques lower their times, they will become most enthusiastic.

Activities for Everyone

Practices and Workouts

Fun relays — inner tube, T-shirt, etc.

Videotaping

Letting the team member having a birthday determine the main set

Social Functions

Recognition and awards banquet

After practice dinners, breakfasts, etc.

Midnight swims

Clinics

Stroke introduction

Lectures

Bringing in another coach

Challenges

Distance clubs in which swimmers accumulate 100, 200, or 300 miles or more in a pool log

Recognition of continuous swimming workouts (for example, 50 straight workouts)

USMS postal events (meets by mail)

Coaches shouldn't let swimmers say that they are too old to change—all it takes is a willingness to try on the swimmers' part and patience on theirs.

Tell coaches to pay close attention to complaints of muscle soreness. Some of the soreness may be due to lack of conditioning or fatigue; however, improper arm and leg movements may also be the cause. Complaints of continuous pain in the deltoids and biceps should alert coaches to swimmers who are pulling their arms straight or pulling out of alignment. If swimmers have persistent arm pains that do not go away during normal practice, coaches should observe them closely for improper stroke movements, since constant repetition of a fault may lead to tendinitis.

Using Land Exercises

Both flexibility and strength training should be part of training for swimmers. Ask coaches to develop a series of slow stretching movements involving the major joint areas for warm-up and cool-down. Tell them not to rush swimmers through the warm-up, since proper stretching before each workout can prevent injury.

It's been said that "nothing is better than swimming for swimming," but there are new methods of strength training that can assist swimmers. It used to be that swimmers were never permitted near a gym or a weight room! Now, workouts with free weights, as well as with Nautilus and Cybex pulling devices designed to make the swimmer stronger, are recommended. Their proper use, particularly by women who have never been involved with athletics, will help swimmers achieve greater success. Of course, there is a danger that participants will overdo it, so coaches should supervise swimmers' work with weights and on various machines.

SPRINGBOARD DIVING

Most of the operation of a springboard diving program is similar to what you would do for other YMCA Swim Lessons, water polo, or synchronized swimming. [For the recreational use of springboard diving, refer *to On the Guard II* (4th ed.) and chapter 10 for information on developing rules and safety procedures.] As for any other program, you will want to be sure you plan properly, provide a safe environment and equipment, and keep appropriate records. You will also want to make sure your instructors and coaches provide adequate supervision and proper instruction and stay current on the skills required. Be sure to warn all participants about any inherent risks involved in participation in your program.

Staff

We recommend that instructors have the following training or certifications: United States Diving coaching progression *or* YMCA Springboard Diving Instructor (not yet available, but coming soon). You should have one instructor for every eight students.

Although general interview questions can be found in chapter 5, here are some more specific ones you might use when talking to springboard diving instructor candidates:

- Describe your background in springboard diving.
- At what levels have you coached diving?
- What training in springboard diving do you have?
- How do you keep the kids active and involved while waiting for their next turn on the board?
- How can you tell if a pool is safe for diving?
- How can you tell if a board should not be used?
- What is a safe diving envelope for a one-meter board?

After you have hired an instructor, you will want to provide in-service training on topics such as these:

- Spotting techniques
- Diving progressions
- Land drills

Since you probably won't have more than one or two diving instructors on staff, encourage diving instructors from other area YMCAs to meet together. They may want to consider meeting before or after local mock competitions or novice league competitions.

Facility and Equipment Needs

Be sure your facility meets the requirements for a safe diving program, with appropriate pool depths and a proper diving envelope (see figure 17.3).

You will need one board for each class of eight. The only equipment needed beyond the pool and diving boards is gymnastic mats.

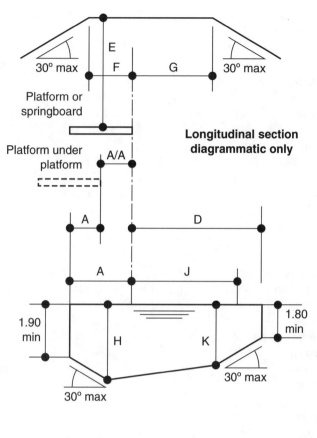

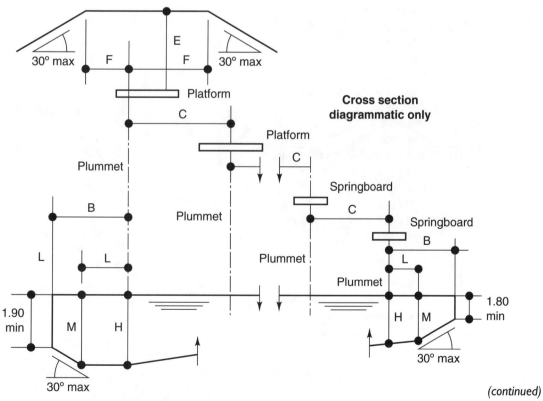

(continued)

Figure 17.3 Sample pool dimensions and equipment.

	Horizontal	Vertical
Length	16'	
Width	1'8"	
Height	3'4"	

	Horizontal	Vertical
Plummet back to pool wall		
Designation	A-1	
Minimum	5'	
Preferred	6'1"	
Plummet to pool wall at side		
Designation	B-1	
Minimum	8'3"	
Preferred	8'3"	
Plummet to adjacent plummet		
Designation	C-11	
Minimum	6'7"	
Preferred	7'1"	
Plummet to pool wall at head		
Designation	D-1	
Minimum	29'7"	
Preferred	29'7"	
On plummet from board to ceiling		
Designation		E-1
Minimum		16'5"
Preferred		16'5"
Clear overhead behind and each side of plummet		
Designation	F-1	E-1
Minimum	8'3"	16'5"
Preferred	8'3"	16'5"
Clear overhead ahead of plummet		
Designation	G-1	E-1
Minimum	16'5"	16'5"
Preferred	16'5"	16'5"
Depth of water at plummet (minimum required)		
Designation		H-1
Minimum		11'
Preferred		11'6"
Distance and depth ahead of plummet		
Designation	J-1	K-1
Minimum	16'5"	10'10"
Preferred	16'5"	11'2"
Distance and depth each side of plummet		
Designation	L-1	M-1
Minimum	5'	10'10"
Preferred	9'11"	11'2"
Maximum slope to reduce dimensions beyond full requirements		
Pool depth	30 degrees	
Ceiling height	30 degrees	

Figure 17.3 *(continued)*

Questions

Here are some common questions asked by those who want to participate in springboard diving:

- Is your diving program safe for my child?
- Should my child wear earplugs in class?
- If my child has tubes implanted in his or her ears, can he or she still participate in diving?

Have answers for these questions, and review them with your front-desk staff and other aquatics staff members.

Here are some ideas for improving your springboard diving program:

- Require participants to have a minimum swimming ability of Minnow level.
- Make sure that kids have lots of time on task, and that they are active and involved during classes.
- Provide a recognition system for participants' achievements as they progress through skills.
- Always have students warm up at the beginning of each class.
- Give participants a task to perform while waiting for their turns, such as modeling the skills they will be doing next.
- Hold novice competitions between classes or with other neighboring YMCA diving programs at the end of each session.
- Consider getting involved with the United States Diving future champions program.
- Offer the right balance of classes at times that allow students to progress and participate at the right levels.

For more information on springboard diving, contact United States Diving, 317-237-5252 or **www.usdiving.org.** These are two of their manuals:

- *U.S. Diving Safety Training Manual* (2nd ed.)
- Official Rules and Code of United States Diving, Inc. 2000-2001

ADDITIONAL RESOURCES

This list gives you some additional sources for information on competitive swimming:

- *Principles of YMCA Competitive Swimming and Diving*
- *YMCA Swim Coach Participant Manual*
- American Swim Coaches Association (ASCA), 800-356-2722
- **www.swiminfo.com**
- YMCA of the USA Medical Advisory Statement on Youth Strength Training
- *Swimming World* periodical, 310-607-9956

BIBLIOGRAPHY

Horn, Thelma S. 1982. What motivates competitive youth swimmers? The Michigan Swim Study. *Spotlight on Youth Sports*, 5(1)(Spring): 1, 3.

Aquatics Programs for People With Disabilities

The YMCA welcomes all people, regardless of their differences. One of those differences may be disabilities. In this chapter, we give you some background on the laws that reduced barriers to participation by people with disabilities and the benefits of aquatics programs for them. We then describe the types of programs possible, including school-related programs that operate under Public Law 94-142. This is followed by sections on program planning, leadership, and necessary facilities and equipment. Additional sections cover suggestions for working with those with disabilities, safety precautions, and health considerations (Behrman, 1987; Horvat, 1990; Miller & Bachrach, 1995; Smith & Luckasson, 1992; Stevens, 1985; Torney & Clayton, 1981).

HISTORY OF LEGISLATION

In recent history, a number of laws have been passed that make discrimination against individuals with disabilities illegal; however, YMCAs have always welcomed people with disabilities and continue to do so today. In the past, people with disabilities were given separate instruction and special classes, but today they are more likely to be included in regular classes.

In 1973, the U.S. government enacted the Rehabilitation Act (Public Law 93-112). Section 504 of this law states that "no otherwise qualified handicapped individual shall solely by reason of his handicap be excluded from participation or denied benefits of or be subjected to discrimination under any program receiving federal assistance." This generally applies to public education, but it also extends to athletics and includes a provision for barrier-free access to programs. This concept was further strengthened in 1975 by the passage of the Education for All Handicapped Children Act (Public Law 92-142), which provided for children to receive an appropriate free public education and be educated in the least restrictive environment. This allows parents the right to be part of the decision-making process, and mandated that students receive services from age 3 through 21. Currently this law is called the Individuals With Disabilities Education Act (IDEA pp. 105-17) and has been amended a number of times since 1975.

In 1990, the Americans With Disabilities Act (Public Law 101-336) expanded these civil rights to include equal access for all people with disabilities to transportation, public accommodations, state and local government services, employment, and telecommunications. This includes physical access to buildings as well as access to programs.

Under the Americans With Disabilities Act, the YMCA is classified as a public accommodation, the same as theaters, restaurants, retail stores, hospitals, day care centers, private schools, and parks. The YMCA is not given an exemption as a religious organization because it is not substantially controlled by a church. Providing access to programs means much more than having a ramp at the front door for wheelchair users. It means that the program admission criteria do not discriminate based on disability, that no additional restrictions are imposed on participants with a disability, and that reasonable accommodations are made to allow participation. It also means that the YMCA must take the necessary steps to provide auxiliary aids and services, such as large-print materials, Braille, and sign language interpreters to make its goods and services accessible to people with disabilities. The YMCA does not need to provide accommodations when doing so would cause "undue hardship" to the organization.

Although the spirit of the law says individuals with disabilities must be integrated into programs, this integration works only if everyone involved has a positive attitude and cooperates. With proper education and realistic expectations, everyone wins when a person with a disability is included in a class such as YMCA Swim Lessons. The attitudes, skills, and knowledge of the teacher, the parents, the YMCA administrator, and especially the students will determine the success or failure of such integrated programs.

Levels of inclusion range from separate programs to full inclusion and supports in between. Including children with disabilities in regular classes helps them meet the needs that all children have: to make friends, to stretch their minds, to broaden their horizons, and to help them build self-esteem by developing their abilities. They often have fewer opportunities to fulfill these needs than do other children. It also benefits the students without disabilities by giving them the opportunity to learn more about diversity and caring about others. By explaining what the disabilities are in simple terms and answering students' questions about them, instructors can help them understand, accept, and interact with those who have disabilities.

BENEFITS OF AQUATICS FOR PEOPLE WITH DISABILITIES

Swimming is a logical, effective, and supportable community program for improving the acceptance, self-esteem, and physical and mental health of individuals with disabilities. Aquatics programs for those with disabilities have several advantages.

- Swimming and other aquatic activities have become so popular that many communities now have appropriate facilities. Opportunities for training qualified leaders are also readily available. Upgrading instructional skills and modifying existing facilities can be done in practical, cost-effective ways.

- Regardless of the nature or severity of the disability, an appropriate water activity can usually be found. Aquatics covers a wide range of activities from shallow-water wading to competitive racing, synchronized swimming, and underwater sports. Water exercise, sports, games, and therapeutic water activities are available to people with widely varying skill levels. With proper training—perhaps in a pool first—and with adequate equipment and suitable attire, including United States Coast Guard-approved PFDs, many people with disabilities can participate in canoeing, boating, kayaking, waterskiing, and other water activities.

Water provides buoyancy. Gravitational forces are reduced substantially in water so that parts of the body can be moved with less muscular effort. Muscle tone and coordination can be improved, and differences among individuals are less apparent.

- Aquatics programs can enhance participants' self-esteem. Accomplishing even the simplest skill can bring a measure of success. For some people with disabilities, the most important accomplishment in the world may be to walk alone for the first time—in the water.

- Aquatics develops physical fitness, strength, endurance, flexibility, balance, and mobility. This may improve mental and emotional health as well as physical health.

- Aquatics provides an excellent opportunity for personal adjustment. Participants learn to relate to others in an acceptable manner. School, club, and community activities, as well as other special events, are open to those in aquatics programs. These activities help to improve social consciousness, establish friendships, and prepare participants for greater involvement in the community.

- Water activities help to improve perception and vocabulary. Participants in aquatics programs also learn to identify colors, shapes, sizes, and the words associated with various activities.

- Water activities are democratic. They focus on ability rather than disability and emphasize mutual acceptance and inclusion.

- Water activities are fun.

Aquatics programs can promote physical fitness and well-being for individuals with disabilities of all ages. Many of these programs need no special equipment—although some equipment such as buoyancy belts and webbed gloves may be fun—and can be set up even in limited areas of water.

TYPES OF PROGRAMS

Programs may be designed for various purposes. Some of the most common are the following:

- *Therapy sessions.* These sessions must be under the leadership of a licensed or registered therapist, who should work under a physician's direction. The individual program prescription should be developed through a team approach; with the consent of appropriate medical personnel, therapy program participants can also engage in fitness, instructional, and recreational water programs.

Another type of therapy session can have socialization as its goal. Mental health agencies, health and human resource departments, physicians, drug and alcohol centers, or other social services may refer participants. Therapeutic recreational programs should be planned, implemented, and evaluated regularly by the coordinators of the program.

- *Instructional programs.* These are programs that assist people in acquiring the skills needed to feel comfortable in and to move through the water. Adaptations of the skills taught in YMCA Swim Lessons programs may be made.

- *Recreation programs.* Such programs have become increasingly popular for people with disabilities. Aquatics recreation programs are ideal for participants who want to exercise, socialize, and relax.

As a safety measure, keep in mind that those participating in aquatics recreation or leisure programs might not mention that they have any specific conditions or disabilities or are taking medications.

• *Water fitness programs.* These programs involve those with disabilities in mainstream as well as separate activities. Such exercise can help participants feel and look better. Water exercise is an ideal way to improve muscle tone, flexibility, and posture. It increases endurance and range of motion, helps manage weight, releases stress, and develops cardiovascular fitness. See the *YMCA Water Fitness for Health* manual for additional information on creating water fitness programs as well as training instructors on making exercise modifications based on the participants' abilities.

Your YMCA may also choose to work with schools to provide physical activity for children with disabilities. In that case, you will have to follow the procedures mandated by Public Law 94-142 to develop individualized programs.

PROGRAM PLANNING

Aquatics programs for people with disabilities succeed because of detailed planning by many segments of the community. Begin by developing a strategic plan for your adapted programs and include a mission statement, vision, principles, and goals and strategic objectives. Follow the program development process as described in chapter 2 to help you get started. Also review your YMCA's policy relating to programs and activities for people with disabilities. A sample policy is given in figure 18.1.

In your planning, include careful evaluation of the suitability, accessibility, availability, and safety of facilities; the availability of trained supervisory and support personnel; transportation; public relations; and, of course, financing. When possible, get the input of current and potential program participants.

Contact schools, health agencies, child-find programs, Birth to 3 programs, recreational departments, and special-interest groups to reach people with disabilities and to learn about needs within the community. Interdisciplinary coalitions and councils have become common and formal ways for developing interagency communication about programs, services, program support, and advocacy (Lepore, Gayle & Stevens, 1998) are available. You can also develop your own informal network by communicating with peers and colleagues in other organizations. Also use print and electronic media such as newspapers, magazines, church bulletins, radio, and television to identify people with disabilities who are not involved with other community programs. Making personal contact with potential participants, parents, and guardians, as well as professionals, can generate and sustain interest in your program.

Now let's briefly look at other steps in planning: creating a sponsoring group, finding appropriate transportation and adequate funding, and developing and evaluating programs.

Sponsoring Group

Forming a sponsoring group consisting of a broad spectrum of community representatives with an interest in people with disabilities, program participants, and their families can greatly facilitate planning for adapted aquatics programs. This group can serve as a program initiator and catalyst. Subcommittees within the sponsoring group or individual members with special expertise can take responsibility for financing, public relations, record keeping, program content, evaluation, recruitment, and leadership training. The YMCA, because of its philosophy and tradition, is an excellent sponsoring organization. Other community members who can be asked to

I. Introduction

This policy has been developed to provide staff and volunteers with direction and guidance in developing programs and services for people with disabilities. This policy is not meant to provide limitations but to ensure careful and thoughtful planning for the development and implementation of programming.

Staff and volunteers who wish to establish new programs for people with disabilities must develop a written proposal that is consistent with this policy and present it to the Program Committee for approval.

II. Constituency

It is the policy of the YMCA to serve all individuals without regard to race, sex, nationality, religion, disability, or other classification protected by law. All individuals participating in a YMCA's programs and using a YMCA's facilities must subscribe to that YMCA's principles and purposes and agree to conduct themselves in accordance therewith.

III. Program

It is the intent of the YMCA to mainstream people with disabilities into regular programs and activities as often as possible. Recognizing limitations due to the individual's disability is important, and the YMCA will adapt a program activity, staffing, and facility to reasonably accommodate the individual's disability so that the person might fully benefit from the activity or experience.

It is recommended in every instance that each family member and the person with the disability tour the facility with the appropriate YMCA program director. This provides them with an opportunity to inspect the program, facilities, and staff. This also allows the staff to ascertain what will need to be done to enhance this individual's experience within the program.

Staff need to communicate clearly with the person and the family what is involved in the program. Staff should share specific program adaptations that have already been implemented for people with disabilities and explore further requirements.

When appropriate, activities and programs for people with specific disabilities may be scheduled. These might include the YMCA's becoming involved in the Special Olympics Program, organizing a Wheelchair Basketball League, or providing programs for schools and other community organizations serving people with certain disabilities.

IV. Organization

The Program Committee has been designated with the responsibility of programming for people with disabilities. The committee is responsible to the Board of Directors and includes people with disabilities.

V. Staffing

A Program Director has been assigned the responsibility for coordinating the YMCA's efforts to serve people with disabilities. However, all staff are expected to be involved in serving people with disabilities. Training will be provided to assist staff in obtaining the knowledge they need to serve people with disabilities effectively.

Through the family interviewing process, it is important to determine the level of staffing required to serve each individual with a disability. Can the person be mainstreamed into the program with the current staffing? Will a one-on-one relationship be needed? Is there another alternative between these two options?

In either case, this needs to be clearly determined by asking specific questions in regard to the individual's needs. These might include mobility, changing clothes, use of rest rooms, following or understanding directions, signing, special behaviors, etc.

(continued)

Figure 18.1   Sample policy relating to programs and activities for people with disabilities.

One-on-one staffing should be brought to the attention of the respective class instructor immediately. The one-on-one staffing structure may be limited by session, the number of trained staff and volunteers, and enrollment.

VI. Facilities

Although all facilities are accessible, special arrangements may be needed to enhance the individual's ability to negotiate the facilities. Frequently, activity areas of special interest to the participant may need to be adapted for him or her. Staff are encouraged to consult with the Property Manager to ensure that the adaptations can be made.

Staff are reminded to check all facilities frequently to be sure that they are clear of hazards and obstacles that might be of danger to all participants, including people with disabilities.

VII. Safety Issues

Although it is the association's aim to provide a full, enriching experience for people with disabilities, it is important to recognize that not everybody can participate in every activity at the same level. It is also important for staff to recognize that they often times need to make the decision with regard to participation in a specific activity.

Physical limitations or restrictions noted on medical history forms will be adhered to at all times. There will be no exceptions. Staff members who are unsure of an individual's ability to participate in an activity should consult with their immediate supervisor prior to the activity.

VIII. Medical Needs

Where an individual discloses a disability or a disability is obvious that could impact the program, staff must be alert for special medical needs and potential reasonable accommodations during the family interview process and explore those issues with the individual and, as appropriate, the family. The individual and family should be informed of the emergency medical services available to the YMCA.

If one-on-one services are needed, staff must know the level of personal assistance needed by the individual so that there are no surprises on the first day of the individual's participation in an activity.

IX. Finances

Budget needs must be considered when developing a new program for people with disabilities. A revenue and expense statement must be developed for each new and existing program annually. Existing programs that allow for one-on-one staffing must budget for these staff costs.

Collaborative programs with other organizations also require an annual budget detailing the YMCA's expenses and revenues.

X. Records and Reports

Through good record keeping and regular reports, the staff will keep the Program Committee and Board of Directors informed of their work with people with disabilities.

XI. Relationships

The staff and Program Committee will work with other departments, committees and groups within the YMCA to ensure that the best possible services are provided for people with disabilities. Efforts will also be made to establish positive relationships with other organizations within the community that are serving people with disabilities.

XII. Review, Evaluation, and Revision

This policy will be reviewed annually by the Program Committee and will be revised as needed.

Figure 18.1   (continued).

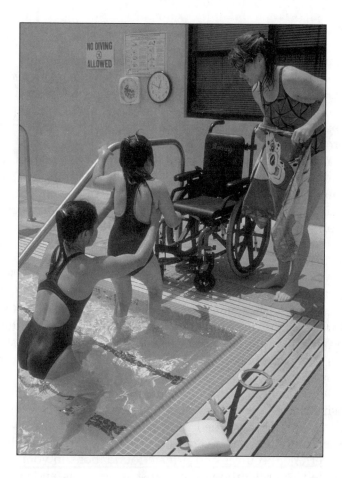

join the committee include interested consumers, family members, physicians, and allied health personnel such as social workers, therapeutic recreation specialists, adapted physical educators, educators, and therapists.

Transportation

Finding adequate practical transportation can mean the difference between a program's success and failure. Local transportation authorities and private businesses in the area may be able to assist with transportation. Schools may have specially equipped buses or vans. Dial-a-Van, Care-a-Van, the local Retired Senior Volunteer Program, service clubs, and even taxicab companies may be able to help with special arrangements. (Check to see if use of care vans requires having a licensed therapist on staff.) Many YMCAs already own vehicles for program use that can be adapted or have arrangements with nursing homes whose vans are equipped to accommodate wheelchairs.

The vehicles used for transportation must be insured and safe. They should be able to accommodate such equipment as crutches and wheelchairs comfortably. Specially trained drivers are essential to successfully transporting disabled people who require assistance. They must be licensed to handle the vehicles and know how to assist the participants in entering and exiting in the safest and most comfortable manner.

For participants who can drive or get a ride to the YMCA, make sure accessible parking spaces are clearly marked and allow participants easy access to the building and pool. See that assistants are available to help participants from their vehicles to the facility site, if needed.

Funding

Aquatics programs for people with disabilities should not be any more expensive than other aquatics programs. However, while many people with disabilities can be mainstreamed, you may have to consider making facility adaptations and hiring additional trained personnel when budgeting for these aquatics programs. Only when you have adequate funding and an approved, realistic budget should you start such programs.

You may be able to obtain funding from a variety of sources, including your YMCA annual campaign, just like any of your other programs. You can also investigate city, county, and state funds; school funds; federal funding; and funding from private foundations, and make appropriate applications. Occasionally, organizations already working with special-needs groups will share their facilities; this can prove to be cost-effective. In addition, allowing other groups to use YMCA facilities in exchange for resources or for a fee can provide further funding.

Many participants can pay their own fees and assist in supporting the program. Fees for service and educational allotments may provide funding. Third-party payments from labor unions and industry, Medicaid, Medicare, Social Security, and insurance companies may underwrite some costs. For industrial injury claims, an appropriate volunteer or staff person should approach the state agency handling workers' compensation. You will need to investigate the procedures involved with third party payments.

A good rule is to ask for what you need. Organizations or individuals may establish scholarships for disabled program participants when they are told a need exists. Grants may be awarded from matching funds already raised by the community. Such funds may be awarded dollar for dollar or in other ways. Check with local government sources and private foundations in your area about grants available. United Way allocations, revenue-sharing funds, and vendor contributions are additional sources of funding.

Program Development

Once you have defined your program, the amount of collaboration desired, and the general goals of the program, develop a specific curriculum. Whether the thrust of your programs is educational or not, you need to develop a curriculum that includes the program's philosophy, goals, scope, and sequence of skills. Such a curriculum gives the program direction and continuity. Center your curriculum around aquatic skills and their application in the lives of individuals with a particular disability. Ask yourself, "Are the goals relevant to the current needs of the target group of the program?"

Also think through the logistics of the program and answer the following questions:

- Do we have an adequate number of assistants to help with moving and changing participants in the pool and locker room, as well as during the program?
- Do we have a process in place to learn about the participants and make sure we are prepared to serve them effectively?
- Do we have the proper equipment needed to serve the participants?
- Are staff prepared and trained to work with the group? Where can they get additional training and support?
- Do we have proper storage for wheelchairs while participants are in the pool?

Here are some additional suggestions for program development:

- Know all personnel. Hire mature, well-informed staff, both paid and volunteer, who know the program and progressions. Besides knowing how to adapt the program, they also should understand how to facilitate interaction between individuals with and without disabilities. See that program staff maintain clear accountability and communication with personnel from institutions and groups involved with the aquatics program.
- Make sure you develop an emergency plan for handling individuals with disabilities.
- Know the facility. Maintain accessibility for students and know when and where to accommodate and adapt.
- Involve people with disabilities in planning and decision making.
- Promote independence.
- Mandate confidentiality among all staff (including volunteers) working with individuals with disabilities.

Some participants with disabilities require no adaptations in facilities or programs, so you may follow the same process as for any other program. For others, special programs must be designed to meet individual needs. Either way, most people can master most aquatic skills. However, every participant will master skills in a different way, depending on the person's ability and how well accommodations can be made. Ability and determination are keys to mastering water skills.

With patience and understanding, instructors can guide and assist participants in achieving success. Innovative instructors can help participants to learn their own way and at their own pace. When one approach does not work, another approach and adaptation can be found. Each person's needs must be considered individually, even in group instruction.

For additional information, see *YMCA Swim Lessons: Teaching Swimming Fundamentals, YMCA Water Fitness for Health,* and *Adapted Aquatics Programming: A Professional Guide,* which are available from the YMCA Program Store. An instructor certification program, YMCA Swim Lessons: Individuals With Disabilities Instructor, is also available. Contact the YMCA of the USA for more information.

Program Evaluation

You must evaluate your program to be sure that it is meeting the goals you set and that it is safe, effective, relevant, and age-appropriate. Through ongoing evaluations, you can quickly uncover issues and problem areas that need to be addressed. Use a process similar to the one described in chapter 2 on program evaluation by getting feedback from parents, instructors, and students, as well as any collaborating agency personnel when possible. Figure 18.2 is a customer satisfaction survey, a sample of the kind of tool you can use to obtain specific feedback about your adapted program.

The Program Evaluation Form (figure 18.3) can be used to examine the processes and practices of your organization and staff when providing appropriate aquatic services for individuals with disabilities. Use this checklist as a general guide for observing an overall program.

You will also want to be sure your instructors are implementing the program effectively. Figure 18.4 is a sample observation form for evaluating instructors.

Help us measure the success of this aquatics program. Check one box for each of the numbered categories. Please explain "disagree" and "strongly disagree" ratings. If you have ideas as to how we might improve the program, please share them with us.

	Strongly agree	Agree	Disagree	Strongly disagree	Unable to judge
1. Facilities met my accessibility needs.	☐	☐	☐	☐	☐
2. Facilities were well kept.	☐	☐	☐	☐	☐
3. Facilities were conducive to learning.	☐	☐	☐	☐	☐
4. It was easy to join this program.	☐	☐	☐	☐	☐
5. I felt comfortable with the process of being assessed and discussing goals.	☐	☐	☐	☐	☐
6. Ongoing assessment was shared with participants.	☐	☐	☐	☐	☐
7. Program staff collaborated with others effectively.	☐	☐	☐	☐	☐
8. Communication lines were always open.	☐	☐	☐	☐	☐
9. Individualized aquatics program plans were developed with me and, if appropriate, significant others.	☐	☐	☐	☐	☐
10. The atmosphere of the classes was positive and conducive to learning.	☐	☐	☐	☐	☐
11. The instructor provided specific goals to be achieved at each session.	☐	☐	☐	☐	☐
12. The instructor provided ample opportunity to practice.	☐	☐	☐	☐	☐
13. There was positive interaction among individuals with varying abilities.	☐	☐	☐	☐	☐
14. Instructor adapted activities and tasks to individuals' levels of performance.	☐	☐	☐	☐	☐
15. Instructor communicated in preferred mode.	☐	☐	☐	☐	☐
16. Instructor included me in the entire session.	☐	☐	☐	☐	☐
17. Instructor chose activities that helped me meet my goals.	☐	☐	☐	☐	☐
18. Enough equipment was available during sessions.	☐	☐	☐	☐	☐
19. Equipment was of good quality.	☐	☐	☐	☐	☐

Reasons for disagreeing with any statement: _____

Suggestions for improvement: _____

_____

Figure 18.2 Sample user survey.

Respond "yes" or "no" to each of the statements. "No" answers could indicate areas for improvement.

Assessment, Placement, and Individualized Program Plans

Y N 1. The aquatic staff has an established procedure for accommodating individuals with disabilities.

Y N 2. The aquatic program provides a continuum of placements, including segregated, partially included, and totally included settings for aquatic participation and instruction.

Y N 3. Aquatic assessment is conducted by an adapted aquatic specialist is conjunction with other professional if warranted (regular aquatic instructor, therapists, or the like).

Y N 4. The adapted aquatic specialist uses an observation instrument for assessment.

Y N 5. The aquatic personnel attend team meetings to present information when appropriate.

Y N 6. All members of a transdisciplinary team of professionals, parents, caregivers, significant others, and participant have voices in placement, goals, and objectives.

Y N 7. Individual programs are evaluated at least four times per year.

Y N 8. The individual plan includes present level of performance, annual goals, rationale for goals, short-term objectives, including projected dates to start and finish, and criteria for evaluation.

Instruction and Programming

Y N 1. The adapted aquatic program is periodically reviewed by outside expert evaluators.

Y N 2. A curriculum manual is available describing overall program goals, philosophy, rationale, benefits, assumptions, and aquatic instructional services for individuals with disabilities.

Y N 3. Aquatic instruction for individuals with disabilities takes place under the guidance of certified adapted aquatic instructors.

Y N 4. Adapted aquatic instruction for individuals with severe disabilities takes place with one support person per participant.

Y N 5. The content of the adapted aquatic program contains a variety of swimming, water safety, and leisure time aquatic activities.

Y N 6. Instructors base aquatics instruction on individual goals as outlined in the Individualized Program Plan.

Y N 7. Individuals with disabilities included in regular aquatic classes have the proper learning, emotional, and physical support as defined by the IAPP.

Y N 8. The program focuses on what an individual with disabilities needs to participate now and in the future in lifetime and leisure pursuits.

Y N 9. Aquatic programs for individuals with disabilities include goals for strengthening self-esteem.

Y N 10. The organization gives individuals with disabilities who can succeed in regular competitive athletics opportunities to do so.

Personnel

Y N 1. The organization leader ensures that staff and participants in the program are prepared to embrace the diversity of abilities of individuals with disabilities.

Y N 2. Sufficient number of qualified personnel are available to meet the needs of individuals with disabilities.

Y N 3. Certified adapted aquatic instructors deliver adapted services and instruction to individuals with disabilities.

Y N 4. Administrators understand the scope of adapted aquatic services.

Y N 5. Administrators ensure that rugular aquatic instructors have at least one inservice training session each year on adapted aquatics concepts by specialists in this area.

Y N 6. Administrators ensure that instructor aides have appropriate inservice training each year by an adapted aquatic specialist.

Y N 7. Administrators encourage aquatic instructors who want to improve knowledge in the area of adapted aquatics.

Y N 8. Administrators grant release time for adapted aquatic instructors to attend team meetings.

Y N 9. Administrators understand the difference between adapted aquatics and aquatic therapy.

Y N 10. Staff maintains communication with parents, caregivers, and significant others.

Y N 11. Staff maintains communication with other professionals.

Y N 12. Instructors provide education to encourage family and caregiver involvement.

Figure 18.3 Sample program evaluation form.

Functions of an Adapted Aquatics Instructor During Class

Instructor's name _____ Date_____

Evaluator's name _____

Rate the instructor on each item on a scale from 1 (very *ineffective*) to 5 (very effective).

Item	1	2	3	4	5	Comments
Reviews previous skills.						
Reviews prerequisite physical, cognitive, and affective skills for new skill.						
States lessons' goals and objectives.						
Uses task-analyzed teaching progressions.						
Provides proper explanations and demonstrations.						
Uses concrete examples.						
Uses key terms and cues.						
Checks for participants' understanding.						
Includes all participants in instruction.						
Modifies tasks when too easy or too hard.						
Displays enthusiasm for task presented.						
Uses a variety of communication modes.						
Brings participants back on task if off-task.						
Allows ample time for practice.						
Responds to all participants at a high rate.						
Gives tasks to participants that meet their individual goals.						
Structures practice so that participants spend a high percentage of time engaged in motor activity.						
Aims for high success rate.						
Provides general corrective feedback.						
Gives specific corrective feedback.						
Uses positive reinforcement.						
Uses applied behavioral analysis principles when necessary.						

(continued)

Figure 18.4 Sample instructor evaluation form.

Item	1	2	3	4	5	Comments
Uses routines for participants who need them.						
Directs assistants to perform specific tasks.						
Offers safety tips.						
Motivates participants to learn new activities.						
Makes smooth transitions from one activity or space to the next.						
Applies rules consistently.						
Promotes positive self-image of all participants.						
Keeps all students in sight at all times.						
Safety concern for students is evident in organizational skills and activities in class.						
Recognizes, demonstrates and celebrates YMCA core values with students.						

Figure 18.4 *(continued)*

LEADERSHIP

To achieve excellence in programming, devote time and effort to finding good staff. Establish ongoing leadership recruitment, selection, and training. First, you will need someone to be in charge of your adapted program or programs. That could be you or an aquatics instructor with training and experience in working with people with disabilities. If you have a large number of adapted programs, you may also have a head instructor who supervises other instructors. You also will need aquatics instructors and assistants, as well as lifeguards. Finally, you will want to offer specific ongoing training to staff so as to provide a quality program.

Program Supervisor

Certain skills, knowledge, and competencies are necessary for the person in charge of the adapted program to be successful in working with individuals with disabilities. These include the following:

- Experience in programs at a pool, camp, beach, agency, or school as an aide, instructor, or supervisor.
- A thorough knowledge of skills and progressions and the ability to break down skills into small steps. Skills should be evaluated on a regular basis.
- An understanding of each participant's specific problems and how the person has adjusted to various disabilities. This helps establish rapport and facilitates individual program planning.

- Ability to communicate with participants—verbally and nonverbally—and to establish rapport.
- Ability to communicate with other support team members, including medical and allied medical professionals, school personnel, social workers, parents and families, and other agency personnel. Communication is an ongoing process, and confidentiality is a must.
- Ability to assess and understand specific disabilities and to explain to staff necessary modifications in teaching sequences or methods.
- Training in CPR, first aid, and handling of seizures.
- An understanding of the necessity for continuing pre-service and in-service training.
- Practical experience in using communication aids—hearing aids, sign language—as well as wheelchairs, prosthetic devices, lifts, and transfers.
- Imagination, originality, creativity, and empathy.

This person should obtain certification in the YMCA Aquatic Management Course as well as related YMCA instructor certifications. Be sure to provide the person with individual opportunities to grow, stretch, and further develop her or his skills.

Head Instructor/Master Teacher

Head instructors should hold a specialist instructor certification as a YMCA Swim Lessons: Individuals with Disabilities Instructor as well as YMCA Swim Lessons: Parent-Child, Preschool, and Youth and Adult certifications. Head instructors may also hold additional specialist instructor and trainer ratings and are recommended to have 100 hours or more of experience in aquatics for people with disabilities. Head instructors should be mature and have good judgment. They should also have a sense of humor, enthusiasm, and patience, an ability to get along with people of all ages and abilities, talent in keeping records, skill at setting and implementing goals, and the ability to constructively critique programs and people. Also important is the ability to reward and recognize teachers, aides, students, and volunteers for attaining goals.

People who may fall into the category of master teacher are those who have worked continuously in adapted aquatics for a number of years and who have proven their leadership capabilities in teaching, program development, and program implementation. These individuals may be recognized locally or nationally and often become excellent resource people. This is not a YMCA certification area but a designation of demonstrated ability and knowledge.

Aquatics Instructors

Before starting the program, you need to be sure you have an adequate number of aquatics instructors/volunteer instructors who are trained or willing to be trained. The ratios needed depend on individuals and programs.

You need to be sure your instructors have the following required skills and training in addition to that of swimming instruction:

1. Knowledge of special conditions and ability to network, ask questions, and obtain answers from knowledgeable people
2. Initiative and imagination
3. Patience and understanding

4. Ability to develop Individualized Program and Individualized Educational Plans

5. Ability to teach

6. Ability to work with aquatics assistants and volunteers

7. Safety and emergency preparedness

8. Knowledge of the requirements of special conditions and common effects of medications

9. Ability to follow record-keeping and reporting procedures

10. Certification as a YMCA Swim Lessons Individuals With Disabilities Instructor.

Records and evaluations may include the following:

- Written data on students compiled before class starts from medical personnel, parents/guardians, educators, service providers, and participants, providing a detailed profile for setting skills, progressions, and goals for each student
- Daily records and evaluations
- Answers from professional advisors to direct questions about each student's abilities and potential
- Application forms, certification forms, progress sheets, and other forms developed for each program
- Program and attendance statistics
- Evaluations made measuring fitness, skills, and development, including
    - physical fitness and ability to perform skills
    - social skills, such as the ability to work individually, to work in a group, and to relate to people of various ages and abilities

These records are kept confidential and are available only to team members. When appropriate, information can be shared with consultants, referring agencies, teachers, families, and participants. Records and information on participants' individual progress should be retained, and attendance records and accident forms should be held for seven years.

Support Staff

You can recruit potential class aides and volunteers from other YMCA volunteer groups, your swim team or other teen leadership programs (swim team advisory committee or Scuba travel clubs in the YMCA), local high schools, colleges and universities with either physical or occupational therapy programs, or local Special Olympics groups.

Select support staff, such as volunteers and assistants, on the basis of their desire to contribute to a successful program and their ability to work well with people who have disabilities. The support staff must perform under the strict guidance of the instructor. Since detailed records of participants' attitudes, reactions, and progress should be kept and regularly maintained, a single staff member should be responsible for them. A computer can help. The records are particularly valuable in updating individual programs developed for participants as required by IDEA.

The YMCA provides a variety of opportunities for pre-service and in-service training. Give support staff who are interested a chance to attend institutes and training sessions to gain and update skills essential in working with people with disabilities.

Lifeguards

Lifeguards for pool or waterfront activities for people with disabilities need a "third eye." Extra awareness and a thorough knowledge of health concerns and special equipment are essential. These lifeguards should know what to expect, be able to assess class participants, and be trained to cope with such concerns as pool accessibility, seizures, cardiac problems, and behavior problems. Choose guards for their ability to work under stress. Conduct orientations for lifeguards who will be guarding people with disabilities, and make instructors responsible for updating guards about special problems.

Staff Training

All staff should be in sincere accord with the program objectives: the improvement of the physical skills and mental outlook of people with disabilities by means of tailored individual and group experiences in water, either through integrated or segregated programs. Staff members should have the knowledge and expertise to deal effectively with various situations that can arise in an aquatics environment, and safety and emergency procedures must be understood by everyone concerned with the program. Staff should also know how to facilitate interaction among members and should encourage individuals without disabilities to interact appropriately with individuals with disabilities.

Offer continued pre-service and in-service training for all staff. Train your staff in the proper procedures relating to the following:

- Lifts and transfers
- Helping participants in the locker room and shower area
- Education in awareness of disabilities
- Background material on aquatics orientation
- Description of swim skills to be used and adaptations
- Encouragement of volunteers to take YMCA certification courses
- Safety

In addition, if you are working with school systems, make all aquatics personnel involved with participants or record keeping aware of the provisions of IDEA and how those provisions affect aquatics programs.

Aquatics instructors and support staff should consider obtaining additional certification as a YMCA Swim Lessons: Individuals with Disabilities Instructor.

FACILITIES, EQUIPMENT, AND SUPPLIES

In this section, we explain and show you how to apply specific information to ensure that your facilities, equipment, and supplies are adequate. As you read, keep in mind that the environment of your program must be safe and accessible, as well as lend itself to successful and satisfying experiences for both participants and instructors. You must be familiar with guidelines for accessibility, state and local health codes for aquatics facilities, resources for equipment, and supplies that facilitate aquatics participation.

As discussed earlier, the Americans With Disabilities Act has mandated that facilities be accessible to individuals with disabilities, and you must follow federal guidelines to make sure your facility complies with the law. Some requirements are very specific, such as standard minimum requirements for widths of doorways and halls, and some are somewhat vague, such as the need for one form of access into the pool. The Access Board of the U.S. Architectural and Transportation Barriers Compliance Board (ATBCB) is the federal agency responsible for the development of design guidelines for accessibility. The Recreation Access Advisory Committee was appointed to provide advice to the Access Board on accessible recreation environments. After the publication of the ADA Accessibility Guidelines for Buildings and Facilities (Federal Register, 1991), the Recreation Access Advisory Committee published its recommendations for recreational facilities and outdoor-developed areas (Recreation Access Advisory Committee, 1994), which included four pages on aquatics facilities. In September 1995, the ATBCB awarded a research contract to the National Center on Accessibility (NCA) to identify and evaluate methods of access to swimming pools by individuals with disabilities (National Center on Accessibility, 1996). In September 1996, the NCA committee submitted its recommendations to the ATBCB.

The recommendations for swimming pool accessibility in this chapter are based on this report. Key specifications are referenced throughout this chapter. You may reference additional specifications from the report "National Center on Accessibility—Swimming Pool Accessibility." But although there are standards for access, recognize that no single pool design will satisfy all the demands of a community. There are facilities designed around competitive, therapeutic, portable, recreational, freestanding, sunken, partially sunken, and deck-level pools. More challenging areas of accessibility—lakes, rivers, and oceanfront—play an important role when providing individuals with disabilities the opportunity to make the transition into the broader world of aquatics that naturally exists in society.

Flotation devices, lifts, transfer equipment, and motivational equipment such as toys, rafts, and tubes give you more instructional strategy options, but they cannot replace quality instruction. Don't let equipment availability be the determining factor in placing an individual in a segregated or integrated program. Good pedagogical practices mandate that individuals with disabilities are entitled to appropriate equipment and supplies in an aquatic setting, just as they are in a more traditional classroom or recreational program. Of course, equipment and supplies needed for individuals with disabilities vary with the abilities of each participant.

Facilities

The types of facilities available for adapted aquatics programs vary as much as do program purposes, goals, and participants. Facilities come in all shapes and sizes, from 10-yard therapeutic pools to 25-yard pools, from 3-foot-deep pools for water-walking to 16-foot-deep diving wells. Although the various purposes of an aquatics program may lend themselves to a specific facility design, most aquatics facilities have locker rooms or changing areas, a pool deck and pool, means of entering and exiting the pool, and storage areas.

Community facilities operated by local governments and agencies serve a variety of uses, from competition to water-walking. Although they may be accessible, they may or may not be usable or desirable. Therapeutic facilities operated by rehabilitation hospitals, private therapists, and residential agencies are generally built with a single purpose and may have greater accessibility, utility, and desirability for individuals with disabilities but may not be open to the general public. Current design trends for most facilities are for multiple uses, combining recreational, instructional, competitive, and therapeutic needs into a single facility design. However, conditions for every one of the uses may be compromised.

The Americans With Disabilities Act is arguably the most significant piece of legislation to affect facility construction in the last 25 years. It asserts that accessibility features should allow independent use by people with disabilities but should interfere as little as possible with swimmers without disabilities using the pool (Mace, 1993).

Accessibility

What is accessibility? Accessibility removes architectural barriers, ensuring the participants' ability to gain easy access to the venue. Close parking with sufficient room for vehicles, visible and safe flow of pedestrian traffic, curb cuts, and generally easy movement outside the facility, as well as easy access to and movement inside the facility, enhance accessibility. Other examples are adequate parking, user-friendly entrance–exit doorways, proper signs, ramps, elevators, open meeting areas, and Braille on doorway entrances to offices, activity areas, and bathrooms (see table 18.1). Remember, the Americans With Disabilities Act requires all places of public accommodation, such as camps, playgrounds, auditoriums, fitness centers, and commu-

Table 18.1	Examples of Accessibility Guidelines for Buildings and Facilities
Required minimum number of accessible parking spaces	1 spot in lot with 1-25 spaces 2 spots in lot with 26-50 spaces 2% of total in lots with 51-100 spaces
Access aisles adjacent to accessible parking spaces	60 in. minimum
Curb ramps	Minimum width = 36 in.
Slope and rise	Least possible, but maximum slope of ramp in new construction is 1:12 ratio.
Handrails	If ramp has a rise of 6 in. or more or a horizontal projection of 72 in. or more, handrails must be on both sides.
Wheelchair passages	32 in. at a point (such as a doorway); 36 in. at a continuous area (such as a hallway, accessible route, or deck) 60 in. for 2 wheelchairs to be able to pass; 60 in. for a 180-degree turning space
Thresholds at doorways	Not to exceed 3/4 in. for exterior sliding doors or 1/2 in. other types
Toilets	17 in. to 19 in. to top of toilet seat
Showers	Seat shall be provided 17 in. to 19 in. from floor and extend full depth of stall. Grab bars are necessary. See ADA guidelines for specifications. Controls operable with one hand and not requiring tight grasping, pinching, or twisting of wrist. Shower unit with a hose at least 60 in. that converts to handheld and stationary. Curbs in shower no higher than 1/2 in.

Adapted from Department of Justice, Office of the Attorney General, 1991.

nity recreational facilities, to provide the same goods and services, in the most integrated setting appropriate, to individuals with disabilities as they do to individuals without disabilities. Another important concept of this law includes providing reasonable accommodations in communication, transportation, and programming.

To ensure accessibility, your aquatics facility should have an Americans With Disabilities Act committee that is familiar with standards and federal guidelines conduct a compliance check by applying these guidelines. Individuals with disabilities from the community and participants in the program should be on this committee. Both general and adapted aquatics instructors should have representatives on the committee to provide input regarding accessibility issues. You can find other practical ideas for implementing the requirements of the ADA in the book *Leisure Opportunities for Individuals With Disabilities,* edited by Grosse and Thompson (1993), including the following:

1. Review current policies for admission to programs, registration procedures, health information forms, and other documents to guarantee that the language in the forms or admission requirements does not discriminate in any way.

2. Review the training program for new employees. Disseminate information regarding nondiscriminatory language, procedures, and ways to assist individuals with disabilities in a respectful manner.

3. Develop resources in the community and on staff for using communication aids, sign language, and lifts and for assisting with wheelchairs and transfers. Keep in a convenient location the names and phone numbers of advocates in the community, as well as interpreters for people who are deaf. Call on these resources immediately in the event of communication or physical accessibility issues.

4. Review safety procedures and considerations for individuals with a variety of disabilities, and have a "walk- and wheelthrough" of your facilities with people who have a variety of disabilities to ensure that your organization has addressed all aspects of safety.

Administrators of aquatics facilities should know what the terms "readily accessible" and "readily achievable" mean in relation to the ADA. Along with accessibility issues, the committee must address usability, which is the ability of participants with disabilities to participate in the general programs of the facility, not simply to move through the building. To create a high degree of usability, ensure that your program accommodates participants with disabilities by adapting instruction, activities, and equipment and modifying supplies.

Making your program accessible and usable means that you provide individuals with disabilities the aquatic services you offer to individuals without disabilities. Make it your goal to adapt existing programs or create new programs that are as close as possible to regular circumstances in society. Then ensure that staff members are made aware of the needs of those with disabilities, are trained to meet those needs in a personable and respectful manner, and are made aware of the need to treat individuals with disabilities as valuable consumers of your organization's services.

What else can you do? Work to make the general conditions more usable. For example, keep air and water temperatures adequately warm, offer times to swim that are not overcrowded, and provide appropriate safety and supervision in an environment without attitudes that create barriers. Your efforts will pay off as you create a program more desirable to those with disabilities.

Locker Room

The locker room can be a place of great frustration for individuals with disabilities. Factors such as inadequate lighting or lockers with combinations can impede independence for those with arthritis, poor fine motor control, or upper body amputations. Such factors do not motivate individuals with disabilities to use a facility. Many other factors may inhibit independence as well, such as benches cemented into the floor in front of lockers, shower area ledges or lips that limit access for participants in wheelchairs, and a lack of Braille signs on lockers and entrances and exits. Because this is the first area a participant must conquer in the aquatics experience, your YMCA must adapt its locker rooms to increase participants' independence, safety, and success. Fortunately, since ADA guidelines relative to physical education, recreation, and aquatics facilities have been published, it is easier to know exactly what to do (Grosse & Thompson, 1993). Here are the recommended requirements:

- *Entry and exit doors.* Entry and exit doors shall have a minimum clear opening of 32 inches wide, with doors opening to 90 degrees, a minimum five-foot-long level clearance in the direction of door swing, and easy-to-open doors requiring less than five pounds of pressure to open (Federal Register, 1991).

- *Locker room spacing.* Pathways to the locker area should be wide enough for two wheelchairs to pass each other, should be clear of protruding objects, and should not have benches in front of every locker. Adequate room for storage of wheelchairs is necessary if participants transfer out of their chairs into aquatics/shower chairs.

- *Sign posting.* Post Braille maps and signs (directions to the shower, lockers, bathroom, and pool) on the wall outside the doors, not on the doors themselves, so that no one is injured by an opening door while reading the Braille.

- *Floor surface/handrails.* Nonslip floor surfaces are preferable, such as indoor-outdoor carpeting strips or rubberized matting. Handrails are recommended for those ambulatory participants who may have poor balance when their feet or crutches are wet.

- *Lockers.* Lockers should have handles that are large, thick, and easy to manipulate. Key or touch pad locks may be easier than combination locks. Locker hooks and shelves should be about 34 inches high. Some horizontal locker space approximately three feet off the ground is a nice addition to conventional vertical lockers (Canadian Red Cross, 1980).

- *Hair dryers, soap dispensers/towels, mirrors.* Hair dryers should be placed at varying heights to enable those in wheelchairs to use them. Soap dispensers and towels should be no more than 34 inches from the floor and mirrors no more than 40 inches from the floor (Grosse & Thompson, 1993).

- *Toilet.* A toilet stall must be large enough for transfers, a minimum of 51 inches wide.

- *Showers.* Showers should have nonskid floors and be void of lips to cross over. A shower bench, handrails, and handheld shower heads are the most convenient features. A stall whose shower head is stationary should be four feet high, with the controls about three feet high. Water should be thermostatically controlled by easy-to-turn valves with long handles and brightly colored raised numbers to indicate temperatures around the valve. A seat shower system is commercially available that caregivers and aides can use to help shower an individual who is dependent without the caregiver getting wet. In addition, this system incorporates water jets attached to a mobile shower seat that surround the participant and can be placed over any water drain. Standard shower chairs should also be available for those who want to wheel into the shower or down an in-pool ramp.

• *Changing areas.* Wide benches, changing tables (at wheelchair-seat height), or mats should be available for dressing areas. Overhead heat bulbs and changing areas that are not drafty are a plus.

If your YMCA cannot provide accessible, usable, and desirable space in the general locker room, you must provide a separate or private area, such as a family changing room, in which caregivers of the opposite sex can assist individuals with disabilities.

Pool Area

Unique architectural design can help a multipurpose aquatics facility meet the needs of many diverse groups. Although the uses and purposes of a pool should drive its design, often it is the dollars budgeted for the project that dictate the size, shape, and amenities. Aquatics instructors often are not included as part of the aquatics facility construction project team, and therefore they must work with what is there. In this section, we describe ideal pool decks, access components of a pool, and the ideal pool itself. For more information regarding planning, design, and construction of a therapeutic pool facility, see Dieffenbach (1991).

• *Pool Deck.* A pool deck may be flush with the gutters or several inches higher than the gutters and water. If not flush, it should not be more than 12 inches above the waterline (American Red Cross, 1977) for safe and easy entry. Individuals with disabilities require pool decks that are free from clutter and wide enough to accommodate wheelchair storage, additional shower chairs, crutches, transfer equipment, flotation devices, seizure mats, and pedestrian traffic.

At any given time, multiuse facilities have a lot of equipment and supplies on the pool deck. Consider the following suggestions as a minimum for deck safety:

a. Floors around the pool should be nonslip but nonabrasive.

b. Surfaces should slope down slightly to facilitate drainage (Golland, 1981).

c. Decks should be kept clean and safe by banning outdoor shoes on them.

d. Place rubberized flow-through safety mat tiles or other sanitary, slip-resistant tiles pieced together over the deck, especially along high-traffic areas from shower to pool edge. Mop-on products can create antiskid surfaces on wet areas as well.

The point at which the deck meets the pool edge should have depth markings and contrasting colors and textures. Contrast is especially important if the deck is flush with the gutter system. For pools constructed with a transfer wall, the top surface should be 12 to 15 inches wide, allowing participants to transfer directly from their wheelchairs to the wall and into the pool. In these types of pools, shown in figure 18.5, the wall is raised 17 inches above the deck (National Center on Accessibility, 1996), about the height of a wheelchair seat. The deck in this case is below the level of water as accessed by a dry ramp, or the pool deck may have been dug lower than the ledge. To further enhance pool entry, the water level should be as close as possible to the top of the transfer wall.

In addition to clutter problems, narrow decks pose difficulty for individuals with visual and orthopedic mobility concerns who use crutches, canes, walkers, or wheelchairs. Especially at risk are those individuals with neuromuscular disorders who require the use of a power wheelchair or crutches. The anxiety caused by being on a

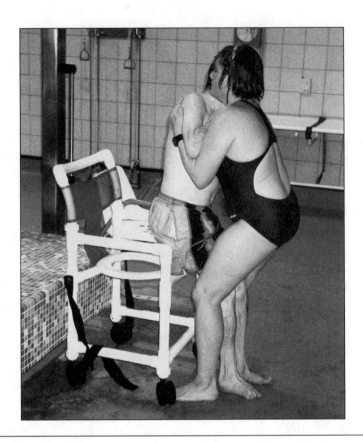

Figure 18.5   A transfer wall.

pool deck is enough to elevate already abnormally high muscle tone. Fears of running into an obstacle course or maneuvering through narrow spots on a narrow deck, close to the water's edge, add to the tension. Such trepidation, compounded by poor deck maintenance, could cause an accident, such as an individual inadvertently driving a wheelchair into people, obstacles, or the pool, or slipping and falling.

• *Pool.* Characteristics of the pool that should be checked include methods of entry and exit; the depth, width, and length of the pool; and water temperature and quality.

• *Entry and exit.* First, your facility must enable participants to make transitions between the pool deck or wheelchair and the water safely, especially for individuals who harbor some anxiety about the water. In addition, individuals with severe cognitive involvement may not recognize that a change from land to water is necessary; thus, you must ensure that such participants are instructed to enter and exit at the appropriate location. The first objective is to get the individual safely into the water by offering encouragement and clear explanations of what is happening (Boulter, 1992; Bradtke, 1979). Provide a facility that offers maximal independent entrance, use, and exit for all participants, while drawing as little attention as possible to the process (Osinski, 1993). Because of differing abilities among participants, however, your program may require more than one mode for safe and dignified entrances and exits.

A variety of facility designs lend themselves to safe access. Wet ramps, dry ramps, and gradual steps with handrails are examples of built-in methods of transferring into the pool. Dry ramps are constructed into the pool deck outside of the pool, and wet ramps connect the deck directly to the water. Regardless of which model is chosen, the National Center on Accessibility (1996) recommends that a ramp should meet the following specifications:

    a. Maximum slope of the pool ramp shall be 1:12 (one-inch rise per horizontal foot).

    b. Minimum clear width of the ramp shall be 36 inches.

    c. Handrails shall be provided at heights of 16 to 26 inches and 34 to 38 inches on both sides of the ramp.

• *Wet ramps.* Wet ramps (figure 18.6) should be located in shallow water away from swimming lanes and have a nonslip, nonabrasive surface that uses color and texture or curbing to indicate the edges (Mace, 1993). To use a wet ramp, participants can walk, crawl, scoot, or use an aquatics chair to gradually enter the water.

• *Dry ramps.* Dry ramps (figure 18.7) provide a gradual slope on the outside of an in-ground pool, bringing the pool deck below the water surface. They provide a transfer point for those who use wheelchairs and for participants who have trouble bending down to sit on a pool deck or using a ladder or steps.

Avoid inset ladders as much as possible. These ladders, with their steps in the wall of the pool, are difficult to navigate for individuals with poor strength, visual-motor

Figure 18.6   Wet ramp.

Figure 18.7   Dry ramp.

coordination, or balance, those with arthritis or other joint dysfunction, and children. Gradually sloping steps (figure 18.8) are a helpful adaptation for many participants using the pool, including senior citizens. Although used extensively in in-ground backyard pools, sloping steps are rarely built into indoor community pools because they take up almost an entire lane of space. But you can purchase portable stairs, ramps, and transfer tiers as movable access modes (see the "Equipment and Supplies" section of this chapter).

•   *Shape, depth, width, and length.* Pool shape, depth, width, and length should be of primary concern. Multiuse pools will have a variety of structural shapes, such as rectangular, oval, round, square, L-shaped, and Z-shaped. Depths, lengths, and widths

Figure 18.8   Built-in gradual slope stairs.

vary even more than shapes. Teaching pools generally have about 40 percent shallow and 60 percent deep water, using an evenly sloping bottom. "Slopes in the shallow end should not exceed 1 in. per horizontal foot. A more gradual slope of 1 in. for each 18 or 20 in. horizontal measure is preferred" (American Red Cross, 1977, p. 113). The depth may vary by a sloping floor, by lanes of differing depths, or actual four- to six-inch steps as wide as the entire bottom of the pool up to the five-foot area. Shallow-water pools, two to four feet deep, are ideal for teaching children. Pools adapted for individuals with disabilities, in which caregivers and aquatics instructors must provide support, should have a surface area of which two-thirds of the water depth is four and a half feet or less (American Red Cross, 1977). If your pool is less than four and a half feet deep, however, you may need to limit lap swimming and underwater activities.

Movable pool floors and movable bulkheads are other ways to adapt community and therapeutic pools to multiple uses. Movable pool bottoms, often called hydraulic pool floors, can be installed during pool construction or retrofitted in an existing pool. This feature can be installed so it encompasses the entire pool bottom or only a section of the pool floor. The floor is constructed of reinforced concrete with a nonslip tile finish. A section or an entire pool floor can be raised or lowered by hydraulic cylinders to any water depth for instruction. If only a section of the floor is raised, various safety design factors eliminate the possibility of entrapment, and the movable floor does indeed create a multipurpose pool. Since you can position such a floor at various levels, it is an excellent way to accommodate children, individuals of short stature, those who cannot stand, and inexperienced swimmers. Individuals using wheelchairs can be transferred from shower chairs directly onto the raised floor and lowered directly into the water where they can swim or float out of the chair (see figure 18.9). When the pool is not in use, you can raise the pool floor to deck level, eliminating the risk of individuals reentering the water, maintaining pool temperature, limiting water evaporation, and converting the pool area into an all-purpose room available for many nonaquatics events.

Figure 18.9 Movable pool floor.

Although movable floors offer a great deal of flexibility and accommodation, the initial money outlay is large. Movable bulkheads can shrink very large pools into smaller areas to accommodate various group sizes. The distinct separation that bulkheads afford allow you to safely run multiple activities concurrently.

• *Water quality and temperature.* As you probably know, pool water treatment disinfects the water to control communicable diseases and balances the water's pH to prevent pool scaling and corroded equipment (Edlich et al., 1988). Water disinfection is important to reduce the risk of patrons catching potential communicable diseases such as rashes, ear infections, and conjunctivitis. The most commonly used disinfection agents are chlorine, chlorine compounds, bromine, PHMB (polyhexamethylene biguanide), copper and silver ions, and ozone. Trained staff members must maintain water balance, controlling water mineral concentration to eliminate pool and equipment damage by monitoring water temperature, pH, total alkalinity, calcium hardness, and total dissolved solids (Edlich et al., 1988).

The water quality of a therapeutic pool is difficult to maintain. These pools are normally kept between 84 and 94 degrees Fahrenheit, which is a higher temperature than is used in multipurpose pools. Unfortunately, water temperature above 84 degrees affects mineral balance (calcium) and the amount of disinfectant needed. Many warm-water pools are disinfected with bromine or metal ions, as these chemicals dissipate more slowly than chlorine in warm water.

If you work in a warm-water pool, you should be concerned with water sanitation and quality since body pores open at high water temperatures, making individuals with low or weak immune systems more susceptible to infection (Osinski, 1989). Persons infected with human immunodeficiency virus (HIV) may pass this virus into swimming pools or whirlpools, but dilution (even in the absence of a chemical germicide) is adequate to kill the pathology of most viruses—the risk of transmission is so miniscule as to be immeasurable (Edlich et al., 1988). Heat and chlorine help destroy HIV, but hepatitis B and C (HBV and HCV) viruses are more durable (Skaros, 1993). Avoiding contact with blood or body fluids is the most effective means of protecting yourself from HBV and HCV; adequate chlorine or other sanitizing agents can ensure that HIV and common communicable diseases that cause skin, eye, and ear irritation will not be problems.

Equipment and Supplies

Proper equipment and supplies are as important for classes serving individuals with disabilities as they are for the general population. *Equipment* refers to items of a relatively fixed nature, such as portable entrance stairs, hydraulic lifts, and tot docks, whereas *supplies* are those nondurable items that have a limited period of use, such as kickboards and flotation devices (Dauer & Pangrazi, 1986). When planning the budget, consider the life span of each piece, keeping in mind that equipment tends to require more maintenance, periodic replacement, and is higher priced. If your aquatics program is to accomplish its objectives, then you must have enough equipment available for individuals with disabilities to dress, enter, participate, and exit the pool in as independent and timely a manner as possible. Moreover, adequate supplies should be available so that participants do not waste instructional time waiting for equipment or supplies.

Six basic reasons to use adapted equipment and supplies in adapted aquatics include the following: (1) entrance and exit requirements, (2) safety, (3) support, (4) propulsion, (5) fitness, and, when it comes to children, (6) motivation (Crawford, 1988; Heckathorn, 1980). In the following sections, we'll address these six categories as well as equipment storage.

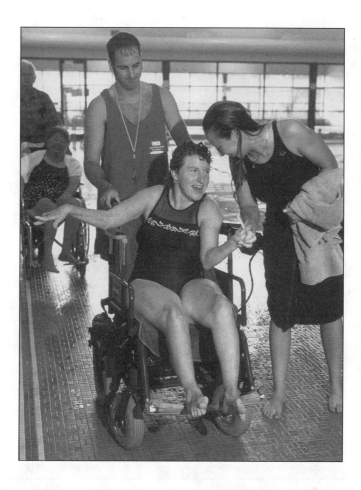

Entrance and Exit Equipment and Supplies

Lifts, portable ramps, stairs, and ladders are the most important items for transferring into and out of the water when no equipment is built into the facility.

- *Lifts.* Lifts often provide the primary means for individuals with severe orthopedic disabilities to access the pool. In addition, those with acute disabilities, such as patients who have just had surgery, may also find lifts helpful in providing access. Lifts operate by suspending, pivoting, lowering, and raising the participant. There are water-powered systems (figure 18.10), water-hydraulic systems (figure 18.11), mechanical lifts, and fully automated lifts. Some lift models require a second party to operate, whereas others can be operated by the participant, resulting in a more independent aquatic experience. The National Center on Accessibility (1996) recommends that pool lifts be used that facilitate independent usage. Independent usage is most facilitated when hand controls are located at the front edge of the seat, are operational with one hand, do not require tight grasping, and require five pounds or less of force to operate. Lifts require little space and vary in price from several hundred to thousands of dollars. Most require some type of pool deck modification. Many decks, however, have a permanent sleeve with a portable lift (figure 18.12). When using a removable device, the device must remain in place until all participants have exited the pool. When not in place, a sign must be posted instructing potential users on how to ask for assistance with the lift (National Center on Accessibility, 1996).

- *Ramps, stairs, and ladders.* Portable ramps, stairs, and ladders are fit to match water depth and deck proportions. Typical materials are stainless steel, PVC, and fiberglass. Figure 18.13 depicts a portable stair that fits flush to the wall and floor in

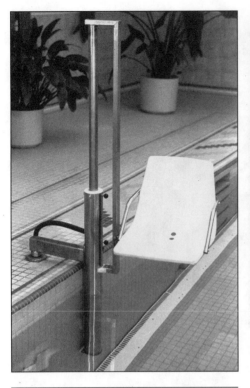

Figure 18.10 Water-powered lift from Aquatic Access.

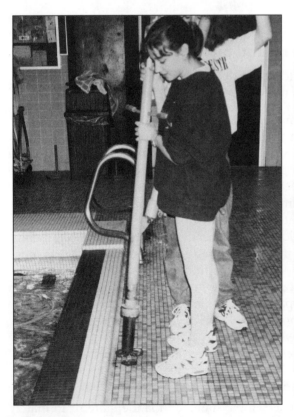

Figure 18.11 Hoyer Lift.

Figure 18.12 Permanent sleeve for a removable lift is one option for accessibility.

Figure 18.13 Portable stairs are easier to use than built-in ladders.

the corner of the pool. These portable steps serve anyone who cannot effectively negotiate a vertical ladder. They should be slip resistant, have a minimum width of 36 inches, and have treads no less than 11 inches deep.

If the pool has a wet ramp, a movable floor, or zero-depth entry as the accessible means of entry and exit, an aquatics chair with push rims must be provided. The aquatics chair should measure 17 inches above the deck, be 19 inches wide at the seat, and have footrests and armrests that can be moved out of the way (National Center on Accessibility, 1996).

- *Transfer steps.* For individuals who have good upper body use but cannot negotiate stairs or ladders because of lower body involvement, the transfer tier (figure 18.14) can facilitate more independent pool access. Participants transfer from a wheelchair onto the upper step, then lower themselves into the pool step-by-step. They reverse the process to exit the pool. The transfer tier requires no facility renovation and should feature nonskid tread strips, have no sharp edges, and should be nonabrasive. Clear deck space of 60 by 60 inches should be adjacent to the surface of the transfer steps, and the transfer surface should be 17 inches above the deck. The last step into the water should be at least 18 inches below the surface of the water, and one handrail should be provided (National Center on Accessibility, 1996).

Safety Equipment and Supplies

In addition to typical pool safety equipment and supplies, such as a shepherd's crook or reaching pole, ring buoys, first aid kits, rescue tubes, and backboards, a few gym mats and some waterproof mats might be warranted when individuals with disabilities are patrons. Boosting oneself out of the water with lower body paralysis requires an individual to lie face down on the pool deck and drag the lower body over the edge, possibly causing abrasions. Gymnasium mats placed on the deck and

Figure 18.14   Transfer Tier by Triad Technology.

slightly overhanging the edge enhance safe transfers (figure 18.15) (Nearing, Johansen, & Vevea 1995). Waterproof aquamats made of closed-cell foam are helpful to have around for individuals who are having a seizure or need to rest after one.

Support Equipment and Supplies

A wide variety of flotation devices, including personal flotation devices, pull buoys, wet vests, dumbbell floats, and sectional rafts, give instructors an extra "hand" when working with individuals who are dependent on others to stay above the water (see figure 18.16). Flotation devices ensure safety, eliminate fear, provide support, and help participants maintain a level position in the water (Heckathorn, 1980). There are flotation devices for head support, especially useful for swimmers with muscular dystrophy; full-body flotation devices for swimmers with quadriplegia or severe multiple disabilities; and handheld flotation devices for balance while water-walking. Flotation devices also help keep the ears out of the water for participants with serious ear problems. Specially designed swimsuits by Speedo and other companies provide in-suit inflation bladders to support the swimmer. Because flotation devices help to support, stabilize, and facilitate movement, they may open a new world to individuals with mobility impairments, allowing freedom of movement not possible on land.

Although flotation devices are useful, they pose several problems for individuals with disabilities. For example, they may impair independence if swimmers rely on them too long after they should have progressed to independent, unaided swimming. Dunn describes more severe problems in the article "PFD's for the Handicapped: A Question of Responsibility" (1981). A research study at the University of Minnesota's Duluth School of Medicine tested personal flotation devices on individuals with disabilities and found PFDs difficult to put on and hard to fasten. In addition, they did not help maintain a good surface position because of variations in body buoyancy and density caused by muscle atrophy, amputations, and decreased

Figure 18.15   A mat placed on the pool deck can alleviate bruises and abrasions during transfer.

Figure 18.16   Flotation equipment.

bone density. Researchers found that standard PFDs positioned swimmers with disabilities too far on the back and some did not keep the mouth far enough above the water surface.

Unfortunately, however, because of the difference in body types of people with disabilities, it would be very expensive to research this issue, as a tailor-made PFD would have to be made for each person. Therefore, if your participants use flotation devices for support, you must provide proper supervision, even if the PFDs are Coast Guard–approved. The Flotation Suit for the Disabled (not Coast Guard–approved, however) is specially made for the needs of individuals with disabilities. You can add or take off various pieces, depending on flotation needs, body control, and safety issues. "When using flotation aids, most of the flotation must center over the lungs and upper chest, not around the stomach or solely across the back" (Shurte, 1981, p. 2).

Propulsion Equipment and Supplies

Forward movement in the water is affected by a swimmer's physical ability, body shape, and efficiency of swim stroke (Andersen, 1988). The first step to efficient propulsion is to devise flotation or other support to put the body in the most streamlined and balanced position possible. If the participant is still having difficulty with propulsion, instructors should try other devices. Thong hand paddles increase the surface area of the hands and press against the water for propulsive efficiency, as do fins; however, overuse of hand paddles can cause shoulder injuries. Swimmers with lower body amputations can use prosthetics designed for the water and swim fins that are directly attached to prosthetic sockets (Marano & DeMarco, 1984). Those who have part or all of their arms missing may be able to use a swimming hand prosthesis or Plexiglas paddles attached to the residual stump. For specific ideas for using these devices, see Paciorek and Jones (1994) and Summerford (1993).

Fitness Equipment and Supplies

The increase in the number of participants in water fitness classes has increased the number of products available for water fitness training. Underwater treadmills, aquacycles, water workout stations, and aquaexercise steps provide cardiovascular conditioning, muscle toning, and strength training. Water fitness participants also use supportive and resistive equipment and supplies in the water that are handheld, pushed, or pulled, such as finger and hand paddles, balance bar floats, upright flotation vests and wraps, aquashoes, webbed gloves, waterproof ankle and wrist weights, workout fins, buoyancy cuffs, aquacollars, and buoyancy belts. Instructors should encourage participants to use hand paddles cautiously, as these devices may contribute to shoulder injury if overused or improperly used.

Over the last few years, companies have developed dozens of pieces of equipment and a variety of supplies to facilitate fitness, and many are geared toward water rehabilitation. Peruse equipment and supply catalogs to compare prices and materials.

Motivational Equipment and Supplies

The developmental levels, interests, and attention spans of children require a different approach to aquatics instruction and recreation. Attractive, brightly colored equipment, nontoxic and sturdy supplies, toys, flotation devices, and balls will help instructors devise instructional strategies that focus on fun. Other devices children might use under close supervision include swim belts, bubbles, and squares, many of which come with modules to increase or decrease flotation. Foam rafts offer kicking fun and relaxation, as well as a central place to play in the pool. They are more durable than blow-up rafts and can support more weight. Water logs, also known as water noodles or woggles, are hefty, flexible buoyant logs that encourage water exploration and kicking in a fun way. In addition, hoops, inner tubes, diving rings, disks, water basketball games, goggles, fins, nose clips, and swim caps are useful. Check to make sure none of your participants is allergic to latex before giving them equipment.

The Wet Wrap by D.K. Douglas Co., Inc., is a wet suit vest to wrap around the body for added warmth; it can be used with both adults and children. In multipurpose pools in which the water temperature is less than 85 degrees Fahrenheit, the Wet Wrap and its partner, Wet Pants, are useful for participants with poor internal heat production systems, those with low body fat (as often is the case for individuals with cerebral palsy), and children who don't move enough to keep warm. The Wet Wrap is easy to put on, as it does not have to be pulled over the head.

Storage of Equipment and Supplies

You should have sufficient supplies available to safely conduct your adapted aquatics classes. Advanced planning by instructors who will be using the supplies simultaneously is critical to instructing without delays and to accounting for equipment at all times. Valuable instruction time is often lost when equipment is in disrepair, suddenly borrowed by another instructor, or lost in storage.

To prevent these problems, ensure that all equipment and supplies are marked and remarked at regular intervals with an indelible marker. Maintain an accurate inventory of all equipment and supplies in storage and make it available to every instructor. Despite these efforts, expect a reasonable turnover of equipment, reflecting this in replacement schedules. Restrict use of such equipment to classes and organized recreation programs, avoiding the damage and loss that inevitably result from use in open recreation and outside group activities.

Establish a system for storage, repair, and issuing of equipment and supplies. Label shelves and bins, and ensure appropriate ventilation to prevent mildewing. Insist that all instructors and participants accept responsibility for the care and storage of equipment.

Finally, designate an additional area for storage of wheelchairs, crutches, canes, braces, and the like, during class times. This will keep the deck free of objects that may further impair the mobility of participants.

WORKING WITH PEOPLE WITH DISABILITIES

You will want your staff to approach people with disabilities in ways that show respect and accommodate problems in a dignified manner. In this section, we give some suggestions on how to communicate with people with disabilities, how to address them properly, and how to teach them.

Sometimes people are uncomfortable around individuals with disabilities because they don't know how to act or what to say. Here are some general tips you can pass along to your staff to make communicating easier.

Part of treating people with disabilities respectfully is addressing them appropriately. The following suggestions are good guidelines.

When you talk about people with disabilities, use the phrase *people with disabilities* rather than *disabled people* or *the disabled*. This stresses that they are people first and that the disability is secondary. Use the word *handicap* to mean something in the environment that causes a problem for someone with a disability; a set of stairs would be a handicap to someone using a wheelchair. Avoid using euphemisms that may be in fashion, such as *physically challenged* or *special*. Most people with disabilities think these terms are not correct and are demeaning.

Some terms appropriate for describing specific types of disabilities are the following:

- Someone with extensive hearing loss is *deaf,* but someone with any type of hearing loss can be described as being *hard of hearing.*

- The word *blind* usually means extensive loss of vision, but either *blind* or *visually impaired* are acceptable words for all levels of loss of vision.

- Any severe mental or physical disorder that began before the person was 22 and will continue is called a *developmental disability.* Examples of such disorders would be cerebral palsy or mental retardation.

- To describe someone who has any form of mental illness, use the phrase *person with a mental disability.*

- People who do not have disabilities should be called *nondisabled,* rather than *normal* or *healthy.*

Don't look at or portray people with disabilities as being either superhuman or tragic. They just want to be regarded as others are.

Finally, here are some practical ideas for teaching people with disabilities:

- Before the class begins, discuss issues of bowel and bladder management with those whose disabilities may affect it.

- Approach each child as an individual, and involve the child and the caregiver in your planning.

- Keep a cautious watch on students with disabilities for possible dangers or physical difficulties.

NATIONAL ORGANIZATION ON
DISABILITY
www.nod.org

1. First and most important—people with disabilities, like everyone else, deserve to be treated with dignity and respect. People with disabilities have different personalities and different preferences about how to do things. To find out what a person prefers, ask.

2. When you meet someone with a disability, it is appropriate to shake hands—even if a person has limited hand use or artificial limbs. Simply touch hands (or the person's prosthesis) to acknowledge his/her presence. Shaking the left hand is also fine.

3. Always ask before you assist a person with a disability, and then listen carefully to any instructions. Do not interfere with a person's full control over his/her own assistive devices. For example, before you push someone who uses a wheelchair, make sure to ask if he or she wants to be pushed. Likewise, never move crutches or communication boards out of the reach of their owners without permission.

4. Remember, most people with disabilities want to serve as well as be served and enjoy assisting others.

5. Usually people with disabilities do not want to make the origin or details of their disability the first topic of conversation. In general, it's best not to ask personal questions until you've become real friends.

6. Be considerate of the extra time it might take a person with a disability to get some things done.

7. Speak directly to the person with a disability rather than to a companion or sign language interpreter who may be along.

8. Relax. Don't be embarrassed to use common expressions such as "I've got to run now," "See you later," or "Have you heard about" even if the person doesn't run, see, or hear well. People with disabilities use these phrases all the time.

9. Some terms that might have sounded acceptable in the past, such as "crippled," "deaf and dumb," and "wheelchair-bound" are no longer accepted by people with disabilities. Many have negative associations. Instead say "person with a disability," "Mary is deaf (or hard of hearing)," "Denise uses a wheelchair," and "Joe has mental retardation." This type of language focuses on the person first, and the disability afterward.

10. Avoid excessive praise when people with disabilities accomplish normal tasks. Living with a disability is an adjustment, one most people have to make at some point in their lives, and it does not require exaggerated compliments.

11. Don't lean on a person's wheelchair—it is considered an extension of personal space.

12. When you talk to a person in a wheelchair for more than a few minutes, try to sit down so that you will be at eye level with that person.
13. Don't pet a guide or companion dog while it's working.
14. Give unhurried attention to a person who has difficulty speaking. Don't pretend to understand when you don't — ask the person to repeat what they said.
15. Speak calmly, slowly, and directly to a person who is hard of hearing. Don't shout or speak in the person's ear. Your facial expressions, gestures, and body movements help in understanding. If you're not certain that you've been understood, write your message.
16. Greet a person who is visually impaired by telling the person your name and where you are. When you offer walking assistance, let the person take your arm and then tell him or her when you are approaching inclines or turning right or left.
17. Be aware that there are many people with disabilities that are not apparent. Just because you cannot see a disability does not mean it doesn't exist.
18. Help make community events available to everyone. Hold them in wheelchair accessible locations. This makes it easier for everyone!

For more etiquette tips and for tips on specific disabilities go to **http://www.epva.org/DownLoad/disaet.pdf** or call the Eastern Paralyzed Veterans of America at 800-444-0120 for a free booklet entitled "Disability Etiquette." (Funding for preparation of this guide provided by AETNA.)

- Make sure that students have adequate breath control.
- Eliminate noise and distractions when possible.
- When you explain or demonstrate, talk slowly and distinctly. Teach one thing at a time, and keep progressions simple.
- Don't keep students in one position for too long.
- Expect students with disabilities to work at skills to their capacities. Try to accomplish something each lesson.
- Focus on what a person with a disability can do, not what he or she can't do. Adapt strokes, use aquatics equipment, and try different methods as necessary to accommodate students.
- Have an aide or parent in the water to assist if it will help students participate more fully.
- If any problems develop, seek help.
- Be accepting and caring.
- Stay patient and firm.
- Provide plenty of praise and enthusiasm. Make class fun!
- Teach individuals without disabilities how to interact with individuals with disabilities. For example, YMCA instructors can teach children without disabilities that it is okay to ask a child with a disability to stay out of their personal space if they ask appropriately, and show them how to do so.

SAFETY

Just as in any aquatics program, you should see that your staff and participants are taught safety procedures at the beginning of each session and that those procedures are reinforced daily. We describe some general precautions for all staff, plus some related to lifeguarding.

General Precautions

Make certain at least one trained lifeguard is on deck, regardless of the student-teacher ratio. Program safety and students' abilities should determine the ratio of guards to students. Also make sure staff and lifeguards are ready to respond to emergencies relating to CPR, first aid, and procedures for aiding participants having seizures.

Here are some additional general safety precautions for your staff:

• Make certain the student always knows what you are trying to do. Stabilize or lock all equipment, furniture, wheelchairs, and devices to prevent tipping, slipping, or moving. Safety belts or their equivalent facilitate handling students while ensuring safety in the performance of the task.

• Be prepared to prevent falls. Make certain no sharp obstacles are in the vicinity, and learn the proper procedures for reporting accidents. Prepare and file accident reports carefully.

• Take care not to bump the limbs or feet of people with paralysis. Their skin can break down easily and decubitus sores can form. These students may need to wear socks for protection, and caution should be taken during entry into and exit from the pool, as well as during pool activities.

• Take care not to cause bone injuries. A characteristic of certain disabilities is fragile, easily broken or fractured bones. Because of osteoporosis, the frail elderly may be vulnerable to breaks and fractures.

• Know how to transfer students of any type and size. For protection, always keep fundamental body mechanics in mind when lifting or transferring someone. Stay close to the center of gravity of the body part or person being moved. Maintain a straight spine and bent knees, and use your legs rather than your back to lift, move, or hold a load. For safety, instruct another person in how best to help in transferring participants.

• Be alert for signs of stress in participants. Reaching safety may be particularly difficult for students with problems such as cramping, spasms, uncontrolled movements in the extremities, chills, an inability to get rid of water splashed into the mouth, and an inability to recover from a position in the water. Stress may include chest pain, pain radiating to other extremities, unease and restlessness, irregular breathing, and pale or clammy skin. Students under stress may lose their balance from diving or being underwater for a long period of time.

• Know the participants. Use current information forms and keep them readily available. All records—attendance, medical information, incident and accident reports, progress reports, records of recognition and awards, and other forms applicable to a program—should be completely updated and easily located for every student.

• Recognize common disabilities. Know their characteristics and what to look for. Students may have obvious problems or may wear medic alert tags. If a disability is difficult to pinpoint, ask the swimmer or attendant about the nature of the disability.

HEALTH CONSIDERATIONS

To ensure that participants are comfortable and safe during classes, consider the following points:

- *Pool.* The water temperature in classes for people with disabilities is often 83 degrees Fahrenheit or higher. Warmer temperatures increase the opportunity for bacterial growth, so water should be chlorinated, filtered, and checked often to ensure proper chemistry. If the temperature is over 86 degrees, treat immediately. An adequate turnover of water, depending on the bather load, is essential. The pool should have a good filter-purification system and, when possible, a heating system capable of raising water temperatures quickly.

- *Whirlpools and hot tubs.* Although whirlpools and hot tubs are wonderful relaxation aids, bacteria grow rapidly because of the heat and movement of the water. These facilities must be monitored carefully and checked frequently. They should only be used with a physician's consent, and they are generally contraindicated for people with heart conditions, young children, pregnant women, and people with multiple sclerosis, for whom heat may be debilitating.

- *Air temperature.* Ideally, air temperature and flow should be controlled to prevent evaporation chilling (four degrees higher than the pool temperature) when a student leaves the water. A place for hanging towels and robes should be provided in the pool area so students are dry and warm when on deck. Radiant heat has been installed in some pool ceilings; a good location is above the waiting area, where towels and robes also can be left.

- *Incontinence.* Some students may be incontinent, and they must take precautions to prevent urine or fecal matter from entering the pool. Swimmers may use special rubber pants with tight-fitting leg bands; many are very careful about preventing potentially embarrassing situations. Those with catheters and colostomy bags should clamp them off during pool time. Provide appropriate containers in the dressing and bathroom areas for diapers, colostomy bags, and other such items. Follow your facility's fecal contamination procedures.

- *Emergency plans.* All aquatics facilities should have an emergency pool evacuation plan. Practice emergency procedures regularly and post emergency numbers clearly. Teach all students how to get in and out of the pool in an emergency; staff assistance may be needed. For example, three short whistles can mean "clear the pool." Swimmers who cannot hear whistles or see warning signs should have a buddy or volunteer who lets them know when they must leave the pool, get to safety, or take whatever action is necessary. Practice and use emergency procedures with discretion. Have special emergency plans to handle people who have epileptic seizures or those who become violent.

- *Medical treatment.* Some swimmers may be using various drugs and medications; others may have disabilities with such symptoms as seizures or loss of consciousness. Review participants' health records regularly to be aware of new drugs, prescribed drug side effects, new symptoms, or any physical changes. Speak to physicians, families, professional personnel at institutions, school officials, and participants as frequently as necessary to protect student safety. Staff members oriented to safety and health considerations who have recently completed CPR and first aid updates and understand the possible effects of medication and treatment of seizures, asthma attacks, dizziness, and other conditions should successfully cope with any special situation. Only qualified people should be assigned to dispense medication to individuals; medication should be secured in a place handy to the pool.

For more information on specific disabilities, refer to the resources listed next. You also can sign up for one of the YMCA's related courses. Working With People With Disabilities is a basic course that provides an overview of different disabilities. The YMCA Swim Lessons: Individuals With Disabilities Instructor course goes into more depth on how to work in aquatics classes with people who have disabilities.

RESOURCES

Contact these organizations for more information that can help you with your adapted aquatics programs:

ADA Technical Assistance Information, 800-466-4232 (V/TDD)

American Association on Mental Retardation, 800-424-3688

American Foundation for the Blind, 800-232-5463

Asthma and Allergy Foundation of America, 800-727-8463

Attention Deficit Disorder Association, 800-487-2282

Disability Rights Education and Defense Fund, Inc., 800-466-4232

Epilepsy Foundation of America, 800-332-1000

Hearing Information Center, 800-622-3277

National AIDS Information Clearinghouse, 800-458-5231

National Easter Seal Society, 800-221-6827

National Head Injury Foundation, 800-444-6443

National Rehabilitation Information Clearinghouse/ABLEDATA, 800-346-2742 (V/TDD)

National Spinal Cord Injury Association, 800-962-9629

Spina Bifida Association of America, 800-621-3141

United Cerebral Palsy Association, 800-872-5827 (V/TDD)

Resources available from the YMCA Program Store (800-747-0089) include the following:

- *On the Guard II* (4th ed.)
- YMCA Water Fitness for Health
- *Adapted Aquatics Programming*
- YMCA Swim Lessons: Teaching Swimming Fundamentals
- YMCA Swim Lessons: The Youth and Adult Aquatic Program Manual
- YMCA Swim Lessons: The Parent/Child and Preschool Aquatic Program Manual

YMCA certification and training available include these:

- YMCA Swim Lessons: Individuals With Disabilities Instructor/Trainer
- YMCA Water Fitness Instructor/Trainer
- YMCA Active Older Adult Water Fitness Instructor/Trainer
- Working With People With Disabilities Instructor/Trainer

Additional YMCA of USA resources are available on the Web site or by contacting the YMCA of the USA at 800-872-9622.

BIBLIOGRAPHY

American Red Cross. 1977. *Adapted aquatics.* Garden City, NY: Doubleday.

Andersen, L. 1988. Swimming to win. In *Training guide to cerebral palsy sports,* edited by J.A. Jones, pp. 68-88. Champaign, IL: Human Kinetics.

Behrman, Richard, E., ed. 1987. *Nelson textbook of pediatrics.* Philadelphia: W.B. Saunders.

Boulter, P. 1992. Using hydrotherapy: Maximizing benefits. *Nursing Standard,* 7(4): 25-27.

Bradtke, J.S. 1979. Adapted devices for aquatic activities. *Practical Pointers,* 3(1): 1-5.

Canadian Red Cross. 1980. *Adapted aquatics recertification.* Ottawa, ON: Canadian Red Cross.

Crawford, M. 1988. Adapted aquatics programming for persons with severe disabilities: An overview of current best practice standards. In *Adapted physical education: A comprehensive resource manual of definition, assessment, programming, and future predictions,* 3rd ed., edited by P. Bishop, pp. 193-213. Kearney, NE: Educational Systems Associates.

Dauer, V., and Pangrazi, R. 1986. *Dynamic physical education for elementary school children,* 2nd ed. Minneapolis: Burgess.

Dieffenbach, L. 1991. Aquatic therapy services. *Clinical Management,* 11(1): 74-78.

Dunn, K. 1981. PFD's for the handicapped: A question of responsibility. *The Physician and Sportsmedicine,* 9(8): 147-152.

Edlich, R.F., Becker, D.G., Phung, D., McClelland, W.A., and Day, S.G. 1988. Water treatment of hydrotherapy exercise pools. *Journal of Burn Care Therapy,* 9(5): 510-515.

Federal Register. 1991. *PL 101-336, Title III of the Americans With Disabilities Act,* July 26.

Golland, A. 1981. Basic hydrotherapy. *Physiotherapy,* 67(9): 258-262.

Goodwill Industries International. 1996. *People with disabilities terminology guide.* Bethesda, MD: Goodwill Industries.

Grosse, S.J., and Thompson, D., eds. 1993. *Leisure opportunities for individuals with disabilities: Legal issues.* Reston, VA: AAHPERD.

Heckathorn, J. 1980. *Strokes and strokes.* Reston, VA: AAHPERD.

Horvat, Michael. 1990. *Physical education and sport for exceptional students.* Dubuque, IA: William C. Brown.

Lepore, Monica, G. William Gayle, and Shawn Stevens. 1998. *Adapted aquatics programming: A professional guide.* Champaign, IL: Human Kinetics.

Mace, R.L. 1993. Making pools accessible. *Athletic Business,* 17(8): 34-36.

Marano, C., and E. DeMarco. 1984. A new design and construction for a swimming prosthesis. *Orthotics and Prosthetics,* 38(1): 45-49.

Miller, Freeman, and Steven J. Bachrach. 1995. *Cerebral palsy: A complete guide for caregiving.* Baltimore: Johns Hopkins University Press.

National Center on Accessibility. 1996. National Center on Accessibility—Swimming pool accessibility.

Nearing, R.J., D.A.K. Johansen, and C. Vevea, C. 1995. Gymnastics mats in the pool? *Palaestra,* 11(2): 22-30, 64.

Osinski, A. 1989. Warm water pool and spa problems. *The National Aquatics Journal,* Winter: 12-13, 15.

Osinski, A. 1993. Modifying public swimming pools to comply with provisions of the Americans With Disabilities Act. *Palaestra,* 9:13-18.

Paciorek, M.J., and J.A. Jones. 1994. *Sports and recreation for the disabled: A resource manual,* 2nd ed. Indianapolis: Masters Press.

Recreation Access Advisory Committee. 1994. *Recommendations for accessibility guidelines: Recreational facilities and outdoor developed areas.* Washington, DC: U.S. Architectural and Transportation Barriers Compliance Board.

Shurte, B. 1981. Adapted aquatics bulletin #101. Ann Arbor, MI: Danmar Products.

Skaros, S. 1993. Bloodborne pathogens and contagion risks for aquatic personnel. *National Aquatic Journal*, 9: 3.

Smith, Deborah Deutsch, and Ruth Luckasson. 1992. *Introduction to special education: Teaching in an age of challenge*. Needham Heights, MA: Allyn and Bacon.

Stevens, Suzanne H. 1985. *Classroom success for the learning disabled*. Winston-Salem, NC: John F. Blair.

Summerford, C.F. 1993. Apparatus used in teaching swimming to quadriplegic amputees. *Palaestra*, Spring: 54-57.

Torney, John A., Jr., and Robert D. Clayton. 1981. *Teaching aquatics*. Minneapolis, MN: Burgess Publishing Company.

YMCA Camp Waterfronts

Y MCA camps may use a variety of water areas for waterfront activities—streams, rivers, ponds, lakes, oceans, or tidal waters. Each type of waterfront location poses different problems and planning issues; however, some basic principles can be applied to waterfront planning that pertain to all sites or can be adapted to specific situations.

Critical factors to consider in advance planning for waterfront use include these:

- The safety of all campers and camp personnel
- The best conditions for instruction
- The ability to provide effective supervision
- The health of campers and staff
- Access for emergencies
- The ability to communicate with EMTs

We begin with what to look for in a good waterfront site and, once you've chosen a site, how to set it up. We also give you suggestions on how to run the site, what equipment you'll need, and how to maintain the site and equipment. From there we turn to the administrative issues of staffing and budgeting, then look at waterfront programming. The last section of this chapter is a complete curriculum for boating programs, including sections on rowing, paddlesports, sailing, waterskiing, and motorboating.

CHARACTERISTICS OF A GOOD WATERFRONT SITE

When you are deciding on where to locate waterfront activities, check for access to the site, slope gradients, soil composition and stability, surface drainage, water depths and currents, and water quality. The following information is a basic waterfront guide. For additional information on developing a waterfront site contact the YMCA of the USA or the American Camping Association.

Access to the Site

The best siting is relatively close to the main part of the camp program and living areas, although this may not always be possible. If private property is near the site, find out who the owners are and whether their proximity will cause a problem for site use.

You should have a way to control access to the waterfront area, ideally a natural barrier or fencing. However, if no such barrier exists, you can set up a control post with an attendant to control access (see "Controlled Access" later in this chapter). It's also helpful if there is a road directly to the waterfront site, making it easier to move equipment to and from the site and allowing emergency vehicles access.

Slope Gradients

Look for a place where the shoreline gradually descends to the beach, rather than a steep drop. The slope of the bottom below the waterline should also be gradual and as flat as possible, ideally 2 to 5 percent. Avoid sudden changes in grades or drop-offs in the zero- to five-foot depth.

Perform pre- and post impoundment studies to ensure that the gradients are acceptable. Consider daily, seasonal, and yearly water level fluctuations due to irrigation, flood control, evaporation, power generation use, tides, currents, or other factors. Do a detailed inspection of the underwater portion of the beach prior to opening each season to identify sinkholes, depressions, or dangerous drift material. Keep records of these inspections on file, and take any corrective actions needed prior to opening the beach.

Soil Composition and Stability

Ideally, the bottom of the waterway should be composed of sand or gravel. It should be free of weeds, broken glass, cans, and sharp rocks and objects. Do not locate the site in an area in which extensive siltation occurs or is expected to occur.

Surface Drainage

Pay particular attention to surface drainage when planning and designing a swimming beach. As surface runoff should not be allowed to drain across the beach, you will need to divert runoff from any area upland of the beach (including runoff from parking areas or from commercial agriculture). Methods of diversion include grassed swales, terracing, inlets, and landscaped walls. Choose methods that complement the beach development and minimize impact to the site. If possible, locate the outfall of diversion downstream from the swimming beach. Make sure that erosion and drainage from your beach site will not be hazardous to surrounding land or water areas. Check with local Department of Natural Resources (DNR) officials that regulate usage of water and areas near water for procedures and usually for permission to make adjustments either to the beach or water area. (You can also contact the Army Corps of Engineers for further information on diverting runoff.) Find out what the restrictions and considerations are and obtain permits before you make any adjustments, rather than starting the project and then having to stop it, as well as possibly incurring a fine.

Water Depth and Currents

Here are examples of water depth for swimming:

- Nonswimmers area, 2.5 to 3.5 feet
- Intermediate swimmers area, 3.5 to 6 feet
- Advanced swimmers area, 3.5 to 12 feet

Make sure that these depths are consistent across all seasons during which there are aquatic activities. Avoid using areas of unknown depths. Be sure to mark the depths clearly. If you are considering using a stream, large lake, or ocean beach, make sure that the existing currents, including undertow, are no more than two miles an hour.

Water Quality

Check that water quality is acceptable for swimming. Collect water samples monthly during the summer or according to your state regulations. Have them analyzed, and coordinate your efforts with the appropriate state agencies. The water should be clear, clean (free from contamination), in adequate quantity, and in a reasonable temperature range. Remember that as summer proceeds, contamination levels increase. Drought conditions will make them even worse.

Make sure there is adequate water circulation to ensure continued acceptable water quality and to assist in removing surface debris that may deposit on the beach. Although barriers and coves generally offer the best protection against wind and wave action, avoid dead-water coves.

Plan your beach to avoid fuel spillage from boats, sewage, industrial outfalls, and boat wakes. Locate it upstream from any boat ramp or marina to minimize the consequences of possible fuel spills.

Check the area for any marine life or vegetation that might be annoying or harmful to swimmers; if there is a problem, place the site elsewhere. Also do not locate your beach where large groups of waterfowl congregate, as the birds may carry diseases. To help prevent waterfowl from gathering on your beach, keep the area free of litter, and don't allow anyone to feed the birds. As waterfowl like large open areas, plant shrubs and hedges or string lines overhead to make the area less welcoming for them.

Here is a checklist of questions to consider in selecting a waterfront location, for all sites and for specific types of sites:

All Bodies of Water

- ✔ How much does the water level fluctuate throughout the entire camping season?
- ✔ What is the average temperature of the water during the camping season?
- ✔ What is the temperature range?
- ✔ If it is a small body of water, how constant is the water flow under all weather conditions during the season it is to be used?
- ✔ What are the riparian rights (rights for use of the water and surrounding area)?
- ✔ Can an unlimited amount of water be withdrawn?
- ✔ What restrictions are already established?
- ✔ What is the nature of the bottom?
- ✔ Have the results of frequent water analysis tests proved satisfactory for swimming?
- ✔ To what extent would other users of the body of water interfere with camp activities?
- ✔ Who are the owners of adjacent properties, and what interference would there be from them, if any?
- ✔ Will the beach and shallow water accommodate necessary equipment satisfactorily?

✔ Can heavy floating equipment be beached and shored up for winter storage?

✔ Is there appropriate depth for diving (minimum of 9 feet deep from the dock when less than 18 inches above water level and 12 feet from any greater height)?

✔ Is there sufficient water clarity to permit suitable swimming?

✔ Is the bottom likely to be covered with broken glass, tin cans, fishhooks, and other debris each spring?

✔ What are the local, state, and federal regulations?

Lake (natural and seminatural)

✔ What is the average depth and the depth of the deepest parts?

✔ Who owns the lake, shares it, or controls it?

✔ Is the water stagnant, or do natural currents and make-up water keep the water in the area fresh?

✔ Can the water level be altered artificially? If so, by whom? How?

✔ Has the water source for a reasonable distance been surveyed for possible unnatural sources of pollution?

✔ Can the water level be lowered in the winter to prevent ice damage to piers and other equipment?

River

✔ How constant is its flow and level during the camping season?

✔ Is there a frequent history of flash floods during the camping season? What is the potential for flooding?

✔ How strong is the current? Are there silt deposits or shifting channels? Is it safe for swimming?

✔ To what extent will other organizations and the public interfere with camp activities?

Tidal Waters

✔ What are the mean high- and low-water marks?

✔ Is the area sufficiently protected from storms to warrant the placing of equipment?

✔ Is the area equally usable at low tide as well as high tide? If it is not usable during one of the tides, can other activities be planned?

✔ Are there any channel or tidal currents that may make the area unsafe?

✔ How close are the nearest port authority, harbor police, and Coast Guard station?

✔ What are the dangers of marine life (jellyfish, stingrays, etc.)?

✔ How difficult will it be to keep free of seaweed and debris?

See figure 19.1 for a reference.

CAMP WATERFRONT LAYOUT

Once you have selected a location, make sure the layout of the camp waterfront is safe and healthy for campers, allows for proper supervision, and aids instruction. Develop a system for restricting access and for keeping track of campers. Divide the waterfront into separate areas for different activities. Plan to build safe and sturdy

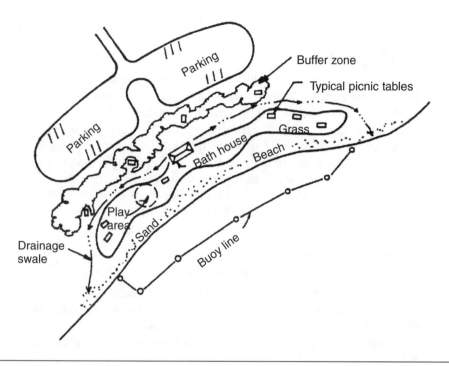

Figure 19.1 Sample beach layout design.

docks, piers, and walkways, as well as sufficient boat storage. Take into consideration sanitation and lifeguarding concerns also. Finally, think about whether a waterfront office would be helpful to your staff. A few comments are included for camps that have pools rather than a waterfront.

Controlled Access

You need to have some type of access control for the waterfront. A staff member will need to stand at a check-in/check-out post and act as an attendant. You should also have some type of system for keeping track of who is in or out of the water and for restricting those with limited aquatic skills to certain areas for swimming and boating.

One example is a tag system. Each camper and staff member is asked to take a swim qualification evaluation at the beginning of each session. You then issue a colored band and tag to each person according to the person's abilities. Here are some sample criteria:

Blue Chip (Advanced)
- Feetfirst entry
- 100-yard swim demonstrating a good resting stroke and one minute treading water
- Minnow level and above

White Chip (Intermediate)
- Feetfirst entry
- 25-yard swim, change positions from front to back and return to beginning
- Guppy level

Red Chip (Beginner)

- Beginners and nonswimmers

You may also apply boating skill criteria for those who will be boating.

The colored bands allow lifeguards to easily see if people are in the correct areas for their abilities. Guards will be expected to warn those who are not.

The colored tags can be used to keep track of who is in the water at any given time. For swimmers, this can be paired with a buddy system so lifeguards can periodically check the accuracy of the system. Each person who enters the water must put the tag on a "buddy board." That person must enter with a "buddy," a swimmer of the same swim classification. Each swimmer must stay within 10 feet of her or his buddy at all times. When a guard blows a whistle, swimmers do one of the following:

- They sit on the dock, deck or sand, hold hands with their buddy, and raise their joined hands to be counted. They hold hands until the count is over.

- They stop where they are in shallow water, grab their buddy's hand, and raise their joined hands high in the air. (Some camps have campers stand next to the dock.) Those who are in deeper water can either move to shallow water or move to the closest floating object (such as a raft) and hang on to that, then raise their buddy's hand.

If the guard's count shows that a swimmer is missing, he or she can ask all campers and staff to exit the water and turn in their tags. The tag that isn't turned in should show who is missing. Lifeguards can then follow standard procedures for a missing-person emergency (see *On the Guard II*, 4th ed.). For information on other such systems, see chapter 11.

Activity Areas

Divide your waterfront site into at least three separate areas for swimming, diving, and small craft use; if you teach waterskiing or windsurfing, you need an additional area to allow enough room to conduct these activities safely. The size of each area will depend on the number of campers you expect to use each one, now and in the near future.

Do not allow small craft activities—canoeing, sailing, windsurfing, rowing, and kayaking—in the same area as swimming, and do not moor small craft off swimming docks. The risk is that the small craft will float into the swimming lines and the swimming perimeter, especially if winds are high or gusty or the participants are beginners. Also, having more than one activity near the swimming area diverts lifeguards' attention from the swimmers.

The swimming area should be large enough to avoid overcrowding and to provide for safety. In natural waters such as a lake or stream, allow at least 50 square feet of usable water area per swimmer.

In the diving area, leave at least 14 feet between boards and 16 feet between boards and walkways. For a one-meter board, the water should be a minimum of 12 feet deep for at least 18 to 25 feet from the edge of the dock. (While the established minimum water depth for use of a one-meter board is 11.5 feet, the extra depth allows for a small variance in an uneven bottom in open-water areas.)

Each season, recheck the bottom depth, as it can change due to wave action and water fluctuation. Also, hidden objects such as logs may have been dragged in over the winter, especially if there is any ice movement on the lake. (This process would be in addition to your regular waterfront checks throughout your season.)

Mark the swimming area and divisions between areas using buoy markers and buoy lines or foam-filled floated pipelines. Place brightly colored (orange or yellow) floats every 5 to 10 feet on buoy lines or at all angles when PVC pipe is used. You also may choose to use lemons or seines, small floats that attach to cords, to mark the areas. The lemons are made of wood, cork, or plastic and may be white or painted a bright color. They are hung on treated, durable cording. Plastic floats that lock onto the line with a twist are very useful, especially if there is a lot of wave action. The floats cannot slide together, and they should be evenly spaced. Lines are usually one-quarter or one-half inch in diameter, depending on the size of the area and the diameter of the inner lines between docks and the shallow and deep water and the outer lines that mark the swim area perimeter. Post depth gauge poles at regular intervals no more than 25 feet apart along dividing lines.

Ideally, buoy lines are placed in water that is not more than five feet deep. However, if water fluctuations occur, place the buoy lines in relation to the mean water level. If the water level fluctuates a lot, use buoy lines that can be adjusted easily.

Place a minimum of two warning buoys or floating signs marked with the "Boats Keep Out," "Designated Swimming Area," or "Slow, No Wake" symbol spaced at 200-foot intervals. Locate them so they provide adequate warning to vessels approaching 100 to 300 feet from the swimming area buoy lines. Check with your local DNR for their specific rules. For example, the minimum distance that boats need to observe from a swimming area differs depending on the state. You will also want to check how far out your swimming area can be. Usually this distance is marked from the shoreline out.

Docks and Piers

Build sturdy docks using wood, plastic, aluminum, or steel (keep in mind that steel may get too hot to walk on barefoot during the summer). Firmly base them on or in the bottom or firmly tether or attach them to shore so they can withstand waves, currents, and storm action. In some cases, you may use Styrofoam or barrels to support the docking. Consult with engineers during the initial planning of all docks to ensure they are built for safety.

Use a nonslip deck surface on all docks, and keep them free of nails, slivers, and projections. Place depth markers on the docks. Do not build the surface of a dock or pier more than two feet above the water level and preferably at 18 inches. Construct fixed platforms, piers, runways, and floats with an airspace of at least one foot underneath. Use only as much underwater construction as is needed to strongly support them. Design all braces, struts, and other supporting elements so they cannot entangle or trap swimmers beneath the structure. If you are in a flood plain or water levels change during the season, build fixed piers with movable underpinnings.

Docks can be built in a variety of letter formations: F, L, E, A, T, H, and others. Figure 19.2 shows examples of two such dock formation layouts.

We recommend that you have separate docks for swimmers and small craft to avoid accidents with swimmers; we also recommend separate fishing docks for fishing, casting, and fly-fishing instruction. Keep boating docks downwind to prevent them from floating into the swim area. Swimming docks should have one ladder for every 20 swimmers. Ladders should be at least two feet wide with nonslip rungs. The docks should also have handholds one foot from the ladders that swimmers can use as nonobstructing grasping devices.

For river and tidal waters where the water level rises and falls, we recommend floating docks with hinged poles or ramps for securing the docks to shore. We also recommend floating cribs where beach bottoms are treacherous.

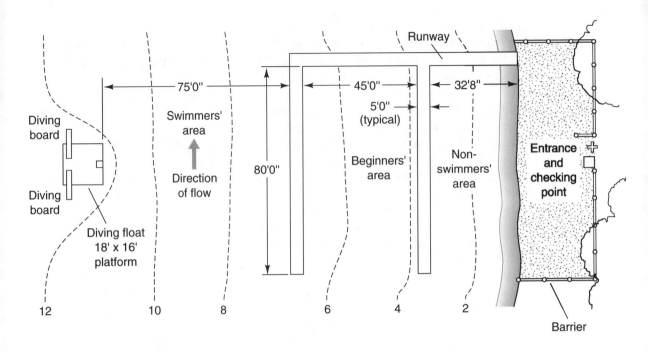

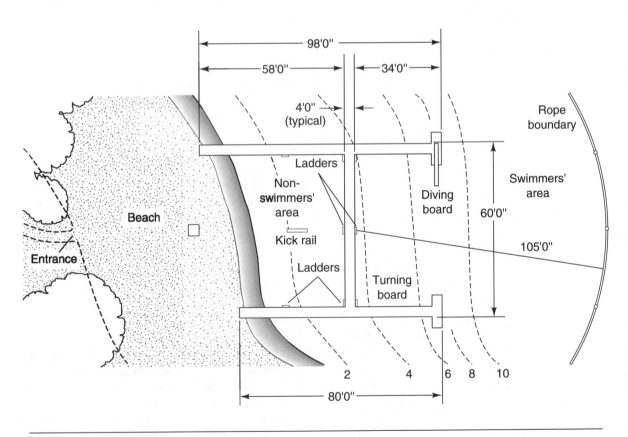

Figure 19.2 Example dock formation layouts.

After the camp season, you may have to take docks (regular or floating) out of the water if you are in a climate with winter storms and ice. If it is possible to lower the water level during the winter, you can use permanent footings to support cribs, which reduces the work and maintenance costs.

Walkways

Build walkways at least four feet wide and cross-planked to reduce the danger of bathers picking up splinters. Space the planks one-quarter inch apart to allow for drainage, and use planks with their edges planed with sufficient beveling to prevent splintering. Several walkway surfaces are available that can also be used.

Boat Storage

Mooring depends on the boats and the camp. Some camps prefer to moor their boats on the water; others may not have room to do so due to DNR regulations regarding the number of boats allowed to be moored on the water. In such cases, camps bring their boats on shore, following guidelines specific to each craft. For motorized boats such as ski boats, you may choose to either moor them or put them on lifts at the end of the period or day to allow them to drain and dry.

Set up separate storage and launching areas for canoes, kayaks, rowboats, paddleboats, motorboats, and sailboats. Be sure to keep the mooring and launching areas for motorcraft and sailboats separate. Create a small craft control system in which all watercraft are under the supervision of assigned staff. Have a method for locking or securing all small craft easily and quickly. Provide a lockable, readily accessible waterfront building in which all boating and canoeing equipment can be stored. Check with the American Camping Association (ACA) and your state regulatory agency for any additional procedures you may need to follow.

Keep rescue boats in a special location that is strategically located to reach all points on the waterfront. Label rescue boats for their usage and paint them in a high-visibility color. These boats should have removable seats to meet rescue requirements for injuries.

Sanitation

Provide convenient sanitation that is not hazardous to the site itself. Furnish proper and adequate toilet facilities near the waterfront that are located conveniently so campers will use them before and during waterfront activities. Waterfront toilets, showers, and the water supply should meet your state's department of health regulations, and septic systems and waste disposal should be in accordance with local and state laws. Avoid draining effluent above ground or near a lake, stream, or other water sources or areas. Do not allow horses, dogs, or other domestic animals on the beach or in the water in the waterfront area or water sources that run into it.

Make sure drinking water (which may be in an insulated cooler) or a water fountain is available in the waterfront area. This will allow campers and staff to drink water regularly and maintain proper hydration. Maintain the cleanliness of the waterfront area. Eliminate any hazards from breakage or waste.

Lifeguarding

The YMCA of the USA has these general guidelines for the number of lifeguards needed for camp waterfronts:

For nonswimmer/beginners: one guard to 10 swimmers

For intermediate swimmers: one guard to 14 swimmers

For advanced swimmers: one guard to 20 swimmers

Besides considering these guidelines, also take into consideration the water and bottom conditions, as well as the other guidelines in appendix 4 when determining how many lifeguards are needed. In areas where there are no docks, assign lifeguards in boats. Check with the ACA and your state regulatory agency for their requirements as well.

Large waterfronts should have a lifeguard tower that overlooks the entire waterfront area. Place it so the guard does not need to turn her or his head in order to see the entire area and can readily and quickly direct or render assistance. Situate the tower at least 15 feet above the water level and in the center of waterfront activity, not too far from the water's edge. Do not allow this tower to be used for diving or any other activities. In addition to lifeguards, other camp staff can help supervise waterfront activities as needed. See the YMCA of the USA Aquatics Guidelines in appendix 4 for more about this topic.

Waterfront Office

A waterfront office will be helpful to your staff. It will allow them to have a small desk and file for keeping records. First aid and emergency response equipment and supplies can be stored there, as well as equipment such as paddleboards, poles, fins, masks, snorkel, spare line, markers, floats, and life jackets.

Pools

Some camps may have pools rather than waterfronts. If your camp does, follow all the recommendations about pools in chapters 10 through 12. Be sure to operate the pool according to your local municipal, county, and state regulations. The pool should be located in a well-drained area; check for possible drainage problems daily.

WATERFRONT SITE CONTROL

Once your site is up and running, you will need to continue your efforts to ensure the safety and health of all campers and staff through sound maintenance, regular supervision, and vigilant observation. Here are some suggestions regard water supply and site condition, weather conditions, sanitation, and safety and control practices.

Water Supply and Site Condition

- Check the waterfront bottom daily for debris, obstructions, erosion, or other changes (often due to storms). Look for changing sand, wave, current, or tide conditions.

- Check regularly for marine life or vegetation that could be bothersome or dangerous to swimmers.
- Check regularly that the water supply—stream, lake, ocean, or pool—is free from pollution in accordance with the standards of the state health department.
- Test the water regularly, and keep permanent records of the results.
- Have procedures in place for staff to follow to take quick action when strong storms or flooding occur. This will help keep campers safe and prevent the loss of docks, boats, and equipment.
- On the trail, allow campers to swim in and use only water that has been tested in advance.

Weather Conditions

- Check water temperature daily.
- Listen to a weather radio and observe weather conditions routinely to assess storms or swift changes in weather and weather predictions. Use such information to guide out-of-camp canoe and boating trips, small craft use on the waterfront, and swimming activities. Consider purchasing a lightning detector.
- Along tidal waters and ocean areas, regularly check the barometer readings as well as U.S. Coast Guard or U.S. Weather Bureau warnings for small craft use, high waves, or dangerous currents.
- Establish and practice an emergency plan for severe weather in the event campers are already on the water.
- Do not allow any aquatics activity during thunderstorms.
- Designate shelter areas near the waterfront for use in case of wind or thunderstorms.
- Remove all small craft from the waterfront areas during thunderstorms or windstorms.
- Following storms, watch along streams and rivers for flooding conditions.

Sanitation

- Keep the toilet, shower, and dressing room facilities clean, orderly, and sanitary throughout the day.
- If any campers or staff members should not be permitted to swim or engage in waterfront activities, give the waterfront director and staff notice. Also inform them if this situation is temporary due to a medical condition or permanent. If possible, meet with staff and identify such swimmers. Consider providing a place for nonswimmers to sit, such as a picnic table.
- Place a responsible staff member on duty at the buddy board entrance to inspect all bathers for such things as skin disorders, open lesions, and cleanliness. Campers who are overheated should cool down before entering cool water.
- Prohibit the common use of towels, drinking cups, bathing suits, combs, hairbrushes, and other toilet articles.

Safety and Control Practices

- Allow swimmers, campers, and staff alike to swim only in areas appropriate for their ability classifications.
- Allow only swimming or diving activities to occur in the designated swimming and diving areas.
- Conduct waterskiing in areas away from swimming and small craft operation. Provide protected storage for all equipment.
- Make sure that the waterfront director and staff have the ability to clear the waterfront safely and quickly through the control system in the event of an emergency or the need for a missing-person drill or rescue.
- Make sure that rescue squads and rescue equipment and craft are readily available and can gain access to the waterfront in case of an emergency. Train staff in lifeboat and rescue procedures so they can use those procedures readily in case of an emergency on the waterfront.
- Establish a working communication system among several waterfront areas—swimming, small craft, and outpost (raft in the water).
- Station at least one lifeguard or lookout on the dock for each class that is in session. (Lookouts are individuals who are trained as a YMCA Aquatic Safety Assistant or in basic water rescue but are not allowed to make rescues in the water. They can notify lifeguards if they notice a problem.) Depending on the activity, such as use of an inflatable, you may need additional guards in the water to supervise.
- Identify fishing and nonfishing areas.
- Prepare in advance for rescue and safety procedures for boating and swimming areas. Practice these procedures regularly.
- Make sure that equipment is safely stored.
- Take steps to ensure the safety of campers during mooring or docking.
- Devise a system for collecting and returning lost and found items each day.

WATERFRONT EQUIPMENT

The waterfront equipment you choose for your YMCA camp will depend on both your programming and safety needs. Camp directors and waterfront directors need to be sure they have the basic safety equipment present and available for all waterfront activities. This is true whether the waterfront location is owned by the YMCA or is being rented or used by agreement with the property owner.

Here is a list of basic equipment for the waterfront:

- *Life jackets/PFDs* (personal flotation devices) must be U.S. Coast Guard-approved. They are mandatory for everyone using boats, canoes, sailboats, and powerboats or for any activity outside of the swimming area. Careful storage and maintenance of jackets will measurably cut down on damage and waste. See *On the Guard II* (4th ed.) or *YMCA Swim Lessons: The Youth and Adult Aquatic Program Manual* for more on fitting PFDs.
- *Rescue tubes and buoys* are necessary equipment for all lifeguards.

- *A ring buoy* with 60 feet of rope should be readily available for rescue purposes and lifesaving practice.
- *Ten- to 15-foot reaching poles* are needed by lifeguards for reaching rescues.
- A *first aid kit*, fully stocked and regularly maintained, is needed for medical emergencies.
- *Other necessary rescue equipment* includes a backboard with head restraints, an automatic external defibrillator (AED), and supplemental oxygen.
- *Paddle boards*, also known as rescue boards, can be used by lifeguards to transport victims in light to moderate surf.
- *Rafts* may be used as part of the camp waterfront layout. They may be set on Styrofoam flats, drums, collapsible piers resting on metal shoes, or permanently anchored piers.
- *Rowboats* are a basic program and safety piece of equipment for the waterfront. Choose 14- or 16-foot rowboats, narrow enough for young campers to row. Plan to have five to six rowboats per 100 campers.
- *Canoes* come in a variety of sizes and materials. Choose 15- to 17-foot canoes. To ensure maximum safety, select canoes on the basis of the anticipated program use and the age and ability of the program participants.
- *Kayaks* come in a variety of sizes, designs, shapes, and materials. Select the type of kayak based on the type of program, age, and ability of program participants.
- *Paddles and oars* should be provided in numbers commensurate with the number of canoes and rowboats. Provide extras for safety and maintenance purposes.
- *Sailboats* come in a wide variety of designs, shapes, and sizes. Take into account the size of the available waterfront area—pond, lake, river, tidal waters—when determining the kind of sailboat to secure. Sailboats for three to five persons are usually desirable. The boat's suitability for use in basic sailing instruction is also an important qualifier. Provide separate docking facilities for small dinghies as well as larger sailboats, free from canoe and rowboat activities. Remove sails daily, dry them, wrap them, and place them in a weather-protected area. Carefully store all equipment between seasons. Sailboat maintenance requires steady attention; plastic, fiberglass, or plywood hulls are frequently used that need to be checked for cracks and leaking and repaired if necessary.
- *Instructional flotation devices* such as kickboards, belts, and water logs are used for instructional classes for campers. Use YMCA Swim Lessons program information as the guide for their use.

Other equipment commonly found at camp waterfronts includes these items:

- Surfboards
- Water skis
- A powerboat for water safety supervision
- A powerboat for waterskiing and instruction
- Marking anchors and buoys for small craft supervision
- Water thermometers, water scoops
- Lanterns
- Throwbags

To give you a feel for how many to purchase of each item, here's a sample equipment list for 100 campers (Gabrielsen, Spears, and Gabrielsen, 1968):

- Lemons (seines): one to every three feet of cording (about 100)
- Cording: 300-500 feet
- Boats: five to six rowboats available for about 20 campers
- Canoes: four to five to hold 12-15 campers
- Sailboats: two to hold six campers
- Oars: 15-20
- Paddles: 12-16
- Ring buoys: three
- Rescue buoys: two
- Rescue tubes: six

Note: For instructional flotation devices, the variety of types and number depend on how many classes are offered at a time. For example, 12 to 24 may be sufficient for three classes. Have one per student in beginning classes. For waterskiing equipment (skis, ropes, life jackets, motorboats), the number of each depends on the number of skiers, the size of the skiers (some skis are better for smaller campers), and the skiers' level of experience (two skis vs. slalom skis vs. trick skis vs. wakeboards). A general rule of thumb is to have at least two pair of skis per boat: one for the skier in the water and one for the skier waiting to go. Have at least two ropes per boat; the type will depend on the kind of skiing being done. For life jackets, have one for the skier on the water and one for each person in the boat (driver and observer). The law usually requires an additional one, but this differs from state to state.

Here's a sample list of camp administration equipment:

- A communication system that connects with the camp office, nurse, and EMS (telephone and radio)
- Rescue equipment (rescue tubes, fanny packs, resuscitation masks, suction device, bag valve mask, AED, oxygen cylinder)
- A check-in/check-out board or buddy board (carefully designed and clearly marked)
- Colored wristbands and tags for the buddy system
- A checker's stand for the buddy system check during waterfront activities
- Equipment and storage shed
- Camp waterfront office with a place for storage, first aid equipment, special rescue equipment, and communication equipment (radio, phone, bull horn, etc.)
- Special gong, bell, or horn for emergencies
- A loudspeaker or air horn for instruction and safety
- Clipboards for instructors
- A bulletin board for announcements, camper progress charts, rules, procedures (Ideally this should be sheltered from the rain and placed so that it does not obscure the view of the waterfront.)
- Program materials (cards, emblems, ribbons, skill sheets, and manuals) for instructors and campers
- Lockers for storage of waterfront gear and supplies
- Drying racks for towels and swimsuits

- Racks for storage and maintenance
- Kneeling pads for canoes
- Sailing and boat-washing equipment
- Waste and trash barrels
- A rake and shovel for waterfront cleanup
- A stopwatch and clock
- Whistles for the buddy check, emergencies, and lifeguards
- A weather radio
- Fuel supplies and maintenance equipment tools for motors and boats

Maintain all equipment in workable order. Place a red tag on faulty equipment or assign a designated place in the boathouse, guard shack, or storage room for such equipment. Devise a system that designates which equipment is to be repaired and which is to be thrown away. Provide proper storage for the equipment when it is not in use. Have a plan to store all program equipment under lock and key, with a protection plan to eliminate vandalism. The waterfront director and staff should be constantly looking for potential problems. Create an identification system for all waterfront equipment using identification numbers that should not be removed. Mark each piece of equipment (boats, safety materials) with the camp logo and an identification number. Take an inventory of all camp waterfront equipment prior to and after the camping season. Check it during the camping season also to facilitate planning and make sure adequate supplies are available to carry out program activities safely.

WATERFRONT MAINTENANCE

With careful planning, you can avoid waste and ensure regular maintenance of waterfront equipment. Having the staff do regular daily and weekly checks under the guidance of the waterfront director is the key to keeping all waterfront equipment in top shape and ready when needed. You can use camp waterfront equipment year

after year if it is properly maintained. Poor storage practices, inappropriate use of equipment, and carelessness can waste a lot of equipment.

When you plan for waterfront maintenance, take the following into consideration:

- A yearly maintenance plan for equipment and facilities (painting, repair, treatment)
- Breakdown and storage during the off-season and repair before setting up the dock and facilities for the waterfront
- Beach reconditioning
- Removing potential hazards or damage from storms
- Daily maintenance of the whole waterfront area for cleanliness and removal of waste
- Repair of equipment and facilities according to a daily check system
- Planning for replacement of equipment, motors, and other supplies
- Careful purchasing for durability and cost of repair or replacement

Camp waterfront maintenance can become increasingly difficult if camps get larger or if poor systems and practices are in operation. The camp waterfront and equipment should be orderly, attractive, clean, and well cared for. Campers and staff will respect a well-organized camp waterfront in which all equipment and facilities are in good condition.

STAFFING

On the waterfront, the head person is the camp waterfront director. He or she is responsible for caring for the waterfront area and for waterfront programming. Many other types of staff may be there too.

Camp Waterfront Director

The camp waterfront director is directly responsible to the camp director. This person plans, organizes, teaches, supervises, and coordinates all waterfront activities. The waterfront director is responsible for controlling and regulating all phases of the waterfront program, using trained and capable leadership to carry out the program and maintenance functions safely.

Here are the five core components of the waterfront director position:

1. Aquatic sports and activities
   - YMCA Swim Lessons, skin diving, snorkeling, YMCA Scuba, synchronized swimming, springboard diving, water polo, water fitness, waterskiing, kneeboarding, surfing
2. Recreational swimming and specialty events (stunts and games; exhibitions and water shows; competitive events such as speed swimming, water polo, lifeguarding, boating, synchronized swimming)
   - Small craft—boating (basic and advanced), canoeing (basic and advanced), sailing (basic and advanced), kayaking, windsurfing
3. Water safety—aquatic safety (Teen Leadership Program, Porpoise, Advanced Aquatic Safety, YMCA Aquatic Safety Assistant)

4. YMCA Lifeguarding
5. Waterfront administration

- Planning—program scheduling, lesson plans
- Maintenance—equipment, docks, small craft, motorcraft
- Supervision—training and appraisal

Camp waterfront directors should be aware of their responsibility for the safety, health, welfare, and progress of all campers and camp staff participating in waterfront programs.

They should have a comprehensive knowledge of aquatics, with special consideration for the camp waterfront setting, and they should have completed thorough training in all components.

Camp waterfront directors should possess effective training skills and be good teachers. They should have the human relations skills to effectively coach the waterfront staff and develop their esprit de corps, as well as to be sensitive to campers' needs and interests.

Maintaining discipline and consistent and effective rule enforcement is another integral part of the waterfront director's role. See chapter 11 on rule enforcement. By intelligently understanding and handling youth, directors can alleviate most discipline problems.

Recommended qualifications for a camp waterfront director include the following:

- Be at least age 21
- Have YMCA certifications as a lifeguard and YMCA Swim Lessons instructor and in YMCA Aquatic Management (preferred certifications are as a YMCA Lifeguard Instructor and a YMCA Swim Lessons Youth and Adult Trainer)
- Have taken the Program Trainer Orientation
- Be certified in CPR-Pro and first aid (instructor rating preferred)

A sample job description can be found on the YMCA of the USA web site.

Other Waterfront Staff

Although camp waterfront staff positions will vary according to the size of the camp and the kinds of facilities, equipment, and programs provided, some of the basic waterfront staff assignments include these:

- Assistant waterfront director
- Small craft director
- Sailing instructor
- Boating and/or canoeing instructor
- Swimming instructor
- Skiing instructor
- Head lifeguard
- Lifeguards
- YMCA Scuba instructor

Depending on how staff assignments are made, some of these positions may be held by staff with other assignments in camp. For example, cabin counselors may have activity positions as instructors in the waterfront areas. Some waterfront positions may be full time. In some camps, an assistant waterfront director carries specialty responsibilities.

Waterfront staff should be trained and certified in their specific areas of responsibility—YMCA Lifeguard, YMCA Swim Lessons Youth and Adult Instructor, and small craft certification from a nationally recognized small craft organization. The number of personnel needed for classes should follow the YMCA of the USA Aquatics Guidelines (see appendix 4).

Here are some additional ideas on precamp and in-service training for waterfront staff and for encouraging good staff to return to camp each year.

Training

Hold a precamp training that includes orientation similar to that listed in chapter 5, as well as opportunities for team building, recreation, and learning about other camp departments. If staff members need certification training, you may need to schedule additional time for that, but encourage staff to obtain their certification training prior to coming to camp. As an added incentive, offer to pay for the training.

All camp staff should be trained in basic water safety, including the YMCA Staff Aquatic Safety training program. In addition, they should receive special instruction in waterfront hazards and safety procedures. You need to tell staff how they will be alerted to an emergency, when to start emergency procedures, and what to do with campers in the event of an emergency. Hold practices and tests in the use of boats, canoes, and other rescue procedures with all camp staff. Classify all staff members who plan to use waterfront facilities and equipment according to their abilities in swimming, boating, and canoeing. If necessary, provide them with instruction in these activities.

Provide staff with a list of rules and regulations that puts the waterfront standards of conduct "on record." Post copies in cabins and at the waterfront so counselors and campers can refer to them easily.

Provide in-service training according to the recommendations listed in chapter 5. Hold waterfront staff meetings regularly and frequently enough to facilitate effective administration. Schedule the meetings for times that least interfere with ongoing camp programs and during which staff members should not be fatigued.

Staff Continuity

Having waterfront staff return each year is economical and reduces the amount of training necessary. When interviewing, ask candidates if they think they may want to work for more than one year. Sufficient continuity of staff from year to year provides stability and cohesion. Strive to have at least 50 percent of your staff return each year.

Talk to those staff members that you would like to see return about the types of training that would be helpful for them to obtain during the school year. Give them recommendations for places where they can receive the training. Encourage them to connect with local YMCAs where they will be spending the school year. This will give them additional opportunities to connect to the YMCA and develop their skills.

BUDGET

The camp director does the budgeting for the camp waterfront program, working closely with the camp waterfront director to determine the operational program and equipment needs for a given year. The camp waterfront director is responsible for carrying out the program and operation within the allocated budget. She or he needs to be able to work effectively with the maintenance director, the camp waterfront staff, and the camp director to run the operation economically and to provide sound stewardship of funds and equipment.

Factors in the overall camp budget related to annual waterfront operations include the following:

- Personnel salaries
- Capital outlay for new equipment
- Capital expense for new facilities
- Maintenance of waterfront equipment
- Maintenance of facilities
- Replacement of equipment and supplies
- Maintenance of motors, boats, canoes, lifesaving equipment, life jackets
- Program materials
- Recognition for camper achievement
- Fuel supplies for powerboating, waterskiing, etc.
- Safety equipment
- Snorkeling/Scuba equipment for search-and-rescue drills and lifeguarding

Most waterfront budgeting is related to expenses for equipment, facilities, and maintenance. In many camps, waterfront income may be derived from extra charges for specialty programs such as waterskiing or powerboating.

The camp waterfront director must work closely with all waterfront staff to provide preventive maintenance for all equipment, to eliminate unnecessary loss or destruction of equipment, and to ensure careful use of facilities and equipment. He or she should order supplies carefully to minimize waste and should try to anticipate needs before the session opens or well in advance of an activity. Refer to chapter 7 for more details on effective fiscal development and control.

These items should be considered for inclusion in the waterfront budget:

Personnel (depending on the staff structure needed by the camp)

- Waterfront director
- Assistant waterfront director
- Small craft director
- Head lifeguard
- Lifeguards
- Swim instructors
- Boating instructors (canoeing, rowing, sailing)

Waterfront Equipment and Supplies

- Paddles
- Oars
- Sails
- Skis
- Life jackets

- Rescue equipment
  - Rescue tubes
  - Backboards
  - AEDs
  - First aid equipment
  - Reach poles
  - Ring buoys
  - Air horns
- Perimeter markers and buoys

Waterfront Maintenance and Repairs

- Special repair services
- Program supplies
- Equipment replacement (PFDs, paddles and oars, sails and boat parts, etc.)
- Fuel supplies for powerboats

Capital Equipment

- Canoes/kayaks
- Sailboats
- Powerboats
- Rowboats
- Trailers
- Storage racks
- Docks
- Waterfront office

CAMP WATERFRONT PROGRAMMING

YMCA camp waterfront programming should provide a balanced variety of activities and camper experiences. Advance planning can ensure quality programming that will generate enthusiasm for and interest in the waterfront for campers and staff alike. By coordinating waterfront activities with the total camp program plan, you can integrate those activities into campers' program experiences.

A productive YMCA camp waterfront program will do the following:

1. Enable campers to become skilled swimmers and to enjoy a variety of waterfront activities, including games, stunts, and competitive events

2. Help campers become conscious of safety in all waterfront activities, including the use of watercraft, and develop safety skills in the use of lifesaving equipment and survival methods

3. Develop campers' skills and feelings of enjoyment in the use of watercraft through such activities as boating, sailing, canoeing, and waterskiing

4. Support lifelong skills development and appreciation for waterfront activities among campers and staff that will contribute to physical fitness, satisfying leisure, and the challenge of adventure

Here is a sample of the types of camp waterfront activities possible:

YMCA Aquatics Programs
- YMCA Swim Lessons
- YMCA Lifeguarding
- YMCA Synchronized Swimming
- YMCA Water Polo
- YMCA Springboard Diving
- YMCA Scuba/Skindiving
- YMCA Aquatic Safety Programs

  - YMCA Splash
  - YMCA Aquatic Leadership Program
  - YMCA Aquatic Safety and Advanced Personal Safety and Survival
  - YMCA Aquatic Safety Assistant

- Small craft programs

  - Boating and rowing programs
  - Canoeing (in camp and on trips)
  - Sailing
  - Windsurfing
  - Powerboating

- Special events

  - Water carnivals
  - Competitive events
  - Water shows
  - International games
  - Olympic events
  - Water polo, water basketball, water volleyball, water games and contests

- Lifeguarding, water safety, and overall waterfront safety

  - Educational activities (land drills for all)
  - Emergency practice drills for storms, lost campers, etc.
  - Small craft safety for all (equipment, knowledge of craft, emergency procedures)
  - Buddy check
  - Swimmer classification
  - Requirements for use of watercraft and for swimming only in certain areas

- Special waterfront skill instruction

  - Fishing (bait casting, fly casting, cleaning fish, recreational fishing)
  - Waterskiing
  - Skin diving, snorkeling, and scuba
  - Synchronized swimming
  - Competitive swimming
  - Special needs

- Games and fun activities
  - Relay races
  - Theme events (Pirate Day, water shows, etc.)
  - Water carnival

The camp waterfront program can be educational as well as meet safety and recreation needs. You need to balance program scheduling to meet the needs of individuals, small groups, and large groups. You also need to foster progression in skill achievement and provide adventurous program experiences to motivate and satisfy campers. Consider the ages, skills, and capabilities of campers and staff in program planning and in the design of lesson plans and learning units for waterfront activities. Finally, consider the length of stay of campers in the camp setting as well.

When you schedule activities for the waterfront, consider these factors:

1. The number and kinds of waterfront facilities and equipment available
2. The climate and weather (temperature, storms)
3. The time of day and length of periods in the water
4. Safety factors related to supervision, observation, policies, and practices
5. The qualifications of camp waterfront staff and their availability
6. The ages and capabilities of the campers and the number of campers
7. The purpose and objectives of program activities on the waterfront
8. How the waterfront program relates to the total camping program
9. Provision of both informal recreation and formal skills instruction
10. Basic instruction in skills and safety fundamentals and progression in experiences
11. Safety of the program
12. Creativity of your program

Keep these principles of health and safety in mind as you schedule:

• Plan to have two swimming periods a day, one instructional and one recreational. Allow enough time for transition between camp areas and changing of clothes.

• Evaluate and assign campers and staff to a swimming category on the first day of camp. Skills and abilities should be based on the YMCA Swim Lessons programs.

• Do not allow swimming or boating activities during thunderstorms or storms with high winds.

• Allow evening swimming only under properly lighted conditions of daylight standards. Never allow deep-water swimming at night.

• Explain basic safety procedures to all campers and staff on the first day of camp, with regular reminders during the camp period.

• Use a buddy check system with swimmers.

• Make sure qualified instructors are available to lead swimming and small craft activities.

• Require everyone (staff and campers) to wear a life jacket when using small craft (rowboats, canoes, sailboats, windsurf boards, and motorboats).

• Provide both instructional and recreational swims daily, with campers participating in the waterfront areas designated for their skills as evaluated.

- Make sure lifeguards are in their assigned positions and ready to supervise before campers or small craft users proceed with their activities.

- Organize waterfront groups and activities so that they do not interfere with each other, such as swimming and small craft use.

- Keep the instructor-student ratio consistent with age, skills, and activity. See the YMCA of the USA Aquatics Guidelines in appendix 4.

- Design competitive programs and special waterfront events to include campers of all swimming capabilities in some way.

- Apply discipline as strictly to recreational swimming and small craft activities as during instruction (see the YMCA intranet site for sample disciplinary forms).

- Display waterfront program schedules and interpretative materials daily where campers and staff can see them clearly and easily.

- Schedule nonswimmers' and basic swimmers' instructional periods for the late morning or early afternoon to take advantage of warmer temperatures.

- See that staff members use good instruction methods and procedures in working with campers on the waterfront. Staff should follow lesson plans with specific objectives, understand leadership styles, be willing to help those with special needs, and be alert to safety concerns.

- Plan skiing activities for earlier in the day and later in the afternoon, as winds may be lighter then and the water easier to learn on.

Figure 19.3 shows a sample schedule.

Special events can give all campers a chance to come together in a single fun activity. Such activities can include competitive events, water shows or carnivals, international games or Olympic events, and games such as water polo, water basketball, water volleyball, and other water games and contests. On these occasions, campers

Sample Daily Waterfront Schedule

8:30—9:00 a.m.	Maintenance (clean up waterfront, empty boats after rain, check water turbidity)
9:00 a.m.	Instruction period I (boating, canoeing, sailing, lifesaving, upper levels of YMCA Swim Lessons)
10:00 a.m.	Instruction period II (motor boating, water skiing, sailing, middle levels of YMCA Swim Lessons)
11:00 a.m.	Instructional period III (beginning levels of YMCA Swim Lessons)
12:00 p.m.—12:15 p.m.	Lifeguard and staff swim
2:30 p.m.—3:30 p.m.	Cabin activity period I (boating, canoeing, fishing), recreational swim
3:30 p.m.	Lifeguard and staff swim
4:00—5:00 p.m.	Cabin activity period II (boating, canoeing, fishing), recreational swim
6:45—7:45 p.m.	Recreational boating, canoeing, and fishing Swimming games and water carnivals if daylight permits

Figure 19.3 Sample daily waterfront schedule.

can be recognized for their accomplishments and parents can come to see what their children have learned. Here are some tips on special event planning:

- If parents are invited to a special water show, try to alter the regular waterfront schedule as little as possible. Make sure that spectators will be able to observe the event safely.
- If awards are to be given, try to make them during arts and crafts instead of using commercial ones.
- Incorporate water safety instruction and education into water special events for parents and visitors.

Finally, on bad weather days or when the water is unsafe for swimming due to contamination, tides, or currents, your staff will still have many things to do around the waterfront. Plan ahead and develop procedures to make these days productive. Some activities that can be performed during these times include the following:

- Do indoor instructional activities and games with campers.
- Clean storerooms.
- Repair equipment (e.g., canoe paddles, rowlocks).
- Inventory equipment.
- Make sure reports are up to date.
- Hold staff meetings.
- Hold in-service training.
- Run staff team-building activities.

Some camps may assign waterfront staff to assist other camp staff with special rainy-day programming or to help with cabin groups.

BOATING PROGRAMS

The rest of this chapter focuses on boating programs, first on general areas of consideration, then on five different types of boating: rowing, paddlesports, sailing, waterskiing, and motorboating. This is updated information taken from *Camp Boating* by the American Camping Association.

General Information

When you consider including a boating program in your camp, you need to look at five areas: equipment, supervision, prerequisites to participation, policies and regulations, and emergency planning and procedures.

Equipment

Each camp may have unique requirements depending on the site where activities take place, the type or class of boat(s) being used, and whether or not any motorized vessels are being utilized. Regardless of these factors, the following guidelines concerning equipment should be considered.

- *Boats:* The following rules apply with boats.
    1. Federal regulations require registration of all motor-powered vessels, and some states require *all* vessels, motorized or not, to be numbered. At a minimum,

all vessels equipped with propulsion machinery must be registered in the state of principal use (with some exceptions for private lakes), and the registration number must then be displayed on each side of the forward half of the vessel. The owner/operator must carry a valid certificate of number whenever the vessel is in use.

2. Federal and state equipment and carriage laws must be followed. Table 19.1 shows the federal minimum requirements for motorboats.

3. It is highly recommended that all motor-powered vessels carry an alternative means of propulsion such as paddles or oars, an anchor, a bailing device, and a first aid kit.

4. All boats, sailboats, canoes, rowboats, and the like, must carry a wearable PFD (Type I, II, or III) for each person on board or being towed; a Type IV (throwable device) is not considered sufficient as the primary PFD. PFDs must be worn at all times. (This may not be true for pontoons.) Figure 19.4 shows PFD types.

5. Boats that are 16 feet or greater in length must also carry one Type IV (throwable device) per boat. Canoes and kayaks greater than 16 feet are exempted from carriage of the additional Type IV.

- *Facility:* The following rules apply to facility management.

1. Rescue and safety equipment should be easily accessible to instructors and safety personnel. At a minimum, rescue equipment should include the following items:

> Long backboard with four straps
>
> Cervical collar and head immobilizer
>
> General first aid kit (including supplemental oxygen and AED, biohazard kit)
>
> Ring buoy or other throwable device
>
> Rescue paddleboard
>
> Bullhorn/airhorn
>
> Reaching device (pole, shepherd's crook, etc.)
>
> Some form of two-way communication (radio, telephone) (Access to 911 is critical.)
>
> Designated safety boat (When water site allows, this boat should be motorized.)

2. When possible, boating activities should take place within view of an elevated observation point. On small bodies of water, a guard chair may be sufficient. Ideally, this point should be visible to all participants and can be used for posting flags or sounding horns when recall is necessary.

3. Some form of communication or recall system, visible or audible to all participants, should be in place. Options for emergency communication include nautical or other flags, two-way radios for use on large bodies of water, handheld bullhorns for small ponds or lakes, and whistles for use on rivers. Signals from these systems can be used to activate emergency procedures.

4. For purposes of general instruction, each boating activity should have its own designated area, either by location or through scheduling, and all boating activities should take place away from swimming areas.

Table 19.1   **Federal Requirements for Motorboats**

	Vessel length (ft)			
	less than 16	**16-26**	**26-40**	**40-65**
Certificate of number	X	X	X	X
State numbering	X	X	X	X
Certificate of documentation		X	X	X
Lifejackets (a)	X	X	X	X
Lifejackets (b)		X	X	X
Visual distress signal	X	X	X	X
Fire extinguishers	X	X	X	X
Ventilation	X	X	X	X
Backfire flame	X	X	X	X
Sound producing devices	X	X	X	X
Navigational lights	X	X	X	X
FCC radio license	N/A	N/A	N/A	N/A
Oil pollution placard			X	X
Garbage placard			X	X
Marine sanitation device			X	X
Navigational rules			X	X

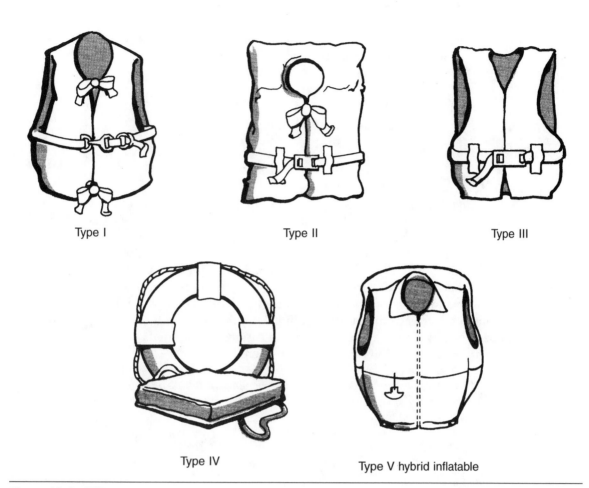

Type I

Type II

Type III

Type IV

Type V hybrid inflatable

Figure 19.4 PFD types.

5. Occupational Safety and Health Administration (OSHA) regulations pertaining to the storage and use of fuel and other hazardous materials must be enforced for camps using motor-powered vessels. You will also want to check with your DNR for other rules and regulations. At a minimum, the following guidelines should be implemented:

    ✔ All containers should be clearly marked with the type or mix of fuel they hold.

    ✔ Tanks and containers should be sealed when not in use.

    ✔ Pump nozzles should be fitted with a collar that prevents fumes from escaping.

    ✔ Spills of more than five gallons must be reported to the local Environmental Pollution Agency, Coast Guard, or hazardous materials authority.

    ✔ Spent batteries should be treated as hazardous waste and, if possible, recycled.

    ✔ Signs forbidding smoking should be posted where fuel is dispensed.

    ✔ Access to fuel should be restricted, and only those trained to dispense it should do so.

    ✔ Portable tanks should be filled off the vessel.

    ✔ Fuel should be stored and dispensed only in well-ventilated areas.

6. Facility policies and procedures should be posted in a prominent place and should include the following information:

> Hours of operation
>
> General rules
>
> Accounting and recall system plans
>
> Staff use policy

Supervision

• *Staff qualifications:* Ideally, staff should be hired who have received instructor training in the specific craft from a national certifying agency. Being an experienced boater does not guarantee competency in teaching, nor does experience in teaching guarantee mastery of boating skills. Fortunately, most instructor training programs require demonstration of proficiency in both teaching and skills. Unfortunately, the number and types of certification programs offered are not nearly as varied as the number and types of boating activities available. Therefore, reliance upon documented experience in specific boating activities is often the deciding factor when hiring staff. When evaluating the qualifications of potential boating staff members, the following questions should be considered:

Is there documentation of experience or demonstration of proficiency in the specific type of activity? Having the ability to row a boat does not mean that a person also has the ability to sail.

Is there documentation of experience in the specific boating environment to be used? Paddling on Class II rivers requires experience beyond that required for paddling on flat water. Sailing on the ocean is significantly different than lake sailing.

Is there documentation of leadership and instructional ability?

If the staff member will be participating in or leading a trip, has she or he participated in or led similar trips?

1. Demonstration of proficiency in the type of craft being used at camp should be required of all instructors, whether certified or not. Assuming that staff members are familiar with camp boats can create otherwise avoidable risks. Even within disciplines there are a wide variety of boat designs, which can cause subtle (and sometimes great) differences in the rigging or handling of the craft.

2. Many states require a boating safety education course for anyone operating a motor-powered boat. Courses are available in all states, and the cost, if any, is minimal. It is recommended that anyone given the responsibility of operating a motorboat, even those used for fishing, take part in this inexpensive training. Operators should demonstrate proficiency in boat handling before carrying campers on board.

3. If safety boats (sometimes called chase or rescue boats) are utilized, proficiency in their use should be demonstrated, and individuals responsible for operating safety boats, ski boats, or any other motorized vessel must comply with any federal and state education requirements.

4. If boating activities take place on coastal waters, the Great Lakes, territorial seas, or any waters connected to them (e.g., the Mississippi River), motorboat operators are subject to Coast Guard licensing requirements. If students are

ferried to boats, if waterskiing takes place, or if large sailboats with auxiliary power are used, staff operators may need to obtain a *6-pak* license issued by the Coast Guard. If a camp utilizes motor-powered vessels on any of the mentioned water sites, it needs to contact the Coast Guard to find out about licensing requirements for staff.

5. In addition to the appropriate boating certification or license, instructors should have current first aid and CPR certification appropriate to the age group with which they will be working. Knowledge of water-based spinal injury management through either lifeguard, emergency water safety, or in-service training should be also be required. Rescue skills and emergency procedures specific to the environment and the activity being taught or supervised should be practiced and demonstrated routinely.

   • *Supervision ratios:* Ratios appropriate to each boating activity need to be established in writing. Recommended ratios for specific activities can be found in the individual boating sections of this chapter. Some campers may require constant assistance or supervision to more fully participate in a boating activity. Individuals providing this additional support should not be counted as instructional staff. It is important that personnel used in this capacity receive proper orientation to the boats and appropriate safety training prior to working with campers.

State boating agencies should be able to direct staff to available courses (many are home study). Another option is to call 800-336-BOAT for information about boater education.

Prerequisites to Participation

The majority of boating-related deaths involve drowning; camp operators need to do all they can to reduce this statistic and to ensure the safety of those who receive training. An individual's swimming ability, while not a precluding factor by itself, should be weighed heavily when determining to what extent that person will be participating in boating activities. Obviously, comfort in the water and swimming ability become greater issues for those participating in waterskiing than for those taking a pleasure cruise on a pontoon boat.

1. Nonswimmers should never be permitted to boat alone, and all participants, staff and campers, regardless of swimming ability, should be required to wear a U.S. Coast Guard–approved PFD (life jacket) during boating activities. While camps may be able to enforce this rule, a large number of recreational boaters do not wear PFDs on the water. For this reason, teaching campers how to put on a life jacket while in the water becomes a critical element of any boating safety curriculum.

2. Both campers and staff should participate in an aquatic skills safety check before taking part in any boating activity. The test should include the following elements:

Swimming

✔ Treading water in clothing appropriate to the boating activity

✔ Donning a PFD while in a water environment similar to the one that will be used

3. Campers should not be excluded from participating in boating due to a disability. When working with campers with disabilities, the type and severity of the disability should be taken into account when conducting the aquatic safety check. The aquatic skills check for campers with disabilities has two primary functions: (1) to assess the individual's degree of comfort in the water, and (2) to determine which type of flotation device is most appropriate for the individual.

- *Recreational programs:* Due to limited amounts of time and the desire to expose campers to as many activities as possible, many camps offer a short orientation to the boats rather than an extensive curriculum. The following questions should be considered before deciding to offer boating as a recreational program only:

  Will activities be taking place in a protected environment where instructors/supervisors will be able to reach campers and boats with limited effort?

  Will novice boaters be paired with staff members or experienced campers or will they be left to their own devices?

  Is it difficult to maneuver the craft safely without extensive instruction?

  How easy (or difficult) is it to capsize or swamp the boats being used? How easy (or difficult) is it to initiate self-rescue in the boats being used?

When the boating program of a camp is focused on recreation rather than instruction, the content of the orientation session takes on extra importance. If campers will not be receiving formal instruction, they must still receive training in basic safe boating principles, and prerequisites to recreational use must be established. After participating in an aquatic skills check and prior to using the craft, all persons permitted to use boats should be provided with the following training:

- *Safety procedures:* Site-specific policies and guidelines including recall and accounting systems, emergency procedures, and the proper use of PFDs
- *Boarding, debarking, trimming, and basic movement procedures:* Three points of contact, weight low in the boat and evenly distributed
- *Capsize or swamping and recovery:* Maintaining contact with the boat, righting the boat, reentry
- *Instructional programs:* If campers are taught how to operate or skipper a boat independently, the level of emphasis placed on swimming ability cannot be too high.

When determining prerequisite skills for instructional programs, consider the following:

Characteristics of the water environment such as depth, presence of waves or currents, visibility, and temperature

Stability and rescue ability of the craft

Swimming, treading, or strength required to self-rescue

Instructor/rescue personnel-to-camper ratio

As campers advance their boating skills, prerequisites to higher levels of instruction also become necessary. For example, campers taking part in canoeing or kayaking should master fundamental skills before embarking on a river trip; sailors should be well versed in basic principles before tackling the complex rules and techniques required in racing; and waterskiing participants should exhibit strength and endurance on two skis before attempting slalom skills. Once prerequisites to the various levels of instruction have been established, they must be strictly maintained to ensure a high degree of safety.

Suggested skills checks for both recreational and instructional purposes are contained in the individual boating sections. Recommended prerequisites for different levels of instruction are also outlined.

Policies and Regulations

Education of staff and campers is the best way to prevent situations leading to property damage, injury, or death. Camp policies and procedures related to boating programs must be presented in an effective way during staff training and the introductory sessions of camper instruction. In addition to adopting standard operating procedures, camps need to document when and how those procedures are to be implemented. Naturally, each camp will have rules and regulations specific to its site and program, but the following general policies should be in effect and communicated to staff and campers.

1. Personal flotation devices should be worn by all staff and campers involved in boating activities. A PFD can save a life, but only if it is worn properly!

2. Any time campers are boating, at least one trained adult supervisor/instructor should also be on the water, preferably in a safety boat.

3. An accounting system appropriate to the camp and the activity being conducted should be in place. Keeping track of how many campers and boats are on the water is integral to safety. Boating staff should be able to tell, at any time, if campers assigned to them are on shore or on the water. For small programs using only two or three boats, this accounting may be done visually, but for camps with more boats, a buddy board similar to those used during swimming activities may be a more appropriate means of accounting for people and boats.

4. A clear-the-water or recall system for all boats should be understood by all and responded to immediately. Flags, whistles, horns, or two-way radios in safety boats are particularly effective means of recall. If visible contact with all boats is not possible, two-way radios are recommended. If large bodies of water are used, campers should know which signals call for a return to camp and which announce a more serious situation, such as a lightning storm, during which it may be safest to proceed to the nearest point of land.

5. Distress signals for campers should be established and rehearsed. Waving a paddle in a circular motion is appropriate for paddlers. When there is no extra equipment to extend the camper's reach, waving both arms in an up-and-down motion can be a signal indicating assistance is required. Campers should understand that these signals are to be used only in distress situations.

6. All staff and campers should wear clothing appropriate to the boating activity and the weather. This includes sunscreen, shoes, and hats when warranted.

7. Hours of operation should be established. As a rule, boating activities should not be permitted before dawn or after dusk unless campers and staff are trained in night navigation techniques and the boats are properly equipped with running lights and any other required equipment.

8. Throwing anything overboard should be strictly prohibited. This includes water balloons, which can damage engines, kill fish and birds, and pollute the lake, river, or ocean bottom.

9. To ensure that all necessary items are present and in working order, a daily inspection of the facility and all equipment should occur, and a log should be kept of all maintenance done.

Items to be checked include these:

All rescue and safety equipment

All training boats and related equipment such as paddles, oars, sails, rigging, and motors

All safety boats and their motors

All PFDs (check especially for filling that may be hardened or waterlogged, tears, or worn areas)

Docks, floats, ramps, beaches, and other access points

Emergency Planning

Use the information in chapter 9 of this manual as a resource as you develop emergency action plans.

No matter how well maintained the equipment, no matter how well conceived the regulating policies, and no matter how vigilant the supervision, situations requiring prompt action do occasionally arise. To prepare effectively for emergency situations, camps must develop *emergency action plans*. When developing these plans, potential problems and possible responses should be identified. Relationships with local boating organizations, emergency medical services, and the local boating law enforcement agency should be established. The policies and procedures of these groups should be reviewed before developing camp plans.

In an effective emergency action plan, individual staff responsibilities are spelled out, and situations are rehearsed by both campers and staff. If it doesn't work in rehearsal, it won't work in a crisis! Consider the following scenarios when developing these plans:

- Missing camper—both on and off the water
- Camper distress calls
- Lightning or other severe weather situations
- Capsized/swamped boats
- Injured boater
- Near drowning
- Actual drowning
- Spinal injury close to shore and away from the mainland

The next five sections will cover rowing, paddlesports, sailing, waterskiing, and motorboating.

Rowing

A rowboat can be a wonderful boat for elementary safety education. The fundamental safety principles learned on this craft will transfer easily to other boats found in camp and elsewhere. The problem arises when seeking competent instructional staff. Although it is one of the most popular small craft activities in camps, there are few options other than in-service training for qualification of rowing staff.

In addition to being used during formal boating instruction and recreation, rowboats (and other craft) are often used during activities such as fishing, or they are employed by lifeguards as rescue craft or on-the-water guard stations. Even when they are engaged in these types of endeavors, where "boating" is the secondary activity, it remains imperative that campers and staff be trained in proper craft handling and safety.

The curriculum contained in this section is not only appropriate for use as a general camper course of study, but level one is also suitable when orienting campers to the boats they will be using during other activities, and skills contained throughout the curriculum are relevant to in-service training for safety personnel who will be staffing boat stations.

Facility and equipment

In addition to the guidelines offered in the general information section, a number of facility and equipment needs are specific to rowing.

1. When possible, rowboats should be equipped with open or ring-type rowlocks rather than fixed oarlocks. Although many skills can be taught with fixed oars, feathering and other more advanced techniques require an open lock. See figure 19.4 for various types of oarlocks.

2. When selecting equipment, attention should be paid to oar size. In general, a boat with a beam of 55 inches or less requires oars six to six and one-half feet in length. Rowboats with a beam greater than 55 inches should use oars approximately seven feet in length.

3. Each rowboat should be equipped with a bailing device such as a cut-off milk jug.

4. Painters (lines or ropes) on both the bow and stern are helpful in case a boat needs to be towed and when students are being instructed how to secure a boat to a dock or mooring.

5. Other recommended equipment includes a light anchor and an extra oar.

6. Type II or III PFDs are appropriate for rowing, but the Type III is recommended due to ease of movement.

Supervision

With the exception of the Boy Scouts of America, there are currently no national agencies certifying instructors in rowing. Although the American Rowing Association certifies rowing coaches, their emphasis is on competitive crew shell rowing, not the basic rowing that occurs in most camps. Many lifeguards and swim instructors receive limited instruction in the handling of rowboats, but this is no substitute for focused training and experience. Because finding qualified staff is so difficult, the following guidelines should be used as criteria when evaluating instructor eligibility:

1. The individual should be at least 18 years old.

2. He or she should have advanced swimming ability, preferably lifeguard or YMCA Aquatic Safety Assistant training.

3. He or she should demonstrate all curriculum components in the boats used by the campers and should have a thorough working knowledge of boating nomenclature and safety.

An *instructor-to-camper* ratio of no more than 1:10 should be observed in rowing activities. To provide appropriate supervision, an *instructor-to-boat* ratio of 1:5 should also be observed. Placing 2 campers per boat is appropriate, but assigning 10 campers to 10 different boats will require an extra instructor.

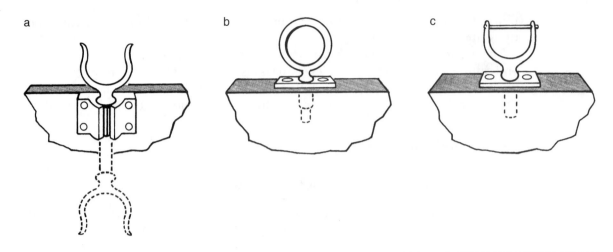

Figure 19.5a-c Types of rowlocks: *(a)* open socket, *(b)* ring, *(c)* pin-type.

Prerequisites to participation

Recreational Programs

Unlike canoes and sailboats, which can capsize easily, rowboats are generally stable in the water. For this reason, with rowing activities, campers need not have as high a degree of comfort in the water as they do for other boating activities. However, campers permitted to independently try rowboats during recreational periods should meet the following prerequisites:

✔ Ability to tread water and swim in rowing clothes (if permitted to boat in deep water)

✔ Height sufficient to stand in water (if boating in shallow water)

If campers are unable to initiate self-rescue due to disabilities or other factors, a trained staff member should accompany them in the boat.

Instructional Programs

Since comfort in the water is intrinsic to safe boating, campers who are given extended instruction in how to row should be competent swimmers. Since level two of this curriculum includes capsizing and swamping, campers receiving instruction beyond level one should meet the following minimal prerequisites:

✔ Swim (any stroke) for at least 50 yards

✔ Tread water for five minutes in rowing clothes

✔ Put on a life jacket in deep water

> All participants in rowing programs should wear PFDs whenever they are afloat or near the water.

Safety

Attention should be paid to wind and wave action; rowboats may become unstable and difficult to handle in adverse conditions. Protected water, small lakes, bays, and flat-water rivers are the best environments for conducting rowing activities.

Rowing Curriculum Guidelines

There are three levels to this rowing curriculum: beginning, intermediate, and advanced. Mastery of level one skills should be sufficient for those using rowboats to supplement other programs. When safety personnel use rowboats, they should be competent at level three. To minimize risk, prior to on-the-water practice, campers at any level of instruction should participate in an orientation session that reinforces the basic safety principles introduced in level one.

Basic Rowing—Level One

By the completion of level one, rowers will be familiar with general boating nomenclature and safety principles. They will be able to safely enter and exit a rowboat, and they will be able to launch, row, land, and secure the craft.

Theory

Course logistics: Introductions, meeting times, proper attire for class, etc.

Safety: Site-specific policies and guidelines, recall and accounting systems, emergency procedures, local weather patterns, and proper use of PFDs.

Procedures in case of swamp or capsize: Stay with boat until help arrives.

Equipment: Basic nomenclature (see figures 19.5 and 19.6).

Skills

Loading: Three points of contact, shoulders within gunwales, weight low and evenly distributed, position(s) in boat

Body position and posture: Feet braced fairly close together; trunk erect with shoulders squared and head up; oars gripped so that forearms and backs of hands are aligned, knuckles in line with the edge of the blade

Trim: Effect of ballast

Stroke: Catch, pull, finish, recover; effort concentrated early in pull, trunk positioned into layback during pull and rocked back during recovery and catch

Backing water: Push, finish, recovery

Turns: Dressed or trailing oars, right and left turns

Changing position: One person at a time, three points of contact, shoulders within gunwales, weight low and evenly distributed

Landing at beach or mooring: Leeward side of pier if possible, bow into wind or current, shipping oars, securing boat and equipment

Basic knots: Bowline, square knot, clove hitch, and any knots pertinent to craft

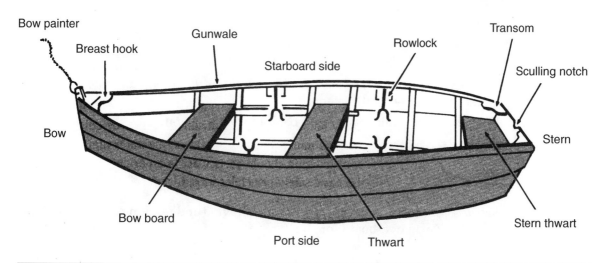

Figure 19.6   Rowboat.

Intermediate Rowing—Level Two

Once campers are familiar with boating safety fundamentals, they will be ready to attempt some of the more advanced rowing techniques found in level two.

Prerequisites to Instruction

To participate at level two of rowing, campers should be able to row to a designated mark, round it, return to shore, and secure the boat successfully. They should be able to answer questions about such basic safety tenets as three points of contact, staying with the boat in case of capsize, and how to properly wear a PFD. By the completion of level two, campers will be able to maneuver a rowboat in confined and open areas. They will demonstrate proper procedures during capsize or swamping situations.

Theory

Course logistics: See level one.

Safety: See level one.

Skills

Feathering: Wrist position during catch phase of pull and after the finish. (Feathering can only be achieved with open and ring-type rowlocks.)

Alternate stroking: Paddling, paired oars, tandem oars, tandem oars with coxswain, sculling (if sculling notch is available).

Stopping and holding position in water: Trail oars in water, push on oars in trailing position, one leg braced under thwart for support.

Maneuvering in confined area: Pivots, pulling and backing with opposite oars.

Boarding and debarking from various environments: Piers vs. beach vs. mooring.

Capsize/swamping recovery: Staying with the boat, reentry, hand paddling, bailing.

Advanced Rowing—Level Three

Prerequisites to Instruction

Campers participating in rowing instruction at level three should be confident swimmers. They should be able to perform all level one and level two skills independently. By the completion of level three, campers will be self-reliant rowers, able to assist others in situations of distress.

Theory

Course logistics: See level one.

Safety: See level one.

Advanced nomenclature and marlinespike seamanship: Different hull types, whipping and splicing lines, other knots.

Rules of the road: Sailboats, motorboats, approaching craft.

Skills

Anchoring: Different anchor types, from bow only

Towing: Securing craft, towing another craft, being towed

Rescue/safety: Assisting a tired swimmer, throwing and reaching assists from boat, assisting man overboard into boat

• *A few notes about sliding-seat rowing:* With the advent of indoor rowing machines, the outdoor sport of crew shell rowing has also grown in popularity. Although most camps do not offer rowing of this sort, some are adding single-seat shells to their fleets. Although it employs many of the same techniques as traditional rowing, sliding-seat rowing is its own unique sport and should be treated as such. Due to the extreme instability of shells, sliding-seat rowing should be restricted to calm, protected waters. For the same reason, campers participating in this type of rowing should be capable swimmers. Type III PFDs are the best for crew shell rowing since ease of movement is crucial to proper technique.

Camps interested in including sliding-seat rowing in their program should contact U.S. Rowing for information about proper instructional techniques and practices. In addition to the requisite safety instruction, sliding-seat curricula should include instruction in the following areas:

Trim: The effect of ballast

Launching: Carrying shells on land, embarking from a pier

Stroke technique: Hand position, catch, pull, finish, feather, recover

Turning: Oar position, pivots

Rescue/safety: Self-rescue in a shell, how to be assisted in a shell

Racing: Rules, techniques, and such

Paddlesport: Canoeing and Kayaking

Paddling, in both canoes and kayaks, is the number-one boating activity found in camps. Although the majority of programs take place on the flat water of a lake, many camps offer extended river trips, and some actually prepare campers to shoot the rapids on a Class II or Class III river. The possibilities for programming are endless.

The natural inclination in paddlesport is to designate flat water as the environment for beginning paddlers, moving water as the place where intermediate skills can best be practiced, and white water as the domain of those with advanced abilities. While it is true that paddlers should not attempt moving or white water until they have command of the prior environment, many camp instructional programs never venture beyond flat water. Camps should not feel limited by their water site. As any experienced paddler will tell you, flat water is where skills and maneuvers need to be mastered. Perfecting fundamental skills can take a lifetime, and the more time spent practicing, the better.

For the purposes of this curriculum, level one and level two skills should be taught and practiced in a flatwater environment. Level three is an introduction to moving-water paddling. The moving-water curriculum in this module is not intended to prepare paddlers for anything beyond a Class I river, one with few obstructions and only small waves and riffles. More extreme white water has been left out for two distinct reasons: (1) The majority of camps offering canoe/kayak instruction never venture into water more difficult than that described earlier, and (2) the training and experience required of whitewater instructors is much more comprehensive than that required of flat- or moving-water instructors. If camps are running whitewater programs, the background of the staff should be extensive enough to allow them to design an instructional program appropriate to the needs of the camp.

Facility and equipment

In addition to the guidelines offered in the general information section, there are a number of facility and equipment needs specific to paddlesport.

1. The most common boat types found in camps are tandem and solo open-decked canoes and kayaks. Even with this narrowing factor, there are literally hundreds of canoe and kayak designs from which to choose. The choice can often be overwhelming, but the following questions should be considered when selecting canoes and kayaks for use in camps:

   What are the physical requirements of the campers? Smaller children and those with physical disabilities may benefit from a boat with more stability (determined by the shape of the hull).

   Will the boat be used for instructional purposes only, or will it be loaded with gear during extended river trips?

   On what type of water will the boat be used? If moving water is used, a craft with increased maneuverability is beneficial, and if whitewater paddling is done, decked canoes and kayaks are the best choice. Aluminum boats are best on lakes or slow-moving water with no obstacles, and those made with resins, fiberglass, nylon, or polypropylene can be used on all types of water.

2. During daily equipment inspections, each canoe or kayak should be checked for adequate flotation. To keep boats from sinking when swamped, inflatable airbags, Styrofoam, and other aids are often used. Check to make sure craft flotation is in good repair, properly attached, and inflated. Thwarts and seat rivets should also be checked for sharp edges.

3. Paddles should be chosen with function in mind. High-performance paddles are lighter and usually less durable. Heavier, more durable paddles are more appropriate for wilderness tripping. Attention should also be paid to paddle size. For most paddles, if the grip is eye level to the paddler while the tip is resting on the ground, it will be effective.

4. Type III PFDs are the most appropriate for paddling activities due to the degree of maneuverability they provide.

5. Helmets should be used on moving water when there is a probability of tipping. Those using decked canoes or kayaks should always wear helmets.

Both the American Canoe Association's *Instructional Manual* and the annual Buyer's Guide published in *Canoe Magazine* are excellent resources when determining what type of boat is most appropriate for your camp's needs.

Supervision

Paddling instructors should hold certification from either the American Canoe Association, the American Red Cross, or another national certifying agency. Instructors should hold certification appropriate to the degree of water being used. It can be assumed that those qualified to teach on white water have the expertise necessary to teach on moving and flat water, but instructors with only flat- or moving-water instructional training will not necessarily be qualified to teach on white water. All instructors, whether certified or not, should demonstrate proficiency in the craft used by campers. A proficiency check should include the following skills:

- Capsize with self-rescue
- Maneuvering the boat through an obstacle course or gates
- Rolling (if kayaks are used)
- Ability to rescue others in the water environment used

In paddlesport, the maximum number of boats supervised by any one instructor should be five. In addition, the maximum number of campers supervised by any one instructor should be five.

Prerequisites to participation

Recreational Programs

Canoes are excellent boats for introducing campers to the pleasure of small craft activities. However, when novices paddle, even on flat water, capsize is inevitable; on moving water, the potential for being swept away from instructors or safety personnel increases the danger. Therefore, recreational paddling, where there is little time for orientation, must take place on flat water only. Before being permitted to use canoes recreationally, campers should receive the following minimal orientation:

Procedures for embarking and debarking

Procedures for capsize and self-rescue

Basic strokes and paddling

Campers should also have a degree of comfort and swimming ability appropriate to the depth of the water. If campers cannot swim at all, or if they have disabilities that preclude self-rescue, they should be partnered with qualified staff members in tandem canoes.

If kayaks are used, the requirements must be modified somewhat. In addition to following the guidelines stated earlier, campers permitted to use kayaks during recreational periods should be able to demonstrate the following skills:

✔ Underwater swimming ability

✔ Wet exit from overturned kayak

Instructional Programs

All participants in paddling programs should wear PFDs whenever they are afloat or near the water.

While students engaged in paddling instruction are learning such techniques as proper body position and boat lean, they will inevitably capsize. In kayaking, *rolling* contributes to the need for comfort and swimming ability. If campers will be receiving extensive instruction in canoeing or kayaking, they should meet the following prerequisites:

✔ Swim (any stroke) for at least 50 yards

✔ Tread water for five minutes in canoeing clothes

✔ Put on a life jacket in deep water

Safety

1. If tripping will take place, it is imperative that a float plan, including departure and return times, planned routes, and a list of participants, be filed.

2. The American Whitewater Affiliation has developed a safety code related to paddlesport. Copies of the code can be found in most canoe instruction books and are available from the American Canoe Association in pamphlet form. The safety code should be required reading for all paddling instructors and for campers who will be involved in moving-water instruction and/or tripping programs.

Paddlesport Curriculum Guidelines

If your camp offers instruction in canoeing or kayaking, the curriculum presented in this section will be helpful. Although many camps will never move beyond the flatwater curriculum presented here, the emphasis placed on this basic level of instruction cannot be too high, for it is here that campers will learn the fundamental skills necessary to pursuing further instruction.

With the wide variety of boats available, it would be impossible to write detailed plans for each. This curriculum has been written with tandem and solo flatwater canoes and slalom kayaks in mind. Skills indigenous to tandem or solo operation have been clearly marked, and kayaking is written as a separate course. The Fundamentals of Moving Water Paddling curriculum guidelines are appropriate for use with either canoes or kayaks.

Although the skills presented in this curriculum can be applied to large canoes, coastal kayaks, or any other boat with paddling as its base, it is important to remember that each boat has a unique handling response, and campers and staff alike will need ample time to orient themselves to various boat designs.

Although campers may be ready for level two or three instruction, they may not have paddled for some time, or they may have received their original training at a different site or in a different boat. To minimize risk, prior to on-the-water practice, campers at any level of instruction should participate in an orientation session that reinforces the basic safety tenets introduced at level one.

Flatwater Open Canoe—Level One

The objective of this level is that by the completion of the basic canoe course, campers will be familiar with the safety issues surrounding canoeing, and they will be able to initiate self-rescue. They will be able to maneuver a canoe in a straight line on flat water.

Theory

Course logistics: Introductions, meeting times, proper attire for class, and such

Safety: Site-specific open-water policies and guidelines, recall and accounting systems, emergency procedures, local weather patterns, proper use of PFDs, and rescue priorities (people, boats, equipment)

Equipment: Basic nomenclature of boat and paddle (see figure 19.7); knee pads, hat, bailer, whistle

Orientation to the boat: Loading and unloading (racking and unracking), carries, entering and exiting the canoe and movement on board, positions in the canoe (when appropriate to kneel, sit, or stand), posture, rocking (balance), debarking and embarking

Tandem canoe responsibilities: Paddles on opposite sides, changing position

Content—Skills

Strokes: Forward, back, draw, push away, stern rudder, cross-draw, forward sweep, reverse sweep, pry; balance, boat lean, body mechanics, coordination and fluidity

Maneuvers: Pivots, sideslips, forward straight, and reverse straight; coordination, correct use of stroke, body position

Rescue: Hand paddling, deep-water exit, reentry, self-rescue, shakeouts

Knots: Truckers hitch, square, sheet bend, figure eight, bowline, and butterfly

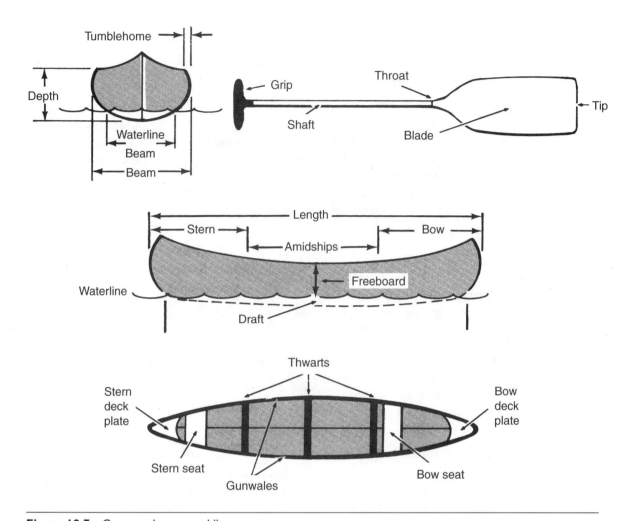

Figure 19.7 Canoe and canoe paddle.

Flatwater Open Canoe—Level Two

Once campers have a sense of comfort and stability in the canoe, they will be ready to attempt maneuvers requiring more control and fluidity of movement.

Prerequisites to Instruction

Campers should be able to demonstrate all level one skills. If solo canoes are used, campers should be able to perform all skills independently. If tandem canoes are used, proper technique in both the bow and stern positions should be observed. By completion of level two, campers will be self-reliant flatwater paddlers. They will be able to maneuver a canoe through designated courses with precision and ease. They will be able to participate effectively during assisted rescues.

Theory

Course logistics: See level one

Safety: See level one; hypothermia and hyperthermia

Equipment: Different canoe types, characteristics (stem, rocker, flare, symmetry, bottom), rescue equipment (throw rope/bag, etc.)

Skills

Strokes: Review and command of level one strokes; duffek, cross-duffek, braces (high and low), sculls, J-stroke; balance, boat lean, body mechanics, coordination and fluidity

Additional strokes for solo canoes: C-stroke, compound reverse stroke, compound reverse sweep, cross-forward

Maneuvers: Turns, forward straight with J-stroke, figure eight, S-turns, dock landings

Maneuvering in a confined area: Obstacle course, slalom gates; coordination, correct use of stroke, body position

Rescue: Canoe over canoe, sling rescue

Flatwater Slalom Kayak—Level One

Prerequisites to Instruction

For safety's sake, students should master a wet exit with a skirt and an alert signal (three taps) before proceeding with the general curriculum. By the completion of the level one kayak course, campers will be familiar with the safety issues surrounding kayaking, and they will be able to initiate self-rescue. They will be able to maneuver a kayak in a straight line on flat water.

Theory

Course logistics: Introductions, meeting times, proper attire for class, and such

Safety: Site-specific open-water policies and guidelines, recall and accounting systems, emergency procedures, local weather patterns, proper use of PFDs, and rescue priorities (people, boats, equipment)

Equipment: Basic nomenclature of kayak and paddle (see figure 19.8), spray skirt, helmet

Orientation to the boat: Loading and unloading (racking and unracking), carries, entering and exiting the kayak, positions and fitting, debarking and embarking, emptying the kayak of water

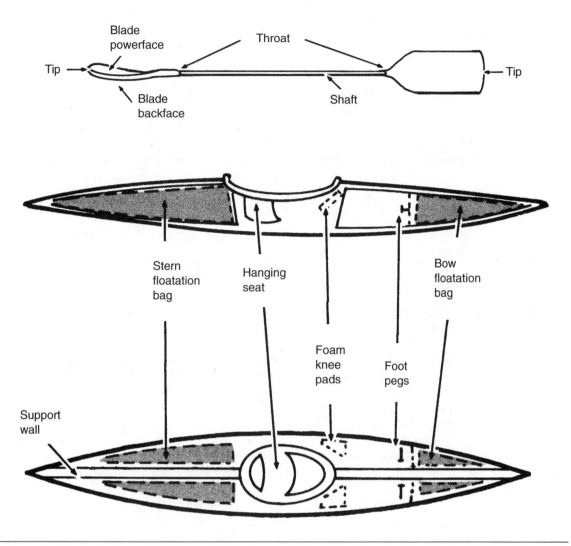

Figure 19.8 Kayak and kayak paddle.

Skills

Strokes: Forward, back, draw, rudder, forward and reverse sweep; balance, boat lean, body mechanics, coordination and fluidity

Maneuvers: Pivots, sideslips, forward straight, reverse straight; coordination, correct use of stroke, body position

Rescue: Hand paddling, wet exit, reentry, buddy rescue, eskimo rescue, self-rescue

Knots: Truckers hitch, square, sheet bend, figure eight, bowline, and butterfly

Flatwater Slalom Kayak—Level Two

Prerequisites to Instruction

Campers should be able to demonstrate all level one skills. By completion of level two, campers will be self-reliant flatwater paddlers. They will be able to maneuver a kayak through designated courses with precision and ease. They will be able to effectively participate during assisted rescues.

Theory

Course logistics: See level one.

Safety: See level one; hypothermia and hyperthermia.

Equipment: Different kayak types, characteristics (rocker, flare, symmetry, bottom), rescue equipment (throw rope/bag, etc.).

Skills

Strokes: Review and command of level one strokes; duffek, braces (high and low), sculls; balance, boat lean, body mechanics, coordination and fluidity

Maneuvers: Turns, forward straight, dock landings, S-turns, figure eight; coordination, correct use of stroke, body position

Maneuvering in a confined area: Obstacle course, slalom gates; coordination, correct use of stroke, body position

Rescue: Kayak over kayak, kayak to kayak, and sling rescue

Fundamentals of Moving Water Paddling (Canoe or Kayak)— Level Three

Often the motivation for taking a paddling course is the goal of participating in a river trip. Campers who can demonstrate all skills and maneuvers outlined in levels one and two should be physically ready to take on this challenge. However, before embarking on an extended trip, they need to be given opportunities to practice the skills they will be using. The skills introduced in the moving-water course should be rehearsed on flat water and then in a controlled moving-water environment before campers put them into practice on a trip.

Prerequisites to Instruction

Campers should be able to maneuver the boat through a designated course with coordination and fluidity of movement on flat water. They should be able to initiate self-rescue and effectively participate in assisted rescues. By the completion of level three, campers will be able to identify potential hazards and will be able to successfully avoid obstacles while paddling on moving water. They will have the ability to initiate self-rescue on moving water, and they will be able to participate effectively in assisted rescues.

Theory

Course logistics: Introductions, meeting times, proper attire for class, and such

Safety: Open-water guidelines, waterway policies, helmet wearing, river signals for accounting, recall, and other communication, rescue priorities (people, boats, equipment)

Hazards: American Whitewater Affiliation Safety Code, dams, strainers, high water

River classification: Moving-water classifications, whitewater classifications (see table 19.2)

Characteristics of current: Surface features, upstream vs. downstream vs. rocks, eddies, ledges, hydraulics, strainers, horizon line, water color, waves, water sounds, river bends

Scouting: From boat vs. land

Entry and exit points to waterway: Determining safety

Table 19.2   International Scale of River Difficulty*

	Moving water classifications
Class A:	Water flowing under two miles per hour.
Class B:	Water flowing two to four miles per hour.
Class C:	Water flowing greater than four miles per hour.
	White water classifications
Class I: Easy	Fast moving water with riffles and small waves. Few obstructions, all obvious and easily missed with little training. Risk to swimmers is slight; self-rescue is easy.
	White water classifications
Class II: Novice	Straightforward rapids with wide, clear channels that are evident without scouting. Occasional maneuvering may be required, but rocks and medium-sized waves are easily missed by trained paddlers. Swimmers are seldom injured and group assistance, while helpful, is seldom needed. Rapids that are at the upper end of this difficulty range are designated "Class II+".
Class III: Intermediate	Rapids with moderate, irregular waves which may be difficult to avoid and which can swamp an open canoe. Complex maneuvers in fast current and good boat control in tight passages or around ledges are often required; large waves or strainers may be present but are easily avoided. Strong eddies and powerful current effects can be found, particularly on large-volume rivers. Scouting is advisable for inexperienced parties. Injuries while swimming are rare; self-rescue is usually easy, but group assistance may be required to avoid long swims. Rapids that are at the lower or upper end of this difficulty range are designated "Class III-" or "Class III+" respectively.
Class IV: Advanced	Intense, powerful, but predictable rapids requiring precise boat handling in turbulent water. Depending on the character of the river, it may feature large, unavoidable waves and holes or constricted passages demanding fast maneuvers under pressure. A fast, reliable eddy turn may be needed to initiate maneuvers, scout rapids, or rest. Rapids may require "must" moves above dangerous hazards. Scouting may be necessary the first time down. Risk of injury to swimmers is only moderate to high, and water conditions may make self-rescue difficult. Group assistance for rescue is often essential but requires practiced skills. A strong eskimo roll is highly recommended. Rapids that are at the upper end of this difficulty range are designated "Class IV-" or "Class IV+" respectively.
Class V: Expert	Extremely long, obstructed, or very violent rapids that expose a paddler to added risks. Drops may contain large, unavoidable waves and holes or steep, congested chutes with complex, demanding routes. Rapids may continue for long distances between pools, demanding a high level of fitness. What eddies exist may be small, turbulent, or difficult to reach. At the high end of the scale, several of these factors may be combined. Scouting is recommended but may be difficult. Swims are dangerous, and rescue is often difficult even for experts. A very reliable eskimo roll,

(continued)

Table 19.2 *(continued)*	
Class V: Expert	proper equipment, extensive experience, and practiced rescue skills are essential. Because of the large range of difficulty that exists beyond class IV, class V is an open-ended, multiple-level scale designated by class 5.0, 5.1, 5.2, etc. Each of these levels is an order of magnitude more difficult than the last example: increasing difficulty from class 5.0 to class 5.1 is a similar order of magnitude as increasing from class IV to class V.
Class VI: Extreme and exploratory	These runs have almost never been attempted and often exemplify the extremes of difficulty, unpredictability, and danger. The consequences of errors are very severe and rescue may be impossible. For teams of experts only, at favorable water levels, after close personal inspection and taking all precautions. After a class VI rapids has been run many times, its rating may be changed to an appropriate class 5.x rating.

Used with permission of the White Water Affiliation.

Trip planning: Group organization, at least three boats, lead vs. sweep, spacing

River etiquette: Give boat in current right-of-way, give all chance to play, move over in eddy, respect rights of landowners and fishermen

Skills

Strokes: Review and practice of all with particular emphasis on stationary strokes

Rolls (kayaks only): It is suggested that the participant be introduced to rolls on flat water with the opportunity to attempt them in moving water; proficiency is not required

Rescue: Bump rescue, towing rescue, rapid swimming, throw bag rescue

River reading: Identifying surface characteristics, hazards, and features

Portage: Correct carrying techniques, entry and exit points

Sailing

Sailing is one of the most popular boating activities found in camps. If your camp offers instruction in sailing on either dinghies (small boats with a center or dagger board) or keelboats (large sailboats with a fixed keel), you will benefit from the curriculum guidelines found in this section. Boardsailing, while utilizing many of the same principles as traditional sailing, requires a different set of skills and is not covered.

The curriculum contained in this section has been written with dinghies in mind. Although the skill progression for keelboat sailing is the same, certain skills and techniques unique to sailing keelboats are not covered in depth.

Facility and equipment

In addition to the guidelines offered in the general information section, there are a number of facility and equipment needs specific to the sport of sailing.

1. There are hundreds of different types of boats and many sailboat classes, each with its own distinct characteristics. The choice of sailboats used in camp boating programs is an important one and should be based on the following factors:

   The age, height, and weight of the sailors: Do campers have the size sufficient to safely skipper a boat independently?

The rescue ability of the sailboat: Will campers be able to self-rescue in case of capsize, or will capsize recovery require staff and/or equipment to complete?

The environment where sailing activities take place: Are currents or cold water present? What are the normal weather and wind patterns like?

2. During daily equipment checks, each sailboat should be checked for adequate flotation. Most boats have built-in buoyancy to keep from sinking and to aid in capsize recovery. Drain plugs and flotation bags (if used) should be inspected before sailing, and all ropes should be checked for fraying.

3. Type II or Type III PFDs are the most appropriate for sailing activities. Most small sailboats require agility by the skipper and crew. Type III PFDs allow for more ease of movement.

4. In addition to moorings or docks for boat storage, adequate storage space for sails and other equipment is necessary. A cool, dry space is needed for sails to dry properly and to stay dry when not in use.

Supervision

Small boat (dinghy) sailing instructors should hold certification from U.S. Sailing or another national certifying agency. If sailboards or keelboats are used, instructors should have specialized training in their use. U.S. Sailing offers instructor certification in small boats (dinghies) as well as keelboats and windsurfing (boardsailing). All instructors, whether certified or not, should demonstrate proficiency in the sailboat(s) used by campers. A proficiency check should include the following skills:

✔ Rigging the boat

✔ Marlinespike seamanship (knot tying)

✔ Leaving the dock, mooring, or beach

✔ Demonstrating all points of sail, including the safety position

✔ Capsizing and recovering (unless large keelboats are used)

✔ Returning to the dock

✔ Derigging the boat

An *instructor-to-student* ratio of 1:6 is recommended for beginning sailing instruction. As students become more proficient and confident, this ratio will change. Factors that can affect the ratio include the following:

Age, ability level, and maturity of campers. Older, more accomplished sailors will not require as strict supervision as beginners.

Type of boat used (self-rescue vs. non-self-rescue). What will happen to supervision if an instructor has to spend time righting a capsized boat?

The number of campers per boat. Even if boats carry six campers, the instructor-to-camper ratio should remain the same.

The sailing environment. Is the sailing area protected, or can students move out to open water easily?

For beginning instruction, a *safety boat-to-sailboat* ratio of 1:6 is also recommended. If each sailboat holds more than one or two sailors, this ratio may need to be modified. Check the capacity limits of safety boats to determine if they will be able to accommodate a full complement of stranded campers.

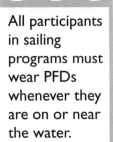

All participants in sailing programs must wear PFDs whenever they are on or near the water.

Recreational Programs

Sailing safely requires more than a cursory introduction to the craft. Capsizes are an accepted part of sailing, particularly when dinghies are used. At a minimum, campers permitted to use sailboats without a qualified staff member on the boat should meet the following prerequisites:

✔ Swim (any stroke) for at least 50 yards

✔ Tread water for five minutes in sailing clothes

✔ Right a capsized boat

✔ Demonstrate the safety position

If swimming ability is limited, or if campers have disabilities significant enough to impede self-rescue, then a qualified staff member should be present on the boat.

Instructional Programs

As stated earlier, capsizes may frequently occur during sailing. Because of this, the ability to swim becomes a necessary skill for those who will be learning how to skipper sailboats independently. Before receiving sailing instruction, campers should meet the following prerequisites:

✔ Swim (any stroke) for at least 50 yards

✔ Tread water for five minutes in sailing clothes

✔ Put on a life jacket in deep water

Safety

1. All sailing activities, especially boat launching and mast stepping, must be prohibited where overhead power lines exist.

2. Unlike boats using manual propulsion, the force of the wind can cause sailboats to cover a long distance in a small amount of time. This, combined with beginning sailors' difficulty maneuvering upwind, can cause even three or four sailboats to spread out over a great amount of space. For this reason, depending on the size of the sailing area, it is highly recommended that sailing instructors or supervisors utilize motorized safety boats during instructional and recreational sailing. For the same reason, two-way radios can be extremely useful for communication between safety boats and shore personnel.

Sailing Curriculum Guidelines

There are three levels to this sailing curriculum: basic, intermediate, and advanced. Generally, only camps specializing in sailing will have the opportunity to explore the intermediate and advanced curriculum. However, camps offering instruction in sailing should be covering all elements contained in level one. The fundamental skills covered in the basic course will give campers a solid base for further instruction.

Although campers may be ready for the intermediate or advanced curriculum, they may not have sailed for some time, or they may have received their original training in a different environment or on different boats. To minimize risk, prior to on-the-water practice, campers at any level of instruction should participate in an orientation session that reinforces the safety tenets and self-rescue procedures introduced at level one.

Basic Sailing—Level One

By the completion of level one sailing, campers should be able to leave the dock or mooring area safely, demonstrate all points of sail, and return to the dock. Emphasis should be placed on doing rather than identifying.

Theory

Course logistics: Introductions, meeting times, proper attire for class, etc.

Safety: Site-specific policies and guidelines, recall and accounting systems, emergency procedures, local weather patterns, and proper use of PFDs

Procedures in case of capsize: Stay with boat, avoid swimming under the hull or sails, weight concentrated on centerboard, or if boat can't be righted, climb on hull

Equipment: Basic nomenclature. Figure 19.9 presents a lateen-rigged boat and figure 19.10 a sloop-rigged boat

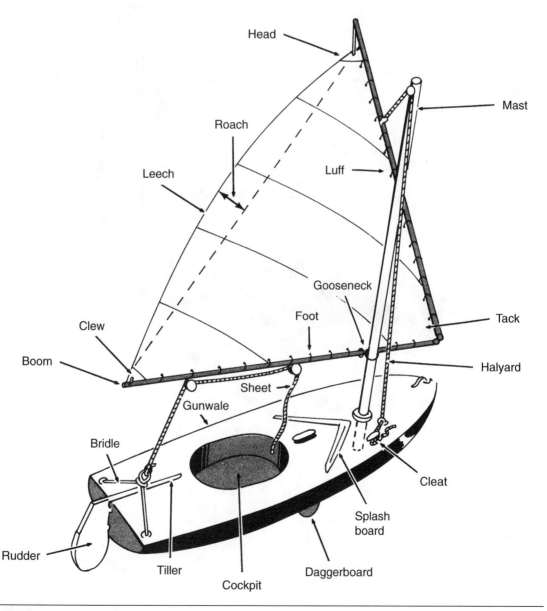

Figure 19.9 Lateen-rigged boat.

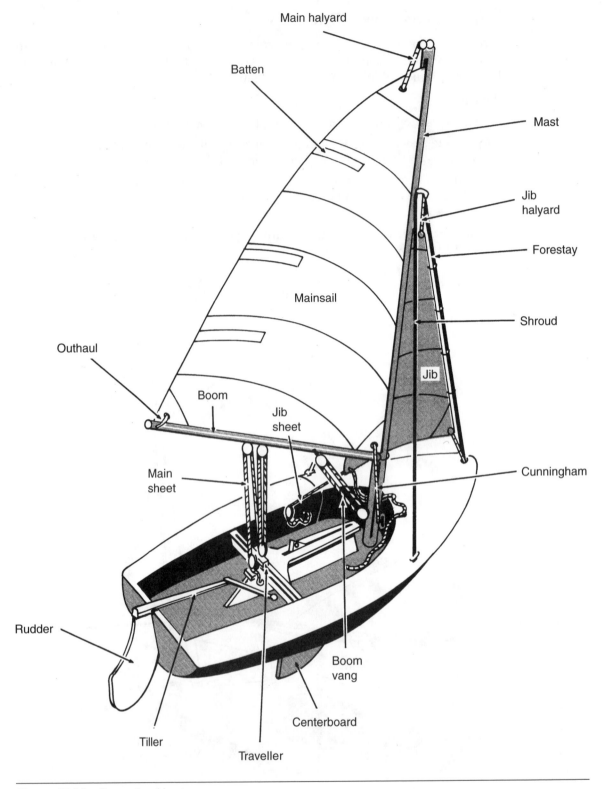

Figure 19.10 Sloop-rigged boat.

Skills

Basic marlinespike seamanship: Bowline, figure eight, two half hitches, square knot, cleating

Rigging the boat: Centerboard, rudder, sails, battens, halyards, sheets, etc.

Leaving dock or mooring: Determining wind direction and speed, determining current direction and speed, entering the boat, raising sails, leaving dock, sail trim, maneuverability, departure plan, backing sails, tacks, jibes, boat handling

Starting and stopping: Sail trim, body position, response time (include two methods for stopping)

Safety position: Point of sail, sail trim, response time, holding position

Tacking: Steering, course heading, sail trim, body movements, helmsman/crew communication

Jibing: Steering, course heading, sail trim, body movements, helmsman/crew communication

Sailing a rectangular course: Steering, boat speed, sail trim, tacks and jibes, body position, body movement, helmsman/crew communication

Man overboard (MOB): Communication, recovery plan, sequence of maneuvers, boat handling, course sailed, pickup approach, bringing MOB aboard

Maneuvering in confined area: Communication, boat handling, avoiding obstacles, tiller toward trouble, general right-of-way, sail trim, course sailed

Capsize recovery: Recovery method (scoop method for two people), sequence of maneuvers, exiting and entering boat, communication, maintaining contact with boat, PFD properly worn

Returning to dock or mooring: Approach plan, maneuverability, boat handling, sail trim, tacks and jibes, use of glide zone, backing mainsail, tying to dock or mooring, lowering sails

Derigging boat: Sail folding, stowing equipment, securing and tying down boat

Intermediate Sailing—Level Two

Once campers have mastered the skills in level one, they will be ready to learn more about the theory of sailing. Although these concepts are introduced earlier, mastery should not be expected until campers have achieved a degree of confidence in the boat and are able to apply the principles to their growing awareness of the boat and how it responds to the water, the air, and the movements of their bodies.

Prerequisites to Intermediate Instruction

Campers should be able to demonstrate all level one skills. If single-handed boats are used, campers should be able to perform skills independently. If boats requiring crew are used, performance as the skipper is the prerequisite; however, crewing skills are required as well. By the completion of the intermediate level of sailing, campers will be self-reliant sailors, able to demonstrate all basic skills generally mistake-free. They will be able to identify what skills they are demonstrating and when various principles are applicable.

Theory

Course logistics: See level one

Safety: See level one

Equipment: Additional nomenclature

Rules of the road: Starboard vs. port, leeward vs. windward, sailing vs. tacking or jibing, slowing vs. overtaking, sailboat vs. powerboat, rowboat/paddleboat vs. sailboat

Points of sail: No-go zone, beating, reaching, running

Navigation: Sailing various courses, reading nautical charts

Skills

Knots: Clove hitch, rolling hitch, square knot, sheet bend

General seamanship: Anchoring, reefing, maintenance

Crewing techniques: Communication, balance, jib work, sail controls

Heavy wind techniques: Sail controls, traveler, body placement

Depending on the boats being used, the following skills can also be introduced at the intermediate level:

Trapeze: Rigging, techniques, tacking, jibing

Sail controls: Outhaul, cunningham, boom vang

Spinnakers: Nomenclature, control lines, setting, jibing, takedown

Advanced Sailing—Level Three

Much of the thrill in the sport of sailing comes from racing. Whether in a regatta or a spontaneous match race, the challenge of capturing the wind in a more effective manner than another skipper is a temptation few sailors, at any level, can resist. Racing can be introduced during basic instruction, but thorough understanding of rules and techniques should not be expected until campers have mastered fundamental skills.

Prerequisites to Instruction

Based on instructor evaluation, campers should demonstrate self-reliance and confidence as both skipper and crew. They should demonstrate understanding of concepts and skills introduced at level two that relate to the boats being used. By the completion of the advanced level of sailing, campers will have the skills and knowledge necessary to participate in competition.

Theory

Course logistics: See level one

Safety: See level one

Additional nomenclature: Different sail shapes and hull types, classes of boats available

Courses used in racing: Triangular, oval, etc.

Tactics: Tuning, rules, protests, sportsmanship

Skills

Marlinespike seamanship: Whipping and splicing lines

Starting: Signals, position, restarts

Different legs: Sail trim, centerboard position, boat balance

Rounding marks: Windward marks, leeward marks, buoy room

Finishing

Waterskiing

Due to the nature of the sport of waterskiing, those who participate should be knowledgeable about fundamentals of boating safety. People who practice the sport of waterskiing are often called upon to drive for friends and family members who also want a chance to ski. Reinforcement of correct skiing techniques, observation of proper driving by camp instructional staff, and daily practice of boating safety principles will influence campers as they apply the skills they learn in camp to a lifetime of boating.

Facility and equipment

In choosing or designating boats for waterskiing activities, the following design specifications should be considered:

1. Water surface is best if calm and protected from wind and boat traffic.
2. The engine should have sufficient horsepower (25 mph for average ski instruction for youth and adults).
3. Ropes should be attached to the boat via a tow pylon or transom mounts. Pylons are the safest option, holding the towrope above the motor and helping prevent the line from becoming entangled in the propeller.
4. In addition to carrying a trained observer, ski boats should be equipped with a wide-angle rearview mirror for the driver.
5. The boat should have a steering wheel, speed indicator, and seating set so an observer can face the rear to watch the skier.
6. Accessibility to the boat from the water should be provided via a ladder, boarding platform, or low gunwales.
7. Water ski boats should have a low freeboard for better visibility while towing a skier, for approaching a fallen skier, and for ease of getting in and out of the water.
8. Towropes should be approximately 75 feet in length. Shorter ropes may be used for kneeboarding, trick skiing, tubing, and wakeboarding. Ropes should be checked for nicks and knots daily and should be replaced when these appear. Ropes also should be replaced annually or once they begin to fray or show signs of wear. Knots shouldn't be used for shortening ropes, as they can reduce a rope's strength by half, and ropes with unbreakable knots shouldn't be used at all. Rope length should be altered at the pylon.
9. Handles should have molded-rubber end caps and should be easily gripped.
10. Depending on the skill level and needs of both campers and staff, the following should be standard equipment: multiple combo pairs with adjustable bindings; at least one ski designed for slalom skiing (can be from a combo pair, but should have a pocket on the back directly behind the front binding); one pair of trick skis; one kneeboard; trainer skis (if young or extremely lightweight campers are being taught)
11. Skiers should wear only U.S. Coast Guard–approved Type III PFDs specifically designed for waterskiing. The water ski PDF should be vest type or open front type with proper straps to ensure a good fit.
12. Daily equipment checks should include inspecting towropes for frayed fibers, cuts, knots, or other weaknesses. Skis should be checked for loose hardware and splits in the foot bindings.

Supervision

Water ski instructors should hold instructor certification. Currently, USA Water Ski is the only national organization providing water ski certification. The Level I Instructor Course through USA Water Ski *requires* that all participants demonstrate practical boat driving and safety skills, teaching skills, and skiing skills. It is also recommended that instructors have a First Class Ski Rating from a USA Water Ski judge. For more information on USA Water Ski Instructor courses, contact USA Water Ski at 863-324-4341 or **www.usawaterski.org.**

If water ski instructors have boat-driving responsibilities, they should complete a National Association of State Boating Law Administrators (NASBLA)–approved boating safety course through the United States Power Squadrons, United States Coast Guard Auxiliary, or one of the state boating agencies. If there is mandatory education for motorboat operators in your state, a completion certificate from one of these courses will meet that requirement. Contact your local DNR for boater education requirements. The fees for these courses, if any, are negligible, and many can be completed through home study. After completing education, drivers/instructors should demonstrate boat-handling proficiency in the craft used at camp. One of the passengers on each towboat must be a trained observer, able to either drive the boat or effect a rescue in case of emergency.

Instructor-to-student ratios are determined by the passenger capacity and the age of the participants in the boat. Generally, a ratio of 1:4 should be established. Onshore ratios can be higher. Ski staff should have training in injury rescue and deep-water backboarding. Back injuries are common for skiers.

Prerequisites to participation

Recreational and Instructional Programs

Since waterskiing requires the camper to spend a great deal of time in the water as opposed to the boat, swimming ability is essential for participants. At a minimum, campers involved in waterskiing activities should meet the following minimal prerequisites:

✔ Swim (any stroke) at least 50 yards

✔ Tread water for at least five minutes

✔ Put on and take off a PFD in deep water

✔ On dry land, pull up from a sitting to a standing position with the use of a ski handle (Tying the rope to a tree or holding the rope while the camper does this works really well.)

✔ Demonstrate proper skier hand signals

With the advent of specially adapted equipment, more and more people with disabilities are enjoying the sport of waterskiing. Campers with physical disabilities who will be waterskiing should have a higher degree of comfort in the water and should, with the aid of a PFD, be able to support themselves with their heads above the water.

Safety

1. Skiing activities should take place at least 100 feet from shore and in water that is at least nine feet deep. Be sure to check local requirements. The boat traveling 15-25 mph should be able to move in a relatively straight path for a minute or more with large sweeping turns at either end (2,000-2,400 feet in length, 250-300 feet in width).

2. When a skier falls, the driver should automatically bring the boat into neutral until it has slowed down and the rope has cleared the skier, in the event the skier is entangled in the rope. The driver should slow the boat down well before getting back to the skier, then idle at least 12 feet from the skier.

3. Downed skiers should always be approached on the driver's side of the boat, in full view of the driver.

4. Downed skiers should never be picked up with the engine running.

5. Injured skiers should never be transported on the boat platform.

6. Lines and skis should be stored in a cool, dry area. Extended exposure to the sun may cause towlines to deteriorate and ski bindings to dry out, split, and crack.

7. Check local ordinances concerning dropped skis. This practice may be prohibited in some areas. If dropping is permitted, attempt to drop near the dock or shore. An added suggestion for dropped skis is to spray the bottom of the skis with a line of bright spray paint, particularly if they are black on the bottom. It makes them easier to spot from the boat, especially if it's windy.

Waterskiing Curriculum Guidelines

The three levels in this waterskiing curriculum include two-ski, slalom, kneeboard, and trick skiing. Since students will demonstrate varying levels of skiing aptitude, some may progress well beyond what is presented. Properly trained instructors should be capable of taking those students through the more advanced skills listed at the end of level three. Whether or not these skills are included in a camp's curriculum should be an administrative decision based on sophistication of available equipment, water site, and staff expertise.

> All waterskiing participants should wear PFDs at all times, whether skiing or riding in the boat.

Although traditional skiing is emphasized, kneeboarding may be more appropriate for some campers. Before letting campers attempt slalom or trick skiing, however, two-ski skills should be mastered. With any new skills, dryland instruction should precede on-the-water practice.

Making assumptions that campers are ready to try a new skill can be dangerous. Before attempting any new skill on the water, campers should run through the skill sequence in a dryland rehearsal. At any level of instruction, campers should participate in an orientation session that reinforces the safety guidelines introduced in level one.

Basic Waterskiing—Level One

By the completion of the basic waterskiing course, campers will be able to understand the safety rules and demonstrate all skier hand signals. They will be able to start and stop on two skis (or kneeboard), and they will be able to follow the boat within the wake while on two skis (or kneeboard). Skills may be limited to skis or kneeboard, or done on both. They should also be able to cut their wakes (aggressively cross their wakes with a moderate amount of speed).

Theory

Course logistics: Introductions, meeting times, proper attire for class, etc.

Safety: Site-specific policies, guidelines, and rules of conduct while in the boat, techniques for falling, skier hand signals with emphasis on "Okay after a fall" signal

Equipment: Skis and bindings, towlines and handles, boom (if used)

Skills—Two Skis

Skier hand signals: See figure 19.11.

Carrying and caring for equipment appropriately: Always carry skis by their sides, not the bindings, and do not drag the equipment in the sand. If equipment is carried by the bindings, it tends to rip them. Also, store equipment in appropriate racks and *not* in the sand. This allows it to dry appropriately, and sand tends to wear on equipment.

Putting on skis: Knees to chest, feet in bindings, treading water. Sometimes it's easier to tell participants to lie back on their life vest when putting on skis (use the vest to help them float and not fight the water), maintaining balance in the cannonball position.

Starting: Overhand grip on handle, knees bent, arms straight and wrapped around the knees, holding the tow bar, head up, communication with driver sequence from sitting to standing, timing with boat pull, legs only. (Use the term "Hit it" to start, *not* "Go," which sounds too much like "No.")

Riding skis in straight line: Head up, back straight, knees bent, arms straight, skis about shoulder-width apart. It's easier for beginners to get out of the water if

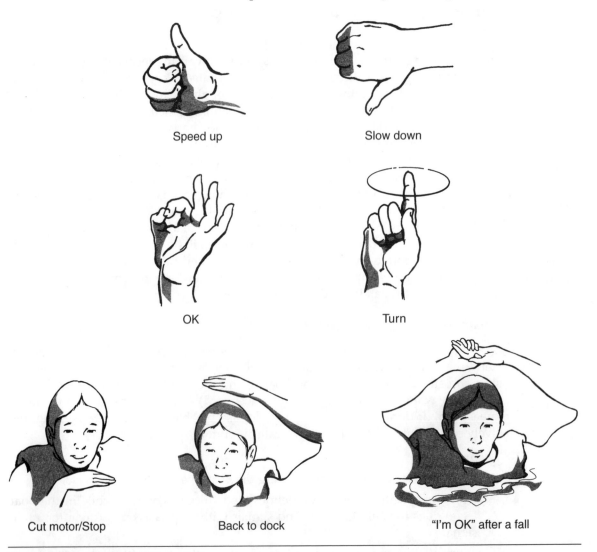

Speed up   Slow down

OK   Turn

Cut motor/Stop   Back to dock   "I'm OK" after a fall

Figure 19.11 Skier hand signals.

their arms are bent. They have the tendency to pull the rope toward them, trying to pull themselves up against the boat instead of letting the boat pull them up.

Riding one minute without falling: Campers should be able to ride at least one minute without falling, including maintaining control behind the boat while the boat turns 180 degrees (back toward shore).

Wake crossing: Beginning skiers need to learn to control their skis. They can learn to cross the wakes rather than weave in between the wakes, even if they have just learned to get up on the skis. The rule of thumb is that a beginner should be able to cross the wakes six times (three times on each side of the boat) before graduating to the next level. Beginners should use good body position and point their knees in the direction they want to go. This automatically puts the skis on edge and pressure on the outside ski.

Stopping: Stay behind boat, let go of rope, sink slowly or brake by sitting and dragging hands, give "okay" signal, take off skis.

Answering safety questions: Campers should be able to answer basic safety information such as the following:

Q: What do you do if you are coming into a dock or beach area too fast?

A: Sit down and drag your hands in the water.

Q: What must you always wear when waterskiing?

A: A life jacket.

Q: What do you do if you fall in the water and see another boat (besides the boat pulling you) coming toward you?

A: Take a ski and hold it high in the air to make yourself more visible to the boat.

Kneeboard

Skier hand signals: See figure 19.11.

Starting: Overhand or baseball grip, communication with driver, timing with boat pull, progression to kneeling position, attachment of strap

Riding in straight line: Body position, balance

Weaving within wake: Body position, leaning in the desired direction (This puts pressure on the outside edge of the board and takes the skier in the direction she or he wants to go.)

Stopping: Stay behind boat, let go of rope, sink slowly or brake by sitting and dragging hands, detach strap, give "okay" signal

Intermediate Waterskiing—Level Two

While some campers will be content merely getting up and skiing on two skis, others will want to experiment with moving in and out of the wake, and many will want to attempt slalom skiing.

Prerequisites to Instruction

Campers should be able to consistently start and remain riding for at least one minute on two skis or a kneeboard. Before attempting slalom skiing, campers should be stable on two skis, be able to cross in and out of the wake in good control, and show a desire to continue instruction. By the completion of level two, campers will be able to remain skiing on two skis (or a kneeboard) for extended periods. If they choose to continue, they will be able to drop a ski and slalom ski within the wake.

Theory

Course logistics: See level one.

Safety: See level one.

Skills—Two Skis

Skier hand signals: Be able to demonstrate these while being towed.

Wake crossing: Knees bent, sharp angle to wake, speed

Skills—Slalom

Skier's salute: Head up, gradual weight shift to one foot, opposite ski lifted out of water, toes up (This should be done on both sides to determine which foot is actually stronger.)

Dropping a ski: Before attempting to drop a ski, the skier should loosen the binding enough so that the foot will slip out easily when dropped. Correct body position, weight shift, ski drop, free foot drag, back foot placement. (Have the skier bring the free foot behind the calf of the ski leg and follow the calf down and backward to the pocket. If the skier can't get the foot in the pocket, he or she can just place the foot on top of the pocket.)

Skills—Kneeboard

Skier hand signals: Be able to demonstrate these while being towed.

Wake crossing: Baseball grip on handle, board tip up, maximum horizontal momentum, stay on edge

Advanced Waterskiing—Level Three

Prerequisites to Instruction

Campers should be able to consistently cut their wakes on two skis and drop a ski and ride on a slalom ski for extended periods. If they are focusing on kneeboarding, they should be able to cross in and out of the wake in a controlled manner. By the completion of level three waterskiing, campers will be confident slalom skiers, will be able to cross in and out of the wake in a controlled manner, and will know how to cut wakes in a simulated slalom course. If they are focusing on trick skiing, they will be able to complete a side slide in both directions, perform a 180-degree turn, and perform a single 360-degree turn. If kneeboarding is the focus, elementary wake jumping and side slides will be accomplished.

Theory

Course logistics: See level one.

Safety: See level one.

Skills—Slalom

Starting on slalom ski: Proper body position, ski leg knee bent up to the chest, free leg extended out and behind. (This can also be taught with a foot in the pocket, but it is usually more difficult to learn because of the associated drag in the water. It takes more effort to get out of the water.) Body weight evenly distributed over ski, timing with boat pull, free foot drag, back foot placement.

Wake crossing: Baseball grip, putting the ski on edge by applying weight to the side of the ski in the desired direction, knees bent, sharp angle to wake, speed.

Skills—Trick Skiing

Starting: Overhand grip on handle, knees bent, arms straight, head up, communication with driver, sequence from sitting to standing, timing with boat pull, legs only

Skiing in straight line: Knees bent, weight on the balls of the feet, back straight, head up, handle held in overhand grip at waist level

Wake crossing: Knees bent, sharp angle to wake, speed

Side slide: Even pull on rope, release of hand leading the turn, skis slightly spread (shoulder-width apart), weight should be on the balls of the feet, arms bent (both hands remain on the towbar), handle at waist level near the hip facing the boat, 90-degree turn by skis (body turns, head faces the boat), vertical body position (head up, arms bent and into the waist, back straight, knees bent)

180-degree turn front to back, with hold: The 180 is the next trick to learn after the side slide. Body position is the same, although the head and shoulders lead the turn (the 180 shouldn't be done from the side slide. This trick is easier to learn if you do it from the front), handle close to body at waist level near the small of the back during the turn, regrip handle, proper body position, slight lean away from boat, head up (eyes focused on the tree line).

180-degree turn back to front: Release of hand, rope arm bent and handle close to body, regrip handle

360-degree turn: Continuation of 180-degree turn, smooth pull on rope, proper body position, rope close to body at waist level

Skills—Kneeboard

Side slide: Overhand grip, body and board turn at same time, handle to hip, weight shifted away from boat, 90-degree angle to boat, head up

Wake jumping: Shortened rope, speed, board position on takeoff and landing, inward pull on rope, upward body thrust, rope control

Additional Skills

Depending on the equipment available, the expertise of the staff, the time allotted for instruction, and most important, the ability level of the students, the following skills may be appropriate. It is essential that campers master fundamentals before attempting any of the skills listed here.

Slalom	Kneeboard
Slalom course	Aerials
Kneeboard slalom course	Trick
Helicopters	**Other**
Multiple turns	Barefoot
Single ski tricks	Shoe skis, disc
Wake tricks	Jumping
	Wakeboarding

Motorboating

The number of camps offering motorboating instruction to campers is small compared to those offering other boating activities. The expense of insuring and maintaining motor-powered vessels makes motorboating infeasible for many camps. However, when camps do utilize motorboats, the opportunity exists for campers to learn boat-handling and other safety skills while under supervision. This controlled learning situation is preferred to the trial-and-error method intrinsic to self-instruction. Campers will carry the proper techniques and safety skills they learned in camp through a lifetime of recreational boating.

Even if motorboating instruction is not offered to campers, many camps utilize motor-powered vessels for cruising and as safety boats. If staff responsible for the operation of motor-powered vessels have no practical boat-handling experience, the curriculum guidelines contained in this section are appropriate to use during in-service training.

Facility and equipment

Many of the special equipment needs of motorboating programs are listed in the "General Information" section. When boats are used for instruction, operators must still abide by all state and federal registration regulations and carriage requirements. Check with the appropriate boating authority for regulations in your state.

Supervision

Instructor training courses in motorboating are difficult to locate, but some are available through the United States Power Squadrons and the United States Coast Guard Auxiliary. Because these classes are restricted to members of the respective organizations, camp personnel may not be able to attend. You may want to check with these organizations to see if staff may attend instructor classes. Also, some state DNR programs offer boating safety courses for instructors.

If instructor certification is not possible, motorboating instructors should be required to complete an NASBLA-approved boating safety course through one of the organizations or state boating agencies listed earlier. The fees for these courses, if any, are negligible, and many can be completed through home study. If there is mandatory education for motorboat operators in your state, a completion certificate from one of these courses will meet that requirement. Motorboating instructors should be at least 18 years old and, whether certified or not, should demonstrate boat-handling skills in the craft used at camp. A proficiency check should include the following skills:

Fueling, if it is a required job function

Launching and landing

Troubleshooting

Proper steering and throttle control

Instructional experience of some type

Prerequisites to participation

Recreational Programs

Safe motorboating requires extended practice and knowledge of the principles surrounding boating. Prior to solo operation, campers and staff given motorboat driving privileges should meet the following prerequisites:

Meet any state age requirements

✔ Demonstrate maturity

✔ Swim at least 50 yards (any stroke)

✔ Tread water for five minutes in boating clothes

✔ Put on a PFD in deep water

✔ Successfully complete all level one curriculum components while under strict supervision

Instructional Programs

In addition to any age restrictions imposed by the state, campers who will be learning to operate motorboats should meet the following requirements:

✔ Demonstrate maturity

✔ Swim at least 50 yards (any stroke)

✔ Tread water for five minutes in boating clothes

✔ Put on a PFD in deep water

✔ Complete a different boating course (e.g., sailing or canoeing) (This will help the camper understand the hazards motorboats can create for other boats.)

General safety

1. Except when approaching or leaving a dock or mooring, motorboats should not be operated closer than 200 feet from shore. When boats are within 200 feet of shore, they should not travel faster than 10 miles per hour.

2. Running through a safety checklist should be a standard part of each outing. Operators should be trained to check the following details:

✔ Has a *float plan* been filed? Are camp personnel aware that the boat will be on the water?

✔ Are people on board wearing properly fitted PFDs and shoes?

✔ Is the operator alert, sober, and ready?

• *Equipment safety:*

✔ Is there an approved, charged fire extinguisher on board?

✔ Is there a working bell or whistle on boats that require them? A sound-producing device on smaller boats?

✔ Are there paddles or oars for alternative propulsion?

✔ Is there a bailing device?

✔ Is there an anchor and anchor line?

✔ Is there a tool kit containing spare parts?

✔ Are there approved PFDs for everyone on board, plus one additional? (Check state guidelines for regulations in your area.)

Boat safety

✔ Are fuel tanks full, and have tanks and fuel lines been checked for leaks?

✔ Is the boat plug in?

✔ Is all gear stowed properly?

✔ Are the motor and propeller in good working order?

Motorboating Curriculum Guidelines

There are three levels to this motorboating curriculum: beginning, intermediate, and advanced. Although campers or staff may seem ready for intermediate or advanced instruction, they may have received their original training on different boats or in a different setting. For this reason, those at the more advanced levels should participate in an orientation session that reinforces the basic curriculum prior to on-the-water practice of new skills.

Beginning Motorboating—Level One

By the completion of level one of motorboating instruction, campers will be able to control the steering and throttle of a small power-driven boat. They will know how to complete safety checks before operation, and they will follow safety regulations.

Theory

Course logistics: Introductions, meeting times, proper attire for class, etc.

Safety: Site-specific policies and guidelines, recall and accounting systems, procedures in case of capsize, signals for distress, and proper use of PFDs

Regulations: Speed, rules of the road (right-of-way), distance, riding on decks or gunwales, capacity, negligent operation

Equipment: Types of boats used at camp, basic nomenclature as appropriate, capacity plates, required equipment

How mechanisms of boat work: Steering system, engine control, and handling characteristics

Skills

Knots: Bowline, clove hitch, clove hitch with two half hitches, cleating

Boarding: Balancing, loading, safety checklist

Engine starting and stopping: Fuel system and how to attach, engine kill, choke, stopping the engine

Getting under way: Leaving and returning to pier, dock, or mooring, no wake, maneuvering in a confined area, steering, throttle control, right-of-way

Turns: Steering and throttle control, right-of-way

Operating in waves and wakes: Response time, steering, throttle control, maneuvering ability

Returning to dock: Steering, throttle control, stopping distance, securing boat

Intermediate Motorboating—Level Two

Prerequisites to Instruction

Before participating at level two, campers should master all level one skills, and they should be able to answer questions about basic safety regulations and required equipment. They should be able to operate independently, in a controlled manner, the steering and throttle mechanisms of the training boat. By the completion of level two of motorboating, campers will be able to demonstrate correct right-of-way and boating etiquette. They will be able to maneuver in confined areas, and they will be able to safely retrieve a man overboard.

Theory

Course logistics: See level one.

Safety: Review of entire level one curriculum, navigational aids, markers.

Equipment: Anchor types, PFD types, different hull shapes.

Skills

Maneuvering in a confined area: Steering and throttle control, right-of-way, no wake, turning in own length

Man overboard: Throwing device, approaching to leeward side, motor cut, victim in over stern

Advanced docking skills: Boat lifts, slips, confined areas, mooring

Anchoring: Setting, retrieving

Advanced Motorboating—Level Three

Many camps will not have the facilities or equipment necessary for application of some level three skills. If this is the case, discussion of the topics during classroom sessions can still be very valuable. If campers are properly introduced to the concepts, they will be more likely to implement them correctly later.

Prerequisites to Instruction

Before participating at level three of motorboating instruction, campers should be skilled in the operation of the craft. They should consistently demonstrate common sense when boating, following right-of-way rules and proper boating etiquette. By the completion of level three of motorboating instruction, campers will be able to assist other vessels of the same size, and they will know the procedures for securing additional help. They will know how to care for a boat properly, and they will be able to identify and correct common maintenance and operational problems.

Theory

Course logistics: See level one.

Safety: Review level one and two curriculum.

Equipment: Compass, trailer and hitch and their maintenance.

Accident reporting: U.S. Coast Guard regulations.

Communication: Ship-to-shore radio procedures, navigation lights, whistle signals.

Skills

Towing: Other vessels, skiers.

Launching and retrieving: Trailer safety.

Maintenance: Engine care, fueling procedures, care and cleaning of hull, troubleshooting, winter storage.

Piloting and navigation: Compass and chart reading, communication, navigational aids.

BIBLIOGRAPHY

Gabrielsen, M. Alexander, Betty Spears, and B. W. Gabrielsen. 1968. *Aquatics handbook* (2nd ed.). Englewood Cliffs, NJ: Prentice-Hall.

Scuba Programs

Many people, both young and old, yearn for underwater exploration. The mystery and fantasy of what lies beneath the water's surface has intrigued countless civilizations. Today, through equipment designed by Jacques Cousteau, millions of divers participate in underwater exploration through the use of scuba (self-contained underwater breathing apparatus) equipment.

To participate in scuba diving, one must first be properly trained by a certified scuba instructor. This includes academic study, the development of physical skills, and training in actual diving environments (open water). When a diver has successfully passed the course requirements, she or he receives a scuba certification card, also known as a "c-card." This allows the diver to go diving, rent scuba equipment, and participate in advanced dive training.

Many scuba certification agencies exist worldwide, most of which are in the United States:

YMCA—Young Men's Christian Association National Scuba Program

NAUI—National Association of Underwater Instructors

PADI—Professional Association of Diving Instructors

NASDS—National Association of Scuba Diving Schools

SSI—Scuba Schools International

IDEA—International Diving Educators Association

PDIC—Professional Diving Instructors Corporation

NASE—National Association of Scuba Educators

Each of these agencies is responsible for developing and maintaining scuba training and certification standards for its own instructors to follow when they are teaching any type of scuba-related course. The certification agencies are also responsible for issuing scuba c-cards after successful training and testing have taken place. Each of these agencies has different standards for training and education. These differences in standards may be profound and are often a reflection of the mission and philosophy of the agency or organization.

So how do the YMCA's scuba standards differ from those of other agencies, and why are those standards so strong? Here are a few categories in which the YMCA's standards differ from those of other agencies:

Classroom Training

- *Instruction.* Some agencies allow students to be "self-taught" through home-study programs in which students watch videos or navigate through CD-ROMs. The instructor is there only to answer questions from the video, administer tests, and do in-water work. YMCA Scuba maintains the vital role of the instructor by having strong academic standards and allowing instructors to tailor their presentations to the level of their audience. Videos, textbooks, and other media are used only to supplement instructors' teaching. YMCA Scuba instructors are educators, trainers, and mentors.

- *Academics.* Some agencies give beginning students bite-sized bits of information, just enough to get a c-card, then promote more "advanced knowledge" in numerous specialty courses. Many agencies also compel their instructors to downplay more serious topics to avoid frightening or scaring away students. This is especially common for agencies that support retail dive centers or dive shops, where profit is essential. YMCA Scuba provides thorough and comprehensive academics in all levels of courses. Most beginning certified divers (Open Water Scuba Diver) in the United States do not take advanced scuba courses after their initial course. YMCA Scuba recognizes this. When divers receive YMCA Open Water Scuba Diver certification, they may dive in a vast array of diving locations throughout the world. In YMCA Scuba, we take academics seriously, but we teach them in a fun and supportive manner that students enjoy. YMCA Scuba requires an 80 percent minimum grade to pass the final closed-book exam, the highest requirement in the dive industry.

- *Hours.* Many agencies follow a "modular" training design. This often means that once a module is completed, the instructor goes immediately to the next module regardless of contact time with students. This is attractive to retail interests that are paying instructors per hour or that have to rent classrooms or facilities. This is the reason they run two- or three-day scuba courses. The YMCA has a 12-hour minimum for classroom work. This allows us to deliver a greater amount of academic content to a wide range of students—whether they are fast or slow learners. The minimum hours requirement also reduces the temptation to cut corners to save time or money.

Pool Training

- *Skills.* Many agencies teach only those skills that have "practical applications" when diving, so they don't "bother" the students with any other skills. YMCA instructors present multiple skills and techniques to accomplish goals through multitasking, progressive skill development, and repetition. Students become accustomed to being underwater and feel comfortable there.

- *Hours.* Here again, many agencies follow a "modular" training design. Once a skill is completed, the instructor may go immediately to the next skill without practicing or refining it or presenting alternative exercises. YMCA Scuba maintains a 12-hour minimum on pool hours.

Swimming Requirements

Some agencies downplay the importance of swimming ability to be able to scuba dive. Although this may be necessary for divers with disabilities, it allows those who have few aquatic skills or who have a fear of the water to sign up for the course. The YMCA has both entry and exit swim tests. First, we want to make sure a student is in the right course. If a student is uncomfortable in the water, then perhaps a YMCA Swim Lessons or a YMCA Snorkeling class is a better option. Second, we want students to have a baseline against which they can measure the improvement in their aquatics abilities from the beginning to the end of the course.

Student-to-Instructor Ratios

YMCA Scuba maintains very conservative student-to-instructor ratios. For pool sessions, we have a 10:1 ratio (10 students to 1 instructor). In the open-water dive sites, we have a 6:1 ratio. Most other agencies maintain less conservative ratios in both the pool and open water.

Minimum Age

Some agencies have reduced the minimum age for participating in diving from 12 years to 10 or 8, or in some cases, they have no minimum age. YMCA of the USA's Medical Advisory Committee reviewed and reaffirmed the following minimum age requirements for participating in scuba programs taught at YMCAs, as set forth in the *YMCA Scuba Standards and Procedures Manual (2000)*:

- 12-14 years of age for Junior Diver Certification programs (which require parent participation and supervision)
- 15 years of age or older for Open Water Scuba Diver or other scuba certification programs

The recommendation is based on the fact that there is insufficient scientific evidence to support the position that children under the age of 12 are mentally and physically mature enough to participate safely in scuba training. Children under 12 do not have the intellectual, social, motor/physical, and language development to deal with the complex concepts, judgments, and skills necessary for safely participating in scuba diving activities. YMCA Scuba encourages children under the age of 12 to participate in YMCA Snorkeling and YMCA Skin Diving programs. These programs offer significant underwater exploration, learning, games, and activities.

No other scuba training agency stands for the mission and philosophies of the YMCA. YMCA Scuba is dedicated to developing the individual's spirit, mind, and body through comprehensive academics and strong skills. A competent, skilled, and proficient diver is a safe diver. A safe diver is a comfortable diver who will enjoy years of quality diving.

YMCA SCUBA PROGRAMMING

Because of a demand for safety, YMCA of the USA introduced its scuba program training standards in 1959. YMCA Scuba led the diving industry with several firsts, including the first national scuba instructor training course and the first scuba rescue course. In the 40 years since its inception, YMCA Scuba has continued to provide the highest level of community-oriented education for divers and instructors based on the principles of the YMCA triangle: the spirit, the mind, and the body. These principles are the core philosophy of the YMCA, and YMCA Scuba bases all training and programs on these ideals.

From the very beginning of this nationally certified sport, the YMCA Scuba program has taken the lead in developing safe, educated, well-trained sport divers. YMCA Scuba education and training is designed to teach divers to enjoy the sport while showing them how to minimize the risks involved.

YMCA Scuba offers training standards and certification for over 40 scuba courses. Courses vary in hours, prerequisites, course content, skill development, open-water

diving opportunities, and instructor credentials to teach. All course particulars, guide-lines, and standards are available in the *YMCA Scuba Standards and Procedures Manual, 2000 Edition*. The following is a list of common YMCA Scuba courses and their descriptions.

Snorkeling (Non-scuba)

YMCA Snorkeling introduces individuals and families to the sport of snorkeling. There is no age requirement; snorkeling is a recreational activity that can be shared by the whole family. Allowing people to examine underwater magic from above, snorkeling appeals to those planning a vacation in warm, tropical waters or others simply wanting to enjoy another aquatics activity.

Skin Diving (Non-scuba)

YMCA Skin Diving is designed for swimmers and snorkelers who want to expand their aquatics exploration. With its simple equipment and basic techniques, swimmers will find this course to be enjoyable and challenging. The underwater world is a fascinating place that can be discovered with a minimal amount of effort and the use of a mask, fins, and snorkel.

Open Water Diver

Learning to scuba dive is safe, affordable, and requires a modest amount of training. An entry-level certification course takes approximately 32 hours to complete during

day or evening classes over a few weekends to several weeks. To earn a scuba certification, participants attend classroom sessions and practice essential diving skills
in a pool. Finally, they test their knowledge on a written exam and apply their skills
during training dives in a lake, quarry, spring, or ocean. Upon successful course
completion, participants receive a certification card that identifies them as divers,
allowing them to rent scuba equipment, participate in advanced training, and explore exotic diving destinations.

Open Water II Diver

YMCA Open Water II is designed to give certified scuba divers additional open-
water dives. This guided experience is important for new divers who want more
training before going out on their own and diving without supervision.

Advanced Open Water Diver

The YMCA Advanced Open Water Diver course is for divers wanting to expand
their knowledge and diving experience to include varied diving environments and
an introduction to specialty diving.

Specialty Courses

A number of hobbies can be integrated into scuba diving, ones that require the ability to move in an underwater environment. Our specialty courses permit the diver
to gain comprehensive abilities in virtually any field of aquatic endeavor. They include the following:

Aquatic environmentalist	Public safety diver
Boat diver	Reef ecology
Cavern diver	Research diver
Computer-assisted diver	Search and recovery
Dry suit diver	Scuba Lifesaving and Accident
Equipment service	Management (SLAM) rescue
Ice diver	Underwater archaeology
Night diver	Underwater navigation
Nitrox diver	Underwater photographer
Oxygen provider	Wreck diver

Leadership Courses

Scuba leadership positions include divemaster, assistant instructor, and instructor.

Divemaster

A certified YMCA Divemaster provides on-site leadership for groups of certified
divers during recreational sport diving or for students during training under the
direct supervision of a YMCA Scuba Instructor. Divemasters conduct tours and supervise diving activities. Divemasters can work at dive resorts, on dive boats, and in
dive shops all over the world.

Assistant Instructor

YMCA Assistant Instructor certification is a required step in the development toward YMCA Scuba Instructor. Assistant instructors may teach the YMCA Snorkeling and Skin Diving courses. During the open-water courses, assistant instructors assist in classroom training, pool training, and open-water dives under the direct supervision of the instructor.

Instructor

In 1959, the YMCA developed scuba training standards for instructors. These standards remain the most thorough and comprehensive in the diving industry today.

When it comes to scuba certification, trust is an important aspect of training. YMCA Scuba instructors follow the philosophy of the YMCA by building divers' self-esteem and nurturing their personal growth. YMCA leadership prides itself on maintaining values. In a sport such as scuba diving, those participating need to have good values, moral character, and ethics. YMCA Scuba instructors instill character development in their students by promoting caring, honesty, respect, and responsibility during dive training.

Instructor certification permits an individual to teach scuba students how to become competent divers. The instructor promotes safe diving and upholds the standards of YMCA Scuba. The instructor also teaches many specialty and leadership courses.

Divers With Disabilities

YMCA Scuba is committed to the concepts and principles of the YMCA, including the development of the spirit, the mind, and the body. In keeping with the YMCA's philosophy, YMCA Scuba does not allow discrimination against people with disabilities in any of its programs, including skin diving and scuba. YMCA Scuba allows instructors flexibility in the administration of teaching standards so as to reasonably accommodate the needs of students with disabilities. Based on each student's ability to meet the requirements and challenges of the program successfully, instructors must determine if any conditions should be placed on the diver. These conditions will determine the level of certification the diver can achieve.

Springfield College

Springfield College offers academic credit toward a bachelor's degree for successful certification as an open-water diver and instructor. Located in Springfield, Massachusetts, Springfield College has a distinguished history as an official YMCA educational institution. The academic credit earned through this process can be used in a Springfield College degree program or applied as transfer credit toward a bachelor's degree at most colleges in the United States.

International Recognition

CMAS (Confederation Mondiale Des Activities Subaquatiques), also known as the World Underwater Federation, is the only worldwide diving organization. It is composed of some 14,000 diving clubs, 82 national federations, and 4.5 million divers. CMAS international certification cards are issued by equivalence in 82 countries and at all levels for both divers and instructors. CMAS certification confers the following benefits:

- Global acceptance and international recognition
- Permission to dive in countries where authorization is needed
- Ability to rent equipment and refill cylinders abroad
- Ease in joining international diving groups

In 1980, YMCA Scuba became a federation of the World Underwater Federation (CMAS), thus giving our instructors and divers the ability to obtain this international certification as well. Because of our high standards, YMCA Scuba remains the only scuba certification organization in the United States that offers the CMAS international certification card.

To receive a CMAS international certification card or instructor certification, divers or instructors must submit the following:

- Name and current address
- A copy of the current YMCA Scuba certification card (front and back)
- Registration fee, payable to the YMCA of the USA (by check or credit card authorization)

Now that you know what the YMCA Scuba program has to offer, it's time to think about whether it is a program that you want in your YMCA. (As always, feel free to contact the YMCA of USA Scuba office for more information or to answer specific scuba programming questions.)

DECIDING WHETHER TO OFFER YMCA SCUBA

Today, over 30 percent of all YMCAs offer scuba programming. Several international YMCA federations have modeled their own scuba programs after the YMCA of the USA's Scuba program. But is it right for your YMCA? Ask yourself these questions when planning to offer scuba at your YMCA:

Is there a demand in your community for scuba training and/or a dive club?

Test the interest within your membership by posting an interest flyer in your YMCA. Try to assess the amount of interest outside the YMCA as well. You may be surprised, as YMCAs have flourishing scuba programs in towns that have few or no dive sites near them. Most divers dive abroad but are trained locally. The fact is that anyone who wants to enjoy a lifetime of scuba activities must be trained and certified.

Is there a dive shop in the area?

When your YMCA offers scuba programming, your instructor will have to secure scuba equipment for students to use during the course. This is especially true for beginner-level courses, as more advanced divers usually spend several hundred or thousands of dollars on equipment. A local dive shop can assist your instructor by providing rental equipment and the many air tank refills that scuba tanks (cylinders) need during a course.

When determining whether a local dive shop should become a "preferred vendor" for your YMCA, consider the following questions:

1. Is their management professional?
2. Do they have a good reputation?
3. Is their shop and their rental equipment clean?

4. Do their staff act professionally?

5. Is their way of doing business in line with the YMCA values of caring, honesty, respect, and responsibility?

6. Are they cutthroat competitors, or are they fair, open, and honest?

7. What air purity guidelines do they follow? When were their air compressors, delivery systems, and storage tanks last inspected?

8. Is their staff trained by equipment manufacturers to perform equipment care and maintenance? Do they keep records of equipment maintenance?

9. What is the scope of their general liability store policy? What professional liability insurance policy do their instructors hold? (It must be $1 million minimum coverage.) Does the store/instructor have product liability insurance? Most important, is the YMCA listed as an additional insured on the professional liability policy?

Does your facility (or another facility you have access to) have a pool over six feet deep?

Some scuba skills can be taught in lap pools in water as shallow as four to six feet deep. However, deeper water is essential for developing skills involving pressure changes and water entries. If your YMCA has only a lap pool, you can still offer scuba programming as long as some pool sessions can be conducted at a deeper-water facility.

Does your facility have adequate space and time for scuba programs?

This depends on the number of courses your YMCA would like to offer. Most YMCAs offer the beginning scuba diver training course called Open Water Diver. This course requires a minimum of 12 hours of classroom and 12 hours of pool instruction. The space needed depends on the number of participants. See "Scuba Programs Management" for more ideas on scheduling and facility management.

Offering YMCA Scuba is an asset to your overall comprehensive aquatics program for your members and community. Here are several reasons why:

- Classes and scuba clubs can help people grow as members of the YMCA.

- The program is progressive and provides many specialty and leadership opportunities.

- It brings in individuals who are interested in scuba but who may not be aware of the YMCA's aquatics, program, and membership opportunities.

- Scuba affords those who participate in other aquatics programs an opportunity for cross-training and new learning.

- It is an adventure program that appeals to many people, including older teens and families.

SCUBA PROGRAMS MANAGEMENT

If you decide that you want a scuba program at your YMCA, you will first need to find a good scuba instructor. You'll also want to think about program promotion, scheduling, course costs, and budgeting. This section will also provide you with ideas on how to deal with common instructor and student complaints and some tips on running a quality scuba program.

Selecting a Scuba Instructor

Selecting an instructor to teach skin diving and scuba diving is the same as selecting an instructor to teach any other aquatics course or program. Your criteria for hiring other staff should also be applicable to hiring a scuba instructor. Here are three possible options for finding a scuba instructor:

- *Option 1: Train existing staff.* If your YMCA has a staff member or volunteer who is an avid scuba diver with leadership qualities, you may want to ask him or her to take the necessary scuba leadership courses to become a scuba instructor. However, training to become a scuba instructor is quite involved: hundreds of dives are required, hundreds of training hours, and many costs. Also, to develop as a YMCA Scuba leader, that person would need to learn from other YMCA Scuba instructors and trainers.

- *Option 2: Find a YMCA-certified instructor.* It may be easier for you to find an existing local YMCA Scuba instructor. Such a person will know the latest YMCA Scuba standards and guidelines, will have professional liability insurance, and will have met the annual renewal requirements. To find a currently certified YMCA Scuba instructor, contact the YMCA of the USA Scuba program or visit the YMCA Scuba Web page at **www.ymcascuba.org.** Search "Find an Instructor," a directory of YMCA Scuba instructors organized alphabetically by state.

- *Option 3: Have an existing instructor cross over.* If you do not have a local YMCA Scuba instructor and don't want to train a scuba instructor candidate from your facility, your next option will be to find a local scuba instructor trained through another organization and have her or him cross over to YMCA Scuba. The best place to look for one is at dive shops. Many dive shops not only sell scuba equipment and sponsor dive trips, but they also offer scuba training and certification. Some independent scuba instructors may teach at colleges, universities, high schools, recreation centers, or apartment complexes, or they may teach privately. Regardless of where they work, these instructors should have certifications and credentials from one of the scuba certification organizations.

If a local scuba instructor is not YMCA certified, he or she can take a YMCA Scuba instructor crossover course. Once that person is a successfully certified and active YMCA Scuba instructor, he or she can run official YMCA Scuba courses.

A YMCA Scuba instructor should be highly trained and highly educated. She or he should teach scuba through the mission of the YMCA: To put Christian principles into practice through programs that build healthy spirit, mind, and body for all. A YMCA Scuba instructor promotes the YMCA by highlighting the values of caring, honesty, respect, and responsibility.

Becoming and then maintaining active (current) status as a scuba instructor can be costly. Thus, you should recognize these costs when negotiating course fees and payment to the instructor. Here is a sample of the course costs to become a scuba instructor:

Scuba Instructor Course Costs

1. Become an Open Water Scuba Diver	$150-450
2. Take an Advanced Open Water Diver course	$125-500
3. Purchase a complete scuba system for divers	$850-1,200

4. Become certified in Scuba Lifesaving and Accident Management (SLAM)	$75-200
5. Become certified in CPR, first aid, and oxygen provider	$150-250
6. Take a Divemaster course	$75-200
7. Purchase equipment for leadership (first aid, oxygen, books)	$50-450
8. Take an Assistant Instructor course	$75-200
9. Take an Instructor Institute	$325-1,200

Here is a sample of annual expenses for an instructor:

1. Annual instructor renewal (per agency)	$100-200
2. Annual professional liability insurance policy	$425-500
3. Continuing education courses	$25-100
4. Upkeep of equipment	$50-200+

Here are some sample questions to ask potential staff instructor candidates to determine their qualifications for working at the YMCA:

1. What is your personal philosophy on teaching scuba?
2. How long are your courses typically?
3. How many students have you certified? Do you have student references that we may contact?
4. How is the development of an individual's spirit, mind, and body accomplished through scuba courses?
5. How would you promote the YMCA to your students who are not members?

Because many scuba instructors come from outside the YMCA, you may have to consider whether it's better to have your instructor become a staff member or simply contract with that individual to provide instruction services. We suggest that you not allow an instructor or dive shop to rent the YMCA's pool, for reasons we will explain shortly.

Staff Member

Hiring a scuba instructor as a YMCA staff member has many advantages. A hired instructor is a "part" of the local YMCA. Other staff will interact with the scuba instructor and be familiar with the courses offered. The instructor will "talk the talk" and promote the mission of the YMCA, and the YMCA will have financial control of the program through structured course fees. Quality is also assured, as the aquatics or program director knows the instructor is following YMCA Scuba training standards and procedures. A staff scuba instructor may volunteer for other events such as these:

- Giving the "I Tried Scuba" introduction to scuba diving during YMCA open houses
- Demonstrating scuba rescues to lifeguard trainees in the YMCA lifeguard training courses
- Assisting in scuba-related fundraisers

Contracted Instructors

Contracted scuba instructors may never feel they are part of the YMCA, and staff-related functions may not include contracted individuals. As contracted instructors are not very involved in the local YMCA, staff may not know them or their courses. Also, a conflict of interest may arise if instructors solicit members to take courses outside the YMCA, sell equipment, and so on.

If you plan to use the contracted employee option, be sure you follow your association's independent contractor procedures. Mutually agree on and state the following in your contract:

- Pay
- Training standards
- Textbooks
- Certifications issued and procedures
- Dos and don'ts
- Emergency procedures

Instructors Renting the Pool

Renting a YMCA pool to a dive shop or independent scuba instructor may expose you to several risks:

- You may bring up potential property tax issues because a for-profit entity (dive shop or instructor) is conducting its business on not-for-profit property (YMCA). For further information on tax challenge issues in YMCAs, contact the YMCA of the USA Office of the General Counsel. The fees the dive shop or instructor pays to the YMCA may also be taxable.

- A conflict of interest may arise if an instructor is soliciting members to enroll in courses outside the YMCA, offering dive trips not condoned by the YMCA, or selling scuba equipment.

- The programming conducted in the YMCA's pool may include training standards not condoned by the YMCA of the USA. These may include standards, practices, and/or trends promoted by other scuba certification agencies, such as allowing children under 12 years of age to participate in scuba and/or offering "abbreviated/short" courses.

Here are some scenarios in which renting the pool to an instructor could cause a problem:

- A non-YMCA-certified instructor rents the pool at a local YMCA and solicits children of any age to try scuba in the pool, even breathing compressed air in the deep end.

- The instructor renting the pool damages the pool deck tiles and tells no one.

- The instructor renting the pool teaches three classes at once, violating multiple standards, but the aquatics director has no idea that profound violations are occurring.

- The instructor renting the pool solicits YMCA members to buy scuba equipment, take courses at the shop, or purchase dive travel.

- The instructor renting the pool invites friends or people who just bought equipment from the dive shop to come by the YMCA and get wet during the next course.

As the instructor is teaching, these people come into the pool and use scuba gear without ever signing class waivers and releases (which should always include the name of the YMCA in the "hold harmless" release).

• The instructor renting the pool holds a new class every weekend, offering abbreviated training. An accident then occurs with a diver, who is also a YMCA member, after the course is completed. The YMCA can be included in a legal suit. YMCA directors are questioned by lawyers as to why they allowed abbreviated training to occur at their YMCA when the YMCA of the USA Scuba standards do not permit it. The lawyers say their client heard that the YMCA has great scuba training, and being a member herself, she joined the class she saw training every weekend thinking that it was a YMCA Scuba class.

Promotional Ideas

To get good participation in your scuba program (as with any YMCA program), you will have to spread the word to your members. Also, as scuba programs may not be offered elsewhere in your community, you'll want to let the people in your community know about them too.

One method of program promotion is flyers. They can be as inexpensive or as expensive as you like. A simple one-page, black-and-white flyer can give people enough information to get them interested. You can mail, post, or stack flyers that people can read to help them decide to sign up for the next scuba classes. Your flyer should include the following points:

• *What the members will do:* Members will take classes for YMCA Scuba certification in whatever course topic is offered. These classes will include classroom lectures and pool sessions. Students will learn both academic information and underwater skills so they can safely, successfully, and enjoyably participate in scuba diving activities.

• *What the members will receive (once the course is successfully completed):* Members will receive superior dive training leading to a YMCA Scuba certification card.

• *Who is teaching the course:* The name and possibly the contact information for the instructor(s) teaching the course can be included on the flyers.

• *How much the course will cost:* As there are so many costs associated with scuba courses (see "Course Costs and Budgeting"), try to list *all* course costs that the students will be required to pay. "Hidden costs" are not fair to those signing up for any program, and therefore costs should be explained beforehand. Payment of additional course costs is negotiated between the YMCA and the scuba instructor. If students are required to purchase additional items (dive tables, textbooks, watch, etc.) or pay for additional services (an open-water dive trip), then include that in the course advertising materials.

• *When the course is conducted:* Not only should a flyer include the beginning and ending dates for the course, but it should also list the times for classroom, pool, and open-water sessions.

When you create a flyer, start with something catchy to attract the reader, such as this:

Thirsty for excitement? Try scuba! Explore the underwater world of nature through the use of scuba—Self-Contained Underwater Breathing Apparatus.

Then add the course description given to you by the YMCA Scuba instructor or organization that is running the scuba course at your YMCA.

Keep your target markets in mind as you write the flyer. Some potential participants may be middle-aged or older adults with mediocre to good swimming skills who want to obtain certification for vacation purposes. Younger scuba participants are adventure seekers who engage in other thrill-seeking sports such as rock climbing and jet skiing. Be sure to promote the benefits of your course to them:

- Excitement, adventure, and freedom
- The wonder of underwater sea life
- The opportunity to take an exotic vacation while completing certification
- The safety of the program and the certifications of staff
- Equipment supplied or discounts on equipment available

Besides making the flyers available at your YMCA, provide them to travel agencies, outdoor shops, and sporting goods stores.

In addition to flyers, advertise the course in your own YMCA program brochure. If you are working with a dive shop, the shop may advertise in the newspaper and put up posters around your YMCA. Other ways to get the word out include cable TV announcements and press releases. You might ask the dive shop to run a free "I Tried Scuba" program during your special events.

To keep your front-desk staff aware of the details of your scuba program, supply them with a front-desk brochure.

Scheduling

Scheduling any course that has particular facility requirements, such as a pool or a classroom, can be challenging. You can schedule scuba courses in several ways. Here are some scheduling tips for scuba facility management:

- Schedule scuba courses during "off-peak" times 8:00-10:00 P.M. Nights are popular, as well as weekends.
- Schedule courses before or after YMCA operating hours, when appropriate (proper staffing is required).
- See that classrooms are conducive to learning; that is, they have the proper lighting, minimal distractions, and visual aid equipment.
- Schedule scuba classes at times when there are minimal distractions. This does not mean that scuba classes can't share the pool with other aquatics programs. However, scheduling a scuba class at the same time as a water aerobics class may prove to be problematic because of the loud music used in the aerobics class and the instructor's verbal commands.
- Partition scuba classes away from other aquatics programs. Lap swimmers or even lifeguard courses can share the pool with scuba classes, but reserve lanes for scuba only. Provide access to both shallow and deep water for scuba training. Do not allow divers to wander under lap swimmers or into other aquatics programs areas.

See table 20.1 for some examples of the pool and classroom time you'll need for scuba courses.

Table 20.1	Scuba Class and Pool Time Sample

Open Water Diver (Entry-level course)

4-8 weeks (average)

32 hours recommended

12 hours pool

12 hours classroom

8 hours open water

Class scheduling

4 weeks	8 weeks
Mon. Lecture 3 hrs	Mon. Lecture 1.5 hrs
Wed. Pool 3 hrs	Wed. Pool 1.5 hrs
OR	OR
Thurs. Lecture 3 hrs	Thurs. Lecture 1.5hrs
Sun. Pool 3 hrs	Sun. Pool 1.5 hrs
OR	
Tues. Lecture/Pool 4 hrs	
Thur. Lecture/Pool 4 hrs	

Course Costs and Budgeting

Scuba diving, by nature, is not an inexpensive hobby. Many people look for cost-cutting measures to getting their certification cards (c-cards). Often dive shops will advertise ridiculously low-cost specials that have hidden costs. After those costs are added up, the special isn't such a bargain after all.

Although YMCAs need to remain somewhat competitive in their pricing, keep in mind that YMCA Scuba programming offers more comprehensive training, knowledge, and skill development than many other programs. Often YMCA Scuba training will be conducted over a longer time period than other scuba certification courses. This is good, as the more time a diver is in the water and has contact with the instructor, the more learning and development can take place. So how should you price scuba training courses? Let's take a look at the costs.

1. *Instructor pay:* You may compensate scuba instructors for their teaching and expertise in several ways: per student, per class, per hour, and so on. Whatever way you negotiate it, keep in mind that the instructor has some annual costs associated with remaining a current (or active) instructor with a scuba certification organization. Just becoming a scuba instructor can cost several hundreds to thousands of dollars. Thus, be reasonable and fair when negotiating with instructors for pay.

2. *Equipment rental:* Each student will be required to use a scuba unit during courses. Beginning divers cannot purchase their own scuba equipment (tank, regulator, and buoyancy compensator) without first being trained and certified, so the instructor or facility must make equipment available. This is often accomplished by renting equipment.

Most often a local dive shop will have the amount of equipment necessary to rent to an entire class. Dive shops keep detailed service records on their equipment, and they have personnel trained by the equipment manufacturers to work on scuba systems. Sometimes an independent instructor may have enough sets of equipment to supply a class. However, keep in mind that the instructor must have special training and credentials to service scuba equipment. In some cases, YMCAs own sets of equipment for use during the course. Again, the equipment must be properly serviced.

Scuba equipment may be rented for the pool only or for the pool and open water. In some cases, dive shops may give discounts when you rent equipment for several weeks. A rough guideline is that a diver should be able to rent a complete scuba unit (tank, regulator, and buoyancy compensator) for about $30 a weekend. However, many dive shops consider their class rental equipment overhead and incorporate its costs into course fees, and thus they do not charge separate rental costs. Obviously, the lower the cost of renting equipment, the lower the course costs would be.

Here is the YMCA Scuba minimum student scuba system: the equipment required to be worn by the student to perform the open-water skills. This equipment includes, as a minimum: mask, snorkel, fins, scuba cylinder and valve, buoyancy compensator with low-pressure power inflator, regulator with primary and alternate air source (active scuba air delivery system), submersible pressure gauge, weight ballast system, timing device, depth gauge, and wet suit (if appropriate). (Dry suits are not permitted for entry-level open-water training unless specialized dry suit training is completed before open-water dives.) Additional desirable (but not required) equipment includes compass/direction monitor and Sport Diving Tables.

3. *Air tank refills*: Filling scuba tanks with air is often included in equipment rental costs. However, if the instructor or the YMCA owns the equipment, then the instructor has to go to a dive shop to get the tanks filled. Tank fills range from free to $5 for air and perhaps more for specialized gas mixes such as Nitrox.

4. *Textbook, workbook, and learning materials*: Students are required to have resources from which they study and learn. Any resources that cover the academic content included in the *YMCA Scuba Standards and Procedures Manual* are acceptable, and other dive certification organizations have student resources. However, using other organizations' materials often confuses students about the brand of course being offered. If it is a YMCA Scuba course using NAUI books, then students may question whether the course is a YMCA course. YMCA Scuba recommends that instructors use *Scuba Diving: A Trailside Guide*, available through the YMCA Program Store (Item no. 0-393319-44-X). Here are some sample resources with their price ranges:

Textbook (*Scuba Diving*)	$20
Workbook (to accompany textbooks)	$5-8
Dive tables (YMCA Scuba Sport Diving Tables)	$4-8
Dive log book	$5-15

Most YMCA Scuba materials are available from the YMCA Program Store.

5. *Certification fee*: Certification fees for most YMCA Scuba courses and specialty courses are $12 per certification.

6. *Required student gear**: Students may be required to purchase items that are fitted personally to them and thus may not be shared or rented. These items include mask, snorkel, fins, and an underwater timing device such as a water-resistant watch. Here are price ranges for this equipment:

Mask:	$25-75
Snorkel:	$10-40
Fins:	$30-125 (Booties $20-40)
Watch:	$30-200

*This is paid for by the student and should not be entered into the YMCA course costs.

7. *Checkout dives:* Students must dive in an open-water diving environment before being certified. These open-water "checkout dives" are commonly held at local dive sites such as lakes, springs, sinkholes, quarries, rivers, beaches, and oceans. Some sites have access charges, and paying for parking at a local lake or even paying for two days of boat dives is part of the checkout dive costs. Sometimes it is appropriate to take new students to warm-water diving destinations so they have a pleasurable experience their first time diving. In this case, planning dive trip travel and accommodation costs is a must. Here are estimated costs:

State parks, quarries, sinks, lakes, etc.	Free-$30
Two-tank boat dive	$25-80

8. *Classroom/pool fees:* Some YMCAs charge programs facility usage fees or rental fees. However, it is not a good idea for a YMCA to charge fees for its own in-house programs by making an instructor pay a portion of the YMCA Scuba class fee to the facility. It also is not a good idea to have an outside group rent the YMCA's facilities for scuba. As mentioned earlier, this can jeopardize the YMCA's tax-exempt property status.

9. *Miscellaneous costs:* These include the following:

Advertising

Equipment replacement and maintenance

Handouts

Visual aids

Safety equipment (first aid, oxygen, "soft-shot" weights)

Mailings

Expected surplus after breaking even

Once you have listed the cost for each of the previous items, analyze different average numbers of students and locate the break-even point. For example, you may find that with 6 students all costs are met and with 10 students there is excess money. Your agreement with the instructor will determine how the excess or loss will be shared. You must charge the students at a rate that will provide enough revenue so that the class meets students' expectations, based on the size of the course you intend to market, yet remains competitive. If you feel you will have fewer than 6 students in your courses, the charges will need to be higher to cover the costs than if you expect to average 10 students.

The YMCA should always collect course fees, not the instructor or the dive shop. If you allow the instructor or dive shop to collect them, you have little control over accounting. Here are some ways this arrangement could go wrong:

• The instructor pays the YMCA for six divers enrolled in the course, but there are eight students in the water. When asked by the aquatics director why there are two extra divers, the instructor says that those are his assistants. However, the two divers are in fact assistants in training who have paid him so they could learn how to become assistant instructors or divemasters. The instructor has no intention of paying the YMCA for them because they are his "assistants."

• Four divers are enrolled and paid for, but the aquatics director notices there are five students in the class. The instructor states that the extra student is making up a pool session he missed. What the aquatics director does not know is that the instructor charges for make-up sessions and does not pay the YMCA.

- An instructor is supposed to pay the YMCA at the end of the course. However, two students drop out before the last class because of illness, so the instructor does not pay for them because they do not show up on the certification forms.

The YMCA should collect the fees, then be responsible for paying the instructor(s) and any other agreed-on costs. You can choose to pay the instructor per student, per hour, or per course, or pay a percentage of fees. You may also contract with the instructor or hire her or him on as staff. (Scuba instructors are rarely volunteers, unless the YMCA is paying for all costs and annual expenses.) Carefully review these choices with your accounting and human resource departments to determine your professional relationship with and payment plan for an instructor.

Despite these warnings, though, it is possible to be flexible in your financial arrangements with instructors when it is to your mutual benefit. In one case, a YMCA Scuba instructor who was being charged a rental fee for the pool by his YMCA felt that, because YMCA standards required 12 hours of pool time, he would have to price the course too high. The instructor argued that since most people were coming through his dive shop to learn scuba, it was likely that most were not members of the YMCA. He would guarantee at least one new YMCA member per class if the YMCA would not charge him rental fees. If he did not get a scuba student to join the YMCA, then he would have to pay the fees. It turns out that over four years, he only had two classes from which he did not generate a new member. In addition, the new members were often couples or families.

Common Problems in Scuba Programs

Here are some common instructor and student problems that you can avoid by recognizing and preparing for them ahead of time.

Instructor Problems

In most instances, scuba instructors are scuba professionals, not YMCA professionals. They have been teaching courses their way for a long time. Now, as they teach within a YMCA setting, they may have to conduct their scheduling, finances, and advertising differently to reflect proper YMCA procedures. Instructors may have the following complaints.

My YMCA does not pay me in a reasonable amount of time.

Scuba courses commonly have many expenses. Either the instructor or the YMCA may pay these program-related costs, which include equipment rental, air tank refills, student textbooks, open-water dive fees, and certification card fees. However, if the YMCA chooses to reimburse an instructor for these costs but does not do so in a timely manner, it places a financial burden on the instructor. One way to handle this is to have the YMCA pay for all associated program expenses directly and then pay the instructor for teaching.

My aquatics director wants me to have a lifeguard on duty during scuba classes, but I am SLAM Rescue certified.

According to the YMCA of the USA *Principles of YMCA Aquatics Manual*, lifeguards are to be present at all times when the facility/pool is in operation. This is part of the YMCA's risk management and accident preparedness plans, and it should not be modified for scuba classes.

Lap swimming keeps getting more hours and more lanes, and it is interfering with my scuba classes.

Facility management is often dictated by the more popular programs that members request.

My YMCA tells me that classes will be canceled if not enough people sign up.

Often, if a YMCA is handling all program costs, including payment to the instructor, the YMCA has the right to maintain registration minimums. However, if an instructor handles course registration, she or he may run a course with only a couple of students.

My aquatics director is leaving and the new aquatics director is not interested in scuba programming.

This may be a stressful situation for instructors, as the new aquatics director might send them on their way or cause other problems. The best way for instructors to handle such a change is to meet with the new aquatics director and offer a proposal. They should show numbers and figures that justify retaining the program. They should also keep letters of appreciation from students to share, and they can offer to volunteer for other YMCA programs (such as helping with YMCA Lifeguarding or conducting "I Tried Scuba" during open houses). Instructors should develop a relationship with the new aquatics director quickly and professionally.

Student Problems

Students may also have some common complaints about scuba classes.

I did not know there would be hidden costs in the scuba class.

When advertising YMCA Scuba courses, disclose all required course costs before the students commit to training. See "Course Costs and Budgeting" for guidelines on scuba programming expenses.

I did not pass the swim evaluation. Can I get my money back?

We strongly recommend that when a student cannot pass the swim evaluation before taking classes, he or she be trained in snorkeling or skin diving. If necessary, you may want to recommend that the student take a YMCA Swim Lessons course. Your local YMCA's policy on payment will dictate if refunds should be made and, if so, how they should be handled.

I was required to get a physical. Is that part of the course?

Each student is required to complete a YMCA Scuba Medical History Questionnaire before any in-water activities. In cases where a positive response (yes) is indicated on the Medical History Questionnaire, the student must receive approval from a physician to dive. Some instructors even require all their students to get a physical and obtain a physician's approval before beginning in-water activities, especially scuba classes.

I still have not received my scuba certification card.

Certifications may take as long as a month to be processed and sent back to the instructors, facilities, or students. Ask instructors to turn in YMCA Scuba Certification Forms immediately after all required coursework has been completed. Tell them not to hold up turning in the forms for an entire class to wait for one student to make up incomplete portions of the course. This delays certification of the rest of the students. One way to reduce pressure from students who want their certifications quickly is to have the instructor issue a temporary card that is good for 30 days and allows the cardholder to go on dive charters, rent scuba equipment, and get air for scuba tanks. Temporary cards are available through YMCA of the USA Scuba.

Tips for Running Scuba Programs

As an aquatics director, take these steps to ensure quality scuba programs and to protect your YMCA from liability:

- Ensure that certifications are turned in promptly after class completion.
- Pass out surveys or questionnaires to participants about their program likes and dislikes and their aquatic interests.
- Make sure your facility is listed as an additional insured on the instructor's professional liability insurance.
- Ensure that student waivers and releases are completed and that the facility is listed on the YMCA Scuba Statement of Understanding Waiver and Release forms.
- Make sure that equipment maintenance records exist for all rented or owned scuba equipment used during the course.
- Do not teach abbreviated courses. As mentioned earlier, some agencies are promoting two- or three-day certification courses for new divers. YMCA Scuba standards maintain a minimum of 12 hours for classroom work, 12 hours for pool work, and approximately 8 hours for open-water checkout dives. This adds up to an approximately 32-hour course for the entry-level scuba diver (Open Water Scuba Diver).

Follow the *Principles of YMCA Aquatics Manual*.

- Have lifeguards on duty during scuba courses.
- Use soft-shot weights. These diving weights use lead shot in a heavy-duty bag instead of molded hard lead. If dropped from a weight belt, these soft-shot weights are easier on participants' feet and toes, as well as on pool tiles.
- Set up rinse stations for rinsing off equipment after pool and open-water sessions.
- Place plastic or rubber pool deck mats at poolside in areas where scuba equipment will be set up and disassembled.
- Have first aid kits and oxygen on hand and available for unexpected diving emergencies. For more information on oxygen use for aquatic emergencies, contact the YMCA of the USA or Divers Alert Network at 800-446-2671, as they specialize in oxygen first aid for scuba accidents.
- Check instructors' and assistants' credentials annually.

The following elements help ensure a successful scuba program:

- A scuba instructor who strongly displays values of caring, honesty, respect, and responsibility.
- A good relationship between the scuba instructor and the aquatics, program, and executive directors.

- A mutually beneficial financial relationship between the scuba instructor and the YMCA.
- Promotion of classes in YMCA materials, flyers, posters, banners, and on a scuba bulletin board. Promotion should occur both inside and outside the YMCA.
- Offering multiple scuba training courses and hosting a scuba club.
- Involving scuba in other YMCA events such as open houses, fundraisers, and lifeguard training.

BIBLIOGRAPHY

YMCA of the USA. 2000. *YMCA scuba standards and procedures (2000 edition)*. Atlanta: YMCA Scuba.

YMCA Synchronized Swimming

Synchronized swimming, or "synchro," is a combination of rhythmic swimming and gymnastics performed in the water, all set to music. Participants must have overall body strength and agility, grace, split-second timing, and the ability to interpret music.

Synchronized swimming has two main components: figures and routines. *Figures* are movements similar to gymnastic skills that are performed in the water. *Routines* are combinations of swimming strokes and propulsion techniques with figures and variations of figures.

We begin by describing the different ways you can use the program: as part of other aquatics programs, as a developmental program, as a competitive program, and for water shows. We then talk about the five areas in which participants need to be prepared to perform synchronized swimming at any level. This is followed by information on staffing and facility and equipment requirements. Next is safety, both in the handling of electrical equipment and in training. We end with a few words on budgeting and additional resources.

PROGRAM OVERVIEW

Although synchronized swimming has been around since the early 1900s, it did not become part of YMCA aquatics programs until the 1970s. In the YMCA Synchronized Swimming program, participants can

- learn the fundamental skills of synchronized swimming and gain an understanding of the sport,
- find opportunities to clarify and develop their personal values, and
- provide service to others through leadership development.

The YMCA program lets all interested participants get involved at the level appropriate to their interest and abilities. Your program can include one or more of the following:

- Integration of basic synchronized swimming activities into other existing programs

- A basic developmental program (YMCA Synchronized Swimming program)
- A competitive program

Participants can also put on water shows and exhibitions.

Aquatics Program Enrichment

Synchronized swimming activities can be incorporated into many other YMCA programs, as well as community groups or organizations. Here are some possibilities:

- YMCA Swim Lessons classes (basic skills are included as part of the progression to each level)
- YMCA Guide/Princess and YMCA Trailblazer/Mate
- YMCA Water Fitness
- YMCA swim teams
- YMCA teen clubs
- School-age child care
- Boy Scout/Girl Scout troops
- Day camp
- High school swim teams
- Active older adult clubs

When talking to the leaders of these programs, you may find some barriers to integrating synchro activities into their programs. Here are some common barriers and solutions:

Barrier	Solution
A perception that the sport is too hard	Connect synchronized swimming to commonly known aquatic skills. If necessary, modify activities for the group.
Getting enough pool time	Look at how a synchronized swimming program can share pool space effectively with other aquatics programs. See if you can get access to other pools.
The expense of the equipment	Purchase only a minimum amount of equipment until the program grows.
Lack of participants	Teach the skills within aquatics classes or as a separate class.

You will want to be able to discuss these barriers with program leaders and offer specific answers to help them.

YMCA Synchronized Swimming Program

YMCA Synchronized Swimming program components include skill development, safety education, sport foundation, and character development.

- *Skill development:* Instruction involves teaching participants sound mechanical principles using innovative instructional techniques, as well as increasing their physical fitness. The skills are divided into three levels and include the components of propulsion, body positions, figures, and routine skills.

• *Personal safety:* Participants are assisted in developing sound safety concepts that are intended to reduce accidents and add to the enjoyment of the sport, including pool safety, physical fitness, proper breathing/breath control, and care of skin and hair.

• *Personal growth:* Each level of achievement contains character development issues such as the following and suggestions for how to deal with them:

a. Trying your best

b. Discipline

c. Winning, losing, and sportsmanship

d. Teamwork and fair play

e. Fair judging and positive attitude

f. Cooperation

It also includes skills important to synchronized swimming, such as moving to rhythms or identifying music themes.

Table 21.1 shows the activities involved at the different levels of the synchronized swimming program.

Synchronized Swimming Competitive Program

You can host novice or mock competitions in-house between different classes or among other YMCAs in your area. If you are interested in competing, be sure to review the "Rules That Govern YMCA Competitive Sports." This should be used as the framework for developing rules for any YMCA youth sport program. For basic information on how to judge synchronized swimming events, see *Synchro Intro* or other resources available from United States Synchronized Swimming (USA Synchro).

You can also be more formal and offer sanctioned competitions. United States Synchronized Swimming, the national governing body for synchronized swimming, provides leadership and resources for the promotion and growth of synchronized swimming. To compete in USA Synchro competitions, teams and members must be registered. They are then eligible to compete at any and all levels of USA Synchro competition. All USA Synchro competitions must be sanctioned by the USA Synchro. Additional certification and training are also available from USA Synchro, including coaching clinics and officials certifications.

Water Shows and Exhibitions

Water shows are popular and can be done in conjunction with your YMCA's open house or other special events. These events are ways to demonstrate and celebrate the students' progress and to show off your program. Your day camp students may want to put on a show for Parents' Night, or it may be an opportunity for your classes to perform for campaigners during your annual sustaining campaign. This can also be a fun activity for children in your Y-Guides and Y-Princesses programs.

Combine participants from several different programs to put on a water show. For example, you could have groups from water fitness, an after-school group, an aquatics leaders club, a Flying Fish class, and synchro classes each do a number to put on a show for friends and families.

Table 21.1 Levels of the YMCA Synchronized Swimming Program

Components	Level 1—Oyster	Level 2—Lobster	Level 3—Dolphin
Propulsion	Front crawl and variations	Backstroke and variations	Side flutter
	Sidestroke and variations	Breaststroke and variations	Eggbeater
	Standard scull, stationary and headfirst sculls	Alligator/barrel sculls	Dolphin scull
	Foot-first scull	Lobster/paddle sculls	Support scull
	Canoe scull, stationary and headfirst	Torpedo	
Body positions	Back layout	Front layout	Vertical tuck
	Tuck	Front pike	Circle (dolphin arch)
	Back pike	Ballet leg	
	Bent knee	Split	
Figures	Log roll	Back pike somersault	Kip
	Back tuck somersault	Front walkover	Porpoise
	Tub and variations	Jumpover	Somersub
	Oyster	Ballet leg	Dolphin
			Dolphin, foot-first
Routine skills	Propulsion combinations	Marching (alternate bent knees to music)	Eggbeater to strokes to eggbeater
	Propulsion with figures	Breaststroke to front pike	Figures to strokes: torpedo, descending, ballet leg
	Floats	Sidestroke to backstroke	Eggbeater to figures: front pike, back tuck, ballet leg
	Swimming with others	Backstroke to ballet leg	
Personal safety	Pool rules and safety	Posture	Proper use of music and sound levels
	Use of goggles and nose clips	Physical fitness	Avoiding overuse injuries
	Proper breath control	Stretching	Paying attention underwater
Personal growth	Always try your best	Cooperation	Sportsmanship
	Discipline	Positive attitude	Teamwork
	Moving to rhythms	Counting music	Identifying themes in music

To prepare for a water show, consider the following:

- Preparation time
- Themes and music
- Casting and choreography
- Costuming
- Practice and performance
- Programs and publicity
- Budget

A resource that may assist you with more detailed planning on water shows is *Synchro Show Biz*, available from USA Synchro.

PREPARATIONS TO "SYNCH"

The following areas—flexibility, strength and core control, dance and movement exploration, music appreciation, and swimming—are important in preparing individuals for any kind of synchronized swimming activities. Your instructors/coaches need to work with participants in these areas regardless of whether they are part of a beginner's program or a team preparing for competition.

Flexibility

Flexibility in the shoulders, back, and hips is important for success and comfort in synchronized swimming activities. The adjusted positions for standard strokes, the variety in arm movements, and the lines created and in constant change in figures and hybrids require that all joints be flexible. Since movements from position to position are not made with the support of a stable base, the movements require active, not passive, flexibility. Stretching helps prepare the joints to be mobile and also protects them from injury. Children are naturally flexible and require less stretching than elderly women and most men.

Strength and Core Control

The core muscles of the body stabilize or anchor and move the center pillar ("tree trunk") of the body while the limbs are describing other forms and are constantly in motion. Strength in the core also allows the trunk to change shape (full spinal mobility) and return to a solid center without undue strain. Swimmers use the pelvic tilt to bring the body into the described "plumb line" required in vertical positions, with an imaginary line running through the ears, shoulders, hips, and ankles.

Dance and Movement Exploration

Dance and movement exploration activities are important because they help the participants understand how music dictates movements. Presentation, creative expression, flexibility, and fluidity of movement are improved through dance activity.

Music Appreciation

Feeling rhythm and following music are important skills for synchronized swimming, as participants must perform movements in synchrony with each other and with the music. The music should dictate the movement, both in tempo and kind. Quick movements should be accompanied by staccato music, long slow movements by flowing music; strong movements should be matched to loud segments, and level swimming to softer segments.

Swimming

Participants can do many synchronized swimming activities without being able to swim or swim well, but they need swimming skills if they are to advance in the sport. Building endurance and perfecting strokes enhances participants' ability to learn and perform synchronized swimming skills.

STAFF

You will want to hire a YMCA Synchronized Swimming Instructor for your synchronized swimming program. Certified instructors have the knowledge and teaching skills necessary to teach a YMCA synchronized swimming class, incorporate synchronized swimming into other YMCA programs, or coach a beginning-level team.

The prerequisites for obtaining certification as a YMCA Synchronized Swimming Instructor include the following:

- A minimum age of 16
- Current YMCA Lifeguard certification (current CPR and first aid certifications must be maintained)
- Certification in Principles of YMCA Aquatic Leadership *or* Basic Aquatic Leadership Course or Fundamentals of YMCA Swim Lessons *or* YMCA Water Fitness Instructor
- Recommended: Certification in Working With 5- to 9-Year-Olds or Working With 10- to 14-Year-Olds, depending on the age group(s) in your program

Instructors must renew their certification every three years and keep their CPR, first aid, and YMCA Lifeguard or YMCA Aquatic Safety Assistant (YASA) certifications current.

You may also want to have a synchronized swimming trainer on your staff. Certified trainers can certify staff members or volunteers in Principles of YMCA Aquatic Leadership and YMCA Synchronized Swimming Instructor.

The prerequisites for becoming a trainer are these:

- A minimum age of 21
- Current YMCA Lifeguard *or* YMCA Aquatic Safety Assistant certification (current CPR and first aid certifications must be maintained)
- Current YMCA Synchronized Swimming Instructor certification with at least 50 hours of experience teaching YMCA Synchronized Swimming after becoming a certified instructor or YMCA Swim Lessons Trainer
- Certification in Principles of YMCA Aquatic Leadership *or* Basic Aquatic Leadership Course *or* Fundamentals of YMCA Swim Lessons
- Certification in Program Trainer Orientation
- A completed trainer candidate application that includes a statement from the executive director verifying that the candidate has taught 300 hours of aquatics that included at least 50 hours of teaching as a certified YMCA Synchronized Swimming Instructor

Note: Successful completion of the trainer course automatically renews the Synchronized Swimming Instructor certification. This certification is valid as long as YMCA Lifeguard or YMCA Aquatic Safety Assistant certification (renewable every two years), YMCA Synchronized Swimming Instructor certification (renewable every three years), and CPR and first aid certifications are kept current.

Once you have hired instructors, you will want to make sure they properly plan for your program. This includes doing lesson and session planning, just as they would in your YMCA Swim Lessons programs. Discuss any questions they may have about developing lesson plans. You may want to evaluate their plans and suggest alternative ideas. Also discuss with your instructors the Personal Growth and Personal Safety activities that can be done within the class so students achieve needed skills.

Observe instructors and remind them to keep their classes developmentally appropriate for the age of the students in the class. Encourage them to discuss and plan what they can do to motivate participation by their age groups. Ask them to describe why their methods would work based on the characteristics of that age group. If instructors need additional information on age-group characteristics, refer them to the *Teaching Swimming Fundamentals* manual.

FACILITY REQUIREMENTS

If you are running a basic program, your facility and equipment needs should be minimal. However, if you want to develop a comprehensive program that includes competition, you may want to know the facility requirements from United States Synchronized Swimming, shown in table 21.2.

EQUIPMENT

Your equipment needs vary depending on your program and situation. Here are some likely ones:

- Music/rhythm system: Tom-tom, tambourine, tapper (a length of pipe and a metal spoon), "boom box," whistle, cassette tapes (both as sold and edited for class use), a transformer, a cassette player (variable-speed), air speakers, underwater speaker(s) with current control box, a microphone, a metronome. (Most useful music has a simple 2/4 or 4/4 count.)
- Floating/swimming devices: Kickboards, pull buoys, fins, gallon-sized plastic bottles with caps, water logs, a pole for coaching figures, a "Synchro Suzie" demo doll.
- Resistance bands for strength training.
- A video camera and a portable TV monitor.

Require swimmers to wear bathing caps (or use some method to keep the hair away from their faces) and nose clips.

SAFE USE OF ELECTRICAL EQUIPMENT

Use of electrical equipment can be hazardous, as it can cause dangerous shocks. The probability of getting shocked in or around a swimming pool is probably somewhat less than it is around a normal home, but a shock in the pool environment is more likely to cause severe damage. This is simply due to the greater opportunity for an electrical current to find a path to ground through the body, where it may produce

Table 21.2 Facility Requirements for a Comprehensive Synchronized Swimming Program

Item	Minimum requirements (national competitions)
Pool depth	An area measuring at least 40' × 40' of not less than 9' in depth
Pool length	25 yards
Pool width	Not less than 40'
Pool markings	Standard lane line markings on pool bottom
Overhead lighting	Sufficient to light area with minimum shadows
Underwater lighting	4 lights, 2 on each side, for 25-yard length
Seating	500 total
Deck open space	6'-10' pool to deck wall width on two sides and at least one end
Pool ladders	One ladder/exit
Dressing rooms	One dressing room with space for at least 100-150 participants; 50-100 lockers, shower and toilet facilities, lavatory and mirror, running water, drinking fountain
Restrooms	Four total: 2 for officials; 2 for participants. Additional restroom facilities for spectators.
Electrical capacity	Sufficient voltage and number of outlets to manage the sound, scoring production, and video equipment
Elevated judges' chairs	Seven
Climate control	Sufficient ventilation to accommodate participants and spectators
Water temperature	No less than 80 degrees Fahrenheit
Water clarity	Sufficient clarity for the bottom of the pool to be clearly visible from all angles and elevations, and in compliance with local health standards
Concessions	An area designated for food service, including seating away from the competition area but within the same facility, and well ventilated and lighted for evening events
Parking	Adequate spaces for all USA Synchro officials
Additional practice areas	Open space (hallways, etc.) out of spectator view and inclement conditions. No additional water area required.
Meeting rooms	Five total with one for each of the following: general meetings, scoring/production, hospitality, press, training/first aid

injury or even death. Consequently, it is essential to take more precautions around the pool.

To protect your staff from harm, ask them to follow the procedures listed here. These will reduce shock hazards, keep them from using equipment in dangerous situations, and warn them about specific problems with various pieces of equipment.

Shock Hazards

Your first effort should be to minimize all possibilities of shock hazard. Some of the steps in this effort include the following:

- Keep electrical equipment away from wet areas.
- Keep electrical equipment away from general traffic areas as much as possible.
- Allow only authorized, dry personnel to touch or operate the equipment.
- Use ground fault circuit interrupter (GFCI) receptacles for all electrical power sources.
- Use double-insulated equipment where possible.
- Use equipment fitted with power cords having three wires (one ground wire) and three-prong plugs unless the unit is double insulated.
- Keep equipment and operating personnel dry.
- Wear dry, rubber-soled shoes when handling equipment on even slightly wet decks.
- Make sure that power cords and extension lines are in good repair, with fully intact insulation and grounding wire.
- Keep extension and power cords off the deck and out of the way where possible. If power cords and speaker extension lines are lying on the ground in traffic areas, cover them with rubber mats or tape them to the deck.
- Never use an underwater speaker with a metal shell without its isolation transformer. Having a metal grounding line from the speaker to a water pipe or electrical conduit will provide an additional safety factor.
- Always treat any electrical equipment that is plugged into an electrical circuit with deep respect, no matter how small it is or what kind of power it uses.

Personal Habits and Precautions

Many of the personal precautions that should be habitual are quite obvious, but much too often they are violated.

- Never adjust the sound equipment from in the pool.
- Never adjust the sound equipment when you are wet.
- Never work with the sound equipment in the rain. If there is no shelter, cover the equipment with plastic, and do not touch any metallic part of the equipment, including the microphone.
- If you must adjust anything while wet, stand on a thick rubber mat and wear rubber gloves or keep a plastic or rubber sheet between you and any metallic part you handle.
- Even under dry conditions, always wear shoes or sandals, preferably with rubber soles.

• Do not touch or hold metal structures (ladder stanchions, diving structures, fencing, etc.) while touching metal parts of the sound system or other electrical equipment.

Special Precautions

Here are precautions for specific types of equipment:

• *Speakers:* Speakers and their extension lines are still an electrical component of the sound system, even though the electrical signal going to them may be relatively weak under normal conditions. It is still possible for life-endangering currents to go out to the speakers if a line short should occur within the amplifier. This means that the speakers, both air and underwater, should be handled with the same respect as the rest of the system.

• *Stereo systems:* Home-type stereo components are usually not safe for the pool environment unless they have been modified with proper safety grounding. In some cases, this is impossible without affecting the performance of the system.

• *Underwater speakers:* Always meticulously follow underwater speaker manufacturers' requirements for installation to ensure complete safety in the speakers' use. Install a dynamic coil or plastic-enclosed speakers, with the parallel fuse/resistor line unit required for the warranty. This is primarily done to prevent burning out the speakers with excessive power, but it also provides protection should a line short occur.

Metal-enclosed speakers should have an impedance-matching isolation transformer between the speaker and the amplifier. This transformer is not only a safety precaution, but it also improves the speakers' performance.

• *Clutter:* Keep power cord and speaker extension line clutter to a minimum:

a. Bind multiple lines together.

b. Tape lines down to cover them.

c. Run multiple speaker lines together as far as possible before branching.

d. When running power lines from a wall outlet to a table holding sound equipment, use a single extension cord with multiple outlets. Coil and bind the lines together under the table.

• *Extension lines:* Use completely sealed extension lines, if possible. Inspect the lines frequently for cuts or abrasions that might expose bare wires. Coil the lines properly, using a wind-up reel if possible. If you use the palm-elbow technique instead, make a figure-eight loop instead of a simple loop.

TRAINING SAFETY

Here are some tips for instructors for synchronized swimming safety:

• Tell swimmers to wear nose clips to protect their sinuses. Whether they are beginners or advanced, encourage swimmers to hold their breath while underwater and breathe out through their mouths when surfacing so as to increase their buoyancy. Allow participants to do their swim workouts/warm-ups without wearing their nose clips.

• Do not encourage excessive breath holding. If students do this while swimming underwater, they often lose consciousness, even though they may look as if they are still functioning.

- Slowly build students' capacity to work without oxygen. They can improve their lung function, although some will be genetically more equipped to do so than others.

- Require students to wear goggles, as movement underwater requires them to see clearly in order to see their relationship to the parts of the pool, the other swimmers, and their own body parts.

- Since many skills require the assistance of another swimmer while holding onto the side, standing on the bottom, or treading water, use a buddy/partner system (see chapter 11). Make every effort to match partners in size and physical strength. Watch to make sure that a swimmer, in an effort to assist, is not holding a partner under the water or manipulating the partner's limbs or body parts beyond their range of motion. Use partners only to provide support until students are ready to move into more advanced levels, in which resistance exercises can be introduced.

- Underwater activity prevails in synchronized swimming, so assign instructors and lifeguards to keep watch on all of the swimmers.

- Stretching and extending limbs while performing figures can cause cramping. Tell students who cramp to work out the cramp and regain normal movement before once extending the area again. Having students stretch before and during class sessions helps avoid muscle cramping.

- If the water is not as warm as it should be for a synchronized swimming class, alternate energetic (laps and games) and quiet (figures and skills) activities.

- You may have to provide additional assistance to very young or elderly swimmers until they are familiar with the movements being taught.

- Pool entries for synchro routines are often made by jumping into the water in groups or in rows, either staggered or all together. Carefully set the timing and spacing of entry to the musical counts, taking the depth of the water into account, so as to guard against foot and back injuries.

BUDGETING

When you put together a budget for your synchronized swimming classes, include the following costs:

- Equipment (see previous section)
- Event supplies such as refreshments, decorations, and printed materials
- Costs for instructors/coaches, not only for instructor or coaching time, but also for certification and in-service training

ADDITIONAL RESOURCES

For more information on synchronized swimming, contact United States Synchronized Swimming at 317-237-5700 or **www.usasynchro.org.** Publications available from them include *Synchro Intro: A Guide to Coaching Recreational Synchronized Swimming* and the *Official Rule Book.*

YMCA Wetball/Water Polo

W ater polo has been a part of the YMCA, on and off, for many years. Currently, the YMCA offers programs for Levels one, two, and three of wetball, a lead-up game for water polo, and uses the *United States Water Polo Level One Coaching Manual* for water polo (see figure 22.1 for an introduction to the game of water polo). Water polo skills are also featured in the YMCA Swim Lessons Youth and Adult Aquatics program.

In this chapter we give an overview of the program, then describe program enrichment and the competitive program in more detail. We briefly discuss the role of the volunteer committee, then turn to the role of coaches and how to hire and support staff. If you run a competitive program, you will also need officials, so we also talk about their roles in the game. We follow this with some safety rules and equipment needs, then discuss methods for promoting your program. Finally, we finish with some administrative tips to help you avoid problems and make your program grow.

PROGRAM OVERVIEW

Those who participate in the YMCA Wetball/Water Polo program can

- learn the fundamental skills of water polo and gain an understanding of the sport;
- find opportunities to clarify and develop personal values;
- provide service to others through leadership development;
- play focused on cooperation, not competition;
- be part of an age-appropriate, progressive program;
- promote their own health; and
- involve their families in the program.

The YMCA program lets all interested participants get involved at the level appropriate for their interest and abilities. Your program can include one or more of the following:

- Integration of basic water polo activities into other existing programs
- A basic developmental program

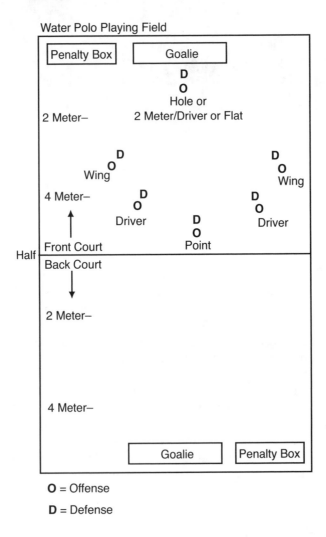

Water Polo Playing Field

O = Offense

D = Defense

1. Positioning:	The basic setup for a polo team is 6 players and 1 goalie in the pool at a time.
2. Start of play:	The beginning of each quarter begins with a sprint to the half. Each team lines up on the wall or 2 meter line to start. When the referee blows the whistle, the two players closest to the referee sprint toward the ball, which is dropped at halfway. The player next to the sprinter also sprints to back them up. The sprinter that reaches the ball first throws the ball back to her or his players to start the play.
	1 2 3 G 4 5 6
3.	**Fouls:** Fouls can be ordinary or major. Ordinary fouls are best understood as minor fouls. Minor fouls are called throughout the game for infringements such as reaching over a player's back if the offensive player isn't holding the ball. Most major fouls occur when a player holds, sinks, or pulls back an opposing player not in control of the ball.

(continued)

Figure 22.1 Introduction to water polo.

4. Free throw: When a player is fouled by a defender (a player on the team defending their goal), he or she receives a free throw. This is a pass that the defender may not block or interfere with in any manner. The player receiving a free throw has three seconds to put the ball in play, either by passing to a teammate, dribbling the ball, or popping it in the air to himself or herself. The ball must be touched by another player after a free throw is awarded prior to a shot being taken.

5. Shot clock: The clock that displays the time of possession in which a team must take a shot (also called a possession clock). Teams have 35 seconds to shoot the ball during each possession. If they do not, the ball will be turned over to the opposing team.

6. Dribble: The method a player uses to swim with the ball.

7. Ejection: A major foul that requires a player to go to the penalty area for 20 seconds (also called a kickout). This results in a 6-on-5 play. The player may return to the game only when the referee or desk waves him or her back in. The player may not push off the wall or deck to do so.

8. Penalty shot: A shot awarded to the offense when a defender commits a major foul within four meters of his or her own goal. Any offensive player currently in the pool (no goalies) may take a free shot at the goal when the referee blows his or her whistle. He or she may take it no closer than four meters, and he or she may not fake or delay. The defending goalie may not move to block the shot until the referee blows his or her whistle.

9. Red: The period of time immediately prior to the expiration of the shot clock or game clock. Some teams yell "red" when either of these clocks indicates 10 seconds or less.

10. Press: A type of defense in which everyone is covered tightly, man-to-man.

11. Zone defense: A type of defense in which players are assigned an area to defend. Defensive players must assume responsibility for covering any offensive players entering their area.

Figure 22.1 *(continued)*

- A competitive program
- A leadership recognition program providing instructor and volunteer training and certification

AQUATICS PROGRAM ENRICHMENT

Water polo can be a great addition to many YMCA programs, as well as some community groups or organizations. Here are some possibilities:

- Swim Lessons (basic skills are included as part of the progression to each level)
- Guide/Princess and Trailblazer/Mates programs
- Water fitness
- Swim teams
- Teen clubs

- School-age child care
- Day camp
- Lifeguarding
- Master swim teams
- Boy Scout/Girl Scout troops
- High school swim teams

You may find some barriers to combining water polo with these other programs. Here are some common ones:

Barrier	Solution
A perception that the sport is too hard	Connect water polo to commonly known aquatic or game skills. If necessary, modify rules for the group.
Getting enough pool time	Look at how a water polo program can share pool space effectively with other aquatics programs. See if you can get access to other pools.
The expense of the equipment	Purchase only a minimum amount of equipment until the program grows.
Lack of participants	Teach the skills within aquatics classes or as a separate class. Play interclass games, rotating teams.
Facility restrictions in indoor/outdoor pools	If your pool has glass enclosures, add netting to keep the ball from hitting the glass or be sure you have shatter-resistant glass.

Discuss these and other types of barriers that could limit the use of water polo programs/activities within other programs and what could be done to break them down.

While many swim teams and their coaches are able to appreciate the skills needed for playing water polo, few communities offer water polo and few swim coaches are familiar with the sport. Many swim coaches have been led to believe that water polo is detrimental to the performance of their swimmers—that it can affect stroke technique or increase the potential for shoulder or knee injury. Hold a presentation to educate swim coaches about water polo. Here is a list of reasons why water polo can be advantageous for swim teams:

Financial	By offering a team sport in addition to your competitive swim club, your program will appeal to a broader range of athletes and actually increase your numbers.
Retention	Water polo adds diversity to your aquatics program, helping to reduce the attrition rate that occurs from age-group burnout.
Conditioning	With proper workouts, water polo can maintain aerobic conditioning, improve anaerobic capacity, and increase the overall strength of your swimmers. The constant stopping, starting, and changing direction involved with the play create conditioning

	benefits difficult to simulate during normal swim practices.
Camaraderie	Water polo promotes an interdependency among swimmers, due to the high degree of teamwork necessary to play the sport.
Athletic agility	Water polo improves overall coordination and hand-eye skills, which will help make your swimmers better athletes.
Coach's sanity	Coaches experience burn out too. Water polo provides you with an opportunity to switch your focus from 10,000-yard workouts to something new, different, and exciting. It also gives you an opportunity for more interaction with your athletes.
Parents' sanity	Variety is important for parents too. With water polo, children are constantly involved with the action and the games run less than an hour.
Mental toughness	A water polo player may experience times during the game when he feels he is too exhausted to move. However, to prevent his opponent from scoring, the player may need to push himself further than he believes possible. This teaches him how to go beyond his perceived limits, giving him added confidence the next time he reaches the same situation.
Water polo aids swimmers	Consider some of the great swimmers who played water polo at a younger age or in college: Roy Saari, Don Schollander, Gary Hall, Brian Goodell, Jill Sterkel, Kurt Krumpholz, Amy Caulkins, John Naber, Mark Spitz, Tim Shaw, Dave and Joe Bottom, Robin Leamy, Joel Thomas, Matt Biondi, and Pablo Morales.

Water polo is fun!

So you can plan when water polo activities can best enhance both sports, here are the typical swim season periods:

- Summer age-group swim team: late May to early August
- High school swim seasons: early February to late May
- Year-round age-group seasons run as follows:

  a. YMCA Short Course: September-March

  b. YMCA Long Course: May-July

  c. USS Short Course: October-March

  d. USS Long Course: April-July

Most high school and college men's water polo seasons run from late August through November. College women's seasons run February through April. Many

U.S. Water Polo programs run throughout the summer months (June through August) where national age-group and open competition is available. Most tournaments are offered throughout the country during these months.

WATER POLO DEVELOPMENTAL PROGRAM

The YMCA has a developmental program for wetball, a lead-up game for water polo. Table 22.1 shows the skills taught, and Table 22.2 describes the guidelines for each of the three levels of wetball.

These are guidelines for the three levels of the YMCA Wetball program. They may be adjusted to work within your pool specifications and swimmers' abilities. Most important, remember that YMCA Wetball is a developmental sport. Coaches should encourage involvement and team play at all times.

If you have a high school water polo team in your area, be sure to contact the coach. Let him or her know you are starting a developmental program and see if she or he can help you with it.

When you orient parents to the Water Polo program, make it clear that, rather than emphasizing competition with others, you will be focusing children's attention on self-improvement, which is developmentally appropriate and mentally healthy for them. Educating parents about this is basic to gaining their acceptance for this approach.

WATER POLO COMPETITIVE PROGRAM (LEAGUES)

Water polo competition is organized locally through national-level events. Use the YMCA "Rules that Govern YMCA Competitive Sports" as the framework for developing rules around any YMCA youth sport program.

In water polo, organized competition (*United States Water Polo Level One Coaching Manual*, p. 48) is coordinated through USA Water Polo (USWP), the national governing body for water polo in the United States. Three types of organized competition exist:

1. Head to head
2. League play
3. Tournament format

The format you choose will depend on the type of program you want to have at your YMCA.

If you would like to organize local competition within the YMCA, you can create leagues of independent YMCAs or offer metro association competition.

Additional information on setting up tournaments can be found in *Organizing Successful Tournaments*, available from the YMCA Program Store (Item no. 0-88011-955-1).

If you want your program to compete outside the YMCA, you will want to obtain information from USWP on how to register your team and find out about other programs in your area. All USWP-registered teams and members are eligible to compete at any and all levels. USWP-registered YMCA teams, programs, and players are also eligible. All USWP competition must be sanctioned by USWP. (Membership and registration is only required if you want your team to be a part of USWP competition.)

Table 22.1	Suggested YMCA Wetball Skills		
Level one	**Level two**	**Level three**
Walk/run in water with recovery	Bounce in water/some swim skills	Swimming proficiency
Catch ball with 2 hands	Catch ball with 2 hands	Catch ball with 1 hand
Throw ball with 2 hands	Throw ball with 1 hand	Throw ball with 1 hand
Dribble ball while walking	Dribble while walking/swimming	Dribble while swimming
Learn positions	Learn positions and be able to move easily to them	Play all positions
Shooting: RB, flip, push	Shoot ball (RB, flip, push, T-up, sweep)	Shoot ball (RB, flip push, T-up, sweep, backhand)
Offense/defense	Offense/defense/fast break/set-up	Offense/defense/fast break/set-up/ 6 on 5 /drills
Vocabulary of water polo	Physical principles and how to use them in water polo	
Pool/locker room rules	Wetball II rules	
The role of the referees and what the flag means		
Wetball I rules		Wetball III/USWP rules
Value sessions theme: "Always try your best."	Value sessions theme: Winning, losing, sportsmanship	Values sessions theme: Leadership, teamwork, and fair play

VOLUNTEER COMMITTEE

Volunteers are important to the success of the program. Once you have decided the type of water polo program your YMCA will have, you can determine your need for volunteers (see chapter 5 for more on recruiting volunteers). You may want to develop a volunteer committee to assist you, much as in a swim team program (see chapter 17). Such a committee is an effective way to involve families in the program.

However, volunteer committees related to competitive teams can easily get out of control. This may be due to poor recruiting, lack of orientation, inadequate supervision, or the committee structure. Stay connected to the committee and attend its meetings.

STAFF

Good coaching is essential to water polo, a sport that is not widely known, so we start by describing what coaches should be prepared to do. We then give some suggestions on what qualities and training to look for in coaching candidates, on interview questions, and on how to monitor and encourage staff after they have been hired

Table 22.2	Wetball Programs		
	YMCA Wetball Level one	**YMCA Wetball Level two**	**YMCA Wetball Level three**
Ages	6 and up	8 and up	9 and up
Playing field	Shallow water (widths approx. 20-40 feet)	Shallow and/or deep water (widths approx. 20-40 feet)	Shallow/deep or all deep (lengths: 25 yards-30 meters)
Swimming ability	None needed	Able to swim 100 yards	Able to swim 500 yards
Number of players	6-15 per coach/instructor 5-7 players in the pool at a time	8-15 per coach/instructor 5-7 players in the pool at a time	8-20 per coach/instructor 7 players in the pool at a time
Skills developed	Pick up the ball, dribbling, passing, shooting, basic rule and game strategies, and game etiquette.	Passing, shooting, offensive and defensive strategies, 6 on 5, and game etiquette.	Passing, shooting, offensive and defensive strategies, 6 on 5, tournament play and U. S. Water Polo rules.
Game description	Level I Wetball is for the novice swimmer, but the game can be played without any swimming ability. The objectives are to introduce basic skills of water polo and correct positioning, and to prepare the player for actual game play. This is achieved through basic drills, game-type activities, and lots of encouragement. Adaptation for this level may be necessary depending on age/skill levels.	Level II Wetball is for the intermediate swimmer. Ideally, a shallow/deep pool is used to allow the swimmers the opportunity to learn to play at both ends. Emphasize offensive and defensive drills, along with actual game involvement. Introduce 6-on-5 play with rules enforced by referees.	Level III Wetball is for the advanced swimmer, and is played preferably, but not necessarily, in an all-deep pool. Swimmers should continue to refine their skills with more advanced drills and play in leagues or tournaments. This level should follow U. S. Water Polo rules, if their skill levels allow. Coaches should encourage equal play among all players, varying positions in order to teach all aspects of the game.
Equipment	Youth Mikasa 6008 water polo ball, small basketball, or nerfball Goals Water polo caps recommended. Goalies should wear water polo caps for protection. Swim caps for all other players as minimum for identification.	Youth Mikasa 6008 water polo ball, small basketball, or nerfball Goals Water polo caps recommended. Goalies should wear water polo caps for protection. Swim caps for all other players as minimum for identification.	Youth Mikasa 6008 water polo ball Goals Water polo caps

The Role of Coaches

The coach is the single most important adult leader for his or her players. He or she is responsible for making sure that team members develop positive attitudes about fair play and respect for others while learning specific sport skills and having fun. The coach teaches players about the rules of the game and helps them develop important values about life. The sport skills themselves are merely tools to achieve something far more significant—helping children reach their full potential.

Good coaches realize that they have a unique opportunity to make a difference in a child's life. Effective YMCA coaches fully support the YMCA Youth Super Sports philosophy in their attitude and behavior at practices, games, and events. The values of fair play, respect for others, and teamwork are encouraged throughout all encounters with team members. Coaches realize their responsibility for making YMCA Youth Super Sports a family program and regularly communicating information to parents, encouraging their involvement through specific activities.

Coaches model a positive attitude toward fitness by providing adequate warm-up and conditioning sessions and discussing healthy lifestyles. They are safety-conscious and knowledgeable about procedures for handling injuries, and they have the planning and organizational skills needed to ensure good use of practice time. They have knowledge of their sport through participation and observation and are enthusiastic individuals, always willing to learn new things. Good coaches are people who enjoy working with and relating to children at a particular skill and age level. They are motivators, teachers, and role models for their players.

Figure 22.2 is a checklist of coaches' responsibilities. For more on coaching, see the *YMCA Youth Super Sports Director's Guide* (3rd ed.).

Hiring and Supporting Staff

When you search for water polo coaches, look for those with these qualities:

- Experience in playing or coaching water polo
- Ability to keep winning in perspective
- Experience in working with children
- Awareness of safety concerns
- Experience in coaching sports

To be trained as a YMCA Wetball/Water Polo Instructor, an individual must be

- at least 16 years old;
- hold current YMCA Lifeguard, CPR (including adult, child, and infant), and first aid certifications; and
- have completed one of the following courses: Fundamentals of Teaching YMCA Swimming or Principles of YMCA Aquatic Leadership or Basic Aquatic Leadership.

We also recommend that a coach be certified as a YMCA Swim Lessons Youth and Adult Instructor. Also, depending on the age group involved in your program, completion of one or more of the following courses is recommended:

- Working with 5- to 9-year-olds
- Working with 10- to 14-year-olds
- Working with 15- to 18-year-olds

General

✔ Attend preseason Coaches' Training.

✔ Participate in the Kickoff, Midseason Event, and End-of-Season Celebration.

✔ Attend family events planned for the team.

✔ Serve as a resource person for clinics.

✔ Share ideas and concerns with the YMCA aquatics director.

Practice Sessions

✔ Make sure parents and team members are aware of the dates, times, and locations of practice sessions and are given adequate notice of changes.

✔ Prepare for practice in advance; develop a lesson plan based on review and progress from previous practices (know what's been covered, what needs to be taught, etc.).

✔ Check the condition of both equipment and site for safety hazards before beginning practice.

✔ Make sure a first aid kit is available at all practice sessions.

✔ Make sure the necessary equipment is available.

✔ Follow outline for practice session, allowing enough time to cover all components.

✔ Allow for as much practice time per individual as possible; avoid making players stand around waiting.

✔ Be aware of the whereabouts of all team members during practice; remain at the site until all players have left (especially if using a non-Y or off-site facility); check with parents of absent players about their children's whereabouts.

✔ Reward 100% attendance at practice.

✔ Get to know team members personally; always call them by name.

✔ Keep a current list of parent contact numbers in case of injury or illness of a child.

✔ Help players set individual goals and work toward these goals.

✔ Teach the skills of the sport and the importance of physical fitness and a healthy lifestyle.

✔ Lead discussions about the values emphasized by the YMCA Youth Super Sports philosophy by asking questions and introducing problems and situations for the players to deal with.

✔ Encourage parent involvement by providing volunteer opportunities for parents and by scheduling a family activity for team members.

✔ During practice scrimmages, have team members take turns officiating.

✔ Maintain a positive attitude and enthusiasm toward practicing.

✔ Inform the assistant coach if you cannot attend a practice, making sure that he or she has the appropriate lesson plan and other necessary information.

✔ Abide by the guidelines for practice sessions as set by the local YMCA.

(continued)

Figure 22.2 Checklist of responsibilities for coaches.

Games

✔ Require team members to arrive early enough for an adequate warm-up prior to the start of the game.

✔ Give a brief pregame talk:

- Put the importance of the game in its proper perspective.
- Remind players of the skills they've been practicing and the individual goals they've set, and encourage them to concentrate on performing these skills rather than on what their opponents may do.
- Emphasize the need to think and play as a team and not to criticize teammates.
- Stress the importance of respecting the officials' decisions.
- Encourage players to have fun.

✔ Demonstrate respect for the officials:

- Don't criticize or insult an official in front of children, parents, or other coaches.
- Don't assume an official intentionally made a mistake.
- Help control parents and spectators during games.
- Make sure that team members cooperate with the officials and understand the importance of the officials' role.
- Ask questions when you don't understand a call; listen and accept what the officials say even when you are sure they are wrong.
- Thank the officials after the game and congratulate them on a job well done.
- Assist the officials in their duties.
- Set an example of good sportsmanship for team members and spectators to follow.

✔ Support players during the game:

- Be enthusiastic and compliment everyone, not just the best players, on their good performances.
- Say something positive about players' performance when taking them out of the game, then give them ideas and suggestions for improvement.
- Don't yell advice from the sidelines; give players a chance to make decisions and learn for themselves.
- Correct the mistakes of your players in a quiet, controlled, and positive tone of voice during timeouts.
- Show respect for opponents whether they are winning or losing and view them as partners in the sport.
- Help players calm down when they lose their tempers by staying calm yourself.

✔ Schedule playing time for team members in accordance with YMCA Youth Super Sports philosophy:

- Every team member plays (at least half of the game) regardless of the score.
- Team members have opportunities to play different positions.

✔ After the game, join team members in congratulating the coaches and players of the other team.

✔ Hold a postgame Team Circle to congratulate players on what they did well and to keep the game's outcome in perspective.

Figure 22.2   *(continued)*

Besides asking the usual interview questions described in chapter 5, use some of the following questions that are specific to water polo coaching:

- Describe a water polo drill that helps players learn how to dribble.
- Describe a lesson plan for a workout.
- How will you rotate players to give them equal time during games and scrimmages?
- How can you encourage players who are not as skilled as others?
- What do you think is the most important part of the game?
- What are some safety issues that you must consider during practice?
- How will you increase participation and build the team?
- What relationships do you have with other water polo teams in the area?

After you've hired a coach and other water polo staff, monitor them:

- Attend practices and games.
- Review practice plans and seasonal plans.
- Review game schedules.
- Encourage staff to learn new techniques, strategies, drills, and teaching methodologies.

In-service training for water polo staff might include the following:

- Practicing scenarios and procedures for handling injuries due to balls
- Discussing skill drills and progressions
- Planning game strategies

Support staff by sending them to clinics and trainings.

OFFICIALS

If you have a competitive water polo program, you may need officials. You can develop your own or contact USWP regional referee representatives or zone representatives for information on referee clinics or the availability of area referees. Normally, officials are parents, coaches, or high school or college students. Most are volunteers.

Be sure to train officials, coaches, and players in the rules of the games. Refer to the USA Water Polo rule book and the YMCA Wetball rules so that everyone is clear on the rules. Discuss key rules regarding common fouls and the importance of observing underwater play and what occurs during transitions.

An official's primary responsibility is to enforce and interpret both the rules of the game and the YMCA Youth Super Sports philosophy. The YMCA official must be able to relate to the players, as well as know the rules of the game. Good officials are critical to the success of every YMCA Youth Super Sports program.

Officiating is an area of expertise that requires knowledge of the rules and strategy of sports in order to control the behavior of players, coaches, and spectators. The official must be able to enforce the rules impartially and control the contest so that the game is a positive experience for players. A good official is consistent, fair, decisive, quick-thinking, helpful, safety-conscious, and positive.

Effective officials maintain control of the game and make it fun for everyone involved. They know the signals and the basic rules, including modifications for younger players. They understand how the YMCA Youth Super Sports philosophy is reinforced by their actions. They see themselves as part of the coaching team, stopping the game occasionally to explain a rule or a call and offering tips on basic skills when the ball is not in play.

Few officials come prepared to perform in this way, although they many have extensive knowledge of the game. In a YMCA Youth Super Sports program, officials must know much more than the rules, and it is your responsibility to see that training is offered and required for officials, even those with experience. All officials need an orientation to the YMCA Youth Super Sports philosophy. That is what makes YMCA Youth Super Sports unique and enables it to fulfill the mission of the organization.

Larger, well-developed programs often divide officials into more than one level, each level having different age, experience, and training requirements. For example, a Level 1 official could be a new official with no experience and a minimum age of 16 years, required to attend the YMCA's Officials' Training and permitted to officiate only with a Level 2 official. A Level 2 official could be an official with at least two years' experience as a YMCA official and a minimum age of 18, required to attend and assist in the leadership of the YMCA's Officials' Training and permitted to officiate at any game. (Experienced, well-trained officials provide good role models for new officials.) Such a progressive program for officials can do much to improve the quality of the program.

Figure 22.3 is a checklist of officials' responsibilities. For more on officiating, see the *YMCA Youth Super Sports Director's Guide* (3rd ed.).

Checklist of Responsibilities for Officials

General

✔ Attend preseason Officials' Training.

✔ Participate in the Kickoff, Midseason Event, and End-of-Season Celebration, making a point to get to know participants. (*Note:* Officials are generally encouraged, but not required, to attend all of these events.)

✔ Serve as a resource person for clinics.

✔ Appear at practice sessions on occasion.

✔ Notify the appropriate person (e.g., YMCA aquatics director, season commissioner, or site coordinator) as early as possible if you cannot fulfill a commitment to officiate.

✔ Share your ideas and concerns with the YMCA aquatic director.

Before the Game

✔ Wear your official shirt, penny, or other designated attire that clearly identifies you as a game official.

✔ Bring a whistle and a coin for the toss.

✔ Arrive at least 15 minutes before the game.

✔ Check the playing area for safety hazards.

✔ Check the condition of game equipment, including scoring and timing devices.

✔ Introduce yourself to other officials and discuss duties and interpretations of the rules. Ground rules may be necessary due to facilities, league rules, and safety considerations.

(continued)

Figure 22.3 Checklist of responsibilities for officials.

✔ Meet with coaches or captains prior to the game to arrange the selection of the end of the pool in accordance with the rules.

✔ Meet with the scorekeeper and timekeeper to clarify their responsibilities.

✔ Make sure a current copy of the rules is readily available.

✔ A few minutes prior to the game, call both teams (players and coaches) together; introduce yourself and any other officials, go over the ground rules, encourage both teams to play a good game, and have them shake hands.

✔ Before starting the game, make sure all officials and coaches are ready and that the timekeeper understands when the clock is to be started and stopped.

✔ Start the game on time.

During the Game

✔ Make safety your number one priority; if an injury occurs, follow established procedures for administering first aid and notifying parents and the YMCA aquatics director.

✔ Keep the game moving; do not allow breaks to last too long.

✔ Be alert, quick, and firm when you make a call; players will notice any indecisiveness and begin to question all your decisions.

✔ Do not stand still; move up and down the playing area so you have a full view of the action.

✔ Inform individuals of infractions and how they were committed; take time to explain the calls and help players who may not understand them.

✔ Enforce the rules in an impartial manner and be consistent.

✔ Make calls appropriate to the age level of the team; older players require tighter officiating.

✔ Communicate clearly with the scorekeeper and timekeeper during the game.

✔ Do not talk with the whistle in your mouth, as this makes it difficult to be understood.

✔ Be sure all signals are clearly visible to the players, coaches, and spectators.

✔ Tactfully discuss questionable calls when it is convenient to consult with the other official.

✔ Stay calm and control your temper when misunderstandings occur. Don't allow yourself to be intimidated. Avoid arguments with players, coaches, or parents. It is not helpful to try to convince a disgruntled player or spectators that you are right and they are wrong.

✔ Keep the game fun and under control from start to finish. In the event of unacceptable conduct by coaches, players, or spectators, give a warning prior to any disciplinary action.

After the Game

✔ Have the two teams line up and shake hands.

✔ Compliment the players and coaches; reinforce what they are doing right.

✔ Be available for 15 minutes after the game to discuss any concerns of the players, coaches, or spectators.

✔ Help clear the playing area.

✔ Secure the game equipment.

✔ Complete any required recordkeeping paperwork with the scorekeeper.

✔ Share any immediate concerns you have with the person to whom you report.

Figure 22.3 *(continued)*

WATER POLO SAFETY RULES

Here are some safety rules from USA Water Polo (1993):

- Never run on the deck.
- Always enter the water feetfirst.
- All goggles come off before the balls enter the pool.
- Proper ear guards must be worn at all times by all players.
- Only safety-certified glasses may be worn.
- Mouthpieces, although not required, are strongly encouraged.
- No punching or dangerous play will be tolerated.
- No jewelry, wristbands, or watches may be worn.
- Stretching, warm-up, and cool-down periods are required every practice and game.
- Fingernails must be trimmed to prevent scratching.
- Don't mismatch players. Younger athletes should be paired against players of similar age, size, strength, and experience.

Be sure your staff members enforce these rules with their players.

EQUIPMENT NEEDS

Here is the equipment you'll need for your water polo program:

- Balls for the correct level (youth, women, men)
- Swim caps
- Goals
- Markers
- Whistles for coaches
- Flags for referees

PROMOTION

Try these ideas to promote your water polo program within and outside the YMCA:

- Advertise to swim team participants and coaches, swim lesson participants, and schools. Develop relationships with area schools.
- Get high school and college water polo players to help out with the program.
- Conduct clinics and workshops on water polo.
- Recruit help from local water polo coaches in establishing your program.

ADMINISTRATIVE TIPS

Here are some common questions people ask about the water polo program. Prepare answers to these questions and share them with your aquatics and front-desk staff.

- What is water polo?
- What is wetball?

- Can the kids transmit diseases by trading swim caps?
- Will the kids get hurt by the ball?

The following are signs that your program is developing some problems:

- Coaches and/or participants are playing too aggressively.
- Participants are not wearing water polo caps with ear guards.
- The program is not growing.
- The coach is not teaching proper technique and strategy but rather is just letting the kids play.
- The coach is not incorporating core values into the program.

Finally, here are some keys to improving your water polo program:

- Hire a coach with experience in either playing or coaching water polo.
- Include water polo skills in the YMCA Swim Lessons for Youth.
- Develop a water sports and games class/event that incorporates water polo.
- Build a relationship with local high school/college water polo teams.
- Have water polo teams present a demonstration at your YMCA.
- Have the appropriate equipment.
- Include water polo during swim team practices.
- Have adequate pool space so that others in the pool aren't hit by the ball.

For more information, contact USA Water Polo at **www.usawaterpolo.com.**

YMCA Aquatics Leadership Program

T he YMCA Aquatic Leadership Program is meant to train young people ages 11 through 15 in various aspects of aquatic leadership and safety. In this fun and exciting program, young people learn aquatic skills and prepare themselves for responsibilities at the pool and in their own lives. Although it is designed for swimmers, it certainly can be adapted for teens who are nonswimmers as well.

The program has five primary goals:

- Leadership
- Service
- Personal growth
- Skill enhancement
- Safety

These goals are achieved through participation in a variety of activities in the 13 core modules, plus involvement in club activities, volunteer service in YMCA aquatics programs, and social activities. The core modules cover the following topics:

- YMCA mission
- Character development
- Leadership
- Diversity
- Communication
- Facility maintenance
- Healthy lifestyles
- Rescue skills
- Aquatic safety
- Swimming skills
- CPR
- First aid
- Job training

Participants evaluate their performance after they finish the learning activities. If the modules include certification courses, then a practical evaluation is included as well. Participants should be given a recognition award for successful completion of each module.

Throughout the program, participants may become involved in any of several program activities, including the following:

- Lifeguard in-service (as an assistant)
- Course teaching (as an assistant)
- YMCA Splash (as an assistant)
- Volunteers for YMCA competitions (swim meets, lifeguarding, water polo, etc.)
- Tournament planning (assist with tournament planning and running it)
- Mentoring programs (either being mentored or mentoring younger children)

Through participation in this program, teens will learn about themselves, about working with others, and about service. It is through this program that teens can explore themselves and develop skills so they may enjoy further exploration of the aquatics field through teaching, lifeguarding, and potential career opportunities. They also learn the attitudes and skills that could one day save a life—theirs or someone else's.

Many of the activities are designed to let teens participate in activities similar to real lifeguards and leaders in a fun, safe, and controlled setting. They experience teamwork and a sense of accomplishment. In this program, trying is rewarded as well as accomplishment, and personal development and improvement are the goals.

CLUB FORMAT

The YMCA Aquatic Leadership Program is run in a club format with adult leadership. This program can help keep swimmers in your program on an ongoing basis, as well as provide a source for future YMCA aquatics instructors or volunteers. It provides members with a chance to develop their leadership skills, provide community service, and create and participate in challenging, exciting adventures. Whether participants are interested in kayaking, boating, synchronized swimming, windsurfing, waterskiing, skin or Scuba diving, search and rescue, or other water activities, the Aquatic Leadership Program can provide a tantalizing introduction to what may become lifelong pursuits.

The program has three major components:

- Educational modules relating to leadership and aquatic skills
- Aquatic activities chosen by members
- Volunteer projects and social events

A sample program format might include the following:

- A monthly club meeting
- Weekly education sessions (modules)
- Monthly (or more) activity sessions
- Volunteer projects and social events

Usually, the program is formed at the beginning of a school year. It can be enlarged by adding new groups every four months or during school breaks. Schedule an information night for parents and kids. This provides an opportunity for parents and kids to meet the program leadership and other participants, as well as to ask questions about the program. Promote the program through your swim program, swim team, and other teen programs at your YMCA.

ADULT LEADERSHIP

Leadership for this program may be paid staff or volunteers. They should expect to serve as coaches and consultants, rather than instructors. Participants should initiate and lead the activities in consultation with the leader.

Adult leaders should be mature, able to relate well to participants, and interested and skilled in aquatic activities. Other essential qualifications include honesty, reliability, and the ability to relate comfortably to parents and to the larger community. Leaders should be good role models.

Program participants themselves may help recruit their own leaders. They may find their teachers, community leaders, and parents more than willing to take on this challenge.

Acting as a leader differs from being an instructor. The leader's role is to assist individual members in reaching their potential and to help them function effectively as a group. For the group to perform effectively, it must meet the following conditions:

- Club members possess a clear sense of the purpose and goals of the group.
- Members develop consistent but flexible operating procedures. A structure is needed, but not a rigid one.
- Members share leadership. The club leader must encourage them to be aware of their duties and to take responsibility for them. When members feel responsible, they will say and do whatever is necessary to help the club move ahead. This creates a sense of belonging, a critical need of older children and teens.
- Members set aside sufficient time to select, plan, implement, and evaluate their activities and analyze their effectiveness as a group.
- Members make decisions efficiently and effectively and frequently can reach consensus.
- The group makes good use of the skills, interests, and talents of all its members.
- The group balances activities between meeting individual needs and group goals.
- Members demonstrate a high degree of commitment to the group.
- Members have a high level of trust in each other, which encourages open communication.
- The group is not dominated by its official leaders or by any other member or group of members.

If you are a leader, you can aid the group in reaching this level of effectiveness by helping members accept leadership roles and learn about responsibility. Give them the responsibility for planning and running activities. You are present just to oversee the program. Be a good role model, and guide and protect members when necessary. Also, since the program is under the direct supervision of the local YMCA, make sure that all club activities are in keeping with local YMCA policies.

To learn more about working with teen clubs, see the *YMCA Teen Leadership Manual* or take the Teen Leadership Director training course.

RECRUITMENT

The core group of members may be recruited from current class members in the Shark and Porpoise levels of the YMCA Swim Lessons program. These members may then bring in classmates, friends, relatives, and others who have a comparable aquatic skill level.

The club can attract members by stressing adventure, something most older children and teenagers find alluring. The members share similar goals and interests and have a club leader or leaders who take a special interest in them personally. Participants are responsible for creating and implementing real adventures for themselves. Under the proper conditions and with appropriate leadership, they can safely enjoy activities and get a genuine sense of accomplishment and personal pride. The pride and joy of belonging to the club comes from sharing of goals, accomplishments, experiences, and fun.

As your club grows, you may want to consider grouping them into different levels based on the ages of your participants.

CLUB DEVELOPMENT

Your club will go through several phases of development, starting with the first meeting and progressing to an initial organization phase, a sampler phase, and a subgroup and service phase.

The First Meeting

In the first meeting, include a general overview of the club's purpose and goals. You, an instructor, or a previously recruited adult volunteer can chair the meeting. Whoever chairs the meeting should stress the following points:

- It offers those who are good swimmers and who are interested in aquatics an opportunity to develop their own program.
- It allows participants to sample a variety of aquatic activities so they can intelligently choose those they like best.
- It allows participants to develop leadership skills.
- It helps participants serve others while enjoying themselves.
- It lets participants create real adventures of their own choosing.
- It provides a healthy atmosphere and social opportunities.
- It develops human potential—spirit, mind, and body.

After each participant has had the opportunity to introduce and talk about him- or herself for a minute, start with a brainstorming session. Ask club members to call out any aquatic activities that come to mind, then list them. It doesn't matter if they do or don't like the suggestions; the idea is to generate a list of possibilities. (Possible activities are unlimited, but could include sailing, skin diving and snorkeling, scuba, competitive swimming, water polo, waterskiing, and aquatics leadership and instruction.) When they have finished, display the list for everyone to see.

Give each participant a stack of index cards. Ask the participants to write the name of each activity at the top of a card, one to a card. Next to the name, they should write one of the following words:

- *Definitely*—This indicates that the person would very much like to pursue this activity.
- *Curious*—This says that the person might want to learn more about the activity and participate in it.
- *Maybe*—This shows that the person would watch this activity but not necessarily participate in it.

Participants should make copies of the cards for themselves, then hand in the originals. These cards should be treated as secret ballots. Participants should not be swayed by friends or neighbors, but rather should give their own opinions.

From this survey, construct a list of activities in order of club members' preference. Also ask club members to sort their copies of the cards, prioritizing the activities by individual preference. Then form small common-interest subgroups based on these preferences. Include no more than 12 people in a group. If more than one group wants to pursue the same activity, have them choose different aspects of the activity. For example, if two groups wanted to do synchronized swimming, one group could pursue the art form and the other group could try the competitive form.

At this meeting, also tell members about the 13 educational modules (see "Core Module Descriptions"). Schedule a weekly meeting at which members will work through each of the modules, starting with the leadership module.

Finally, club members should create general value-focused "house rules" (not rigid, formal rules and regulations) for meetings and activities and set meeting days and times for both the group as a whole and, later, for subgroups.

Initial Organization Phase

This phase takes about three weeks. During this time, club members carry out the following tasks:

- Pinning down specific activities to pursue
- Determining who wants to join which group

- Choosing leaders and researchers within each group to gather information about specific activities in which the group is interested
- Lining up speakers who are experts in the fields of special interest to make presentations

As individuals and groups take on topics to research and speakers to recruit, questions may arise. Bring these to the group for resolution.

Sampler Phase

This next phase takes about three months. During this time, club members do research, gather data, interview people, and contact community groups and organizations. The recruited speakers and presenters make their presentations, which may involve audiovisuals and field trips to observe and try out different activities. Speakers might include yacht club members, lifeguards, professional athletes, or experts from the YMCA.

Subgroup and Service Phase

This final phase also takes about three months. During this period, the club divides into smaller special-interest groups that meet about monthly (or more often if members want to). The club then meets as a whole once a month to plan joint activities, social events, outreach programs, and volunteer efforts, as well as to take care of business matters.

During this phase, each club member should be able to get a good feel for at least three or four activities. Some members may choose to pursue only one or two in depth.

Service projects are also added during this phase. Possibilities are endless, but here are some common ones:

- Helping swim instructors with classes at lower progressive levels
- Working in the pool with children who have disabilities
- Greeting families on the first day of a session to direct them to the pool and classes, hand out swim information, and answer basic questions about the program and facility
- Helping with swim registration
- Running fundraisers for World Service and the club, such as breakfasts, pasta dinners, bingo games, or ice cream socials
- Cleaning up the area around the outdoor pool just before summer opening
- Holding a swim meet with a YMCA in another country by faxing event results to each other
- Attending water shows with groups of senior adults or small children
- Creating a slide show or videotape, if equipment is available, and going on lecture tours of schools, community organizations, and local business groups

Activities such as these may act as a springboard to participation in Leaders Club or other volunteer opportunities.

By this phase, the main club elements should be in place. A sample schedule might look like this:

First Tuesday of the month: Club meeting and activity planning

Saturday mornings: Class relating to one of the modules and program volunteer time

Third Tuesday of the month: Social or service learning project

Monthly or occasionally: Special-interest group activity

SOCIAL ACTIVITIES

Scheduling regular social activities gives kids a fun break and helps keep them interested. Members should decide on their own activities and should be responsible for planning, implementation, and follow-up. Social activities should be held once a month or so throughout the school year for the entire group. At the monthly meetings, the club can vote on and designate committees and individuals to carry out different aspects of the activities. In this way, subgroups can stay involved with each other.

Some possible activities include these:

- Peer-group skills performance in areas such as competitive diving, skin diving, synchronized swimming, and rescue
- Family nights, where club members perform or families and members free swim
- Outings to see water shows or to windsurf or boat

Social activities can also be used as recruitment activities for new members and adult leaders.

RECOGNITION

Many successful clubs use a point system to recognize members for their level of involvement. The aim of the system is not to foster competition, but rather to provide standards by which a club member can measure involvement. One system awards one or more points for each of the following actions:

- Attending club meetings
- Participating in community service projects or volunteer hours
- Participating in fundraising events
- Participating in training events
- Participating in multiclub events
- Writing an article for the club newsletter
- Serving on a committee
- Assuming an official leadership position
- Meeting deadlines for turning in fees or forms
- Paying dues on time
- Serving as a "big brother" or "big sister" to a new member
- Achieving personal best goals and performances in activities through participation in club meetings and practice sessions
- Successful completion of each module
- Recruiting new members

Once you designate the number of points per activity, you can then determine a maximum number of possible points and decide the range of points needed for each level of recognition. Here is one example:

0-20 points = not recognized

21-40 points = a certificate

41-60 points = a T-shirt or pin

61-80 points = a plaque or trophy

Traditionally, recognition is presented at the end of the year, but it can be done on a quarterly or monthly basis as well.

CORE MODULE DESCRIPTIONS

This program has 13 core modules. Each module should be designed for about four hours of activities. The modules can be broken up into smaller sessions or done in one four-hour session. It is up to you to decide how each of the module objectives can be achieved. Once your club members have accomplished the core modules, they can then determine what other modules they would like to add based on their interests.

We recommend that the leadership module be the prerequisite module for all other modules, as well as for participation in other practical activities.

The club leader or other staff or volunteers can lead the modules. They should focus on having the members gain learning and understanding based on each module's objectives. Recognize achievement through feedback and reflection, personal bests, and friendly competitions. Provide members with a chance to set goals and reach for personal best performances, give them positive recognition for improvement and effort, and encourage them to learn more.

This section includes a description of the objectives for each module and a sample list of activities. Complete descriptions of these activities can be found on the YMCA of the USA web site. You can also create your own activities that meet the module objectives.

Module: What Is the YMCA?

Core Objectives

- To gain an understanding of the history of YMCA and aquatics and its effect on how we do things today
- To understand the mission of the YMCA and how it is accomplished each day
- To understand the YMCA's goals, purpose, and objectives for programs and to understand how they are achieved in programs

Suggested Activity

Teach the Principles of YMCA Aquatic Leadership course. Certify those participants who successfully meet the course requirements.

Module: Character Development

Core Objective

- To understand the character development values of caring, honesty, respect, and responsibility and how they apply to our daily lives

Suggested Activities

• Values Discovery—to help participants explore their beliefs and attitudes. It challenges them to make decisions based on their own feelings and experiences. They may begin the process of self-actualization.

• Character Development and Leadership Challenge—to examine their own actions and decisions. This activity describes character development and the YMCA core values, then has participants ask themselves specific questions each time they take action or make a decision. They then consider what consequences that choice will have and whether the results of that choice will help or hurt those who see them as role models. This activity includes a self-assessment that helps participants determine their beliefs and behaviors related to the core values and how they can lead by example.

• Trait Charades—to illustrate the character development trait of respect.

• Self-Concept "Quiz"—to help participants identify qualities they possess and determine how they think of themselves.

• Values Auction—to help participants explore their beliefs and to challenge them to see the difference between what they believe and what they value.

• Credible Heroes—to help participants explore what makes a leader and how they are perceived by others.

• Leaders' Code of Ethics—to help participants develop a code of ethics and conduct to follow when they are involved as assistants in programs.

• Minefields—to establish trust among participants and to understand trusting and the value of being trusted. This activity also emphasizes the need for participants to speak clearly and listen carefully.

Supplemental Resources for Activities:
  YMCA Character Development Starter Kit
  YMCA Character Development Next Steps
  On the Guard II training design

Module: Leadership

Core Objectives
- To help participants understand the difference between a leader and a follower
- To explore participants' leadership skills and have them assess their own profiles
- To understand their role as a program leader and how to assist instructors and other staff

Suggested Activities
- Decision Making—to provide a model to guide making good decisions. This activity will also encourage teens to consider more options in the hope that they will find the best decision for their circumstances. It should help participants become clear thinkers and improve their focus when making decisions.
- Well . . . Maybe . . . Sure . . . I Mean . . . I Would?—to encourage participants to evaluate their decision-making process and to think about situations that they may encounter. It also helps them measure their confidence in making decisions and giving advice.
- Walk in My Shoes—to provide participants with basic skills for informal peer counseling and to help participants understand empathy. They are encouraged to become involved and informed.
- What's My Role?—to help participants understand their job functions and tasks and how to carry out and follow up on assignments while assisting in programs.
- What Is a Leader?—to help participants understand the characteristics of a leader and how they can improve their leadership skills.
- Learning Buddy—to help participants improve their leadership characteristics.
- Speaking Up—to give participants practice in speaking in front of a group and in handling situations.

Module: Diversity

Core Objectives
- To help participants recognize and assess how they relate to and identify with elements of their own ethnic, racial, religious, age, sexual orientation, gender, class, and disability groupings
- To help participants be open to new ideas (culture, food, experiences)
- To help participants appreciate the range of differences (ethnicity, races, religions) without necessarily agreeing with all beliefs and to see the benefits of the differences

Suggested Activities
- Diversity—to assist participants in measuring how much they value diversity and how that affects relationships with other people. We suggest that this session be followed by a communication activity.

- Conflict Styles—to help participants identify their style of conflict management and determine the appropriate use of each style.

- Facility Readiness—to help participants understand how they can improve safety for those with disabilities who want to participate in aquatics programs, and how they can support them.

- Program Awareness—to help leaders observe and understand how programs are developed for specific groups and appreciate the differences in programs and participants.

Module: Communication

Core Objectives
- To help participants understand the importance of effective communication
- To help participants explore their own behavior when communicating and try to improve
- To help participants learn to communicate effectively

Suggested Activities
- "Getting the Red Out"—to teach participants positive ways to diffuse anger.

- Why Do Mosquitoes Buzz in Peoples' Ears?—to develop participants' listening skills and to help them understand that to hear is not necessarily to listen. It will also introduce the concept of different listening levels, such as pleasure, understanding, remembering, and evaluating.

- Reaching Common Ground—to develop respect for others' opinions during discussions or disagreements.

- Are You a Discussion Blocker?—to explore participants' behavior during discussions and discover how to make points effectively.

- Listening—to provide an opportunity for participants to express themselves on specific value issues in an atmosphere of acceptance and open communication.

Module: Aquatics Facility Maintenance

Core Objectives
- To teach participants to identify potential hazards in pools
- To help participants understand basic pool chemistry
- To help participants understand emergency procedures and what they can do to assist in an emergency
- To help participants understand the importance of facility cleanliness

Suggested Activities
- Safety and Facility Checklists—to help participants understand that a number of areas need to be examined to make a pool safe. In this activity, participants learn how to do a basic safety and facility assessment.

- Do I Want to Swim Here?—to help participants understand what it takes for a swimming site to be a safe place to swim.

- Emergency Procedures—to introduce participants to how they should respond to an emergency and what they can do to assist. They look at their homes and see what emergencies they should be prepared for.

• Basic Pool Chemistry—to introduce participants to basic water testing and the types of chemicals needed to make a pool a safe place to swim. Participants are taught safe handling of pool chemicals and precautions for pool chemistry.

Supplemental Resources for Activities

On the Guard II (4th ed.)

YMCA Pool Operations Manual (2nd ed.)

Module: Healthy Lifestyles

Core Objectives

• To help participants understand what a healthy lifestyle is

• To help participants improve their lifestyles and understand how their daily decisions affect their health

Suggested Activities

• Healthy Lifestyles—to help participants explore how lifestyle affects their social, spiritual, intellectual, physical, and emotional wellness.

• Healthy Friends—to reinforce the character development value of caring and teach how to help friends with healthy choices.

• Food Jeopardy—to provide participants with information regarding healthy dietary choices and the importance of diet when dealing with stress.

• Peer Influence—to encourage discussion about peer influence and provide participants with valuable tools to help battle peer influence. Participants will also identify their priorities and learn the difference between beliefs and values.

• Saying No Gracefully—to help participants say no. This will help them avoid stress from becoming overloaded with commitments and resist peer pressure when necessary.

• It All Makes Cents—to help participants understand the importance of balance and knowing your limits.

Supplemental Resource for Activities

On the Guard II training design

Module: Rescue

Core Objective

• To teach participants the skills needed to assist in water rescues and to understand the limits of their abilities

Suggested Activities

Using *On the Guard II* (4th ed.) as your guide, teach the following skills:

• Victim identification: active, passive, spinal, distressed

• Nonswimming rescues

• Swimming rescues: tube rescues only, submerge defense

• Emergency procedures

• Scanning basics

• Communication skills for lifeguards

Supplemental Resource for Activities
    On the Guard II (4th ed.)

Module: Aquatic Safety

Core Objectives
- To help participants learn basic personal safety skills and increase safe practices in aquatic activities
- To teach participants what makes a safe swimming environment

Suggested Activities
- Use *On the Guard II* (4th ed.) to teach personal safety skills (YASA skills).
- Teach the Staff Aquatic Safety Training Program (SAST).
- Use *YMCA Splash* or *Instructor Manual for On the Guard II* (4th ed.) to teach safety in swimming pools, backyard pools, and water parks, at the beach, and while boating.

Supplemental Resources for Activities
    On the Guard II (4th ed.)
    Staff Aquatic Safety Training/Video
    YMCA Splash
    Instructor Manual for On the Guard II (4th ed.)

Module: Swimming Skills

Core Objective
- To help participants improve their swimming skills, including skills in aquatic sports

Suggested Activities
- Stroke Technique—to help participants improve their speed, endurance, and efficiency.
- Aquatic Sport Development—to help participants gain an appreciation of aquatic sports.

Module: CPR

Core Objective
- To teach leaders basic CPR skills

Suggested Activity
- Teach a CPR certification course that includes adult and youth CPR and obstructed airway. Certify those participants who successfully meet the course requirements.

Supplemental Resources for Activities
    American Heart Association (AHA), American Red Cross (ARC), American Safety and Health Institute, or National Safety Council CPR certification program

Module: First Aid

Core Objectives
- To teach participants how to call 9-1-1 and what to expect
- To teach participants basic first aid skills

Suggested Activity
- Teach a first aid certification course that includes basic first aid and universal precautions. Certify those participants who successfully meet the course requirements.

Supplemental Resources for Activities

National Safety Council, American Red Cross, or American Safety and Health Institute first aid certification course

Module: Job Training

Core Objectives
- To help participants understand what it takes to get a job, as well as to keep one.
- To help participants learn what opportunities are open to them based on their skills, desires, and abilities.

Suggested Activities
- Getting a Job—to help participants develop a resume, complete applications, and interview for a job.
- Exploring Career Options—to explore different career opportunities and help participants identify what they need to do now to accomplish their career goals.
- Goal Setting—to teach participants how to set short-term goals, develop long-term goals, and designate benchmarks in order to evaluate and assess progress toward reaching a goal.
- Job Responsibility—to help participants understand the responsibilities of jobs and how to be an effective leader or employee.

Supplemental Resource for Activities

On the Guard II training design

Forty Developmental Assets

This chart lists forty developmental assets that have been identified as forming a foundation for healthy development in adolescents. These forty assets expand on a set of thirty assets that was first articulated in a 1990 report from Search Institute titled *The Troubled Journey: A Portrait of 6th – 12th Grade Youth* and that undergird Search Institute's current asset-building resources. The new assets are shown in bold type. In addition, several of the original thirty assets have been revised, combined, or renamed.

While this framework focuses on teens, developmental assets are important across the entire first two decades of life. Different developmentally appropriate frameworks for other ages of children (infants, toddlers, pre-schoolers, and school-agers) are available at **http://www.ymcausa.org/programs/YouthDev/AssetBuilding.htm** (user name is ymca; password is 9622).

Asset type	Asset name and definition
Support	1. Family support – Family life provides high levels of love and support.
	2. Positive family communication – Young person and her or his parent(s) communicate positively, and young person is willing to seek advice and counsel from parent(s).
	3. Other adult relationships – Young person receives support from three or more nonparent adults.
	4. Caring neighborhood – Young person experiences caring neighbors.
	5. Caring school climate – School provides a caring, encouraging environment.
	6. Parent involvement in schooling – Parent(s) are actively involved in helping young person succeed in school.

Asset type	Asset name and definition
Empowerment	7. Community values youth – Young person perceives that adults in the community value youth.
	8. Youth as resources – Young people are given useful roles in the community.
	9. Service to others – Young person serves in the community one hour or more per week.
	10. Safety – Young person feels safe at home, at school, and in the neighborhood.
Boundaries and Expectations	11. Family boundaries – Family has clear rules and consequences, and monitors the young person's whereabouts.
	12. School boundaries – School provides clear rules and consequences.
	13. Neighborhood boundaries – Neighbors take responsibility for monitoring young people's behavior.
	14. Adult role models – Parent(s) and other adults model positive, responsible behavior.
	15. Positive peer influence – Young person's best friends model responsible behavior.
	16. High expectations – Both parent(s) and teachers encourage the young person to do well.
Constructive Use of Time	17. Creative activities – Young person spends three or more hours per week in lessons or practice in music, theater, or other arts.
	18. Youth programs – Young person spends three or more hours per week in sports, clubs, or organizations at school and/or in the community.
	19. Religious community – Young person spends one or more hours per week in activities in a religious institution.
	20. Time at home – Young person is out with friends "with nothing special to do" two or fewer nights per week.
Commitment to Learning	21. Achievement motivation – Young person is motivated to do well in school.
	22. School engagement – Young person is actively engaged in learning.
	23. Homework – Young person reports doing at least one hour of homework every school day.
	24. Bonding to school – Young person cares about her or his school.
	25. Reading for pleasure – Young person reads for pleasure three or more hours per week.

Positive Values

26. Caring – Young person places high value on helping other people.
27. Equality and social justice – Young person places high value on promoting equality and reducing hunger and poverty.
28. Integrity – Young person acts on convictions and stands up for her or his beliefs.
29. Honesty – Young person "tells the truth even when it is not easy."
30. Responsibility – Young person accepts and takes personal responsibility.
31. Restraint – Young person believes it is important not to be sexually active or to use alcohol or other drugs.

Social Competencies

32. Planning and decision making – Young person knows how to plan ahead and make choices.
33. Interpersonal competence – Young person has empathy, sensitivity, and friendship skills.
34. Cultural competence – Young person has knowledge of and comfort with people of different cultural/racial/ethnic backgrounds.
35. Resistance skills – Young person can resist negative peer pressure and dangerous situations.
36. Peaceful conflict resolution – Young person seeks to resolve conflict nonviolently.

Positive Identity

37. Personal power – Young person feels he or she has control over "things that happen to me."
38. Self-esteem – Young person reports having a high self-esteem.
39. Sense of purpose – Young person reports that "my life has a purpose."
40. Positive view of personal future – Young person is optimistic about her or his personal future.

Child Abuse Identification and Prevention: Recommended Guidelines for YMCAs

STATEMENT OF THE YMCA OF THE USA MEDICAL ADVISORY COMMITTEE:

Child abuse is damage to a child for which there is no "reasonable" explanation. Child abuse includes non-accidental physical injury, neglect, sexual molestation and emotional abuse.

The increasing incidence of reported child abuse has become a critical national concern. Child abuse reporting levels increased 41% from 1988 to 1997. It is a special concern of the YMCA because of the organization's role as an advocate for children and its responsibility for enhancing the personal growth and development of both children and adults in all YMCA programs.

Each YMCA is encouraged to develop a written policy that clearly defines management practices related to prevention of child abuse. This policy should include approved practices for recruiting, training and supervising staff; a code of conduct for staff relationships with children; reporting procedures for incidents when they do occur; and the responsibility to parents on this issue.

To assist YMCAs, the YMCA of the USA has developed a Child Abuse Prevention Training manual. This manual includes two three-hour training designs; one for staff who hire and supervise, and a second for front-line program staff. Sample policies and procedures are included in both designs. Each YMCA received a copy of the manual in 1994. The manual, revised in 1998, now includes an additional piece titled The Next Steps in Child Abuse Prevention. The Next Steps section includes a "how am I doing checklist," refresher training outlines, a justification for policies limiting staff contact with children, confidentiality and responsibility recommendations, information on screening volunteers and more. The revised manual is available from the YMCA Program Store, item no. 0-7360-0754-7. The Next Steps document (included in the manual) is available as a stand-alone piece from the YMCA of the USA, Program Development Unit, 800-972-9622. YMCAs are encouraged to offer Child Abuse Prevention training on a regular basis for all staff.

The following guidelines have been developed to stimulate thinking about the potential for child abuse in YMCA programs and the need to develop a YMCA policy related to this important issue. Common sense and good judgement should guide the development of required procedures. Good management policies and practices will vary based on local situations. Laws differ from state to state. YMCA administrators need to be aware of changing state and local requirements and monitor YMCA programs to ensure that they are in compliance.

Guidelines for Local YMCAs for Staff Recruitment, Training, and Supervision

1. Reference checks on all prospective employees and program volunteers will be conducted, documented and filed prior to employment.

2. Fingerprinting and/or criminal record checks of adults who work in programs that serve children, youth and teens, especially those authorized or required by State law, are included in the employment process.

3. Photographs will be taken of all staff and attached to personnel record for identification at a later time if needed.

4. All new staff and volunteers must participate in an orientation program including written materials explaining YMCA policies, procedures and regulations. They should be aware of legal requirements and by their signature acknowledge having received and read appropriate policies, standards and codes of conduct. Documentation of attendance in the Child Abuse Prevention training should be added to the employee's personnel file. Staff should periodically read and sign again the Code of Conduct and participate in refresher trainings in Child Abuse Prevention.

5. Staff and volunteers working directly with children will be provided information regularly about the signs of possible child abuse. They should be educated about "high risk parents" and "high risk families" (for example, drug addicted, alcohol addicted, mentally ill, unemployed, teenage parents, and parents who were abused themselves as children). Staff training will include approved procedures for responding to the suspicion of abuse.

6. Administrative staff supervising programs involving the care of children will make unannounced visits to each program site to assure that standards, policies, program quality and performance of staff are being maintained. Written reports on these visits will be completed.

Guidelines for Staff Relationships with Children

7. In order to protect YMCA staff, volunteers and program participants, at no time during a YMCA program may a program leader be alone with a single child unobserved by other staff.

8. Young children will never be unsupervised in bathrooms, locker rooms or showers.

9. Staff may not be alone with children they meet in YMCA programs outside of the YMCA. This includes babysitting, sleepovers, and inviting children to their homes. Any exceptions require a written explanation before the fact and are subject to administrator approval.

10. Staff may not date program participants under the age of 18 years of age.

11. YMCA staff and volunteers will not discipline children by use of physical punishment or by failing to provide the necessities of care, such as food and shelter.

12. YMCA staff or volunteers will not verbally or emotionally abuse or punish children.

13. Staff and volunteers providing direct care for very young children will be identified by a badge/name tag or uniform that is familiar to the children with whom they work. Children will be instructed to avoid any person not so identified.

14. Staff and volunteers should be alert to the physical and emotional state of all children each time they report for a program and indicate, in writing, any signs of injury or suspected child abuse.

Guidelines for the YMCA's Responsibilities to Parents

15. Invite parents to serve on interview committees to screen and select staff and volunteers. Caution should be taken in the selection of parents for this function. They should have a through understanding of, and be in agreement with, the YMCA's philosophy and operating procedures.

16. Ask parent(s) to sign a Parent Statement of Understanding, which includes a statement limiting staff and program volunteers in their contact with children and families outside of the YMCA program, and which informs parent of the YMCA's mandate to report suspected cases of child abuse or neglect.

17. Conduct an intake/orientation, with all parents, to share the programs policies and procedures. Be sure to include the pre-employment screening, supervision, code of conduct, training, and other child abuse prevention policies established to protect children.

18. Daily communication should inform parents of their child's health, behavior, positive anecdotes from their day, etc.

19. The YMCA should maintain an open door policy that encourages parents to drop by and observe or share in the program with their child—at any time.

20. The YMCA should offer information on child abuse and parenting, and assistance to parents through workshops, counseling, book and video lending libraries, etc.

21. The YMCA should try to identify families in stress and offer referral information to agencies that can assist them.

22. Through newsletters, conferences, and modeling appropriate interaction skills, the YMCA should inform and educate parents about age appropriate expectations and discipline.

23. The YMCA curriculum should stress children making choices, solving problems, developing a positive self esteem, sharing feelings and practicing their assertiveness skills. The YMCA should encourage parents to reinforce these skills at home as they leave children less vulnerable to maltreatment.

24. The YMCA should sponsor guest speakers who address the issues of child abuse, child abuse prevention, teaching personal safety to children, etc. Administrators should screen all individuals and their materials before allowing them to present.

REPORTING PROCEDURES

In the event that there is an accusation of child abuse, the YMCA will take prompt and immediate action as follows:

25. At the first report or probable cause to believe that child abuse has occurred, the employed staff person it has been reported to will notify the program director, who will then review the incident with the YMCA executive director, or his/her designate. However, if the program director is not immediately available, this review by the supervisor cannot in any way deter the reporting of child abuse by the mandated reporters. Most states mandate each teacher or child care provider to report information they have learned in their professional role regarding suspected child abuse. In most states, mandated reporters are granted immunity from prosecution.

26. The YMCA will make a report in accordance with relevant state or local child abuse reporting requirements and will cooperate to the extent of the law with any legal authority involved.

27. In the event the reported incident(s) involve a program volunteer or employed staff, the executive director will, without exception, suspend the volunteer or staff person from the YMCA.

28. The parents or legal guardian of the child(ren) involved in the alleged incident will be promptly notified in accordance with the directions of the relevant state or local agency.

29. Whether the incident or alleged offense takes place on or off YMCA premises, it will be considered job related (because of the youth-involved nature of the YMCA).

30. Reinstatement of the program volunteer or employed staff person will occur only after all allegations have been cleared to the satisfaction of the persons named in #25 and 26 above.

31. All YMCA staff and volunteers must be sensitive to the need for confidentiality in the handling of this information, and therefore, should only discuss the incident with supervisory staff and the appropriate legal authority.

32. All full-time and part-time employees and program volunteers must read and sign the Child Abuse Reporting Procedures Policy.

Possible Indicators of Abuse

Sexual Abuse—Behavioral Indicators

1. Is reluctant to change clothes in front of others.
2. Is withdrawn.
3. Exhibits unusual sexual behavior and/or knowledge beyond that which is common for his/her developmental stage.
4. Has poor peer relationships.
5. Either avoids or seeks out adults.
6. Is pseudo-mature.
7. Is manipulative.
8. Is self-conscious.
9. Has problems with authority and rules.
10. Exhibits eating disorders.
11. Is self-mutilating.
12. Is obsessively clean.

13. Uses or abuses alcohol and/or other drugs.
14. Exhibits delinquent behavior such as running away from home.
15. Exhibits extreme compliance or defiance.
16. Is fearful or anxious.
17. Exhibits suicidal gestures and/or attempts suicide.
18. Is promiscuous.
19. Engages in fantasy or infantile behavior.
20. Is unwilling to participate in sports activities.
21. Has school difficulties.

Sexual Abuse—Physical Indicators

1. Has pain and/or itching in the genital area.
2. Has bruises or bleeding in the genital area.
3. Has venereal disease.
4. Has swollen private parts.
5. Has difficulty walking or sitting.
6. Has torn, bloody, and/or stained underclothing.
7. Experiences pain when urinating.
8. Is pregnant.
9. Has vaginal or penile discharge.
10. Wets the bed.

Emotional Abuse—Behavioral Indicators

1. Is overly eager to please.
2. Seeks out adult contact.
3. Views abuse as being warranted.
4. Exhibits changes in behavior.
5. Is excessively anxious.
6. Is depressed.
7. Is unwilling to discuss problems.
8. Exhibits aggressive or bizarre behavior.
9. Is withdrawn.
10. Is apathetic.
11. Is passive.
12. Has unprovoked fits of yelling or screaming.
13. Exhibits inconsistent behavior at home and school.
14. Feels responsible for the abuser.
15. Runs away from home.
16. Attempt suicide.
17. Has low self-esteem.
18. Exhibits a gradual impairment of health or personality.
19. Has difficulty sustaining relationships.

20. Has unrealistic goal setting.
21. Is impatient.
22. Is unable to communicate or express his/her feelings, needs, or desires.
23. Sabotages his/her chances of success.
24. Lacks self-confidence.
25. Is self depreciating and has a negative self- image.

Emotional Abuse—Physical Indicators

1. Has a sleep disorder (nightmares or restlessness).
2. Wets the bed.
3. Exhibits developmental lags (stunting his/her physical, emotional, and/or mental growth).
4. Is hyperactive.
5. Exhibits eating disorders.

Physical Abuse—Behavioral Indicators

1. Is wary of adults.
2. Is either extremely aggressive or withdrawn.
3. Is dependent and indiscriminate in his/her attachments.
4. Is uncomfortable when other children cry.
5. Generally controls his/her own crying.
6. Exhibits a drastic behavior change when not with parents or caregiver.
7. Is manipulative.
8. Has poor self-concept.
9. Exhibits delinquent behavior, such as running away from home.
10. Uses or abuses alcohol and/or other drugs.
11. Is self-mutilating.
12. Is frightened of parents, of going home.
13. Is overprotective of or responsible for parents.
14. Exhibits suicidal gestures and/or attempts suicide.
15. Has behavior problems at school.

Physical Abuse—Physical Indicators

1. Has unexplained* bruises or welts, often clustered or in a pattern.
2. Has unexplained* and/or unusual burns (cigarettes, doughnut-shaped, immersion-lines, object-patterned).
3. Has unexplained* bite marks.
4. Has unexplained* fractures or dislocations.
5. Has unexplained* abrasions or lacerations.
6. Wets the bed.

(* Or explanation is inconsistent or improbable.)

Neglect—Behavior Indicators

1. Is truant or tardy to school often or arrives early and stays late.
2. Begs or steals food.
3. Attempts suicide.
4. Uses or abuses alcohol and/or other drugs.
5. Is extremely dependent or detached.
6. Engages in delinquent behavior, such as prostitution or stealing.
7. Appears to be exhausted.
8. State frequent or continual absence of parent or guardian.

Neglect—Physical Indicators

1. Frequently is dirty, unwashed, hungry, or inappropriately dressed.
2. Engages in dangerous activities (possibly because he/she generally is unsupervised).
3. Is tired and listless.
4. Has unattended physical problems.
5. May appear to be over-worked and/or exploited.

Family Characteristics

1. Secrecy
2. Extreme isolation from support systems
3. Role reversal between parent and child
4. Domestic violence in the family
5. Prior incidence of abuse
6. Family involvement in selling drugs

Note: These indicators can also be indicative of emotional dysfunctions that merit investigation for emotional problems and/or being the victims of abuse.

YMCAs are urged to share copies of their management policies related to child abuse with other YMCAs and the YMCA of the USA. A bibliography of printed and audio-visual educational resources for use with parents and children is included in the Next Steps in Child Abuse Prevention, available from the YMCA of the USA, Program Development Unit, 800-872-9622 or the 1998 edition of the Child Abuse Prevention Manual, available from the YMCA Program Store, 800-747-0089.

June, 1989
Revised April, 1996
Revised October, 2000

Aquatic Emergency Preparedness Self-Assessment

To do a self-assessment of your program, answer the questions in the checklist. In the rating column, rate how well you feel your operation is performing in relation to the question, using a scale of 1 (needs work) to 5 (excellent). In the Improvement Strategies column, list some key strategies for improving your assessment in this area. After completing this column, think through who will have responsibility for accomplishing the strategy, the costs involved, and the due date for completion.

	Emergency Preparedness	Y/N	Rating	Improvement strategies
1	Have you established emergency procedures for the following: ✔ Medical ✔ Water ✔ Missing persons ✔ Environmental ✔ Chemical ✔ Mechanical ✔ Facility			
2	When were these procedures last reviewed and updated (if necessary, annually)?			
3	When did all of your staff last practice all of your procedures?			
4	Do you have a reporting process to document practices and a review process for the procedures?			
5	Have you developed a communication plan to use in an emergency? Where is it kept? How often is it reviewed?			

	Emergency Preparedness	**Y/N**	**Rating**	**Improvement strategies**
6	Do you have copies of local/state regulations? Do you document your compliance?			
7	Do you have a plan and contact people to handle the critical stress issues for staff and participants in the event of an emergency? Where is the plan located for reference?			
8	Do you have a lifeguard assessment process and documentation of its implementation? When was the last time lifeguards were evaluated?			
9	Do you hold a regular in-service training program related to emergency drill and staff readiness? How do you ensure all staff attend?			
10	Do you have your lifeguards perform scanning drills as a regular component of your in-service training program?			
11	Are all staff supervisors trained in the *YMCA Staff Aquatic Safety Training Program*? When was the last time you held this training?			
12	Do you adequately budget for emergency preparedness in the following areas: salaries, training, certification, and equipment?			
13	Do you involve your local EMS with emergency drills at least annually? When was the last time this occurred?			
14	Do you have a system of monitoring all staff certification expirations and renewals?			
15	Are all your lifeguards YMCA certified?			
16	When did you last perform an internal or peer regular assessment and evaluation of your operation using your aquatic policy and the YUSA Aquatic guidelines?			
17	Do duty periods for lifeguards provide them with adequate rotation schedules so that they can be vigilant?			
18	Do you have an adequate amount of equipment for executing emergency procedures and for training purposes? (When lifeguard classes are being taught, is there still an adequate amount of equipment available for lifeguards on duty?)			
19	Do you have supplemental oxygen in your facility?			
20	When was the last time you reviewed your aquatic policy, YUSA aquatic guidelines, and local/state regulations?			

	Emergency Preparedness	Y/N	Rating	Improvement strategies
21	Do you inspect your facility, equipment, and air/water quality daily and keep records of them?			
22	Do you have adequate signage in your pool area?			
23	Do you have an AED in your facility based on AHA criteria?			
24	Does senior management review and inspect during off-hours and unannounced? When was the last visit?			
25	Is there a regular and scheduled program of safety drills? Does senior management observe them? Are scenarios used? Are there unannounced drills?			
26	Do lifeguard drills and assessments include an opportunity for guards to show competency in each stage of the emergency response? (Scan zone, assess situation, determine action, perform rescue, remove victim, provide first aid and assist EMS, report process)			
27	Is your first aid and biohazard kit adequately supplied and inspected daily?			

If your total score is:

120 points and above	You're on the right track—Keep up the hard work!
108-119 points	You are doing a lot of things well, but there is more that can be done.
94-107 points	You are doing many things, but with a good plan you could be better.
Below 94	You should consider putting a plan together to improve your policy and procedures to ensure the safety of your participants.

YMCA of the USA Aquatics Guidelines

C onducting quality programs that meet both industry standards and local needs is an ongoing task for the YMCA aquatic program director. The guidelines given in this chapter will help local YMCA staff, key volunteer decision makers, and program participants assess the quality of their aquatics programs. Used as a tool for self-assessment, the guidelines can point out both areas that need improvement and areas of excellence. Meant to be used in conjunction with YMCA of the USA aquatics program manuals, the guidelines have been compiled from suggestions and evaluation instruments contributed by many local YMCAs.

It is important to differentiate between guidelines and standards. **Guidelines** are recommendations from the YMCA of the USA to be considered by local YMCAs. **Standards** are rules or policies governing any particular program that can only be set by the local association. In developing those standards, each YMCA can customize these guidelines to conform to their methods of operation and to the needs and legal requirements of their communities. Input from every level of your organization staff, volunteers, and members is crucial to developing your own standards; quality should be everyone's concern.

The YMCA of the USA develops guidelines as good practices to operate programs. These guidelines can be considered in the legal world to be a guidance for YMCAs as well as the aquatic industry. Local YMCAs can take the YMCA of the USA guidelines and adopt them (with or without modification) to create their association policies, which become their standard of care.

If your association chooses to develop policies that are not in compliance with or modify the YMCA of the USA guidelines, discuss these policies with your board and have the board approve any modification. Make sure that the rationale for the modification is explained in the minutes of the discussion.

When developing your standards, keep in mind that there may be local or state regulations that must legally be met. *All YMCA programs must meet the current laws, codes, or ordinances of their city, county, and state.* Because regulations vary from place to place, each YMCA aquatic director is responsible for knowing and abiding by the requirements in her or his locale.

But instructors also need to be aware that state and local standards may only be minimum requirements for operation and may not fully address the quality of the program desired by participants and the YMCA. The goal of a YMCA should be to offer programs of the highest possible quality.

Development of standards is only a starting point. Once you have set your association's standards, you must measure or test how well your program meets them in order to document that your association is in compliance with them. You will need to create a process to regularly assess programs using the standard benchmarks. Following is a recommended six-step approach, which utilizes an outside validation team:

1. The association CEO or branch executive explains the assessment process to staff and volunteers.
2. The aquatic director, with the help of other staff, conducts a review of all programs using the standards and addresses areas needing improvement.
3. A validation team is recruited from the community. This team may include program participants, experts in aquatics, directors of other aquatic facilities, YMCA board members, or staff from other YMCAs.
4. An orientation is conducted for the validation team to review the association's aquatics program standards.
5. The validation team conducts a review of each program.
6. The validation team reports its findings to the YMCA Board of Directors through the appropriate channels and process.

Using a validation team provides good community publicity for your YMCA. It familiarizes key people with YMCA aquatics programs and impresses upon them your concern for quality.

During assessment, the team should consider each standard to be important and address it at the appropriate staff level. Self-assessment should not only provide an overview of each program but also reinforce the specific standard. The team should rate each guideline on a scale between one and five, with one being noncompliance and five being complete compliance.

After the assessment is completed, staff and volunteers should determine what corrective action, if any, is needed to bring programs in line with your association's standards. A realistic timetable should be established for implementation, and a monitoring system that focuses on achievement should be put in place. Maintaining high quality in programs is an ongoing job; assessment needs to be done regularly to maintain the standards.

N - No
S - Sometimes

	Rating	Comments
A. PHILOSOPHY AND GOALS		
A1. YMCA goals are used to develop the program's long-range goals, short-term objectives, and programs.	3	
A2. The YMCA of the USA's purpose, goals and mission statements are posted in a prominent location in the facilities and in all program brochures and other materials.	1	
A3. The YMCA Aquatics or Health and Fitness Committee and appropriate staff develop a written philosophy and goals, which are shared with the following people: - Staff - Program participants	1	

	Rating	Comments
- Family members of participants - Committees and boards - Appropriate community agencies		
A4. A written aquatic policy addresses the following topics: - Purpose and objectives - Staffing (professional, full- and part-time, and volunteer) - Planning and program priorities - Community relationships - Promotional planning - Policy development (a list of operational policies) - Facilities and equipment - Financial management - Operational evaluation - Health and safety (The aquatic policy may be a section of a larger policy on health and fitness.)	2	not all policies covered
A5. The aquatic policy is reviewed annually, with changes presented to the appropriate body for action.	4	

B. ADMINISTRATION

	Rating	Comments
B1. The local board has authorized a standing committee to be responsible for all aquatics programs (youth and adult). (This committee may be part of a larger committee responsible for all programs or for health and fitness programs.) Its functions and responsibilities are clearly stated in writing.	1	
B2. The committee is composed of members representing program participants, the board of managers, the community, and specialists in the field of aquatics.	1	
B3. Committee members, along with the program director and staff, annually set appropriate goals for all programs and classes.	1	
B4. The staff develops and the board/committee approves an annual budget and follows its guidelines.	5	
B5. An organizational chart shows the person to whom each employee reports, and job descriptions clarify where staff responsibilities fall.	3	
B6. All administrative policies, procedures, and practices are in accordance with state and local regulations (where applicable), including the following: - Licensing requirements - Fire and building codes - Health department regulations	5	

(continued)

	Rating	Comments
- Zoning laws - Operating permits - Transportation regulations (if applicable) - Electrical inspection codes - Other regulations Current copies of state laws and regulations related to swimming pools are available on file to all aquatics staff.		
B7. City, county, or state pool operation and bacteriological reports, if required, are submitted to the government authority, with copies kept on file.	5	
B8. Copies of pertinent or applicable staff certifications are kept on file. These may include current certifications in first aid, CPR, AED, and oxygen administration or as a lifeguard, instructor, or pool operator, as well as other additional requirements such as a pesticide applicator's license.	5	
B9. A written risk-management plan specific to the YMCA, particularly for your aquatics facilities and programs, is established and includes the following aspects: - Identifying and analyzing hazards, natural or manmade - Selecting the best technique for dealing with loss exposure - Maintaining continuous evaluation and follow-up	4	
B10. A public relations plan for interpreting the goals and programs for the community has been written, is revised annually, and is published in your YMCA's aquatics program operations manual.	2	
B11. Staff at the first contact point (phone receptionists, front desk, courtesy counter positions) receive a program orientation and training in public relations, membership retention, specific information relating to aquatic programs, and their role in the aquatic emergency action plan.	3	
B12. A formal procedure is established to promptly handle complaints, suggestions, or inappropriate behavior and is published in your YMCA's aquatics program operations manual.	5	
B13. All program brochures and other informational materials accurately reflect the YMCA aquatics program and its mission.	4	
B14. A detailed plan is developed for all programs that includes the number of sessions per year with starting dates and minimum and maximum enrollment. The plan is reviewed, and, if necessary, revised regularly.	5	
B15. A comprehensive and practical record keeping system is established, and all information is reviewed annually. This	5	

	Rating	Comments

system includes, where applicable, the
following information:

- Attendance
- Payment of fees
- Skill records
- Participant evaluation
- Health screening forms/emergency information
- Informed consent forms
- Pool maintenance records
- Staff training information
- Authorization for release of a child to an adult other than
  a parent
- Accident reports/incident reports (see items F11 and F12)
- Equipment and supplies

B16. A written enrollment and admission program policy is
established and copies are given to program participants or
their parents. It includes, where applicable, the following
items:

- Fee structure and payment policy
- Program information packet including, where applicable,
  the following:

  ✔ Goals Description of program activities and operation
  ✔ The hours of operation
  ✔ Participant-to-staff ratio
  ✔ Staff qualifications
  ✔ Benefits to participants and their families
  ✔ Parental involvement
  ✔ Other YMCA programs and services

- The attendance and illness policy
- Policy regarding refunds, canceled classes, credits, and
  make-ups
- Policy regarding parental observation of classes or
  programs
- An enrollment form that includes the following
  information on the participant:

  ✔ Full name
  ✔ Address
  ✔ Phone number
  ✔ Emergency phone number
  ✔ Participant's or parent signature

- Health screening form
- A non-discrimination clause/policy
- Transportation release (if applicable)

Rating for B16: 4

(continued)

	Rating	Comments
- An authorization for release of a child to an adult other than a parent - Parent options for involvement and volunteer opportunities - A plan for communicating to participants their progress - A policy statement on enrollment of participants with special needs, disabilities, chronic illnesses, medically fragile conditions, and so on - A policy statement on behavior management, including your YMCA's approach to discipline, grounds for enrollment termination, and steps that need to be taken for termination - A financial aid statement		
B17. A written financial assistance policy is established and publicized. Financial assistance is available to program participants who qualify based on your association's ability to secure funds and your charitable duty to reflect your community in the YMCA programs.	4	
B18. Members and participants are required to show proper identification when entering the facility or participating in programs or classes. A checkout procedure is also in place.	4	
B19. The association has a comprehensive insurance plan that covers programs and the staff and volunteers involved in their delivery. It includes, where applicable, the following items: - Comprehensive general liability - Property coverage - Accident coverage - Employer's non-ownership liability - Hired and leased vehicle coverage - Fire, theft, and catastrophe coverage - Motor vehicle coverage - Workmen's compensation - Director's and officers' liability coverage	4	
B20. A written agreement is obtained for the rental of any YMCA facilities and equipment, including vehicles, by non-YMCA groups and for YMCA use of non-YMCA facilities and equipment. The agreement shall include, but not be limited to, the following: - The responsibilities of each party - Fees for use - A "hold harmless" agreement - A certificate of insurance showing that the YMCA is named as an "additional insured" under the general, auto, and umbrella policies - Safety standards, pool rules, and safety equipment	5	

	Rating	Comments
- Help in drafting such an agreement is available from the YMCA of the USA General Counsel office.		

C. LEADERSHIP STAFF/VOLUNTEER

C1. The following are used in the selection and hiring of staff and in the recruitment of volunteers: - Applications - Personal interviews - References (personal/business) - Previous work history - Law enforcement record checks (when appropriate) - Performance observation (and skill check) - A trial performance period (probationary period)		
C2. The YMCA professional director, who supervises the program, is on the official roster of employed staff and has achieved the following: - Twenty-one years of age - A Bachelor's degree in a related field or commensurate experience - YMCA Aquatics Management certification - Current CPR, first aid, AED, and oxygen administration certification - YMCA POOL certification		
C3. All aquatics staff and volunteers conducting programs and classes meet the following criteria: - They are certified as YMCA Specialist Aquatic Instructors (including YMCA Scuba and Competitive Swim programs) for the programs they are teaching or will be within six months of employment (for seasonal programs, 30 days). Noncertified staff are under the direct supervision of a person certified in that particular program until their certification is received. - They are at least 16 years of age or have special approval of the director. - They hold current CPR (obstructed airway, adult, infant, and youth) and first aid certification, and have taken blood-borne pathogen training. - They have the necessary education or training in compliance with national guidelines or guidelines of the specific program and have had opportunity for continued education at least annually.		
C4. All lifeguards and aquatic specialist instructors are given a thorough interview and both a written and practical water skills examination (including lifeguarding, swimming, and water safety skills) prior to employment. Results of the		*(continued)*

	Rating	Comments
examination and copies of current certifications are kept on file as part of the employee's personnel file. An example of pre-hire water skill evaluation for a lifeguard could be a 200 yard continuous swim, surface dive, and recovery of a 10 pound brick from the deep end of the pool; one minute of treading water with a break; and victim rescue, exit and breathing assessment based on a given scenario.		
C5. Lifeguards are evaluated on their ability to perform and maintain all of the required skills and skill tests of their currently held lifeguarding certification. These skills are verified and documented.		
C6. Copies of staff and volunteer certifications (e.g., CPR, first aid, lifeguard, and related instructor certifications) are available for inspection.		
C7. One or more certified YMCA Specialist Aquatic Trainers are on staff to train YMCA instructors according to national YMCA aquatic guidelines.		
C8. Staff will intern or practice teach a minimum of four hours with an experienced staff member before they lead their own classes.		
C9. All aquatic staff are covered within the association's personnel policy as full-time, part-time, or volunteer staff. Individuals operating as independent contractors must meet IRS criteria to qualify as independent contractors. (IRS criteria are available on the YMCA of the USA Web site.)		
C10. All staff and volunteers have signed statements that they have read and understood and have agreed to all matters relating to their job functions, which include the following: - A position description, including environmental factors or specific abilities needed to perform the job - Hours of work - Responsibilities for enforcement of association rules and regulations - Grievance/dismissal policy - Performance appraisal - Salary review** - Vacations** - Tardiness/absences - Training opportunities - Employee benefits - Employee safety procedures - Maintenance of certifications - Conflict of interest policy - Code of conduct		

	Rating	Comments
- Attendance at orientation meeting and receipt of orientation materials (see item C11) These agreements are kept on file. **For employees only, when applicable.		

C11. The following written materials are provided for new staff and volunteers in your YMCA's aquatics program operations manual. The manual should include at least the following:
  - All policies, standards, and operating procedures
  - Job description(s)
  - Statement of YMCA and program purpose, goals, and philosophy
  - Personnel policy, including plans for ongoing supervision, goal setting, performance review, training, and the salary administration plan
  - Specific policies and procedures related to individual programs, such as health and safety, emergency procedures, sun safety, transportation, OSHA rules regarding blood-borne pathogens, and child abuse prevention
  - Program description and fee structure
  - YMCA organizational chart with names
  - Lifeguard/staff conduct guidelines
  - Duty stations
  - Instructional program protocols
  - Substitution procedures
  - Accident reports/incident reports (see items F11 and F12)
  - Bathing code
  - Pool/diving rules
  - Procedures for enforcement of association rules and regulations
Proof of distribution of these materials and orientation is on file.		

C12. The director of aquatics has a written training plan and has participated in relevant training or continuous education within the past year (for example, YMCA of the USA aquatics training, university courses, technical seminars, and so on).		
C13. All program instructors and volunteers reflect an attitude, an image, and values consistent with national YMCA goals and philosophy.		
C14. Staff and volunteers wear neat, professional-looking clothing that is suitable for the activity and that identifies them as YMCA personnel.		
C15. All staff and volunteers receive appropriate recognition for their service.		

(continued)

	Rating	Comments
C16. The aquatics director provides staff and volunteer supervision, staff meetings, in-service training, and opportunities for staff to express themselves on aquatics matters through the following: - Regularly scheduled staff meetings and in-service training - Written job descriptions and performance standards - Planned observation of staff and volunteers - Conferences, including written appraisals - Opportunities for feedback and evaluation - Orientation for all new staff and volunteers - Training related to personal safety issues (sun safety, chemical hazard awareness, OSHA standards on blood-borne pathogens) - Training on and regular practices of safety, emergency procedures, emergency communication system and signals, rescue equipment, and rescues - Activities that help staff and others recover from dealing with an emergency - Regular tests of aquatic skill proficiency and simulated response using rescue and emergency procedures. These tests are documented. - Training opportunities both inside and outside the YMCA. In-service training, staff meetings, and emergency response training are documented and maintained for all staff. The content, length of the meetings/trainings, and attendance are included in the documentation.		
C17. Lifeguards and aquatic specialist instructors are strongly encouraged to maintain a high level of swimming fitness.		
C18. Indoors, lifeguards are not scheduled for continuous duty periods of longer than two hours without at least a 15-minute break. Outdoors, in high temperatures and humidity, the maximum duty period is no more than one hour without a break.		
C19. Instructors teaching scuba for a YMCA are required to have a minimum of $1 million professional liability insurance. Additionally, scuba instructors are certified as S.L.A.M. (Scuba Lifesaving and Accident Management) instructors.		
C20. YMCAs offering scuba lessons shall use and certify the YMCA Scuba program taught by certified and insured YMCA Scuba instructors. Instructor crossover programs are available for YMCAs using instructors certified by agencies other than the YMCA. For information and instructor referrals, contact the national YMCA Scuba office.		

	Rating	Comments
D. PROGRAM CONTENT		
D1. In all program areas where YMCA of the USA aquatics programs exist, YMCA materials and standards are used as a minimum (including YMCA Scuba and competitive swimming programs). If certifications exist in these program areas, the YMCA certification shall be used. Other agency programs are taught only in program areas not covered by the YMCA of the USA.		
D2. The program design includes specific methods and activities to achieve YMCA goals such as the following: - Personal and spiritual growth - Character development - Support and strengthening of families - Appreciation of diversity - Leadership development - Skills development - Health enhancement - Community service - International awareness - Environmental awareness - Having fun		
D3. In line with the YMCA mission, the ultimate goal of aquatics programs is to develop the whole person spiritually, mentally, and physically. In order to achieve this goal, the instructor should have a basic understanding of and respect for the individuality and uniqueness of each student. The teaching methods that are recommended throughout the programs are student-centered. They are designed to help develop each participant's human potential, to encourage his or her awareness of safety in all aspects of the program, and to perfect skills to the best of his or her ability.		
D4. An orientation that includes information on the national YMCA purpose, mission, and goals and local programs and facilities is provided for every new member.		
D5. The instructor/participant ratios are based upon the age of participants, the program offered, the size of the facility, and the other programs offered in the pool at the same time. In general terms, recommended class ratios are as follows: Parent/Child classes...1:10-12 pairs Preschool classes...1:6 Youth classes Polliwogs and Guppies...1:8 Minnows and up...1:10 Adult instructional classes...1:8-12 (depending on the type of		

(continued)

	Rating	Comments
class and the skill level of the participants) Water fitness...1:25 Lifeguard classes...1:20 Arthritis exercise classes...1:20		
D6. Instructional flotation devices are used as teaching aids in all YMCA Swim Lessons instruction.		
D7. A parent orientation is included as part of the first class for parents of children participating in preschool and youth YMCA Swim Lessons programs.		
D8. A system of achievement, skill monitoring, and recognition is used to evaluate progress. Formal testing and pass/fail approaches are not used for instructional classes (excluding lifeguard classes).		
D9. At least one YMCA Splash campaign is conducted each year for the community.		
D10. A current professional staff member who works with competitive swim teams is directly responsible for interaction with the Parents' Committee. The Parents' Committee is a subcommittee of the YMCA board/committee structure. All swim team money is deposited in YMCA accounts.		
D11. YMCA-certified officials are used for competitive swim events.		
D12. Your YMCA participates in a YMCA competitive swimming league whenever possible.		
D13. Aquatic programs for children under the age of 3 should follow the Medical Advisory Committee statement "Aquatic Program Guidelines for Children Under the Age of Three."		

E. FACILITIES AND EQUIPMENT

	Rating	Comments
E1. A copy of your state and local bathing codes and permits are kept on file, reviewed by staff, and, if required, posted for the public to see.		
E2. All sites and facilities are appropriate for the class activity, including equipment and supplies of sufficient quality, quantity, and variety, and are developmentally appropriate for the participants' ages, their abilities and disabilities, and the size of the group.		
E3. All aquatics facilities and equipment are inspected regularly (daily, weekly, monthly, or annually, depending on the area of the facility inspected) for safety by the director of the program (or someone he or she assigns) and judged suitable for use. Records of inspections are kept on file for at least five years.		

	Rating	Comments
E4. A written schedule of preventative maintenance for all facilities and equipment exists, and documentation indicates when the work has been performed, who performed it, and that it was approved.		
E5. All floor and deck surfaces and equipment are cleaned and disinfected on a regular basis and are free of unsafe or hazardous conditions. Proof of maintenance is on file.		
E6. A YMCA POOL-certified operator is on staff to monitor and maintain the disinfection, filtration, and mechanical operation of each aquatic facility to ensure that state and local health department standards are being met. Records are on file as proof of this function, and copies are sent to the state health department as required.		
E7. Measurements of water and air temperature, chemical levels, humidity, pool clarity, and bather load are taken every hour during pool operation. Each pool is tested at both the shallow and deep ends of the pool. This includes pools, spas and wading pools at the facility. The Langelier saturation index water balance is measured weekly and appropriate necessary chemicals added to achieve acceptable water balance. These measurements are recorded in a pool log, which is kept on file for at least five years (or longer if the documentation is relevant to pending litigation).		
E8. The pool area has an emergency lighting system, which is tested monthly. The emergency lighting system, the regular pool lighting, and the mechanical, ventilating, and plumbing systems are maintained in good working condition at all times and are inspected periodically. A schedule of inspections and a written report is on file.		
E9. Periodic inspections of the roof and ceiling by a licensed structural engineer are needed to check for structural safety and signs of corrosion at least every five years. A record of inspections is on file. (*Note:* Suspended ceilings are not recommended for pools.)		
E10. Pool filters are routinely maintained and backwashed in accordance with manufacturer's instructions. A record of maintenance is on file.		
E11. Starting blocks are placed only in the deep end of the pool in no less than five feet of water. They are used only under the direct supervision of a trained competition swimming coach or certified YMCA Swim Lessons Instructor. Safety warnings are posted regarding starting block use. Starting blocks must be removed or capped off to avoid unintended use; if they are in the shallow end, they need to be removed.		

(continued)

	Rating	Comments
E12. All diving boards have two guardrails that extend one foot over the pool. Rails of three-meter boards are enclosed to prevent falling. Ladders or steps are not vertical, but slant at an angle. Diving board fulcrums are locked in a forward position when used for recreational diving. See chapter 10 for information on appropriate minimum water depths for diving.		
E13. Rules, regulations, warning signs, and procedures for use of the swimming pool, locker rooms, and diving areas are permanently mounted in the pool and locker room areas (for example, pool rules are posted near the pool entrance and diving rules near the diving board). Rules are clearly written in positive language and are reviewed with members and participants.		
E14. Material Safety Data Sheets from OSHA are posted in the room or readily available where chemicals are used. Chemicals are clearly identified and stored properly, and a warning sign is posted on the outside of the door.		
E15. For indoor pools, at the water's surface there is a minimum illumination of 30 foot-candles when underwater lighting is on. Without underwater lighting, a minimum illumination of 50 foot-candles is recommended. For outdoor pools, underwater lighting provides 60 foot-candles of illumination measured at the surface.		
E16. A written security plan is developed and implemented. The plan should include methods to keep any unauthorized persons from entering the swimming area when not officially open. This plan addresses both daily and seasonal security concerns.		
E17. For seasonal pools, a sign is posted when the pool has been closed for the season stating that the pool is closed and no lifeguards are on duty.		
E18. A severe weather policy is developed that considers issues such as early identification of storms through weather monitoring, the evacuation of patrons to appropriate sheltered areas, and a communication system to convey instructions. As an example, the National Weater Service recommends if lightning occurs in the area, the indoor or outdoor pool is cleared when either of the following occurs: (1) Cloud-to-ground lightning is observed and less than 30 seconds pass from seeing a flash and hearing thunder from that flash; (2) in-cloud lightning is occurring overhead. The pool can be considered safe to re-occupy 30 minutes after the last lightning is seen or thunder is heard.*		

*National weather service recommendation. (US Dept. of Commerce; National Oceanic and Atmospheric Administration; National Weather Service Forecast Office, 1200 Westheimer Dr., Rm. 101, Norman OK 73069, 12/16/99) Letter from James Purpura, Warning Coordination Meteorologist, National Weather Service and Ron Holle, Lightning Researcher, National Severe Storms Laboratory. Letter to Cleveland County YMCA, Norman OK.

696

	Rating	Comments
E19. Local EMS providers are invited to your facility at least annually to discuss coordination and individual responsibilities in the event of an aquatic emergency. If local EMS providers require any specific or unusual procedures or actions of your facility/staff, ask that they document their request in writing.		
E20. All outdoor pools have perimeter fencing at least six feet high, and eight feet is recommended. Fencing is in good condition and is inspected regularly for protrusions, sharp edges, openings, etc.		
E21. Glass and other breakable materials are not allowed in pool areas.		
E22. Floor surfaces are slip resistant. Freestanding water is removed whenever possible to minimize slips and falls.		
E23. Uneven or not-obvious floor surface level changes are eliminated or made highly visible by being painted in contrasting colors.		
E24. Grates covering floor drains and the pool bottom are tightly secured and flush, requiring tools to remove them. They are in good condition and have no enlarged openings greater than one half-inch.		
E25. All electrical outlets in wet areas have ground fault circuit interrupters.		
E26. There is an electrical inspection every 3 to 5 years to certify the pool area is bonded and grounded.		
E27. All electrical panel circuits are clearly marked and have unobstructed access with at least three feet clearance.		
E28. At least four feet of clearance are around the pool, where the area is free of furniture and equipment. (Lifeguard chairs are not included.)		
E29. There is at least one elevated lifeguard chair for every 2000 feet of water surface area. The chair should be 5 to 6 feet high from the deck at the seat. All lifeguards should be trained to get properly up and down from the chair safely.		

F. HEALTH AND SAFETY

F1. Established accident and emergency procedures are written and posted, and all staff and volunteers are trained to handle emergency situations. The procedures cover the following situations:

- All possible injury emergencies
- Heart attack
- Death

(continued)

	Rating	Comments
- Facility evacuation - Power failure - Natural disasters and severe weather - Chemical leak - Loss of communication capability (downed phone lines, etc.) - OSHA standards on blood-borne pathogens exposure control plan - Drowning or near drowning - Back injuries - Steps for reducing the emotional trauma to staff and others encountering such situations		
F2. Documented regular training sessions are held for all staff and volunteers to review all the safety rules and practice the emergency procedures. Procedures are rehearsed at least every two weeks during peak season and at least once a month at all other times.		
F3. An accessible telephone or emergency alarm system is in the immediate pool area, with posted emergency procedures and numbers. Emergency phone numbers include as a minimum numbers for the police, fire department, poison control, and key staff contacts.		
F4. A participant accident and emergency evacuation plan with clear, precise directions is posted conspicuously near each activity area and in each locker room.		
F5. The following safety equipment is available and within easy access of lifeguard stations at all times: - Rescue tube/rescue buoy, resuscitation mask, and latex gloves for each lifeguard - Reaching poles and shepherd's crook - Soft ring buoys 15 to 18 inches in diameter, attached securely to a length of line sufficient to reach across the width of the pool - Backboard equipped with straps, a head immobilizer, and cervical collars - First aid kit completely stocked to treat all common pool emergencies - Emergency supplemental oxygen (recommended) - AED (recommended) This equipment is in good repair and inspected regularly. Check your local ordinances to determine the number of each piece of equipment that is needed.		
F6. First aid kits, blood-borne pathogen spill kits, bag-valve mask, mechanical suction device, and other first-aid supplies are located in the aquatic facility, and signs are posted to indicate their location.		

	Rating	Comments
F7. First aid materials and equipment are inventoried monthly, and supplies are replaced and updated on a regular basis. A record of inspections is kept on file.		
F8. If AEDs and supplemental oxygen are used, all federal, state, and manufacturer requirements are followed.		
F9. A sign is posted indicating the designated emergency entrance.		
F10. Emergency medical release forms and emergency information are readily accessible to appropriate staff.		
F11. Incident and accident reports are filed immediately after each incident or accident and processed according to standard emergency procedures for your association. Appropriate authorities are informed. Reports are kept on file. (A sample accident report form appears in chapter 9.)		
F12. Incident and accident report forms are available at courtesy and service counters, from off-site instructors, and from staff for reporting injuries, accidents, and other incidents. A procedure is established for promptly informing parents of injuries and explaining the exact circumstances. Reports are forwarded to the supervisor and executive director for review and follow-up. Reports are kept on file.		
F13. Accident and emergency procedures are established for each off-site location in cooperation with the lessee or contracting organization. Procedures are written and included in your YMCA's aquatics program operations manual.		
F14. Procedures for handling suspected child abuse and neglect incidents include documenting and reporting them to child protection services and other procedures as required by your state and local codes. All staff, including volunteers, are trained in these procedures. (See the YMCA of the USA Medical Advisory Committee statement "Child Abuse Identification and Prevention: Recommended Guidelines for YMCAs" in appendix 2.)		
F15. Each YMCA pool is guarded whenever the swimming pool is open for activities, including skill instruction and scuba classes and swim team activities. The lifeguard has no other duties to perform while guarding. He or she conducts a complete inspection of the pool area and pool bottom immediately after each class or recreational swim period. Often, due to many factors, one certified YMCA lifeguard might not be enough. The decision as to the number of lifeguards on duty should be based on these types of factors: - Activity or activities in the pool area (on deck and in the water) - The size and shape of the pool		

(continued)

	Rating	Comments
- Equipment in the pool area (slides, inflatables, and so on) - The bather load - The skill level of the swimmers - Changes in glare from sunlight - High-use areas - Ability to handle emergencies in a proper and effective manner - Meeting or exceeding compliance with applicable state and local codes - Size of zone so each lifeguard can adequately scan his or her assigned zone in 10 seconds and is able to reach any victim in that zone within 10 seconds. Lifeguards on duty are positioned so that they have a full view of the assigned area, above and below the surface of the water. It should be impossible for anyone to enter the pool area without being observed by a lifeguard. Lifeguards should strive to cover their assigned scan zone every 10 seconds and respond to distress situations within 10 seconds.		
F17. Diving board use is supervised and rules are established and prominently posted for the type of diving to occur. For competitive programs, current state and local codes and national governing bodies' regulations for the sport are followed. For recreational programs, see the YMCA of the USA Medical Advisory Committee statement "Diving Board Guidelines for YMCAs."		
F18. Warning signs are posted to indicate there is no diving in shallow water. (For example: Danger! Shallow water. Diving prohibited. Paralysis or death may occur.) A universal warning sign can be used for easier understanding by sight-impaired individuals or by multilingual participants.		
F19. During recreational swims, a procedure is used to determine the swimming ability of those claiming to be swimmers and, if necessary, to assign them to the nonswimmer area. Persons unable to swim one length of the pool (minimum 75 feet) are classified as nonswimmers. Approved personal flotation devices (PFDs) are allowed for use during recreational swims for those individuals who need them, in addition to required adult supervision. Instructional flotation devices (IFDs) are not recommended for use by nonswimmers during recreational swims.		
F20. Children seven years of age or younger are not allowed into an aquatic facility without supervision due to their inability to fully appreciate the dangers of water and other hazards. Older age minimum limits are acceptable based on association needs and policy. No one younger than sixteen years of age is allowed to supervise children.		

	Rating	Comments
F21. A warning sign or pool rules sign is appropriately posted that indicates that "Parents or guardians are responsible for supervising their children. Lifeguards are on duty to enforce rules and to respond in case of emergency." In addition, we recommend that recreational swim pool rules state that young children or nonswimmers should remain within arm's length of a responsible adult at all times.		
F22. A lifeline is in place between the deep and shallow water during recreational swims stretched tight enough to support an adult with his or her head above water.		
F23. When flotation devices are used as teaching aids, all aquatics staff are trained in the use of these devices and other equipment used for swimming instruction.		
F24. Pool water is maintained at strict standards of clarity at all times to permit observation of the bottom of the pool. Floating objects such as kickboards or rubber balls used in instruction or recreational periods are to be removed from the water and stored appropriately immediately after use.		
F25. Water depths are clearly marked on the pool deck and vertical wall at or above the water surface in feet/inches and meters. Markers should be of contrasting color with the deck and wall background and a minimum of four inches high.		
F26. Walking surfaces (decks, steps, and ladders) are constructed or treated in such a way as to render them nonskid and are kept free of obstructions.		
F27. Entrances and exits to the pool have self-closing and lockable doors/gates so that the area can be secured against unauthorized access.		
F28. All windows in the pool area are secured against opening and entry from the outside.		
F29. When the pool is drained for repair or cleaning, signs to that effect are posted on the outside of all doors leading to the pool area, and all doors are kept locked (unless otherwise required by local fire codes).		
F30. If the pool is being cleaned with an automatic vacuum sweeper, the pool is closed and locked from use by swimmers (unless otherwise required by local fire codes).		
F31. For water slides or drop slides, the following precautions are taken: - Lifeguard is stationed near the discharge of the slide and is only responsible for that area of the pool. - A trained staff member is stationed at the top of the slide to control discharge of sliders.		

(continued)

	Rating	Comments
- A sign is posted on the entrance to slides that states that all sliders should not proceed down the slide until instructed to do so by staff. - Slides are inspected daily for loose railings, sharp edges in the flume, loose guards, etc.		
F32. In zero-depth pools, a four-inch- to six-inch-wide line is painted or a floating buoy line is installed across the pool at the two-and-a-half- to three-foot depth mark. This visual marker will help parents and lifeguards keep young children in shallow water.		
F33. During recreational swims, a planned rest period (5-10 minutes) occurs each hour, during which the pool is cleared.		
F34. Lifeguards for outdoor pools are required to wear sunglasses (polarized and block 99 to100% of UV-A and UV-B rays), a hat or visor, and sunscreen (minimum 15 SPF) to protect against the sun's rays. Annual training is provided on sun protection safety and your association's policy regarding the use of sun- protective devices.		
F35. If music is used in the pool area, the volume is adjusted so it does not interfere with the lifeguards' ability to hear someone in distress. Once the maximum acceptable volume level has been determined, it is marked so everyone knows what it is.		
F36. All vehicle operators who transport passengers are 21 years of age, possess an appropriate operator or chauffeur's license, and are experienced in operating the vehicle. In addition, they can provide evidence of an acceptable driving record. An MVR (motor vehicle report) is kept on file. All YMCA vehicle policies are followed.		
F37. A fecal contamination policy is established and procedure in place to document incident and action steps.		
G. HEALTH AND SAFETY NON-YMCA FACILITIES/NON-YMCA GROUPS G1. When programs are managed by the YMCA, swimming takes place only during daylight hours or in appropriately lighted facilities and when one or more certified YMCA lifeguards are on duty. If the YMCA does not manage a program, one or more YMCA staff members are on duty at all times while the group is utilizing the facility.		
G2. During boating activities, every person must *wear* a United States Coast Guard-approved PFD that is in good condition.		

	Rating	Comments
G3. All outside facilities meet appropriate local YMCA program and safety standards. A person approved by the YMCA should regularly inspect the facility and ensure compliance with standards.		
G4. Participants and staff abide by local YMCA safety and behavior standards during off-site competitive swim meets, water carnivals, or other water activities.		
G5. Personnel in other programs that use YMCA pools or other aquatics facilities are trained by YMCA aquatics staff in appropriate aquatic safety skills.		
G6. When outside groups use YMCA facilities (including high school rentals), an appropriate number of YMCA lifeguards are on duty. The program has been reviewed by the YMCA executive and aquatics directors and is consistent with the YMCA's policies. (See also item B20.)		
H. EVALUATION		
H1. Program participants are given regular opportunities to evaluate the programs or classes in which they are involved, with a minimum of one evaluation per session recommended. Parents are asked to evaluate programs for young children.		
H2. All programs are evaluated annually by the Health and Physical Education Committee, the Aquatics Committee, and/or through an assessment process.		
H3. All staff and volunteers are given an opportunity to evaluate the program annually.		
I. CHILD CARE AND CAMPING AQUATIC ACTIVITIES AND PROGRAMS		
I1. The child care/camp director meets with the aquatic director to plan a safe, developmentally appropriate program for the children. The planning discussion includes the following issues: • What is the length of each swim session? • What type of program? (lessons, structured games, recreational swimming) • What are the ages of the children (to help determine instructor-to-student ratios)? • Will all children participate in the aquatic program, and how will you identify who will participate in the swim program? Determine alternate activities for the children who do not swim.		

(continued)

	Rating	Comments

- Discuss how children will be identified as swimmers/ nonswimmers (e.g., wristbands, colored swimming caps) and usage of diving board, flotation devices, inflatables, toys, etc.
- How many lifeguards will be needed? (Consider state and local ordinances, licensing requirements, and local YMCA policy.) How many instructors will be needed?
- What will child care/camp staff be expected to do during aquatic activities (e.g., help children change, supervise children in the water, act as "safety assistants" on deck, conduct restroom runs, supervise locker rooms)?
- When will joint staff training and in-service training sessions be held?
- What are the emergency procedures?
- What are the emergency procedure roles/responsibilities for child care/camp staff?
- What safety orientation and pool/waterfront rules will be reviewed with children?
- Which department pays for expenses related to the camp/ child care use of the pool?
- If the pool/waterfront is to be shared with others, how it will be scheduled?

Review all applicable state and local regulations related to swimming pools/waterfronts, child care, and camping.

12. A written plan is in place for safety considerations (depth of water, starting blocks, number of children in the water, identification of swimmers who cannot swim, staff placement in and out of the water, etc.) Everyone is aware of the plan and emergency procedures (including lost swimmer drills).

13. A camp/child care supervisor is on duty during aquatic activities, in addition to an on-site aquatic supervisor. This is in addition to the appropriate number of lifeguards and other staff necessary to protect the safety of the children. If a center is licensed, required ratios are maintained.

14. If the plan for swimming does not include instruction, conduct games and activities during at least part of the recreational swimming time. (*Note:* When children are involved in activities they are safer and learn additional skills.)

15. An aquatic safety orientation and training session is conducted by well-trained and experienced aquatic staff members for all camp/child care staff who will assist in swimming activities. A session is conducted prior to the camp/child care program and sessions continue throughout the season.

A lost swimmer policy and drill is established and part of the aquatic plan. The lost swimmer drill is reviewed with all staff and practiced on a regular basis throughout the season. (Refer to *On the Guard II: The YMCA Lifeguard Manual.*)

	Rating	Comments
16. Children's emergency information, medications, first aid supplies, and local emergency numbers are readily accessible. If you travel to another site for swimming, the director (or appointed supervisor) brings the records to the off-site location.		
17. Responsibilities for day camp/child care staff, swim instructors, lifeguards, and children are defined. Here is an example for recreational activities:		

17. Responsibilities for day camp/child care staff, swim instructors, lifeguards, and children are defined. Here is an example for recreational activities:

Camp/child care staff
- Watch children at all times, whether they are in the water, locker rooms, or elsewhere.
- Pair up buddies (if buddy system is used).
- Provide behavioral guidance and help to enforce pool/waterfront rules.
- Supervise in locker rooms and on deck.
- Ensure children take thorough soap showers before entering the pool.
- Help children keep track of their clothing.
- Follow your YMCA's policy for proper attire on deck.
- Follow all rules and regulations.
- Alert the lifeguard if assistance is needed.
- Keep track of swimmers who leave the pool/waterfront area.
- Conduct head counts.
- Obey lifeguard decisions and instructions.
- Supervise children not participating in programmed aquatic activities.
- Collect lost and found articles; clean up the deck/beach area.
- Inform aquatic staff if any child has disabilities or requires special attention.
- Know emergency procedures and lost swimmer policy.

Children
- Take care of their clothing and towel.
- Take a thorough soap shower before entering the pool.
- Follow all pool/waterfront rules and procedures.
- Ask permission to leave the pool/waterfront area.
- Stop talking when the whistle blows. ("When the whistle blows, mouths close.")
- Stay with their buddy (if buddy system is used).

Lifeguards
- Guard the pool/waterfront and enforce the rules.
- If not on guard duty at the time, test children, assign them to a swimming area, and give them identifiable bands (or other forms of identifying their swim level).

(continued)

	Rating	Comments

- If not on guard duty at the time, orient swimmers to rules and procedures to follow when in the pool/waterfront area.

Swim instructor

- Teach classes.
- Be certified in the aquatic specialist area in which they are instructing (for example, YMCA Swim Lessons: Youth and Adult Instructor).
- Maintain complete records and complete end-of-session progress reports.

18. The following children-to-staff ratios are maintained when children are in the water (Ratios do not include the lifeguard(s) or supervising child care/camp staff members.):

Instructional swimming

Ages	Ratio
• 0-3	1:1 in the water unless state child care licensing regulations are stricter. Follow YMCA of the USA Aquatic guidelines for children under the age of three.
• Preschool (3-5)	6:1
• Youth (6 and up)	8:1 Polliwog and Guppy levels 10:1 Minnow and up

Recreational swimming

Based on the facility's size and water depth, equipment, and participants' age and ability levels, additional supervision may be required. As a general rule, the ratio should be one lifeguard for every twenty-five campers (age six and over) plus one additional trained day camp staff member who serves as a "safety assistant" on deck to observe swimmers. Children under the age of six should have appropriate supervision in the water based on the instructional class ratios listed above, in addition to lifeguards.

Other camp/child care staff should still be involved with the children playing in the water or be assigned to children who are on the deck or not swimming. [*Note:* Pool design and water depth may affect the number of staff needed (e.g., if the pool is too deep for children to stand, additional staff may be needed and/or flotation devices may be required for children).] Children under the age of six and those with special needs will require additional supervision.

During recreational swimming, the number of nonswimmers (e.g., preschoolers in the water without flotation devices) should be limited or additional staff assigned to increase supervision. All nonswimmers who cannot stand on the bottom of the pool should wear approved flotation devices.

Those designated as "Safety Assistants" (day camp/child care staff members) should be

- under the direct supervision of aquatic personnel;

	Rating	Comments
• oriented to procedures for aquatic safety, the activity, and the site, and be certified in elementary emergency assistance, CPR, and first aid; and • stationed to observe, quickly assist participants, and signal lifeguards if necessary. (*Note:* We recommend that these individuals be certified as YMCA Aquatic Safety Assistants.)		
I9. Entry into and exit from the pool/waterfront is planned to ensure staff always know how many children are with them and where those children are at all times. Head counts are done and/or attendance is taken before children enter the water and prior to their leaving the pool/waterfront area. All children are seated in a standard location before and after aquatic activities.		
I10. Camp/child care staff are aware of and follow each individual pool's/waterfront's operating procedures (if the program utilizes several sites).		
I11. A head count system is used during the recreational swim. During regular periods, all swimmers are called out of the water and the number of swimmers is counted (e.g., every fifteen minutes, after three loud whistle blasts, the children must sit on the side of the pool or deck with their buddies and the children are counted). State or local codes on frequency of head counts are followed.		
I12. If children leave to use the restroom, they check in with staff before re-entering the water. Children are supervised in the restrooms or locker rooms by more than one adult as a child abuse prevention practice.		
I13. Children are required to pass a swim test before being allowed in the deep end of the pool or water. The test should include the ability to swim the length (twenty to twenty-five yards) of the pool/waterfront comfortably without use of flotation devices. The results of testing are documented. Swimmers who are allowed in the deep end are identified by wristbands, caps, etc. The results of testing are documented (e.g., which children can swim, where they can go in the water). All children who do not pass the test are classified as nonswimmers.		
J. NON-YMCA-OWNED SWIMMING FACILITIES AND WATER PARKS		
J1. Day camp and childcare programs use only public/private waterfronts that have a qualified lifeguard(s) on duty. If the programs use waterfronts without lifeguards on duty, the YMCA provides its own lifeguard(s), who must hold proper certification and receive additional site-specific training for that aquatic environment.		

(continued)

	Rating	Comments
J2. Prior to the trip, the day camp/child care director visits with the park staff to walk through the facility to review parking areas, entrances and exits, bathrooms, vending areas, and first aid stations, and to review the proper use of slides and other equipment, emergency procedures, missing child procedures (including intercom announcements regarding lost children), lifeguard/swimmer ratios, etc. Staff write a plan based on this meeting.		
J3. The day camp/child care director discusses with the day camp/child care staff what their responsibilities are while at the facility and any other facility rules. The director emphasizes that they must supervise the children at all times and describes how the children will be grouped and allowed to move around the facility with their group leaders. The director discusses the system that employees at the host facility will use to identify YMCA staff and kids. (See item J7.)		
J4. When the group arrives, they check in with the facility manager or head lifeguard.		
J5. Any child with disabilities or who requires special attention is brought to the attention of the aquatic staff of the aquatic facility.		
J6. Day camp/child care staff do a head count or take attendance regularly, and they give children a rest period (5-10 minutes) every hour.		
J7. Children have identification bands or other means of identifying them as members of the YMCA group. Children stay with a buddy from the time they leave the YMCA until their return. Staff wear the same identifying YMCA attire (T-shirts, visors, etc.) so they can be easily identified as YMCA staff.		
J8. The following medical /first aid precautions are taken: - Emergency information about the children (e.g., descriptions of special conditions) is accessible and is brought to the facility. - A first aid kit is taken to the facility. - A designated adult transports children's medication. - If someone administers medication, he or she should make notes on medical forms for parents to review. - If possible, a YMCA lifeguard or designated "first responder" (in charge of first aid) travels with the group to increase group safety. This person can be in charge of the medical information forms and group first aid kit.		
J9. Facility rules and attraction-rider responsibilities are reviewed with the children. Children are given an introduction to the attractions so they are aware of what to expect		

	Rating	Comments

during the rides. A meeting point is designated in case anyone should get separated from the group. At all times a YMCA staff person is at a designated spot that is known to the facility staff and children. If feasible, a tour of the facility is given to the children before they are allowed to play. Children are shown the designated swimming and picnicking areas and the areas that are off limits.

J10. All other local association field trip guidelines are followed.

K. WATERFRONT SAFETY

In these guidelines, the term *waterfront* will refer to anyplace where open water meets land. This includes both surf and inland aquatic environments, such as rivers, ponds, lakes (natural or artificial), quarries, reservoirs, and ocean beaches.

K1. Waterfront program and facility operations must conform to all local, state, and federal health and safety codes and ordinances. YMCA of the USA aquatic guidelines (where applicable) and applicable American Camping Association standards should still apply. An association policy is developed based on these.

K2. A written policy explaining aquatic operating and emergency procedures is available and is reviewed with all camp and aquatic leadership staff regularly throughout the season. (See *On the Guard II: The YMCA Lifeguard Manual*.)

K3. All waterfront program and facility operations have the following equipment readily available in an appropriate quantity based on the size of the facility and attendance:

- Emergency equipment
- Telephone with emergency numbers posted nearby
- A first aid kit
- Personal protective equipment (e.g., latex gloves, resuscitation masks, eye shields, resuscitation equipment)
- A backboard with straps, plus a head restraint and cervical collars
- A rescue boat or paddle board
- Rescue tubes/buoys
- A mask, fins, and snorkel
- A rescue boat or motorized rescue craft recommended for larger facilities

All equipment is inspected daily.

YMCAs in remote and rural locations should seriously consider having the following available:

- Supplemental oxygen (O2)
- An automatic external defibrillator (AED)
- A first aid room with a bed and refrigeration or ice available

(continued)

	Rating	Comments

- Splints
- Blankets
- A bag valve mask
- A mechanical suction device

Factors to help determine the necessity of this equipment are time and distance away from advanced life support services. A helicopter landing zone location and emergency procedures for helicopter evacuation should be established. Advanced-trained staff (EMT/RN) will be needed on site in these areas. Staff on duty should be trained and certified to use additional medical equipment (O2 or AED), if available.

A telephone or cell phone is readily accessible to the waterfront staff for emergencies. We recommend that staff practice rescue drills and review them with local EMS personnel to maximize efficiency if needed.

Communication equipment is readily available. Examples include flags, a public address system, walkie-talkies, bullhorns, intercoms, cell phones, and telephones. Whistles can be used as a means of communication to swimmers (one blast means listen; two means resume activity; three means get out of the water immediately).

Behavioral rules and warning signs: Rules and warnings are clearly stated on signs and can be understood by swimmers. The signs are adequately secured and in accordance with ANSI sign standards.

Beaches

Beaches are inspected each day to look for unusual hazards and to mitigate hazards (e.g., empty the trashcans to reduce the number of bees). Identify water/bottom conditions such as the following and decide how to deal with them:

- Accuracy of depth markers
- Debris on bottom
- Holes or sandbars
- Currents or tides
- Drains or open storm sewers
- Wave size, direction, and type
- Thermocline conditions and water temperature
- Water/bottom conditions are inspected daily.

Docks

Docks are checked for stability, surface slickness, and protruding splinters, nails or other sharp objects. For diving, springboard diving equipment and the height of the dock and springboards above water (variation of depth due to evaporation and tides/dam water level) are checked.

K4. A lifeguard(s) who is currently YMCA certified is on duty at all times the facility is open. Lifeguards are not given duties unrelated to their public safety function of water surveil-

	Rating	Comments
lance. Sufficient breaks are provided (per aquatic guidelines) throughout shifts.		
In-service training, including child abuse prevention, and training specific to the facility must be provided.		
Lifeguards practice the facility's emergency action plan(s) prior to the opening of the facility and periodically during the season. Lifeguards at any aquatic facility that offers swimming regularly practice lost swimmer drills and submerged victim drills (with mask and fins) in the water with zero visibility.		
Lifeguards are positioned so all areas of the beach, water, docks, and floats are easily observable. Lifeguard staffing is at a level adequate to ensure the distress of any person in a protected swimming area can be quickly recognized and a rescue immediately initiated. Zone coverage is set by policy and clearly stated to all lifeguards via training procedures, policies, and posted directions. Zones require lifeguards to scan no more than 180 degrees and allow lifeguards to reach the victim in 10 seconds. (This means no more than 180 degrees and no farther than a 10-second swim to the farthest point in their zone.) Specific and continual attention must be given to persons swimming underwater, diving, or surface diving.		
A public address system and hand-held megaphones are available to staff to enforce beachfront rules and coordinate an emergency response.		
International staff working in USA camps must "crossover" their aquatic and safety certifications to receive a USA course certification. If they do not obtain USA certification, those staff are assigned to other duties.		
Lifeguard in-service training includes the following in addition to regular training for non-waterfront areas: • Lost bather drills • Boat rescue techniques • Search and recovery in turbid water • The use of mask and fins • Paddleboard rescue techniques • The use of scuba (if lifeguards are certified in scuba and its use is applicable)		
K5. Water Environments		
Swimming areas: These areas are roped off with lines running parallel to shore so swimmers can stay in water of the same depth. The swimmers are informed of the potential hazards and rules of the area. All swimmers are given an orientation prior to their first aquatic experience, including a deep-water test.		

(continued)

	Rating	Comments

The size of the swimming area is limited to a space that can be adequately searched for a known submerged victim in a two-minute time period.

Flotation buoys and warning signs are used to identify water depths or any sudden drop-offs.

If the water is over 13 feet deep, masks, snorkels, and fins are available for lifeguards and additional line is attached to each rescue tube.

The swimming area has limited access. It is fenced and locked appropriately.

Diving areas: No-diving signs are posted when the area does not meet minimum diving depths as indicated in YMCA of the USA aquatic guidelines. Rules and warnings are clearly stated and can be understood by swimmers on signs that are adequately secured and in accordance with ANSI sign standards. Incompatible activities such as boating, water skiing, and fishing are prohibited near swimming areas and are constantly monitored.

Waves: Lifeguards practice preventive lifeguarding, directing potential victims away from beach hazards or waves caused by boats.

Currents: Lifeguards educate swimmers on how to identify currents and how to get out of them. They practice preventive lifeguarding by identifying rip currents and directing swimmers away from them. Clear, understandable warning signs are posted where appropriate.

Piers: Signs are posted on piers and lifeguards issue warnings from piers and mobile units to keep swimmers away from danger areas.

Ocean bottoms: Lifeguards actively warn swimmers of dangers in the area. They discourage dangerous activities such as skim boarding "aerial dismounts," shallow diving, horseplay, pier jumping, or diving under docks.

Flotation devices: (boogie boards, surfboards, skim boards, air mattresses, etc.): Lifeguards educate swimmers on the hazards of these devices and the problems swimmers will face if they lose their flotation devices. Lifeguards take steps to segregate swimming from surfing populations.

Backwash: Lifeguards actively warn beach patrons during times of dangerous backwash.

Aquatic life: Lifeguards educate swimmers on the local aquatic life and the hazards that aquatic life presents. Warning signs are posted during appropriate seasons.

K6. Boating and Small Craft

Small craft: A specific area is designated for small craft, with swimming not allowed in that area. Small craft are not allowed in the swimming area. A swim test is required before anyone uses any small craft. Staff supervising this area should

	Rating	Comments
be trained in small craft safety or in the specific crafts used at the waterfront by a nationally recognized organization.		
Instructors for boating activities are certified as instructors for their crafts by a nationally recognized organization from the United States.		
During all boating activities every boat user must wear a personal flotation device (PFD) that is appropriate to the activity and in good condition. Rescue equipment such as reaching and throwing devices is appropriate to the activity on the craft.		
Staff and boaters are trained to identify hazardous water and weather conditions and to take appropriate actions. All staff and boaters using small craft are trained in handling, trimming, loading, and moving on the craft; the use of lifejackets; and self-rescue in case of capsizing or swamping situations.		
Boaters are not allowed beyond the sight of waterfront guards unless the trip has been planned and approved in advance.		
Aquatic facilities with intensive equipment use (e.g., boats) create an equipment checklist to be used daily to protect against damaged or faulty equipment.		
A properly equipped rescue boat is available and in good working order for emergency retrieval purposes.		
For small craft trips, campers must have appropriate training in packing a small craft, propelling a loaded boat, and trailering.		
K7. Safety systems (e.g., buddy check, tag boards, equipment checkout) are used to help enable lifeguards and safety assistants to quickly account for all participants in swimming and boating activities. All swimmers are evaluated and classified as to their swimming ability. Water tests are given and swimmers are assigned to designated areas or are required to wear appropriate flotation devices.		

REFERENCES FOR ADDITIONAL INFORMATION

American Alliance for Health, Physical Education, Recreation, and Dance. 1997. *Waterfront safety: A position paper of the Aquatic Council.* Reston, VA: American Alliance for Health, Physical Education, Recreation and Dance.

Pohndorf, Richard. 1960. *Camp waterfront programs and management.* New York: Association Press.

The Royal Life Saving Society Canada. 1993. *Alert: Lifeguarding in action.* North York, ON: The Royal Life Saving Society Canada.

United States Lifesaving Association. 1995. *United Stated Lifesaving Association manual of open water lifesaving.* Englewood Cliffs, NJ: Prentice Hall.

YMCA of the USA. 1997. *On the guard II* (4th edition). Champaign, IL: Human Kinetics.

American Camping Association, 765-342-8456.

Index

Note: The italicized *f* and *t* following page numbers refer to figures and tables, respectively.

Additional Resources for Aquatics & Aquatic Safety

See the YMCA Program Store Catalog for details about these additional items for your aquatics and aquatic safety programs, or contact the Program Store, PO Box 5077, Champaign, IL 61825-5077, phone (800) 747-0089. To save time, order by FAX (217) 351-2674.

Aquatics

0-87322-656-9	YMCA Pool Operations Manual (Second Edition)	$25.00

Aquatic Safety

0-88011-742-7	YMCA Splash Kit (book, video)	$35.00
0-7360-3311-4	Staff Aquatic Safety Training Video Package (instructional handout and video)	$20.00

Lifeguarding

0-7360-3976-6	On the Guard II-The YMCA Lifeguard Manual (book & CD-ROM)	$31.00
0-7360-3989-9	Instructor Manual for On the Guard II (book, video, CD-ROM)	$80.00

Swim Lessons

0-7360-0038-0	YMCA Swim Lessons Administrator's Manual	$55.00
0-7360-0044-5	Teaching Swimming Fundamentals	$32.00
0-7360-0254-5	Fundamentals of Teaching YMCA Swim Lessons (video)	$24.95
07360-0048-8	YMCA Swim Lessons: Youth and Adult Aquatic Program Manual	$32.00
0-7360-02553	YMCA Swim Lessons: Youth and Adult Aquatic Program Instructor Training (video)	$24.95
0-7360-0053-4	YMCA Swim Lessons: The Parent/Child and Preschool Aquatic Program Manual	$32.00
0-7360-0256-1	YMCA Swim Lessons: Parent/Child and Preschool Aquatic Program Instructor Training (video)	$24.95
0-7360-0270-7	YMCA Swim Lessons Instructor Training Video Package	$59.95

Arthritis Foundation YMCA Aquatic Program and AFYAP PLUS

0-99-003189-6	Instructor's Guide/Guidelines and Procedures Guide (booklet + 3-ring binder)	$20.00
0-99-003190-X	Trainer's Guide/Recertification Guide	$13.00
0-99-003191-8	Deep Water Instructor's Guide	$3.50
0-99-003192-6	Deep Water Trainer's Guide	$3.50
0-99-003193-4	Juvenile Arthritis Instructor's Guide	$4.00
0-99-003194-2	Juvenile Arthritis Trainer's Guide	$4.00

Aquatics for Special Populations

0-88011-695-1	Adapted Aquatics Programming	$40.00

Water Fitness & Exercise

0-7360-3246-0	YMCA Water Fitness for Health	$35.00
0-99-1998-5	Introduction to the Speedo Aquatic	
0-99-1998-6	Fitness System (video)	$25.00
0-99-001999-3	Specificity of Training and Deep Water Program (video)	$25.00
0-99-002003-7	Tidal Waves (video)	$25.00
0-99-002000-2	Aquatic Step Program (video)	$25.00
0-99-002001-0	Golden Waves 1 (video)	$25.00
0-99-002002-9	Golden Waves 2 (video)	$25.00

Competitive Swimming and Water Polo

0-7360-3452-8	Principles of Competitive Swimming	$28.00
1-884125-00X	United States Water Polo Level One Coaching Manual	$10.00

Scuba Resources

0-7360-4408-6	Scuba Dive Tables (laminated cards)	10/$35.00
0-7360-4476-0	Scuba Diving Log	$7.00
0-87322-132-X	Scuba Lifesaving and Accident Management (Second Edition)	$14.00
0-393-31944-X	Scuba Diving: A Trailside Guide	$18.95